THE BLOOD OF AZRAEL

COLLECTED COMIC STRIPS
from the pages of

BBC
DOCTOR WHO MAGAZINE™

PANINI COMICS

Contents

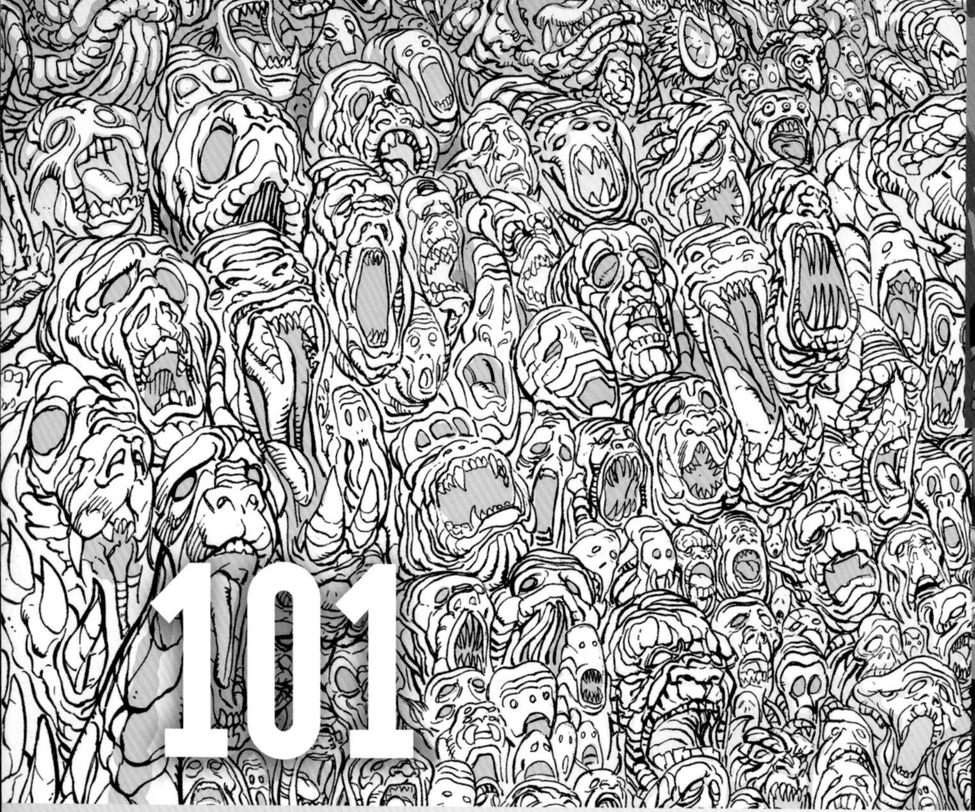
101

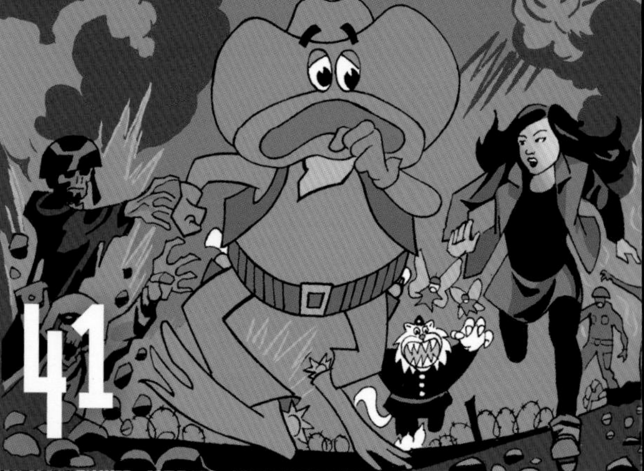
41

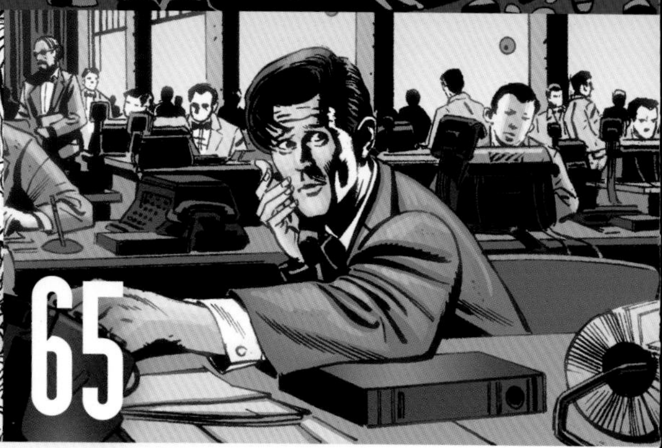
65

Project Editors **TOM SPILSBURY & SCOTT GRAY** Designer **PERI GODBOLD**
Cover pencils and inks by **DAVID A ROACH** Cover colours by **JAMES OFFREDI**

Head of Production **MARK IRVINE** Managing Editor **ALAN O'KEEFE** Managing Director **MIKE RIDDELL**

Special thanks to **MATT SMITH, JENNA COLEMAN, STEVEN MOFFAT, RICHARD ATKINSON, PETER WARE, JOHN AINSWORTH, MARK WRIGHT and all the writers and artists whose work is presented herein.**

MIX
Paper from responsible sources
FSC® C010353
www.fsc.org

Doctor Who Graphic Novel #19: *The Blood of Azrael*. Published by Panini Publishing Ltd. Office of publication: Brockbourne House, 77 Mount Ephraim, Tunbridge Wells, Kent TN4 8BS.

Printed in the UK. ISBN 978-1-84653-625-0

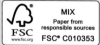

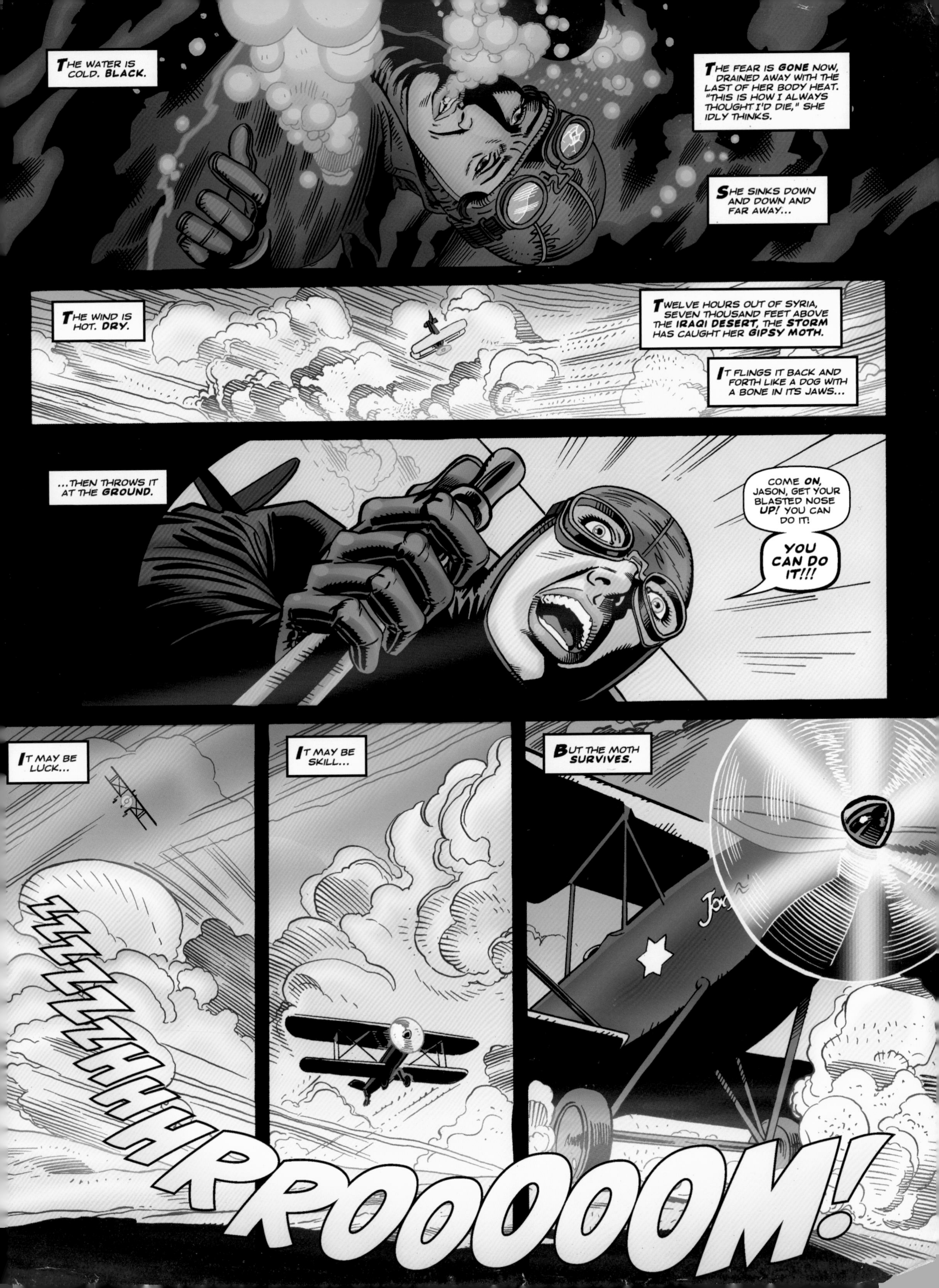
THE WATER IS COLD. BLACK.
THE FEAR IS GONE NOW, DRAINED AWAY WITH THE LAST OF HER BODY HEAT. "THIS IS HOW I ALWAYS THOUGHT I'D DIE," SHE IDLY THINKS.
SHE SINKS DOWN AND DOWN AND FAR AWAY...
THE WIND IS HOT. DRY.
TWELVE HOURS OUT OF SYRIA, SEVEN THOUSAND FEET ABOVE THE IRAQI DESERT, THE STORM HAS CAUGHT HER GIPSY MOTH.
IT FLINGS IT BACK AND FORTH LIKE A DOG WITH A BONE IN ITS JAWS...
...THEN THROWS IT AT THE GROUND.
COME ON, JASON, GET YOUR BLASTED NOSE UP! YOU CAN DO IT!
YOU CAN DO IT!!!
IT MAY BE LUCK...
IT MAY BE SKILL...
BUT THE MOTH SURVIVES.
VVVVHHHHRROOOOOOM!

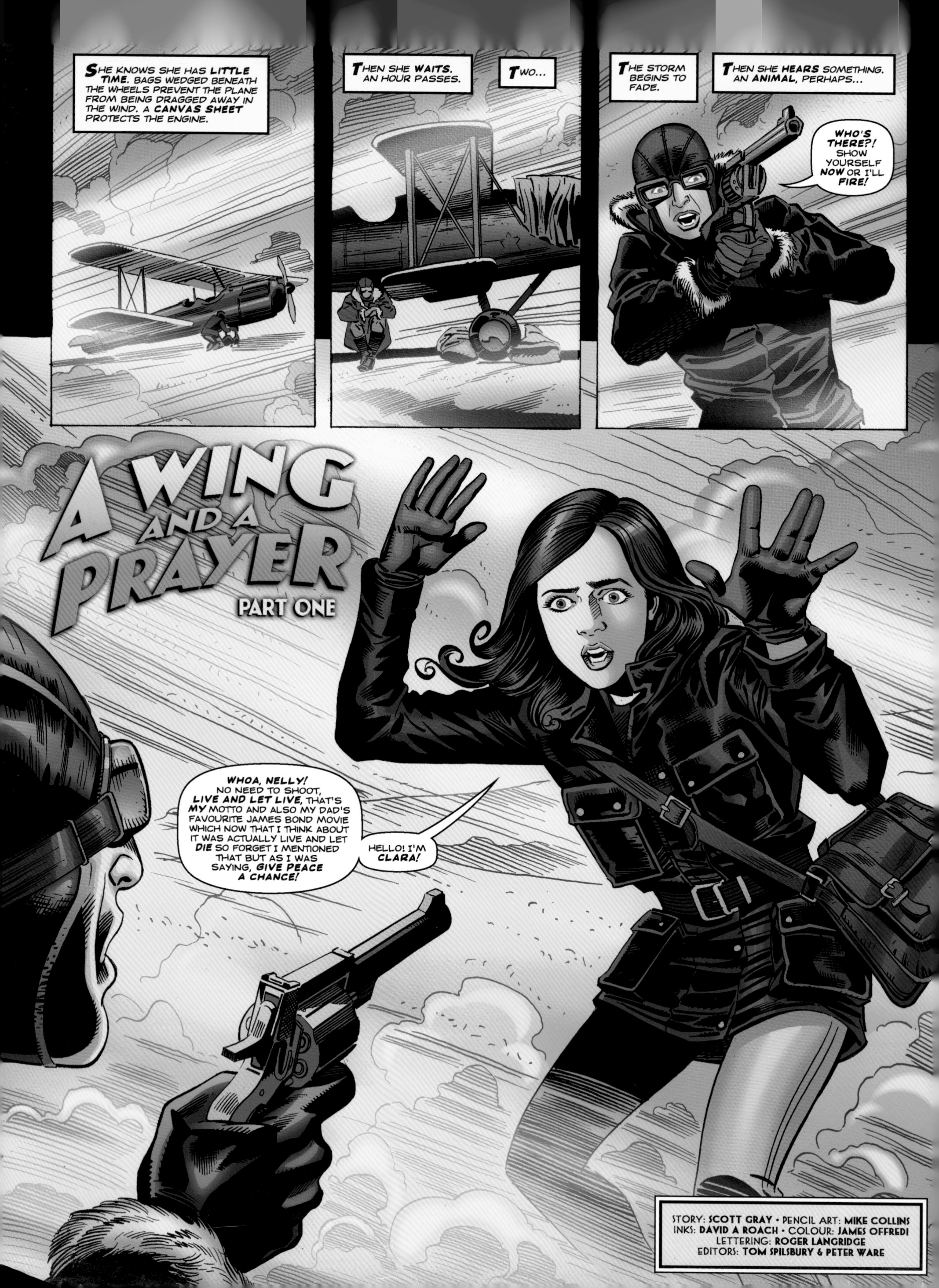
SHE KNOWS SHE HAS LITTLE TIME. BAGS WEDGED BENEATH THE WHEELS PREVENT THE PLANE FROM BEING DRAGGED AWAY IN THE WIND. A CANVAS SHEET PROTECTS THE ENGINE.
THEN SHE WAITS. AN HOUR PASSES.
TWO...
THE STORM BEGINS TO FADE.
THEN SHE HEARS SOMETHING. AN ANIMAL, PERHAPS...
WHO'S THERE?! SHOW YOURSELF NOW OR I'LL FIRE!
A WING AND A PRAYER
PART ONE
WHOA, NELLY! NO NEED TO SHOOT, LIVE AND LET LIVE, THAT'S MY MOTTO AND ALSO MY DAD'S FAVOURITE JAMES BOND MOVIE WHICH NOW THAT I THINK ABOUT IT WAS ACTUALLY LIVE AND LET DIE SO FORGET I MENTIONED THAT BUT AS I WAS SAYING, GIVE PEACE A CHANCE!
HELLO! I'M CLARA!
STORY: SCOTT GRAY • PENCIL ART: MIKE COLLINS
INKS: DAVID A ROACH • COLOUR: JAMES OFFREDI
LETTERING: ROGER LANGRIDGE
EDITORS: TOM SPILSBURY & PETER WARE

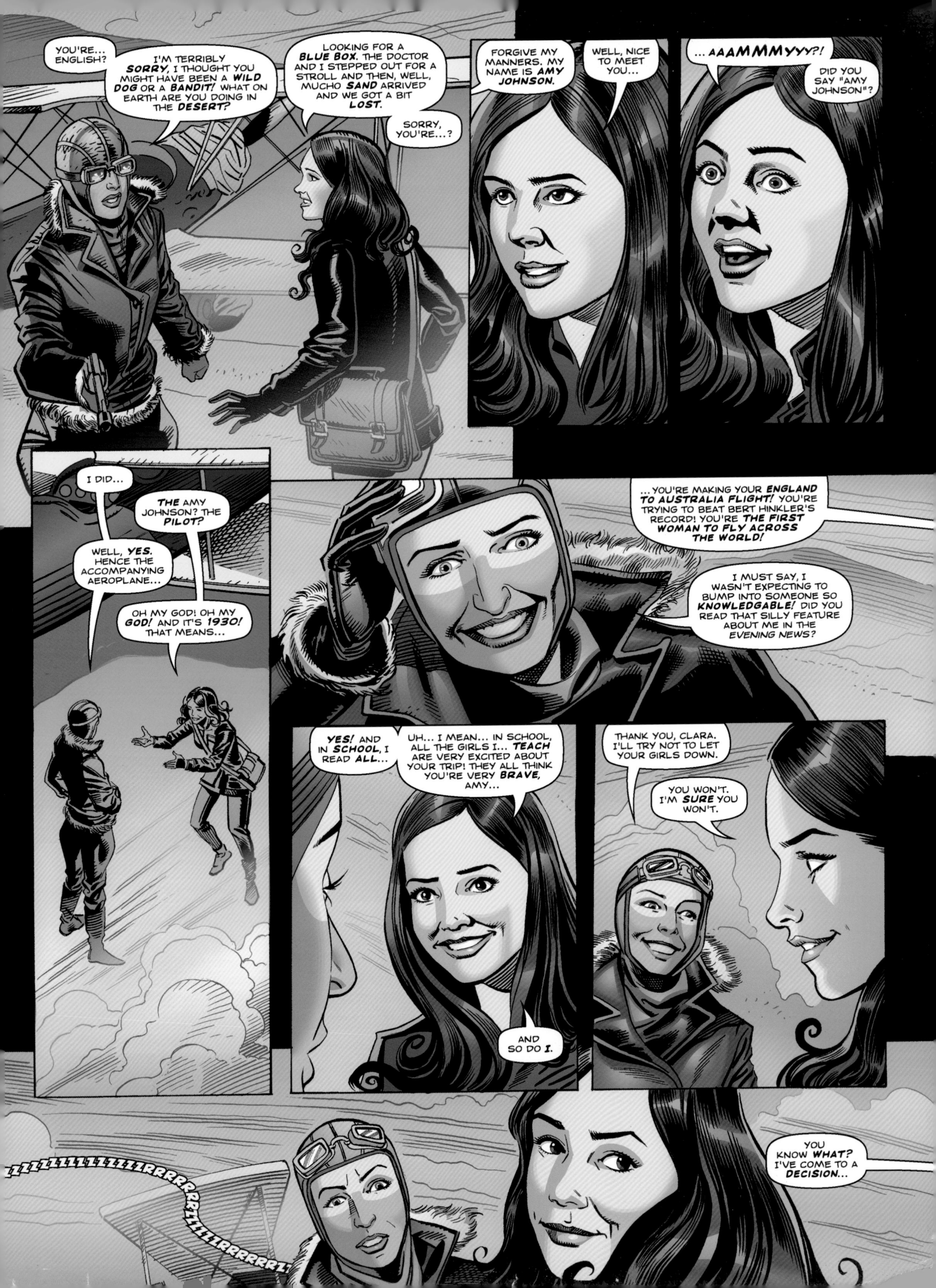

YOU'RE... ENGLISH?
I'M TERRIBLY SORRY, I THOUGHT YOU MIGHT HAVE BEEN A WILD DOG OR A BANDIT! WHAT ON EARTH ARE YOU DOING IN THE DESERT?
LOOKING FOR A BLUE BOX. THE DOCTOR AND I STEPPED OUT FOR A STROLL AND THEN, WELL, MUCHO SAND ARRIVED AND WE GOT A BIT LOST.
SORRY, YOU'RE...?
FORGIVE MY MANNERS. MY NAME IS AMY JOHNSON.
WELL, NICE TO MEET YOU...
...AAAMMMYYY?!
DID YOU SAY "AMY JOHNSON"?
I DID...
THE AMY JOHNSON? THE PILOT?
WELL, YES. HENCE THE ACCOMPANYING AEROPLANE...
OH MY GOD! OH MY GOD! AND IT'S 1930! THAT MEANS...
...YOU'RE MAKING YOUR ENGLAND TO AUSTRALIA FLIGHT! YOU'RE TRYING TO BEAT BERT HINKLER'S RECORD! YOU'RE THE FIRST WOMAN TO FLY ACROSS THE WORLD!
I MUST SAY, I WASN'T EXPECTING TO BUMP INTO SOMEONE SO KNOWLEDGABLE! DID YOU READ THAT SILLY FEATURE ABOUT ME IN THE EVENING NEWS?
YES! AND IN SCHOOL, I READ ALL...
UH... I MEAN... IN SCHOOL, ALL THE GIRLS I... TEACH ARE VERY EXCITED ABOUT YOUR TRIP! THEY ALL THINK YOU'RE VERY BRAVE, AMY...
AND SO DO I.
THANK YOU, CLARA. I'LL TRY NOT TO LET YOUR GIRLS DOWN.
YOU WON'T. I'M SURE YOU WON'T.
ZZZZZZZZZZZZZZZZZRRRRRRRZZZZZZZZZRRRRRRZ
YOU KNOW WHAT? I'VE COME TO A DECISION...

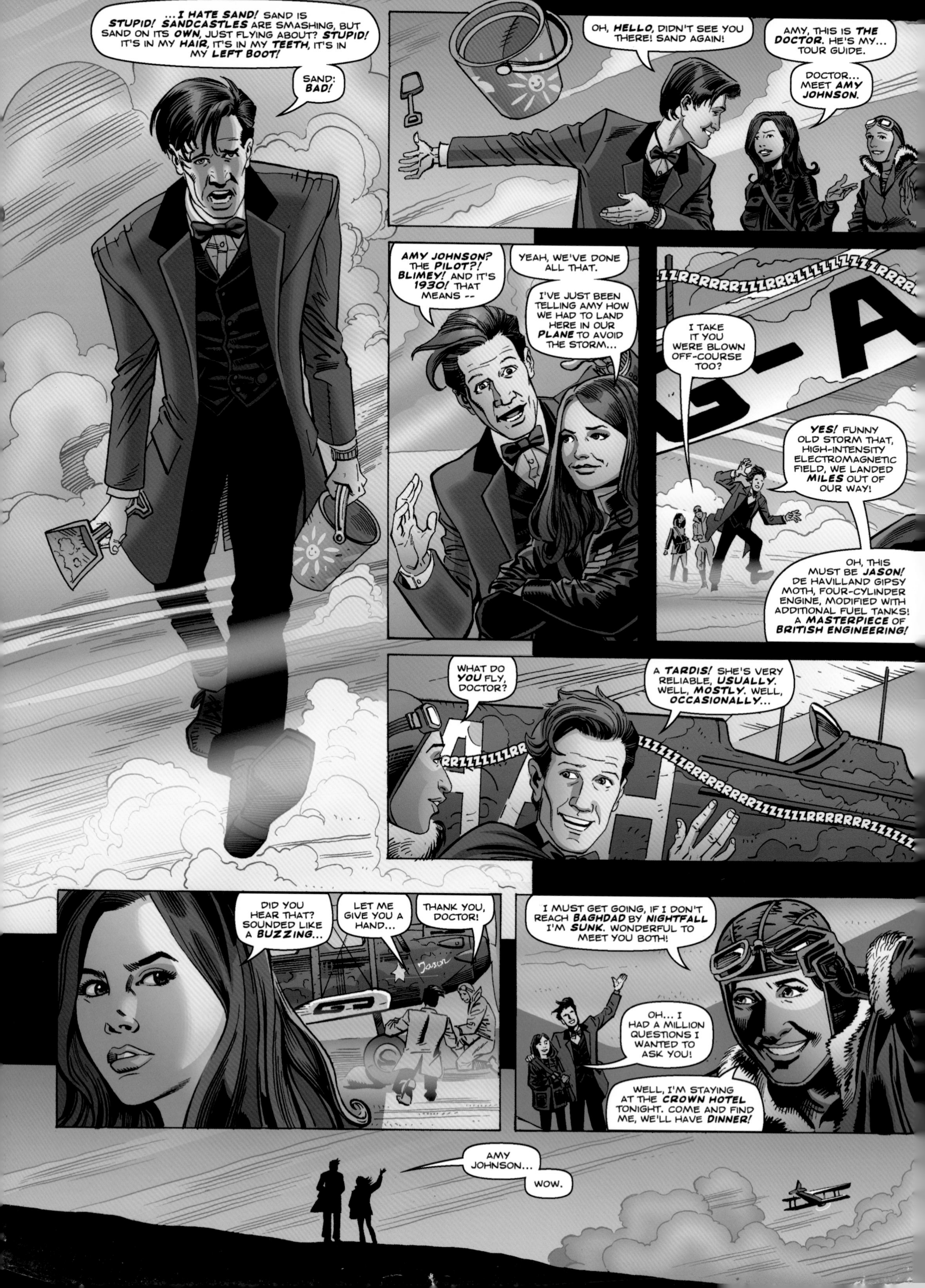

...I HATE SAND! SAND IS STUPID! SANDCASTLES ARE SMASHING, BUT SAND ON ITS OWN, JUST FLYING ABOUT? STUPID! IT'S IN MY HAIR, IT'S IN MY TEETH, IT'S IN MY LEFT BOOT!
SAND: BAD!
OH, HELLO, DIDN'T SEE YOU THERE! SAND AGAIN!
AMY, THIS IS THE DOCTOR. HE'S MY... TOUR GUIDE.
DOCTOR... MEET AMY JOHNSON.
AMY JOHNSON? THE PILOT?! BLIMEY! AND IT'S 1930! THAT MEANS --
YEAH, WE'VE DONE ALL THAT.
I'VE JUST BEEN TELLING AMY HOW WE HAD TO LAND HERE IN OUR PLANE TO AVOID THE STORM...
ZZRRRRRRZZZRRRZZZZRRRZZZZZZZRRRR
I TAKE IT YOU WERE BLOWN OFF-COURSE TOO?
YES! FUNNY OLD STORM THAT, HIGH-INTENSITY ELECTROMAGNETIC FIELD, WE LANDED MILES OUT OF OUR WAY!
OH, THIS MUST BE JASON! DE HAVILLAND GIPSY MOTH, FOUR-CYLINDER ENGINE, MODIFIED WITH ADDITIONAL FUEL TANKS! A MASTERPIECE OF BRITISH ENGINEERING!
WHAT DO YOU FLY, DOCTOR?
A TARDIS! SHE'S VERY RELIABLE, USUALLY. WELL, MOSTLY. WELL, OCCASIONALLY...
RZZZZZZZRR
ZZZZZZRRRRRRRRZZZZZZZZRRRRRRZZZZZ
DID YOU HEAR THAT? SOUNDED LIKE A BUZZING...
LET ME GIVE YOU A HAND...
THANK YOU, DOCTOR!
Jason
I MUST GET GOING, IF I DON'T REACH BAGHDAD BY NIGHTFALL I'M SUNK. WONDERFUL TO MEET YOU BOTH!
OH... I HAD A MILLION QUESTIONS I WANTED TO ASK YOU!
WELL, I'M STAYING AT THE CROWN HOTEL TONIGHT. COME AND FIND ME, WE'LL HAVE DINNER!
AMY JOHNSON...
WOW.

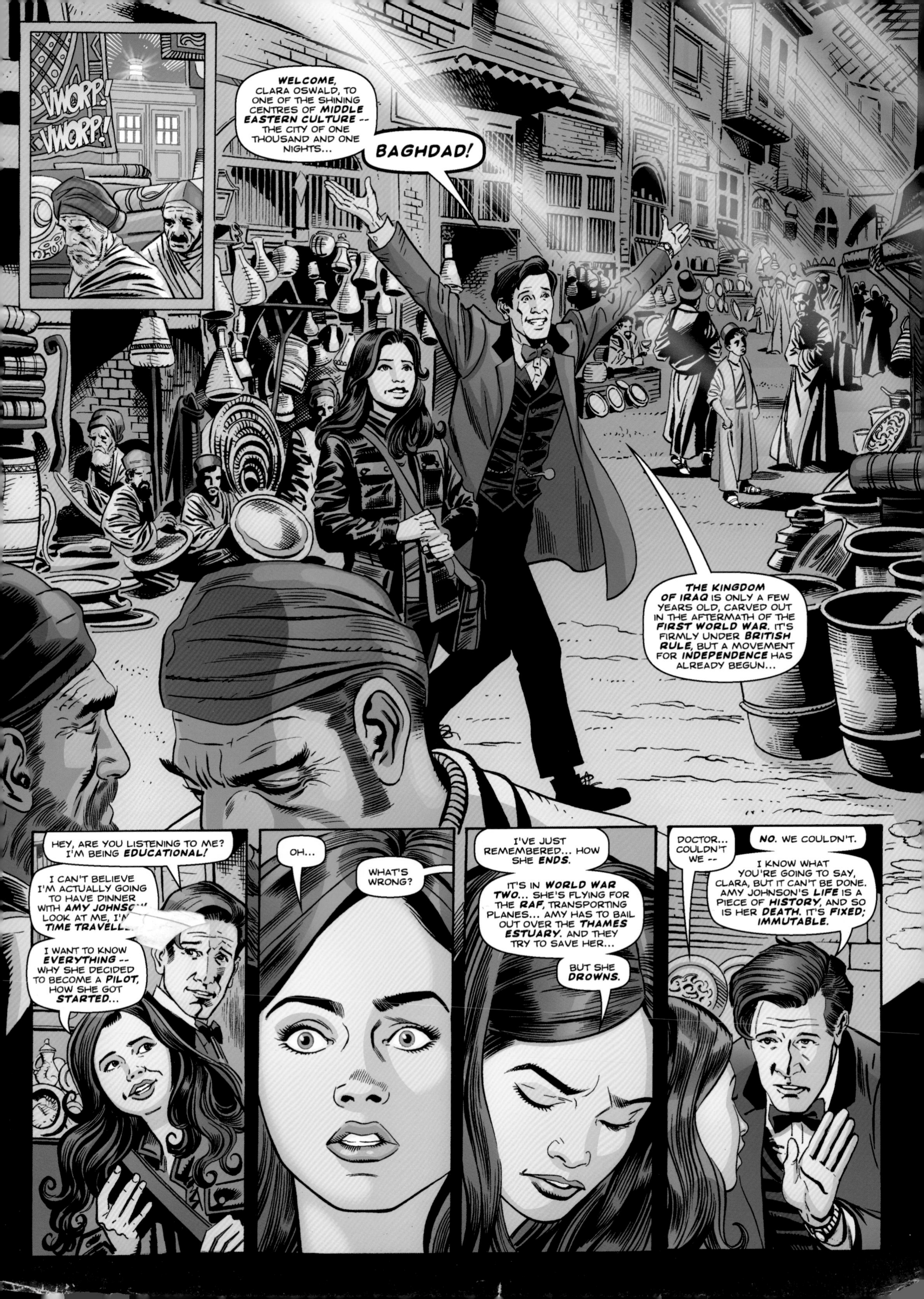
VWORP! VWORP!
WELCOME, CLARA OSWALD, TO ONE OF THE SHINING CENTRES OF MIDDLE EASTERN CULTURE -- THE CITY OF ONE THOUSAND AND ONE NIGHTS...
BAGHDAD!
THE KINGDOM OF IRAQ IS ONLY A FEW YEARS OLD, CARVED OUT IN THE AFTERMATH OF THE FIRST WORLD WAR. IT'S FIRMLY UNDER BRITISH RULE, BUT A MOVEMENT FOR INDEPENDENCE HAS ALREADY BEGUN...
HEY, ARE YOU LISTENING TO ME? I'M BEING EDUCATIONAL!
I CAN'T BELIEVE I'M ACTUALLY GOING TO HAVE DINNER WITH AMY JOHNSON LOOK AT ME, I'M TIME TRAVELL
I WANT TO KNOW EVERYTHING -- WHY SHE DECIDED TO BECOME A PILOT, HOW SHE GOT STARTED...
OH...
WHAT'S WRONG?
I'VE JUST REMEMBERED... HOW SHE ENDS.
IT'S IN WORLD WAR TWO... SHE'S FLYING FOR THE RAF, TRANSPORTING PLANES... AMY HAS TO BAIL OUT OVER THE THAMES ESTUARY. AND THEY TRY TO SAVE HER...
BUT SHE DROWNS.
DOCTOR... COULDN'T WE --
NO. WE COULDN'T.
I KNOW WHAT YOU'RE GOING TO SAY, CLARA, BUT IT CAN'T BE DONE. AMY JOHNSON'S LIFE IS A PIECE OF HISTORY, AND SO IS HER DEATH. IT'S FIXED; IMMUTABLE.

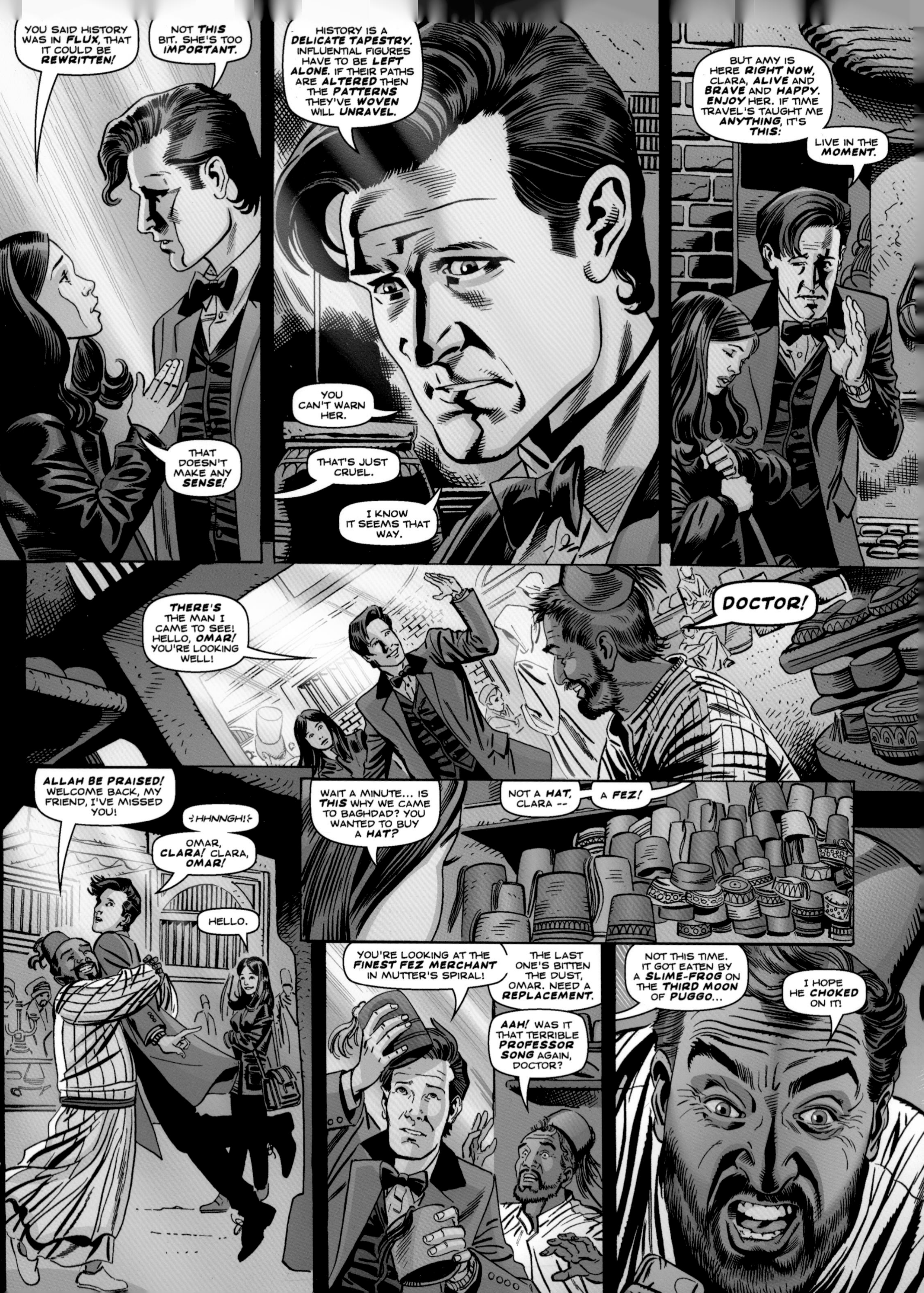

YOU SAID HISTORY WAS IN FLUX, THAT IT COULD BE REWRITTEN!
NOT THIS BIT. SHE'S TOO IMPORTANT.
THAT DOESN'T MAKE ANY SENSE!
HISTORY IS A DELICATE TAPESTRY. INFLUENTIAL FIGURES HAVE TO BE LEFT ALONE. IF THEIR PATHS ARE ALTERED THEN THE PATTERNS THEY'VE WOVEN WILL UNRAVEL.
YOU CAN'T WARN HER.
THAT'S JUST CRUEL.
I KNOW IT SEEMS THAT WAY.
BUT AMY IS HERE RIGHT NOW, CLARA, ALIVE AND BRAVE AND HAPPY. ENJOY HER. IF TIME TRAVEL'S TAUGHT ME ANYTHING, IT'S THIS:
LIVE IN THE MOMENT.
THERE'S THE MAN I CAME TO SEE! HELLO, OMAR! YOU'RE LOOKING WELL!
DOCTOR!
ALLAH BE PRAISED! WELCOME BACK, MY FRIEND, I'VE MISSED YOU!
HHNNGH!
OMAR, CLARA! CLARA, OMAR!
HELLO.
WAIT A MINUTE... IS THIS WHY WE CAME TO BAGHDAD? YOU WANTED TO BUY A HAT?
NOT A HAT, CLARA --
A FEZ!
YOU'RE LOOKING AT THE FINEST FEZ MERCHANT IN MUTTER'S SPIRAL!
THE LAST ONE'S BITTEN THE DUST, OMAR. NEED A REPLACEMENT.
AAH! WAS IT THAT TERRIBLE PROFESSOR SONG AGAIN, DOCTOR?
NOT THIS TIME. IT GOT EATEN BY A SLIME-FROG ON THE THIRD MOON OF PUGGO...
I HOPE HE CHOKED ON IT!

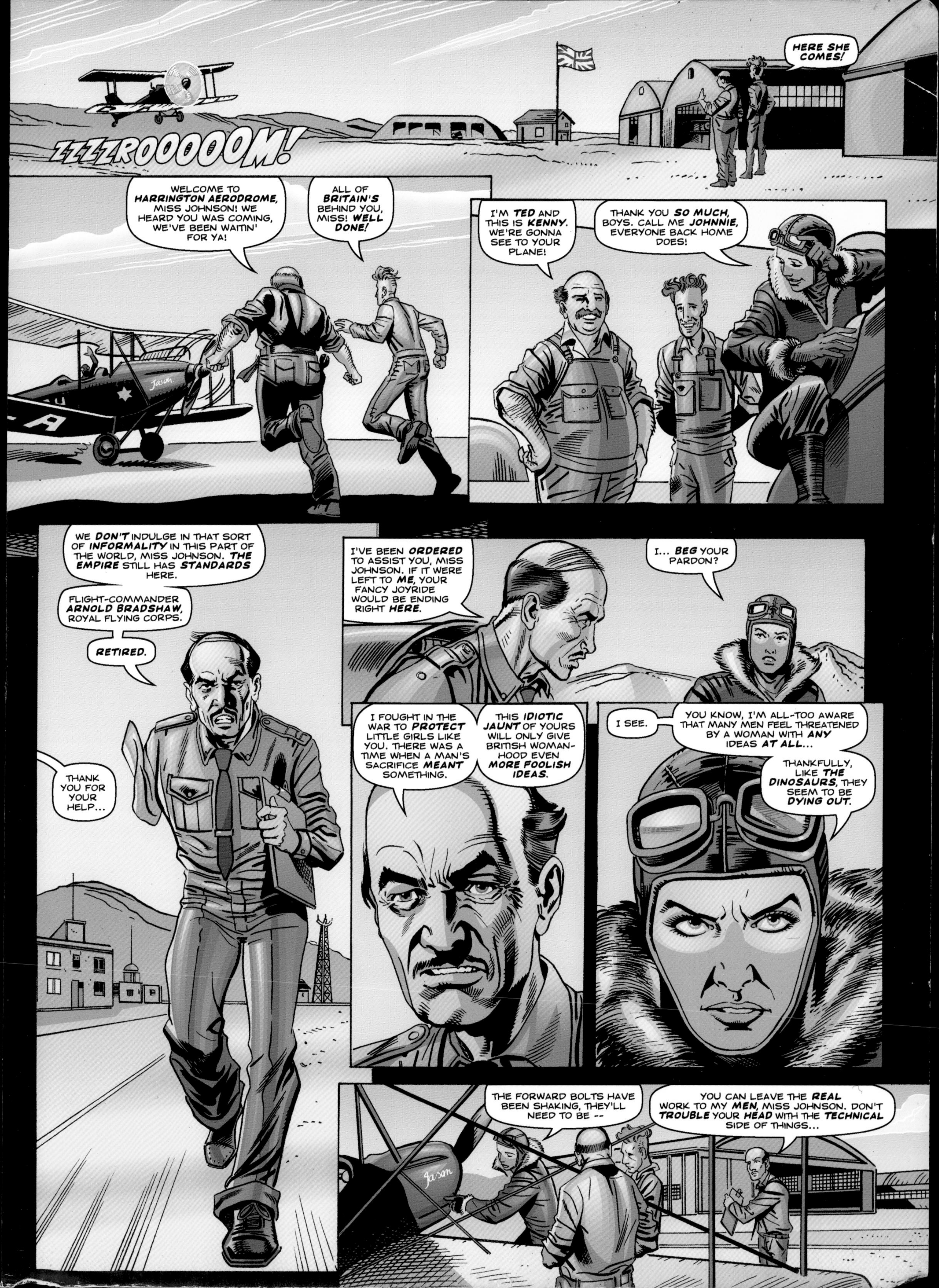
ZZZZROOOOOM!
HERE SHE COMES!
WELCOME TO HARRINGTON AERODROME, MISS JOHNSON! WE HEARD YOU WAS COMING, WE'VE BEEN WAITIN' FOR YA!
ALL OF BRITAIN'S BEHIND YOU, MISS! WELL DONE!
I'M TED AND THIS IS KENNY. WE'RE GONNA SEE TO YOUR PLANE!
THANK YOU SO MUCH, BOYS. CALL ME JOHNNIE, EVERYONE BACK HOME DOES!
WE DON'T INDULGE IN THAT SORT OF INFORMALITY IN THIS PART OF THE WORLD, MISS JOHNSON. THE EMPIRE STILL HAS STANDARDS HERE.
FLIGHT-COMMANDER ARNOLD BRADSHAW, ROYAL FLYING CORPS.
RETIRED.
THANK YOU FOR YOUR HELP...
I'VE BEEN ORDERED TO ASSIST YOU, MISS JOHNSON. IF IT WERE LEFT TO ME, YOUR FANCY JOYRIDE WOULD BE ENDING RIGHT HERE.
I... BEG YOUR PARDON?
I FOUGHT IN THE WAR TO PROTECT LITTLE GIRLS LIKE YOU. THERE WAS A TIME WHEN A MAN'S SACRIFICE MEANT SOMETHING.
THIS IDIOTIC JAUNT OF YOURS WILL ONLY GIVE BRITISH WOMANHOOD EVEN MORE FOOLISH IDEAS.
I SEE.
YOU KNOW, I'M ALL-TOO AWARE THAT MANY MEN FEEL THREATENED BY A WOMAN WITH ANY IDEAS AT ALL...
THANKFULLY, LIKE THE DINOSAURS, THEY SEEM TO BE DYING OUT.
THE FORWARD BOLTS HAVE BEEN SHAKING, THEY'LL NEED TO BE --
YOU CAN LEAVE THE REAL WORK TO MY MEN, MISS JOHNSON. DON'T TROUBLE YOUR HEAD WITH THE TECHNICAL SIDE OF THINGS...

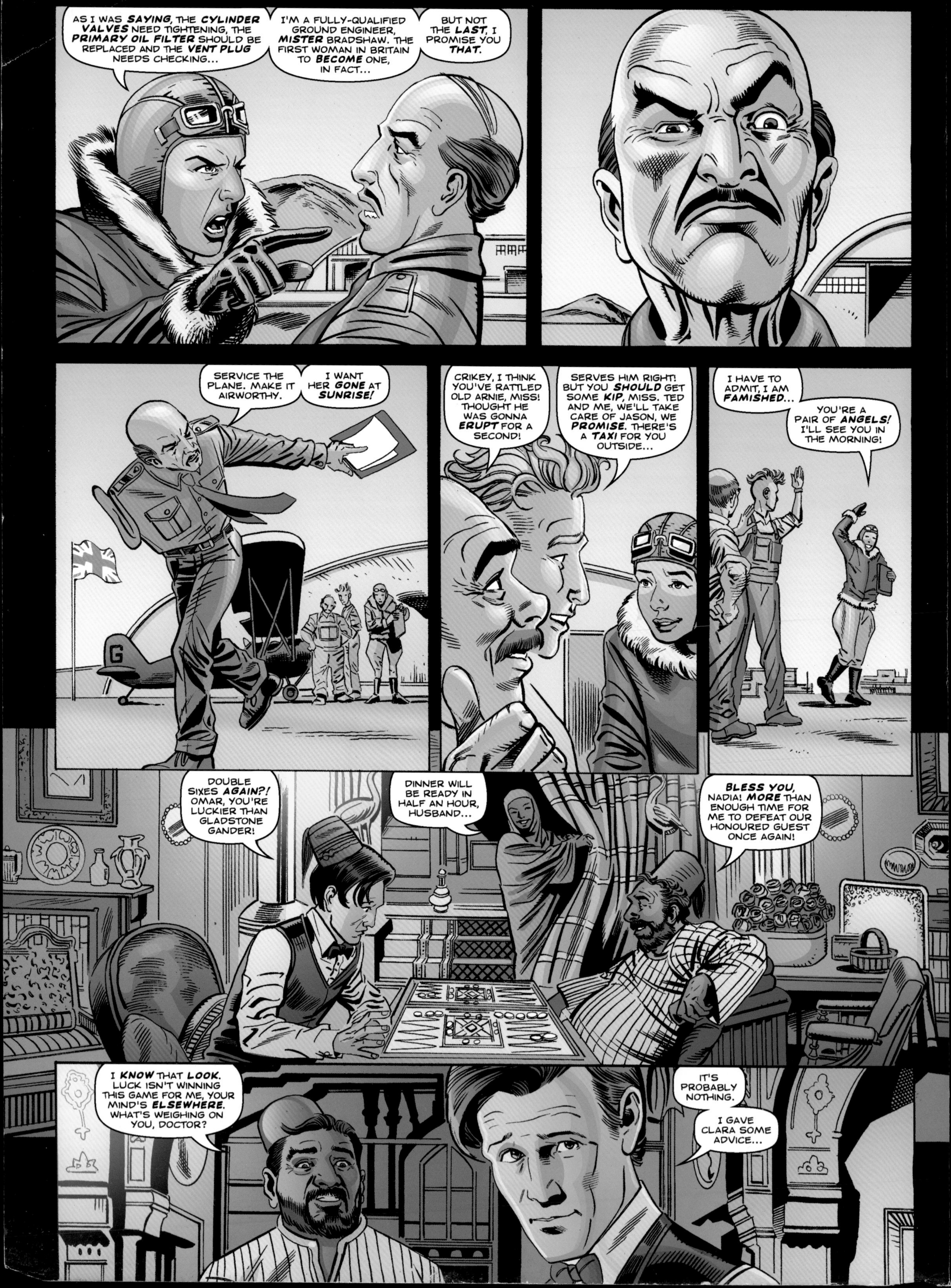
AS I WAS SAYING, THE CYLINDER VALVES NEED TIGHTENING, THE PRIMARY OIL FILTER SHOULD BE REPLACED AND THE VENT PLUG NEEDS CHECKING...
I'M A FULLY-QUALIFIED GROUND ENGINEER, MISTER BRADSHAW. THE FIRST WOMAN IN BRITAIN TO BECOME ONE, IN FACT...
BUT NOT THE LAST, I PROMISE YOU THAT.
SERVICE THE PLANE. MAKE IT AIRWORTHY.
I WANT HER GONE AT SUNRISE!
CRIKEY, I THINK YOU'VE RATTLED OLD ARNIE, MISS! THOUGHT HE WAS GONNA ERUPT FOR A SECOND!
SERVES HIM RIGHT! BUT YOU SHOULD GET SOME KIP, MISS. TED AND ME, WE'LL TAKE CARE OF JASON, WE PROMISE. THERE'S A TAXI FOR YOU OUTSIDE...
I HAVE TO ADMIT, I AM FAMISHED...
YOU'RE A PAIR OF ANGELS! I'LL SEE YOU IN THE MORNING!
DOUBLE SIXES AGAIN?! OMAR, YOU'RE LUCKIER THAN GLADSTONE GANDER!
DINNER WILL BE READY IN HALF AN HOUR, HUSBAND...
BLESS YOU, NADIA! MORE THAN ENOUGH TIME FOR ME TO DEFEAT OUR HONOURED GUEST ONCE AGAIN!
I KNOW THAT LOOK. LUCK ISN'T WINNING THIS GAME FOR ME, YOUR MIND'S ELSEWHERE. WHAT'S WEIGHING ON YOU, DOCTOR?
IT'S PROBABLY NOTHING.
I GAVE CLARA SOME ADVICE...

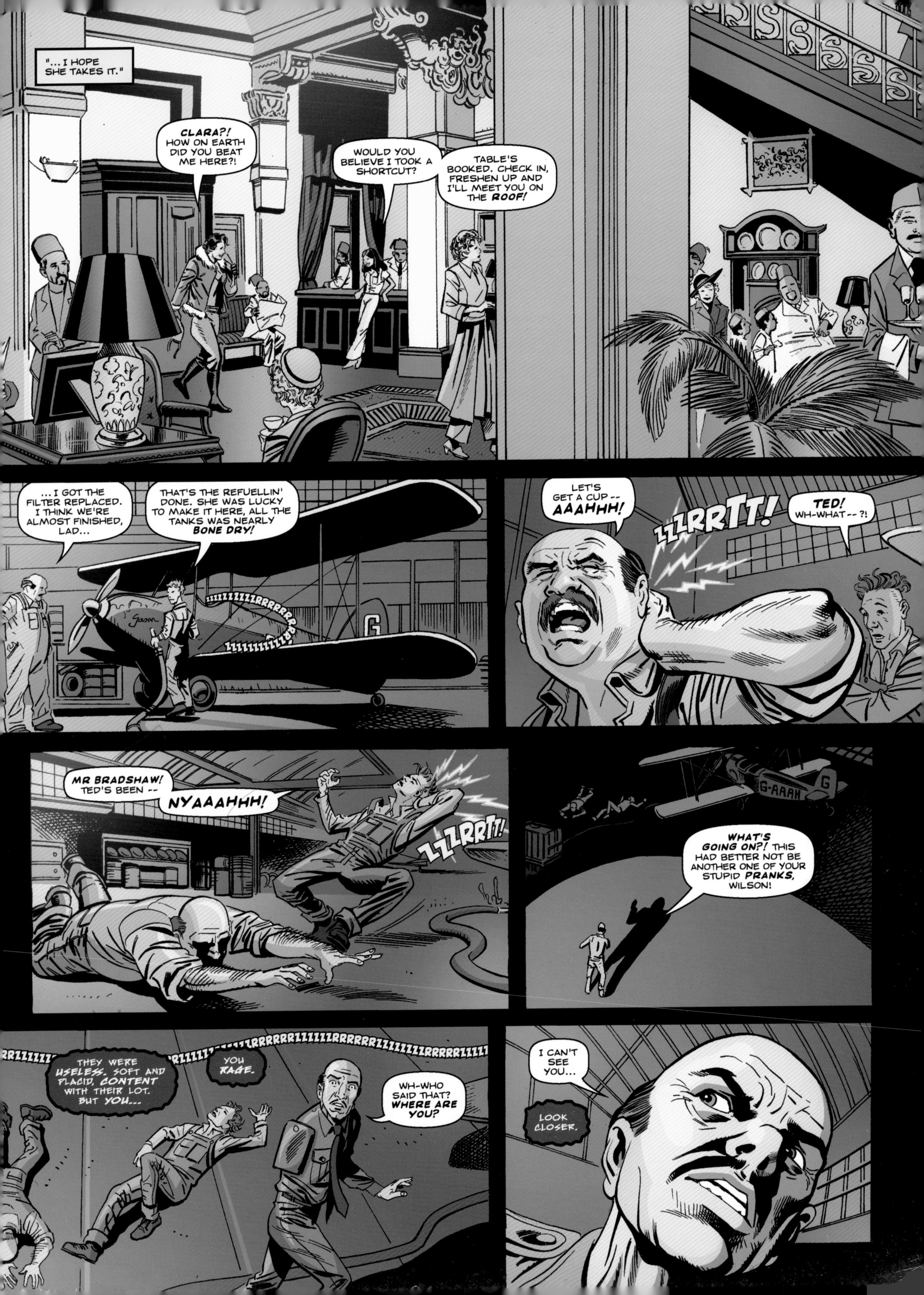
"... I HOPE SHE TAKES IT."
CLARA?! HOW ON EARTH DID YOU BEAT ME HERE?!
WOULD YOU BELIEVE I TOOK A SHORTCUT?
TABLE'S BOOKED. CHECK IN, FRESHEN UP AND I'LL MEET YOU ON THE ROOF!
... I GOT THE FILTER REPLACED. I THINK WE'RE ALMOST FINISHED, LAD...
THAT'S THE REFUELLIN' DONE. SHE WAS LUCKY TO MAKE IT HERE, ALL THE TANKS WAS NEARLY BONE DRY!
LET'S GET A CUP -- AAAHHH!
ZZZRRTT!
TED! WH-WHAT -- ?!
MR BRADSHAW! TED'S BEEN --
NYAAAHHH!
ZZZRRTT!
WHAT'S GOING ON?! THIS HAD BETTER NOT BE ANOTHER ONE OF YOUR STUPID PRANKS, WILSON!
THEY WERE USELESS. SOFT AND PLACID, CONTENT WITH THEIR LOT. BUT YOU...
YOU RAGE.
WH-WHO SAID THAT? WHERE ARE YOU?
I CAN'T SEE YOU...
LOOK CLOSER.

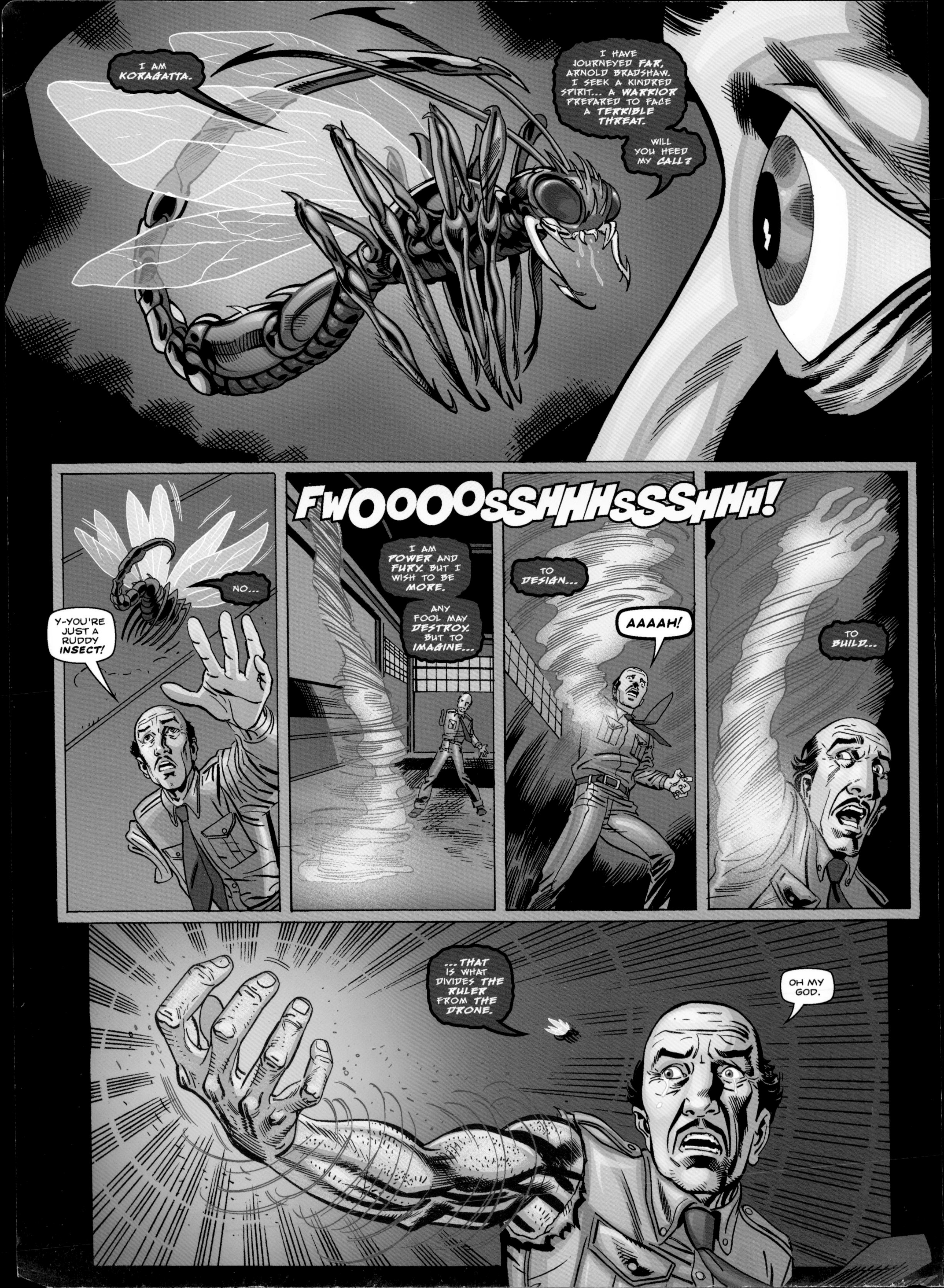
I AM KORAGATTA.
I HAVE JOURNEYED FAR, ARNOLD BRADSHAW. I SEEK A KINDRED SPIRIT... A WARRIOR PREPARED TO FACE A TERRIBLE THREAT.
WILL YOU HEED MY CALL?
Y-YOU'RE JUST A RUDDY INSECT!
NO...
FWOOOOSSHHHSSSHHH!
I AM POWER AND FURY. BUT I WISH TO BE MORE.
ANY FOOL MAY DESTROY. BUT TO IMAGINE...
TO DESIGN...
AAAAH!
TO BUILD...
...THAT IS WHAT DIVIDES THE RULER FROM THE DRONE.
OH MY GOD.

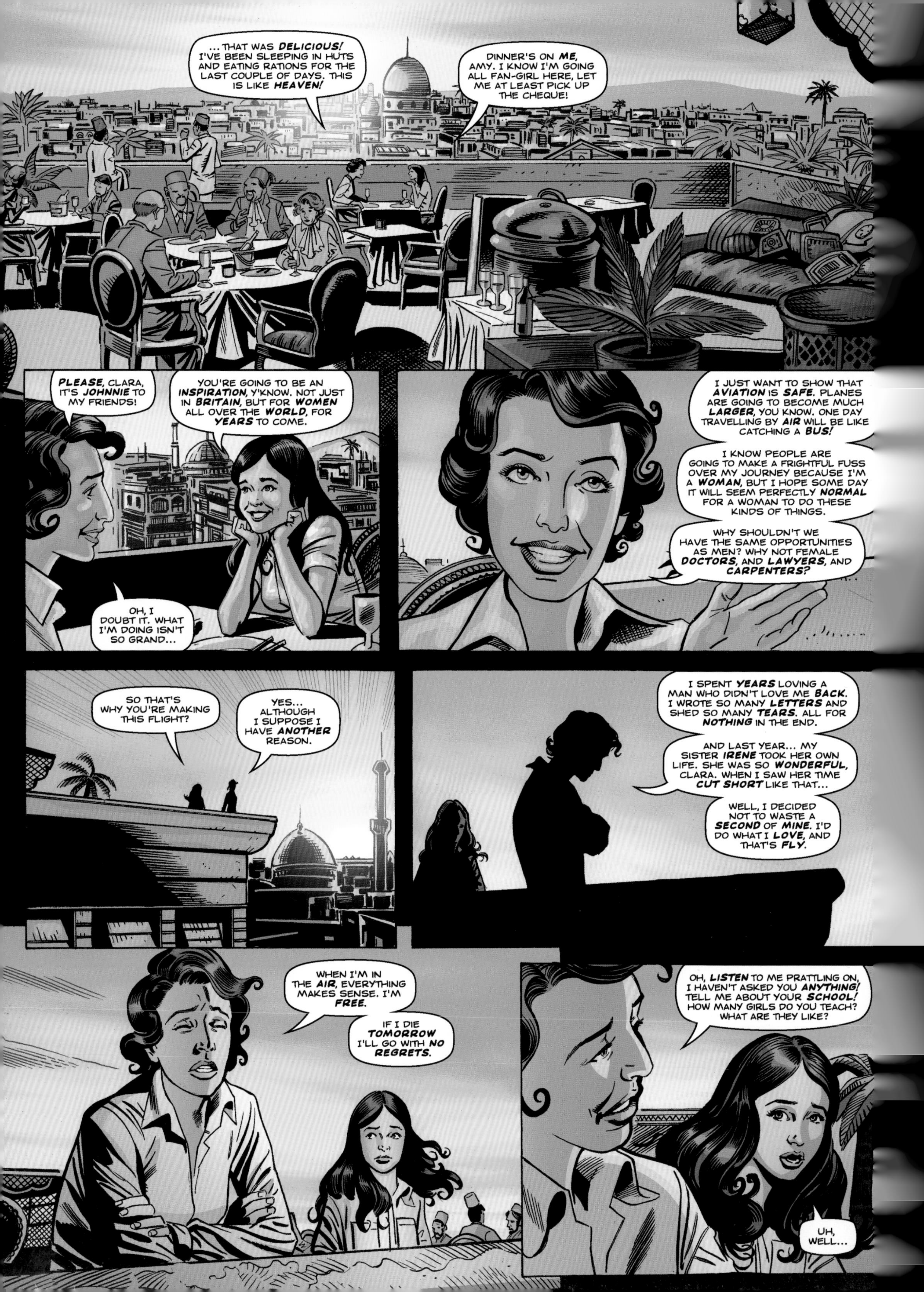
...THAT WAS DELICIOUS! I'VE BEEN SLEEPING IN HUTS AND EATING RATIONS FOR THE LAST COUPLE OF DAYS. THIS IS LIKE HEAVEN!
DINNER'S ON ME, AMY. I KNOW I'M GOING ALL FAN-GIRL HERE, LET ME AT LEAST PICK UP THE CHEQUE!
PLEASE, CLARA, IT'S JOHNNIE TO MY FRIENDS!
YOU'RE GOING TO BE AN INSPIRATION, Y'KNOW. NOT JUST IN BRITAIN, BUT FOR WOMEN ALL OVER THE WORLD, FOR YEARS TO COME.
OH, I DOUBT IT. WHAT I'M DOING ISN'T SO GRAND...
I JUST WANT TO SHOW THAT AVIATION IS SAFE. PLANES ARE GOING TO BECOME MUCH LARGER, YOU KNOW. ONE DAY TRAVELLING BY AIR WILL BE LIKE CATCHING A BUS!
I KNOW PEOPLE ARE GOING TO MAKE A FRIGHTFUL FUSS OVER MY JOURNEY BECAUSE I'M A WOMAN, BUT I HOPE SOME DAY IT WILL SEEM PERFECTLY NORMAL FOR A WOMAN TO DO THESE KINDS OF THINGS.
WHY SHOULDN'T WE HAVE THE SAME OPPORTUNITIES AS MEN? WHY NOT FEMALE DOCTORS, AND LAWYERS, AND CARPENTERS?
SO THAT'S WHY YOU'RE MAKING THIS FLIGHT?
YES... ALTHOUGH I SUPPOSE I HAVE ANOTHER REASON.
I SPENT YEARS LOVING A MAN WHO DIDN'T LOVE ME BACK. I WROTE SO MANY LETTERS AND SHED SO MANY TEARS. ALL FOR NOTHING IN THE END.
AND LAST YEAR... MY SISTER IRENE TOOK HER OWN LIFE. SHE WAS SO WONDERFUL, CLARA. WHEN I SAW HER TIME CUT SHORT LIKE THAT...
WELL, I DECIDED NOT TO WASTE A SECOND OF MINE. I'D DO WHAT I LOVE, AND THAT'S FLY.
WHEN I'M IN THE AIR, EVERYTHING MAKES SENSE. I'M FREE.
IF I DIE TOMORROW I'LL GO WITH NO REGRETS.
OH, LISTEN TO ME PRATTLING ON, I HAVEN'T ASKED YOU ANYTHING! TELL ME ABOUT YOUR SCHOOL! HOW MANY GIRLS DO YOU TEACH? WHAT ARE THEY LIKE?
UH, WELL...

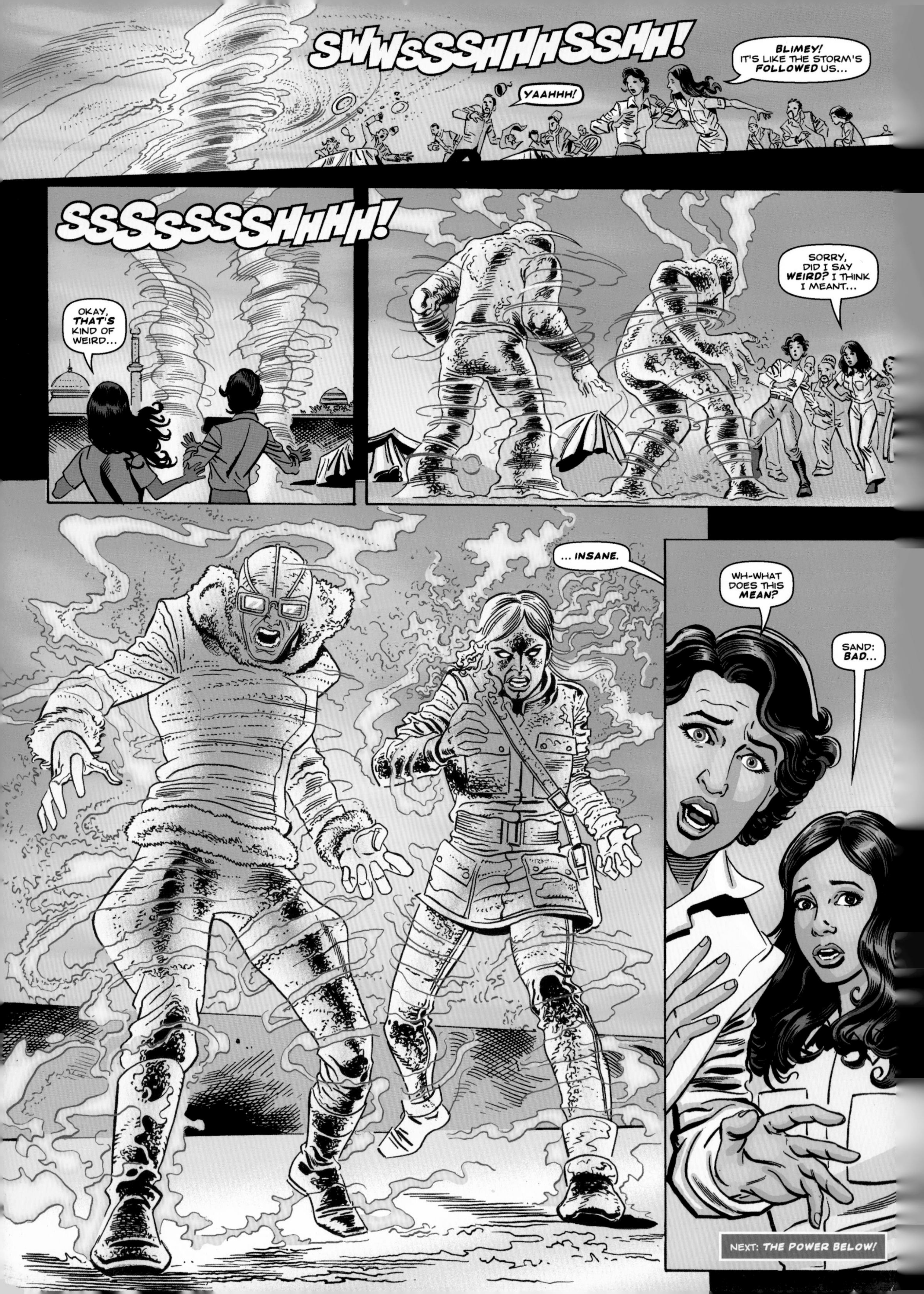
SWWSSSHHHSSHH!
YAAHHH!
BLIMEY! IT'S LIKE THE STORM'S FOLLOWED US...
SSSSSSSSHHHH!
OKAY, THAT'S KIND OF WEIRD...
SORRY, DID I SAY WEIRD? I THINK I MEANT...
... INSANE.
WH-WHAT DOES THIS MEAN?
SAND: BAD...
NEXT: THE POWER BELOW!

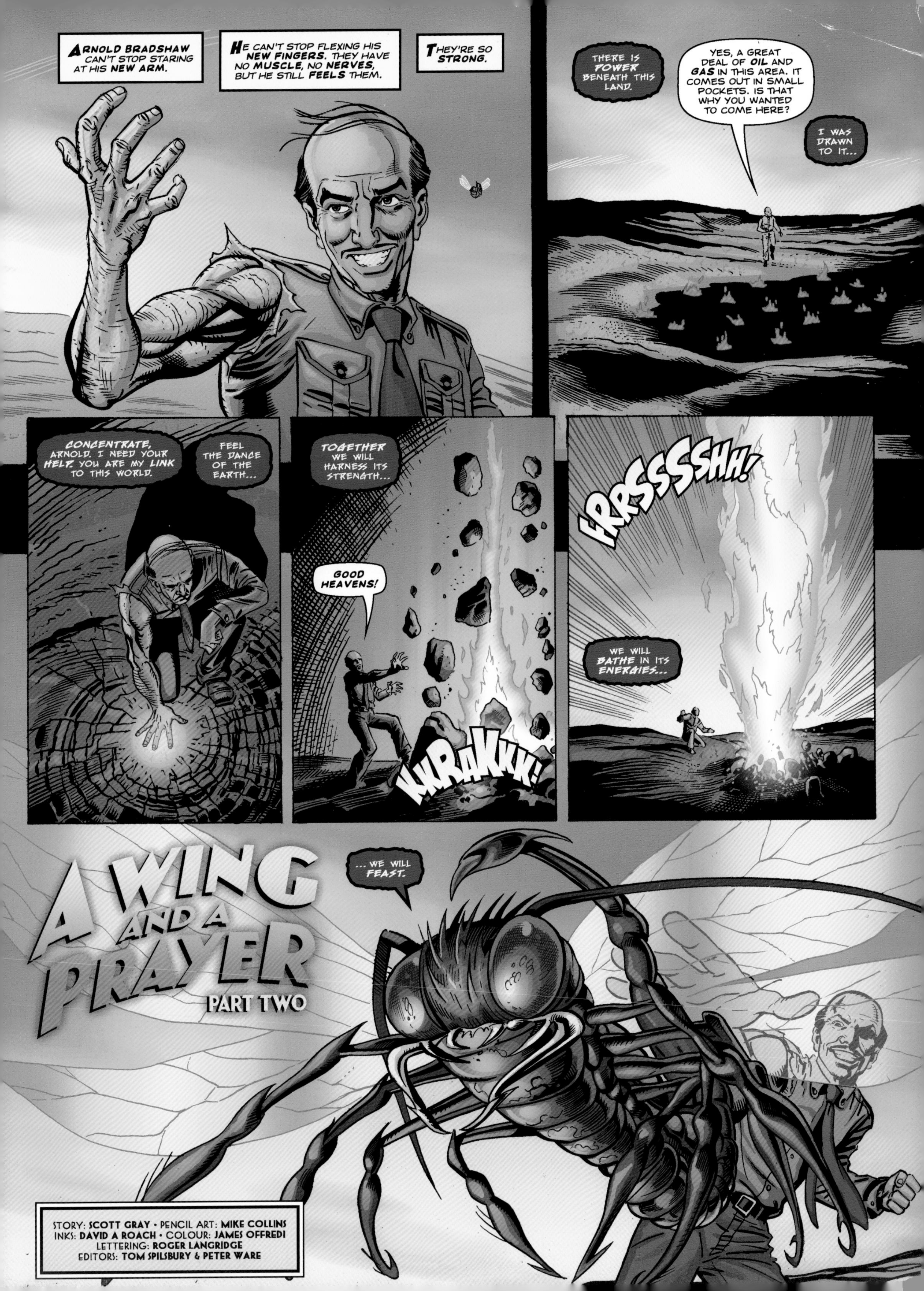
ARNOLD BRADSHAW CAN'T STOP STARING AT HIS NEW ARM.
HE CAN'T STOP FLEXING HIS NEW FINGERS. THEY HAVE NO MUSCLE, NO NERVES, BUT HE STILL FEELS THEM.
THEY'RE SO STRONG.
THERE IS POWER BENEATH THIS LAND.
YES, A GREAT DEAL OF OIL AND GAS IN THIS AREA. IT COMES OUT IN SMALL POCKETS. IS THAT WHY YOU WANTED TO COME HERE?
I WAS DRAWN TO IT...
CONCENTRATE, ARNOLD. I NEED YOUR HELP. YOU ARE MY LINK TO THIS WORLD.
FEEL THE DANCE OF THE EARTH...
TOGETHER WE WILL HARNESS ITS STRENGTH...
GOOD HEAVENS!
KKRAKKK!
FRRSSSSHH!
WE WILL BATHE IN ITS ENERGIES...
...WE WILL FEAST.
A WING AND A PRAYER
PART TWO
STORY: SCOTT GRAY • PENCIL ART: MIKE COLLINS
INKS: DAVID A ROACH • COLOUR: JAMES OFFREDI
LETTERING: ROGER LANGRIDGE
EDITORS: TOM SPILSBURY & PETER WARE

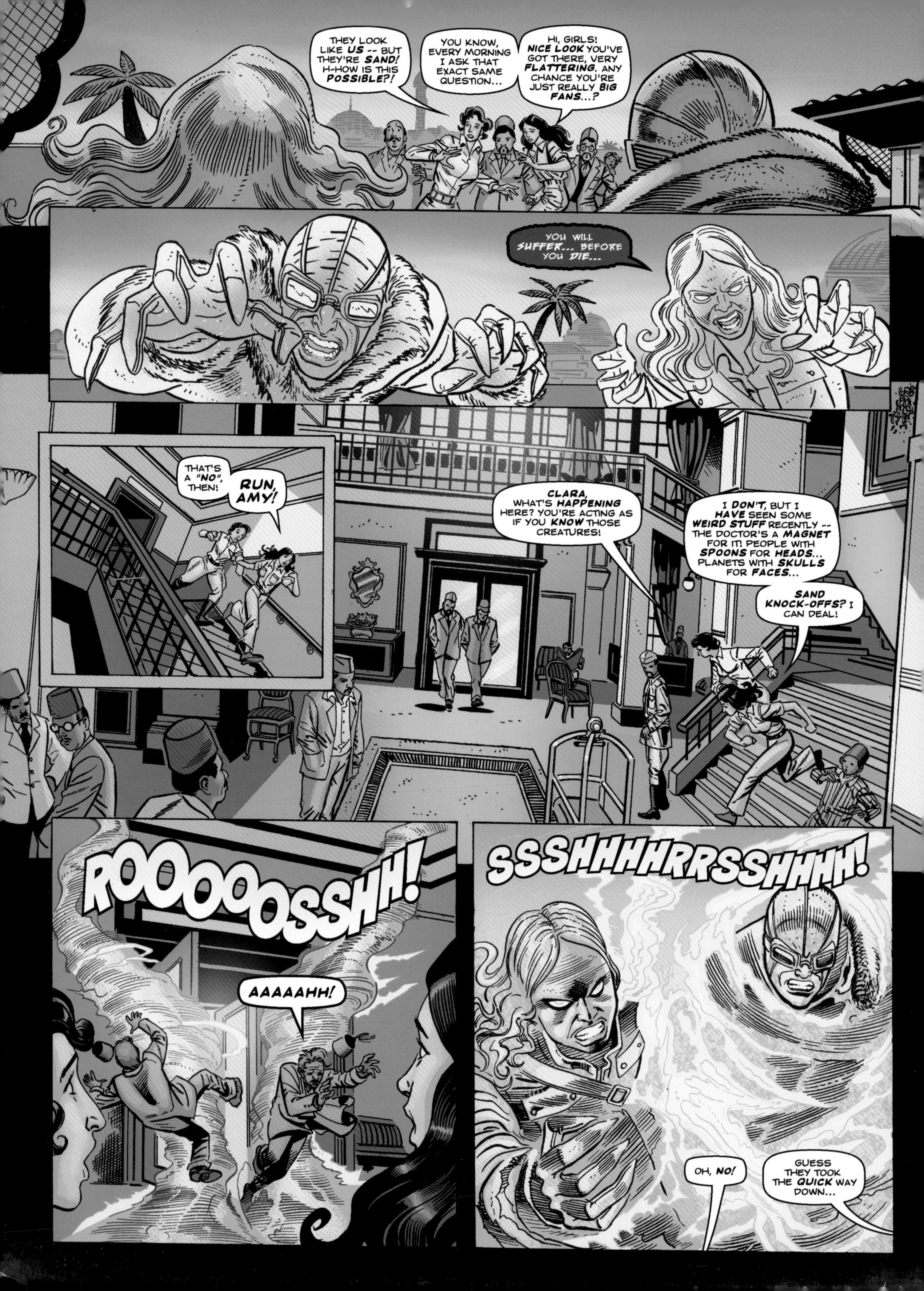

THEY LOOK LIKE US -- BUT THEY'RE SAND! H-HOW IS THIS POSSIBLE?!
YOU KNOW, EVERY MORNING I ASK THAT EXACT SAME QUESTION...
HI, GIRLS! NICE LOOK YOU'VE GOT THERE, VERY FLATTERING. ANY CHANCE YOU'RE JUST REALLY BIG FANS...?
YOU WILL SUFFER... BEFORE YOU DIE...
THAT'S A "NO", THEN!
RUN, AMY!
CLARA, WHAT'S HAPPENING HERE? YOU'RE ACTING AS IF YOU KNOW THOSE CREATURES!
I DON'T, BUT I HAVE SEEN SOME WEIRD STUFF RECENTLY -- THE DOCTOR'S A MAGNET FOR IT! PEOPLE WITH SPOONS FOR HEADS... PLANETS WITH SKULLS FOR FACES...
SAND KNOCK-OFFS? I CAN DEAL!
ROOOOOOSSHH!
AAAAAHH!
SSSHHHHHRRSSHHHH!
OH, NO!
GUESS THEY TOOK THE QUICK WAY DOWN...

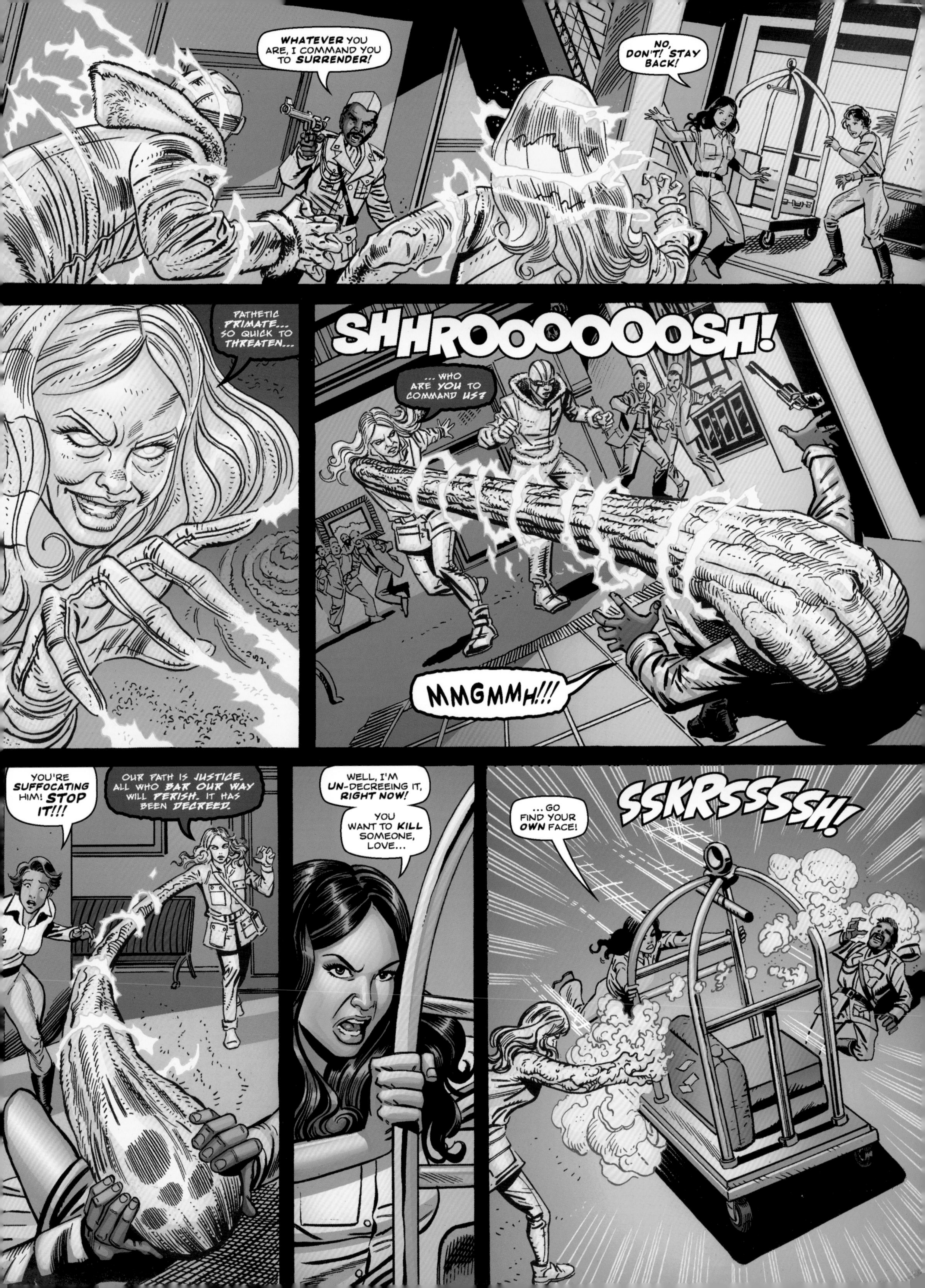

WHATEVER YOU ARE, I COMMAND YOU TO SURRENDER!
NO, DON'T! STAY BACK!
PATHETIC PRIMATE... SO QUICK TO THREATEN...
SHHROOOOOOOSH!
... WHO ARE YOU TO COMMAND US?
MMGMMH!!!
YOU'RE SUFFOCATING HIM! STOP IT!!!
OUR PATH IS JUSTICE. ALL WHO BAR OUR WAY WILL PERISH. IT HAS BEEN DECREED.
WELL, I'M UN-DECREEING IT, RIGHT NOW!
YOU WANT TO KILL SOMEONE, LOVE...
SSKRSSSSH!
... GO FIND YOUR OWN FACE!

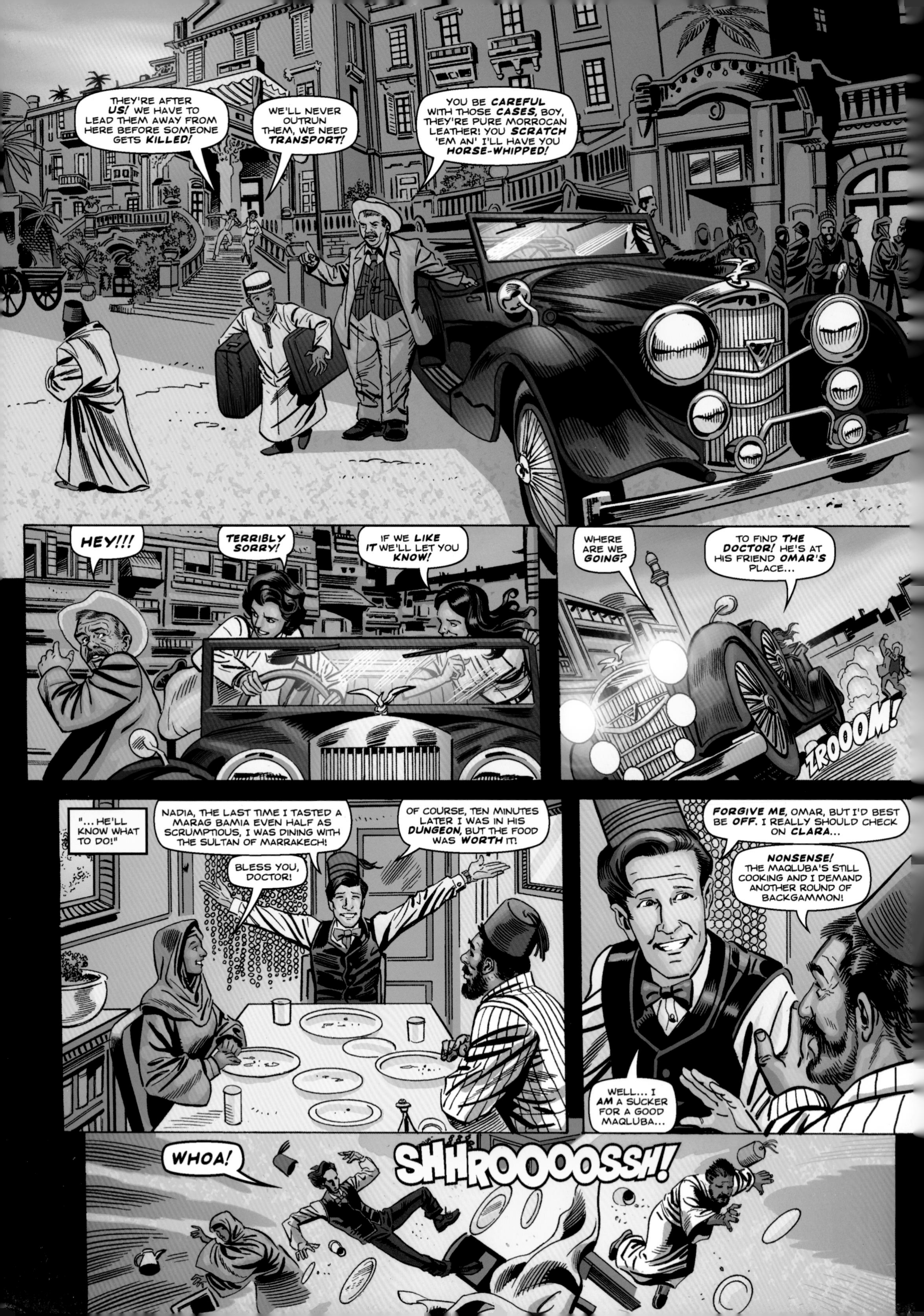
THEY'RE AFTER US! WE HAVE TO LEAD THEM AWAY FROM HERE BEFORE SOMEONE GETS KILLED!
WE'LL NEVER OUTRUN THEM, WE NEED TRANSPORT!
YOU BE CAREFUL WITH THOSE CASES, BOY, THEY'RE PURE MORROCAN LEATHER! YOU SCRATCH 'EM AN' I'LL HAVE YOU HORSE-WHIPPED!
HEY!!!
TERRIBLY SORRY!
IF WE LIKE IT WE'LL LET YOU KNOW!
WHERE ARE WE GOING?
TO FIND THE DOCTOR! HE'S AT HIS FRIEND OMAR'S PLACE...
ZROOOM!
"...HE'LL KNOW WHAT TO DO!"
NADIA, THE LAST TIME I TASTED A MARAG BAMIA EVEN HALF AS SCRUMPTIOUS, I WAS DINING WITH THE SULTAN OF MARRAKECH!
OF COURSE, TEN MINUTES LATER I WAS IN HIS DUNGEON, BUT THE FOOD WAS WORTH IT!
BLESS YOU, DOCTOR!
FORGIVE ME, OMAR, BUT I'D BEST BE OFF. I REALLY SHOULD CHECK ON CLARA...
NONSENSE! THE MAQLUBA'S STILL COOKING AND I DEMAND ANOTHER ROUND OF BACKGAMMON!
WELL... I AM A SUCKER FOR A GOOD MAQLUBA...
WHOA!
SHHROOOOOSSH!

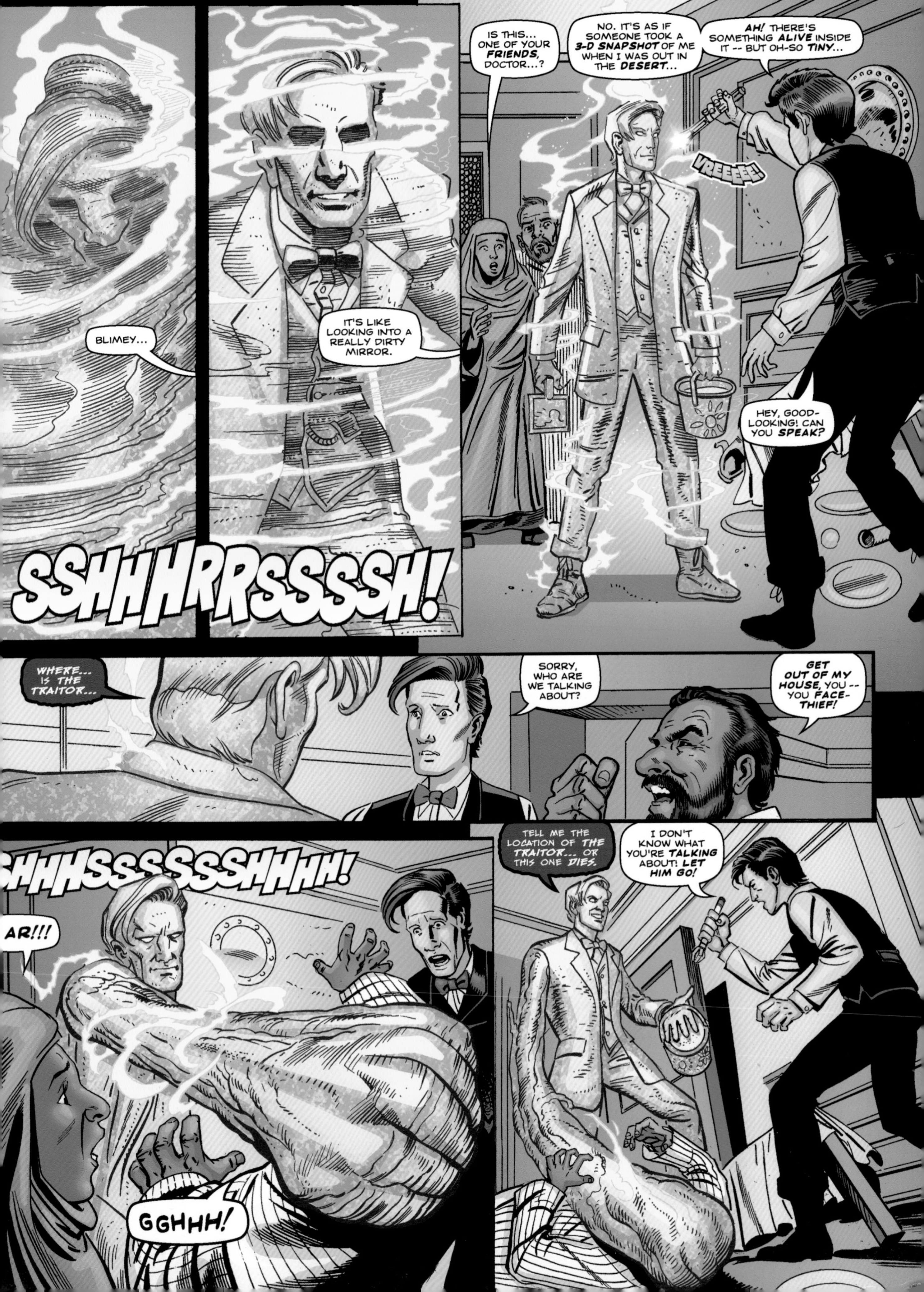
BLIMEY...
IT'S LIKE LOOKING INTO A REALLY DIRTY MIRROR.
SSHHHRRSSSSSH!
IS THIS... ONE OF YOUR FRIENDS, DOCTOR...?
NO. IT'S AS IF SOMEONE TOOK A 3-D SNAPSHOT OF ME WHEN I WAS OUT IN THE DESERT...
AH! THERE'S SOMETHING ALIVE INSIDE IT -- BUT OH-SO TINY...
VREEEEE!
HEY, GOOD-LOOKING! CAN YOU SPEAK?
WHERE... IS THE TRAITOR...
SORRY, WHO ARE WE TALKING ABOUT?
GET OUT OF MY HOUSE, YOU -- YOU FACE-THIEF!
SHHHSSSSSSHHHH!
AR!!!
GGHHH!
TELL ME THE LOCATION OF THE TRAITOR... OR THIS ONE DIES.
I DON'T KNOW WHAT YOU'RE TALKING ABOUT! LET HIM GO!

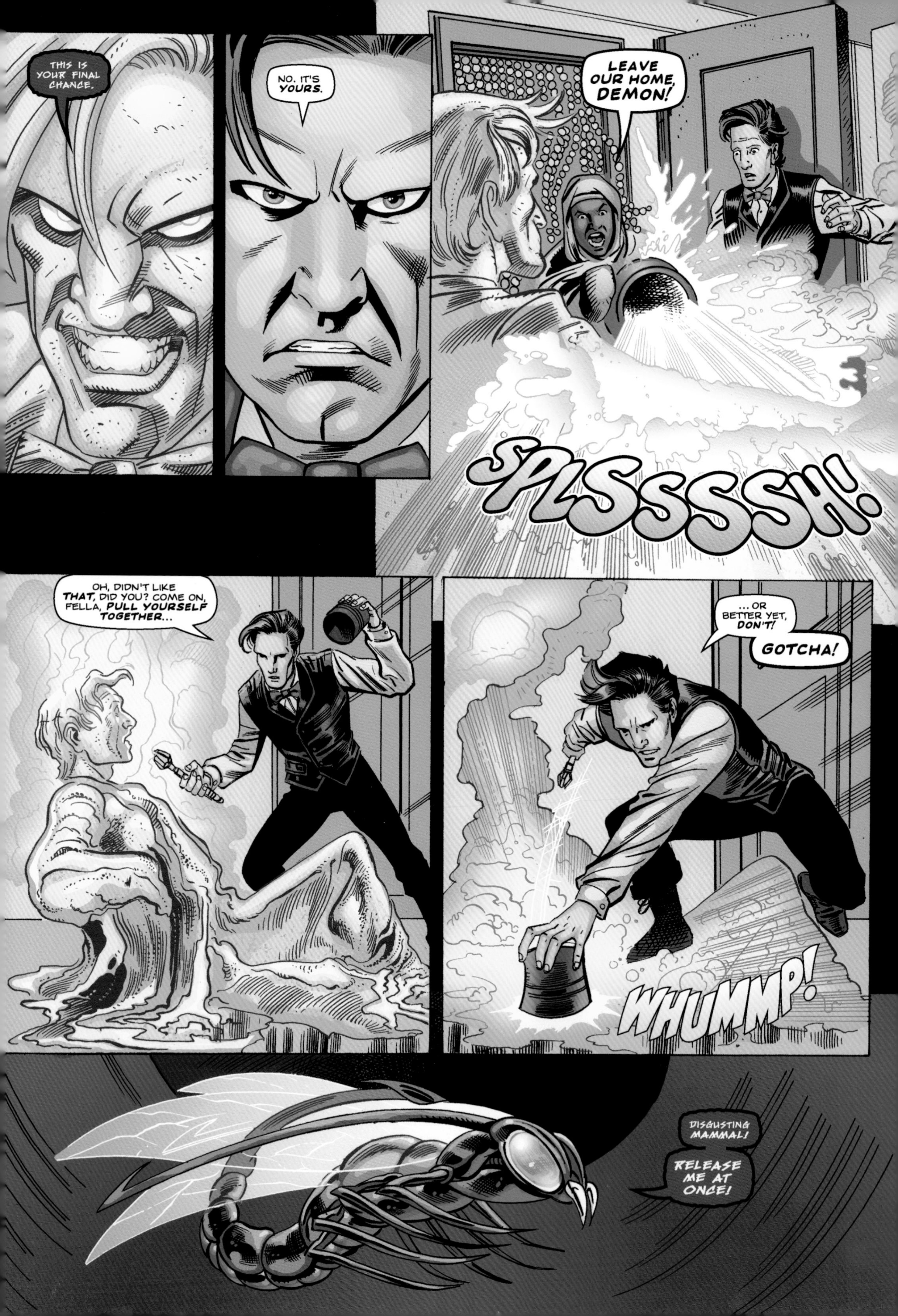
THIS IS YOUR FINAL CHANCE.
NO. IT'S YOURS.
LEAVE OUR HOME, DEMON!
SPLSSSSH!
OH, DIDN'T LIKE THAT, DID YOU? COME ON, FELLA, PULL YOURSELF TOGETHER...
...OR BETTER YET, DON'T!
GOTCHA!
WHUMMP!
DISGUSTING MAMMAL!
RELEASE ME AT ONCE!

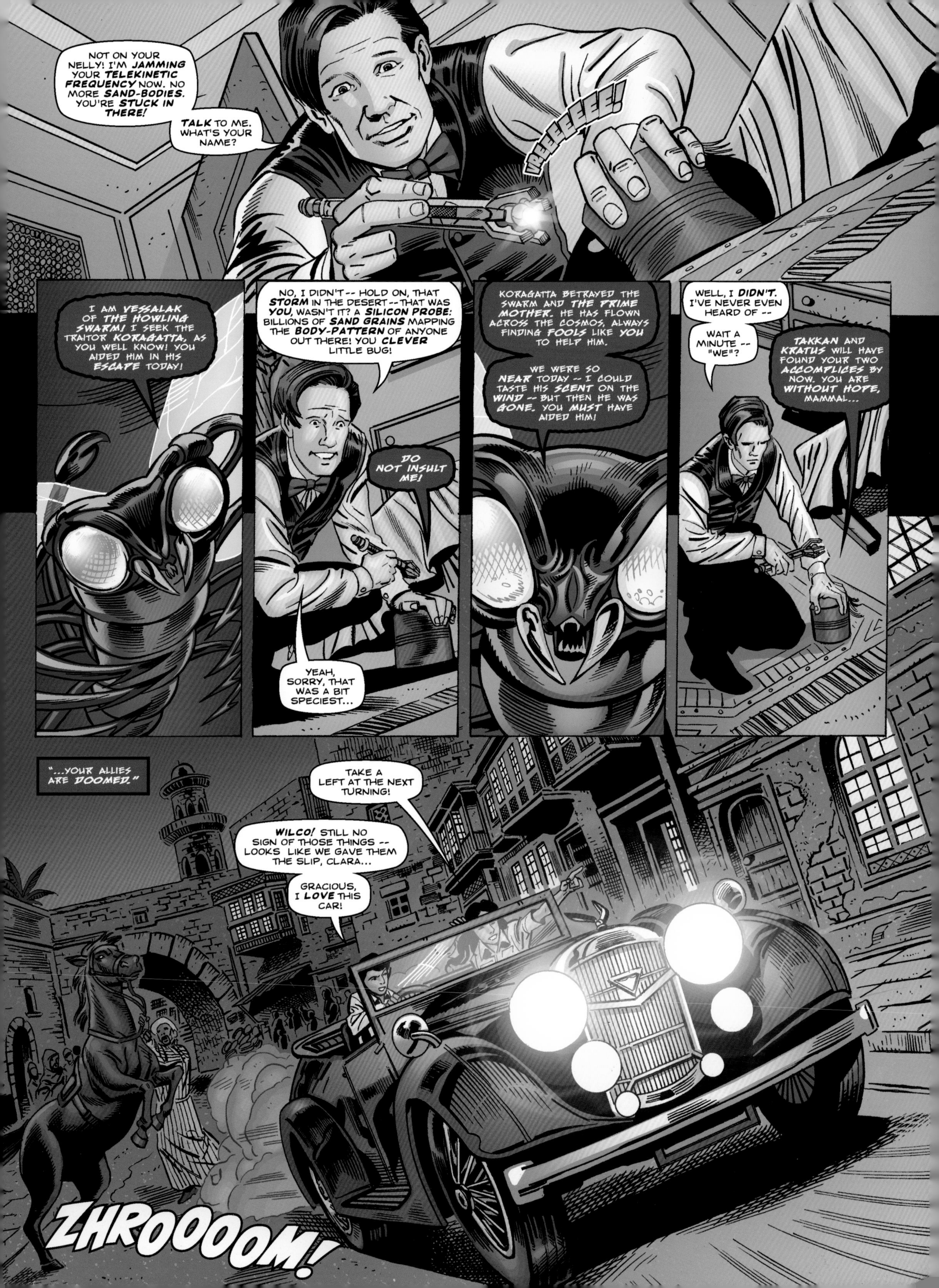
NOT ON YOUR NELLY! I'M JAMMING YOUR TELEKINETIC FREQUENCY NOW. NO MORE SAND-BODIES. YOU'RE STUCK IN THERE!
TALK TO ME. WHAT'S YOUR NAME?
VREEEEEE!
I AM YESSALAK OF THE HOWLING SWARM! I SEEK THE TRAITOR KORAGATTA, AS YOU WELL KNOW! YOU AIDED HIM IN HIS ESCAPE TODAY!
NO, I DIDN'T -- HOLD ON, THAT STORM IN THE DESERT -- THAT WAS YOU, WASN'T IT? A SILICON PROBE: BILLIONS OF SAND GRAINS MAPPING THE BODY-PATTERN OF ANYONE OUT THERE! YOU CLEVER LITTLE BUG!
DO NOT INSULT ME!
YEAH, SORRY, THAT WAS A BIT SPECIEST...
KORAGATTA BETRAYED THE SWARM AND THE PRIME MOTHER. HE HAS FLOWN ACROSS THE COSMOS, ALWAYS FINDING FOOLS LIKE YOU TO HELP HIM.
WE WERE SO NEAR TODAY -- I COULD TASTE HIS SCENT ON THE WIND -- BUT THEN HE WAS GONE. YOU MUST HAVE AIDED HIM!
WELL, I DIDN'T. I'VE NEVER EVEN HEARD OF --
WAIT A MINUTE -- "WE"?
TAKKAN AND KRATUS WILL HAVE FOUND YOUR TWO ACCOMPLICES BY NOW. YOU ARE WITHOUT HOPE, MAMMAL...
"...YOUR ALLIES ARE DOOMED."
TAKE A LEFT AT THE NEXT TURNING!
WILCO! STILL NO SIGN OF THOSE THINGS -- LOOKS LIKE WE GAVE THEM THE SLIP, CLARA...
GRACIOUS, I LOVE THIS CAR!
ZHROOOOM!

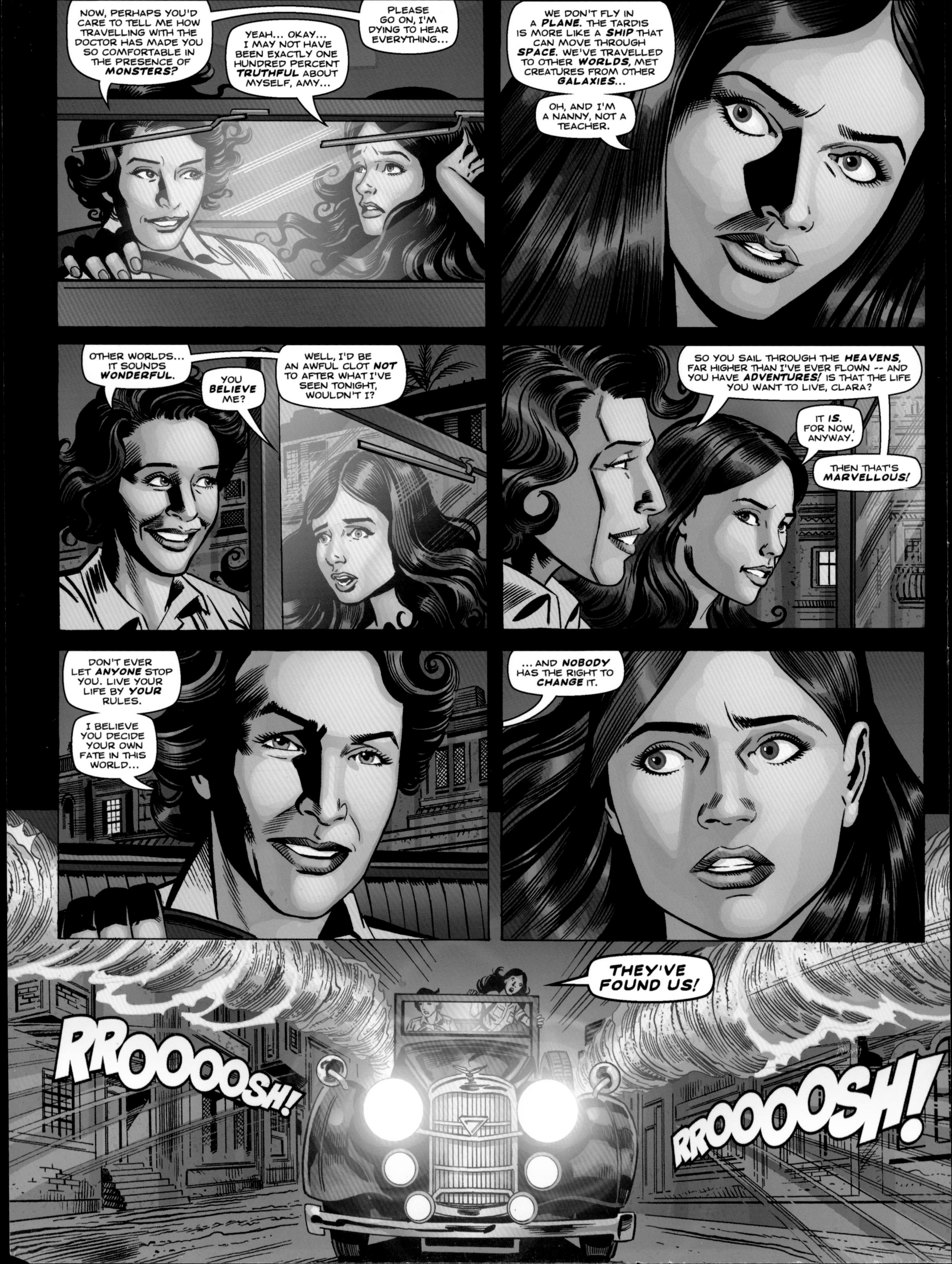

NOW, PERHAPS YOU'D CARE TO TELL ME HOW TRAVELLING WITH THE DOCTOR HAS MADE YOU SO COMFORTABLE IN THE PRESENCE OF MONSTERS?
PLEASE GO ON, I'M DYING TO HEAR EVERYTHING...
YEAH... OKAY... I MAY NOT HAVE BEEN EXACTLY ONE HUNDRED PERCENT TRUTHFUL ABOUT MYSELF, AMY...
WE DON'T FLY IN A PLANE. THE TARDIS IS MORE LIKE A SHIP THAT CAN MOVE THROUGH SPACE. WE'VE TRAVELLED TO OTHER WORLDS, MET CREATURES FROM OTHER GALAXIES...
OH, AND I'M A NANNY, NOT A TEACHER.
OTHER WORLDS... IT SOUNDS WONDERFUL.
YOU BELIEVE ME?
WELL, I'D BE AN AWFUL CLOT NOT TO AFTER WHAT I'VE SEEN TONIGHT, WOULDN'T I?
SO YOU SAIL THROUGH THE HEAVENS, FAR HIGHER THAN I'VE EVER FLOWN -- AND YOU HAVE ADVENTURES! IS THAT THE LIFE YOU WANT TO LIVE, CLARA?
IT IS. FOR NOW, ANYWAY.
THEN THAT'S MARVELLOUS!
DON'T EVER LET ANYONE STOP YOU. LIVE YOUR LIFE BY YOUR RULES.
I BELIEVE YOU DECIDE YOUR OWN FATE IN THIS WORLD...
... AND NOBODY HAS THE RIGHT TO CHANGE IT.
THEY'VE FOUND US!
RROOOOSH!
RROOOOSH!

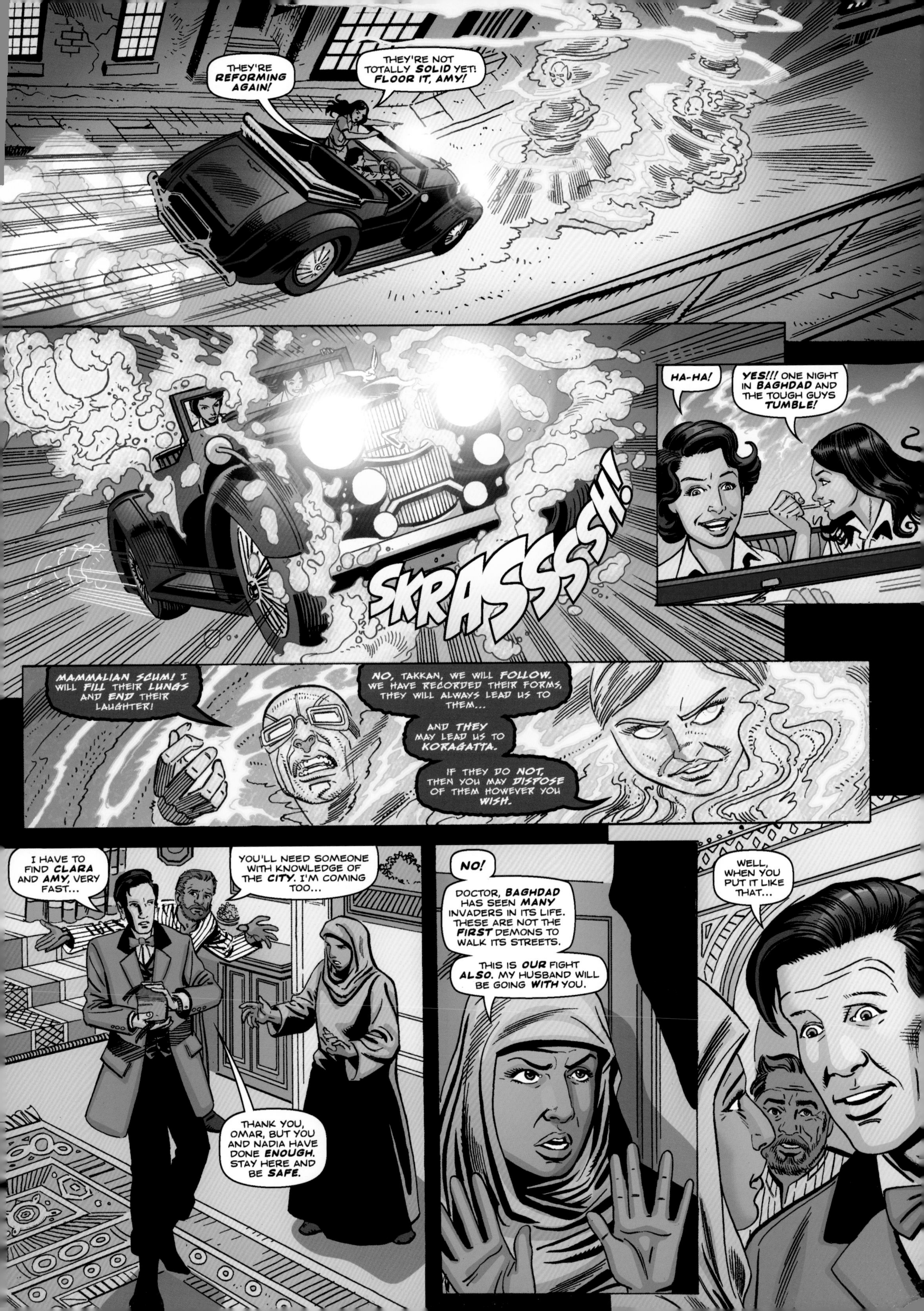

THEY'RE REFORMING AGAIN!
THEY'RE NOT TOTALLY SOLID YET! FLOOR IT, AMY!
SKRASSSSSH!
HA-HA!
YES!!! ONE NIGHT IN BAGHDAD AND THE TOUGH GUYS TUMBLE!
MAMMALIAN SCUM! I WILL FILL THEIR LUNGS AND END THEIR LAUGHTER!
NO, TAKKAN, WE WILL FOLLOW. WE HAVE RECORDED THEIR FORMS, THEY WILL ALWAYS LEAD US TO THEM...
AND THEY MAY LEAD US TO KORAGATTA.
IF THEY DO NOT, THEN YOU MAY DISPOSE OF THEM HOWEVER YOU WISH.
I HAVE TO FIND CLARA AND AMY, VERY FAST...
YOU'LL NEED SOMEONE WITH KNOWLEDGE OF THE CITY. I'M COMING TOO...
THANK YOU, OMAR, BUT YOU AND NADIA HAVE DONE ENOUGH. STAY HERE AND BE SAFE.
NO!
DOCTOR, BAGHDAD HAS SEEN MANY INVADERS IN ITS LIFE. THESE ARE NOT THE FIRST DEMONS TO WALK ITS STREETS.
THIS IS OUR FIGHT ALSO. MY HUSBAND WILL BE GOING WITH YOU.
WELL, WHEN YOU PUT IT LIKE THAT...

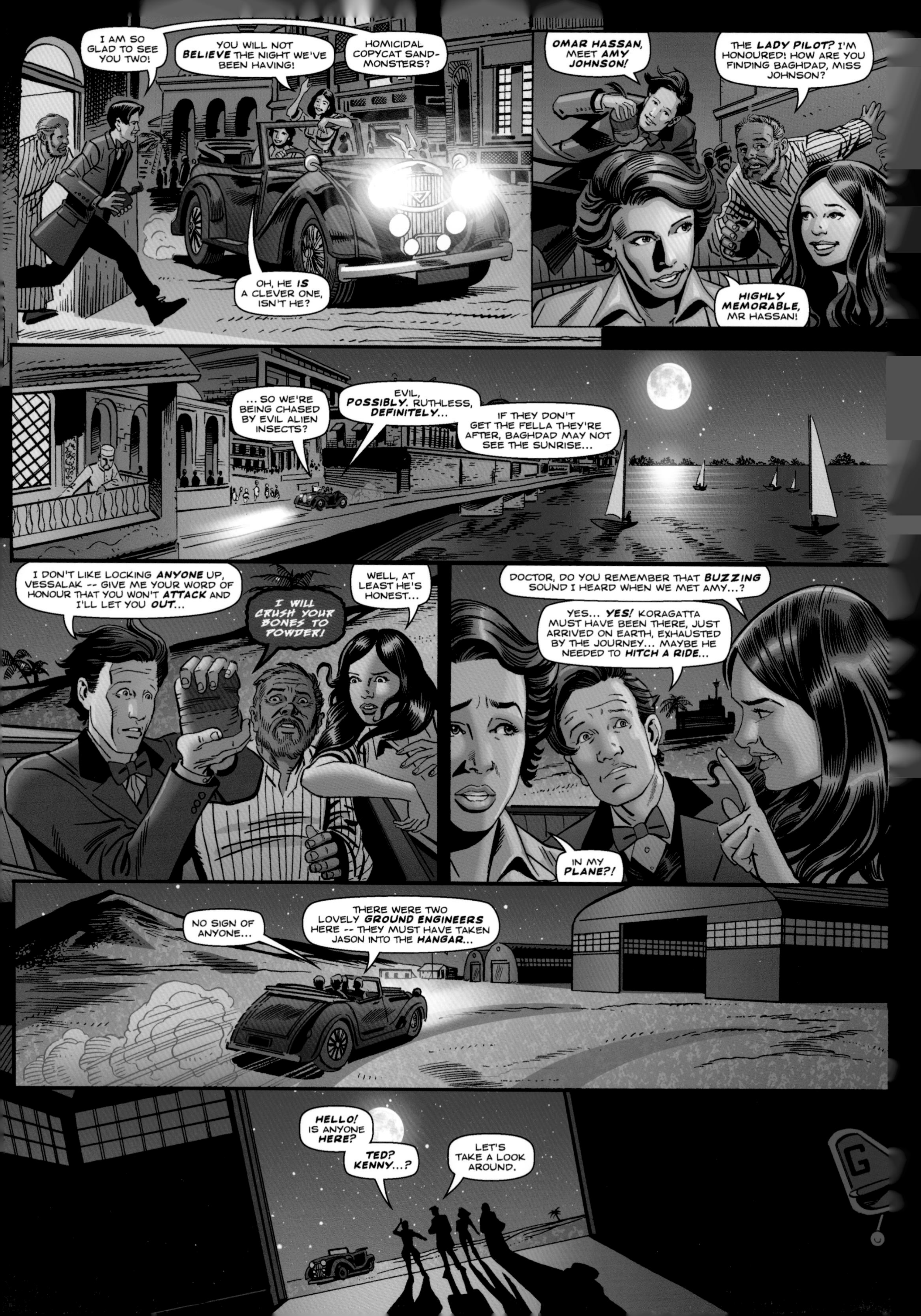

I AM SO GLAD TO SEE YOU TWO!
YOU WILL NOT BELIEVE THE NIGHT WE'VE BEEN HAVING!
HOMICIDAL COPYCAT SAND-MONSTERS?
OH, HE IS A CLEVER ONE, ISN'T HE?
OMAR HASSAN, MEET AMY JOHNSON!
THE LADY PILOT? I'M HONOURED! HOW ARE YOU FINDING BAGHDAD, MISS JOHNSON?
HIGHLY MEMORABLE, MR HASSAN!
... SO WE'RE BEING CHASED BY EVIL ALIEN INSECTS?
EVIL, POSSIBLY. RUTHLESS, DEFINITELY...
IF THEY DON'T GET THE FELLA THEY'RE AFTER, BAGHDAD MAY NOT SEE THE SUNRISE...
I DON'T LIKE LOCKING ANYONE UP, VESSALAK -- GIVE ME YOUR WORD OF HONOUR THAT YOU WON'T ATTACK AND I'LL LET YOU OUT...
I WILL CRUSH YOUR BONES TO POWDER!
WELL, AT LEAST HE'S HONEST...
DOCTOR, DO YOU REMEMBER THAT BUZZING SOUND I HEARD WHEN WE MET AMY...?
YES... YES! KORAGATTA MUST HAVE BEEN THERE, JUST ARRIVED ON EARTH, EXHAUSTED BY THE JOURNEY... MAYBE HE NEEDED TO HITCH A RIDE...
IN MY PLANE?!
NO SIGN OF ANYONE...
THERE WERE TWO LOVELY GROUND ENGINEERS HERE -- THEY MUST HAVE TAKEN JASON INTO THE HANGAR...
HELLO! IS ANYONE HERE?
TED? KENNY...?
LET'S TAKE A LOOK AROUND.

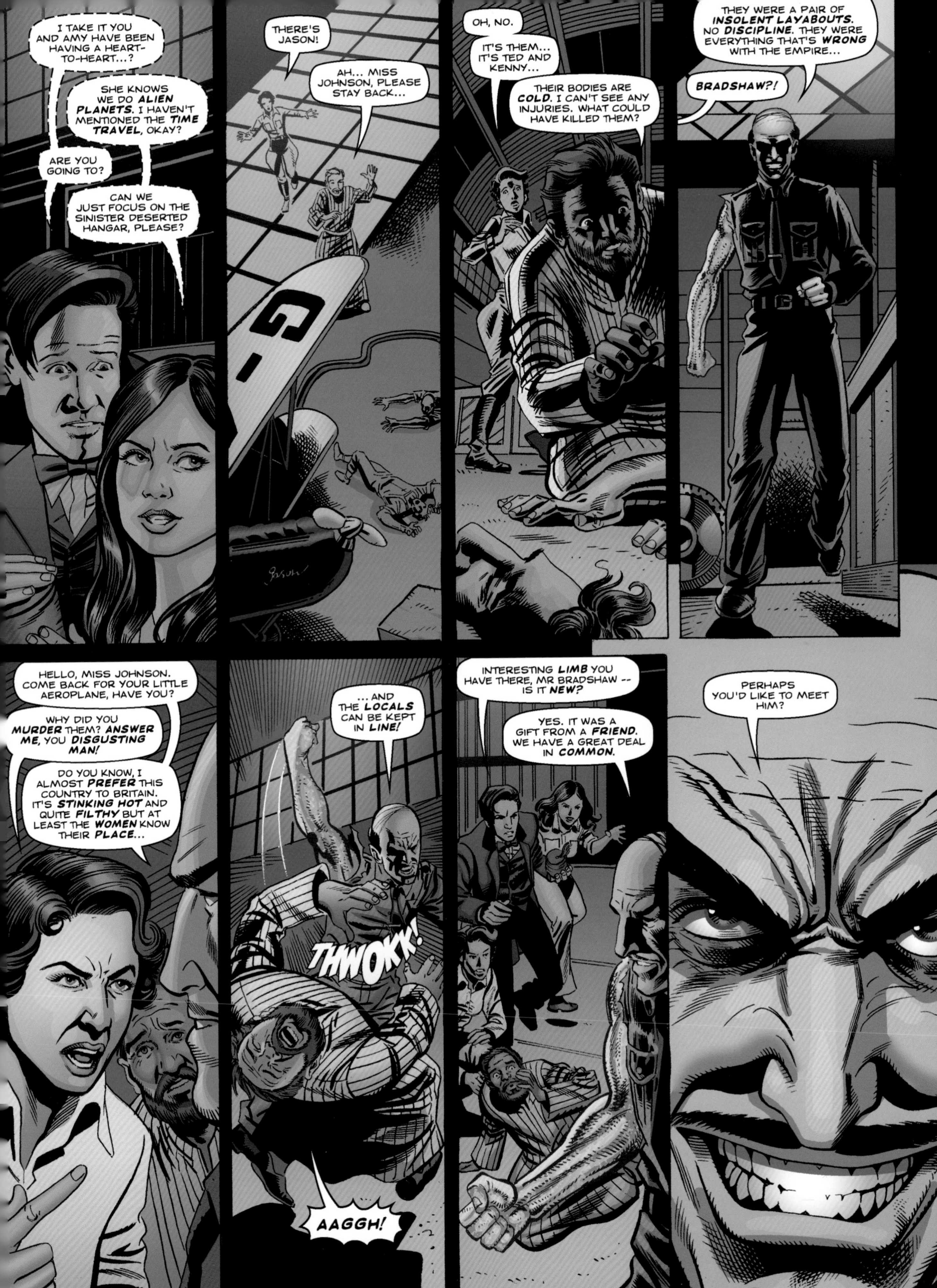
I TAKE IT YOU AND AMY HAVE BEEN HAVING A HEART-TO-HEART...?
SHE KNOWS WE DO ALIEN PLANETS. I HAVEN'T MENTIONED THE TIME TRAVEL, OKAY?
ARE YOU GOING TO?
CAN WE JUST FOCUS ON THE SINISTER DESERTED HANGAR, PLEASE?
THERE'S JASON!
AH... MISS JOHNSON, PLEASE STAY BACK...
OH, NO.
IT'S THEM... IT'S TED AND KENNY...
THEIR BODIES ARE COLD. I CAN'T SEE ANY INJURIES. WHAT COULD HAVE KILLED THEM?
THEY WERE A PAIR OF INSOLENT LAYABOUTS. NO DISCIPLINE. THEY WERE EVERYTHING THAT'S WRONG WITH THE EMPIRE...
BRADSHAW?!
HELLO, MISS JOHNSON. COME BACK FOR YOUR LITTLE AEROPLANE, HAVE YOU?
WHY DID YOU MURDER THEM? ANSWER ME, YOU DISGUSTING MAN!
DO YOU KNOW, I ALMOST PREFER THIS COUNTRY TO BRITAIN. IT'S STINKING HOT AND QUITE FILTHY BUT AT LEAST THE WOMEN KNOW THEIR PLACE...
... AND THE LOCALS CAN BE KEPT IN LINE!
THWOKK!
AAGGH!
INTERESTING LIMB YOU HAVE THERE, MR BRADSHAW -- IS IT NEW?
YES. IT WAS A GIFT FROM A FRIEND. WE HAVE A GREAT DEAL IN COMMON.
PERHAPS YOU'D LIKE TO MEET HIM?

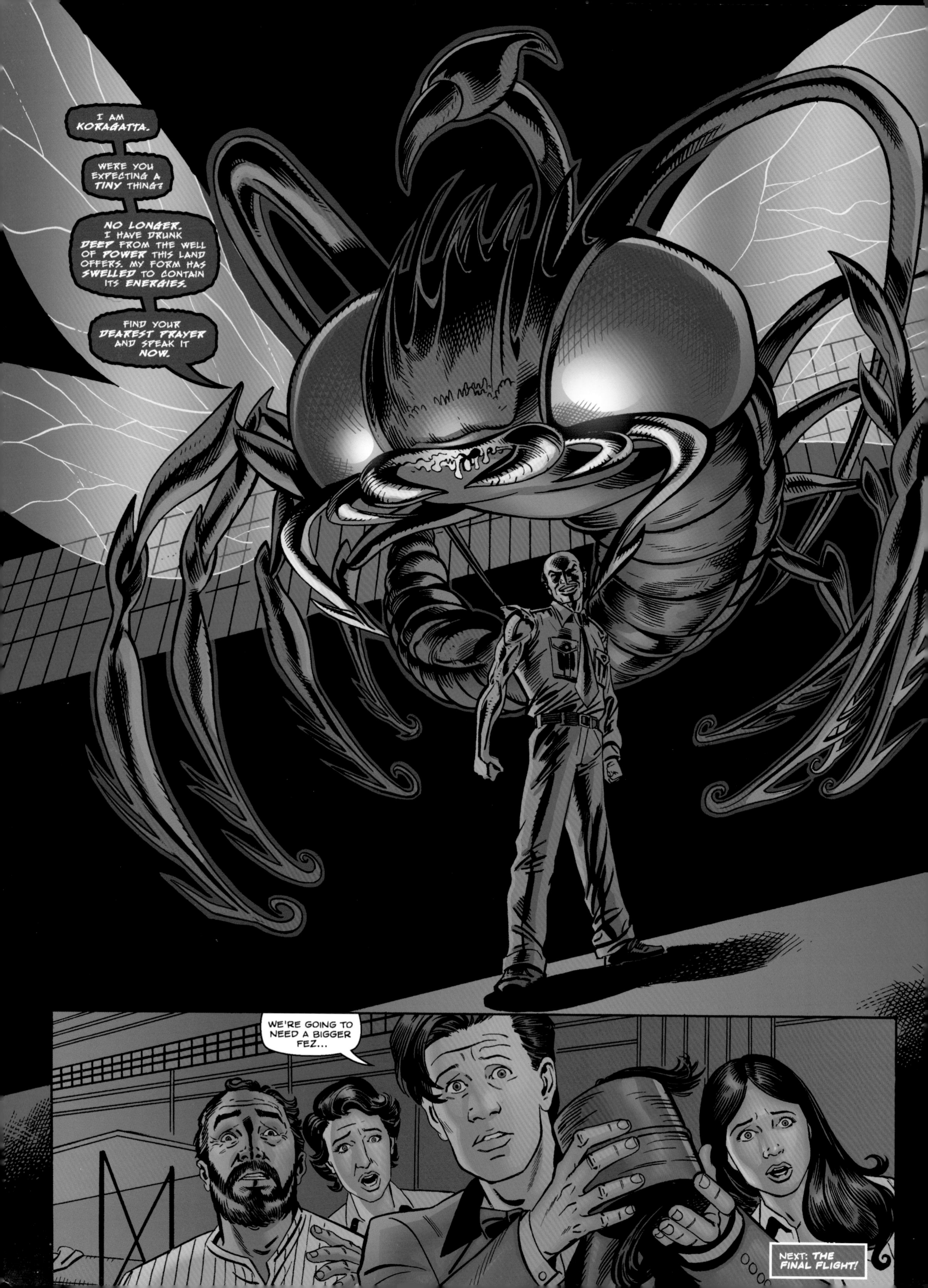
I AM KORAGATTA.
WERE YOU EXPECTING A TINY THING?
NO LONGER. I HAVE DRUNK DEEP FROM THE WELL OF POWER THIS LAND OFFERS. MY FORM HAS SWELLED TO CONTAIN ITS ENERGIES.
FIND YOUR DEAREST PRAYER AND SPEAK IT NOW.
WE'RE GOING TO NEED A BIGGER FEZ...
NEXT: THE FINAL FLIGHT!

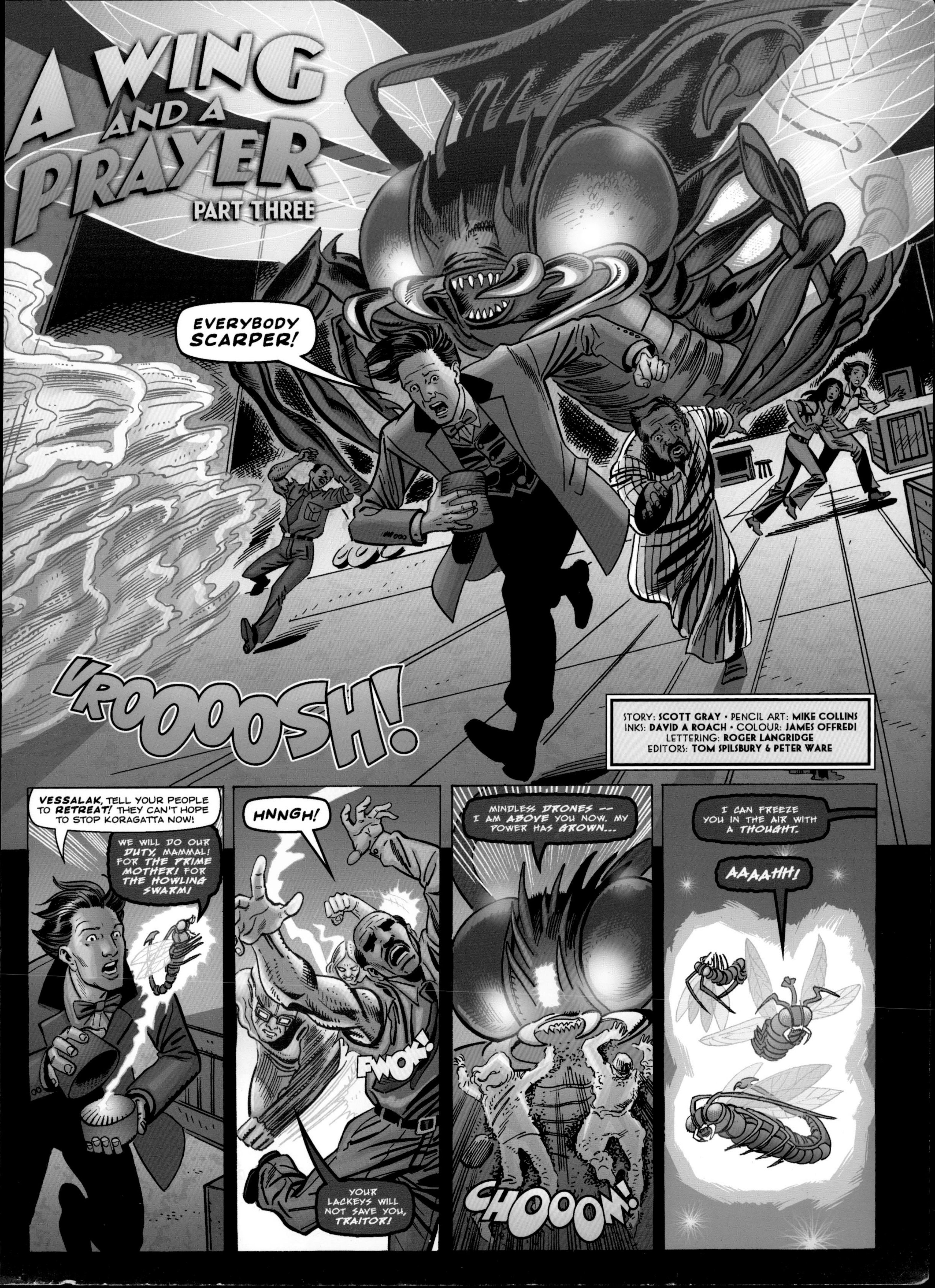

A WING AND A PRAYER
PART THREE
EVERYBODY SCARPER!
VROOOOOSH!
STORY: SCOTT GRAY • PENCIL ART: MIKE COLLINS
INKS: DAVID A ROACH • COLOUR: JAMES OFFREDI
LETTERING: ROGER LANGRIDGE
EDITORS: TOM SPILSBURY & PETER WARE
VESSALAK, TELL YOUR PEOPLE TO RETREAT! THEY CAN'T HOPE TO STOP KORAGATTA NOW!
WE WILL DO OUR DUTY, MAMMAL! FOR THE PRIME MOTHER! FOR THE HOWLING SWARM!
HNNGH!
FWOK!
YOUR LACKEYS WILL NOT SAVE YOU, TRAITOR!
MINDLESS DRONES -- I AM ABOVE YOU NOW. MY POWER HAS GROWN...
CHOOOM!
I CAN FREEZE YOU IN THE AIR WITH A THOUGHT.
AAAAHH!

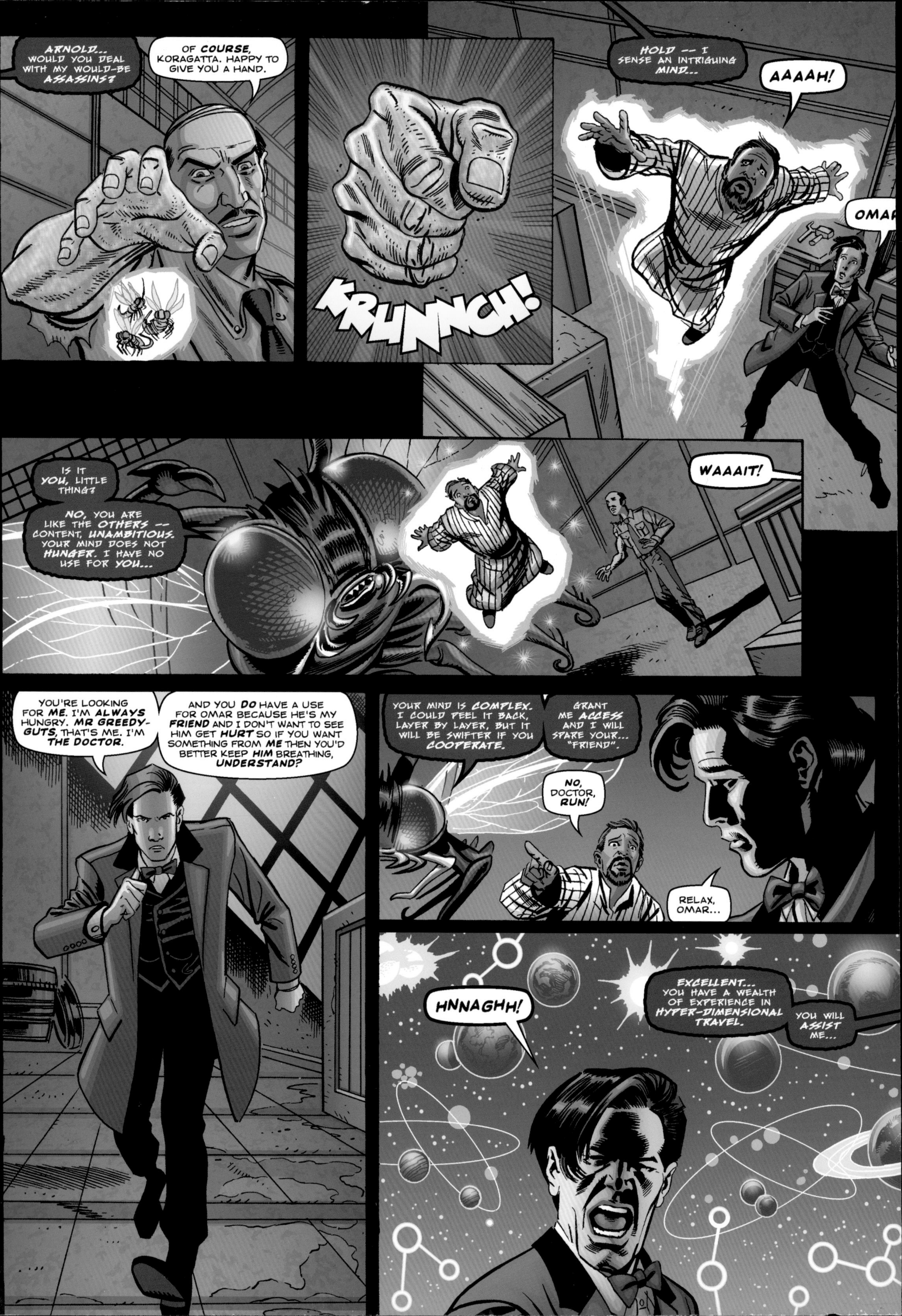
ARNOLD... WOULD YOU DEAL WITH MY WOULD-BE ASSASSINS?
OF COURSE, KORAGATTA. HAPPY TO GIVE YOU A HAND.
KRUNNCH!
HOLD -- I SENSE AN INTRIGUING MIND...
AAAAH!
WAAAIT!
IS IT YOU, LITTLE THING?
NO, YOU ARE LIKE THE OTHERS -- CONTENT, UNAMBITIOUS. YOUR MIND DOES NOT HUNGER. I HAVE NO USE FOR YOU...
YOU'RE LOOKING FOR ME. I'M ALWAYS HUNGRY. MR GREEDY-GUTS, THAT'S ME. I'M THE DOCTOR.
AND YOU DO HAVE A USE FOR OMAR BECAUSE HE'S MY FRIEND AND I DON'T WANT TO SEE HIM GET HURT SO IF YOU WANT SOMETHING FROM ME THEN YOU'D BETTER KEEP HIM BREATHING, UNDERSTAND?
YOUR MIND IS COMPLEX. I COULD PEEL IT BACK, LAYER BY LAYER, BUT IT WILL BE SWIFTER IF YOU COOPERATE.
GRANT ME ACCESS AND I WILL SPARE YOUR... "FRIEND".
NO, DOCTOR, RUN!
RELAX, OMAR...
HNNAGHH!
EXCELLENT... YOU HAVE A WEALTH OF EXPERIENCE IN HYPER-DIMENSIONAL TRAVEL.
YOU WILL ASSIST ME...

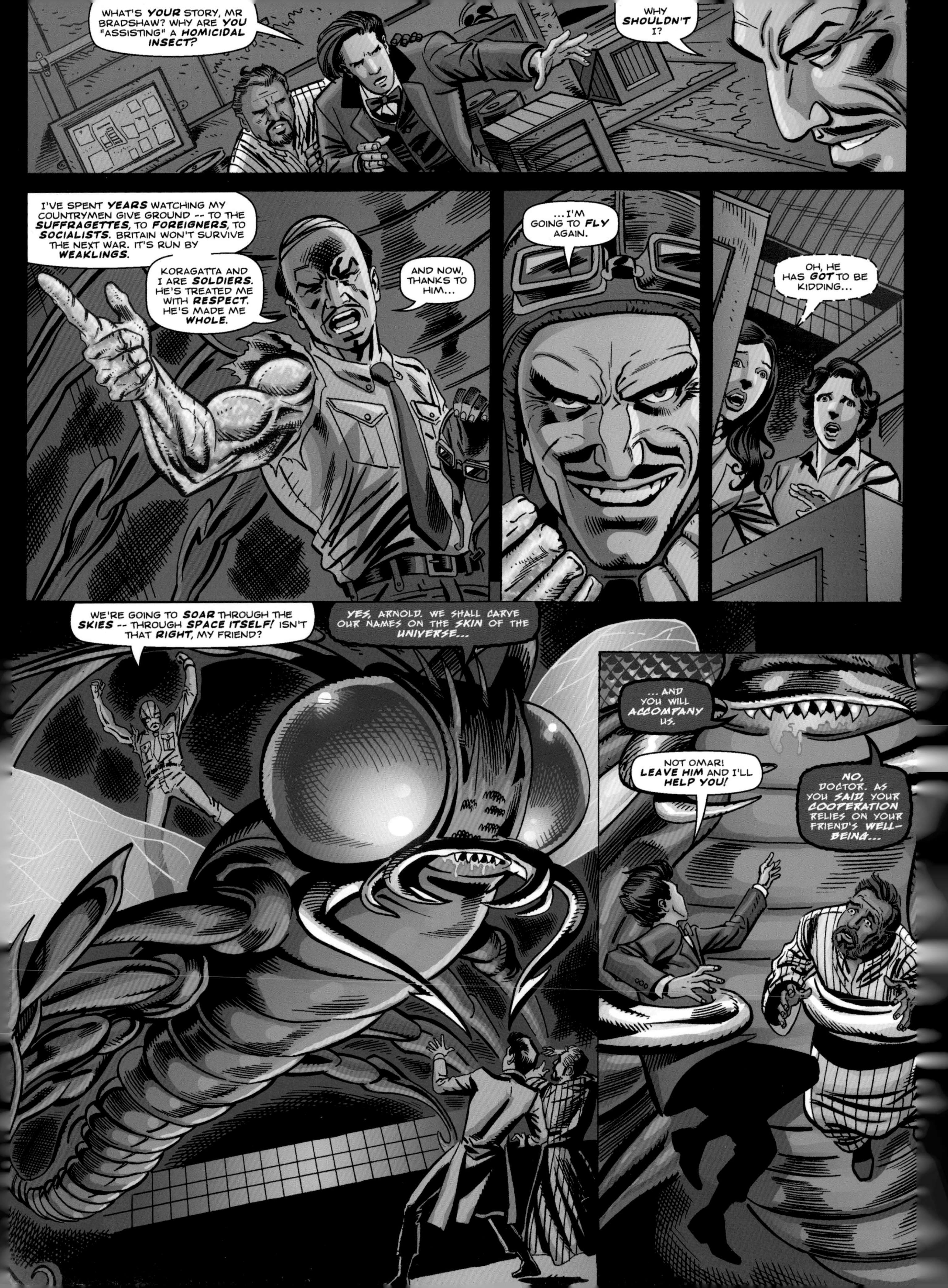

WHAT'S YOUR STORY, MR BRADSHAW? WHY ARE YOU "ASSISTING" A HOMICIDAL INSECT?
WHY SHOULDN'T I?
I'VE SPENT YEARS WATCHING MY COUNTRYMEN GIVE GROUND -- TO THE SUFFRAGETTES, TO FOREIGNERS, TO SOCIALISTS. BRITAIN WON'T SURVIVE THE NEXT WAR. IT'S RUN BY WEAKLINGS.
KORAGATTA AND I ARE SOLDIERS. HE'S TREATED ME WITH RESPECT. HE'S MADE ME WHOLE.
AND NOW, THANKS TO HIM...
...I'M GOING TO FLY AGAIN.
OH, HE HAS GOT TO BE KIDDING...
WE'RE GOING TO SOAR THROUGH THE SKIES -- THROUGH SPACE ITSELF! ISN'T THAT RIGHT, MY FRIEND?
YES, ARNOLD. WE SHALL CARVE OUR NAMES ON THE SKIN OF THE UNIVERSE...
...AND YOU WILL ACCOMPANY US.
NOT OMAR! LEAVE HIM AND I'LL HELP YOU!
NO, DOCTOR. AS YOU SAID, YOUR COOPERATION RELIES ON YOUR FRIEND'S WELL-BEING...

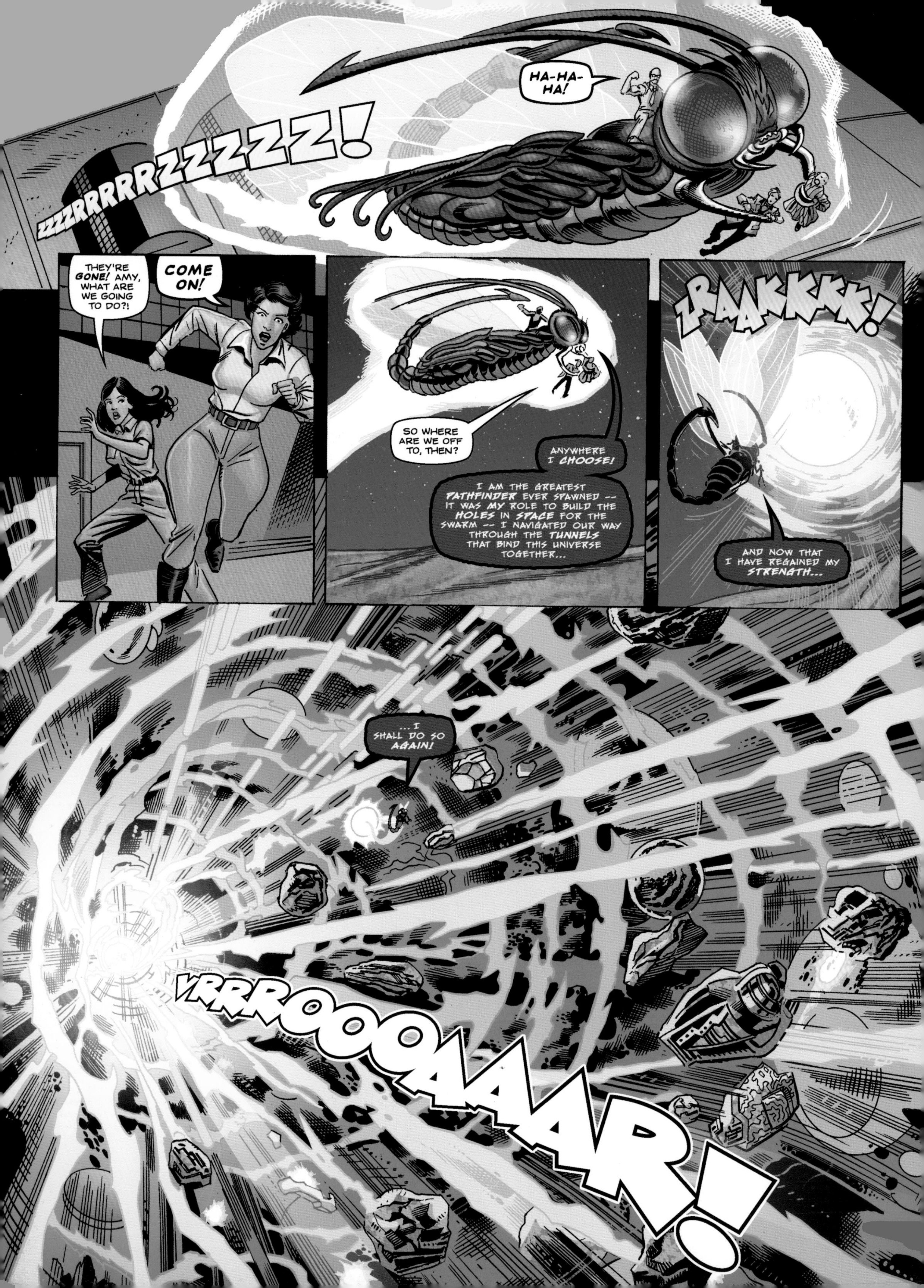

HA-HA-HA!
ZZZRRRRRZZZZZZ!
THEY'RE GONE! AMY, WHAT ARE WE GOING TO DO?!
COME ON!
SO WHERE ARE WE OFF TO, THEN?
ANYWHERE I CHOOSE!
I AM THE GREATEST PATHFINDER EVER SPAWNED -- IT WAS MY ROLE TO BUILD THE HOLES IN SPACE FOR THE SWARM -- I NAVIGATED OUR WAY THROUGH THE TUNNELS THAT BIND THIS UNIVERSE TOGETHER...
ZRAAKKKK!
AND NOW THAT I HAVE REGAINED MY STRENGTH...
...I SHALL DO SO AGAIN!
VRRROOOOAAAAR!

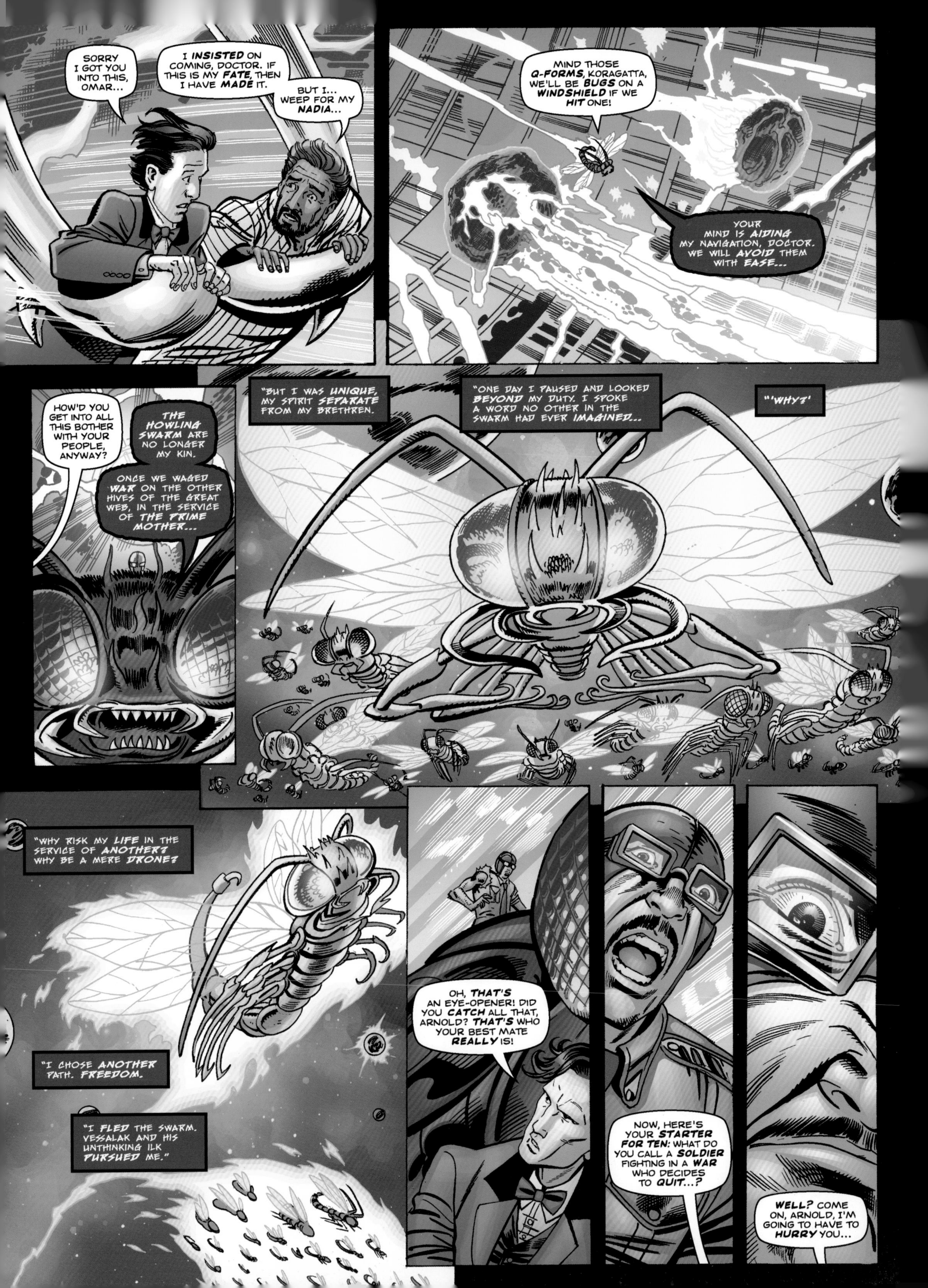
SORRY I GOT YOU INTO THIS, OMAR...
I INSISTED ON COMING, DOCTOR. IF THIS IS MY FATE, THEN I HAVE MADE IT.
BUT I... WEEP FOR MY NADIA...
MIND THOSE Q-FORMS, KORAGATTA, WE'LL BE BUGS ON A WINDSHIELD IF WE HIT ONE!
YOUR MIND IS AIDING MY NAVIGATION, DOCTOR. WE WILL AVOID THEM WITH EASE...
HOW'D YOU GET INTO ALL THIS BOTHER WITH YOUR PEOPLE, ANYWAY?
THE HOWLING SWARM ARE NO LONGER MY KIN.
ONCE WE WAGED WAR ON THE OTHER HIVES OF THE GREAT WEB, IN THE SERVICE OF THE PRIME MOTHER...
"BUT I WAS UNIQUE, MY SPIRIT SEPARATE FROM MY BRETHREN.
"ONE DAY I PAUSED AND LOOKED BEYOND MY DUTY. I SPOKE A WORD NO OTHER IN THE SWARM HAD EVER IMAGINED...
"'WHY?'
"WHY RISK MY LIFE IN THE SERVICE OF ANOTHER? WHY BE A MERE DRONE?
"I CHOSE ANOTHER PATH. FREEDOM.
"I FLED THE SWARM. YESSALAK AND HIS UNTHINKING ILK PURSUED ME."
OH, THAT'S AN EYE-OPENER! DID YOU CATCH ALL THAT, ARNOLD? THAT'S WHO YOUR BEST MATE REALLY IS!
NOW, HERE'S YOUR STARTER FOR TEN: WHAT DO YOU CALL A SOLDIER FIGHTING IN A WAR WHO DECIDES TO QUIT...?
WELL? COME ON, ARNOLD, I'M GOING TO HAVE TO HURRY YOU...

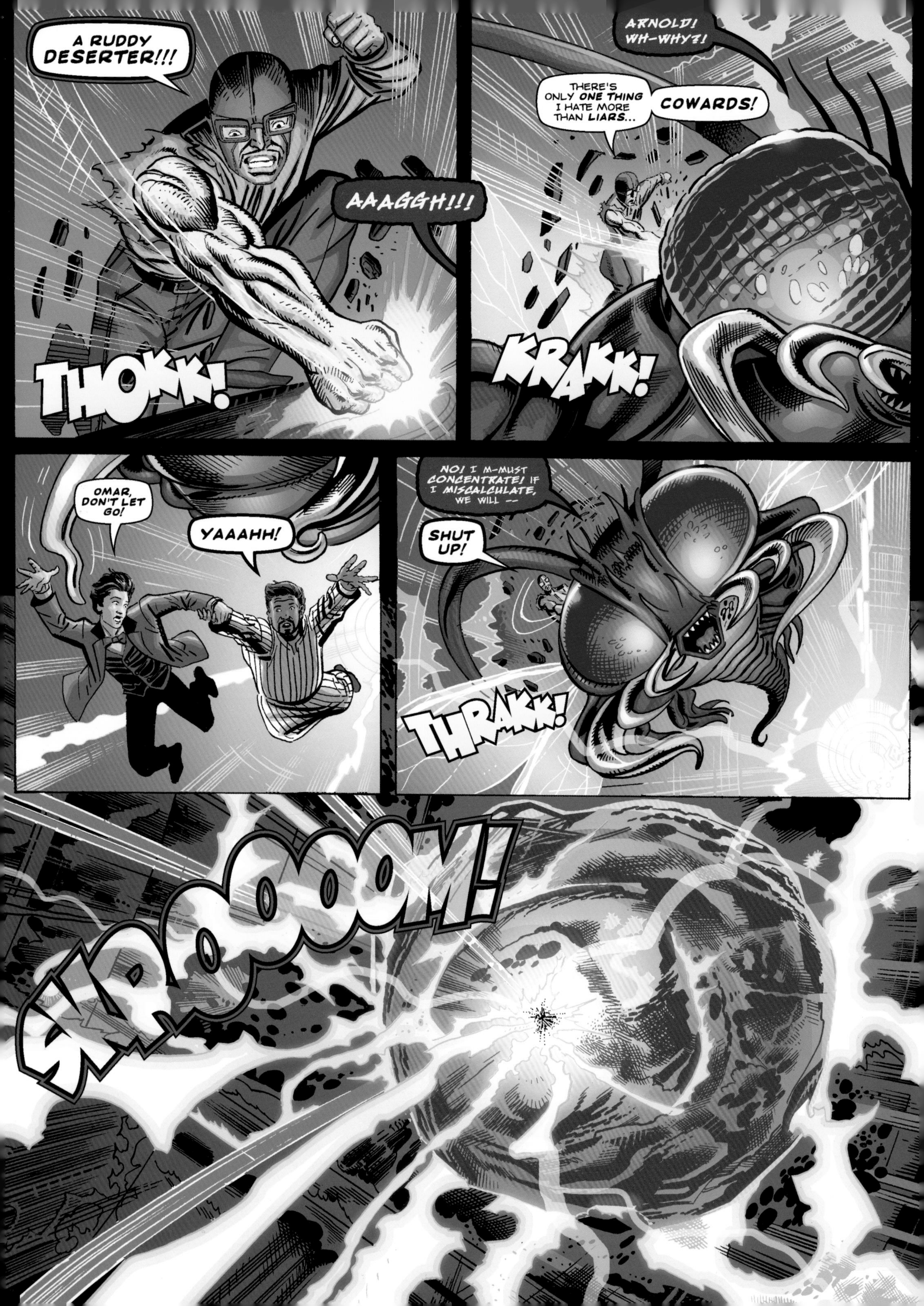
A RUDDY DESERTER!!!
AAAGGH!!!
THOKK!
ARNOLD! WH-WHY?!
THERE'S ONLY ONE THING I HATE MORE THAN LIARS...
COWARDS!
KRAKK!
OMAR, DON'T LET GO!
YAAAHH!
NO! I M-MUST CONCENTRATE! IF I MISCALCULATE, WE WILL --
SHUT UP!
THRAKK!
SKROOOOM!

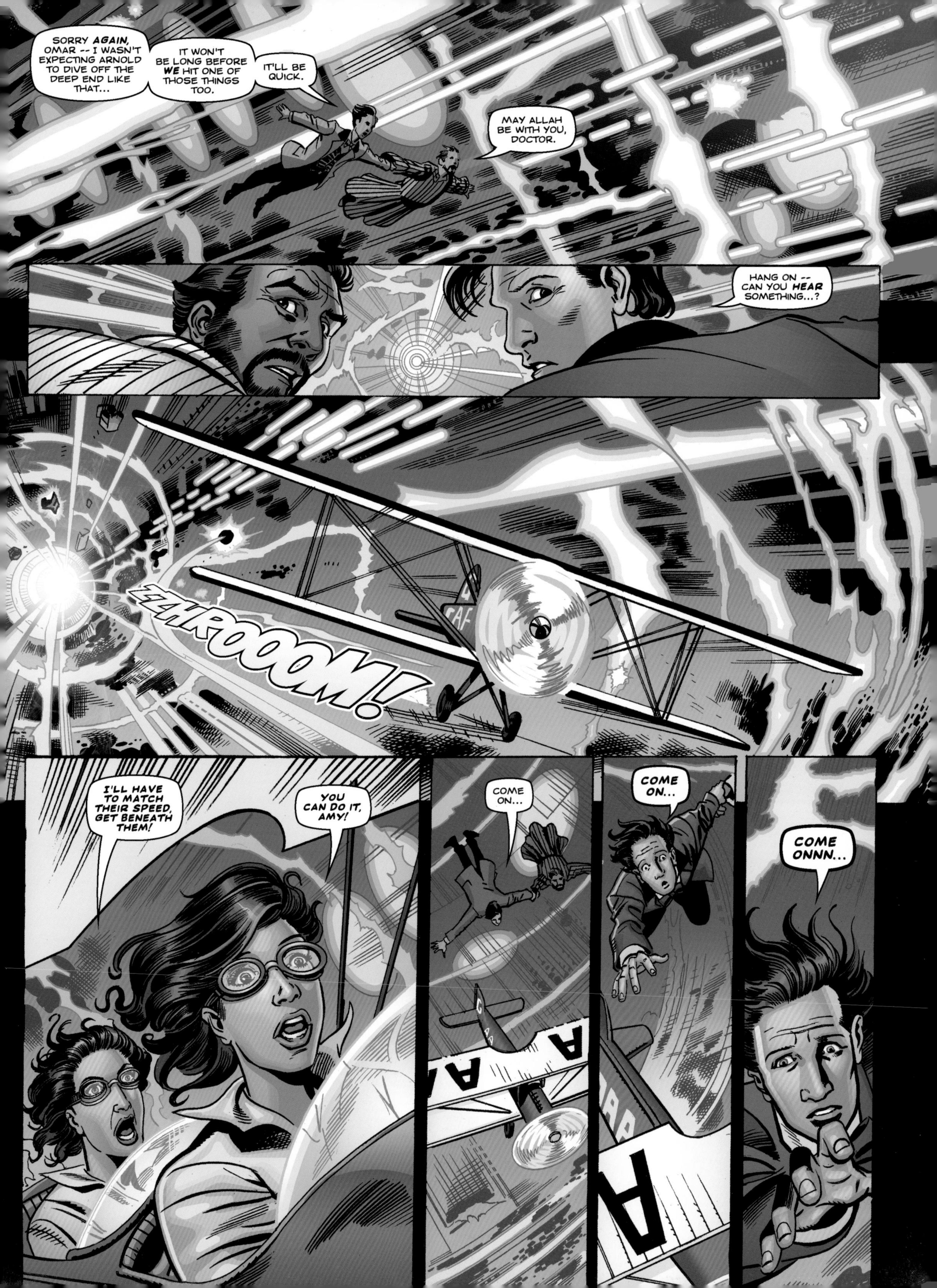

SORRY AGAIN, OMAR -- I WASN'T EXPECTING ARNOLD TO DIVE OFF THE DEEP END LIKE THAT...
IT WON'T BE LONG BEFORE WE HIT ONE OF THOSE THINGS TOO.
IT'LL BE QUICK.
MAY ALLAH BE WITH YOU, DOCTOR.
HANG ON -- CAN YOU HEAR SOMETHING...?
ZZHROOOOM!
I'LL HAVE TO MATCH THEIR SPEED, GET BENEATH THEM!
YOU CAN DO IT, AMY!
COME ON...
COME ON...
COME ONNN...

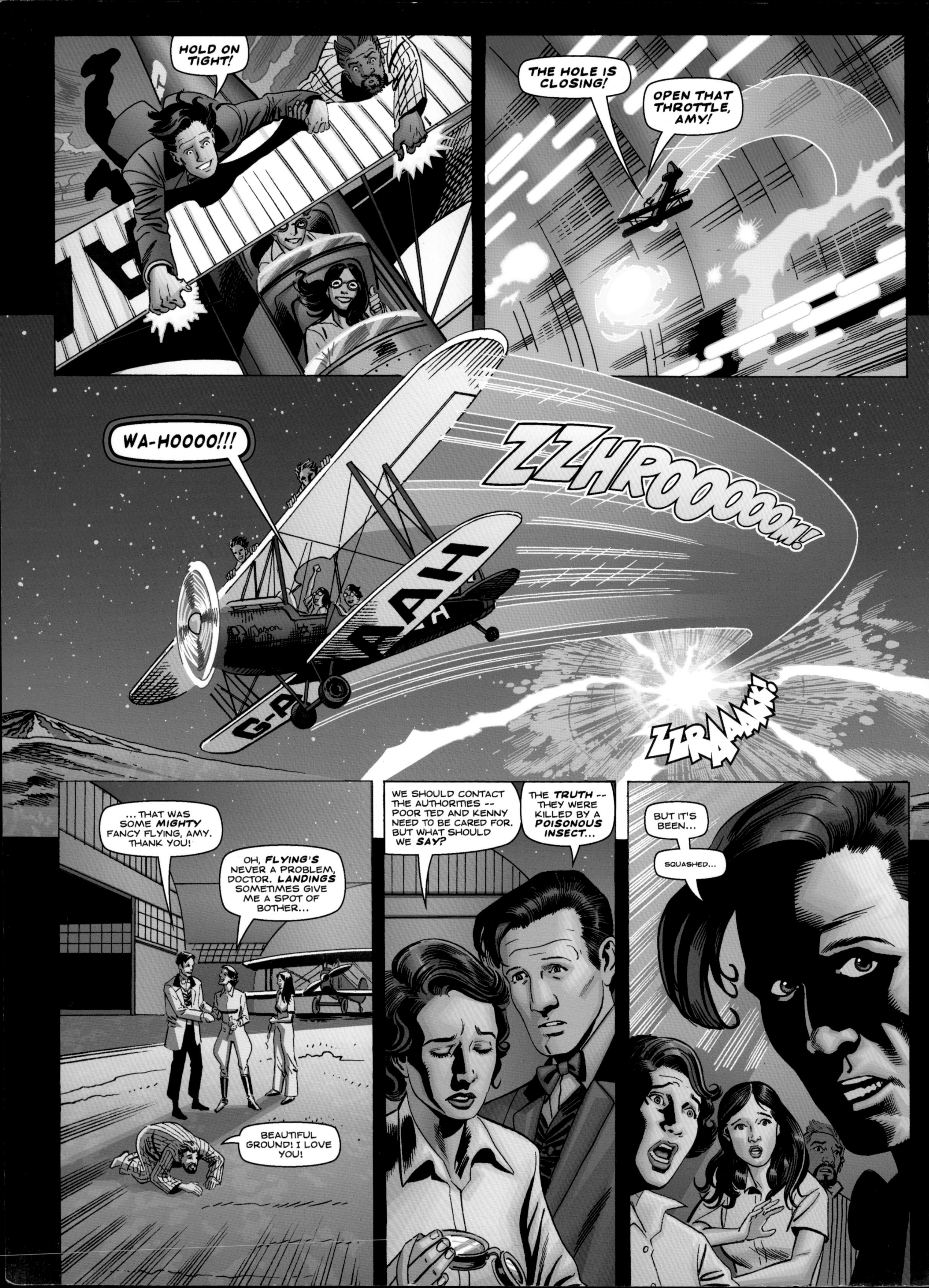
HOLD ON TIGHT!
THE HOLE IS CLOSING!
OPEN THAT THROTTLE, AMY!
WA-HOOOO!!!
ZZHROOOOOOM!
ZZRAAAKK!
...THAT WAS SOME MIGHTY FANCY FLYING, AMY. THANK YOU!
OH, FLYING'S NEVER A PROBLEM, DOCTOR. LANDINGS SOMETIMES GIVE ME A SPOT OF BOTHER...
BEAUTIFUL GROUND! I LOVE YOU!
WE SHOULD CONTACT THE AUTHORITIES -- POOR TED AND KENNY NEED TO BE CARED FOR. BUT WHAT SHOULD WE SAY?
THE TRUTH -- THEY WERE KILLED BY A POISONOUS INSECT...
BUT IT'S BEEN...
SQUASHED...

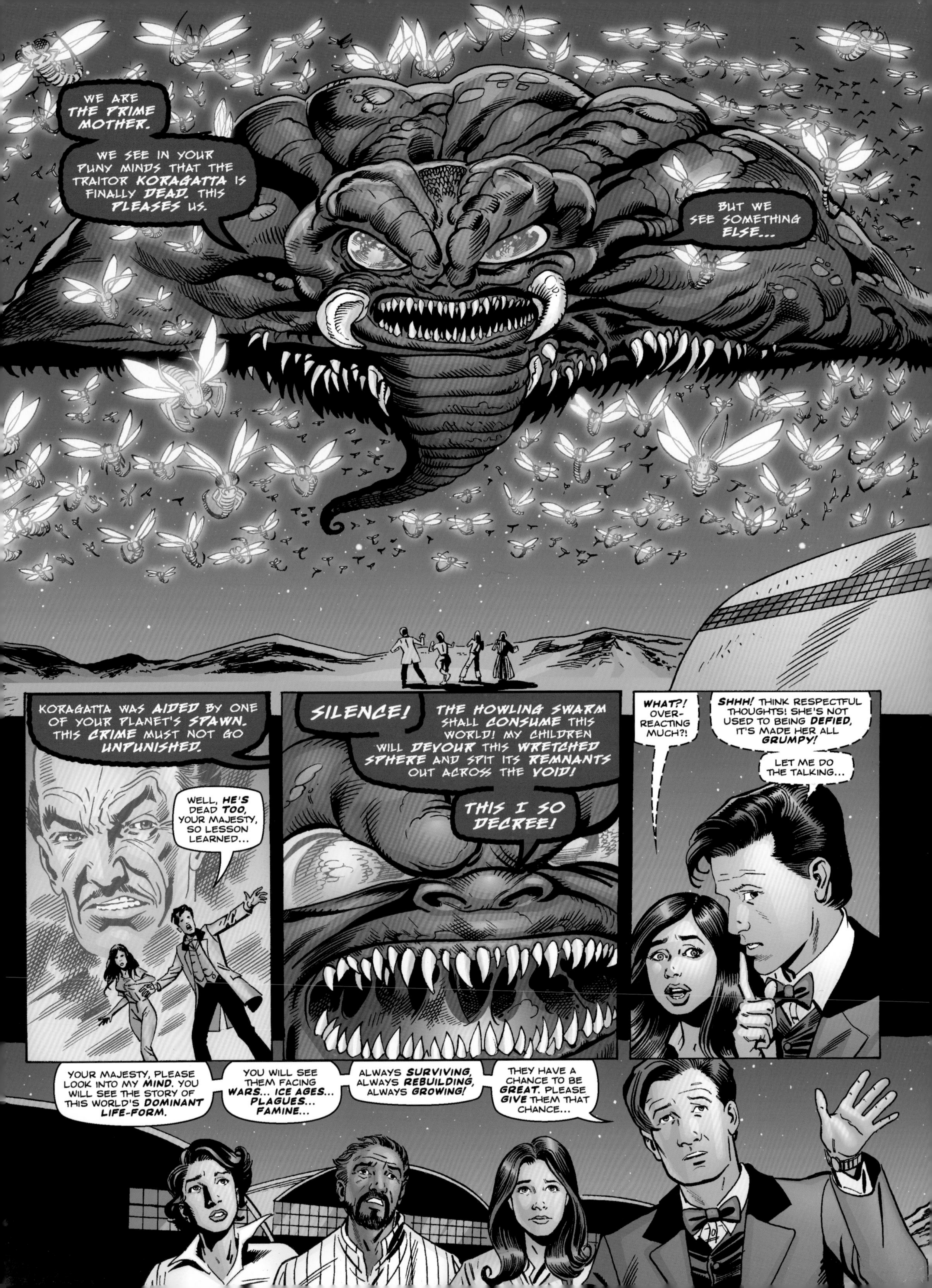
WE ARE THE PRIME MOTHER.
WE SEE IN YOUR PUNY MINDS THAT THE TRAITOR KORAGATTA IS FINALLY DEAD. THIS PLEASES US.
BUT WE SEE SOMETHING ELSE...
KORAGATTA WAS AIDED BY ONE OF YOUR PLANET'S SPAWN. THIS CRIME MUST NOT GO UNPUNISHED.
WELL, HE'S DEAD TOO, YOUR MAJESTY, SO LESSON LEARNED...
SILENCE!
THE HOWLING SWARM SHALL CONSUME THIS WORLD! MY CHILDREN WILL DEVOUR THIS WRETCHED SPHERE AND SPIT ITS REMNANTS OUT ACROSS THE VOID!
THIS I SO DECREE!
WHAT?! OVER-REACTING MUCH?!
SHHH! THINK RESPECTFUL THOUGHTS! SHE'S NOT USED TO BEING DEFIED, IT'S MADE HER ALL GRUMPY!
LET ME DO THE TALKING...
YOUR MAJESTY, PLEASE LOOK INTO MY MIND. YOU WILL SEE THE STORY OF THIS WORLD'S DOMINANT LIFE-FORM.
YOU WILL SEE THEM FACING WARS... ICE AGES... PLAGUES... FAMINE...
ALWAYS SURVIVING, ALWAYS REBUILDING, ALWAYS GROWING!
THEY HAVE A CHANCE TO BE GREAT. PLEASE GIVE THEM THAT CHANCE...

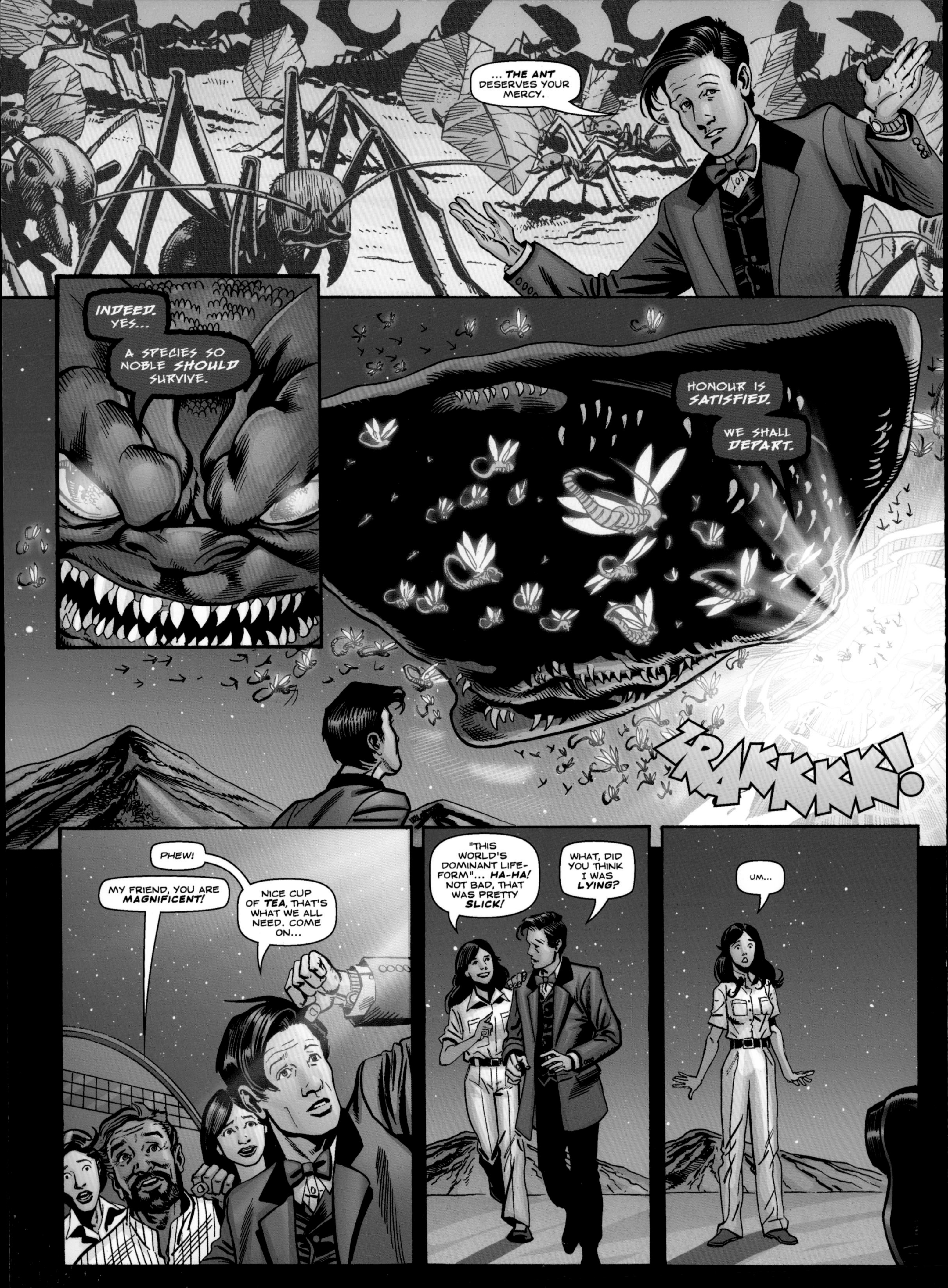
... THE ANT DESERVES YOUR MERCY.
INDEED. YES...
A SPECIES SO NOBLE SHOULD SURVIVE.
HONOUR IS SATISFIED.
WE SHALL DEPART.
FRAKKKK!
PHEW!
MY FRIEND, YOU ARE MAGNIFICENT!
NICE CUP OF TEA, THAT'S WHAT WE ALL NEED. COME ON...
"THIS WORLD'S DOMINANT LIFE-FORM"... HA-HA! NOT BAD, THAT WAS PRETTY SLICK!
WHAT, DID YOU THINK I WAS LYING?
UM...

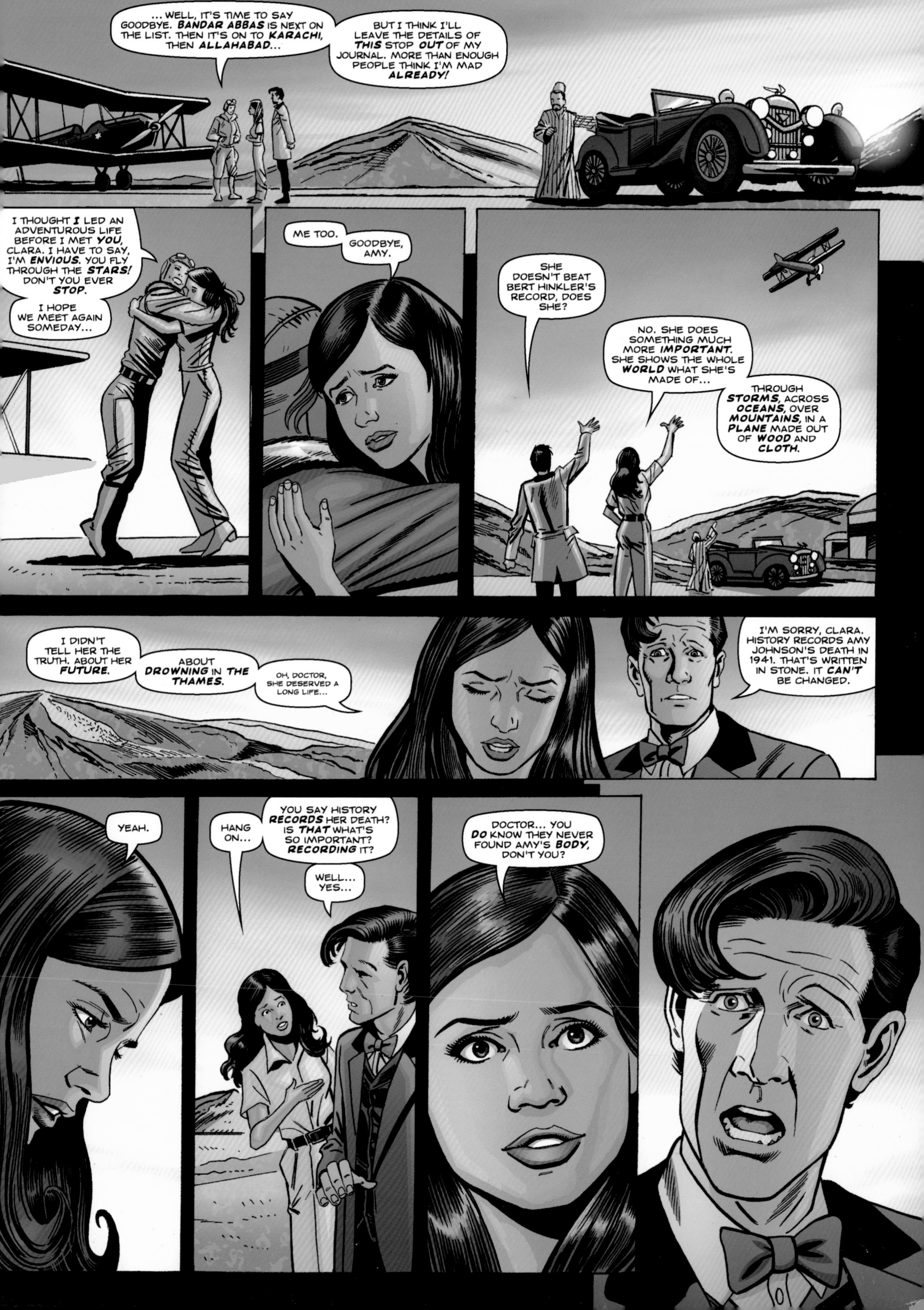

... WELL, IT'S TIME TO SAY GOODBYE. BANDAR ABBAS IS NEXT ON THE LIST. THEN IT'S ON TO KARACHI, THEN ALLAHABAD...
BUT I THINK I'LL LEAVE THE DETAILS OF THIS STOP OUT OF MY JOURNAL. MORE THAN ENOUGH PEOPLE THINK I'M MAD ALREADY!
I THOUGHT I LED AN ADVENTUROUS LIFE BEFORE I MET YOU, CLARA. I HAVE TO SAY, I'M ENVIOUS. YOU FLY THROUGH THE STARS! DON'T YOU EVER STOP.
I HOPE WE MEET AGAIN SOMEDAY...
ME TOO.
GOODBYE, AMY.
SHE DOESN'T BEAT BERT HINKLER'S RECORD, DOES SHE?
NO. SHE DOES SOMETHING MUCH MORE IMPORTANT. SHE SHOWS THE WHOLE WORLD WHAT SHE'S MADE OF...
THROUGH STORMS, ACROSS OCEANS, OVER MOUNTAINS, IN A PLANE MADE OUT OF WOOD AND CLOTH.
I DIDN'T TELL HER THE TRUTH. ABOUT HER FUTURE.
ABOUT DROWNING IN THE THAMES.
OH, DOCTOR, SHE DESERVED A LONG LIFE...
I'M SORRY, CLARA. HISTORY RECORDS AMY JOHNSON'S DEATH IN 1941. THAT'S WRITTEN IN STONE. IT CAN'T BE CHANGED.
YEAH.
HANG ON...
YOU SAY HISTORY RECORDS HER DEATH? IS THAT WHAT'S SO IMPORTANT? RECORDING IT?
WELL... YES...
DOCTOR... YOU DO KNOW THEY NEVER FOUND AMY'S BODY, DON'T YOU?

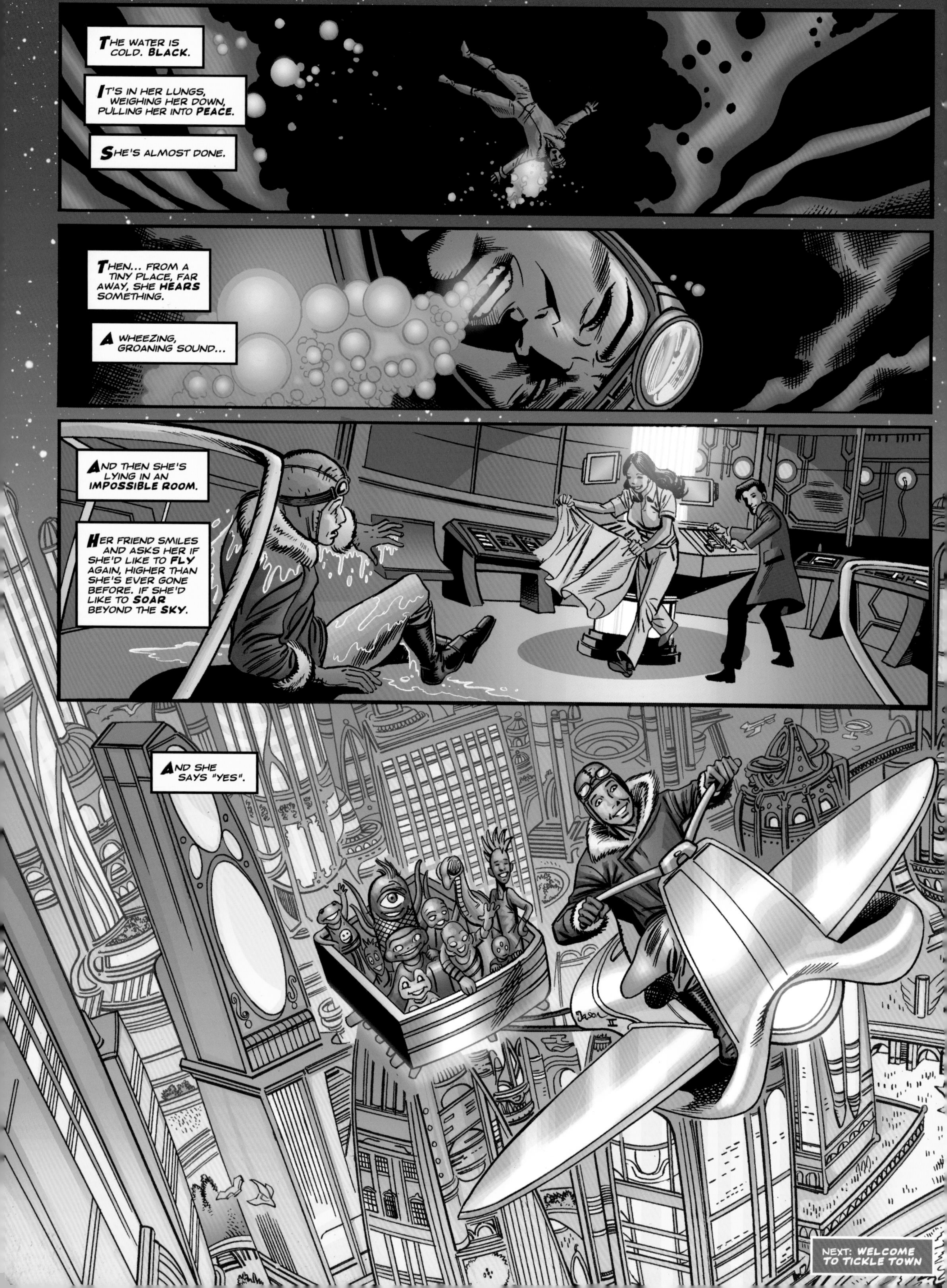
THE WATER IS COLD. BLACK.
IT'S IN HER LUNGS, WEIGHING HER DOWN, PULLING HER INTO PEACE.
SHE'S ALMOST DONE.
THEN... FROM A TINY PLACE, FAR AWAY, SHE HEARS SOMETHING.
A WHEEZING, GROANING SOUND...
AND THEN SHE'S LYING IN AN IMPOSSIBLE ROOM.
HER FRIEND SMILES AND ASKS HER IF SHE'D LIKE TO FLY AGAIN, HIGHER THAN SHE'S EVER GONE BEFORE. IF SHE'D LIKE TO SOAR BEYOND THE SKY.
AND SHE SAYS "YES".
NEXT: WELCOME TO TICKLE TOWN

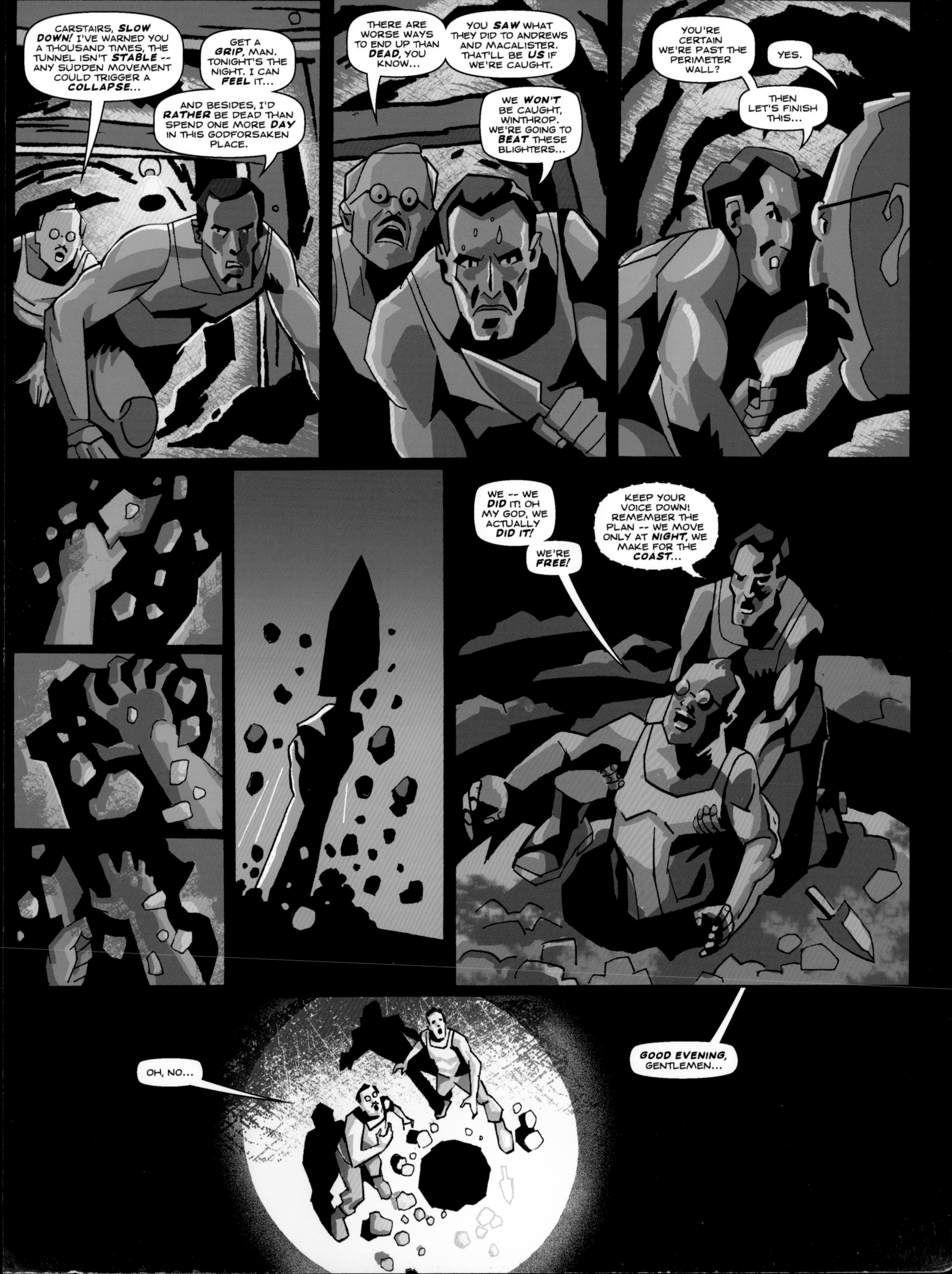
CARSTAIRS, SLOW DOWN! I'VE WARNED YOU A THOUSAND TIMES, THE TUNNEL ISN'T STABLE -- ANY SUDDEN MOVEMENT COULD TRIGGER A COLLAPSE...
GET A GRIP, MAN. TONIGHT'S THE NIGHT. I CAN FEEL IT...
AND BESIDES, I'D RATHER BE DEAD THAN SPEND ONE MORE DAY IN THIS GODFORSAKEN PLACE.
THERE ARE WORSE WAYS TO END UP THAN DEAD, YOU KNOW...
YOU SAW WHAT THEY DID TO ANDREWS AND MACALISTER. THAT'LL BE US IF WE'RE CAUGHT.
WE WON'T BE CAUGHT, WINTHROP. WE'RE GOING TO BEAT THESE BLIGHTERS...
YOU'RE CERTAIN WE'RE PAST THE PERIMETER WALL?
YES.
THEN LET'S FINISH THIS...
WE -- WE DID IT! OH MY GOD, WE ACTUALLY DID IT!
WE'RE FREE!
KEEP YOUR VOICE DOWN! REMEMBER THE PLAN -- WE MOVE ONLY AT NIGHT, WE MAKE FOR THE COAST...
GOOD EVENING, GENTLEMEN...
OH, NO...

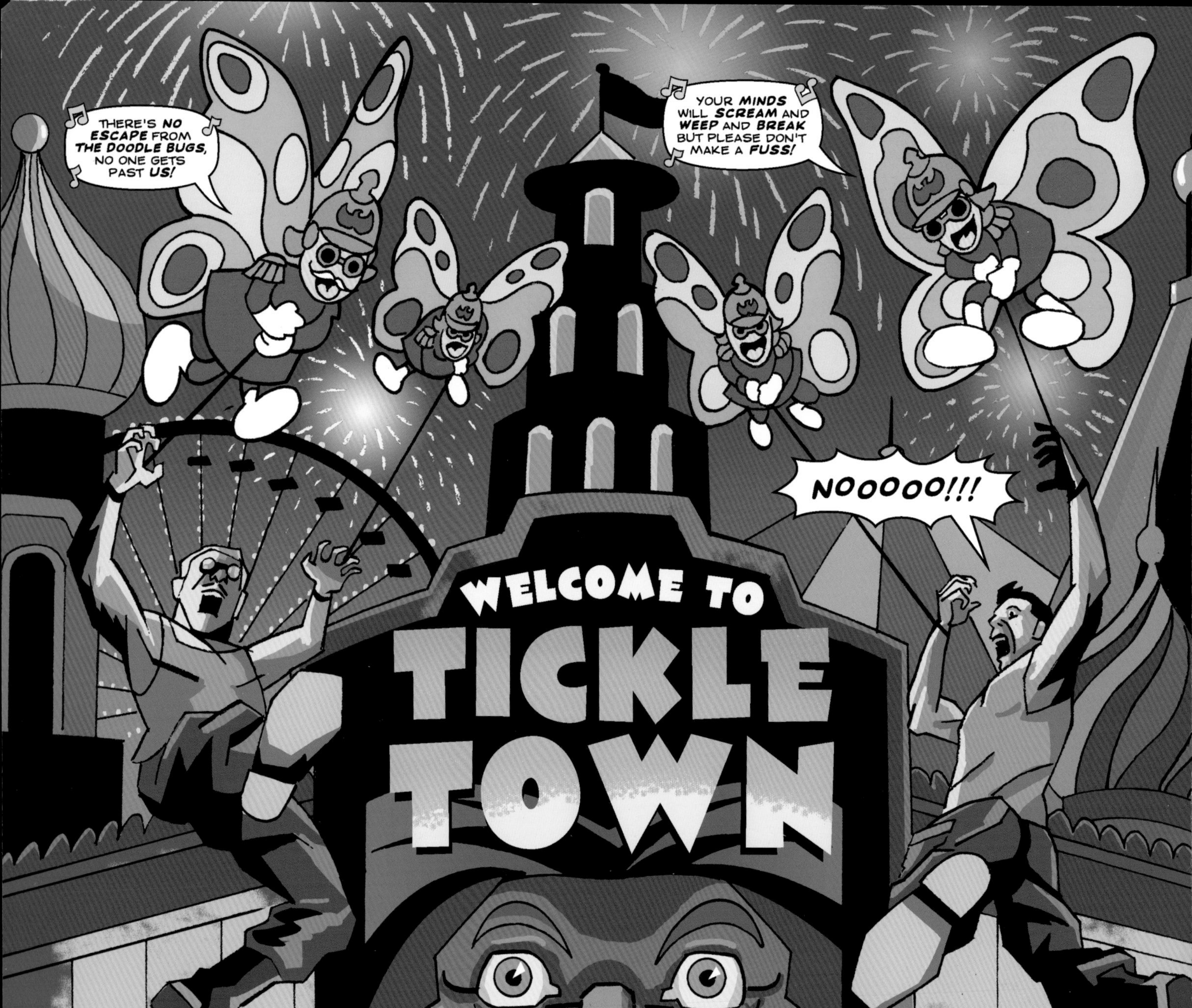
THERE'S NO ESCAPE FROM THE DOODLE BUGS, NO ONE GETS PAST US!
YOUR MINDS WILL SCREAM AND WEEP AND BREAK BUT PLEASE DON'T MAKE A FUSS!
NOOOOO!!!
WELCOME TO
TICKLE TOWN
STORY: SCOTT GRAY
ART & COLOUR: ADRIAN SALMON
LETTERING: ROGER LANGRIDGE
EDITORS: TOM SPILSBURY & PETER WARE

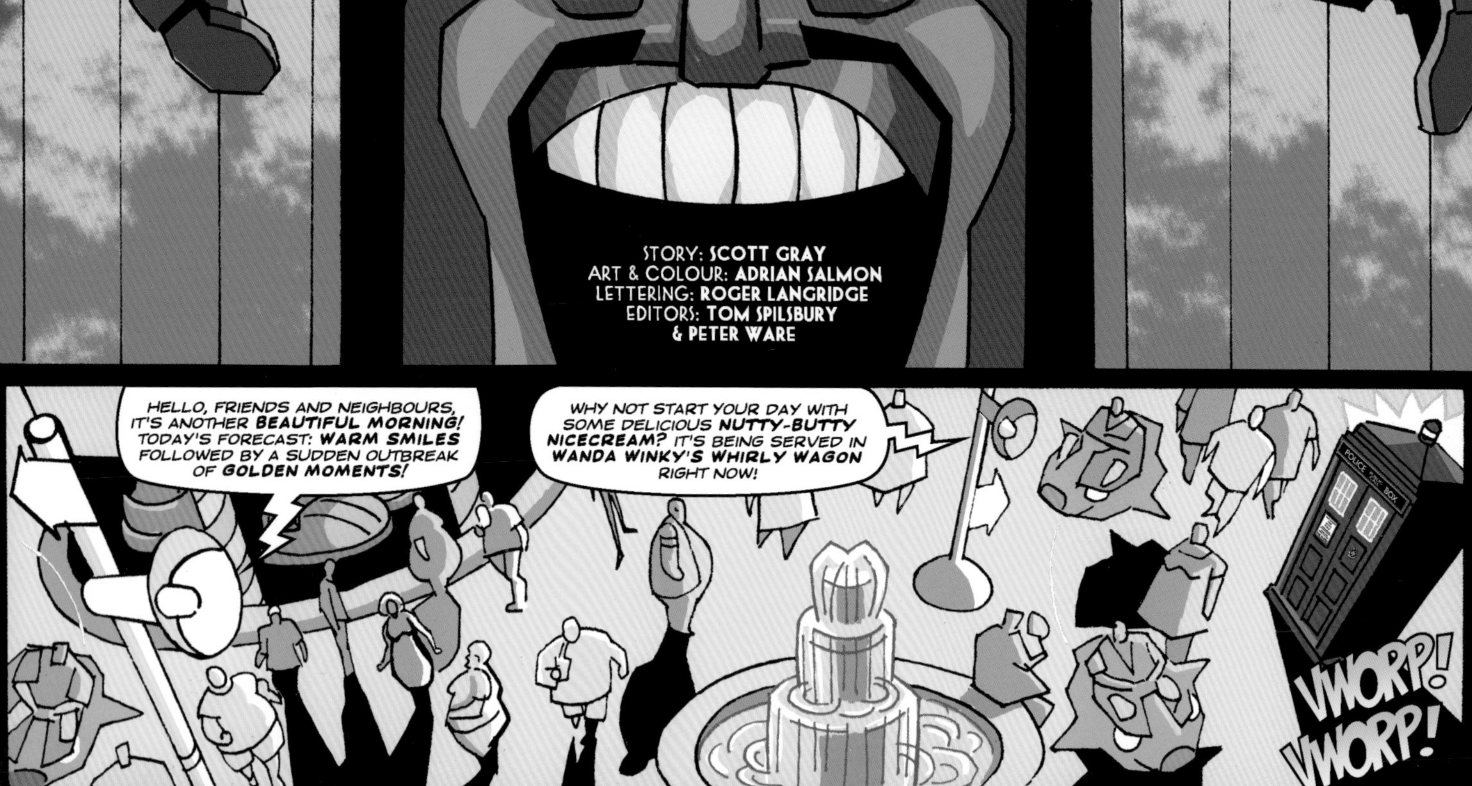
HELLO, FRIENDS AND NEIGHBOURS, IT'S ANOTHER BEAUTIFUL MORNING! TODAY'S FORECAST: WARM SMILES FOLLOWED BY A SUDDEN OUTBREAK OF GOLDEN MOMENTS!
WHY NOT START YOUR DAY WITH SOME DELICIOUS NUTTY-BUTTY NICECREAM? IT'S BEING SERVED IN WANDA WINKY'S WHIRLY WAGON RIGHT NOW!
POLICE BOX
VWORP! VWORP!

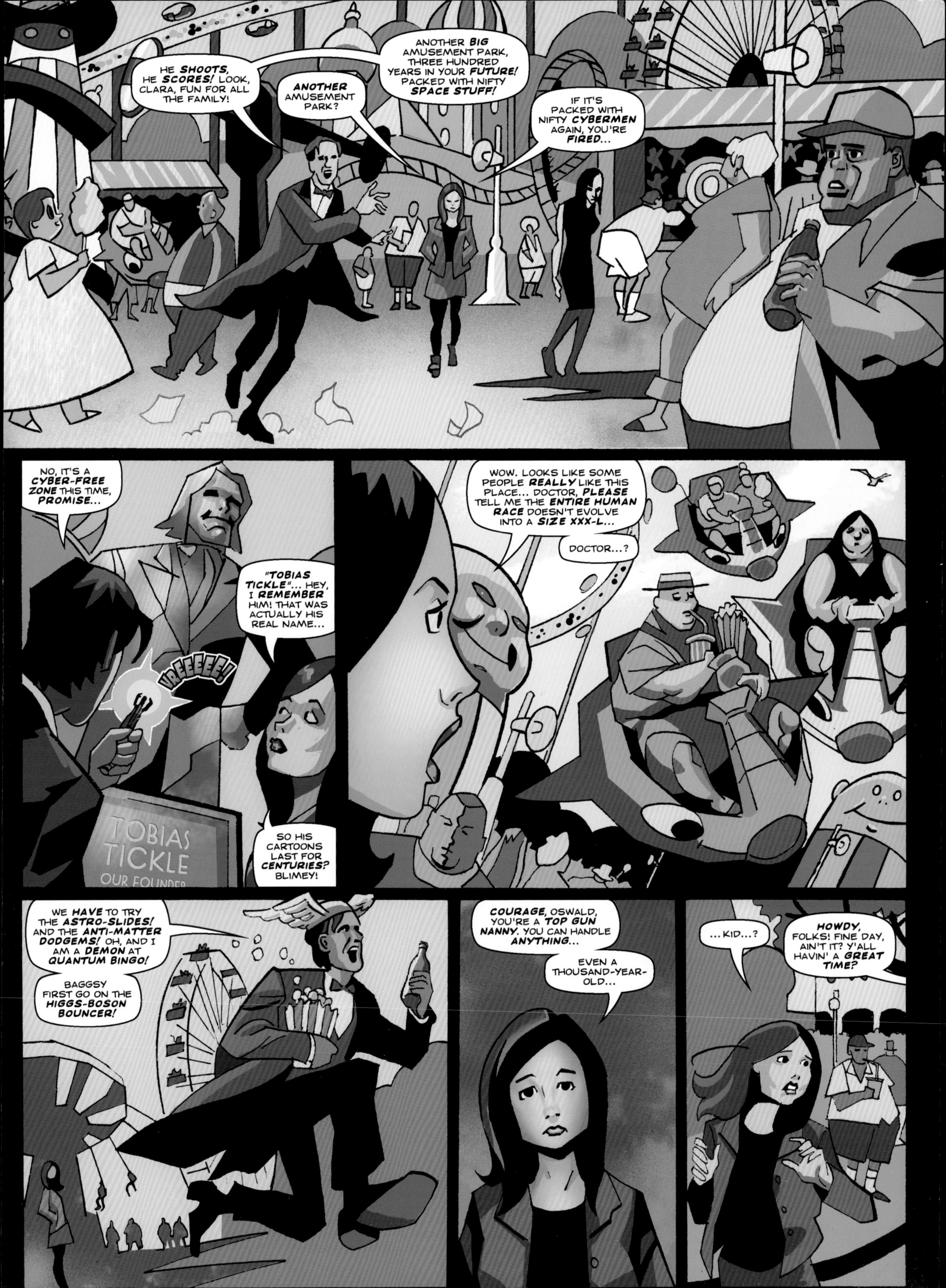
HE SHOOTS, HE SCORES! LOOK, CLARA, FUN FOR ALL THE FAMILY!
ANOTHER AMUSEMENT PARK?
ANOTHER BIG AMUSEMENT PARK, THREE HUNDRED YEARS IN YOUR FUTURE! PACKED WITH NIFTY SPACE STUFF!
IF IT'S PACKED WITH NIFTY CYBERMEN AGAIN, YOU'RE FIRED...
NO, IT'S A CYBER-FREE ZONE THIS TIME, PROMISE...
VREEEEE!
"TOBIAS TICKLE"... HEY, I REMEMBER HIM! THAT WAS ACTUALLY HIS REAL NAME...
TOBIAS TICKLE OUR FOUNDER
SO HIS CARTOONS LAST FOR CENTURIES? BLIMEY!
WOW. LOOKS LIKE SOME PEOPLE REALLY LIKE THIS PLACE... DOCTOR, PLEASE TELL ME THE ENTIRE HUMAN RACE DOESN'T EVOLVE INTO A SIZE XXX-L...
DOCTOR...?
WE HAVE TO TRY THE ASTRO-SLIDES! AND THE ANTI-MATTER DODGEMS! OH, AND I AM A DEMON AT QUANTUM BINGO!
BAGGSY FIRST GO ON THE HIGGS-BOSON BOUNCER!
COURAGE, OSWALD, YOU'RE A TOP GUN NANNY. YOU CAN HANDLE ANYTHING...
EVEN A THOUSAND-YEAR-OLD...
...KID...?
HOWDY, FOLKS! FINE DAY, AIN'T IT? Y'ALL HAVIN' A GREAT TIME?

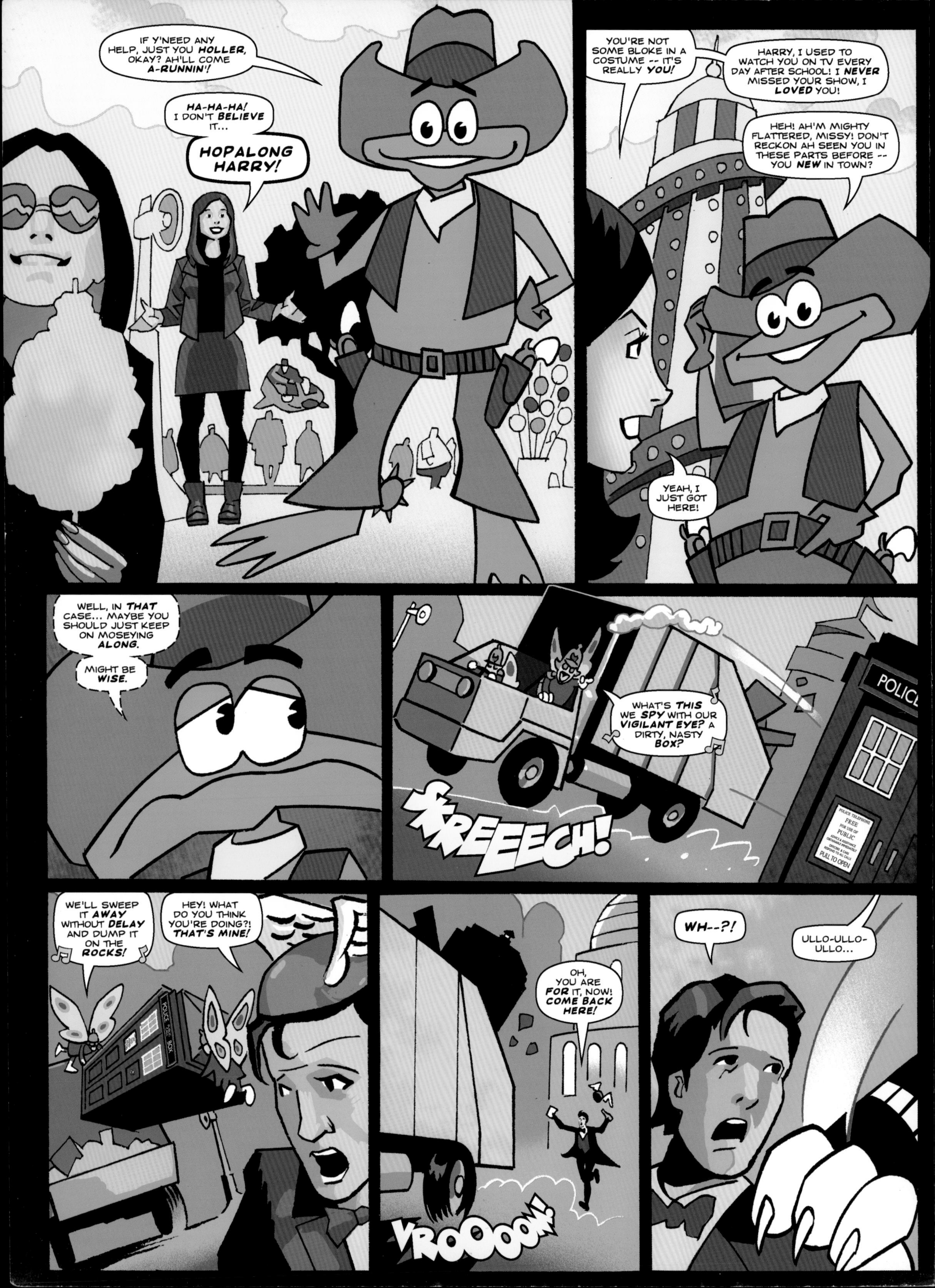
IF Y'NEED ANY HELP, JUST YOU HOLLER, OKAY? AH'LL COME A-RUNNIN'!
HA-HA-HA! I DON'T BELIEVE IT...
HOPALONG HARRY!
YOU'RE NOT SOME BLOKE IN A COSTUME -- IT'S REALLY YOU!
HARRY, I USED TO WATCH YOU ON TV EVERY DAY AFTER SCHOOL! I NEVER MISSED YOUR SHOW, I LOVED YOU!
HEH! AH'M MIGHTY FLATTERED, MISSY! DON'T RECKON AH SEEN YOU IN THESE PARTS BEFORE -- YOU NEW IN TOWN?
YEAH, I JUST GOT HERE!
WELL, IN THAT CASE... MAYBE YOU SHOULD JUST KEEP ON MOSEYING ALONG.
MIGHT BE WISE.
WHAT'S THIS WE SPY WITH OUR VIGILANT EYE? A DIRTY, NASTY BOX?
SKREEEECH!
POLICE
POLICE TELEPHONE FREE FOR USE OF PUBLIC
PULL TO OPEN
WE'LL SWEEP IT AWAY WITHOUT DELAY AND DUMP IT ON THE ROCKS!
HEY! WHAT DO YOU THINK YOU'RE DOING?! THAT'S MINE!
OH, YOU ARE FOR IT, NOW! COME BACK HERE!
VROOOOM!
WH--?!
ULLO-ULLO-ULLO...

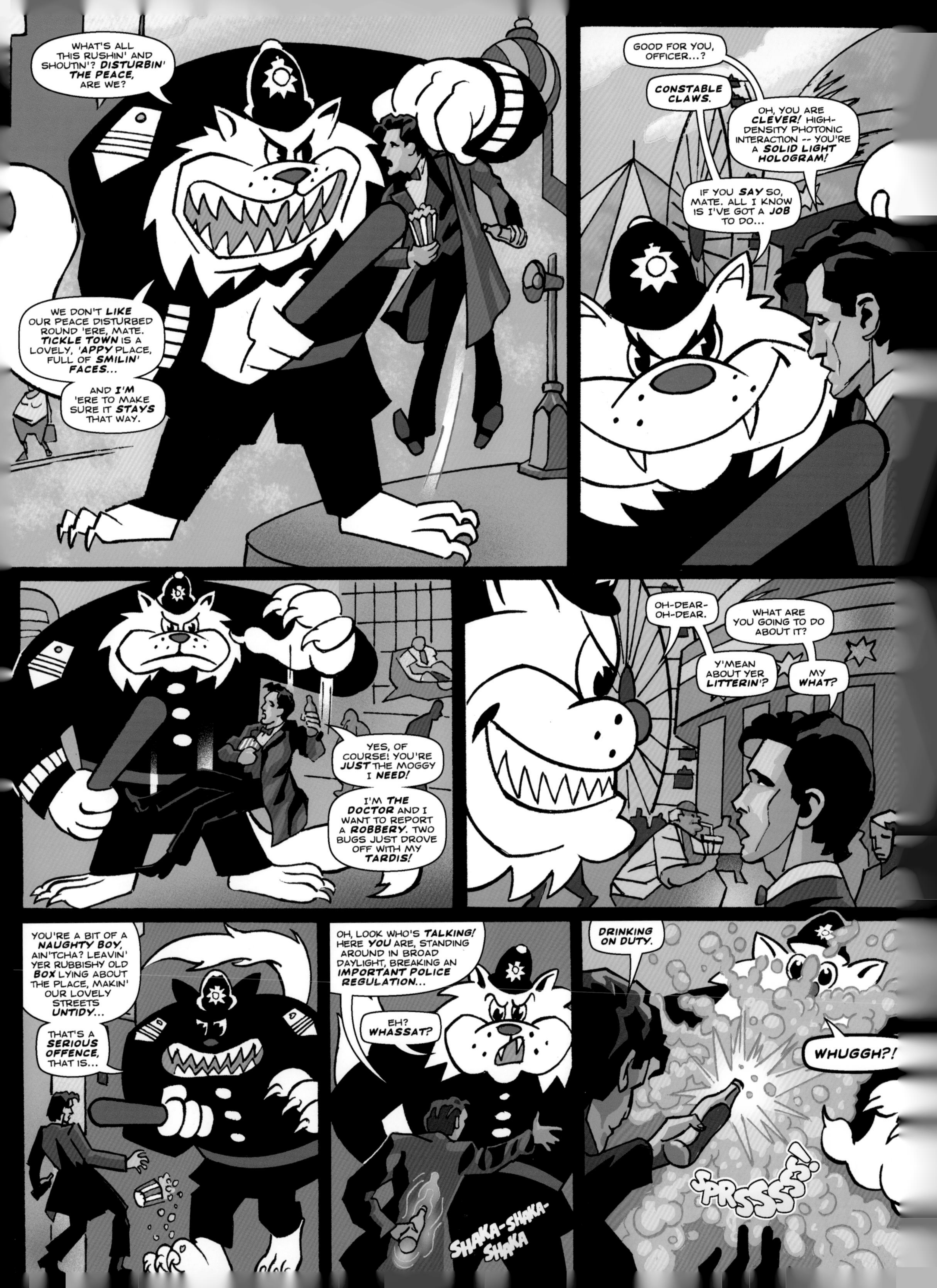

WHAT'S ALL THIS RUSHIN' AND SHOUTIN'? DISTURBIN' THE PEACE, ARE WE?
WE DON'T LIKE OUR PEACE DISTURBED ROUND 'ERE, MATE. TICKLE TOWN IS A LOVELY, 'APPY PLACE, FULL OF SMILIN' FACES...
AND I'M 'ERE TO MAKE SURE IT STAYS THAT WAY.
GOOD FOR YOU, OFFICER...?
CONSTABLE CLAWS.
OH, YOU ARE CLEVER! HIGH-DENSITY PHOTONIC INTERACTION -- YOU'RE A SOLID LIGHT HOLOGRAM!
IF YOU SAY SO, MATE. ALL I KNOW IS I'VE GOT A JOB TO DO...
YES, OF COURSE! YOU'RE JUST THE MOGGY I NEED!
I'M THE DOCTOR AND I WANT TO REPORT A ROBBERY. TWO BUGS JUST DROVE OFF WITH MY TARDIS!
OH-DEAR-OH-DEAR.
WHAT ARE YOU GOING TO DO ABOUT IT?
Y'MEAN ABOUT YER LITTERIN'?
MY WHAT?
YOU'RE A BIT OF A NAUGHTY BOY, AIN'TCHA? LEAVIN' YER RUBBISHY OLD BOX LYING ABOUT THE PLACE, MAKIN' OUR LOVELY STREETS UNTIDY...
THAT'S A SERIOUS OFFENCE, THAT IS...
OH, LOOK WHO'S TALKING! HERE YOU ARE, STANDING AROUND IN BROAD DAYLIGHT, BREAKING AN IMPORTANT POLICE REGULATION...
EH? WHASSAT?
SHAKA-SHAKA-SHAKA
DRINKING ON DUTY.
WHUGGH?!
SPRSSSS!

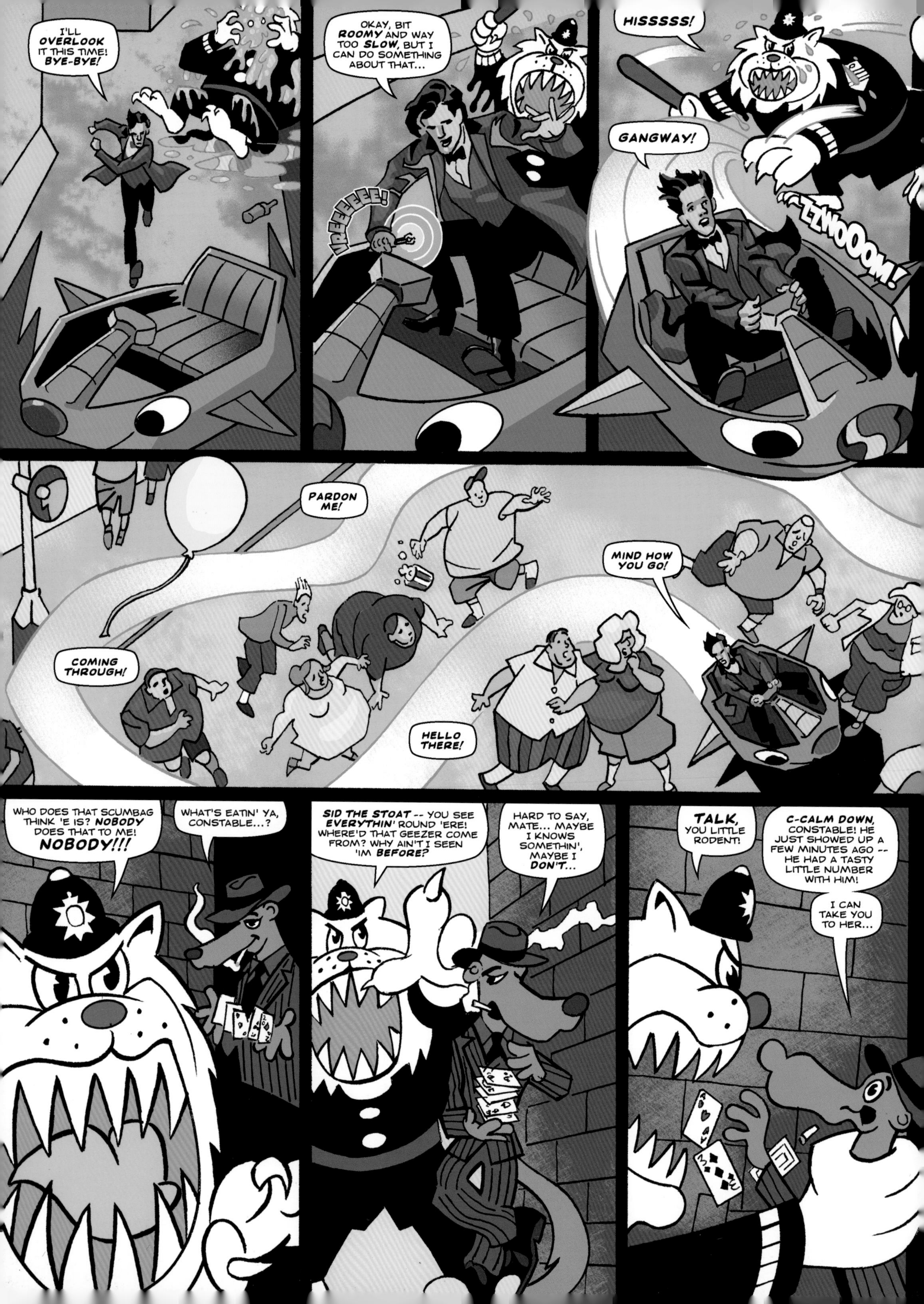
I'LL **OVERLOOK** IT THIS TIME! **BYE-BYE!**
OKAY, BIT **ROOMY** AND WAY TOO **SLOW**, BUT I CAN DO SOMETHING ABOUT THAT...
VREEEEEE!
HISSSSS!
GANGWAY!
-ZZWOOOOM!
PARDON ME!
MIND HOW YOU GO!
COMING THROUGH!
HELLO THERE!
WHO DOES THAT SCUMBAG THINK 'E IS? **NOBODY** DOES THAT TO ME! **NOBODY!!!**
WHAT'S EATIN' YA, CONSTABLE...?
SID THE STOAT -- YOU SEE **EVERYTHIN'** ROUND 'ERE! WHERE'D THAT GEEZER COME FROM? WHY AIN'T I SEEN 'IM **BEFORE?**
HARD TO SAY, MATE... MAYBE I KNOWS SOMETHIN', MAYBE I **DON'T...**
TALK, YOU LITTLE RODENT!
C-CALM DOWN, CONSTABLE! HE JUST SHOWED UP A FEW MINUTES AGO -- HE HAD A TASTY LITTLE NUMBER WITH HIM!
I CAN TAKE YOU TO HER...

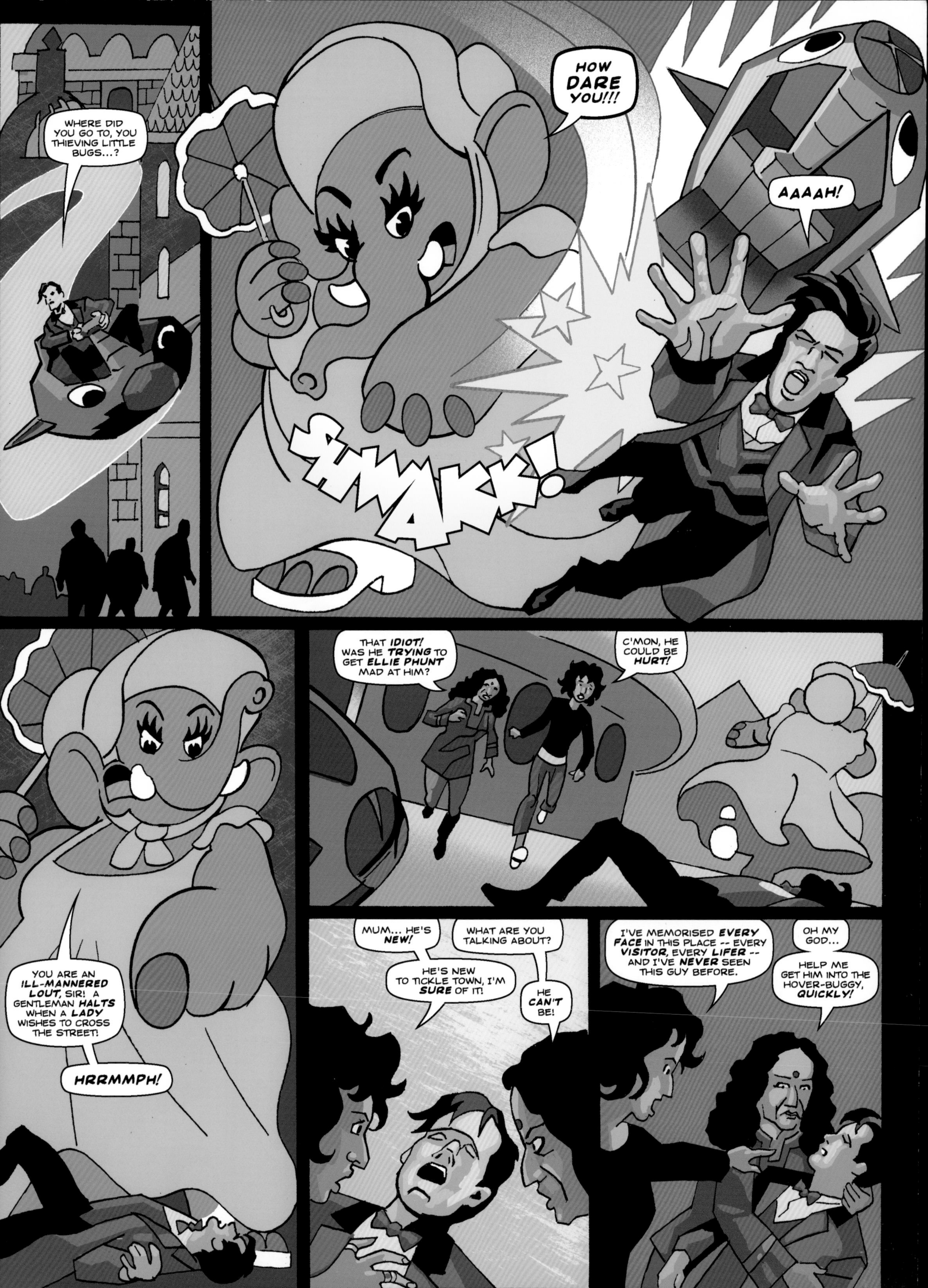
WHERE DID YOU GO TO, YOU THIEVING LITTLE BUGS...?
HOW DARE YOU!!!
AAAAH!
SHWAKK!
YOU ARE AN ILL-MANNERED LOUT, SIR! A GENTLEMAN HALTS WHEN A LADY WISHES TO CROSS THE STREET!
HRRMMPH!
THAT IDIOT! WAS HE TRYING TO GET ELLIE PHUNT MAD AT HIM?
C'MON, HE COULD BE HURT!
MUM... HE'S NEW!
WHAT ARE YOU TALKING ABOUT?
HE'S NEW TO TICKLE TOWN, I'M SURE OF IT!
HE CAN'T BE!
I'VE MEMORISED EVERY FACE IN THIS PLACE -- EVERY VISITOR, EVERY LIFER -- AND I'VE NEVER SEEN THIS GUY BEFORE.
OH MY GOD...
HELP ME GET HIM INTO THE HOVER-BUGGY, QUICKLY!

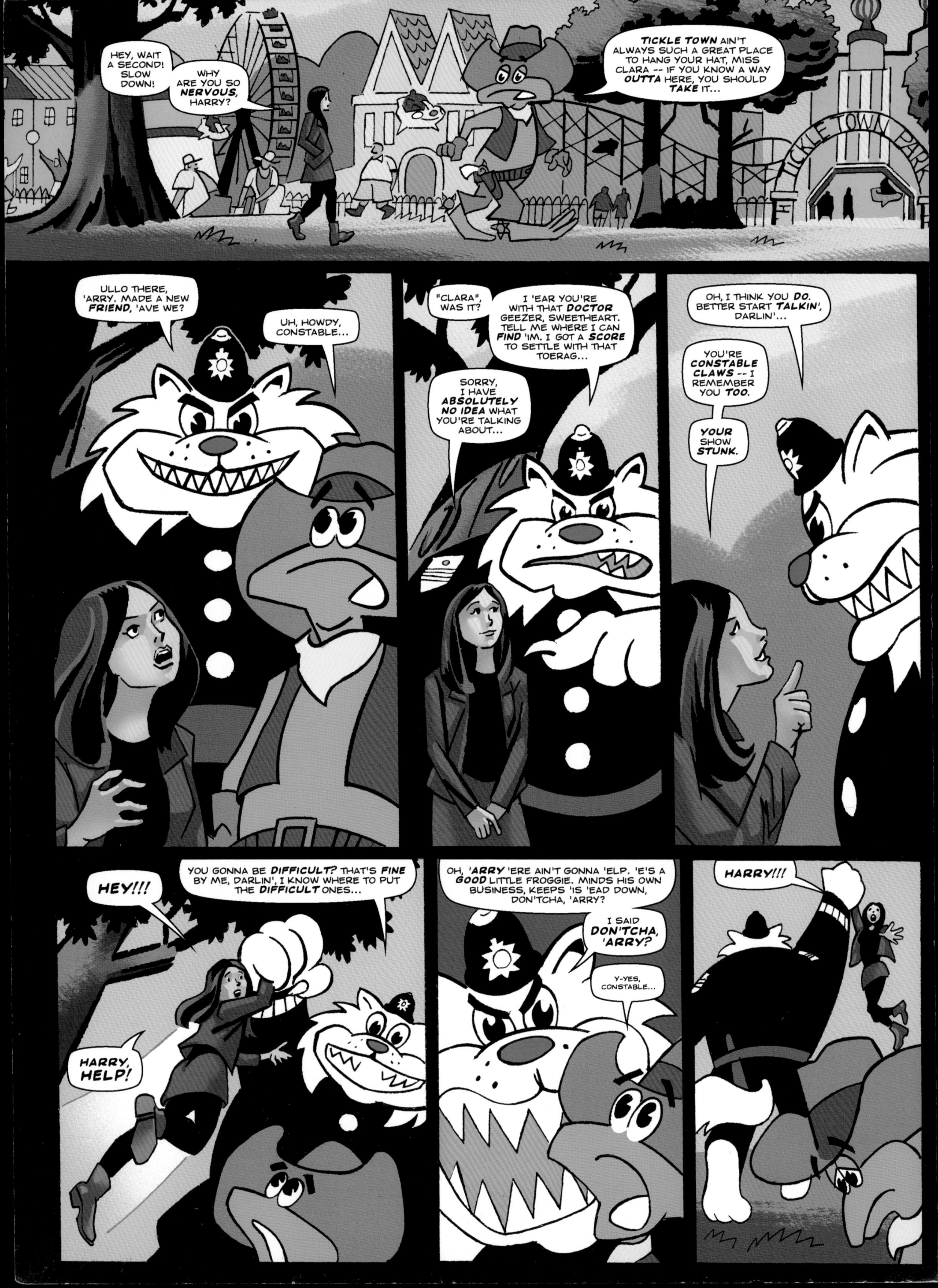
HEY, WAIT A SECOND! SLOW DOWN!
WHY ARE YOU SO NERVOUS, HARRY?
TICKLE TOWN AIN'T ALWAYS SUCH A GREAT PLACE TO HANG YOUR HAT, MISS CLARA -- IF YOU KNOW A WAY OUTTA HERE, YOU SHOULD TAKE IT...
TICKLE TOWN PARK
ULLO THERE, 'ARRY. MADE A NEW FRIEND, 'AVE WE?
UH, HOWDY, CONSTABLE...
"CLARA", WAS IT?
I 'EAR YOU'RE WITH THAT DOCTOR GEEZER, SWEETHEART. TELL ME WHERE I CAN FIND 'IM. I GOT A SCORE TO SETTLE WITH THAT TOERAG...
SORRY, I HAVE ABSOLUTELY NO IDEA WHAT YOU'RE TALKING ABOUT...
OH, I THINK YOU DO. BETTER START TALKIN', DARLIN'...
YOU'RE CONSTABLE CLAWS -- I REMEMBER YOU TOO.
YOUR SHOW STUNK.
HEY!!!
YOU GONNA BE DIFFICULT? THAT'S FINE BY ME, DARLIN', I KNOW WHERE TO PUT THE DIFFICULT ONES...
HARRY, HELP!
OH, 'ARRY 'ERE AIN'T GONNA 'ELP. 'E'S A GOOD LITTLE FROGGIE. MINDS HIS OWN BUSINESS, KEEPS 'IS 'EAD DOWN, DON'TCHA, 'ARRY?
I SAID DON'TCHA, 'ARRY?
Y-YES, CONSTABLE...
HARRY!!!

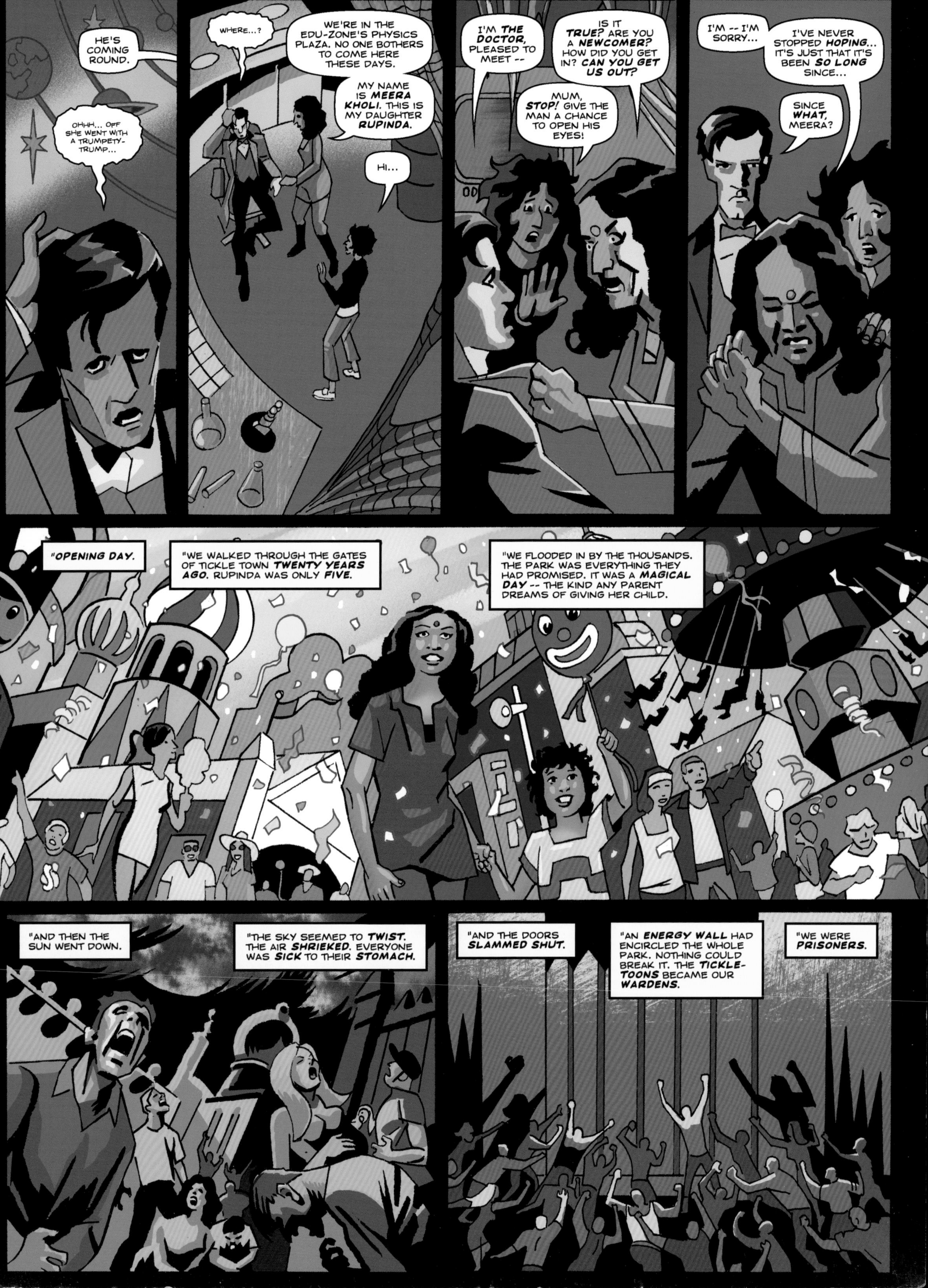
HE'S COMING ROUND.
OHHH... OFF SHE WENT WITH A TRUMPETY-TRUMP...
WHERE...?
WE'RE IN THE EDU-ZONE'S PHYSICS PLAZA. NO ONE BOTHERS TO COME HERE THESE DAYS.
MY NAME IS MEERA KHOLI. THIS IS MY DAUGHTER RUPINDA.
HI...
I'M THE DOCTOR, PLEASED TO MEET --
IS IT TRUE? ARE YOU A NEWCOMER? HOW DID YOU GET IN? CAN YOU GET US OUT?
MUM, STOP! GIVE THE MAN A CHANCE TO OPEN HIS EYES!
I'M -- I'M SORRY...
I'VE NEVER STOPPED HOPING... IT'S JUST THAT IT'S BEEN SO LONG SINCE...
SINCE WHAT, MEERA?
"OPENING DAY.
"WE WALKED THROUGH THE GATES OF TICKLE TOWN TWENTY YEARS AGO. RUPINDA WAS ONLY FIVE.
"WE FLOODED IN BY THE THOUSANDS. THE PARK WAS EVERYTHING THEY HAD PROMISED. IT WAS A MAGICAL DAY -- THE KIND ANY PARENT DREAMS OF GIVING HER CHILD.
"AND THEN THE SUN WENT DOWN.
"THE SKY SEEMED TO TWIST. THE AIR SHRIEKED. EVERYONE WAS SICK TO THEIR STOMACH.
"AND THE DOORS SLAMMED SHUT.
"AN ENERGY WALL HAD ENCIRCLED THE WHOLE PARK. NOTHING COULD BREAK IT. THE TICKLE-TOONS BECAME OUR WARDENS.
"WE WERE PRISONERS.

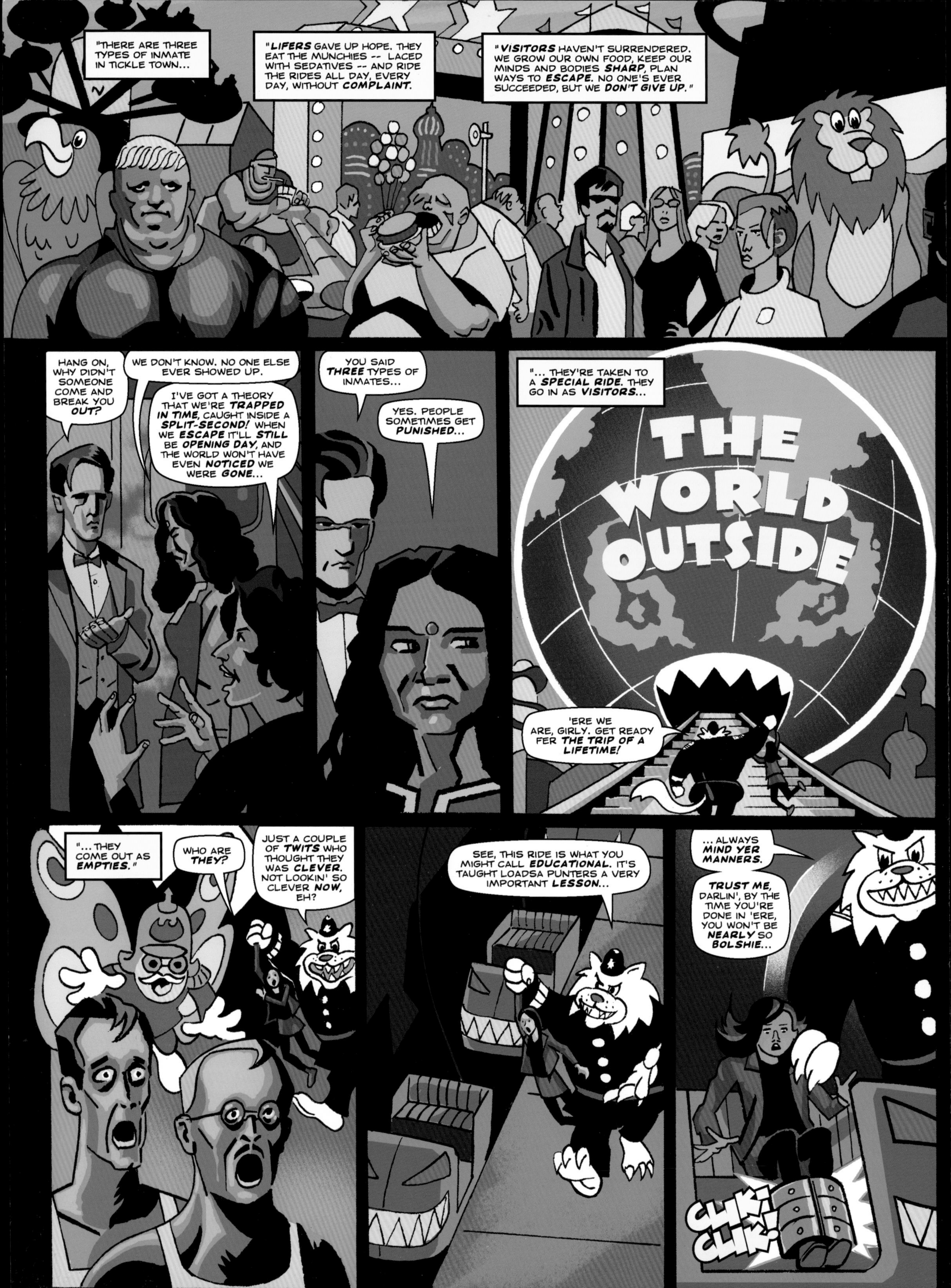
"THERE ARE THREE TYPES OF INMATE IN TICKLE TOWN...
"LIFERS GAVE UP HOPE. THEY EAT THE MUNCHIES -- LACED WITH SEDATIVES -- AND RIDE THE RIDES ALL DAY, EVERY DAY, WITHOUT COMPLAINT.
"VISITORS HAVEN'T SURRENDERED. WE GROW OUR OWN FOOD, KEEP OUR MINDS AND BODIES SHARP, PLAN WAYS TO ESCAPE. NO ONE'S EVER SUCCEEDED, BUT WE DON'T GIVE UP."
HANG ON, WHY DIDN'T SOMEONE COME AND BREAK YOU OUT?
WE DON'T KNOW. NO ONE ELSE EVER SHOWED UP.
I'VE GOT A THEORY THAT WE'RE TRAPPED IN TIME, CAUGHT INSIDE A SPLIT-SECOND! WHEN WE ESCAPE IT'LL STILL BE OPENING DAY, AND THE WORLD WON'T HAVE EVEN NOTICED WE WERE GONE...
YOU SAID THREE TYPES OF INMATES...
YES. PEOPLE SOMETIMES GET PUNISHED...
"... THEY'RE TAKEN TO A SPECIAL RIDE. THEY GO IN AS VISITORS...
THE WORLD OUTSIDE
'ERE WE ARE, GIRLY. GET READY FER THE TRIP OF A LIFETIME!
"... THEY COME OUT AS EMPTIES."
WHO ARE THEY?
JUST A COUPLE OF TWITS WHO THOUGHT THEY WAS CLEVER. NOT LOOKIN' SO CLEVER NOW, EH?
SEE, THIS RIDE IS WHAT YOU MIGHT CALL EDUCATIONAL. IT'S TAUGHT LOADSA PUNTERS A VERY IMPORTANT LESSON...
... ALWAYS MIND YER MANNERS.
TRUST ME, DARLIN', BY THE TIME YOU'RE DONE IN 'ERE, YOU WON'T BE NEARLY SO BOLSHIE...
CLIK! CLIK!

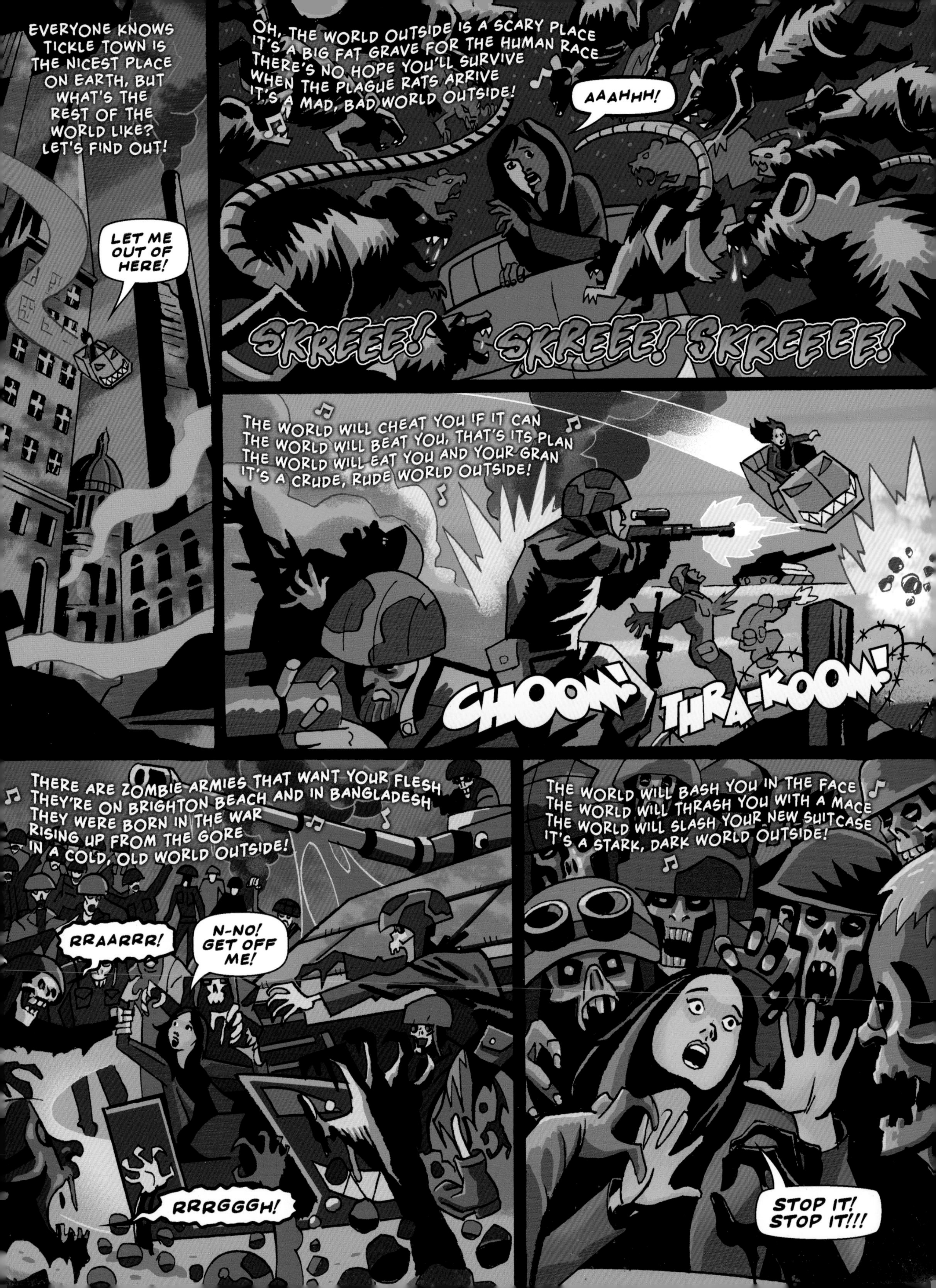
EVERYONE KNOWS TICKLE TOWN IS THE NICEST PLACE ON EARTH, BUT WHAT'S THE REST OF THE WORLD LIKE? LET'S FIND OUT!
LET ME OUT OF HERE!
OH, THE WORLD OUTSIDE IS A SCARY PLACE
IT'S A BIG FAT GRAVE FOR THE HUMAN RACE
THERE'S NO HOPE YOU'LL SURVIVE
WHEN THE PLAGUE RATS ARRIVE
IT'S A MAD, BAD WORLD OUTSIDE!
AAAHHH!
SKREEE! SKREEEE! SKREEEEE!
THE WORLD WILL CHEAT YOU IF IT CAN
THE WORLD WILL BEAT YOU, THAT'S ITS PLAN
THE WORLD WILL EAT YOU AND YOUR GRAN
IT'S A CRUDE, RUDE WORLD OUTSIDE!
CHOOM! THRA-KOOM!
THERE ARE ZOMBIE ARMIES THAT WANT YOUR FLESH
THEY'RE ON BRIGHTON BEACH AND IN BANGLADESH
THEY WERE BORN IN THE WAR
RISING UP FROM THE GORE
IN A COLD, OLD WORLD OUTSIDE!
RRAARRR!
N-NO! GET OFF ME!
RRRGGGH!
THE WORLD WILL BASH YOU IN THE FACE
THE WORLD WILL THRASH YOU WITH A MACE
THE WORLD WILL SLASH YOUR NEW SUITCASE
IT'S A STARK, DARK WORLD OUTSIDE!
STOP IT! STOP IT!!!

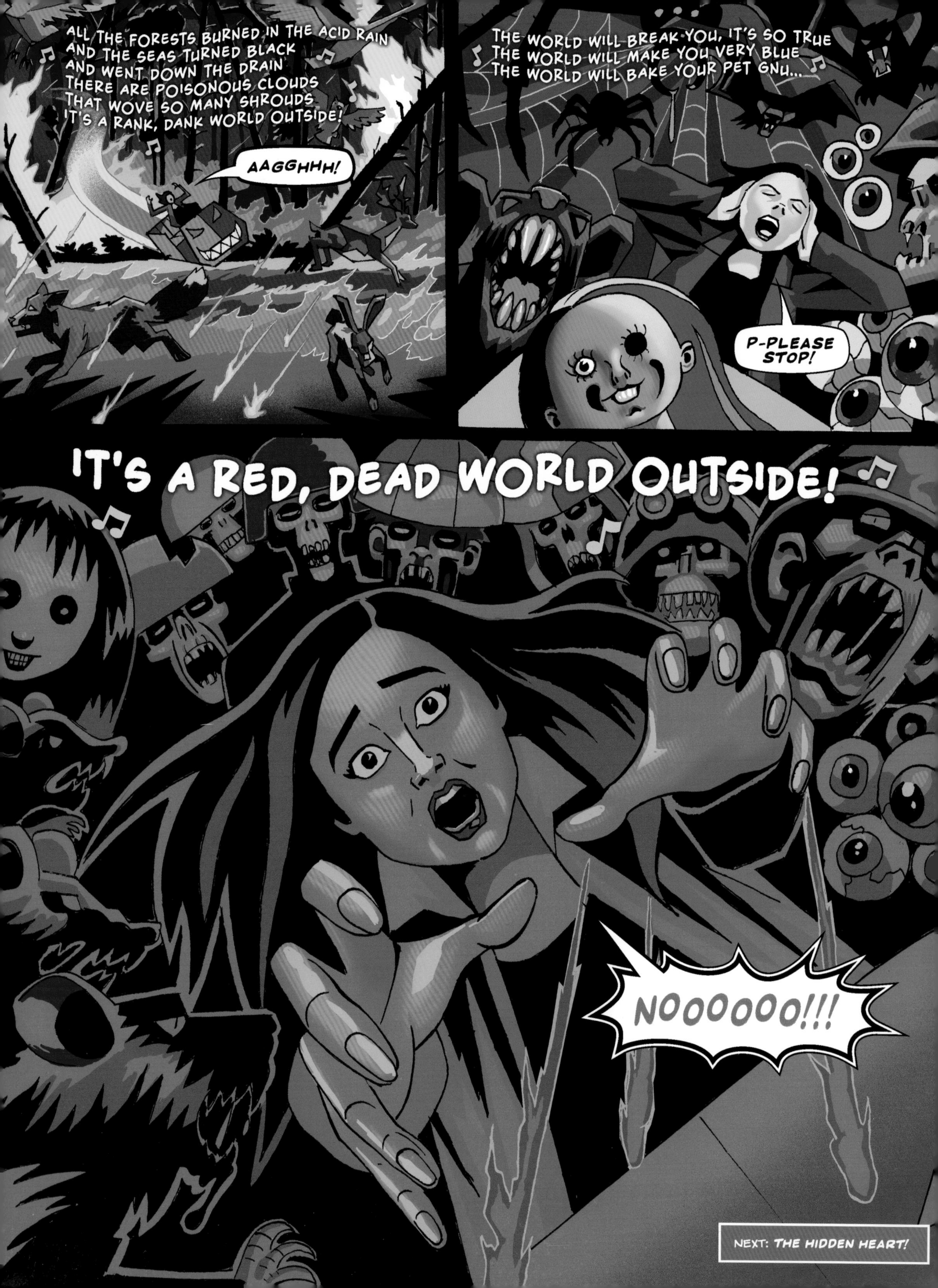
ALL THE FORESTS BURNED IN THE ACID RAIN
AND THE SEAS TURNED BLACK
AND WENT DOWN THE DRAIN
THERE ARE POISONOUS CLOUDS
THAT WOVE SO MANY SHROUDS
IT'S A RANK, DANK WORLD OUTSIDE!
AAGGHHH!
THE WORLD WILL BREAK YOU, IT'S SO TRUE
THE WORLD WILL MAKE YOU VERY BLUE
THE WORLD WILL BAKE YOUR PET GNU...
P-PLEASE STOP!
IT'S A RED, DEAD WORLD OUTSIDE!
NOOOOOO!!!
NEXT: THE HIDDEN HEART!

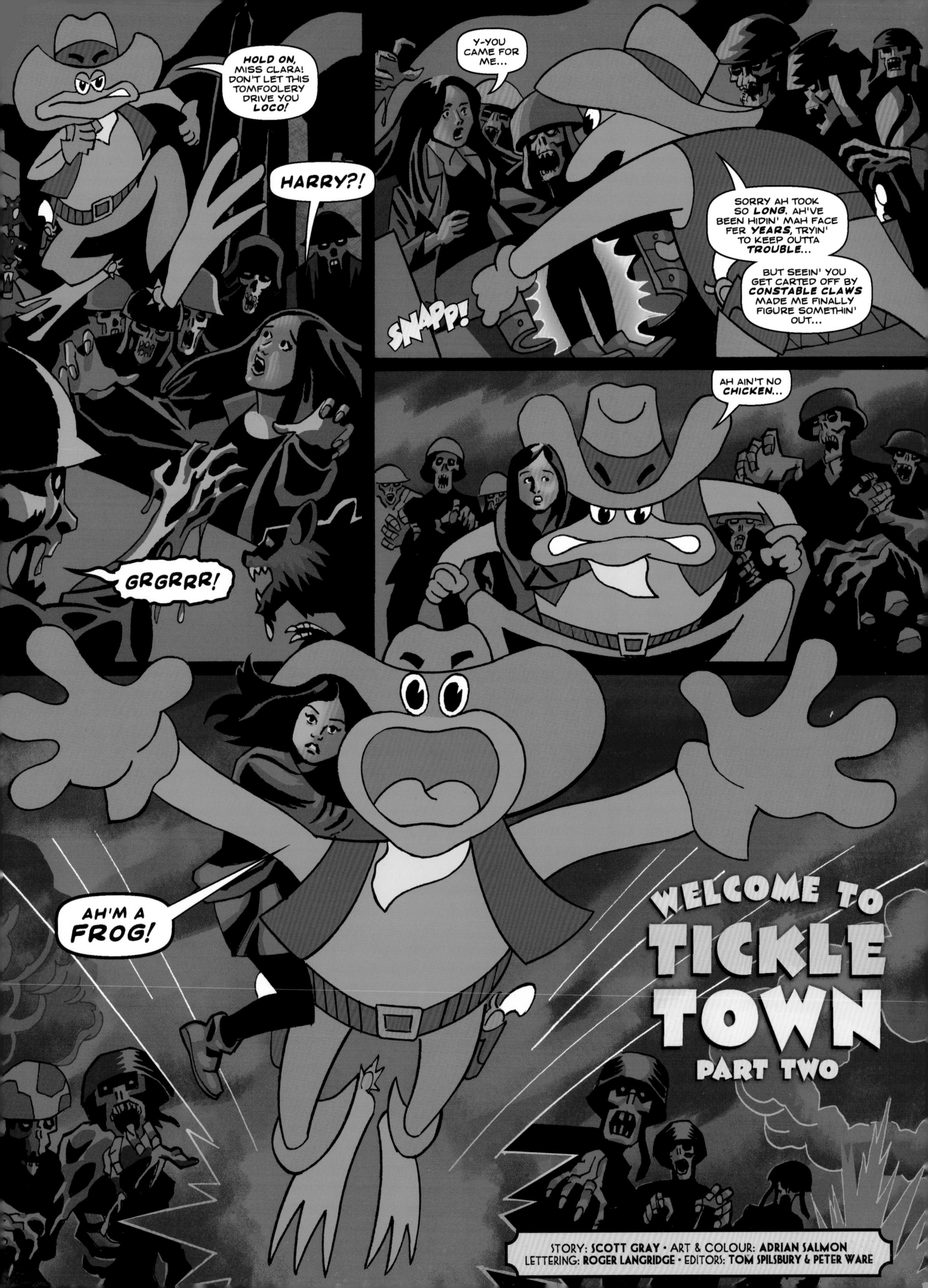

HOLD ON, MISS CLARA! DON'T LET THIS TOMFOOLERY DRIVE YOU LOCO!
HARRY?!
GRGRRR!
Y-YOU CAME FOR ME...
SORRY AH TOOK SO LONG. AH'VE BEEN HIDIN' MAH FACE FER YEARS, TRYIN' TO KEEP OUTTA TROUBLE...
BUT SEEIN' YOU GET CARTED OFF BY CONSTABLE CLAWS MADE ME FINALLY FIGURE SOMETHIN' OUT...
SNAPP!
AH AIN'T NO CHICKEN...
AH'M A FROG!
WELCOME TO TICKLE TOWN
PART TWO
STORY: SCOTT GRAY • ART & COLOUR: ADRIAN SALMON
LETTERING: ROGER LANGRIDGE • EDITORS: TOM SPILSBURY & PETER WARE

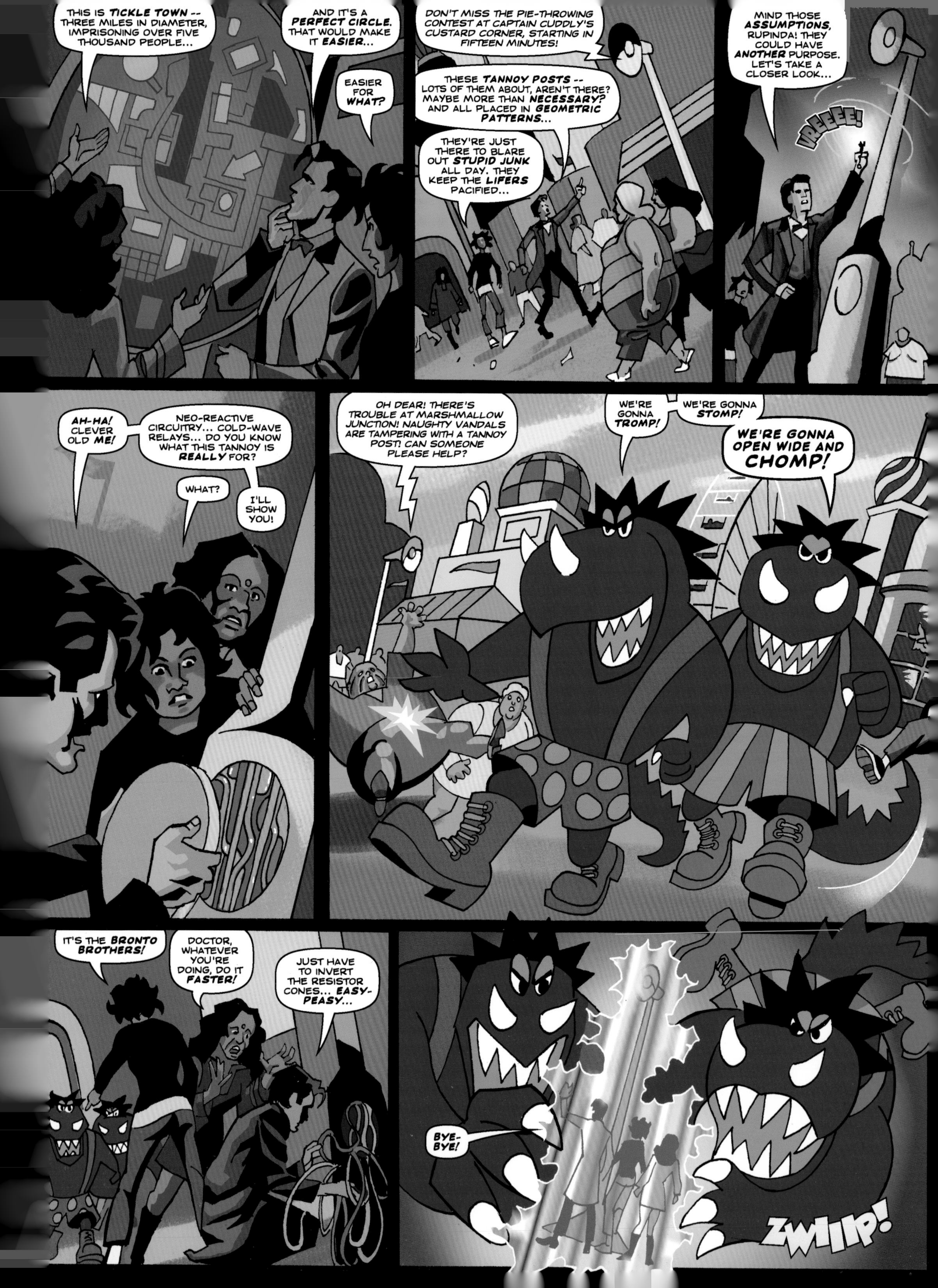
THIS IS TICKLE TOWN -- THREE MILES IN DIAMETER, IMPRISONING OVER FIVE THOUSAND PEOPLE...
AND IT'S A PERFECT CIRCLE. THAT WOULD MAKE IT EASIER...
EASIER FOR WHAT?
DON'T MISS THE PIE-THROWING CONTEST AT CAPTAIN CUDDLY'S CUSTARD CORNER, STARTING IN FIFTEEN MINUTES!
THESE TANNOY POSTS -- LOTS OF THEM ABOUT, AREN'T THERE? MAYBE MORE THAN NECESSARY? AND ALL PLACED IN GEOMETRIC PATTERNS...
THEY'RE JUST THERE TO BLARE OUT STUPID JUNK ALL DAY. THEY KEEP THE LIFERS PACIFIED...
MIND THOSE ASSUMPTIONS, RUPINDA! THEY COULD HAVE ANOTHER PURPOSE. LET'S TAKE A CLOSER LOOK...
VREEEE!
AH-HA! CLEVER OLD ME!
NEO-REACTIVE CIRCUITRY... COLD-WAVE RELAYS... DO YOU KNOW WHAT THIS TANNOY IS REALLY FOR?
WHAT?
I'LL SHOW YOU!
OH DEAR! THERE'S TROUBLE AT MARSHMALLOW JUNCTION! NAUGHTY VANDALS ARE TAMPERING WITH A TANNOY POST! CAN SOMEONE PLEASE HELP?
WE'RE GONNA TROMP!
WE'RE GONNA STOMP!
WE'RE GONNA OPEN WIDE AND CHOMP!
IT'S THE BRONTO BROTHERS!
DOCTOR, WHATEVER YOU'RE DOING, DO IT FASTER!
JUST HAVE TO INVERT THE RESISTOR CONES... EASY-PEASY...
BYE-BYE!
ZWIIIP!

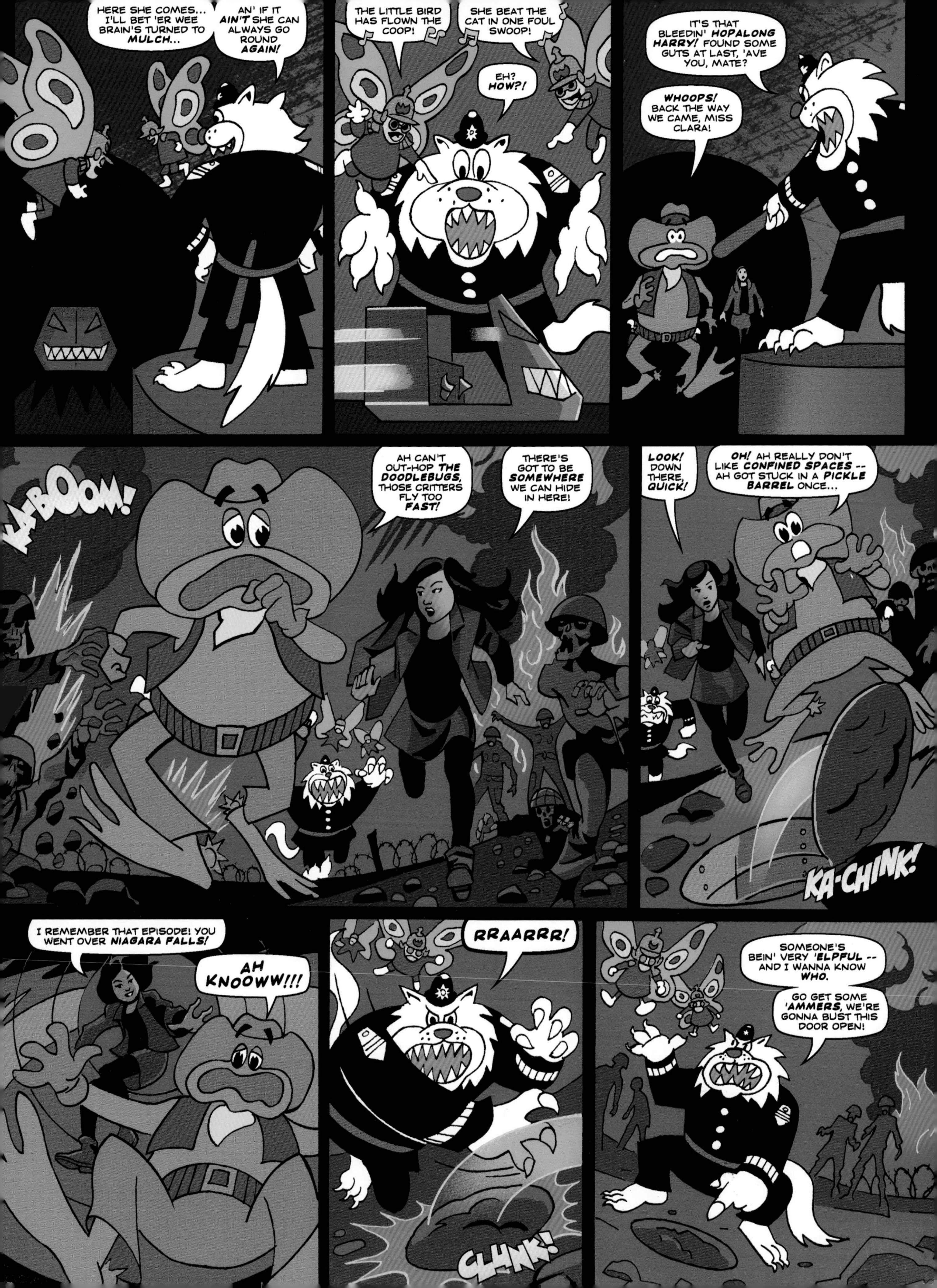
HERE SHE COMES... I'LL BET 'ER WEE BRAIN'S TURNED TO MULCH...
AN' IF IT AIN'T SHE CAN ALWAYS GO ROUND AGAIN!
THE LITTLE BIRD HAS FLOWN THE COOP!
SHE BEAT THE CAT IN ONE FOUL SWOOP!
EH? HOW?!
IT'S THAT BLEEDIN' HOPALONG HARRY! FOUND SOME GUTS AT LAST, 'AVE YOU, MATE?
WHOOPS! BACK THE WAY WE CAME, MISS CLARA!
KA-BOOM!
AH CAN'T OUT-HOP THE DOODLEBUGS, THOSE CRITTERS FLY TOO FAST!
THERE'S GOT TO BE SOMEWHERE WE CAN HIDE IN HERE!
LOOK! DOWN THERE, QUICK!
OH! AH REALLY DON'T LIKE CONFINED SPACES -- AH GOT STUCK IN A PICKLE BARREL ONCE...
KA-CHINK!
I REMEMBER THAT EPISODE! YOU WENT OVER NIAGARA FALLS!
AH KNOOWW!!!
RRAARRR!
CLUNK!
SOMEONE'S BEIN' VERY 'ELPFUL -- AND I WANNA KNOW WHO.
GO GET SOME 'AMMERS, WE'RE GONNA BUST THIS DOOR OPEN!

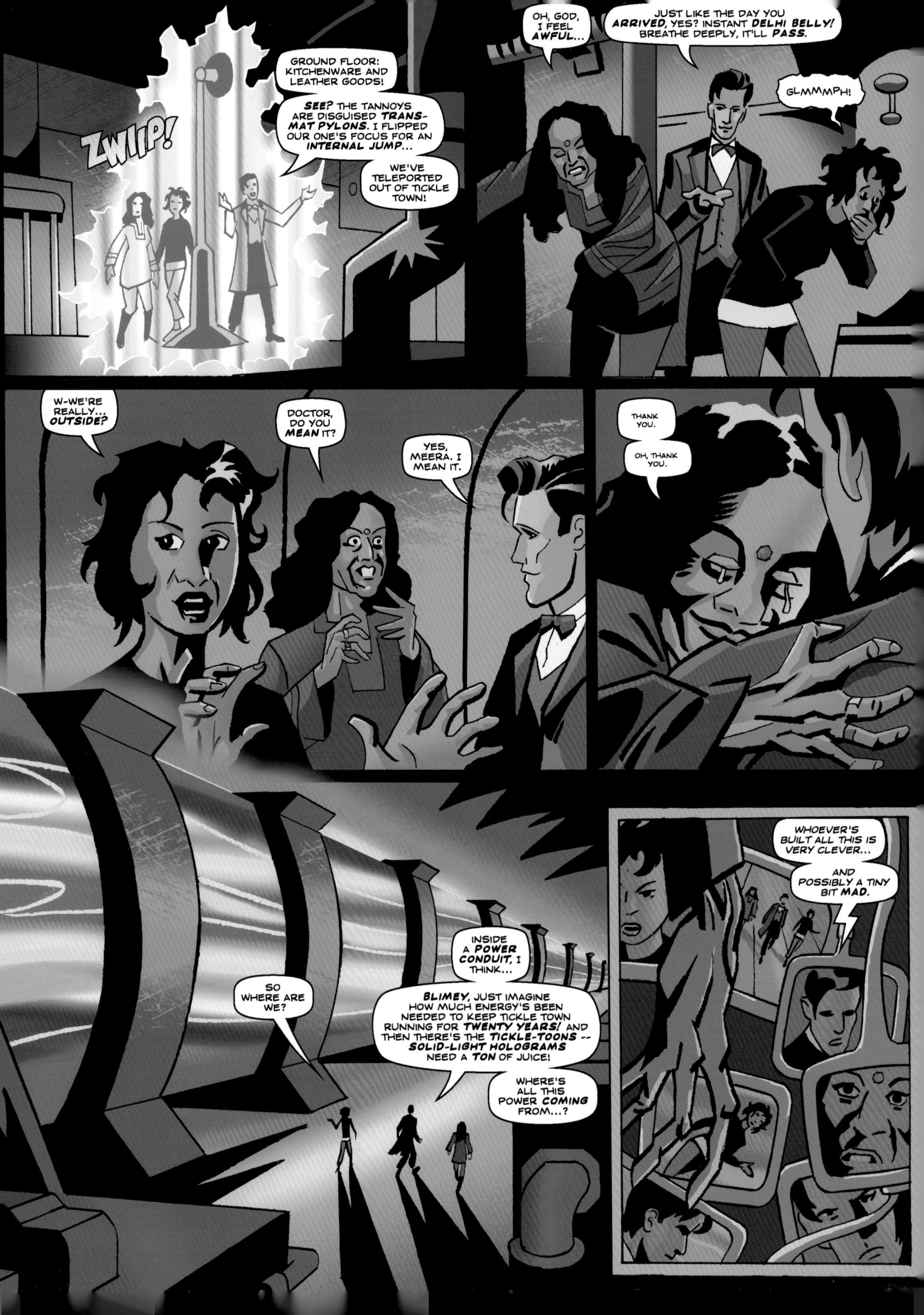
ZWIIP!
GROUND FLOOR: KITCHENWARE AND LEATHER GOODS!
SEE? THE TANNOYS ARE DISGUISED TRANS-MAT PYLONS. I FLIPPED OUR ONE'S FOCUS FOR AN INTERNAL JUMP...
WE'VE TELEPORTED OUT OF TICKLE TOWN!
OH, GOD, I FEEL AWFUL...
JUST LIKE THE DAY YOU ARRIVED, YES? INSTANT DELHI BELLY! BREATHE DEEPLY, IT'LL PASS.
GLMMMPH!
W-WE'RE REALLY... OUTSIDE?
DOCTOR, DO YOU MEAN IT?
YES, MEERA. I MEAN IT.
THANK YOU.
OH, THANK YOU.
SO WHERE ARE WE?
INSIDE A POWER CONDUIT, I THINK...
BLIMEY, JUST IMAGINE HOW MUCH ENERGY'S BEEN NEEDED TO KEEP TICKLE TOWN RUNNING FOR TWENTY YEARS! AND THEN THERE'S THE TICKLE-TOONS -- SOLID-LIGHT HOLOGRAMS NEED A TON OF JUICE!
WHERE'S ALL THIS POWER COMING FROM...?
WHOEVER'S BUILT ALL THIS IS VERY CLEVER...
AND POSSIBLY A TINY BIT MAD.

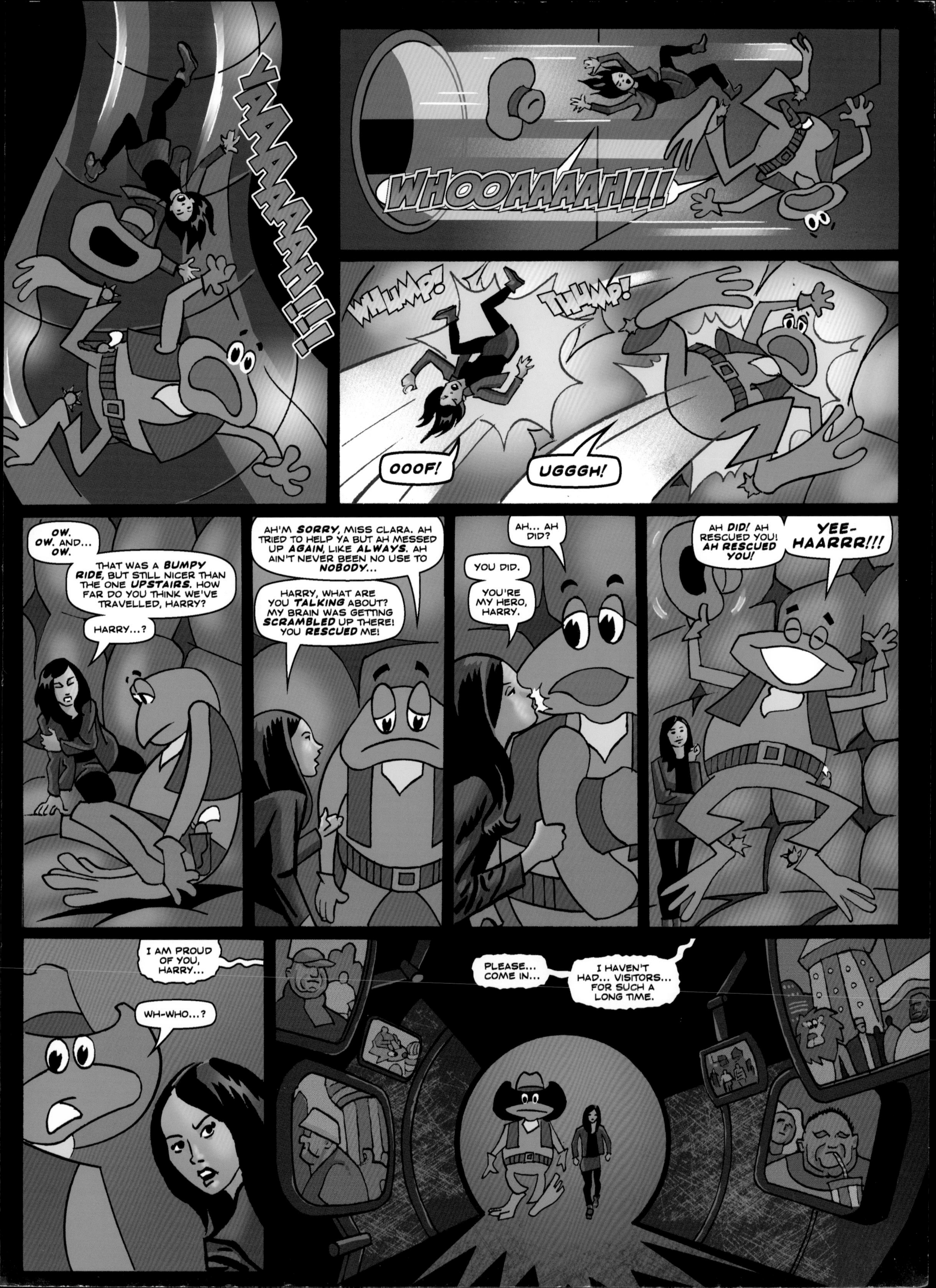
YAAAAAAAAH!!!!
WHOOAAAAAH!!!
WHUMP!
THUMP!
OOOF!
UGGGH!
OW. OW. AND... OW.
THAT WAS A BUMPY RIDE, BUT STILL NICER THAN THE ONE UPSTAIRS. HOW FAR DO YOU THINK WE'VE TRAVELLED, HARRY?
HARRY...?
AH'M SORRY, MISS CLARA. AH TRIED TO HELP YA BUT AH MESSED UP AGAIN, LIKE ALWAYS. AH AIN'T NEVER BEEN NO USE TO NOBODY...
HARRY, WHAT ARE YOU TALKING ABOUT? MY BRAIN WAS GETTING SCRAMBLED UP THERE! YOU RESCUED ME!
AH... AH DID?
YOU DID.
YOU'RE MY HERO, HARRY.
AH DID! AH RESCUED YOU! AH RESCUED YOU!
YEE-HAARRR!!!
I AM PROUD OF YOU, HARRY...
WH-WHO...?
PLEASE... COME IN...
I HAVEN'T HAD... VISITORS... FOR SUCH A LONG TIME.

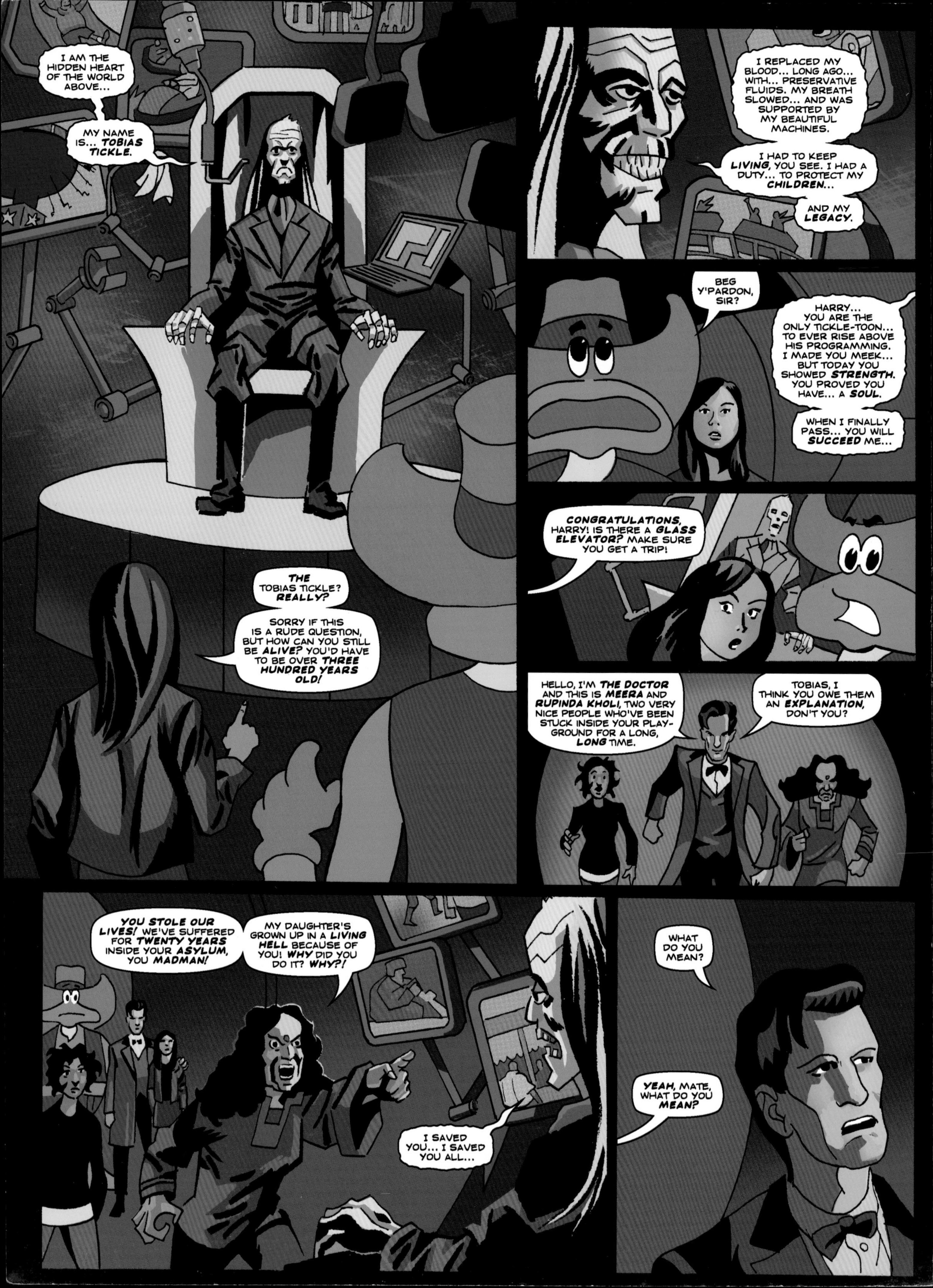
I AM THE HIDDEN HEART OF THE WORLD ABOVE...
MY NAME IS... TOBIAS TICKLE.
THE TOBIAS TICKLE? REALLY?
SORRY IF THIS IS A RUDE QUESTION, BUT HOW CAN YOU STILL BE ALIVE? YOU'D HAVE TO BE OVER THREE HUNDRED YEARS OLD!
I REPLACED MY BLOOD... LONG AGO... WITH... PRESERVATIVE FLUIDS. MY BREATH SLOWED... AND WAS SUPPORTED BY MY BEAUTIFUL MACHINES.
I HAD TO KEEP LIVING, YOU SEE. I HAD A DUTY... TO PROTECT MY CHILDREN...
AND MY LEGACY.
BEG Y'PARDON, SIR?
HARRY... YOU ARE THE ONLY TICKLE-TOON... TO EVER RISE ABOVE HIS PROGRAMMING. I MADE YOU MEEK... BUT TODAY YOU SHOWED STRENGTH. YOU PROVED YOU HAVE... A SOUL.
WHEN I FINALLY PASS... YOU WILL SUCCEED ME...
CONGRATULATIONS, HARRY! IS THERE A GLASS ELEVATOR? MAKE SURE YOU GET A TRIP!
HELLO, I'M THE DOCTOR AND THIS IS MEERA AND RUPINDA KHOLI, TWO VERY NICE PEOPLE WHO'VE BEEN STUCK INSIDE YOUR PLAY-GROUND FOR A LONG, LONG TIME.
TOBIAS, I THINK YOU OWE THEM AN EXPLANATION, DON'T YOU?
YOU STOLE OUR LIVES! WE'VE SUFFERED FOR TWENTY YEARS INSIDE YOUR ASYLUM, YOU MADMAN!
MY DAUGHTER'S GROWN UP IN A LIVING HELL BECAUSE OF YOU! WHY DID YOU DO IT? WHY?!
I SAVED YOU... I SAVED YOU ALL...
WHAT DO YOU MEAN?
YEAH, MATE, WHAT DO YOU MEAN?

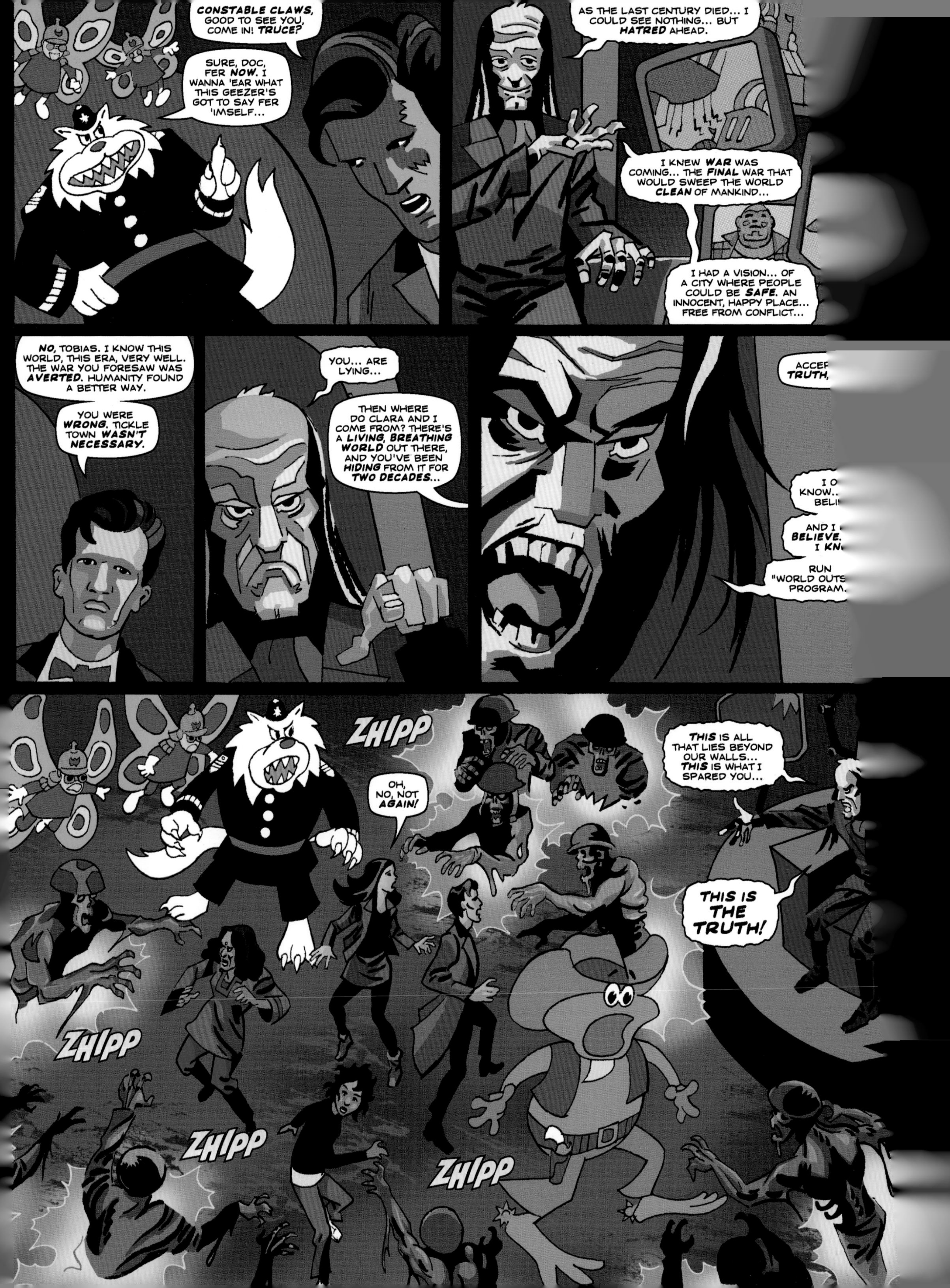

CONSTABLE CLAWS, GOOD TO SEE YOU, COME IN! TRUCE?
SURE, DOC, FER NOW. I WANNA 'EAR WHAT THIS GEEZER'S GOT TO SAY FER 'IMSELF...
AS THE LAST CENTURY DIED... I COULD SEE NOTHING... BUT HATRED AHEAD.
I KNEW WAR WAS COMING... THE FINAL WAR THAT WOULD SWEEP THE WORLD CLEAN OF MANKIND...
I HAD A VISION... OF A CITY WHERE PEOPLE COULD BE SAFE. AN INNOCENT, HAPPY PLACE... FREE FROM CONFLICT...
NO, TOBIAS. I KNOW THIS WORLD, THIS ERA, VERY WELL. THE WAR YOU FORESAW WAS AVERTED. HUMANITY FOUND A BETTER WAY.
YOU WERE WRONG. TICKLE TOWN WASN'T NECESSARY.
YOU... ARE LYING...
THEN WHERE DO CLARA AND I COME FROM? THERE'S A LIVING, BREATHING WORLD OUT THERE, AND YOU'VE BEEN HIDING FROM IT FOR TWO DECADES...
TRUTH,
KNOW...
RUN
PROGRAM.
ZHIPP
OH, NO, NOT AGAIN!
THIS IS ALL THAT LIES BEYOND OUR WALLS... THIS IS WHAT I SPARED YOU...
THIS IS THE TRUTH!
ZHIPP
ZHIPP
ZHIPP

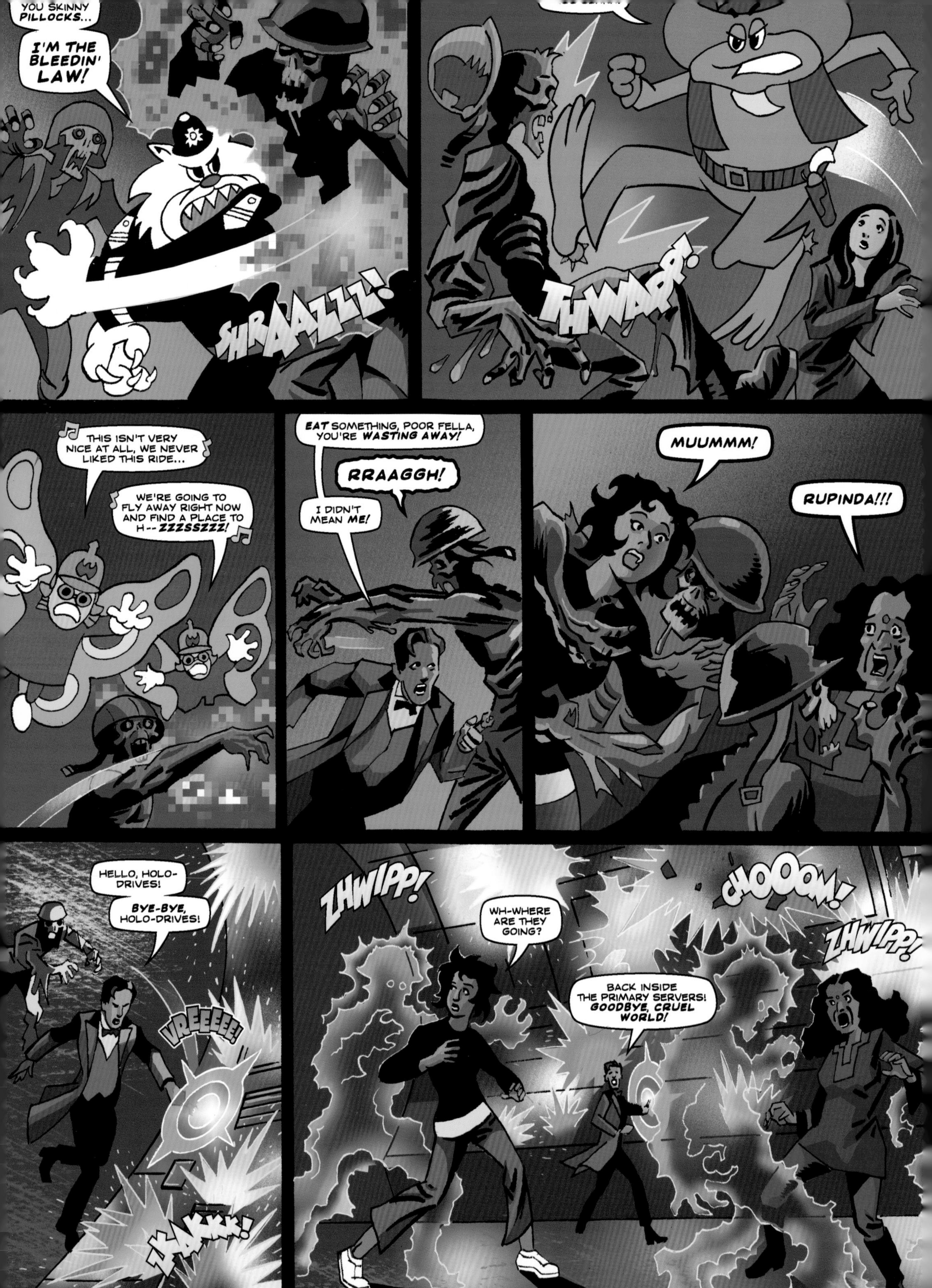
YOU SKINNY PILLOCKS...
I'M THE BLEEDIN' LAW!
SHRAAZZZZ!
THWACK!
THIS ISN'T VERY NICE AT ALL, WE NEVER LIKED THIS RIDE...
WE'RE GOING TO FLY AWAY RIGHT NOW AND FIND A PLACE TO H -- ZZZSSZZZ!
EAT SOMETHING, POOR FELLA, YOU'RE WASTING AWAY!
RRAAGGH!
I DIDN'T MEAN ME!
MUUMMM!
RUPINDA!!!
HELLO, HOLO-DRIVES!
BYE-BYE, HOLO-DRIVES!
VREEEEE!
ZAKKK!
ZHWIPP!
WH-WHERE ARE THEY GOING?
CHOOOM!
ZHWIPP!
BACK INSIDE THE PRIMARY SERVERS! GOODBYE, CRUEL WORLD!

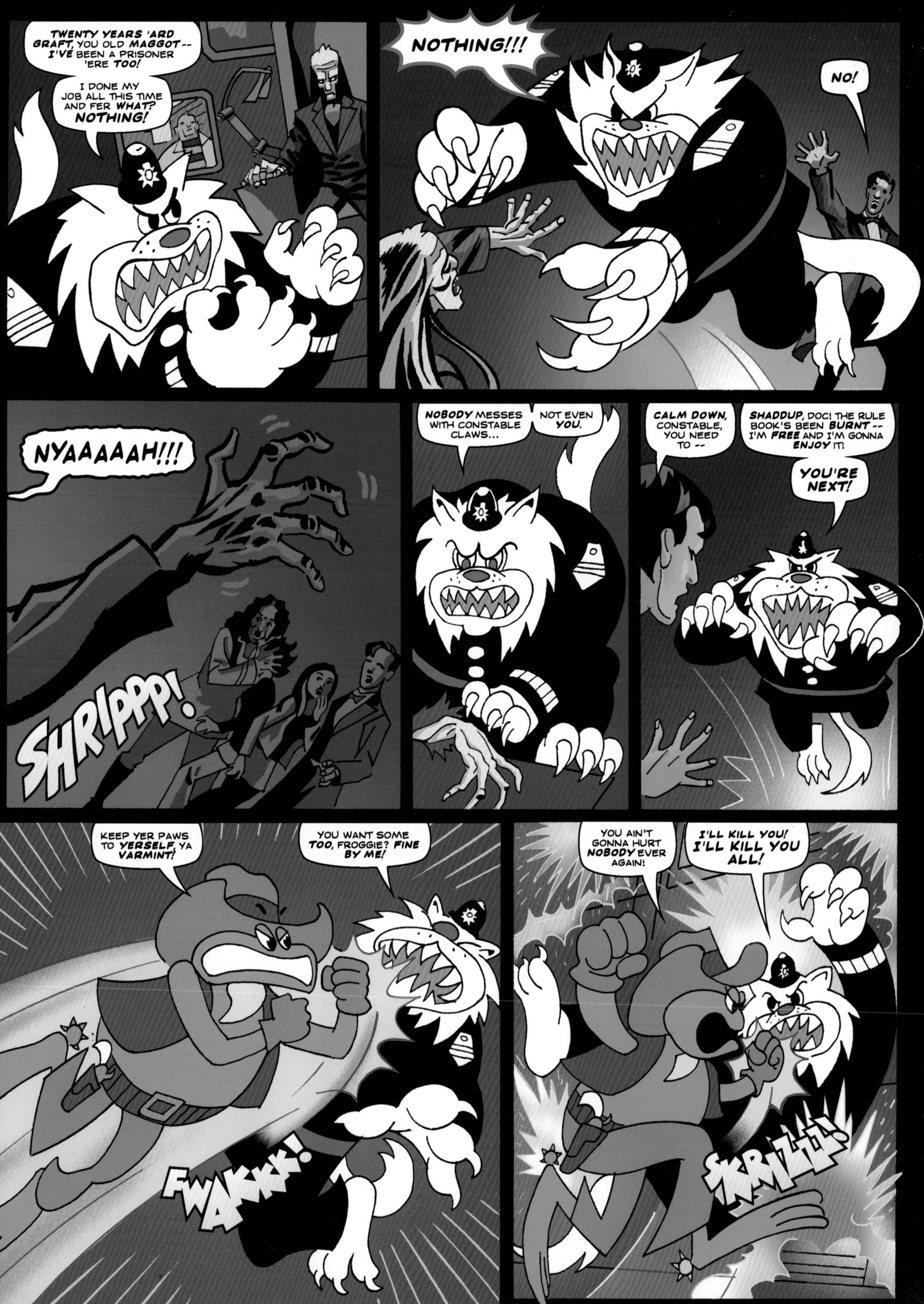

TWENTY YEARS 'ARD GRAFT, YOU OLD MAGGOT -- I'VE BEEN A PRISONER 'ERE TOO!
I DONE MY JOB ALL THIS TIME AND FER WHAT? NOTHING!
NOTHING!!!
NO!
NYAAAAAH!!!
SHRIPPP!
NOBODY MESSES WITH CONSTABLE CLAWS...
NOT EVEN YOU.
CALM DOWN, CONSTABLE, YOU NEED TO --
SHADDUP, DOC! THE RULE BOOK'S BEEN BURNT -- I'M FREE AND I'M GONNA ENJOY IT!
YOU'RE NEXT!
KEEP YER PAWS TO YERSELF, YA VARMINT!
YOU WANT SOME TOO, FROGGIE? FINE BY ME!
FWAKKK!
YOU AIN'T GONNA HURT NOBODY EVER AGAIN!
I'LL KILL YOU! I'LL KILL YOU ALL!
SKRIZZZ!

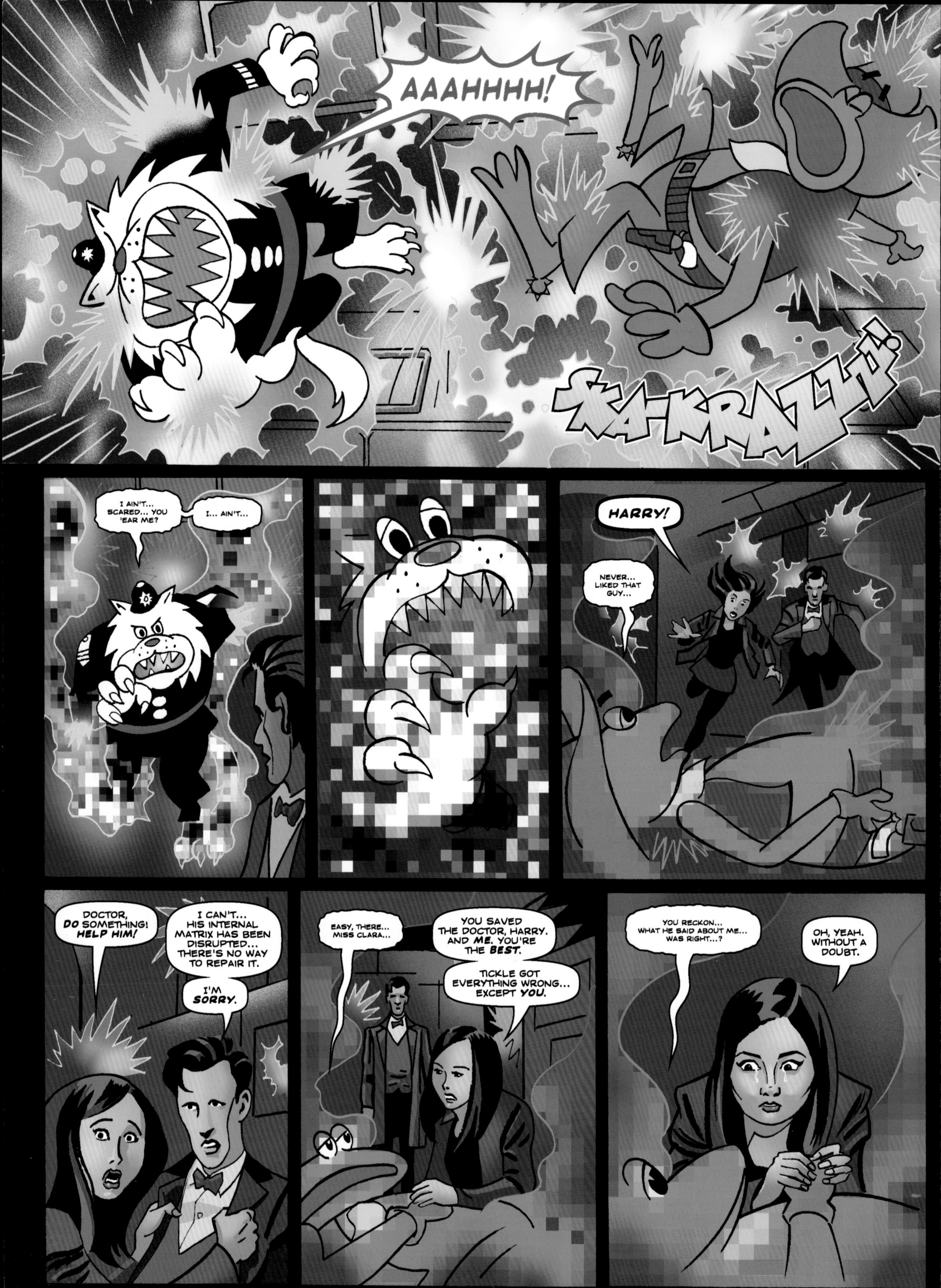
AAAHHHH!
SKA-KRAZZT!
I AIN'T... SCARED... YOU 'EAR ME?
I... AIN'T...
HARRY!
NEVER... LIKED THAT GUY...
DOCTOR, DO SOMETHING! HELP HIM!
I CAN'T... HIS INTERNAL MATRIX HAS BEEN DISRUPTED... THERE'S NO WAY TO REPAIR IT.
I'M SORRY.
EASY, THERE... MISS CLARA...
YOU SAVED THE DOCTOR, HARRY. AND ME. YOU'RE THE BEST.
TICKLE GOT EVERYTHING WRONG... EXCEPT YOU.
YOU RECKON... WHAT HE SAID ABOUT ME... WAS RIGHT...?
OH, YEAH. WITHOUT A DOUBT.

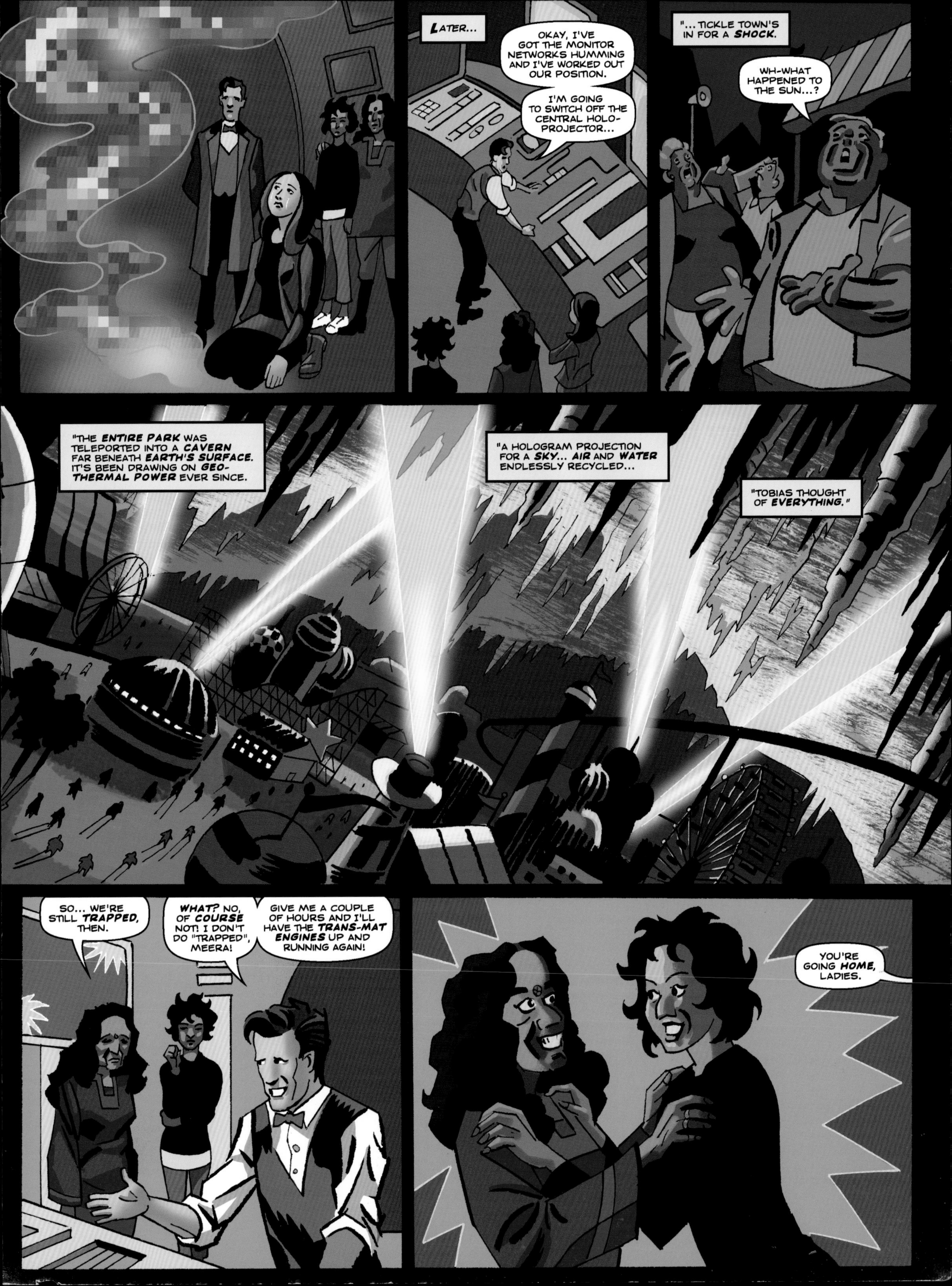
LATER...
OKAY, I'VE GOT THE MONITOR NETWORKS HUMMING AND I'VE WORKED OUT OUR POSITION.
I'M GOING TO SWITCH OFF THE CENTRAL HOLO-PROJECTOR...
"... TICKLE TOWN'S IN FOR A SHOCK.
WH-WHAT HAPPENED TO THE SUN...?
"THE ENTIRE PARK WAS TELEPORTED INTO A CAVERN FAR BENEATH EARTH'S SURFACE. IT'S BEEN DRAWING ON GEO-THERMAL POWER EVER SINCE.
"A HOLOGRAM PROJECTION FOR A SKY... AIR AND WATER ENDLESSLY RECYCLED...
"TOBIAS THOUGHT OF EVERYTHING."
SO... WE'RE STILL TRAPPED, THEN.
WHAT? NO, OF COURSE NOT! I DON'T DO "TRAPPED", MEERA!
GIVE ME A COUPLE OF HOURS AND I'LL HAVE THE TRANS-MAT ENGINES UP AND RUNNING AGAIN!
YOU'RE GOING HOME, LADIES.

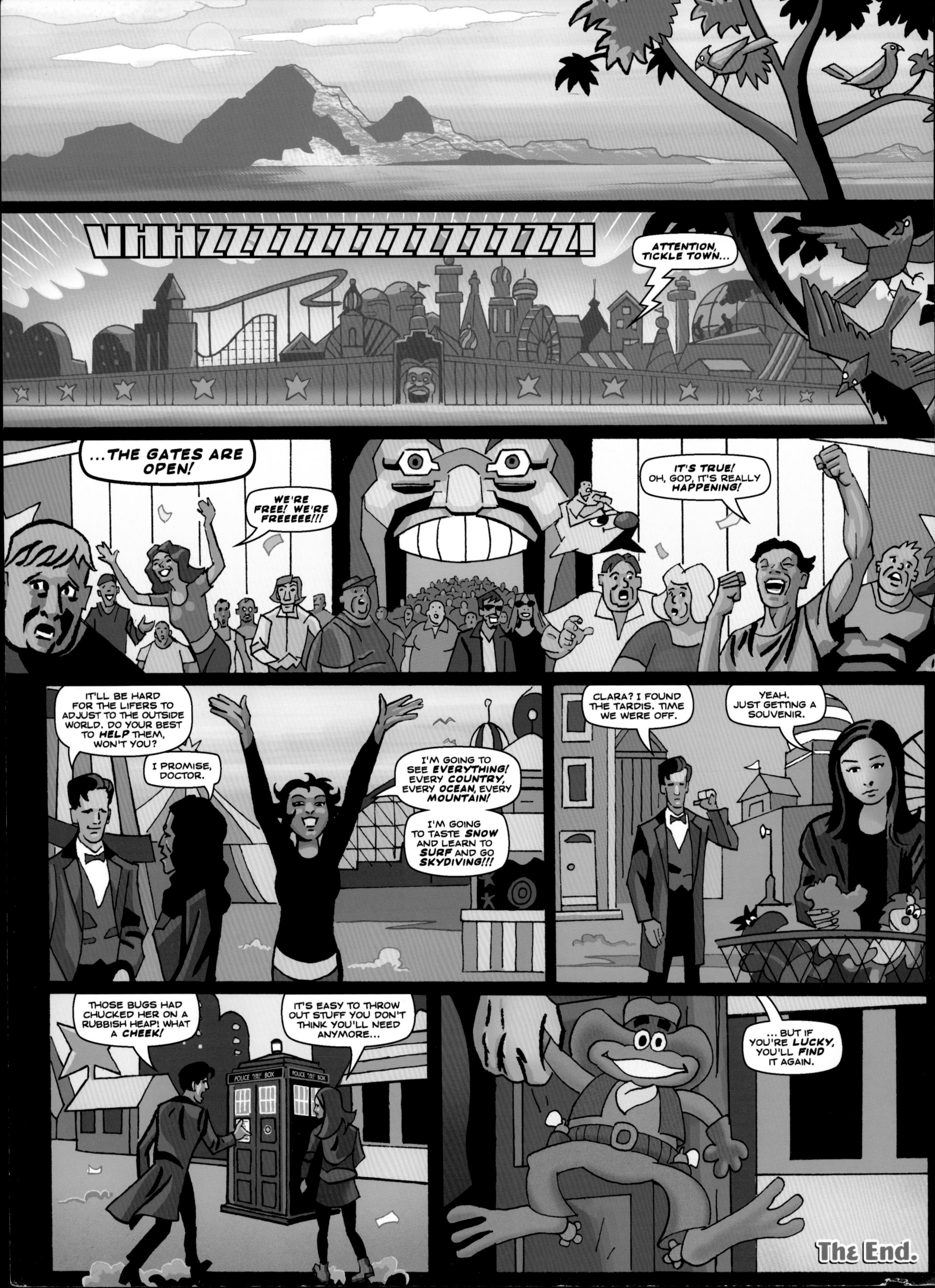
VHHZZZZZZZZZZZZZZZZZ!
ATTENTION, TICKLE TOWN...
...THE GATES ARE OPEN!
WE'RE FREE! WE'RE FREEEEE!!!
IT'S TRUE! OH, GOD, IT'S REALLY HAPPENING!
IT'LL BE HARD FOR THE LIFERS TO ADJUST TO THE OUTSIDE WORLD. DO YOUR BEST TO HELP THEM, WON'T YOU?
I PROMISE, DOCTOR.
I'M GOING TO SEE EVERYTHING! EVERY COUNTRY, EVERY OCEAN, EVERY MOUNTAIN!
I'M GOING TO TASTE SNOW AND LEARN TO SURF AND GO SKYDIVING!!!
CLARA? I FOUND THE TARDIS. TIME WE WERE OFF.
YEAH. JUST GETTING A SOUVENIR.
THOSE BUGS HAD CHUCKED HER ON A RUBBISH HEAP! WHAT A CHEEK!
IT'S EASY TO THROW OUT STUFF YOU DON'T THINK YOU'LL NEED ANYMORE...
POLICE PUBLIC CALL BOX
... BUT IF YOU'RE LUCKY, YOU'LL FIND IT AGAIN.
The End.

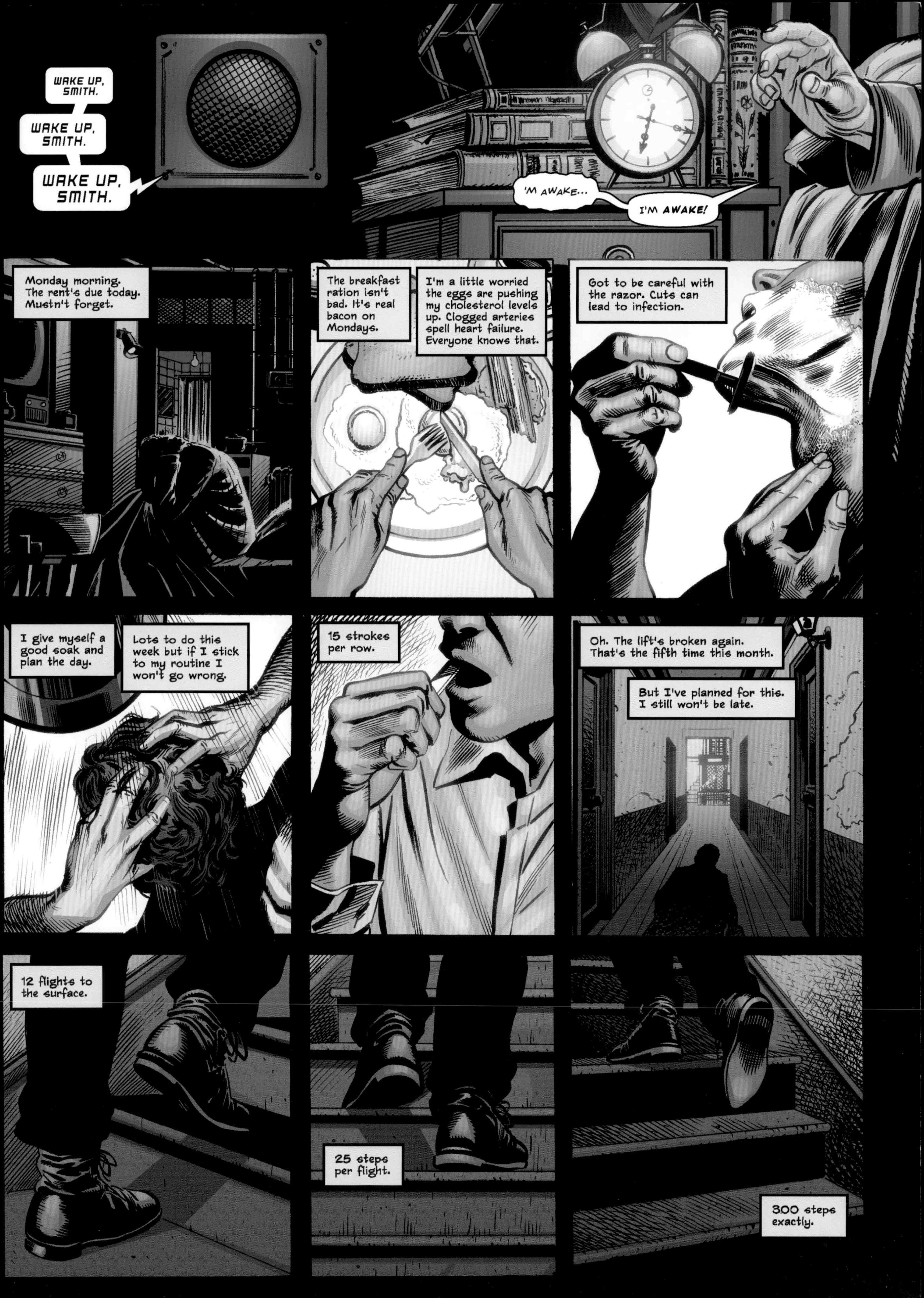
WAKE UP, SMITH.
WAKE UP, SMITH.
WAKE UP, SMITH.
'M AWAKE...
I'M AWAKE!
Monday morning. The rent's due today. Mustn't forget.
The breakfast ration isn't bad. It's real bacon on Mondays.
I'm a little worried the eggs are pushing my cholesterol levels up. Clogged arteries spell heart failure. Everyone knows that.
Got to be careful with the razor. Cuts can lead to infection.
I give myself a good soak and plan the day.
Lots to do this week but if I stick to my routine I won't go wrong.
15 strokes per row.
Oh. The lift's broken again. That's the fifth time this month.
But I've planned for this. I still won't be late.
12 flights to the surface.
25 steps per flight.
300 steps exactly.

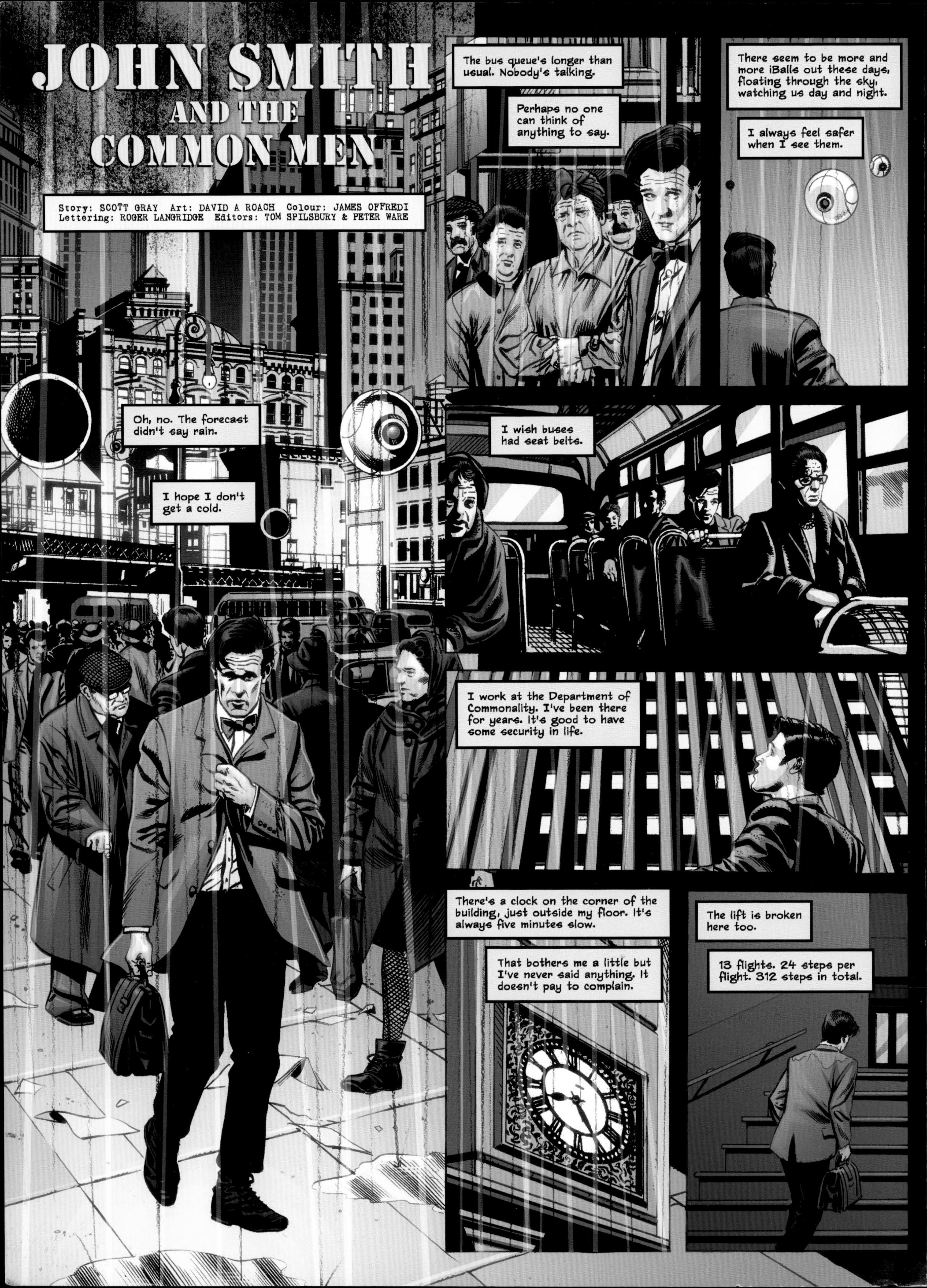
JOHN SMITH AND THE COMMON MEN
Story: SCOTT GRAY Art: DAVID A ROACH Colour: JAMES OFFREDI Lettering: ROGER LANGRIDGE Editors: TOM SPILSBURY & PETER WARE
Oh, no. The forecast didn't say rain.
I hope I don't get a cold.
The bus queue's longer than usual. Nobody's talking.
Perhaps no one can think of anything to say.
There seem to be more and more iBalls out these days, floating through the sky, watching us day and night.
I always feel safer when I see them.
I wish buses had seat belts.
I work at the Department of Commonality. I've been there for years. It's good to have some security in life.
There's a clock on the corner of the building, just outside my floor. It's always five minutes slow.
That bothers me a little but I've never said anything. It doesn't pay to complain.
The lift is broken here too.
13 flights. 24 steps per flight. 312 steps in total.

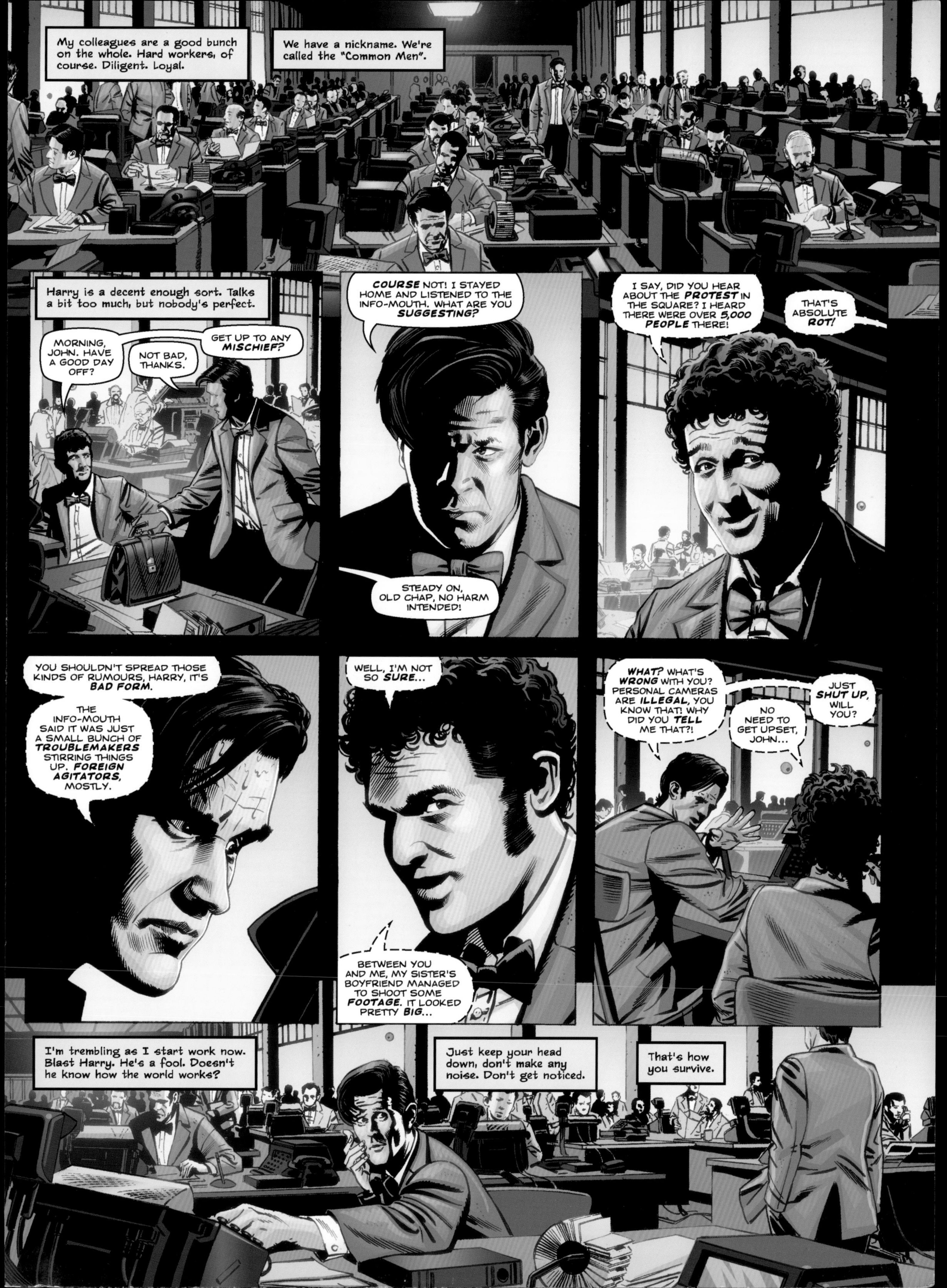

My colleagues are a good bunch on the whole. Hard workers, of course. Diligent. Loyal.
We have a nickname. We're called the "Common Men".
Harry is a decent enough sort. Talks a bit too much, but nobody's perfect.
MORNING, JOHN. HAVE A GOOD DAY OFF?
NOT BAD, THANKS.
GET UP TO ANY MISCHIEF?
COURSE NOT! I STAYED HOME AND LISTENED TO THE INFO-MOUTH. WHAT ARE YOU SUGGESTING?
STEADY ON, OLD CHAP, NO HARM INTENDED!
I SAY, DID YOU HEAR ABOUT THE PROTEST IN THE SQUARE? I HEARD THERE WERE OVER 5,000 PEOPLE THERE!
THAT'S ABSOLUTE ROT!
YOU SHOULDN'T SPREAD THOSE KINDS OF RUMOURS, HARRY, IT'S BAD FORM.
THE INFO-MOUTH SAID IT WAS JUST A SMALL BUNCH OF TROUBLEMAKERS STIRRING THINGS UP. FOREIGN AGITATORS, MOSTLY.
WELL, I'M NOT SO SURE...
BETWEEN YOU AND ME, MY SISTER'S BOYFRIEND MANAGED TO SHOOT SOME FOOTAGE. IT LOOKED PRETTY BIG...
WHAT? WHAT'S WRONG WITH YOU? PERSONAL CAMERAS ARE ILLEGAL, YOU KNOW THAT! WHY DID YOU TELL ME THAT?!
NO NEED TO GET UPSET, JOHN...
JUST SHUT UP, WILL YOU?
I'm trembling as I start work now. Blast Harry. He's a fool. Doesn't he know how the world works?
Just keep your head down, don't make any noise. Don't get noticed.
That's how you survive.

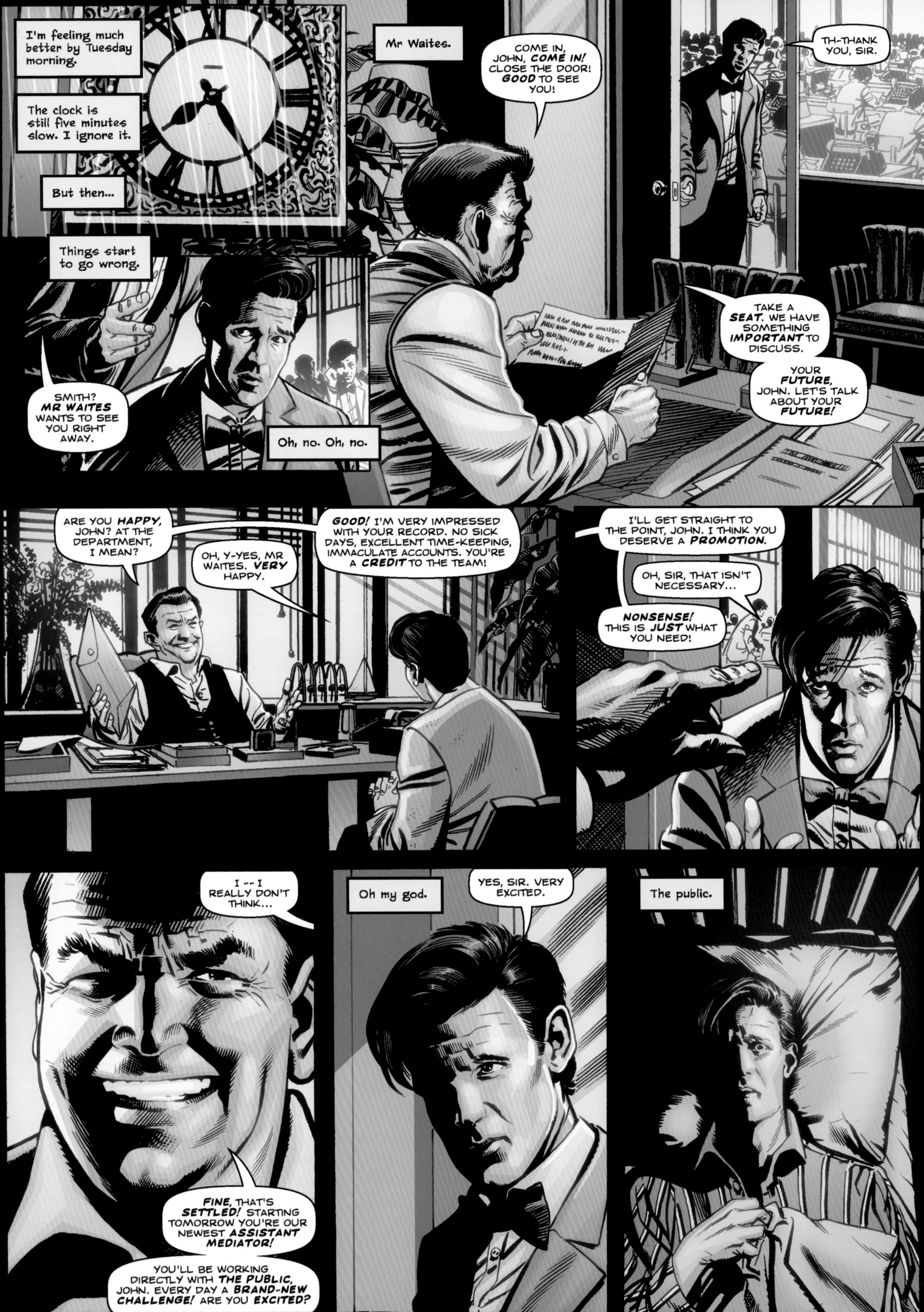
I'm feeling much better by Tuesday morning.
The clock is still five minutes slow. I ignore it.
But then...
Things start to go wrong.
SMITH? MR WAITES WANTS TO SEE YOU RIGHT AWAY.
Oh, no. Oh, no.
Mr Waites.
COME IN, JOHN, COME IN! CLOSE THE DOOR! GOOD TO SEE YOU!
TH-THANK YOU, SIR.
TAKE A SEAT. WE HAVE SOMETHING IMPORTANT TO DISCUSS.
YOUR FUTURE, JOHN. LET'S TALK ABOUT YOUR FUTURE!
ARE YOU HAPPY, JOHN? AT THE DEPARTMENT, I MEAN?
OH, Y-YES, MR WAITES. VERY HAPPY.
GOOD! I'M VERY IMPRESSED WITH YOUR RECORD. NO SICK DAYS, EXCELLENT TIME-KEEPING, IMMACULATE ACCOUNTS. YOU'RE A CREDIT TO THE TEAM!
I'LL GET STRAIGHT TO THE POINT, JOHN. I THINK YOU DESERVE A PROMOTION.
OH, SIR, THAT ISN'T NECESSARY...
NONSENSE! THIS IS JUST WHAT YOU NEED!
I -- I REALLY DON'T THINK...
FINE, THAT'S SETTLED! STARTING TOMORROW YOU'RE OUR NEWEST ASSISTANT MEDIATOR!
YOU'LL BE WORKING DIRECTLY WITH THE PUBLIC, JOHN. EVERY DAY A BRAND-NEW CHALLENGE! ARE YOU EXCITED?
Oh my god.
YES, SIR. VERY EXCITED.
The public.

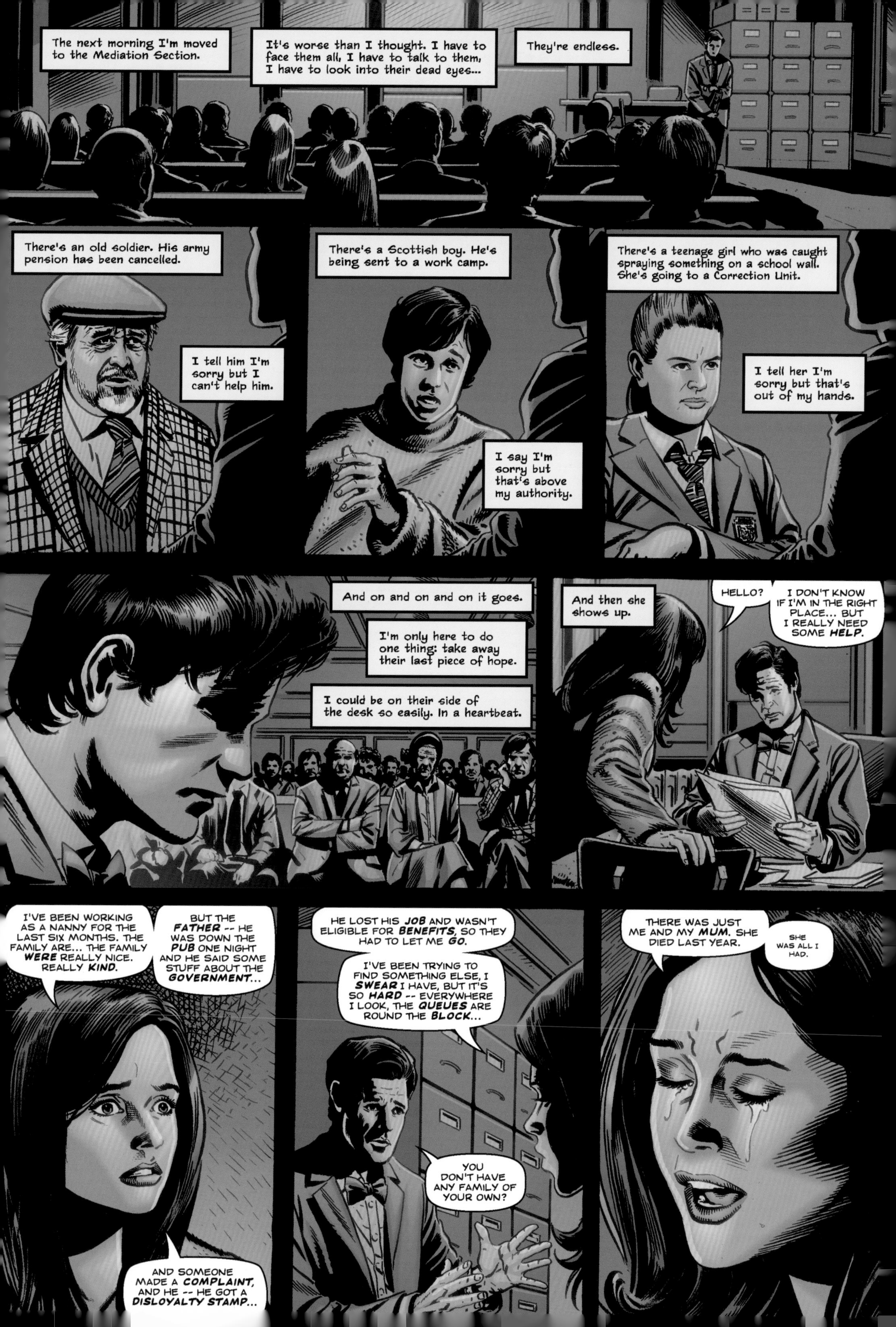

The next morning I'm moved to the Mediation Section.
It's worse than I thought. I have to face them all, I have to talk to them, I have to look into their dead eyes...
They're endless.
There's an old soldier. His army pension has been cancelled.
I tell him I'm sorry but I can't help him.
There's a Scottish boy. He's being sent to a work camp.
I say I'm sorry but that's above my authority.
There's a teenage girl who was caught spraying something on a school wall. She's going to a Correction Unit.
I tell her I'm sorry but that's out of my hands.
And on and on and on it goes.
I'm only here to do one thing: take away their last piece of hope.
I could be on their side of the desk so easily. In a heartbeat.
And then she shows up.
HELLO?
I DON'T KNOW IF I'M IN THE RIGHT PLACE... BUT I REALLY NEED SOME HELP.
I'VE BEEN WORKING AS A NANNY FOR THE LAST SIX MONTHS. THE FAMILY ARE... THE FAMILY WERE REALLY NICE. REALLY KIND.
BUT THE FATHER -- HE WAS DOWN THE PUB ONE NIGHT AND HE SAID SOME STUFF ABOUT THE GOVERNMENT...
AND SOMEONE MADE A COMPLAINT, AND HE -- HE GOT A DISLOYALTY STAMP...
HE LOST HIS JOB AND WASN'T ELIGIBLE FOR BENEFITS, SO THEY HAD TO LET ME GO.
I'VE BEEN TRYING TO FIND SOMETHING ELSE, I SWEAR I HAVE, BUT IT'S SO HARD -- EVERYWHERE I LOOK, THE QUEUES ARE ROUND THE BLOCK...
YOU DON'T HAVE ANY FAMILY OF YOUR OWN?
THERE WAS JUST ME AND MY MUM. SHE DIED LAST YEAR.
SHE WAS ALL I HAD.

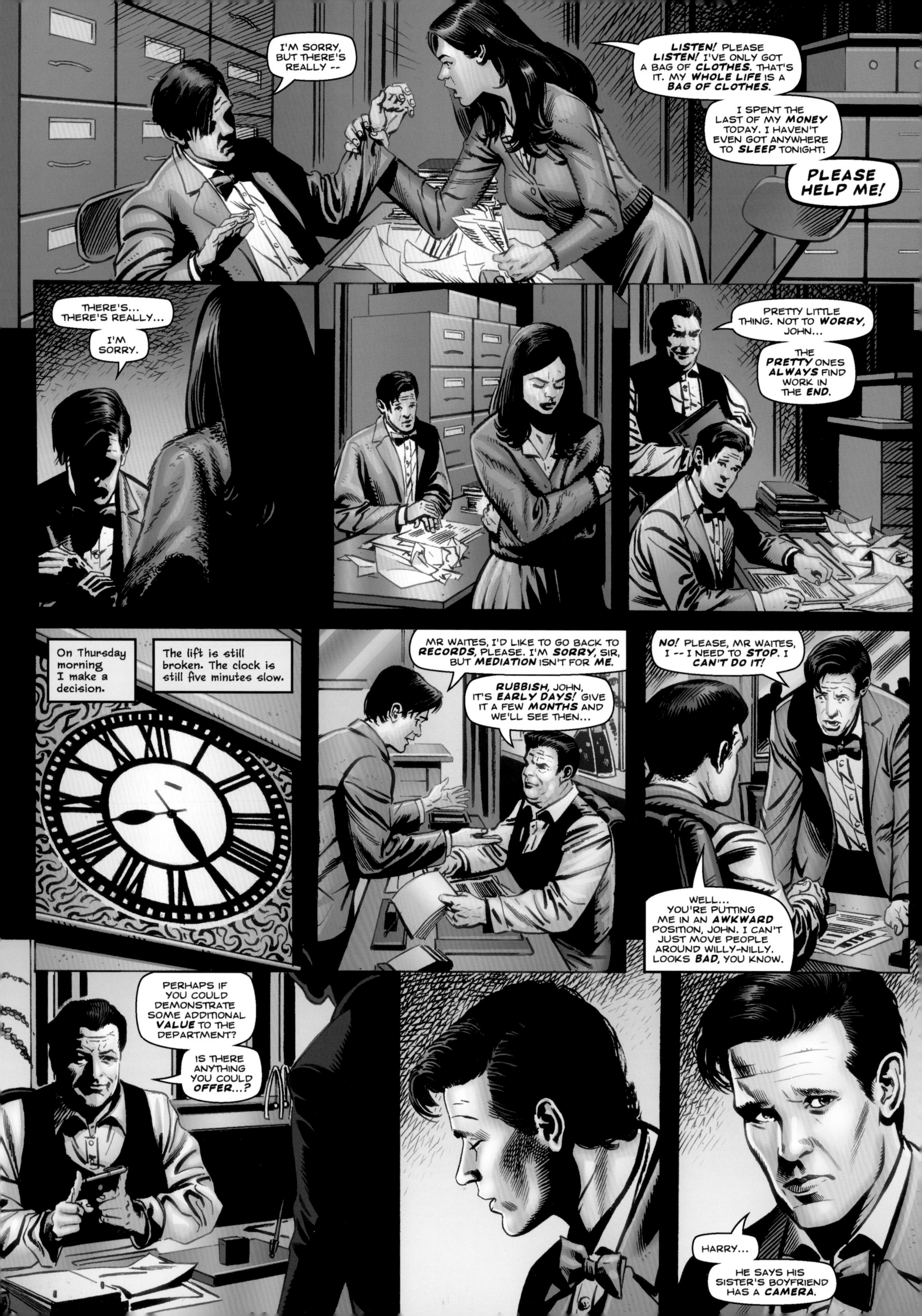

I'M SORRY, BUT THERE'S REALLY --
LISTEN! PLEASE LISTEN! I'VE ONLY GOT A BAG OF CLOTHES. THAT'S IT. MY WHOLE LIFE IS A BAG OF CLOTHES.
I SPENT THE LAST OF MY MONEY TODAY. I HAVEN'T EVEN GOT ANYWHERE TO SLEEP TONIGHT!
PLEASE HELP ME!
THERE'S... THERE'S REALLY...
I'M SORRY.
PRETTY LITTLE THING. NOT TO WORRY, JOHN...
THE PRETTY ONES ALWAYS FIND WORK IN THE END.
On Thursday morning I make a decision.
The lift is still broken. The clock is still five minutes slow.
MR WAITES, I'D LIKE TO GO BACK TO RECORDS, PLEASE. I'M SORRY, SIR, BUT MEDIATION ISN'T FOR ME.
RUBBISH, JOHN, IT'S EARLY DAYS! GIVE IT A FEW MONTHS AND WE'LL SEE THEN...
NO! PLEASE, MR WAITES, I -- I NEED TO STOP. I CAN'T DO IT!
WELL... YOU'RE PUTTING ME IN AN AWKWARD POSITION, JOHN. I CAN'T JUST MOVE PEOPLE AROUND WILLY-NILLY. LOOKS BAD, YOU KNOW.
PERHAPS IF YOU COULD DEMONSTRATE SOME ADDITIONAL VALUE TO THE DEPARTMENT?
IS THERE ANYTHING YOU COULD OFFER...?
HARRY...
HE SAYS HIS SISTER'S BOYFRIEND HAS A CAMERA.

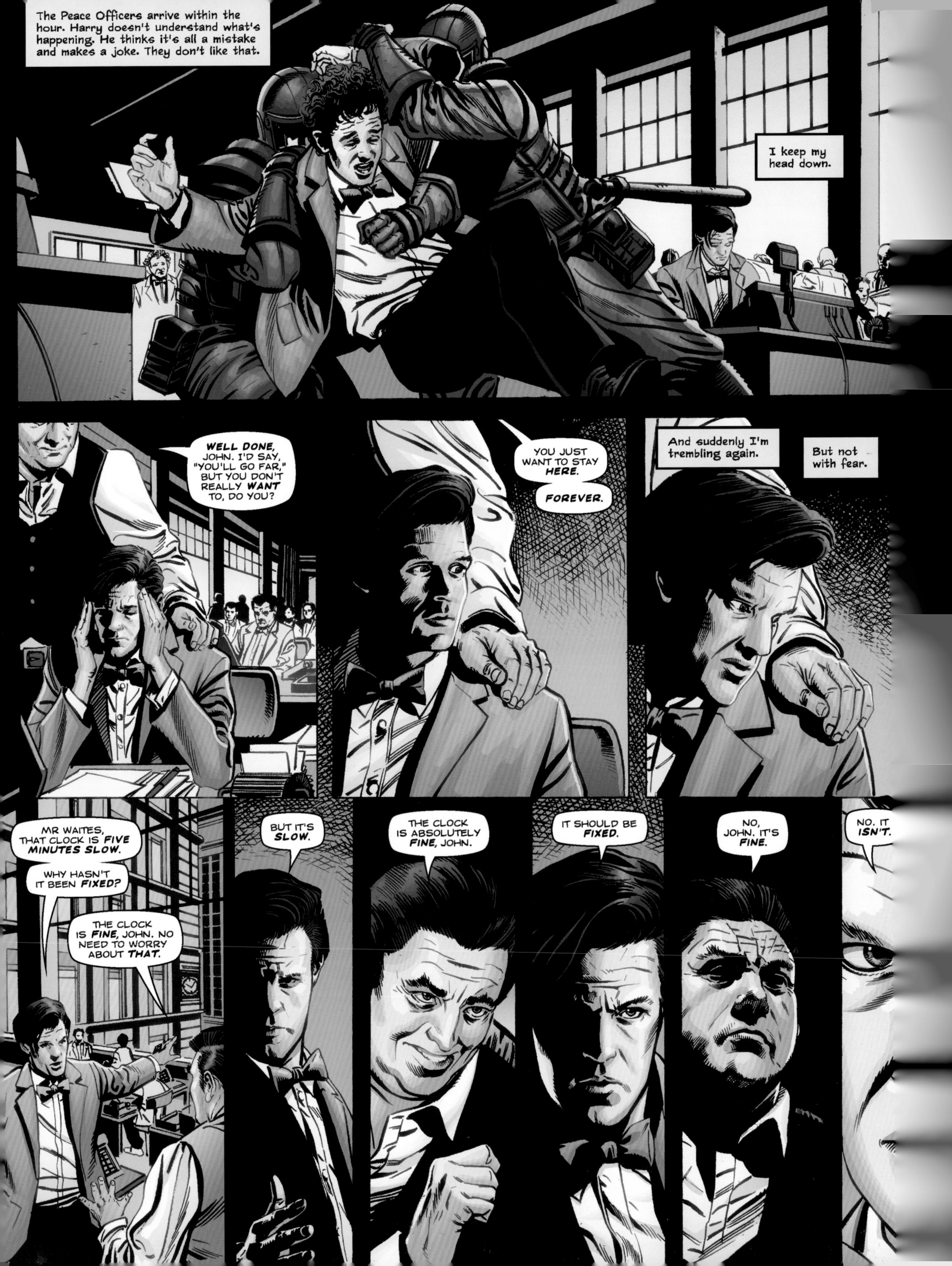

The Peace Officers arrive within the hour. Harry doesn't understand what's happening. He thinks it's all a mistake and makes a joke. They don't like that.
I keep my head down.
WELL DONE, JOHN. I'D SAY, "YOU'LL GO FAR," BUT YOU DON'T REALLY WANT TO, DO YOU?
YOU JUST WANT TO STAY HERE.
FOREVER.
And suddenly I'm trembling again.
But not with fear.
MR WAITES, THAT CLOCK IS FIVE MINUTES SLOW.
WHY HASN'T IT BEEN FIXED?
THE CLOCK IS FINE, JOHN. NO NEED TO WORRY ABOUT THAT.
BUT IT'S SLOW.
THE CLOCK IS ABSOLUTELY FINE, JOHN.
IT SHOULD BE FIXED.
NO, JOHN. IT'S FINE.
NO. IT ISN'T.

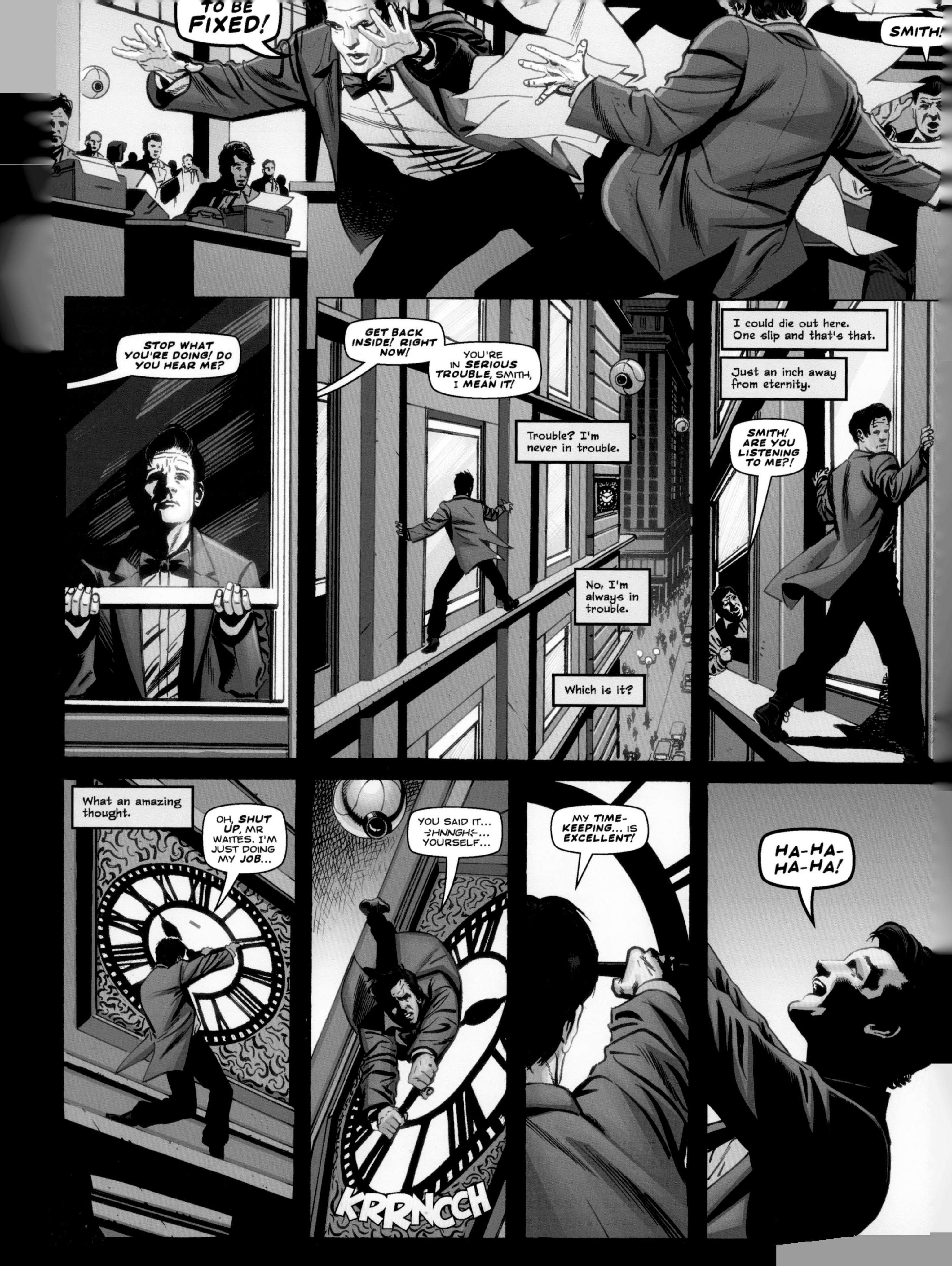
TO BE FIXED!
SMITH!
STOP WHAT YOU'RE DOING! DO YOU HEAR ME?
GET BACK INSIDE! RIGHT NOW!
YOU'RE IN SERIOUS TROUBLE, SMITH, I MEAN IT!
Trouble? I'm never in trouble.
No, I'm always in trouble.
Which is it?
I could die out here. One slip and that's that.
Just an inch away from eternity.
SMITH! ARE YOU LISTENING TO ME?!
What an amazing thought.
OH, SHUT UP, MR WAITES. I'M JUST DOING MY JOB...
YOU SAID IT... HNNGH... YOURSELF...
KRRNCCH
MY TIME-KEEPING... IS EXCELLENT!
HA-HA-HA-HA!

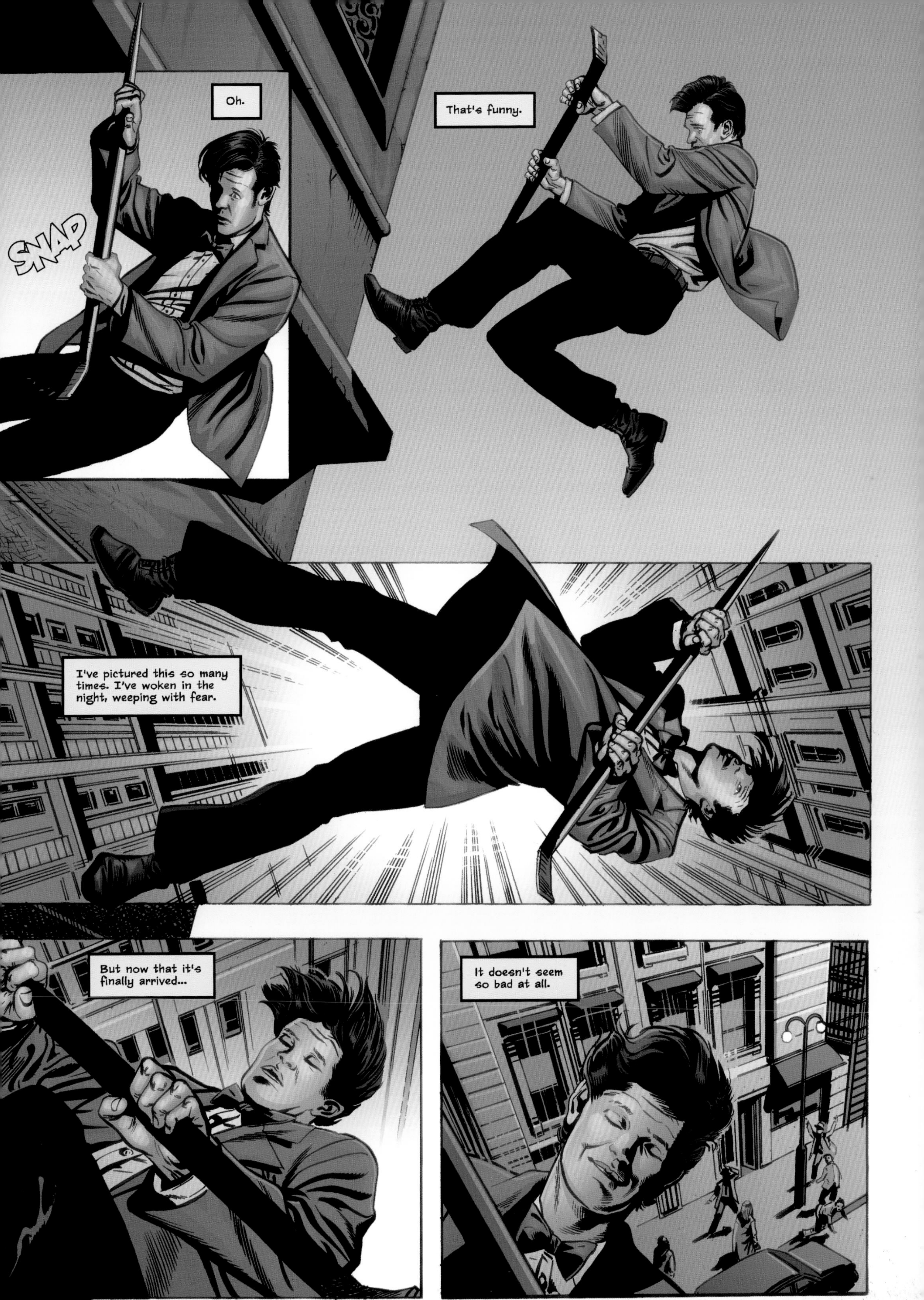
Oh.
SNAP
That's funny.
I've pictured this so many times. I've woken in the night, weeping with fear.
But now that it's finally arrived...
It doesn't seem so bad at all.

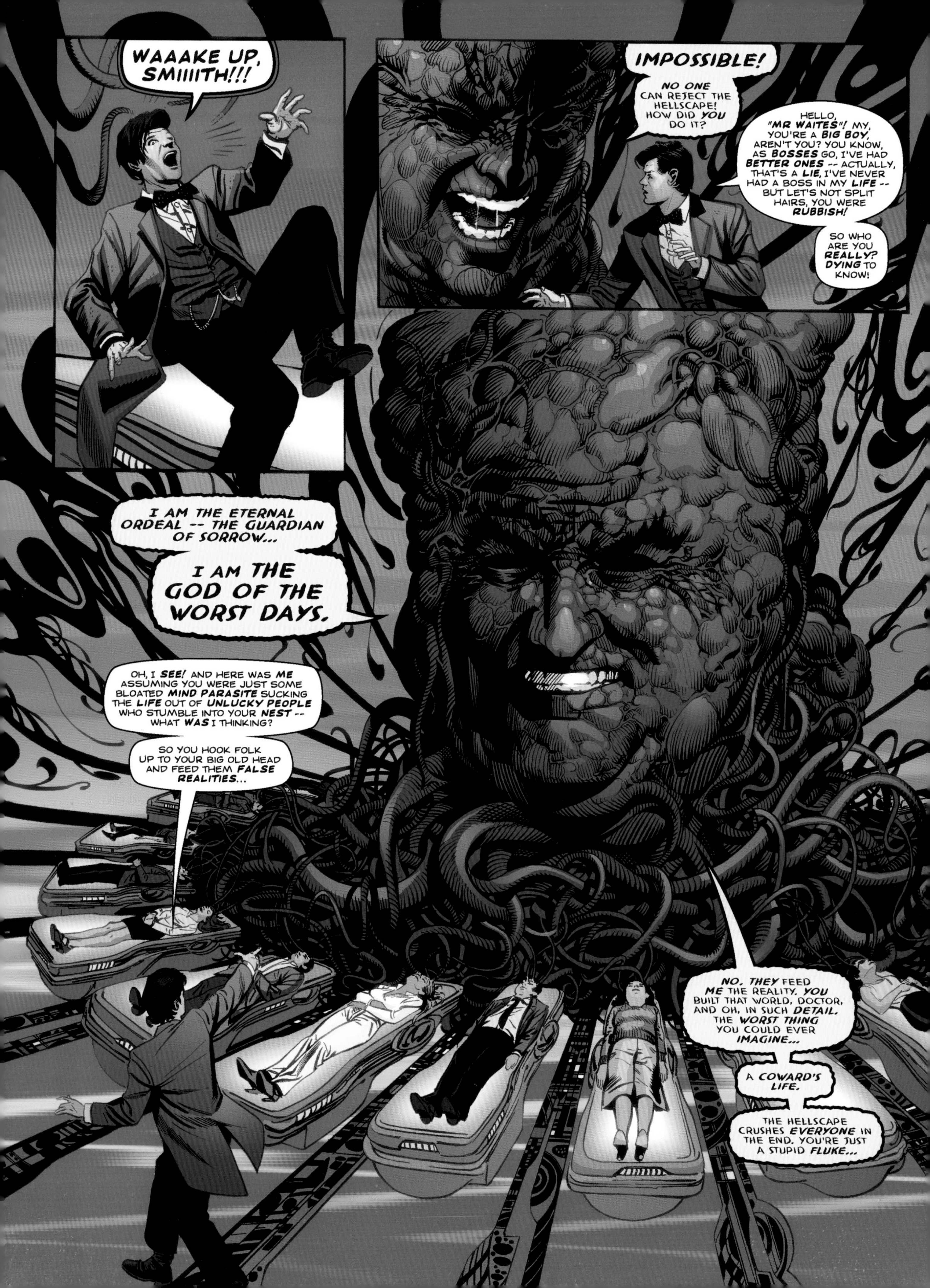
WAAAKE UP, SMIIIITH!!!
IMPOSSIBLE!
NO ONE CAN REJECT THE HELLSCAPE! HOW DID YOU DO IT?
HELLO, "MR WAITES"! MY, YOU'RE A BIG BOY, AREN'T YOU? YOU KNOW, AS BOSSES GO, I'VE HAD BETTER ONES -- ACTUALLY, THAT'S A LIE, I'VE NEVER HAD A BOSS IN MY LIFE -- BUT LET'S NOT SPLIT HAIRS, YOU WERE RUBBISH!
SO WHO ARE YOU REALLY? DYING TO KNOW!
I AM THE ETERNAL ORDEAL -- THE GUARDIAN OF SORROW...
I AM THE GOD OF THE WORST DAYS.
OH, I SEE! AND HERE WAS ME ASSUMING YOU WERE JUST SOME BLOATED MIND PARASITE SUCKING THE LIFE OUT OF UNLUCKY PEOPLE WHO STUMBLE INTO YOUR NEST -- WHAT WAS I THINKING?
SO YOU HOOK FOLK UP TO YOUR BIG OLD HEAD AND FEED THEM FALSE REALITIES...
NO, THEY FEED ME THE REALITY. YOU BUILT THAT WORLD, DOCTOR, AND OH, IN SUCH DETAIL. THE WORST THING YOU COULD EVER IMAGINE...
A COWARD'S LIFE.
THE HELLSCAPE CRUSHES EVERYONE IN THE END. YOU'RE JUST A STUPID FLUKE...

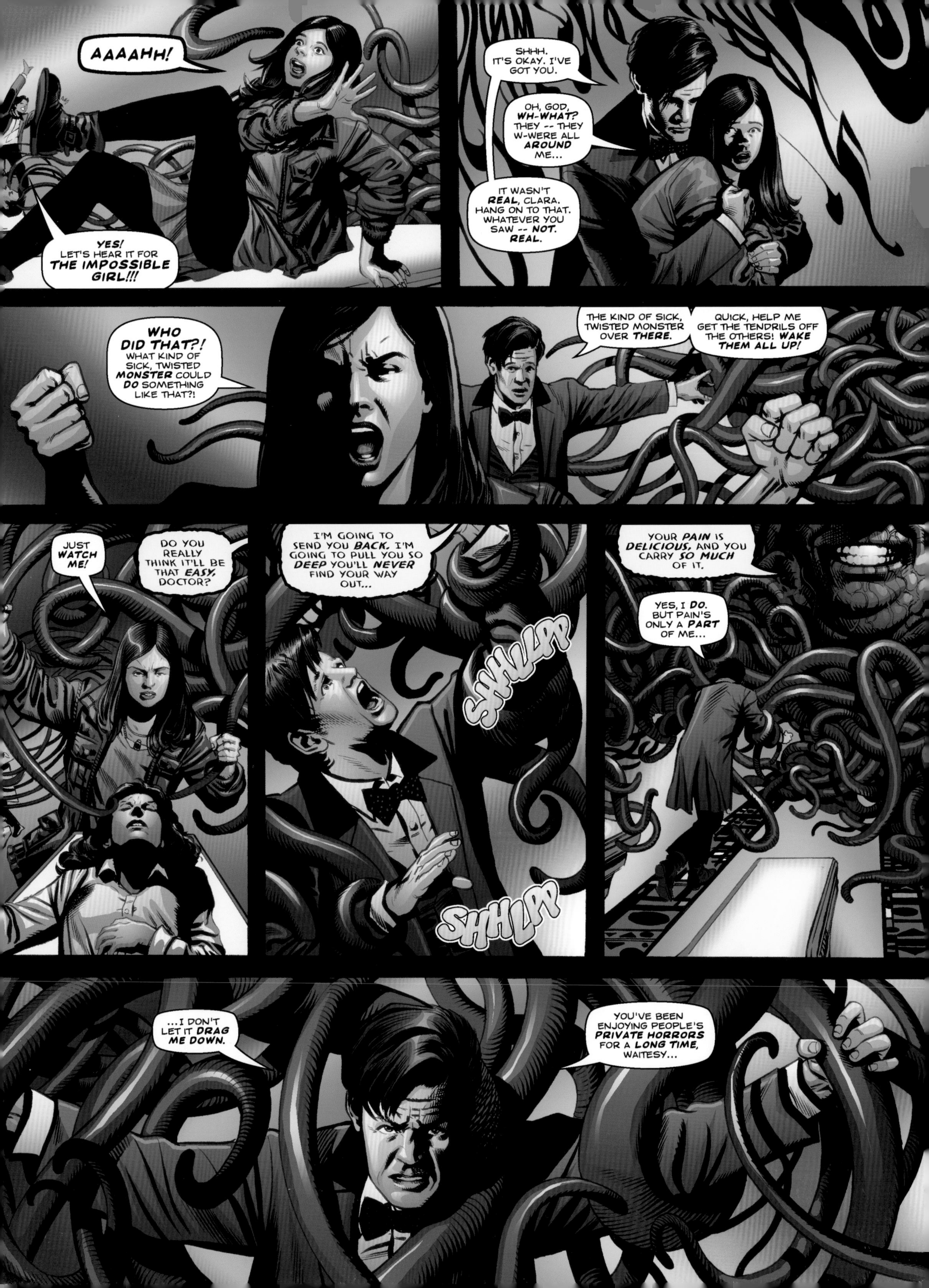
AAAAHH!
YES! LET'S HEAR IT FOR THE IMPOSSIBLE GIRL!!!
SHHH. IT'S OKAY. I'VE GOT YOU.
OH, GOD, WH-WHAT? THEY -- THEY W-WERE ALL AROUND ME...
IT WASN'T REAL, CLARA. HANG ON TO THAT. WHATEVER YOU SAW -- NOT. REAL.
WHO DID THAT?! WHAT KIND OF SICK, TWISTED MONSTER COULD DO SOMETHING LIKE THAT?!
THE KIND OF SICK, TWISTED MONSTER OVER THERE.
QUICK, HELP ME GET THE TENDRILS OFF THE OTHERS! WAKE THEM ALL UP!
JUST WATCH ME!
DO YOU REALLY THINK IT'LL BE THAT EASY, DOCTOR?
I'M GOING TO SEND YOU BACK. I'M GOING TO PULL YOU SO DEEP YOU'LL NEVER FIND YOUR WAY OUT...
SHHLPP
SHHLPP
YOUR PAIN IS DELICIOUS, AND YOU CARRY SO MUCH OF IT.
YES, I DO. BUT PAIN'S ONLY A PART OF ME...
...I DON'T LET IT DRAG ME DOWN.
YOU'VE BEEN ENJOYING PEOPLE'S PRIVATE HORRORS FOR A LONG TIME, WAITESY...

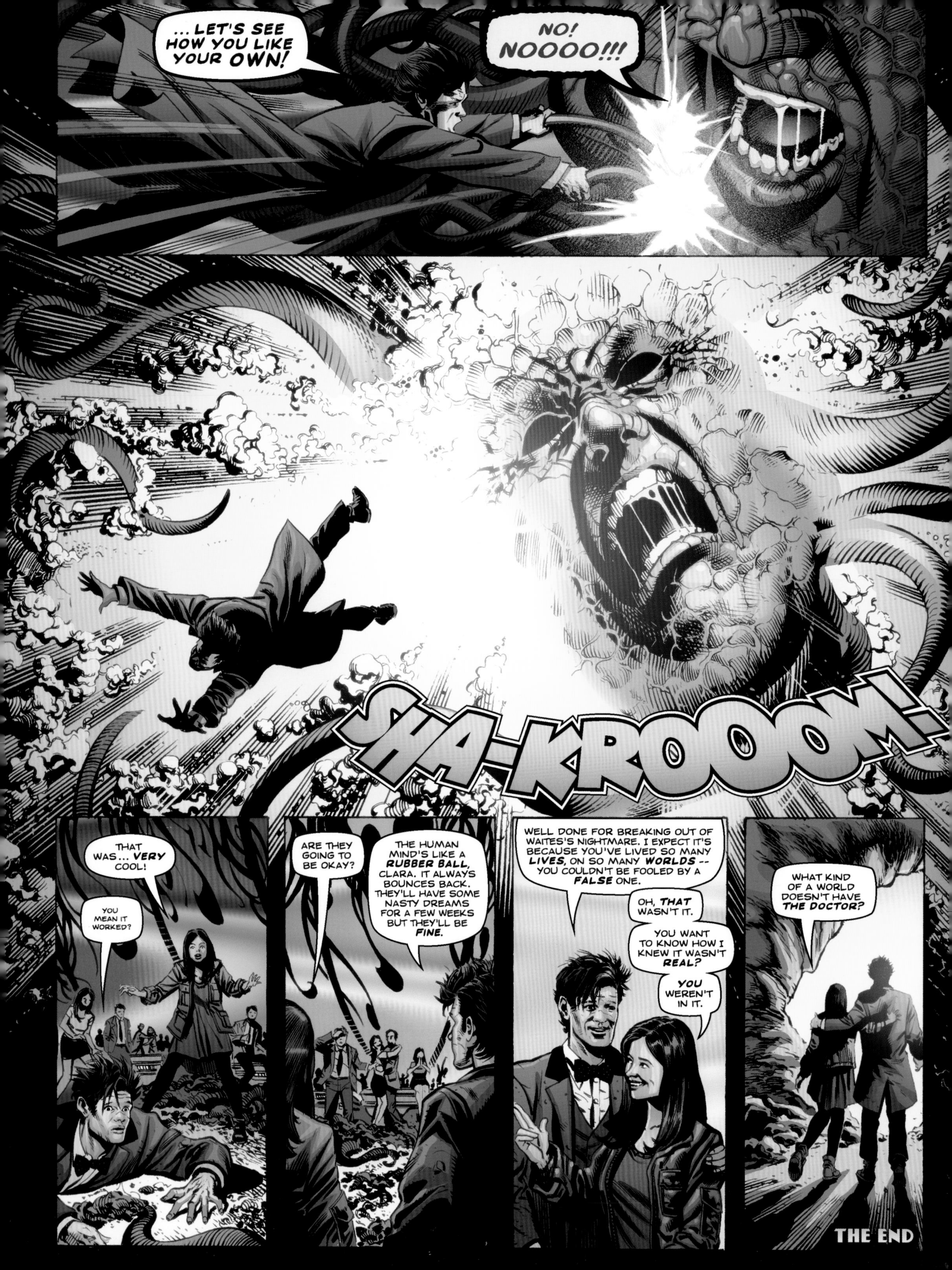
... LET'S SEE HOW YOU LIKE YOUR OWN!
NO! NOOOO!!!
SHA-KROOOM!
THAT WAS... VERY COOL!
YOU MEAN IT WORKED?
ARE THEY GOING TO BE OKAY?
THE HUMAN MIND'S LIKE A RUBBER BALL, CLARA. IT ALWAYS BOUNCES BACK. THEY'LL HAVE SOME NASTY DREAMS FOR A FEW WEEKS BUT THEY'LL BE FINE.
WELL DONE FOR BREAKING OUT OF WAITES'S NIGHTMARE. I EXPECT IT'S BECAUSE YOU'VE LIVED SO MANY LIVES, ON SO MANY WORLDS -- YOU COULDN'T BE FOOLED BY A FALSE ONE.
OH, THAT WASN'T IT.
YOU WANT TO KNOW HOW I KNEW IT WASN'T REAL?
YOU WEREN'T IN IT.
WHAT KIND OF A WORLD DOESN'T HAVE THE DOCTOR?
THE END

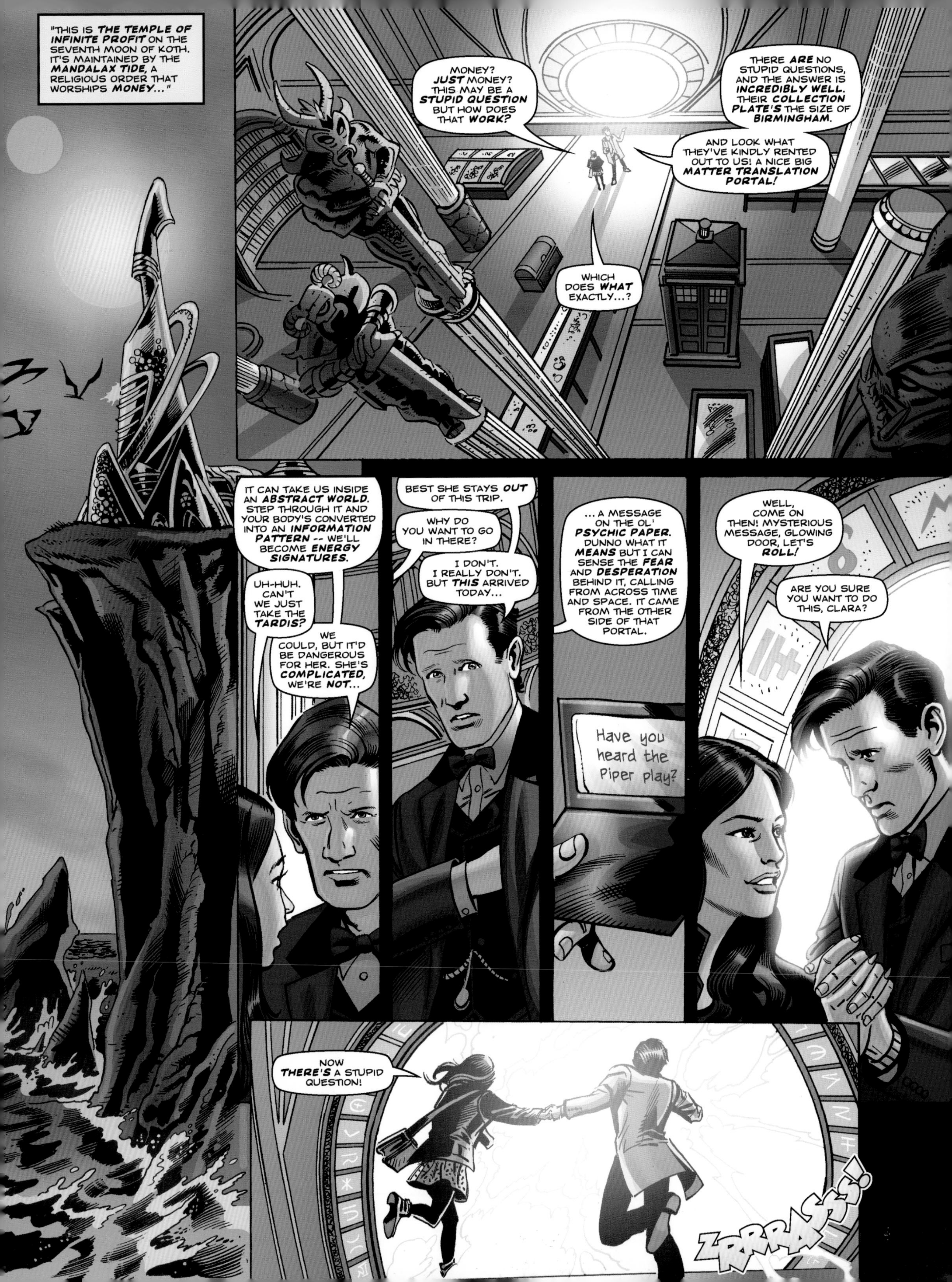
"THIS IS THE TEMPLE OF INFINITE PROFIT ON THE SEVENTH MOON OF KOTH. IT'S MAINTAINED BY THE MANDALAX TIDE, A RELIGIOUS ORDER THAT WORSHIPS MONEY..."
MONEY? JUST MONEY? THIS MAY BE A STUPID QUESTION BUT HOW DOES THAT WORK?
THERE ARE NO STUPID QUESTIONS, AND THE ANSWER IS INCREDIBLY WELL. THEIR COLLECTION PLATE'S THE SIZE OF BIRMINGHAM.
AND LOOK WHAT THEY'VE KINDLY RENTED OUT TO US! A NICE BIG MATTER TRANSLATION PORTAL!
WHICH DOES WHAT EXACTLY...?
IT CAN TAKE US INSIDE AN ABSTRACT WORLD. STEP THROUGH IT AND YOUR BODY'S CONVERTED INTO AN INFORMATION PATTERN -- WE'LL BECOME ENERGY SIGNATURES.
UH-HUH. CAN'T WE JUST TAKE THE TARDIS?
WE COULD, BUT IT'D BE DANGEROUS FOR HER. SHE'S COMPLICATED, WE'RE NOT...
BEST SHE STAYS OUT OF THIS TRIP.
WHY DO YOU WANT TO GO IN THERE?
I DON'T. I REALLY DON'T. BUT THIS ARRIVED TODAY...
... A MESSAGE ON THE OL' PSYCHIC PAPER. DUNNO WHAT IT MEANS BUT I CAN SENSE THE FEAR AND DESPERATION BEHIND IT, CALLING FROM ACROSS TIME AND SPACE. IT CAME FROM THE OTHER SIDE OF THAT PORTAL.
Have you heard the Piper play?
WELL, COME ON THEN! MYSTERIOUS MESSAGE, GLOWING DOOR, LET'S ROLL!
ARE YOU SURE YOU WANT TO DO THIS, CLARA?
NOW THERE'S A STUPID QUESTION!
ZZRRRASSS!

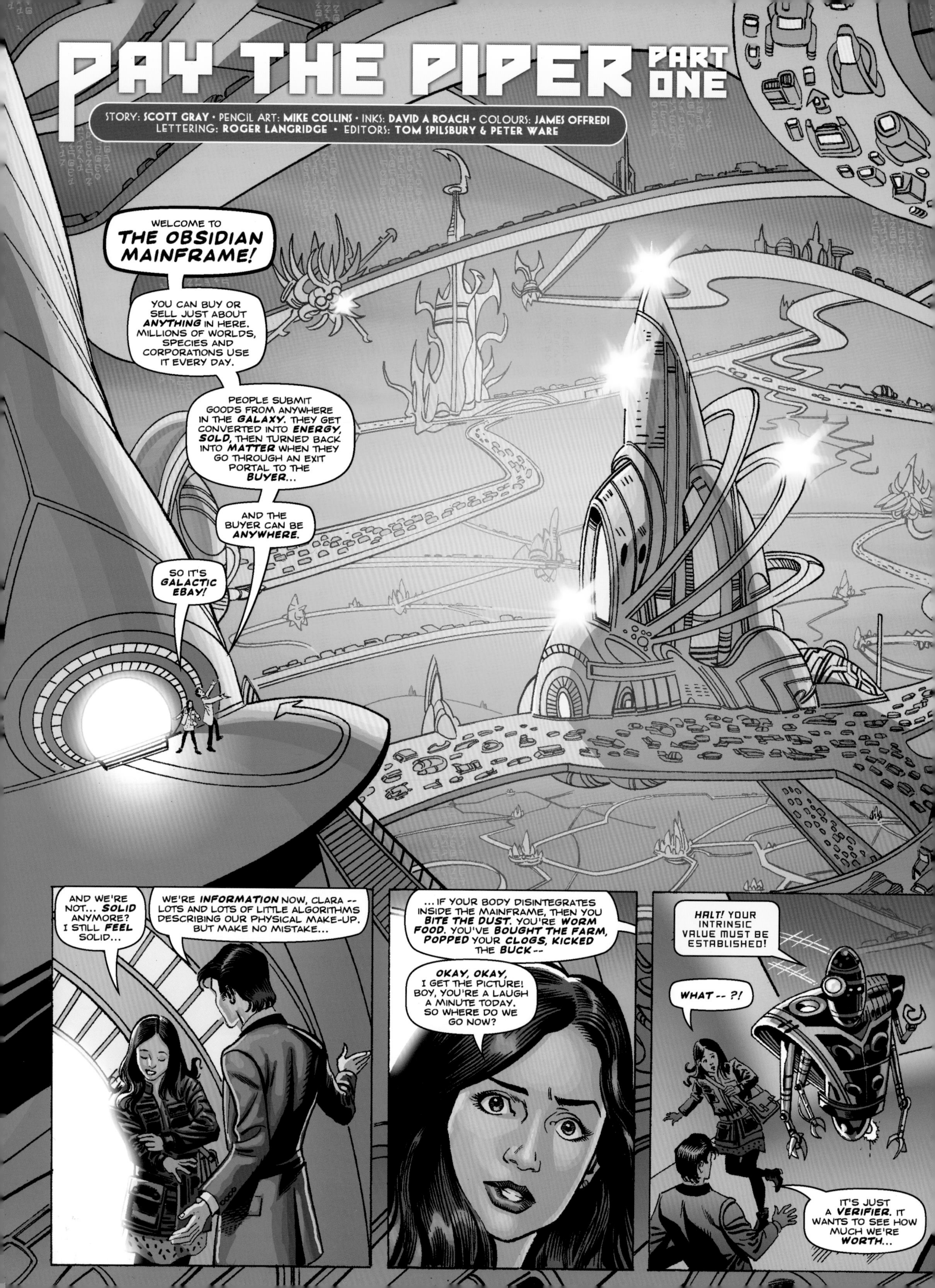

PAY THE PIPER PART ONE
STORY: SCOTT GRAY • PENCIL ART: MIKE COLLINS • INKS: DAVID A ROACH • COLOURS: JAMES OFFREDI
LETTERING: ROGER LANGRIDGE • EDITORS: TOM SPILSBURY & PETER WARE
WELCOME TO THE OBSIDIAN MAINFRAME!
YOU CAN BUY OR SELL JUST ABOUT ANYTHING IN HERE. MILLIONS OF WORLDS, SPECIES AND CORPORATIONS USE IT EVERY DAY.
PEOPLE SUBMIT GOODS FROM ANYWHERE IN THE GALAXY. THEY GET CONVERTED INTO ENERGY, SOLD, THEN TURNED BACK INTO MATTER WHEN THEY GO THROUGH AN EXIT PORTAL TO THE BUYER...
AND THE BUYER CAN BE ANYWHERE.
SO IT'S GALACTIC EBAY!
AND WE'RE NOT... SOLID ANYMORE? I STILL FEEL SOLID...
WE'RE INFORMATION NOW, CLARA -- LOTS AND LOTS OF LITTLE ALGORITHMS DESCRIBING OUR PHYSICAL MAKE-UP. BUT MAKE NO MISTAKE...
... IF YOUR BODY DISINTEGRATES INSIDE THE MAINFRAME, THEN YOU BITE THE DUST. YOU'RE WORM FOOD. YOU'VE BOUGHT THE FARM, POPPED YOUR CLOGS, KICKED THE BUCK--
OKAY, OKAY, I GET THE PICTURE! BOY, YOU'RE A LAUGH A MINUTE TODAY. SO WHERE DO WE GO NOW?
HALT! YOUR INTRINSIC VALUE MUST BE ESTABLISHED!
WHAT -- ?!
IT'S JUST A VERIFIER. IT WANTS TO SEE HOW MUCH WE'RE WORTH...

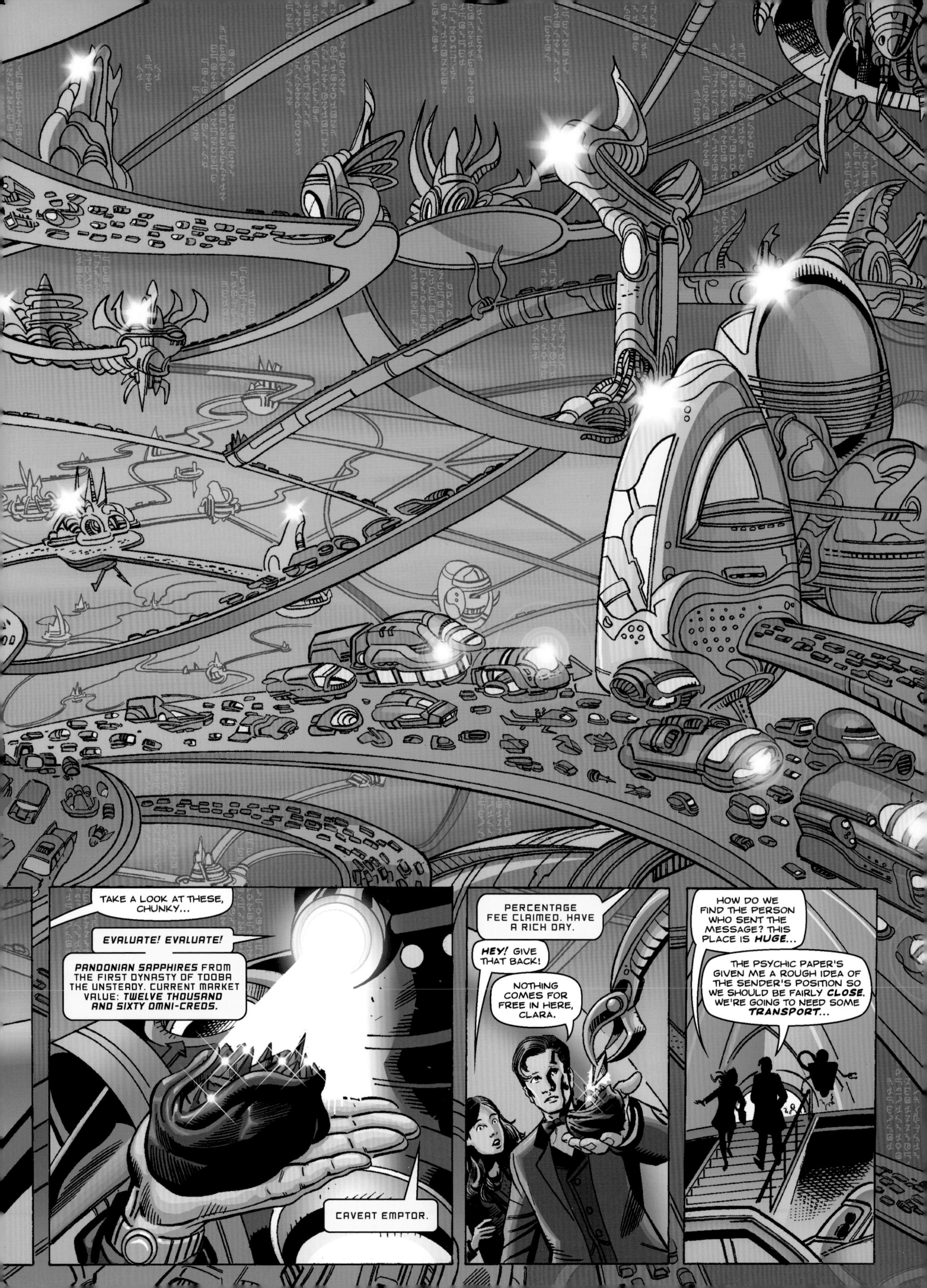

TAKE A LOOK AT THESE, CHUNKY...
EVALUATE! EVALUATE!
PANDONIAN SAPPHIRES FROM THE FIRST DYNASTY OF TOOBA THE UNSTEADY. CURRENT MARKET VALUE: TWELVE THOUSAND AND SIXTY OMNI-CREDS.
CAVEAT EMPTOR.
PERCENTAGE FEE CLAIMED. HAVE A RICH DAY.
HEY! GIVE THAT BACK!
NOTHING COMES FOR FREE IN HERE, CLARA.
HOW DO WE FIND THE PERSON WHO SENT THE MESSAGE? THIS PLACE IS HUGE...
THE PSYCHIC PAPER'S GIVEN ME A ROUGH IDEA OF THE SENDER'S POSITION SO WE SHOULD BE FAIRLY CLOSE. WE'RE GOING TO NEED SOME TRANSPORT...

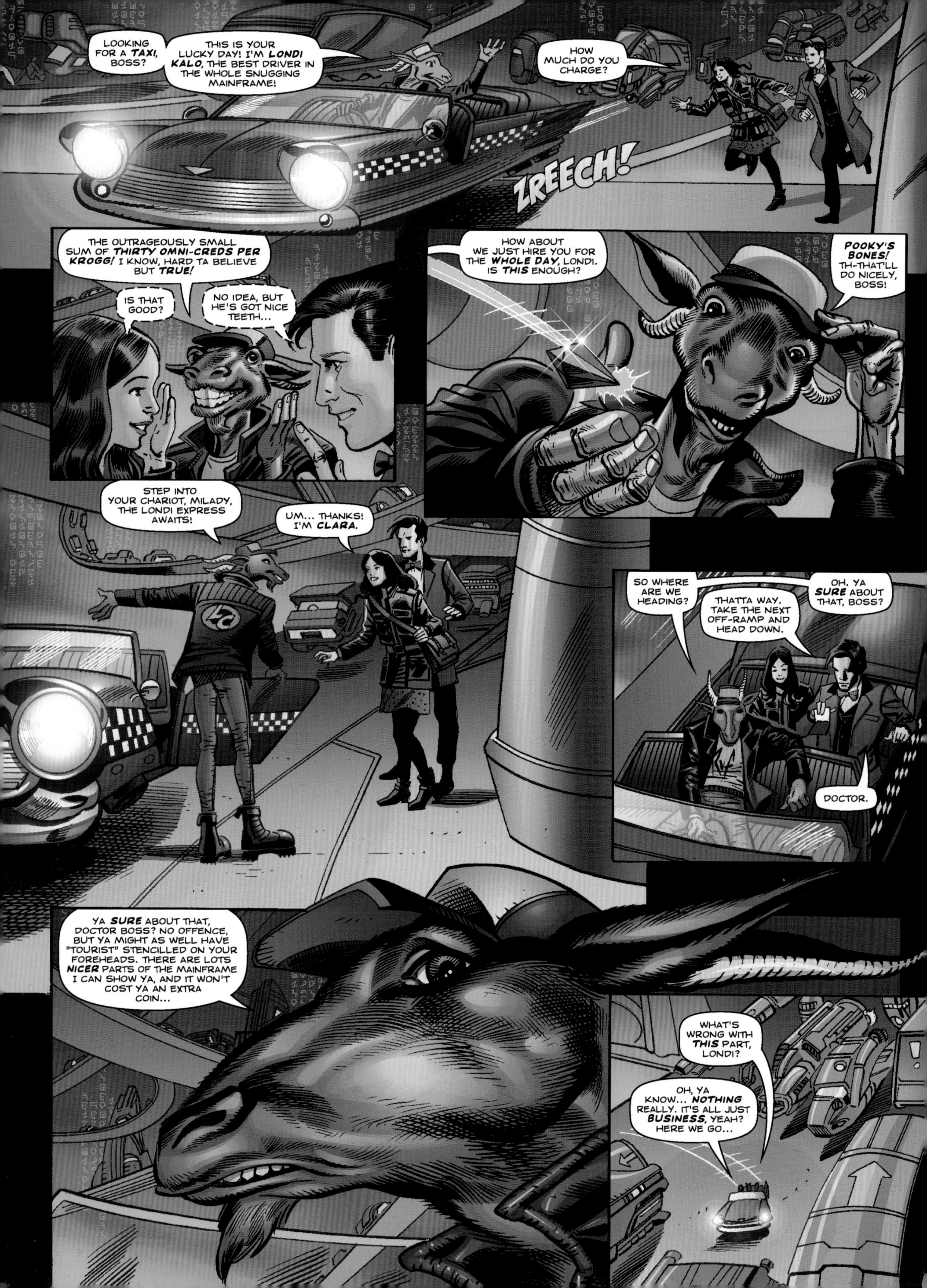
LOOKING FOR A TAXI, BOSS?
THIS IS YOUR LUCKY DAY! I'M LONDI KALO, THE BEST DRIVER IN THE WHOLE SNUGGING MAINFRAME!
HOW MUCH DO YOU CHARGE?
ZREECH!
THE OUTRAGEOUSLY SMALL SUM OF THIRTY OMNI-CREDS PER KROGG! I KNOW, HARD TA BELIEVE BUT TRUE!
IS THAT GOOD?
NO IDEA, BUT HE'S GOT NICE TEETH...
HOW ABOUT WE JUST HIRE YOU FOR THE WHOLE DAY, LONDI. IS THIS ENOUGH?
POOKY'S BONES! TH-THAT'LL DO NICELY, BOSS!
STEP INTO YOUR CHARIOT, MILADY, THE LONDI EXPRESS AWAITS!
UM... THANKS! I'M CLARA.
SO WHERE ARE WE HEADING?
THATTA WAY. TAKE THE NEXT OFF-RAMP AND HEAD DOWN.
OH. YA SURE ABOUT THAT, BOSS?
DOCTOR.
YA SURE ABOUT THAT, DOCTOR BOSS? NO OFFENCE, BUT YA MIGHT AS WELL HAVE "TOURIST" STENCILLED ON YOUR FOREHEADS. THERE ARE LOTS NICER PARTS OF THE MAINFRAME I CAN SHOW YA, AND IT WON'T COST YA AN EXTRA COIN...
WHAT'S WRONG WITH THIS PART, LONDI?
OH, YA KNOW... NOTHING REALLY. IT'S ALL JUST BUSINESS, YEAH? HERE WE GO...

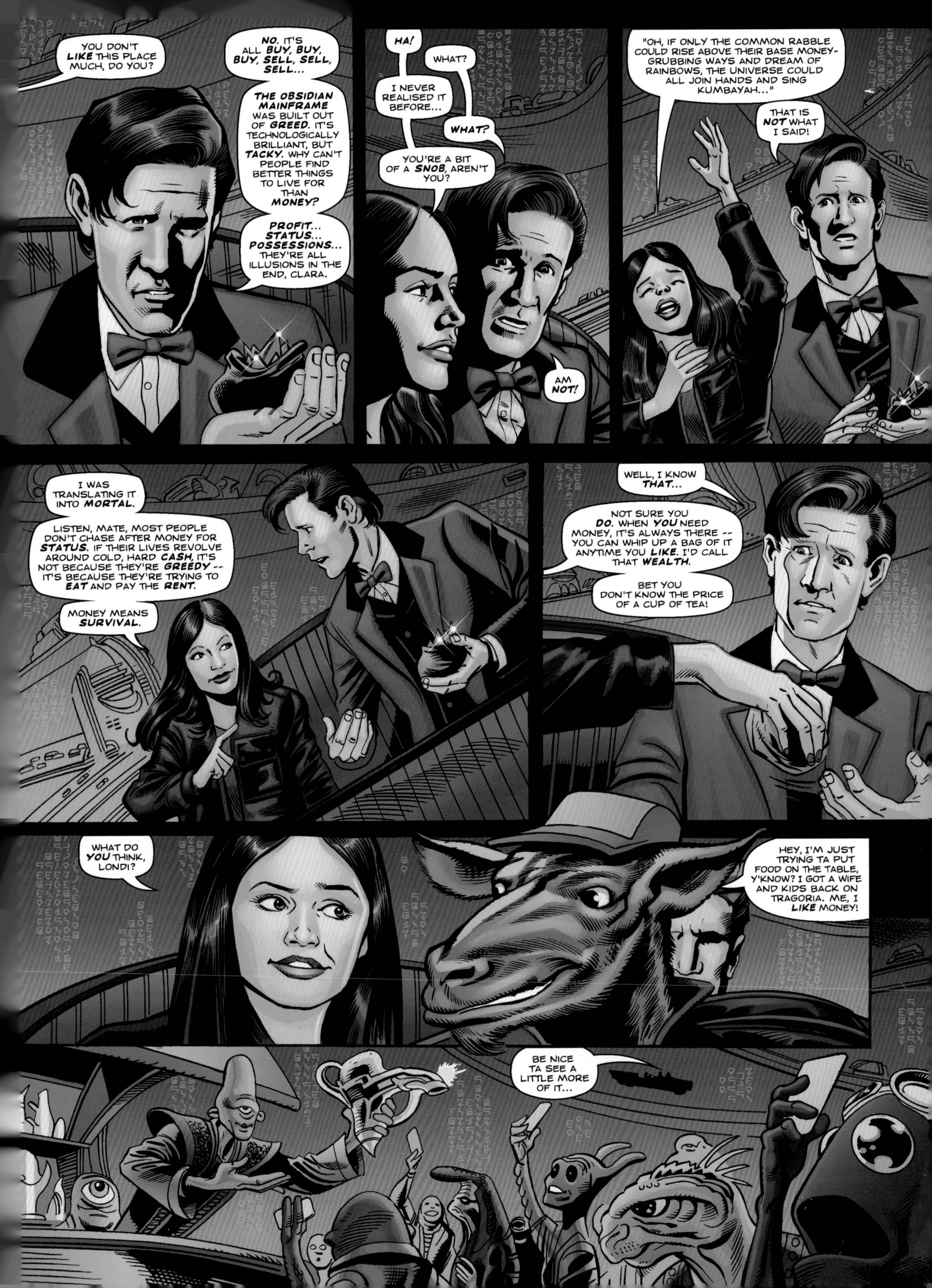

YOU DON'T LIKE THIS PLACE MUCH, DO YOU?
NO. IT'S ALL BUY, BUY, BUY, SELL, SELL, SELL...
THE OBSIDIAN MAINFRAME WAS BUILT OUT OF GREED. IT'S TECHNOLOGICALLY BRILLIANT, BUT TACKY. WHY CAN'T PEOPLE FIND BETTER THINGS TO LIVE FOR THAN MONEY?
PROFIT... STATUS... POSSESSIONS... THEY'RE ALL ILLUSIONS IN THE END, CLARA.
HA!
WHAT?
I NEVER REALISED IT BEFORE...
WHAT?
YOU'RE A BIT OF A SNOB, AREN'T YOU?
AM NOT!
"OH, IF ONLY THE COMMON RABBLE COULD RISE ABOVE THEIR BASE MONEY-GRUBBING WAYS AND DREAM OF RAINBOWS, THE UNIVERSE COULD ALL JOIN HANDS AND SING KUMBAYAH..."
THAT IS NOT WHAT I SAID!
I WAS TRANSLATING IT INTO MORTAL.
LISTEN, MATE, MOST PEOPLE DON'T CHASE AFTER MONEY FOR STATUS. IF THEIR LIVES REVOLVE AROUND COLD, HARD CASH, IT'S NOT BECAUSE THEY'RE GREEDY -- IT'S BECAUSE THEY'RE TRYING TO EAT AND PAY THE RENT.
MONEY MEANS SURVIVAL.
WELL, I KNOW THAT...
NOT SURE YOU DO. WHEN YOU NEED MONEY, IT'S ALWAYS THERE -- YOU CAN WHIP UP A BAG OF IT ANYTIME YOU LIKE. I'D CALL THAT WEALTH.
BET YOU DON'T KNOW THE PRICE OF A CUP OF TEA!
WHAT DO YOU THINK, LONDI?
HEY, I'M JUST TRYING TA PUT FOOD ON THE TABLE, Y'KNOW? I GOT A WIFE AND KIDS BACK ON TRAGORIA. ME, I LIKE MONEY!
BE NICE TA SEE A LITTLE MORE OF IT...

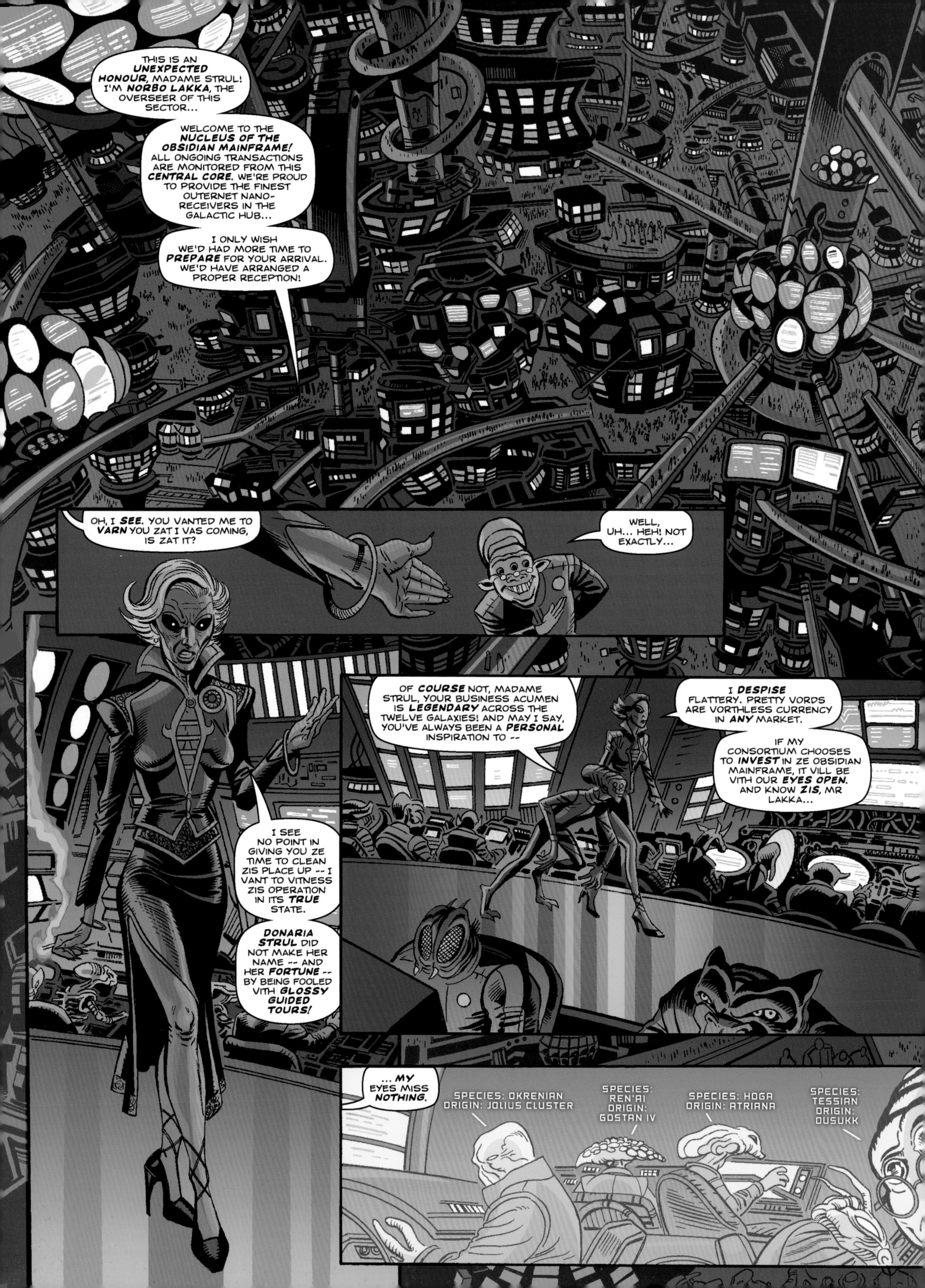
THIS IS AN UNEXPECTED HONOUR, MADAME STRUL! I'M NORBO LAKKA, THE OVERSEER OF THIS SECTOR...
WELCOME TO THE NUCLEUS OF THE OBSIDIAN MAINFRAME! ALL ONGOING TRANSACTIONS ARE MONITORED FROM THIS CENTRAL CORE. WE'RE PROUD TO PROVIDE THE FINEST OUTERNET NANO-RECEIVERS IN THE GALACTIC HUB...
I ONLY WISH WE'D HAD MORE TIME TO PREPARE FOR YOUR ARRIVAL. WE'D HAVE ARRANGED A PROPER RECEPTION!
OH, I SEE. YOU VANTED ME TO VARN YOU ZAT I VAS COMING, IS ZAT IT?
WELL, UH... HEH! NOT EXACTLY...
I SEE NO POINT IN GIVING YOU ZE TIME TO CLEAN ZIS PLACE UP -- I VANT TO VITNESS ZIS OPERATION IN ITS TRUE STATE.
DONARIA STRUL DID NOT MAKE HER NAME -- AND HER FORTUNE -- BY BEING FOOLED VITH GLOSSY GUIDED TOURS!
OF COURSE NOT, MADAME STRUL, YOUR BUSINESS ACUMEN IS LEGENDARY ACROSS THE TWELVE GALAXIES! AND MAY I SAY, YOU'VE ALWAYS BEEN A PERSONAL INSPIRATION TO --
I DESPISE FLATTERY. PRETTY VORDS ARE VORTHLESS CURRENCY IN ANY MARKET.
IF MY CONSORTIUM CHOOSES TO INVEST IN ZE OBSIDIAN MAINFRAME, IT VILL BE VITH OUR EYES OPEN. AND KNOW ZIS, MR LAKKA...
... MY EYES MISS NOTHING.
SPECIES: OKRENIAN ORIGIN: JOLIUS CLUSTER
SPECIES: REN'AI ORIGIN: GOSTAN IV
SPECIES: HOGA ORIGIN: ATRIANA
SPECIES: TESSIAN ORIGIN: DUSUKK

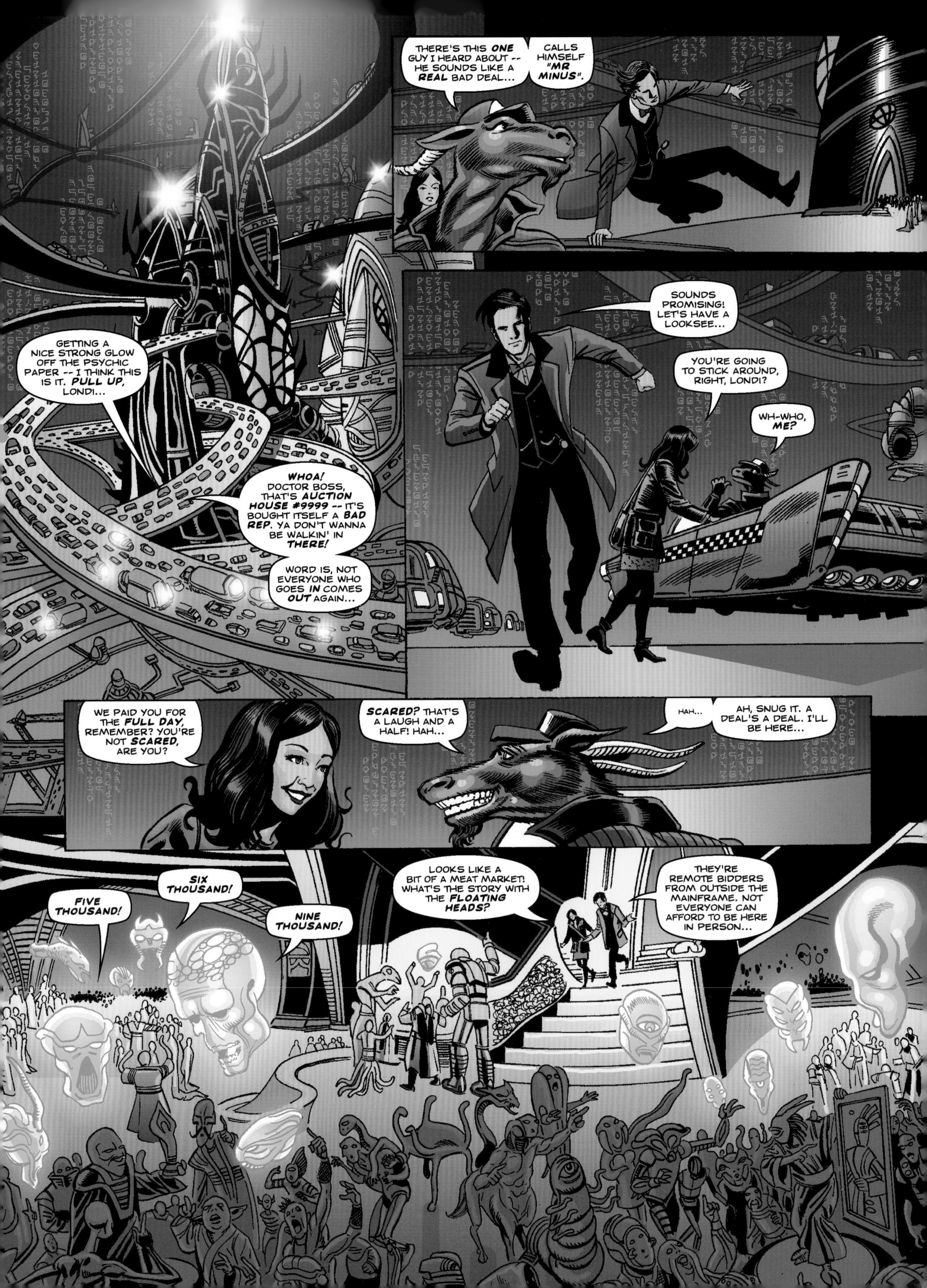

GETTING A NICE STRONG GLOW OFF THE PSYCHIC PAPER -- I THINK THIS IS IT. PULL UP, LONDI...
WHOA! DOCTOR BOSS, THAT'S AUCTION HOUSE #9999 -- IT'S BOUGHT ITSELF A BAD REP. YA DON'T WANNA BE WALKIN' IN THERE!
WORD IS, NOT EVERYONE WHO GOES IN COMES OUT AGAIN...
THERE'S THIS ONE GUY I HEARD ABOUT -- HE SOUNDS LIKE A REAL BAD DEAL...
CALLS HIMSELF "MR MINUS".
SOUNDS PROMISING! LET'S HAVE A LOOKSEE...
YOU'RE GOING TO STICK AROUND, RIGHT, LONDI?
WH-WHO, ME?
WE PAID YOU FOR THE FULL DAY, REMEMBER? YOU'RE NOT SCARED, ARE YOU?
SCARED? THAT'S A LAUGH AND A HALF! HAH...
HAH...
AH, SNUG IT. A DEAL'S A DEAL. I'LL BE HERE...
FIVE THOUSAND!
SIX THOUSAND!
NINE THOUSAND!
LOOKS LIKE A BIT OF A MEAT MARKET! WHAT'S THE STORY WITH THE FLOATING HEADS?
THEY'RE REMOTE BIDDERS FROM OUTSIDE THE MAINFRAME. NOT EVERYONE CAN AFFORD TO BE HERE IN PERSON...

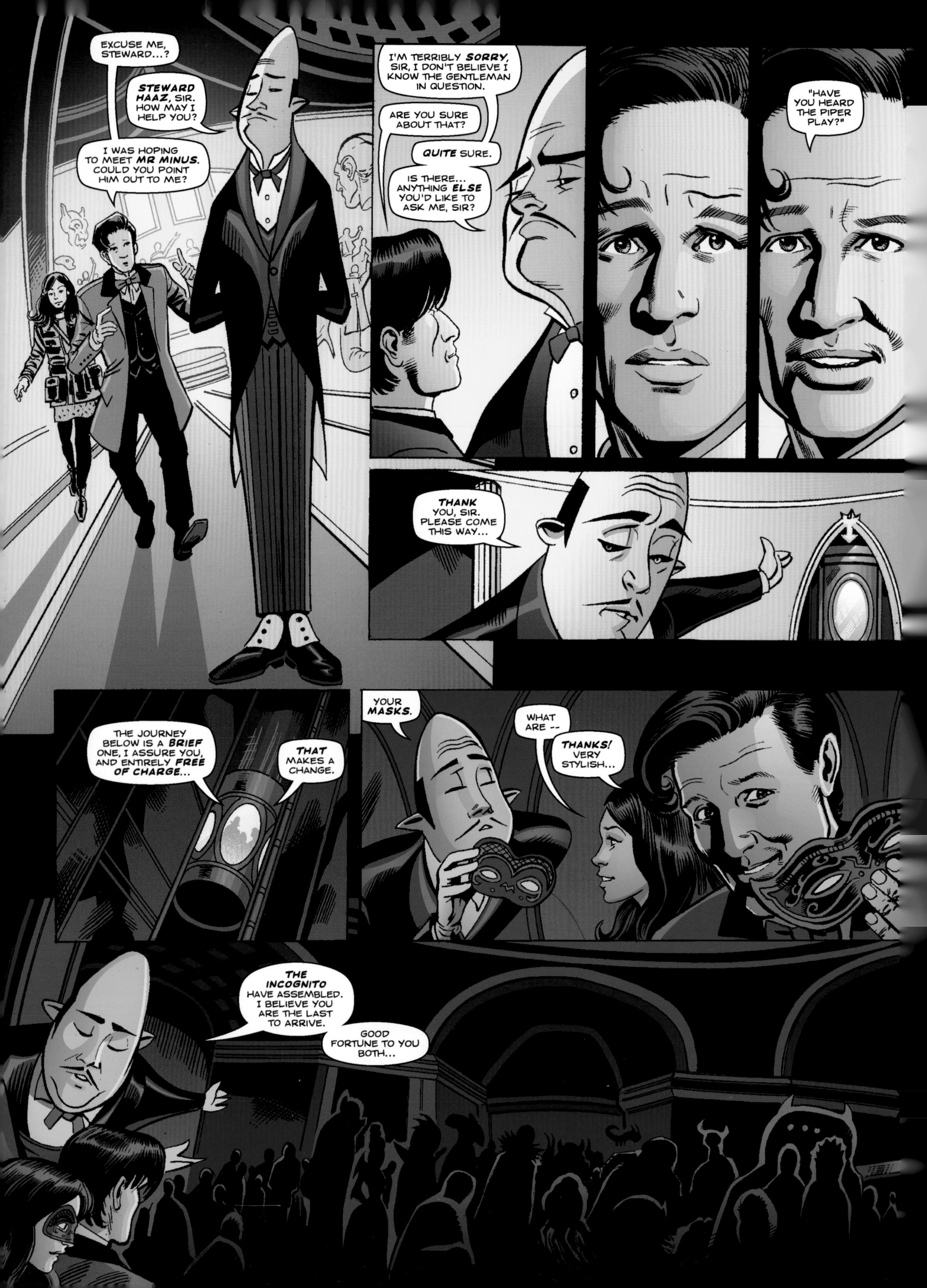
EXCUSE ME, STEWARD...?
STEWARD HAAZ, SIR. HOW MAY I HELP YOU?
I WAS HOPING TO MEET MR MINUS. COULD YOU POINT HIM OUT TO ME?
I'M TERRIBLY SORRY, SIR, I DON'T BELIEVE I KNOW THE GENTLEMAN IN QUESTION.
ARE YOU SURE ABOUT THAT?
QUITE SURE.
IS THERE... ANYTHING ELSE YOU'D LIKE TO ASK ME, SIR?
"HAVE YOU HEARD THE PIPER PLAY?"
THANK YOU, SIR. PLEASE COME THIS WAY...
THE JOURNEY BELOW IS A BRIEF ONE, I ASSURE YOU, AND ENTIRELY FREE OF CHARGE...
THAT MAKES A CHANGE.
YOUR MASKS.
WHAT ARE --
THANKS! VERY STYLISH...
THE INCOGNITO HAVE ASSEMBLED. I BELIEVE YOU ARE THE LAST TO ARRIVE.
GOOD FORTUNE TO YOU BOTH...

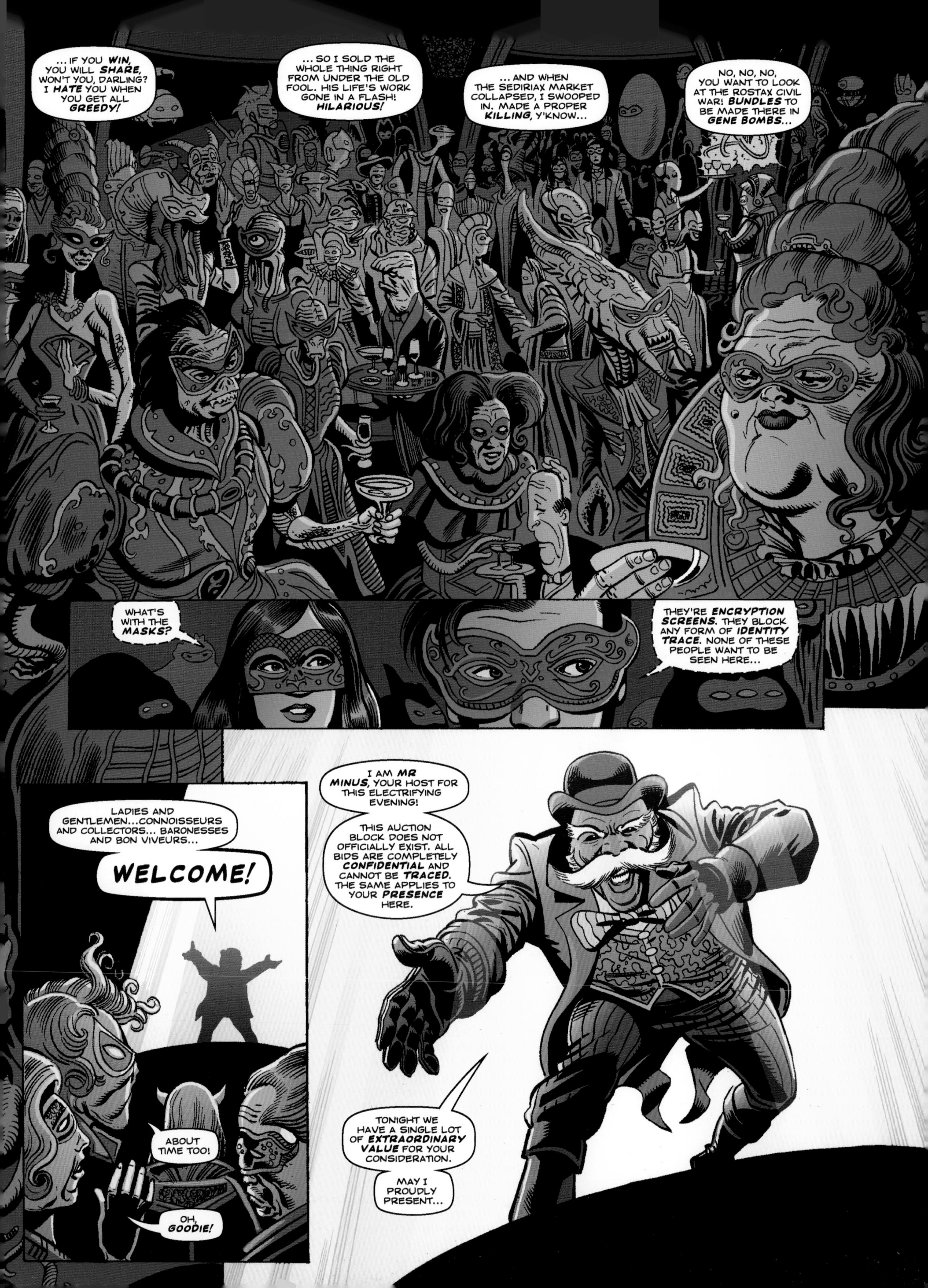

... IF YOU WIN, YOU WILL SHARE, WON'T YOU, DARLING? I HATE YOU WHEN YOU GET ALL GREEDY!
... SO I SOLD THE WHOLE THING RIGHT FROM UNDER THE OLD FOOL. HIS LIFE'S WORK GONE IN A FLASH! HILARIOUS!
... AND WHEN THE SEDIRIAX MARKET COLLAPSED, I SWOOPED IN. MADE A PROPER KILLING, Y'KNOW...
NO, NO, NO, YOU WANT TO LOOK AT THE ROSTAX CIVIL WAR! BUNDLES TO BE MADE THERE IN GENE BOMBS...
WHAT'S WITH THE MASKS?
THEY'RE ENCRYPTION SCREENS. THEY BLOCK ANY FORM OF IDENTITY TRACE. NONE OF THESE PEOPLE WANT TO BE SEEN HERE...
LADIES AND GENTLEMEN...CONNOISSEURS AND COLLECTORS... BARONESSES AND BON VIVEURS...
WELCOME!
ABOUT TIME TOO!
OH, GOODIE!
I AM MR MINUS, YOUR HOST FOR THIS ELECTRIFYING EVENING!
THIS AUCTION BLOCK DOES NOT OFFICIALLY EXIST. ALL BIDS ARE COMPLETELY CONFIDENTIAL AND CANNOT BE TRACED. THE SAME APPLIES TO YOUR PRESENCE HERE.
TONIGHT WE HAVE A SINGLE LOT OF EXTRAORDINARY VALUE FOR YOUR CONSIDERATION.
MAY I PROUDLY PRESENT...

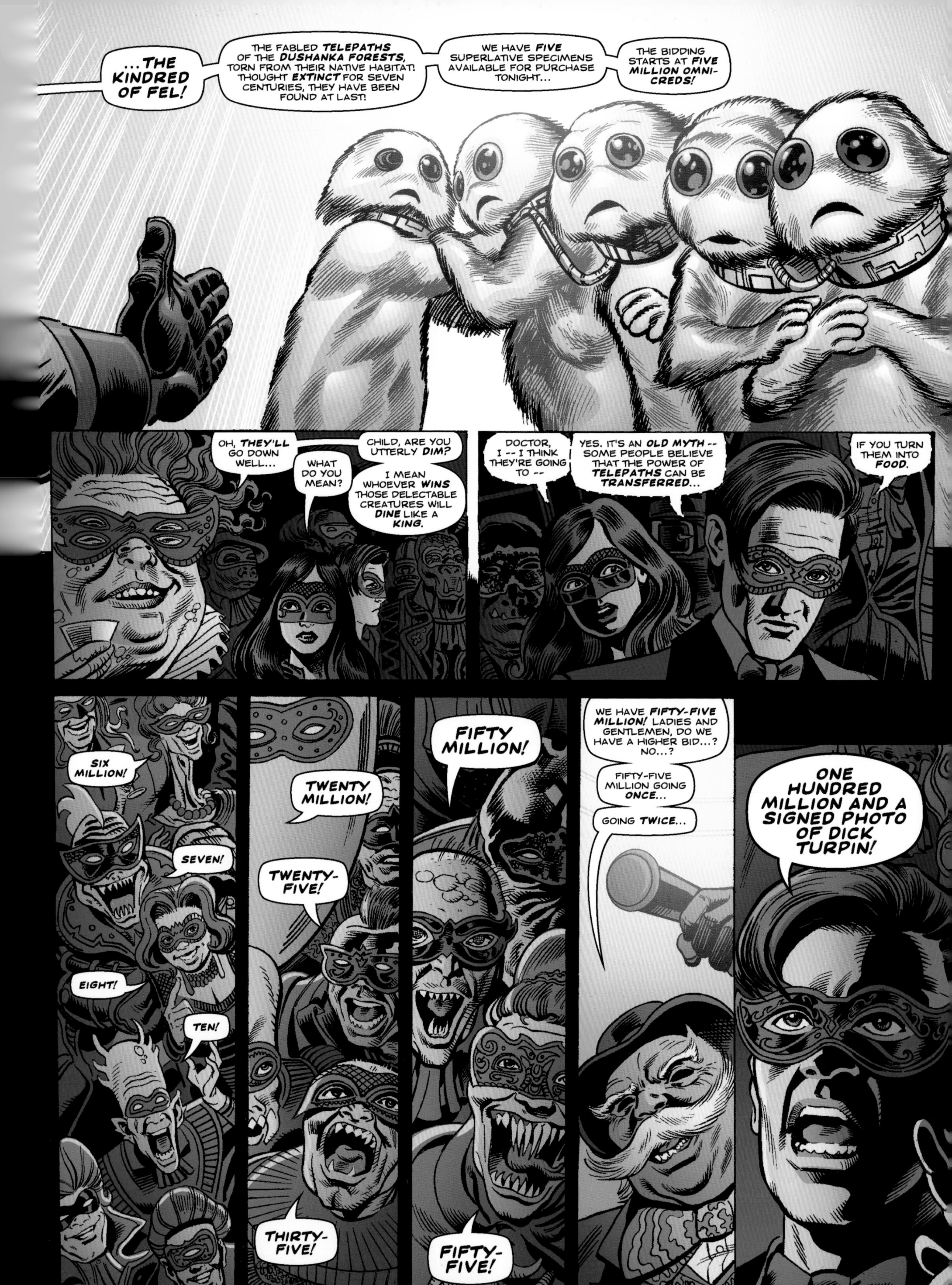
...THE KINDRED OF FEL!
THE FABLED TELEPATHS OF THE DUSHANKA FORESTS, TORN FROM THEIR NATIVE HABITAT! THOUGHT EXTINCT FOR SEVEN CENTURIES, THEY HAVE BEEN FOUND AT LAST!
WE HAVE FIVE SUPERLATIVE SPECIMENS AVAILABLE FOR PURCHASE TONIGHT...
THE BIDDING STARTS AT FIVE MILLION OMNI-CREDS!
OH, THEY'LL GO DOWN WELL...
WHAT DO YOU MEAN?
CHILD, ARE YOU UTTERLY DIM?
I MEAN WHOEVER WINS THOSE DELECTABLE CREATURES WILL DINE LIKE A KING.
DOCTOR, I -- I THINK THEY'RE GOING TO --
YES. IT'S AN OLD MYTH -- SOME PEOPLE BELIEVE THAT THE POWER OF TELEPATHS CAN BE TRANSFERRED...
IF YOU TURN THEM INTO FOOD.
SIX MILLION!
SEVEN!
EIGHT!
TEN!
TWENTY MILLION!
TWENTY-FIVE!
THIRTY-FIVE!
FIFTY MILLION!
FIFTY-FIVE!
WE HAVE FIFTY-FIVE MILLION! LADIES AND GENTLEMEN, DO WE HAVE A HIGHER BID...? NO...?
FIFTY-FIVE MILLION GOING ONCE...
GOING TWICE...
ONE HUNDRED MILLION AND A SIGNED PHOTO OF DICK TURPIN!

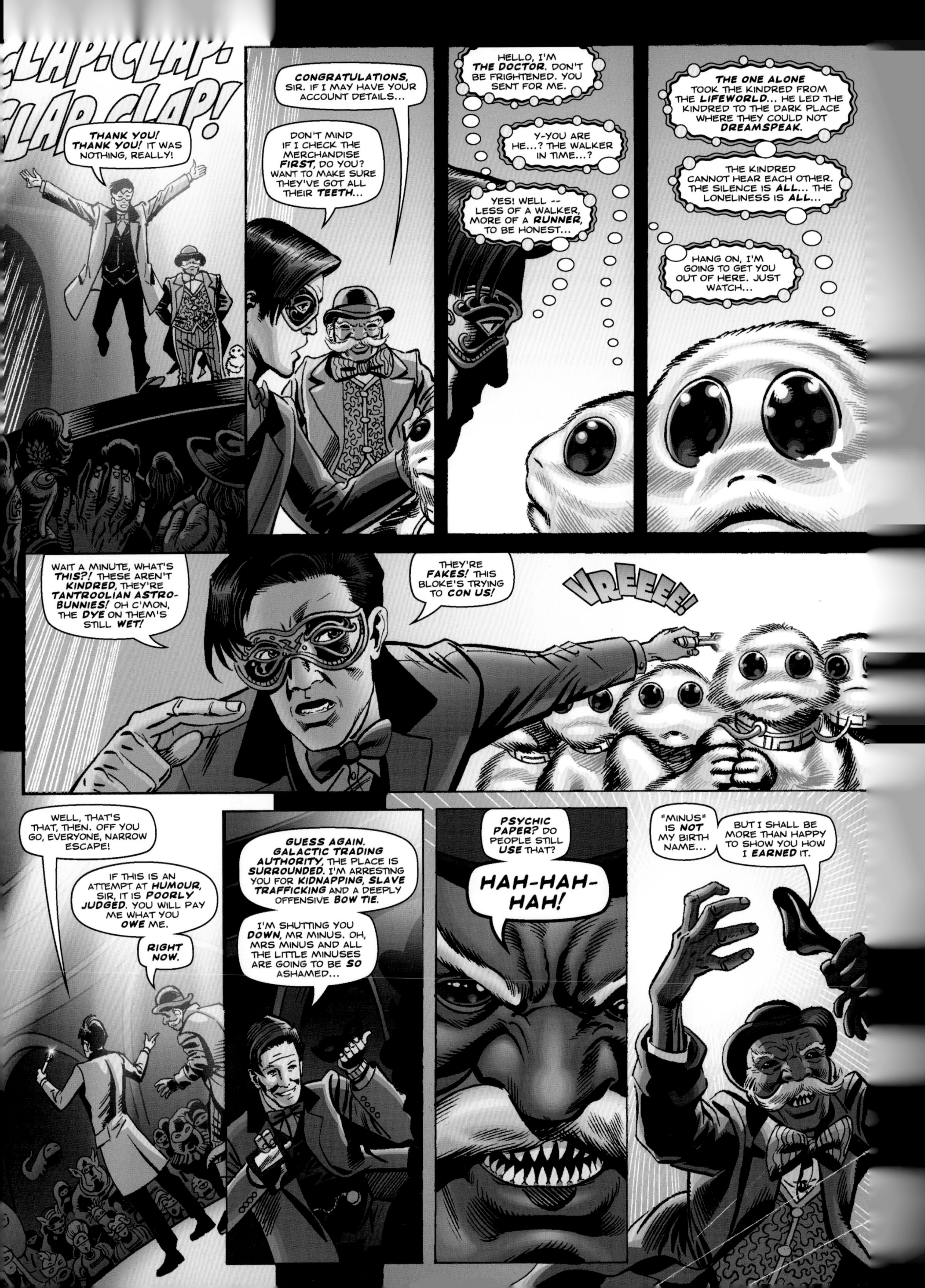

CLAP-CLAP-CLAP-CLAP!
THANK YOU! THANK YOU! IT WAS NOTHING, REALLY!
CONGRATULATIONS, SIR. IF I MAY HAVE YOUR ACCOUNT DETAILS...
DON'T MIND IF I CHECK THE MERCHANDISE FIRST, DO YOU? WANT TO MAKE SURE THEY'VE GOT ALL THEIR TEETH...
HELLO, I'M THE DOCTOR. DON'T BE FRIGHTENED. YOU SENT FOR ME.
Y-YOU ARE HE...? THE WALKER IN TIME...?
YES! WELL -- LESS OF A WALKER, MORE OF A RUNNER, TO BE HONEST...
THE ONE ALONE TOOK THE KINDRED FROM THE LIFEWORLD... HE LED THE KINDRED TO THE DARK PLACE WHERE THEY COULD NOT DREAMSPEAK.
THE KINDRED CANNOT HEAR EACH OTHER. THE SILENCE IS ALL... THE LONELINESS IS ALL...
HANG ON, I'M GOING TO GET YOU OUT OF HERE. JUST WATCH...
WAIT A MINUTE, WHAT'S THIS?! THESE AREN'T KINDRED, THEY'RE TANTROOLIAN ASTRO-BUNNIES! OH C'MON, THE DYE ON THEM'S STILL WET!
THEY'RE FAKES! THIS BLOKE'S TRYING TO CON US!
VREEEE!
WELL, THAT'S THAT, THEN. OFF YOU GO, EVERYONE, NARROW ESCAPE!
IF THIS IS AN ATTEMPT AT HUMOUR, SIR, IT IS POORLY JUDGED. YOU WILL PAY ME WHAT YOU OWE ME.
RIGHT NOW.
GUESS AGAIN. GALACTIC TRADING AUTHORITY, THE PLACE IS SURROUNDED. I'M ARRESTING YOU FOR KIDNAPPING, SLAVE TRAFFICKING AND A DEEPLY OFFENSIVE BOW TIE.
I'M SHUTTING YOU DOWN, MR MINUS. OH, MRS MINUS AND ALL THE LITTLE MINUSES ARE GOING TO BE SO ASHAMED...
PSYCHIC PAPER? DO PEOPLE STILL USE THAT?
HAH-HAH-HAH!
"MINUS" IS NOT MY BIRTH NAME...
BUT I SHALL BE MORE THAN HAPPY TO SHOW YOU HOW I EARNED IT.

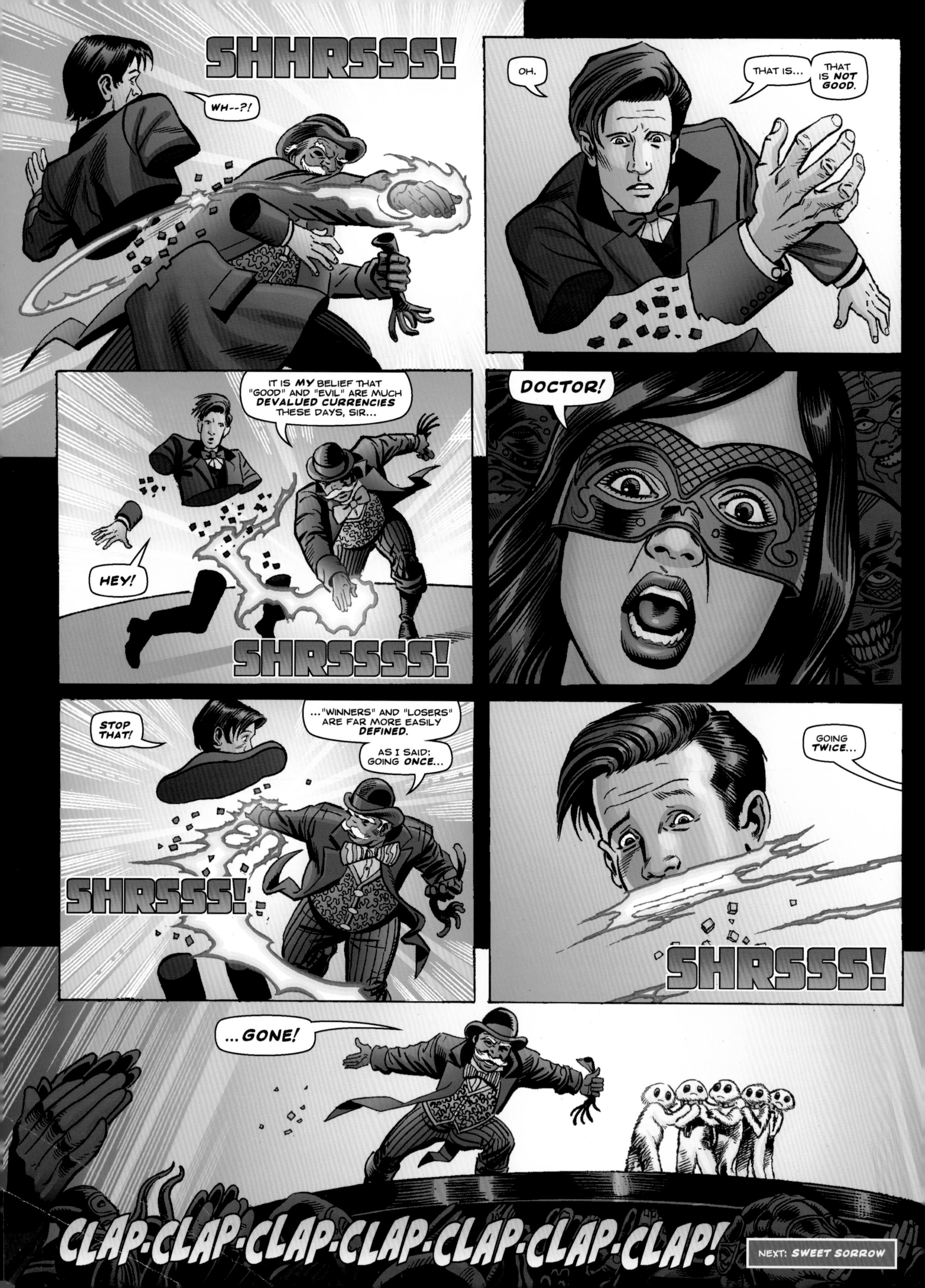

SHHRSSS!
WH--?!
OH.
THAT IS...
THAT IS NOT GOOD.
IT IS MY BELIEF THAT "GOOD" AND "EVIL" ARE MUCH DEVALUED CURRENCIES THESE DAYS, SIR...
HEY!
SHRSSSS!
DOCTOR!
STOP THAT!
..."WINNERS" AND "LOSERS" ARE FAR MORE EASILY DEFINED.
AS I SAID: GOING ONCE...
SHRSSS!
GOING TWICE...
SHRSSS!
...GONE!
CLAP-CLAP-CLAP-CLAP-CLAP-CLAP-CLAP!
NEXT: SWEET SORROW

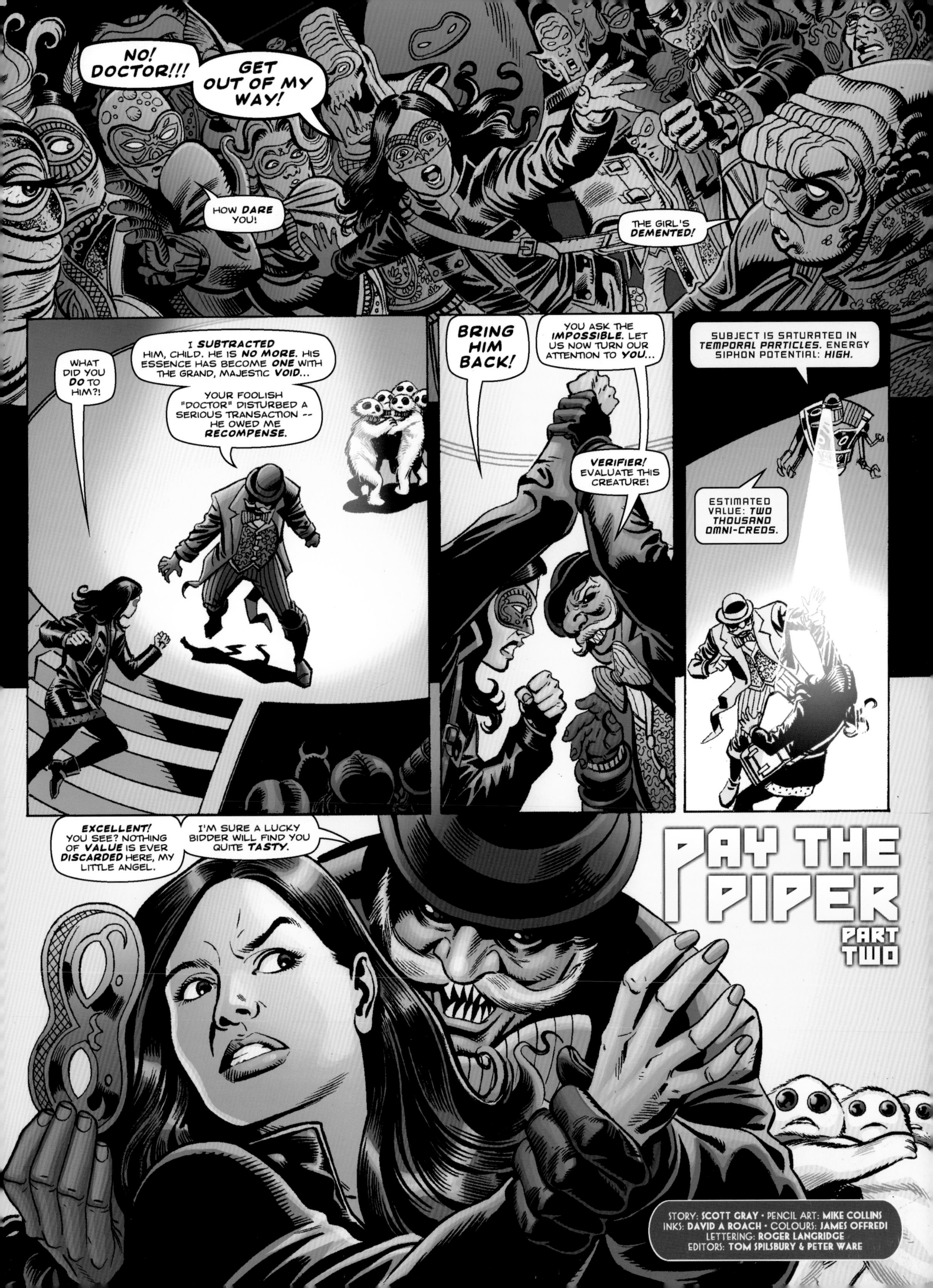
NO! DOCTOR!!!
GET OUT OF MY WAY!
HOW DARE YOU!
THE GIRL'S DEMENTED!
WHAT DID YOU DO TO HIM?!
I SUBTRACTED HIM, CHILD. HE IS NO MORE. HIS ESSENCE HAS BECOME ONE WITH THE GRAND, MAJESTIC VOID...
YOUR FOOLISH "DOCTOR" DISTURBED A SERIOUS TRANSACTION -- HE OWED ME RECOMPENSE.
BRING HIM BACK!
YOU ASK THE IMPOSSIBLE. LET US NOW TURN OUR ATTENTION TO YOU...
VERIFIER! EVALUATE THIS CREATURE!
SUBJECT IS SATURATED IN TEMPORAL PARTICLES. ENERGY SIPHON POTENTIAL: HIGH.
ESTIMATED VALUE: TWO THOUSAND OMNI-CREDS.
EXCELLENT! YOU SEE? NOTHING OF VALUE IS EVER DISCARDED HERE, MY LITTLE ANGEL.
I'M SURE A LUCKY BIDDER WILL FIND YOU QUITE TASTY.
PAY THE PIPER
PART TWO
STORY: SCOTT GRAY • PENCIL ART: MIKE COLLINS
INKS: DAVID A ROACH • COLOURS: JAMES OFFREDI
LETTERING: ROGER LANGRIDGE
EDITORS: TOM SPILSBURY & PETER WARE

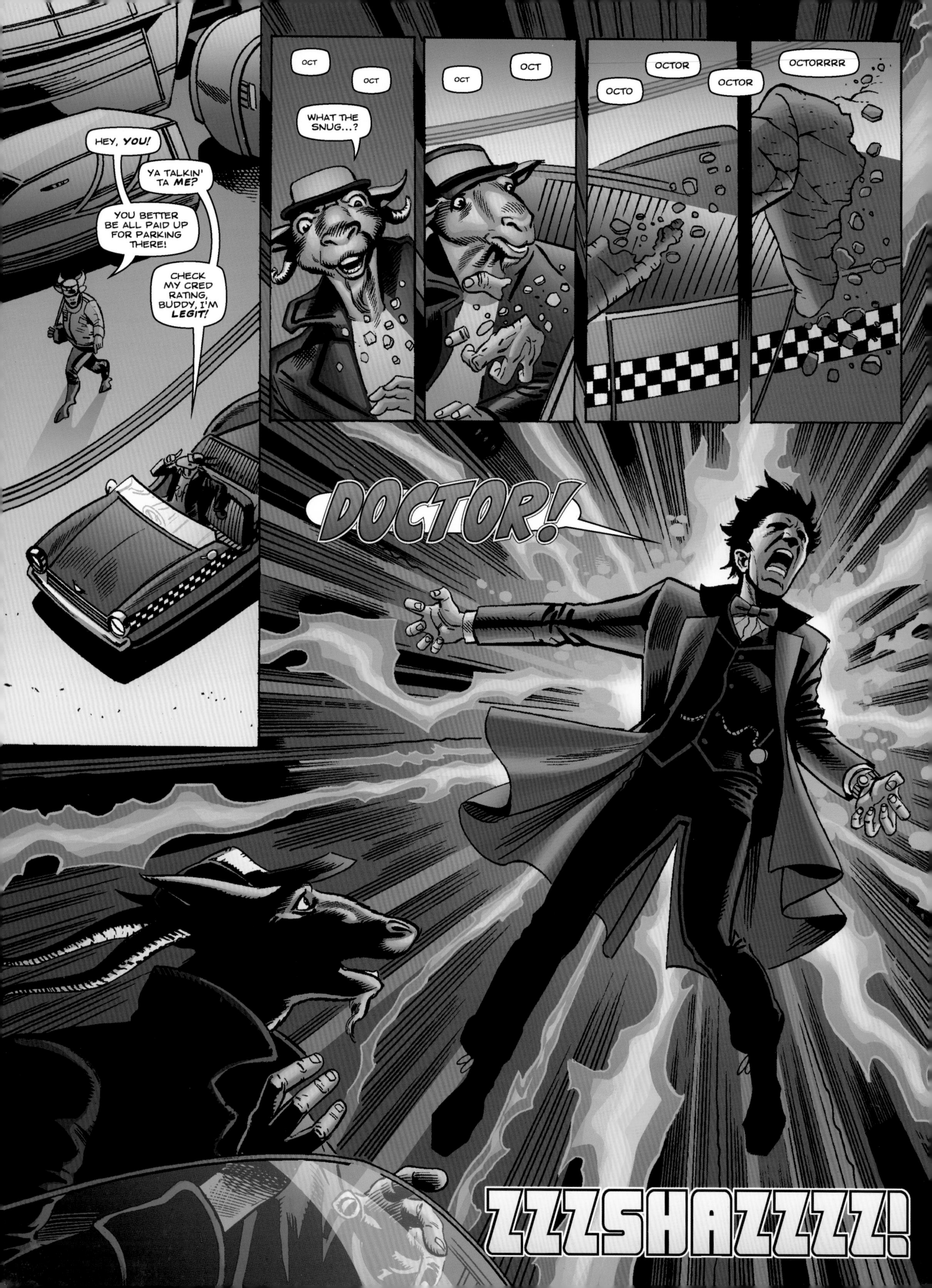

HEY, YOU!
YA TALKIN' TA ME?
YOU BETTER BE ALL PAID UP FOR PARKING THERE!
CHECK MY CRED RATING, BUDDY, I'M LEGIT!
OCT
OCT
WHAT THE SNUG...?
OCT
OCT
OCTO
OCTOR
OCTOR
OCTORRRR
DOCTOR!
ZZZSHAZZZZ!

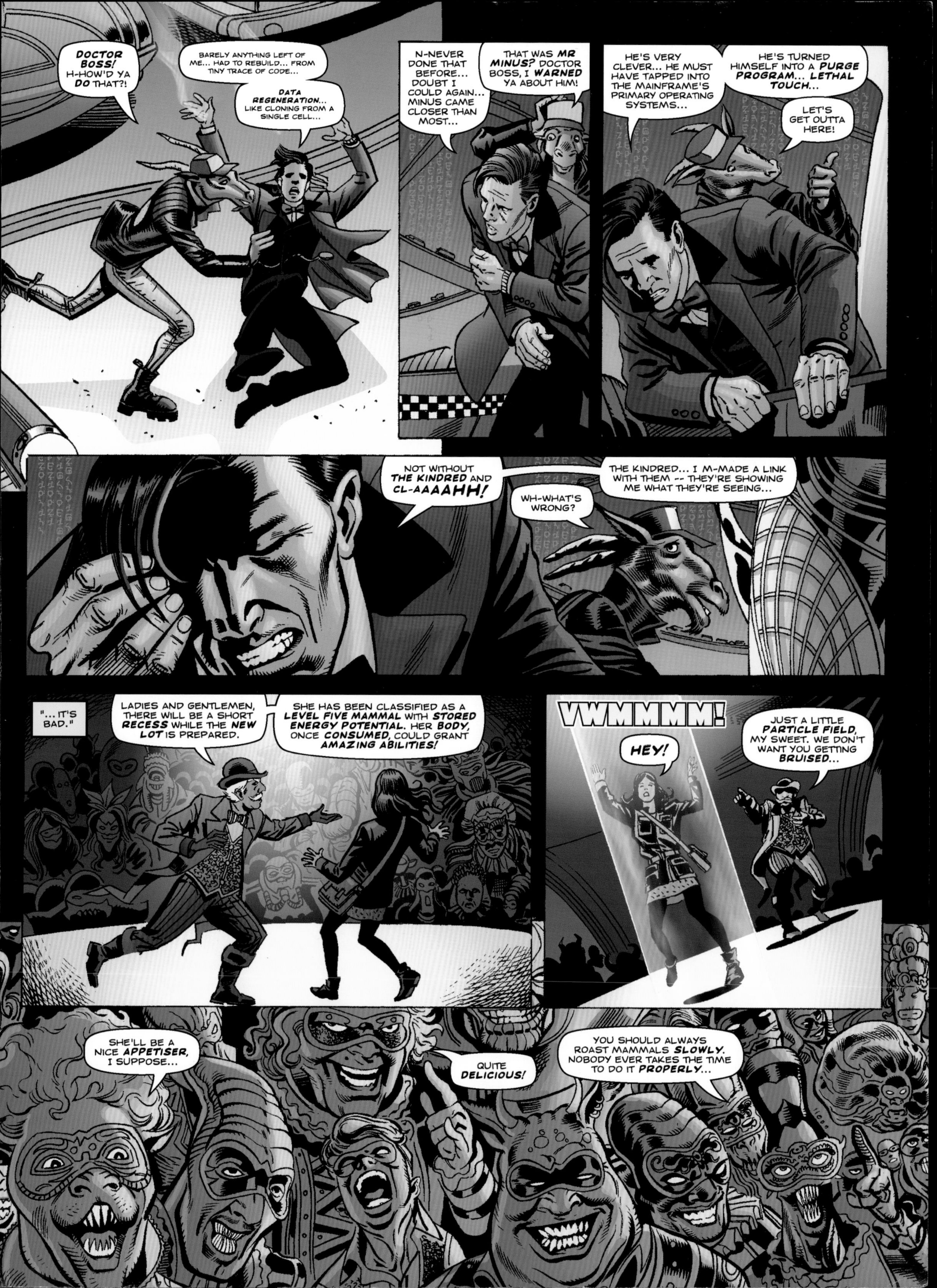
DOCTOR BOSS! H-HOW'D YA DO THAT?!
BARELY ANYTHING LEFT OF ME... HAD TO REBUILD... FROM TINY TRACE OF CODE...
DATA REGENERATION... LIKE CLONING FROM A SINGLE CELL...
N-NEVER DONE THAT BEFORE... DOUBT I COULD AGAIN... MINUS CAME CLOSER THAN MOST...
THAT WAS MR MINUS? DOCTOR BOSS, I WARNED YA ABOUT HIM!
HE'S VERY CLEVER... HE MUST HAVE TAPPED INTO THE MAINFRAME'S PRIMARY OPERATING SYSTEMS...
HE'S TURNED HIMSELF INTO A PURGE PROGRAM... LETHAL TOUCH...
LET'S GET OUTTA HERE!
NOT WITHOUT THE KINDRED AND CL-AAAAHH!
WH-WHAT'S WRONG?
THE KINDRED... I M-MADE A LINK WITH THEM -- THEY'RE SHOWING ME WHAT THEY'RE SEEING...
"... IT'S BAD."
LADIES AND GENTLEMEN, THERE WILL BE A SHORT RECESS WHILE THE NEW LOT IS PREPARED.
SHE HAS BEEN CLASSIFIED AS A LEVEL FIVE MAMMAL WITH STORED ENERGY POTENTIAL. HER BODY, ONCE CONSUMED, COULD GRANT AMAZING ABILITIES!
VWMMMMM!
HEY!
JUST A LITTLE PARTICLE FIELD, MY SWEET. WE DON'T WANT YOU GETTING BRUISED...
SHE'LL BE A NICE APPETISER, I SUPPOSE...
QUITE DELICIOUS!
YOU SHOULD ALWAYS ROAST MAMMALS SLOWLY. NOBODY EVER TAKES THE TIME TO DO IT PROPERLY...

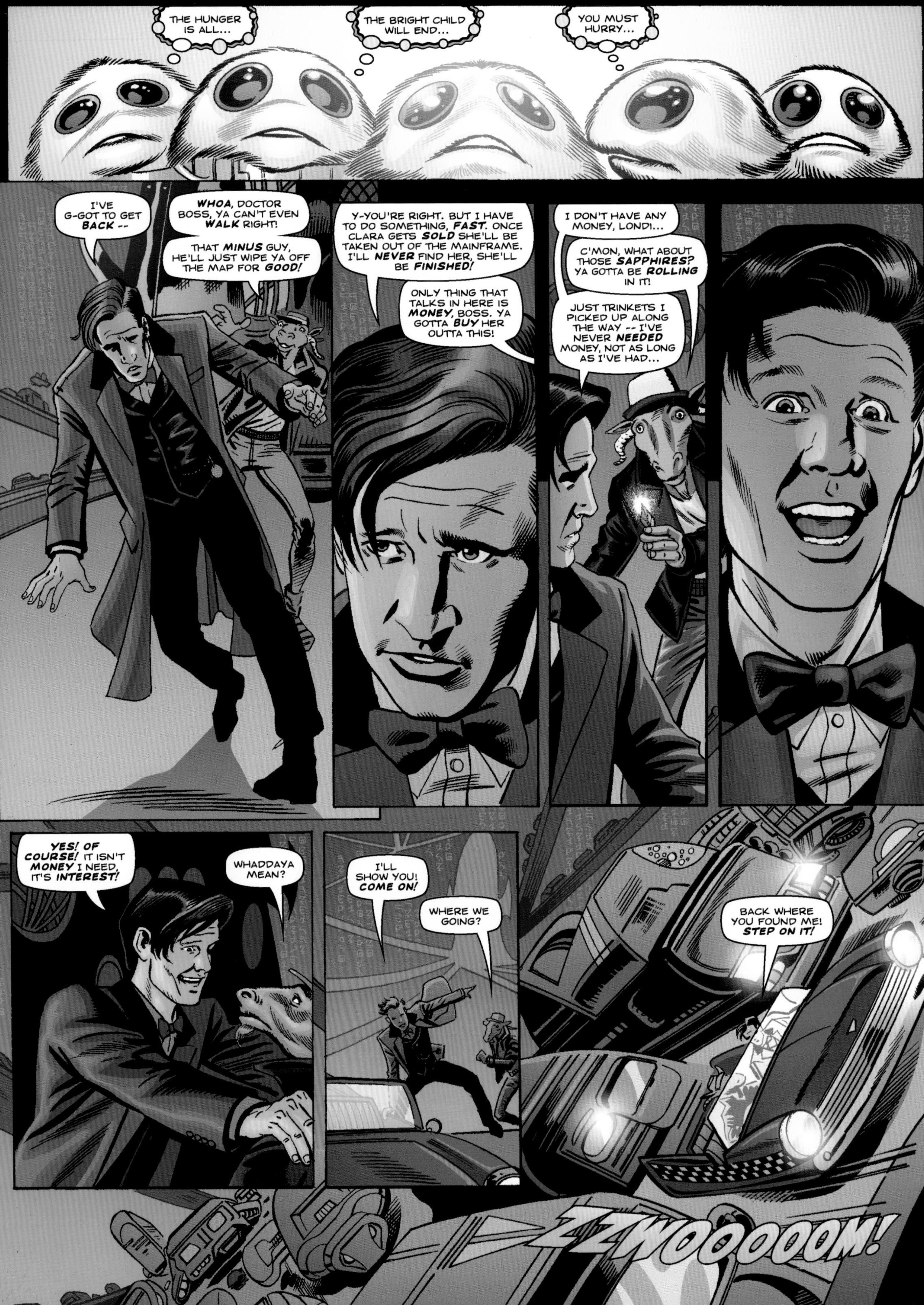
THE HUNGER IS ALL...
THE BRIGHT CHILD WILL END...
YOU MUST HURRY...
I'VE G-GOT TO GET BACK --
WHOA, DOCTOR BOSS, YA CAN'T EVEN WALK RIGHT!
THAT MINUS GUY, HE'LL JUST WIPE YA OFF THE MAP FOR GOOD!
Y-YOU'RE RIGHT. BUT I HAVE TO DO SOMETHING, FAST. ONCE CLARA GETS SOLD SHE'LL BE TAKEN OUT OF THE MAINFRAME. I'LL NEVER FIND HER, SHE'LL BE FINISHED!
ONLY THING THAT TALKS IN HERE IS MONEY, BOSS. YA GOTTA BUY HER OUTTA THIS!
I DON'T HAVE ANY MONEY, LONDI...
C'MON, WHAT ABOUT THOSE SAPPHIRES? YA GOTTA BE ROLLING IN IT!
JUST TRINKETS I PICKED UP ALONG THE WAY -- I'VE NEVER NEEDED MONEY, NOT AS LONG AS I'VE HAD...
YES! OF COURSE! IT ISN'T MONEY I NEED, IT'S INTEREST!
WHADDAYA MEAN?
I'LL SHOW YOU! COME ON!
WHERE WE GOING?
BACK WHERE YOU FOUND ME! STEP ON IT!
ZZWOOOOOM!

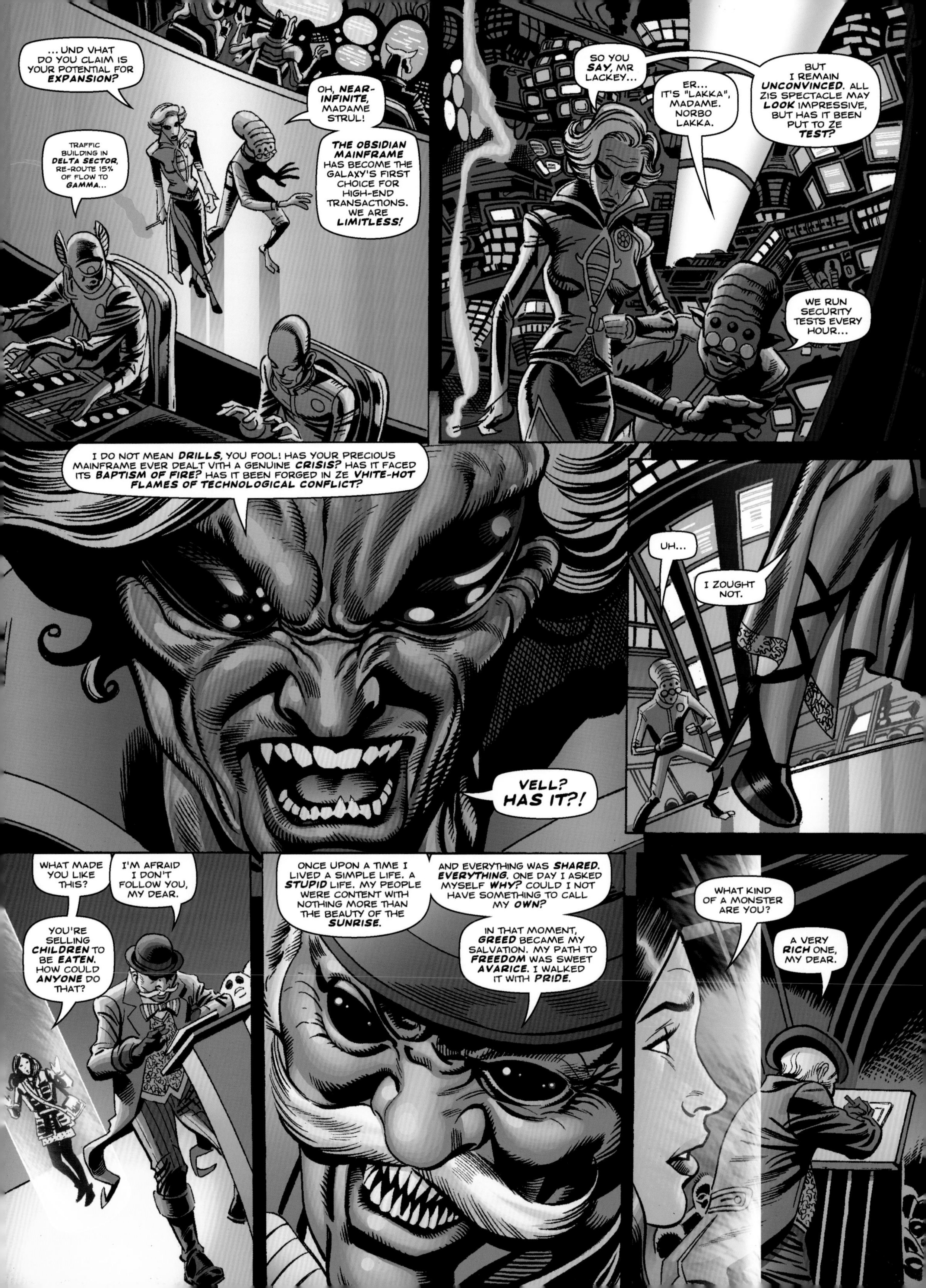

...UND VHAT DO YOU CLAIM IS YOUR POTENTIAL FOR EXPANSION?
OH, NEAR-INFINITE, MADAME STRUL!
TRAFFIC BUILDING IN DELTA SECTOR, RE-ROUTE 15% OF FLOW TO GAMMA...
THE OBSIDIAN MAINFRAME HAS BECOME THE GALAXY'S FIRST CHOICE FOR HIGH-END TRANSACTIONS. WE ARE LIMITLESS!
SO YOU SAY, MR LACKEY...
ER... IT'S "LAKKA", MADAME. NORBO LAKKA.
BUT I REMAIN UNCONVINCED. ALL ZIS SPECTACLE MAY LOOK IMPRESSIVE, BUT HAS IT BEEN PUT TO ZE TEST?
WE RUN SECURITY TESTS EVERY HOUR...
I DO NOT MEAN DRILLS, YOU FOOL! HAS YOUR PRECIOUS MAINFRAME EVER DEALT VITH A GENUINE CRISIS? HAS IT FACED ITS BAPTISM OF FIRE? HAS IT BEEN FORGED IN ZE VHITE-HOT FLAMES OF TECHNOLOGICAL CONFLICT?
VELL? HAS IT?!
UH...
I ZOUGHT NOT.
WHAT MADE YOU LIKE THIS?
I'M AFRAID I DON'T FOLLOW YOU, MY DEAR.
YOU'RE SELLING CHILDREN TO BE EATEN. HOW COULD ANYONE DO THAT?
ONCE UPON A TIME I LIVED A SIMPLE LIFE. A STUPID LIFE. MY PEOPLE WERE CONTENT WITH NOTHING MORE THAN THE BEAUTY OF THE SUNRISE.
AND EVERYTHING WAS SHARED. EVERYTHING. ONE DAY I ASKED MYSELF WHY? COULD I NOT HAVE SOMETHING TO CALL MY OWN?
IN THAT MOMENT, GREED BECAME MY SALVATION. MY PATH TO FREEDOM WAS SWEET AVARICE. I WALKED IT WITH PRIDE.
WHAT KIND OF A MONSTER ARE YOU?
A VERY RICH ONE, MY DEAR.

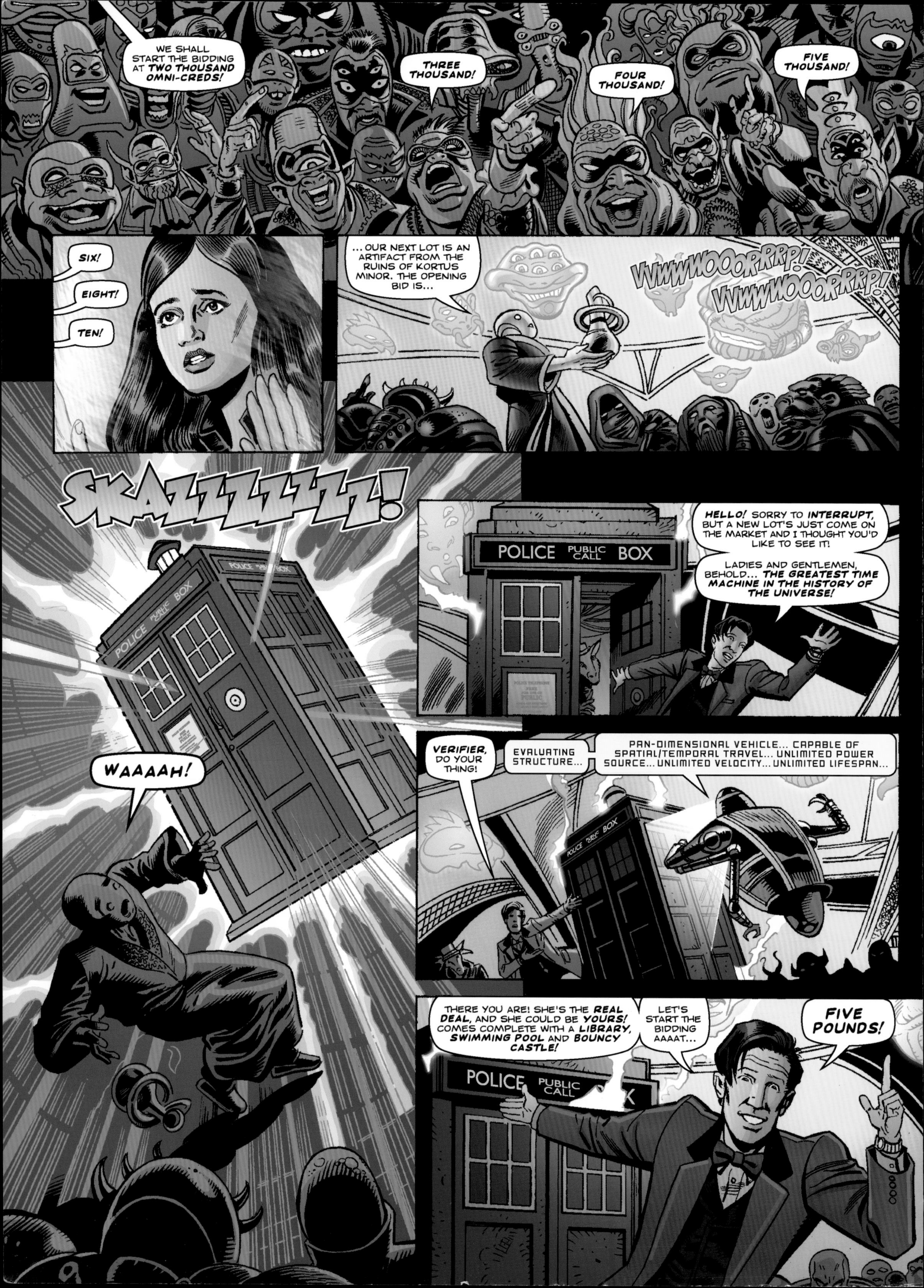

WE SHALL START THE BIDDING AT TWO THOUSAND OMNI-CREDS!
THREE THOUSAND!
FOUR THOUSAND!
FIVE THOUSAND!
SIX!
EIGHT!
TEN!
... OUR NEXT LOT IS AN ARTIFACT FROM THE RUINS OF KORTUS MINOR. THE OPENING BID IS...
VVWWWOOORRRP! VVWWWOOORRRP!
SKAZZZZZZZ!
WAAAAH!
POLICE PUBLIC CALL BOX
HELLO! SORRY TO INTERRUPT, BUT A NEW LOT'S JUST COME ON THE MARKET AND I THOUGHT YOU'D LIKE TO SEE IT!
LADIES AND GENTLEMEN, BEHOLD... THE GREATEST TIME MACHINE IN THE HISTORY OF THE UNIVERSE!
VERIFIER, DO YOUR THING!
EVALUATING STRUCTURE...
PAN-DIMENSIONAL VEHICLE... CAPABLE OF SPATIAL/TEMPORAL TRAVEL... UNLIMITED POWER SOURCE... UNLIMITED VELOCITY... UNLIMITED LIFESPAN...
THERE YOU ARE! SHE'S THE REAL DEAL, AND SHE COULD BE YOURS! COMES COMPLETE WITH A LIBRARY, SWIMMING POOL AND BOUNCY CASTLE!
LET'S START THE BIDDING AAAAT...
FIVE POUNDS!

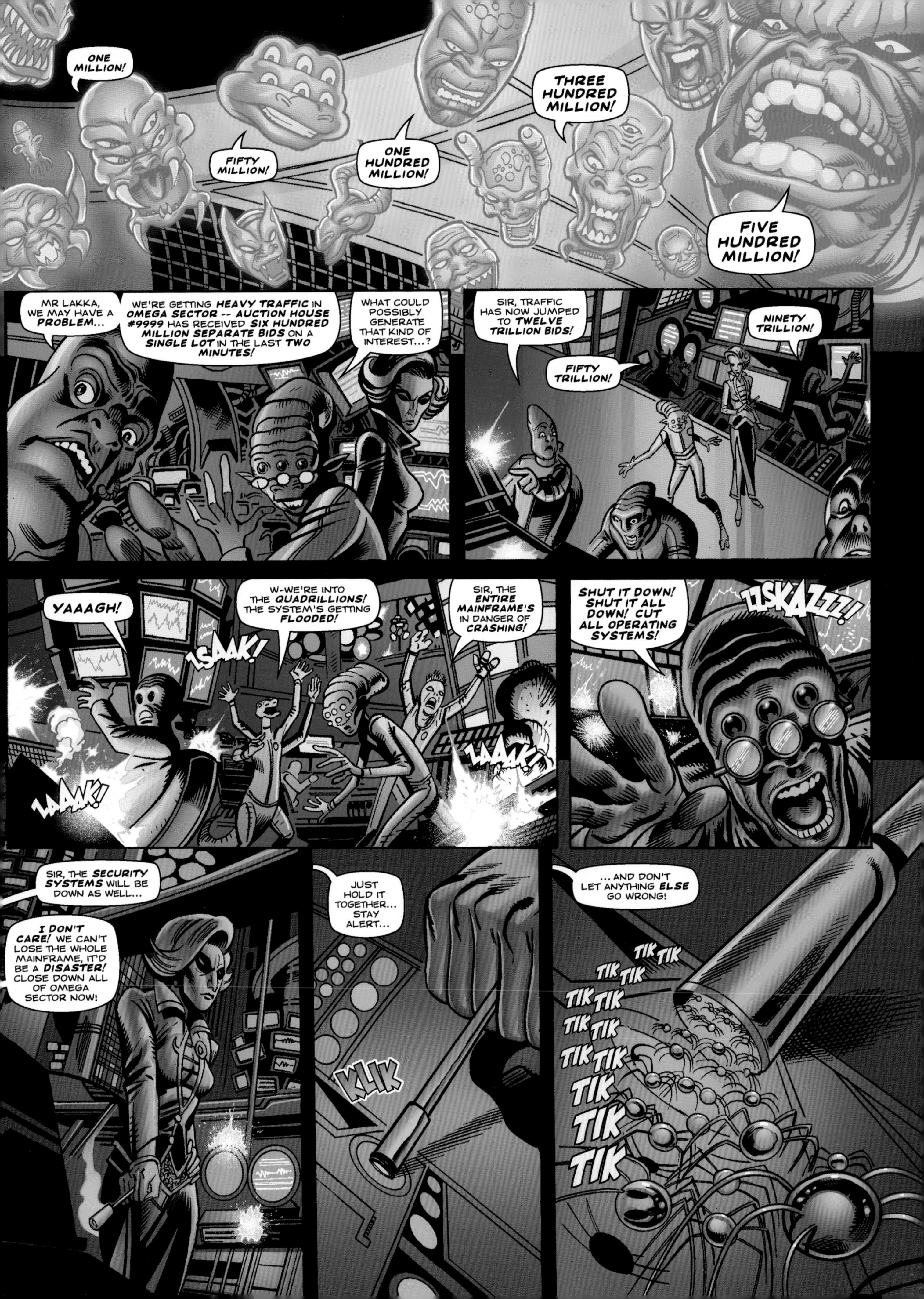
ONE MILLION!
FIFTY MILLION!
ONE HUNDRED MILLION!
THREE HUNDRED MILLION!
FIVE HUNDRED MILLION!
MR LAKKA, WE MAY HAVE A PROBLEM...
WE'RE GETTING HEAVY TRAFFIC IN OMEGA SECTOR -- AUCTION HOUSE #9999 HAS RECEIVED SIX HUNDRED MILLION SEPARATE BIDS ON A SINGLE LOT IN THE LAST TWO MINUTES!
WHAT COULD POSSIBLY GENERATE THAT KIND OF INTEREST...?
SIR, TRAFFIC HAS NOW JUMPED TO TWELVE TRILLION BIDS!
FIFTY TRILLION!
NINETY TRILLION!
YAAAGH!
ZSAAK!
W-WE'RE INTO THE QUADRILLIONS! THE SYSTEM'S GETTING FLOODED!
SIR, THE ENTIRE MAINFRAME'S IN DANGER OF CRASHING!
ZAAAK!
ZAAAK!
SHUT IT DOWN! SHUT IT ALL DOWN! CUT ALL OPERATING SYSTEMS!
ZZSKAZZZ!!
SIR, THE SECURITY SYSTEMS WILL BE DOWN AS WELL...
I DON'T CARE! WE CAN'T LOSE THE WHOLE MAINFRAME, IT'D BE A DISASTER! CLOSE DOWN ALL OF OMEGA SECTOR NOW!
JUST HOLD IT TOGETHER... STAY ALERT...
KLIK
...AND DON'T LET ANYTHING ELSE GO WRONG!
TIK TIK TIK TIK TIK TIK TIK TIK TIK TIK TIK TIK TIK TIK

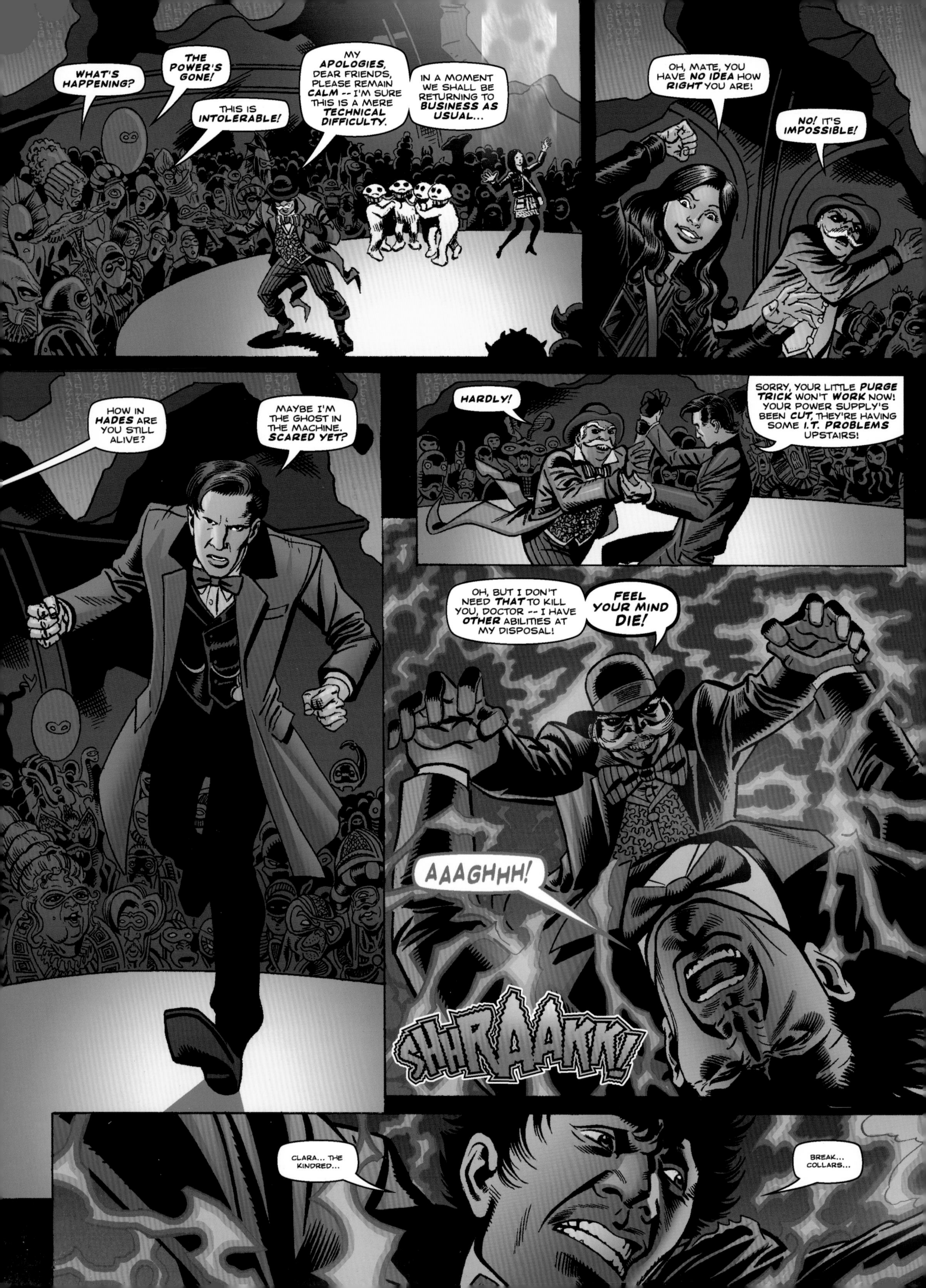
WHAT'S HAPPENING?
THE POWER'S GONE!
THIS IS INTOLERABLE!
MY APOLOGIES, DEAR FRIENDS, PLEASE REMAIN CALM -- I'M SURE THIS IS A MERE TECHNICAL DIFFICULTY.
IN A MOMENT WE SHALL BE RETURNING TO BUSINESS AS USUAL...
OH, MATE, YOU HAVE NO IDEA HOW RIGHT YOU ARE!
NO! IT'S IMPOSSIBLE!
HOW IN HADES ARE YOU STILL ALIVE?
MAYBE I'M THE GHOST IN THE MACHINE. SCARED YET?
HARDLY!
SORRY, YOUR LITTLE PURGE TRICK WON'T WORK NOW! YOUR POWER SUPPLY'S BEEN CUT, THEY'RE HAVING SOME I.T. PROBLEMS UPSTAIRS!
OH, BUT I DON'T NEED THAT TO KILL YOU, DOCTOR -- I HAVE OTHER ABILITIES AT MY DISPOSAL!
FEEL YOUR MIND DIE!
AAAGHHH!
SHHRAAKK!
CLARA... THE KINDRED...
BREAK... COLLARS...

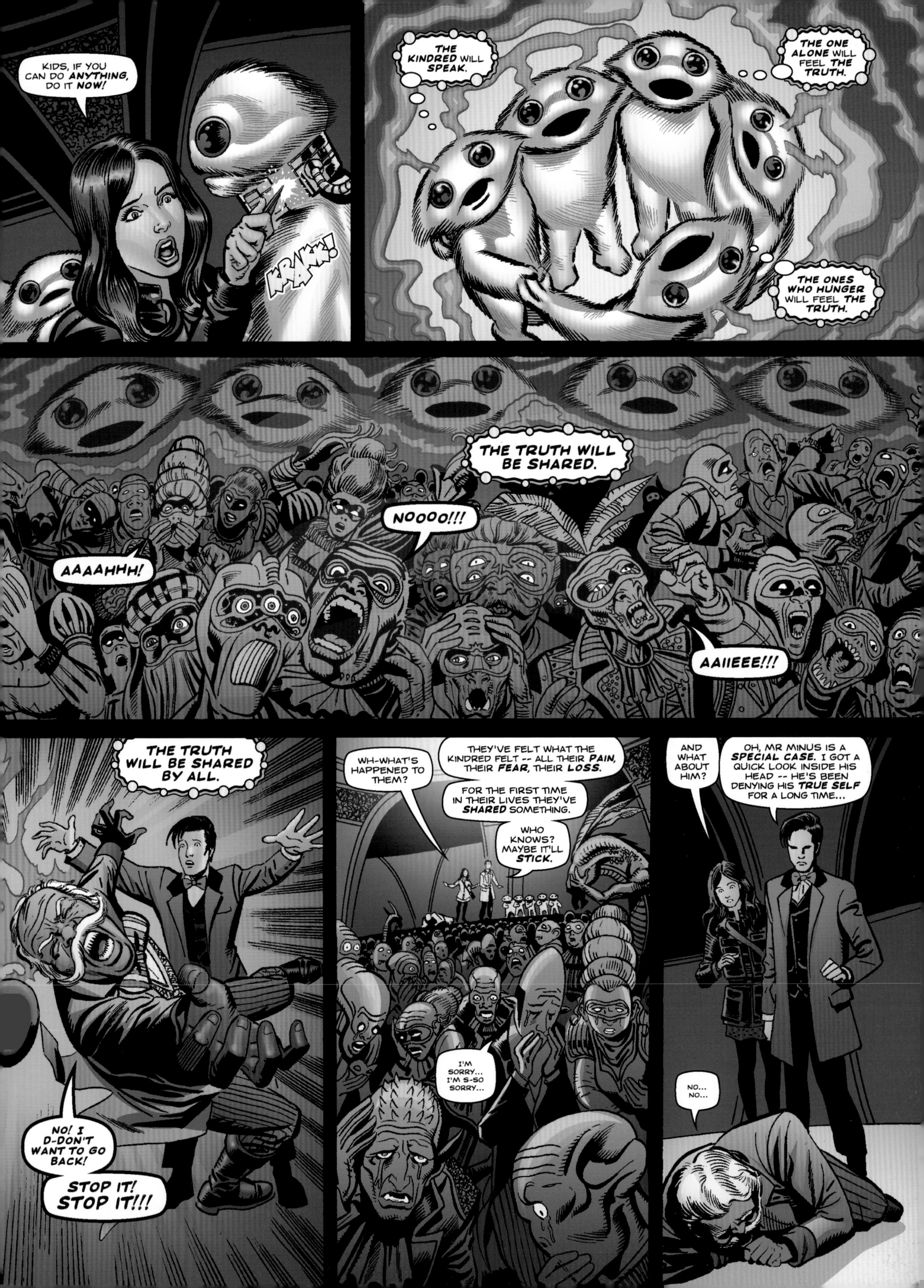
KIDS, IF YOU CAN DO ANYTHING, DO IT NOW!
KRANNK!
THE KINDRED WILL SPEAK.
THE ONE ALONE WILL FEEL THE TRUTH.
THE ONES WHO HUNGER WILL FEEL THE TRUTH.
THE TRUTH WILL BE SHARED.
NOOOO!!!
AAAAHHH!
AAIIEEE!!!
THE TRUTH WILL BE SHARED BY ALL.
NO! I D-DON'T WANT TO GO BACK!
STOP IT! STOP IT!!!
WH-WHAT'S HAPPENED TO THEM?
THEY'VE FELT WHAT THE KINDRED FELT -- ALL THEIR PAIN, THEIR FEAR, THEIR LOSS.
FOR THE FIRST TIME IN THEIR LIVES THEY'VE SHARED SOMETHING.
WHO KNOWS? MAYBE IT'LL STICK.
I'M SORRY... I'M S-SO SORRY...
AND WHAT ABOUT HIM?
OH, MR MINUS IS A SPECIAL CASE. I GOT A QUICK LOOK INSIDE HIS HEAD -- HE'S BEEN DENYING HIS TRUE SELF FOR A LONG TIME...
NO... NO...

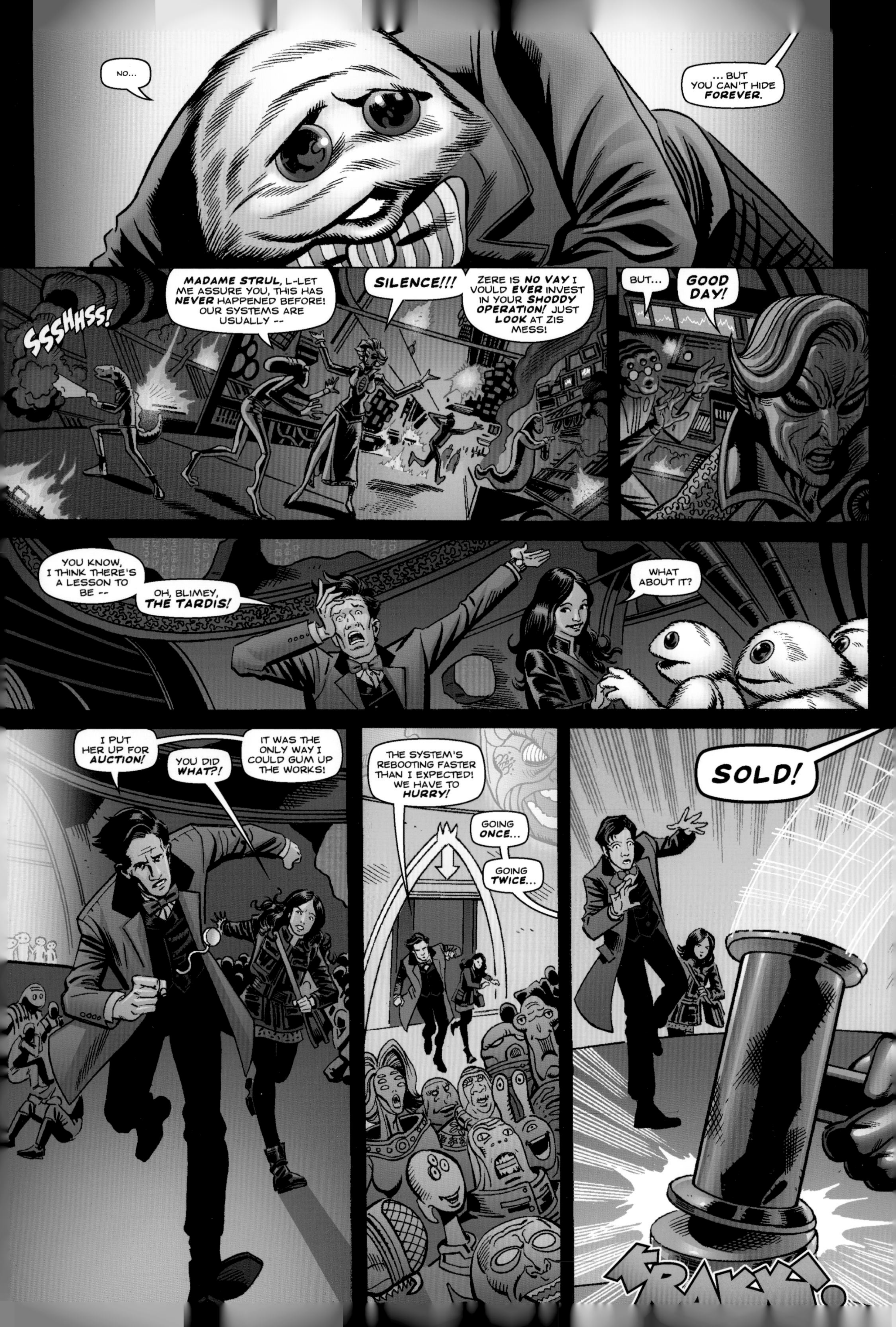

NO...
... BUT YOU CAN'T HIDE FOREVER.
SSSHHSS!
MADAME STRUL, L-LET ME ASSURE YOU, THIS HAS NEVER HAPPENED BEFORE! OUR SYSTEMS ARE USUALLY --
SILENCE!!!
ZERE IS NO VAY I VOULD EVER INVEST IN YOUR SHODDY OPERATION! JUST LOOK AT ZIS MESS!
BUT...
GOOD DAY!
YOU KNOW, I THINK THERE'S A LESSON TO BE --
OH, BLIMEY, THE TARDIS!
WHAT ABOUT IT?
I PUT HER UP FOR AUCTION!
YOU DID WHAT?!
IT WAS THE ONLY WAY I COULD GUM UP THE WORKS!
THE SYSTEM'S REBOOTING FASTER THAN I EXPECTED! WE HAVE TO HURRY!
GOING ONCE...
GOING TWICE...
SOLD!

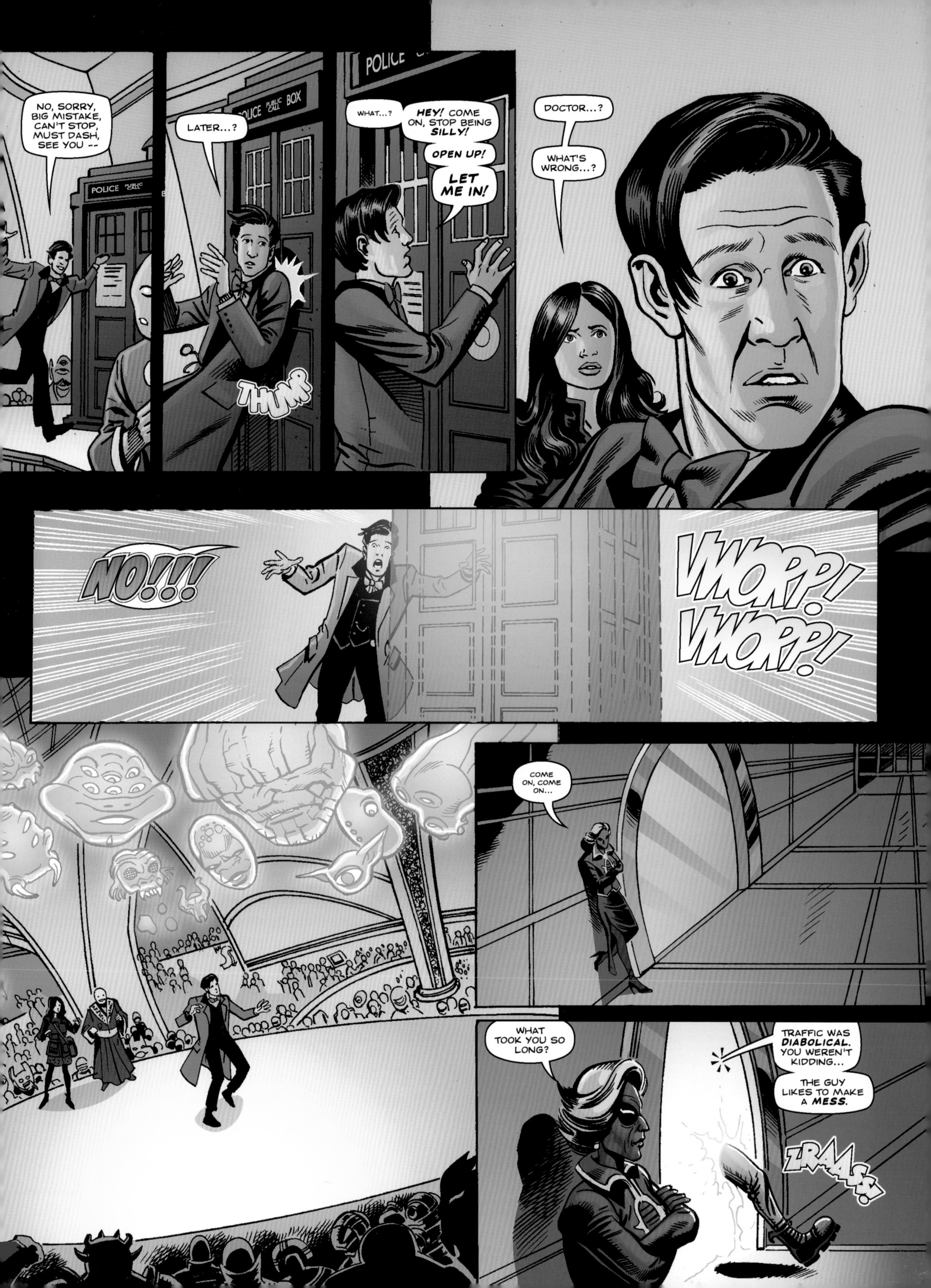
NO, SORRY, BIG MISTAKE, CAN'T STOP, MUST DASH, SEE YOU --
POLICE PUBLIC CALL BOX
LATER...?
THUMP
WHAT...?
HEY! COME ON, STOP BEING SILLY!
OPEN UP!
LET ME IN!
DOCTOR...?
WHAT'S WRONG...?
NO!!!
VWORP! VWORP!
COME ON, COME ON...
WHAT TOOK YOU SO LONG?
TRAFFIC WAS DIABOLICAL. YOU WEREN'T KIDDING...
THE GUY LIKES TO MAKE A MESS.
ZRAASS!

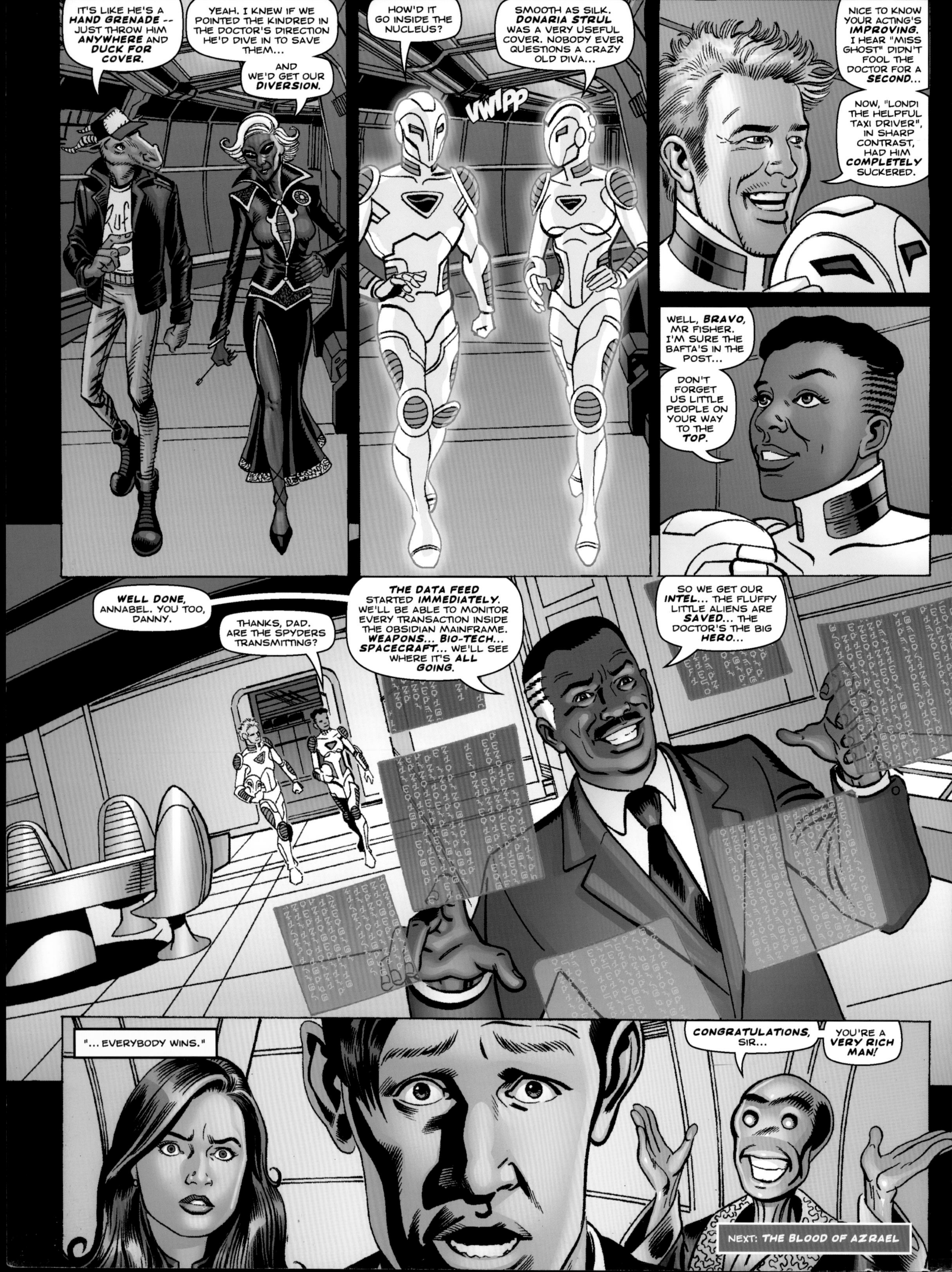
IT'S LIKE HE'S A HAND GRENADE -- JUST THROW HIM ANYWHERE AND DUCK FOR COVER.
YEAH. I KNEW IF WE POINTED THE KINDRED IN THE DOCTOR'S DIRECTION HE'D DIVE IN TO SAVE THEM...
AND WE'D GET OUR DIVERSION.
HOW'D IT GO INSIDE THE NUCLEUS?
SMOOTH AS SILK. DONARIA STRUL WAS A VERY USEFUL COVER. NOBODY EVER QUESTIONS A CRAZY OLD DIVA...
VWIPP
NICE TO KNOW YOUR ACTING'S IMPROVING. I HEAR "MISS GHOST" DIDN'T FOOL THE DOCTOR FOR A SECOND...
NOW, "LONDI THE HELPFUL TAXI DRIVER", IN SHARP CONTRAST, HAD HIM COMPLETELY SUCKERED.
WELL, BRAVO, MR FISHER. I'M SURE THE BAFTA'S IN THE POST...
DON'T FORGET US LITTLE PEOPLE ON YOUR WAY TO THE TOP.
WELL DONE, ANNABEL. YOU TOO, DANNY.
THANKS, DAD. ARE THE SPYDERS TRANSMITTING?
THE DATA FEED STARTED IMMEDIATELY. WE'LL BE ABLE TO MONITOR EVERY TRANSACTION INSIDE THE OBSIDIAN MAINFRAME. WEAPONS... BIO-TECH... SPACECRAFT... WE'LL SEE WHERE IT'S ALL GOING.
SO WE GET OUR INTEL... THE FLUFFY LITTLE ALIENS ARE SAVED... THE DOCTOR'S THE BIG HERO...
"... EVERYBODY WINS."
CONGRATULATIONS, SIR...
YOU'RE A VERY RICH MAN!
NEXT: THE BLOOD OF AZRAEL

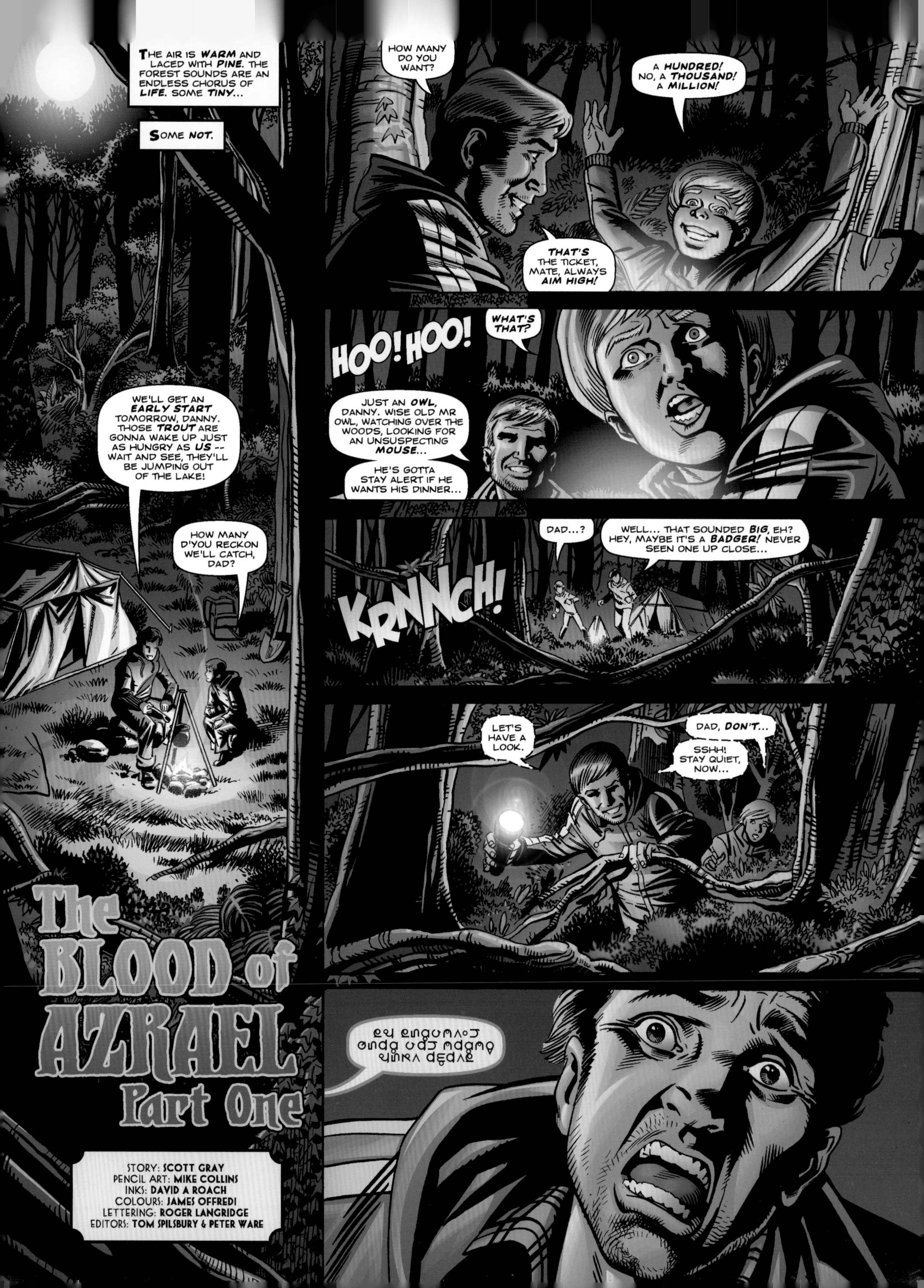

THE AIR IS WARM AND LACED WITH PINE. THE FOREST SOUNDS ARE AN ENDLESS CHORUS OF LIFE. SOME TINY...
SOME NOT.
WE'LL GET AN EARLY START TOMORROW, DANNY. THOSE TROUT ARE GONNA WAKE UP JUST AS HUNGRY AS US -- WAIT AND SEE, THEY'LL BE JUMPING OUT OF THE LAKE!
HOW MANY D'YOU RECKON WE'LL CATCH, DAD?
HOW MANY DO YOU WANT?
A HUNDRED! NO, A THOUSAND! A MILLION!
THAT'S THE TICKET, MATE, ALWAYS AIM HIGH!
HOO! HOO!
WHAT'S THAT?
JUST AN OWL, DANNY. WISE OLD MR OWL, WATCHING OVER THE WOODS, LOOKING FOR AN UNSUSPECTING MOUSE...
HE'S GOTTA STAY ALERT IF HE WANTS HIS DINNER...
KRNNCH!
DAD...?
WELL... THAT SOUNDED BIG, EH? HEY, MAYBE IT'S A BADGER! NEVER SEEN ONE UP CLOSE...
LET'S HAVE A LOOK.
DAD, DON'T...
SSHH! STAY QUIET, NOW...
The BLOOD of AZRAEL
Part One
STORY: SCOTT GRAY
PENCIL ART: MIKE COLLINS
INKS: DAVID A ROACH
COLOURS: JAMES OFFREDI
LETTERING: ROGER LANGRIDGE
EDITORS: TOM SPILSBURY & PETER WARE

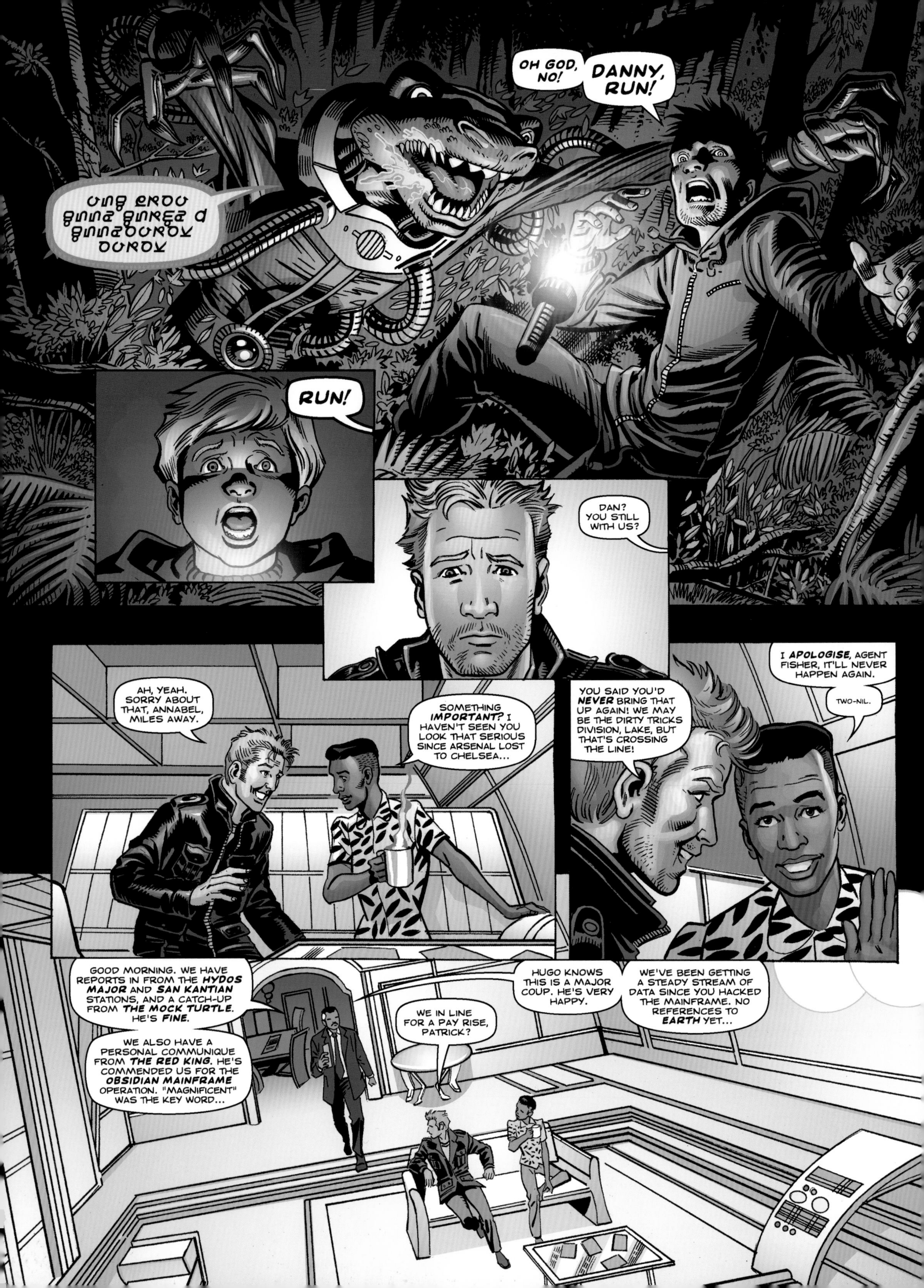
OH GOD, NO!
DANNY, RUN!
RUN!
DAN? YOU STILL WITH US?
AH, YEAH. SORRY ABOUT THAT, ANNABEL, MILES AWAY.
SOMETHING IMPORTANT? I HAVEN'T SEEN YOU LOOK THAT SERIOUS SINCE ARSENAL LOST TO CHELSEA...
YOU SAID YOU'D NEVER BRING THAT UP AGAIN! WE MAY BE THE DIRTY TRICKS DIVISION, LAKE, BUT THAT'S CROSSING THE LINE!
I APOLOGISE, AGENT FISHER, IT'LL NEVER HAPPEN AGAIN.
TWO-NIL.
GOOD MORNING. WE HAVE REPORTS IN FROM THE HYDOS MAJOR AND SAN KANTIAN STATIONS, AND A CATCH-UP FROM THE MOCK TURTLE. HE'S FINE.
WE ALSO HAVE A PERSONAL COMMUNIQUE FROM THE RED KING. HE'S COMMENDED US FOR THE OBSIDIAN MAINFRAME OPERATION. "MAGNIFICENT" WAS THE KEY WORD...
WE IN LINE FOR A PAY RISE, PATRICK?
HUGO KNOWS THIS IS A MAJOR COUP. HE'S VERY HAPPY.
WE'VE BEEN GETTING A STEADY STREAM OF DATA SINCE YOU HACKED THE MAINFRAME. NO REFERENCES TO EARTH YET...

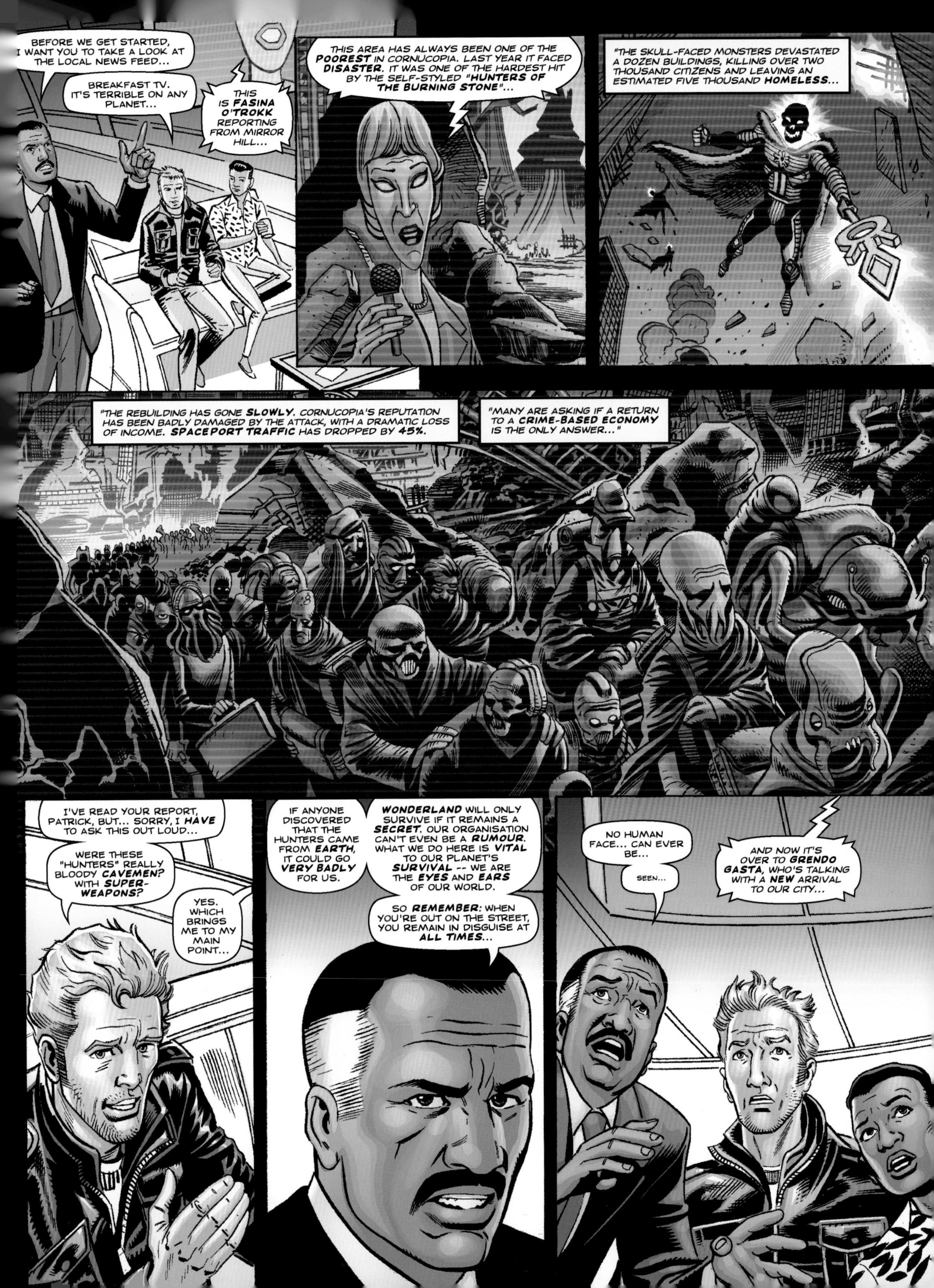

BEFORE WE GET STARTED, I WANT YOU TO TAKE A LOOK AT THE LOCAL NEWS FEED...
BREAKFAST TV. IT'S TERRIBLE ON ANY PLANET...
THIS IS FASINA O'TROKK REPORTING FROM MIRROR HILL...
THIS AREA HAS ALWAYS BEEN ONE OF THE POOREST IN CORNUCOPIA. LAST YEAR IT FACED DISASTER. IT WAS ONE OF THE HARDEST HIT BY THE SELF-STYLED "HUNTERS OF THE BURNING STONE"...
"THE SKULL-FACED MONSTERS DEVASTATED A DOZEN BUILDINGS, KILLING OVER TWO THOUSAND CITIZENS AND LEAVING AN ESTIMATED FIVE THOUSAND HOMELESS...
"THE REBUILDING HAS GONE SLOWLY. CORNUCOPIA'S REPUTATION HAS BEEN BADLY DAMAGED BY THE ATTACK, WITH A DRAMATIC LOSS OF INCOME. SPACEPORT TRAFFIC HAS DROPPED BY 45%.
"MANY ARE ASKING IF A RETURN TO A CRIME-BASED ECONOMY IS THE ONLY ANSWER..."
I'VE READ YOUR REPORT, PATRICK, BUT... SORRY, I HAVE TO ASK THIS OUT LOUD...
WERE THESE "HUNTERS" REALLY BLOODY CAVEMEN? WITH SUPER-WEAPONS?
YES. WHICH BRINGS ME TO MY MAIN POINT...
IF ANYONE DISCOVERED THAT THE HUNTERS CAME FROM EARTH, IT COULD GO VERY BADLY FOR US.
WONDERLAND WILL ONLY SURVIVE IF IT REMAINS A SECRET. OUR ORGANISATION CAN'T EVEN BE A RUMOUR. WHAT WE DO HERE IS VITAL TO OUR PLANET'S SURVIVAL -- WE ARE THE EYES AND EARS OF OUR WORLD.
SO REMEMBER: WHEN YOU'RE OUT ON THE STREET, YOU REMAIN IN DISGUISE AT ALL TIMES...
NO HUMAN FACE... CAN EVER BE...
SEEN...
AND NOW IT'S OVER TO GRENDO GASTA, WHO'S TALKING WITH A NEW ARRIVAL TO OUR CITY...

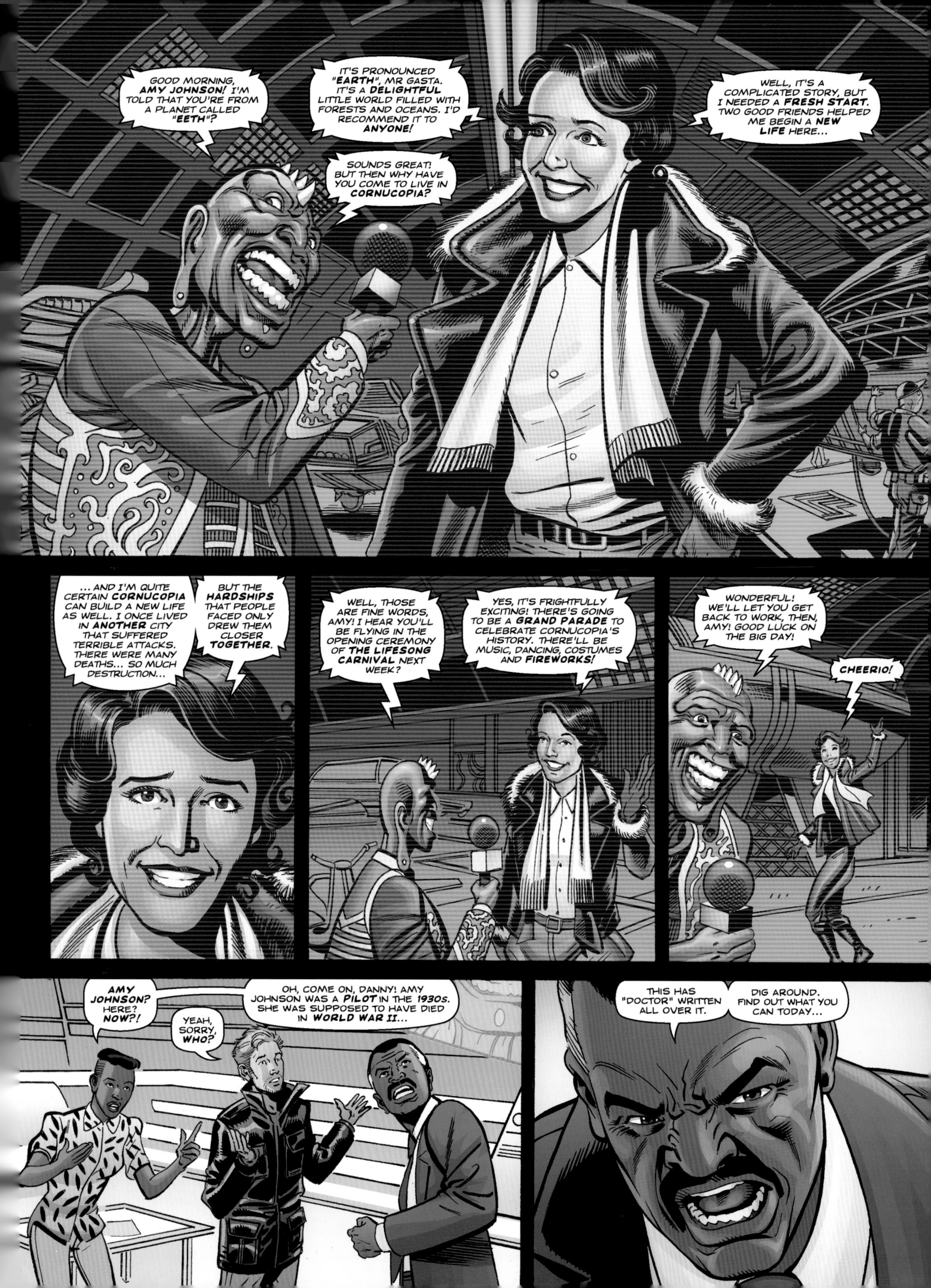

GOOD MORNING, AMY JOHNSON! I'M TOLD THAT YOU'RE FROM A PLANET CALLED "EETH"?
IT'S PRONOUNCED "EARTH", MR GASTA. IT'S A DELIGHTFUL LITTLE WORLD FILLED WITH FORESTS AND OCEANS. I'D RECOMMEND IT TO ANYONE!
SOUNDS GREAT! BUT THEN WHY HAVE YOU COME TO LIVE IN CORNUCOPIA?
WELL, IT'S A COMPLICATED STORY, BUT I NEEDED A FRESH START. TWO GOOD FRIENDS HELPED ME BEGIN A NEW LIFE HERE...
... AND I'M QUITE CERTAIN CORNUCOPIA CAN BUILD A NEW LIFE AS WELL. I ONCE LIVED IN ANOTHER CITY THAT SUFFERED TERRIBLE ATTACKS. THERE WERE MANY DEATHS... SO MUCH DESTRUCTION...
BUT THE HARDSHIPS THAT PEOPLE FACED ONLY DREW THEM CLOSER TOGETHER.
WELL, THOSE ARE FINE WORDS, AMY! I HEAR YOU'LL BE FLYING IN THE OPENING CEREMONY OF THE LIFESONG CARNIVAL NEXT WEEK?
YES, IT'S FRIGHTFULLY EXCITING! THERE'S GOING TO BE A GRAND PARADE TO CELEBRATE CORNUCOPIA'S HISTORY. THERE'LL BE MUSIC, DANCING, COSTUMES AND FIREWORKS!
WONDERFUL! WE'LL LET YOU GET BACK TO WORK, THEN, AMY! GOOD LUCK ON THE BIG DAY!
CHEERIO!
AMY JOHNSON? HERE? NOW?!
YEAH, SORRY, WHO?
OH, COME ON, DANNY! AMY JOHNSON WAS A PILOT IN THE 1930s. SHE WAS SUPPOSED TO HAVE DIED IN WORLD WAR II...
THIS HAS "DOCTOR" WRITTEN ALL OVER IT.
DIG AROUND. FIND OUT WHAT YOU CAN TODAY...

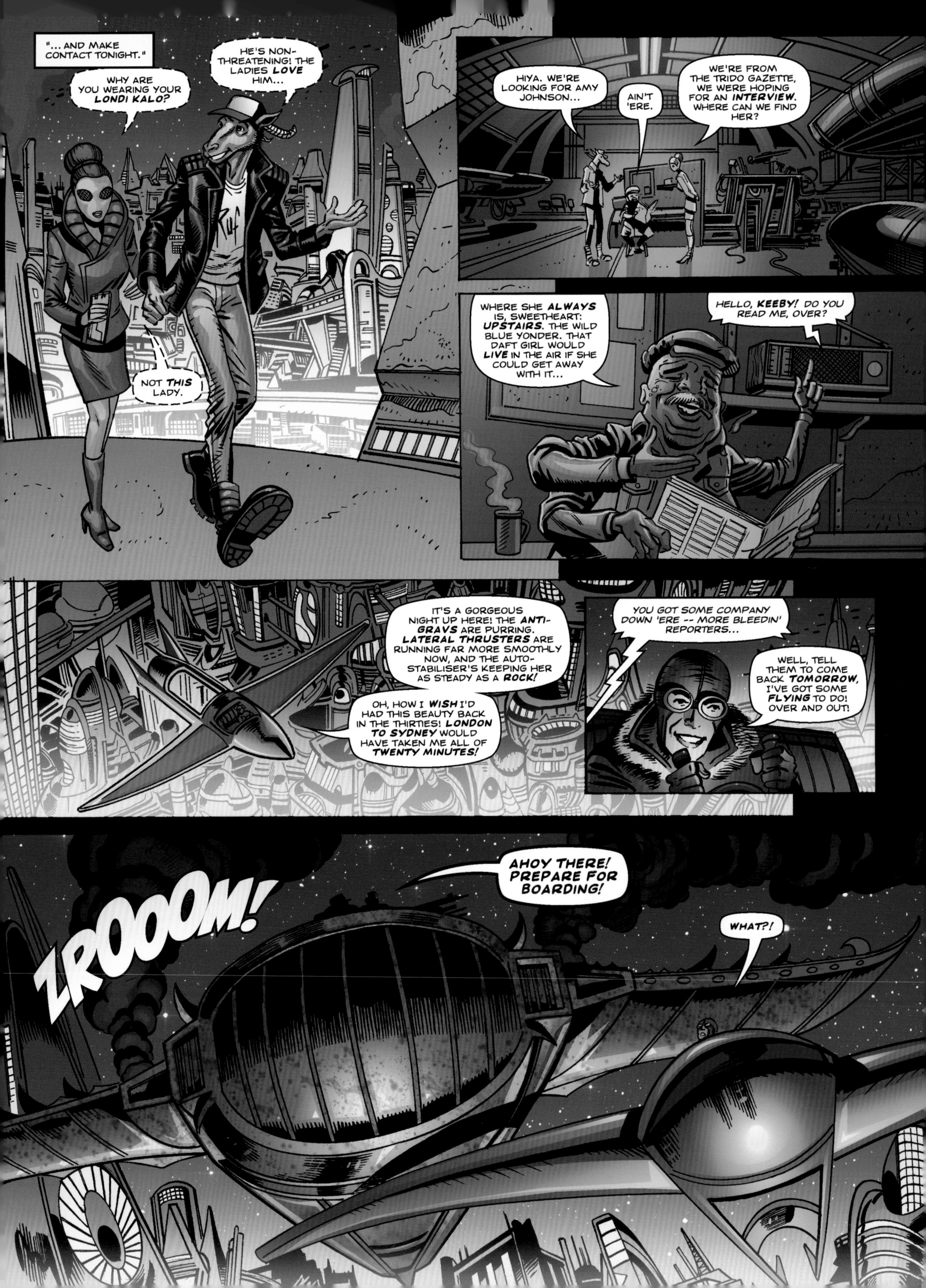
"...AND MAKE CONTACT TONIGHT."
WHY ARE YOU WEARING YOUR LONDI KALO?
HE'S NON-THREATENING! THE LADIES LOVE HIM...
NOT THIS LADY.
HIYA. WE'RE LOOKING FOR AMY JOHNSON...
AIN'T 'ERE.
WE'RE FROM THE TRIDO GAZETTE, WE WERE HOPING FOR AN INTERVIEW. WHERE CAN WE FIND HER?
WHERE SHE ALWAYS IS, SWEETHEART: UPSTAIRS. THE WILD BLUE YONDER. THAT DAFT GIRL WOULD LIVE IN THE AIR IF SHE COULD GET AWAY WITH IT...
HELLO, KEEBY! DO YOU READ ME, OVER?
IT'S A GORGEOUS NIGHT UP HERE! THE ANTI-GRAVS ARE PURRING. LATERAL THRUSTERS ARE RUNNING FAR MORE SMOOTHLY NOW, AND THE AUTO-STABILISER'S KEEPING HER AS STEADY AS A ROCK!
OH, HOW I WISH I'D HAD THIS BEAUTY BACK IN THE THIRTIES! LONDON TO SYDNEY WOULD HAVE TAKEN ME ALL OF TWENTY MINUTES!
YOU GOT SOME COMPANY DOWN 'ERE -- MORE BLEEDIN' REPORTERS...
WELL, TELL THEM TO COME BACK TOMORROW, I'VE GOT SOME FLYING TO DO! OVER AND OUT!
ZROOOM!
AHOY THERE! PREPARE FOR BOARDING!
WHAT?!

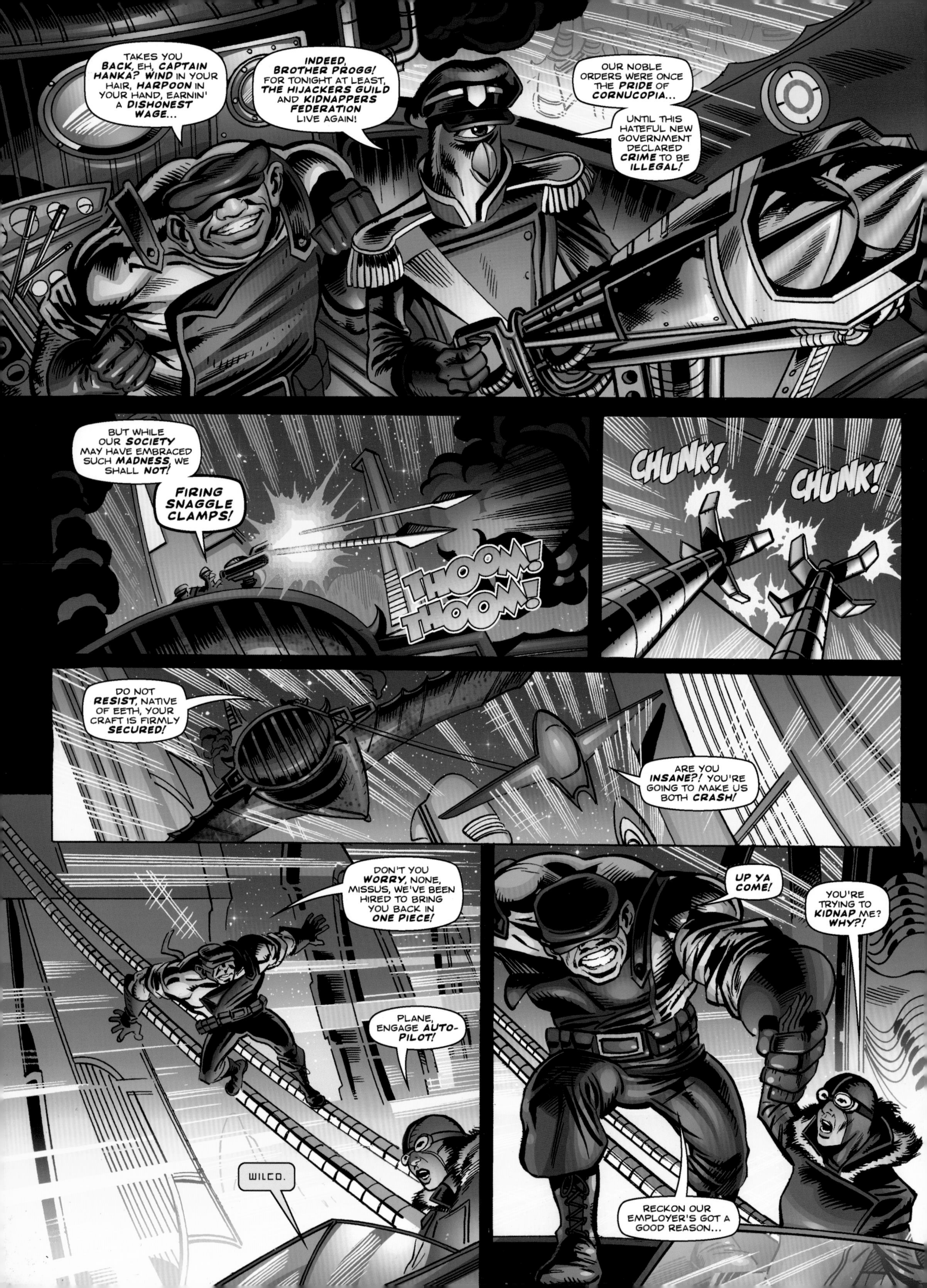

TAKES YOU BACK, EH, CAPTAIN HANKA? WIND IN YOUR HAIR, HARPOON IN YOUR HAND, EARNIN' A DISHONEST WAGE...
INDEED, BROTHER PROGG! FOR TONIGHT AT LEAST, THE HIJACKERS GUILD AND KIDNAPPERS FEDERATION LIVE AGAIN!
OUR NOBLE ORDERS WERE ONCE THE PRIDE OF CORNUCOPIA...
UNTIL THIS HATEFUL NEW GOVERNMENT DECLARED CRIME TO BE ILLEGAL!
BUT WHILE OUR SOCIETY MAY HAVE EMBRACED SUCH MADNESS, WE SHALL NOT!
FIRING SNAGGLE CLAMPS!
THOOM! THOOM!
CHUNK!
CHUNK!
DO NOT RESIST, NATIVE OF EETH, YOUR CRAFT IS FIRMLY SECURED!
ARE YOU INSANE?! YOU'RE GOING TO MAKE US BOTH CRASH!
DON'T YOU WORRY, NONE, MISSUS, WE'VE BEEN HIRED TO BRING YOU BACK IN ONE PIECE!
PLANE, ENGAGE AUTO-PILOT!
WILCO.
UP YA COME!
YOU'RE TRYING TO KIDNAP ME? WHY?!
RECKON OUR EMPLOYER'S GOT A GOOD REASON...

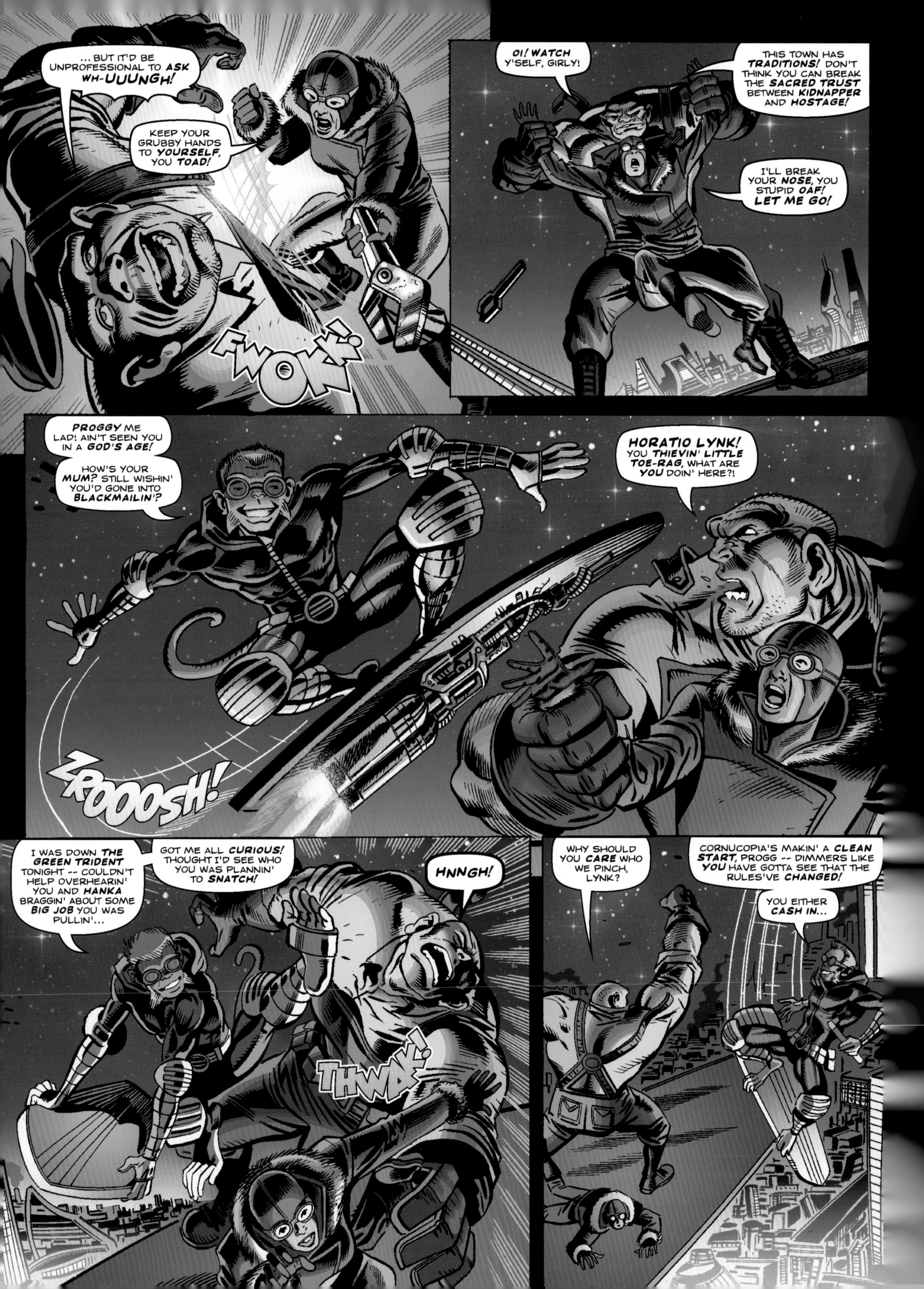
... BUT IT'D BE UNPROFESSIONAL TO ASK WH-UUUNGH!
KEEP YOUR GRUBBY HANDS TO YOURSELF, YOU TOAD!
FWOK!
OI! WATCH Y'SELF, GIRLY!
THIS TOWN HAS TRADITIONS! DON'T THINK YOU CAN BREAK THE SACRED TRUST BETWEEN KIDNAPPER AND HOSTAGE!
I'LL BREAK YOUR NOSE, YOU STUPID OAF! LET ME GO!
PROGGY ME LAD! AIN'T SEEN YOU IN A GOD'S AGE!
HOW'S YOUR MUM? STILL WISHIN' YOU'D GONE INTO BLACKMAILIN'?
HORATIO LYNK! YOU THIEVIN' LITTLE TOE-RAG, WHAT ARE YOU DOIN' HERE?!
ZROOOSH!
I WAS DOWN THE GREEN TRIDENT TONIGHT -- COULDN'T HELP OVERHEARIN' YOU AND HANKA BRAGGIN' ABOUT SOME BIG JOB YOU WAS PULLIN'...
GOT ME ALL CURIOUS! THOUGHT I'D SEE WHO YOU WAS PLANNIN' TO SNATCH!
HNNGH!
THWAK!
WHY SHOULD YOU CARE WHO WE PINCH, LYNK?
CORNUCOPIA'S MAKIN' A CLEAN START, PROGG -- DIMMERS LIKE YOU HAVE GOTTA SEE THAT THE RULES'VE CHANGED!
YOU EITHER CASH IN...

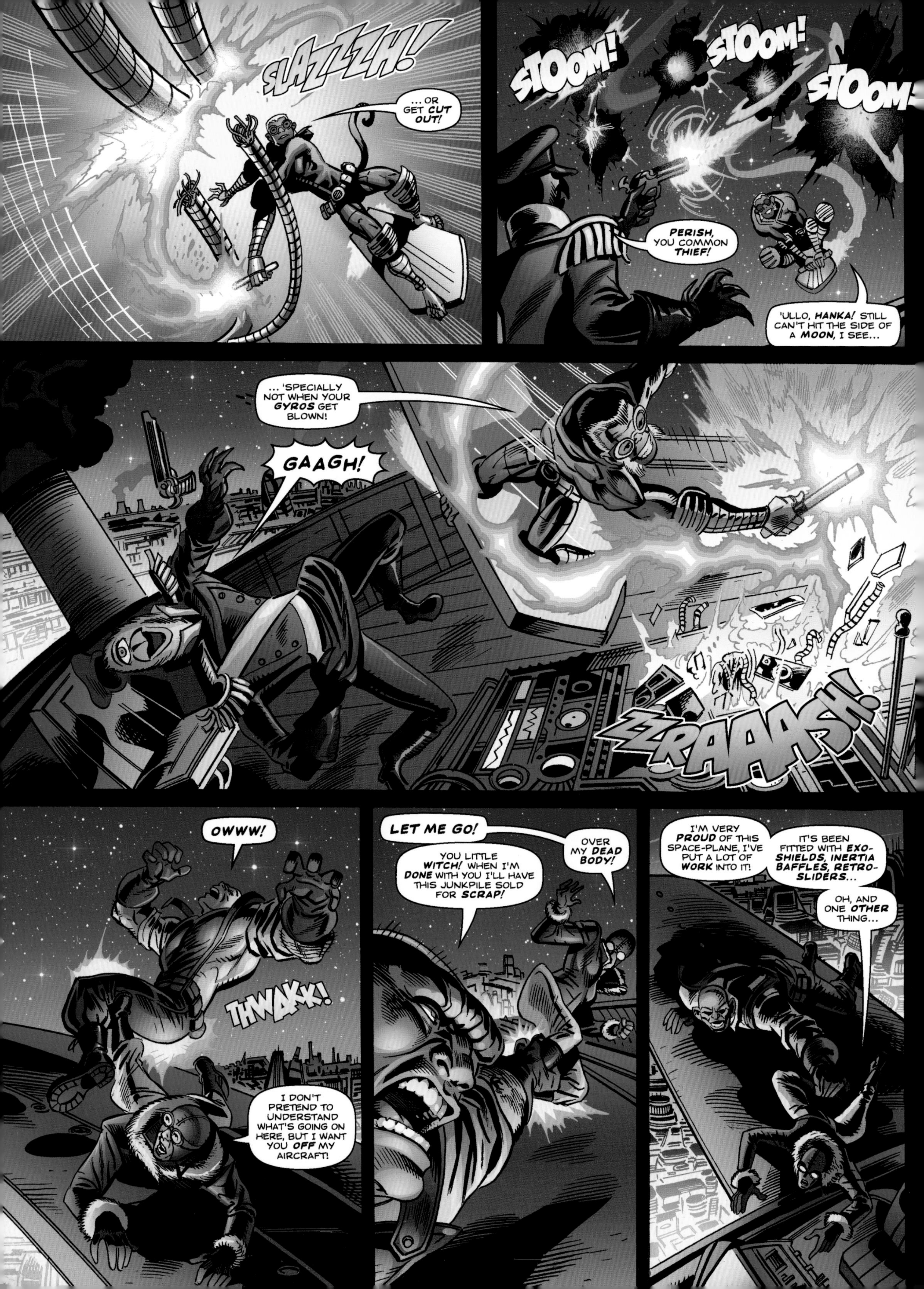
SLAZZZH!
...OR GET CUT OUT!
STOOM! STOOM! STOOM-
PERISH, YOU COMMON THIEF!
'ULLO, HANKA! STILL CAN'T HIT THE SIDE OF A MOON, I SEE...
...'SPECIALLY NOT WHEN YOUR GYROS GET BLOWN!
GAAGH!
ZZRAAAASH!
OWWW!
THWAKK!
I DON'T PRETEND TO UNDERSTAND WHAT'S GOING ON HERE, BUT I WANT YOU OFF MY AIRCRAFT!
LET ME GO!
YOU LITTLE WITCH! WHEN I'M DONE WITH YOU I'LL HAVE THIS JUNKPILE SOLD FOR SCRAP!
OVER MY DEAD BODY!
I'M VERY PROUD OF THIS SPACE-PLANE, I'VE PUT A LOT OF WORK INTO IT!
IT'S BEEN FITTED WITH EXO-SHIELDS, INERTIA BAFFLES, RETRO-SLIDERS...
OH, AND ONE OTHER THING...

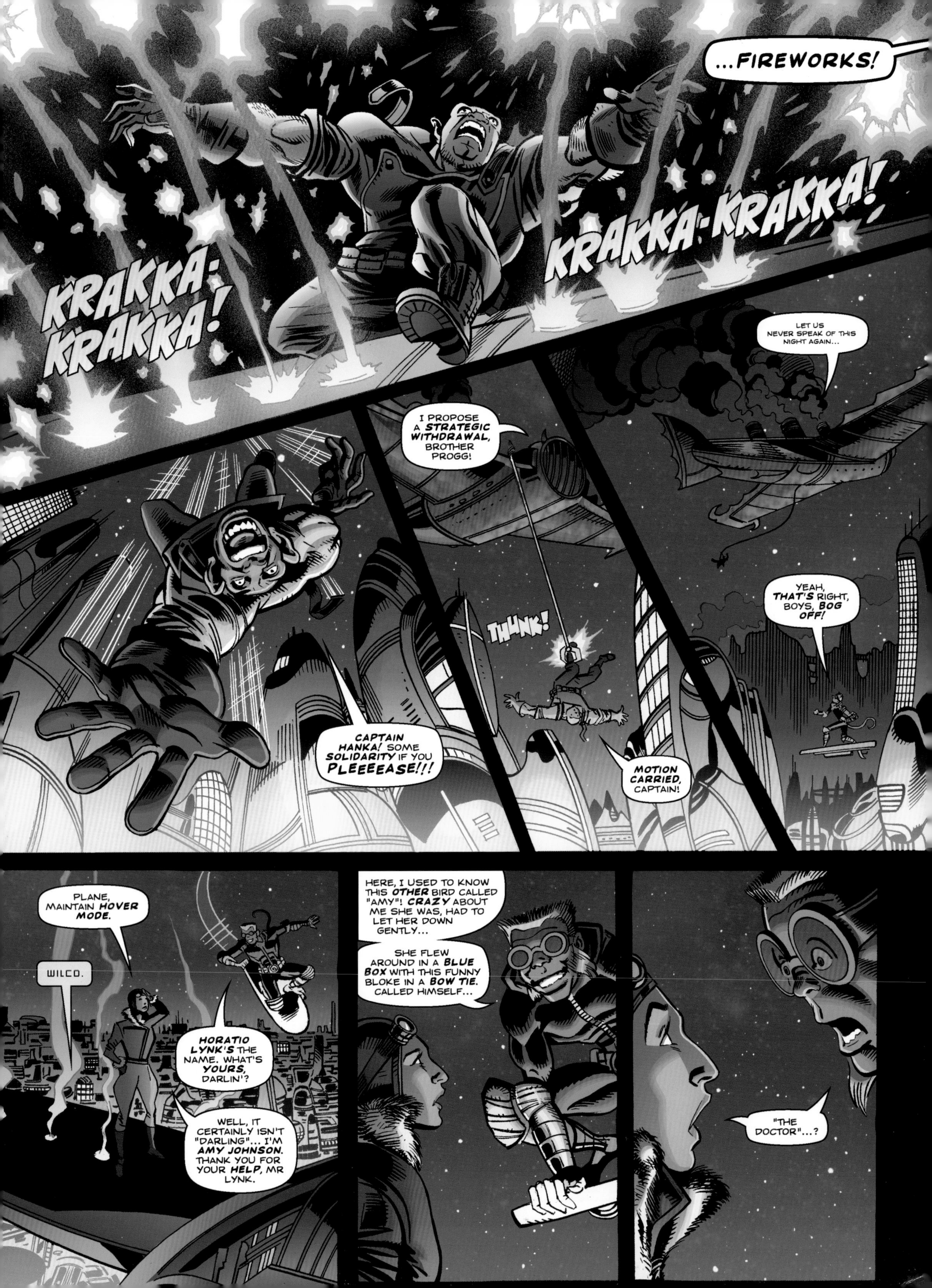

...FIREWORKS!
KRAKKA-KRAKKA!
KRAKKA-KRAKKA!
LET US NEVER SPEAK OF THIS NIGHT AGAIN...
I PROPOSE A STRATEGIC WITHDRAWAL, BROTHER PROGG!
THUNK!
CAPTAIN HANKA! SOME SOLIDARITY IF YOU PLEEEEASE!!!
MOTION CARRIED, CAPTAIN!
YEAH, THAT'S RIGHT, BOYS, BOG OFF!
PLANE, MAINTAIN HOVER MODE.
WILCO.
HORATIO LYNK'S THE NAME. WHAT'S YOURS, DARLIN'?
WELL, IT CERTAINLY ISN'T "DARLING"... I'M AMY JOHNSON. THANK YOU FOR YOUR HELP, MR LYNK.
HERE, I USED TO KNOW THIS OTHER BIRD CALLED "AMY"! CRAZY ABOUT ME SHE WAS, HAD TO LET HER DOWN GENTLY...
SHE FLEW AROUND IN A BLUE BOX WITH THIS FUNNY BLOKE IN A BOW TIE. CALLED HIMSELF...
"THE DOCTOR"...?

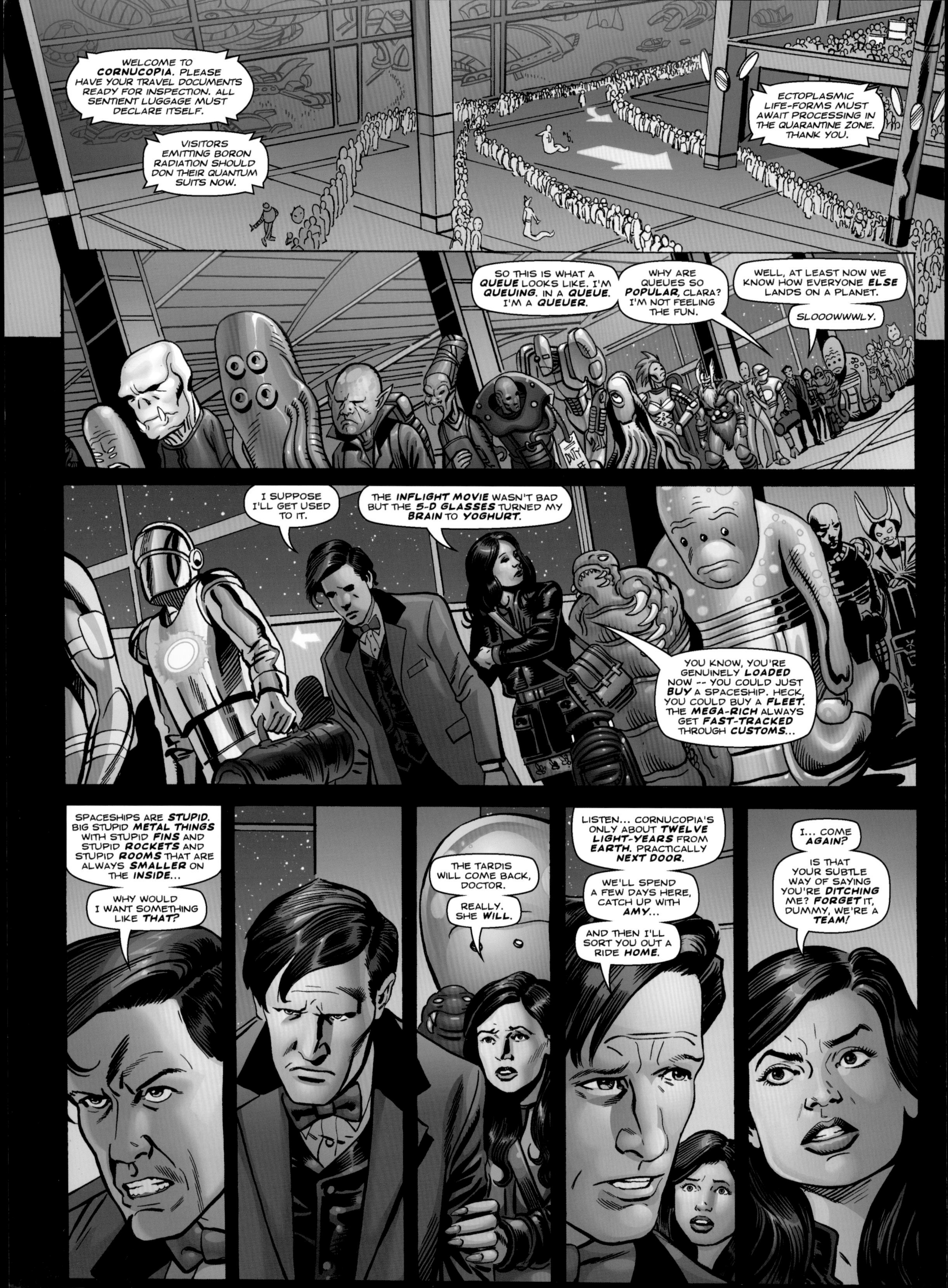
WELCOME TO CORNUCOPIA. PLEASE HAVE YOUR TRAVEL DOCUMENTS READY FOR INSPECTION. ALL SENTIENT LUGGAGE MUST DECLARE ITSELF.
VISITORS EMITTING BORON RADIATION SHOULD DON THEIR QUANTUM SUITS NOW.
ECTOPLASMIC LIFE-FORMS MUST AWAIT PROCESSING IN THE QUARANTINE ZONE. THANK YOU.
SO THIS IS WHAT A QUEUE LOOKS LIKE. I'M QUEUING. IN A QUEUE. I'M A QUEUER.
WHY ARE QUEUES SO POPULAR, CLARA? I'M NOT FEELING THE FUN.
WELL, AT LEAST NOW WE KNOW HOW EVERYONE ELSE LANDS ON A PLANET.
SLOOOWWWLY.
I SUPPOSE I'LL GET USED TO IT.
THE INFLIGHT MOVIE WASN'T BAD BUT THE 5-D GLASSES TURNED MY BRAIN TO YOGHURT.
YOU KNOW, YOU'RE GENUINELY LOADED NOW -- YOU COULD JUST BUY A SPACESHIP. HECK, YOU COULD BUY A FLEET. THE MEGA-RICH ALWAYS GET FAST-TRACKED THROUGH CUSTOMS...
SPACESHIPS ARE STUPID. BIG STUPID METAL THINGS WITH STUPID FINS AND STUPID ROCKETS AND STUPID ROOMS THAT ARE ALWAYS SMALLER ON THE INSIDE...
WHY WOULD I WANT SOMETHING LIKE THAT?
THE TARDIS WILL COME BACK, DOCTOR.
REALLY. SHE WILL.
LISTEN... CORNUCOPIA'S ONLY ABOUT TWELVE LIGHT-YEARS FROM EARTH. PRACTICALLY NEXT DOOR.
WE'LL SPEND A FEW DAYS HERE, CATCH UP WITH AMY...
AND THEN I'LL SORT YOU OUT A RIDE HOME.
I... COME AGAIN?
IS THAT YOUR SUBTLE WAY OF SAYING YOU'RE DITCHING ME? FORGET IT, DUMMY, WE'RE A TEAM!

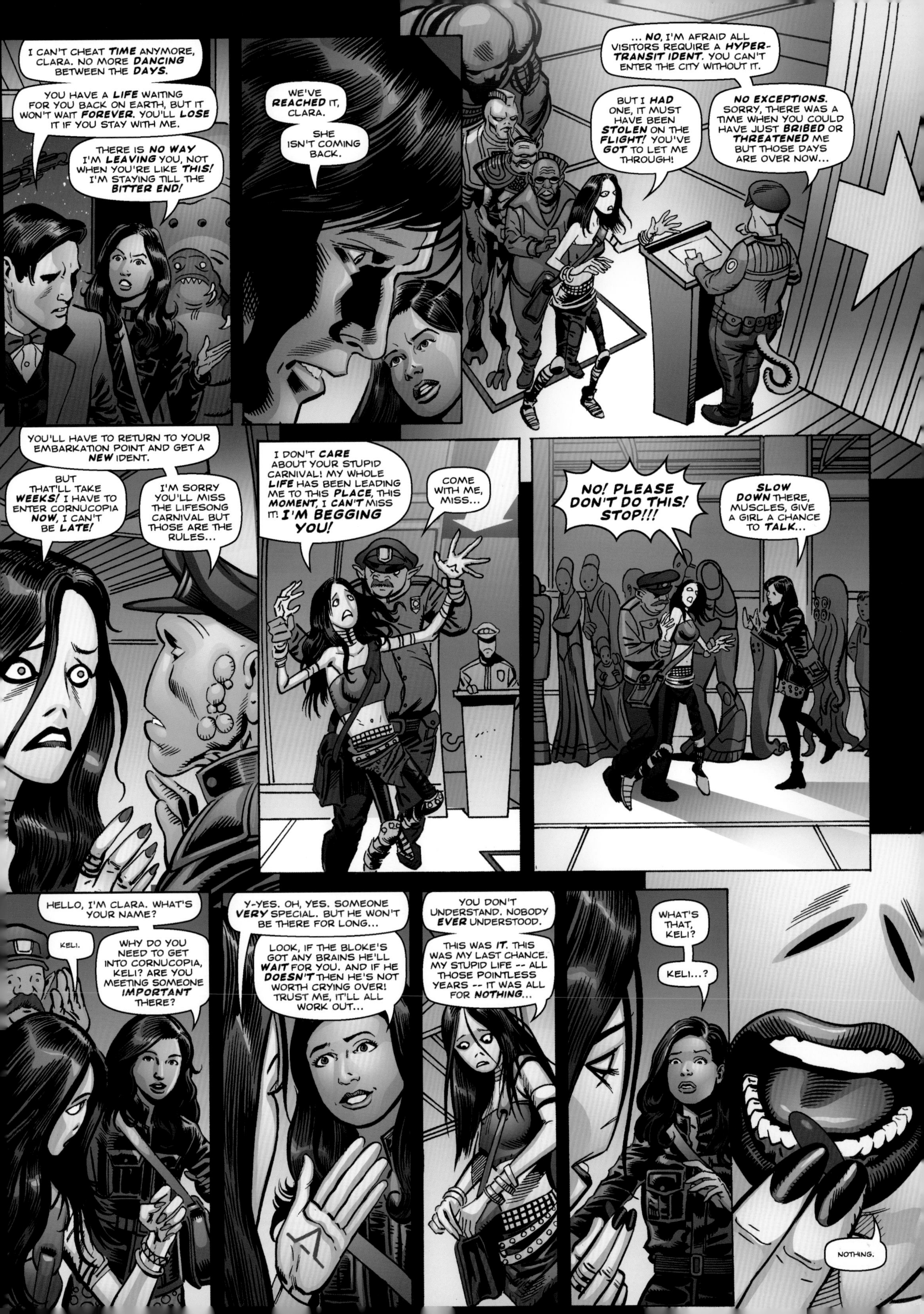

I CAN'T CHEAT TIME ANYMORE, CLARA. NO MORE DANCING BETWEEN THE DAYS.
YOU HAVE A LIFE WAITING FOR YOU BACK ON EARTH, BUT IT WON'T WAIT FOREVER. YOU'LL LOSE IT IF YOU STAY WITH ME.
THERE IS NO WAY I'M LEAVING YOU, NOT WHEN YOU'RE LIKE THIS! I'M STAYING TILL THE BITTER END!
WE'VE REACHED IT, CLARA.
SHE ISN'T COMING BACK.
... NO, I'M AFRAID ALL VISITORS REQUIRE A HYPER-TRANSIT IDENT. YOU CAN'T ENTER THE CITY WITHOUT IT.
BUT I HAD ONE, IT MUST HAVE BEEN STOLEN ON THE FLIGHT! YOU'VE GOT TO LET ME THROUGH!
NO EXCEPTIONS. SORRY, THERE WAS A TIME WHEN YOU COULD HAVE JUST BRIBED OR THREATENED ME BUT THOSE DAYS ARE OVER NOW...
YOU'LL HAVE TO RETURN TO YOUR EMBARKATION POINT AND GET A NEW IDENT.
BUT THAT'LL TAKE WEEKS! I HAVE TO ENTER CORNUCOPIA NOW, I CAN'T BE LATE!
I'M SORRY YOU'LL MISS THE LIFESONG CARNIVAL BUT THOSE ARE THE RULES...
I DON'T CARE ABOUT YOUR STUPID CARNIVAL! MY WHOLE LIFE HAS BEEN LEADING ME TO THIS PLACE, THIS MOMENT, I CAN'T MISS IT! I'M BEGGING YOU!
COME WITH ME, MISS...
NO! PLEASE DON'T DO THIS! STOP!!!
SLOW DOWN THERE, MUSCLES, GIVE A GIRL A CHANCE TO TALK...
HELLO, I'M CLARA. WHAT'S YOUR NAME?
KELI.
WHY DO YOU NEED TO GET INTO CORNUCOPIA, KELI? ARE YOU MEETING SOMEONE IMPORTANT THERE?
Y-YES. OH, YES. SOMEONE VERY SPECIAL. BUT HE WON'T BE THERE FOR LONG...
LOOK, IF THE BLOKE'S GOT ANY BRAINS HE'LL WAIT FOR YOU. AND IF HE DOESN'T THEN HE'S NOT WORTH CRYING OVER! TRUST ME, IT'LL ALL WORK OUT...
YOU DON'T UNDERSTAND. NOBODY EVER UNDERSTOOD.
THIS WAS IT. THIS WAS MY LAST CHANCE. MY STUPID LIFE -- ALL THOSE POINTLESS YEARS -- IT WAS ALL FOR NOTHING...
WHAT'S THAT, KELI?
KELI...?
NOTHING.

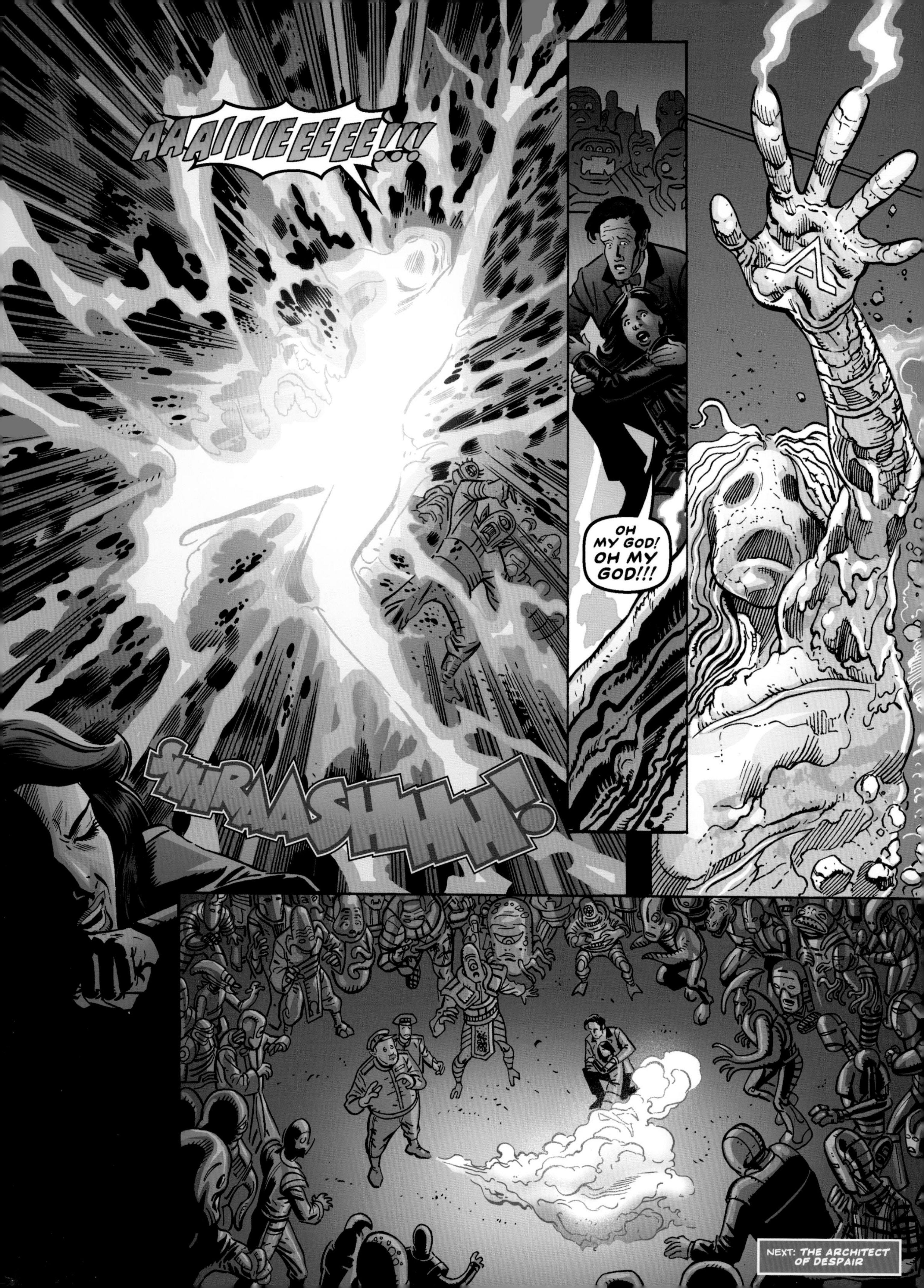

AAAIIIIEEEEEE!!!
OH MY GOD! OH MY GOD!!!
SHHRAASHHHH!
NEXT: THE ARCHITECT OF DESPAIR

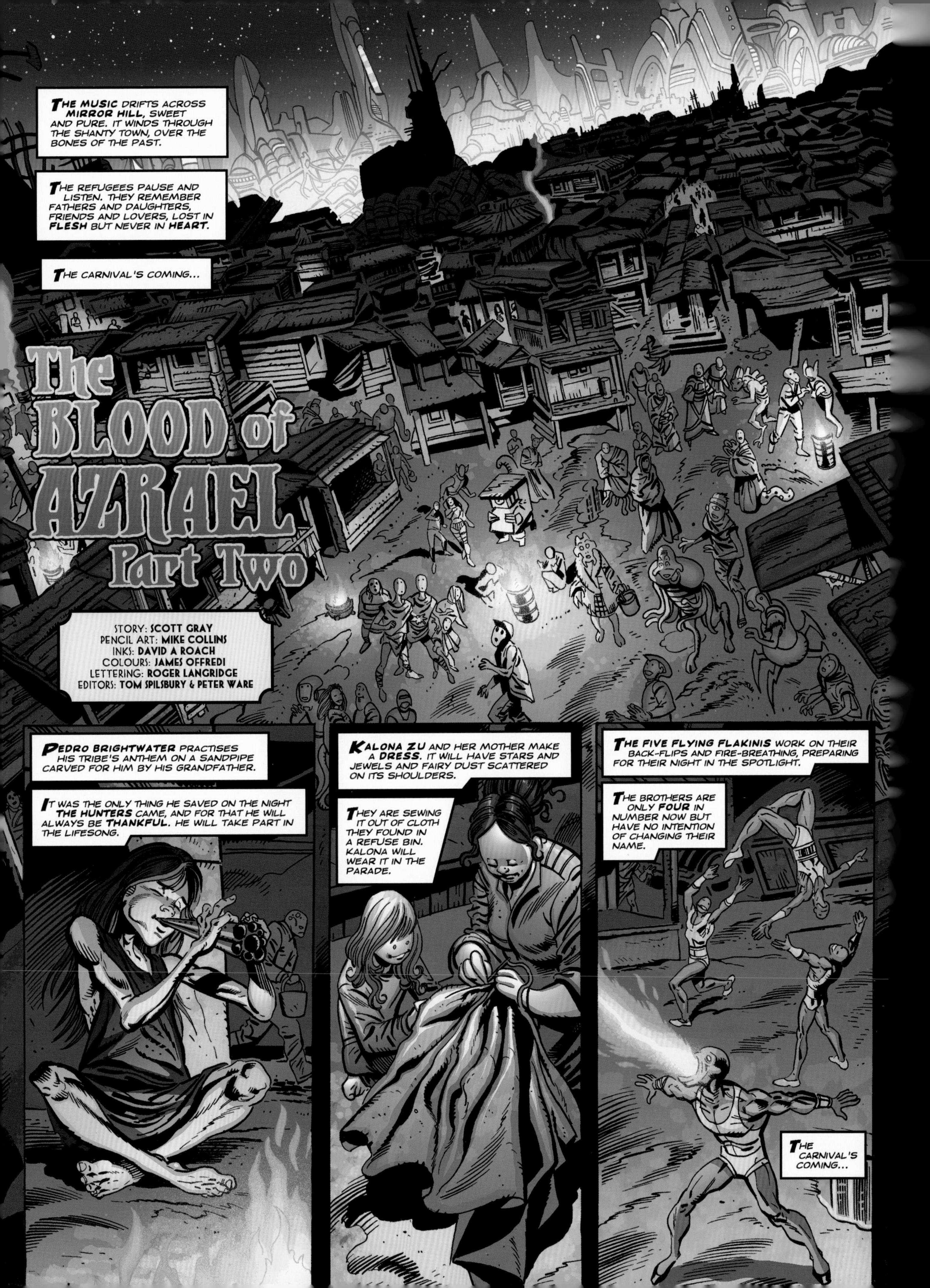
THE MUSIC DRIFTS ACROSS MIRROR HILL, SWEET AND PURE. IT WINDS THROUGH THE SHANTY TOWN, OVER THE BONES OF THE PAST.
THE REFUGEES PAUSE AND LISTEN. THEY REMEMBER FATHERS AND DAUGHTERS, FRIENDS AND LOVERS, LOST IN FLESH BUT NEVER IN HEART.
THE CARNIVAL'S COMING...
The BLOOD of AZRAEL Part Two
STORY: SCOTT GRAY
PENCIL ART: MIKE COLLINS
INKS: DAVID A ROACH
COLOURS: JAMES OFFREDI
LETTERING: ROGER LANGRIDGE
EDITORS: TOM SPILSBURY & PETER WARE
PEDRO BRIGHTWATER PRACTISES HIS TRIBE'S ANTHEM ON A SANDPIPE CARVED FOR HIM BY HIS GRANDFATHER.
IT WAS THE ONLY THING HE SAVED ON THE NIGHT THE HUNTERS CAME, AND FOR THAT HE WILL ALWAYS BE THANKFUL. HE WILL TAKE PART IN THE LIFESONG.
KALONA ZU AND HER MOTHER MAKE A DRESS. IT WILL HAVE STARS AND JEWELS AND FAIRY DUST SCATTERED ON ITS SHOULDERS.
THEY ARE SEWING IT OUT OF CLOTH THEY FOUND IN A REFUSE BIN. KALONA WILL WEAR IT IN THE PARADE.
THE FIVE FLYING FLAKINIS WORK ON THEIR BACK-FLIPS AND FIRE-BREATHING, PREPARING FOR THEIR NIGHT IN THE SPOTLIGHT.
THE BROTHERS ARE ONLY FOUR IN NUMBER NOW BUT HAVE NO INTENTION OF CHANGING THEIR NAME.
THE CARNIVAL'S COMING...

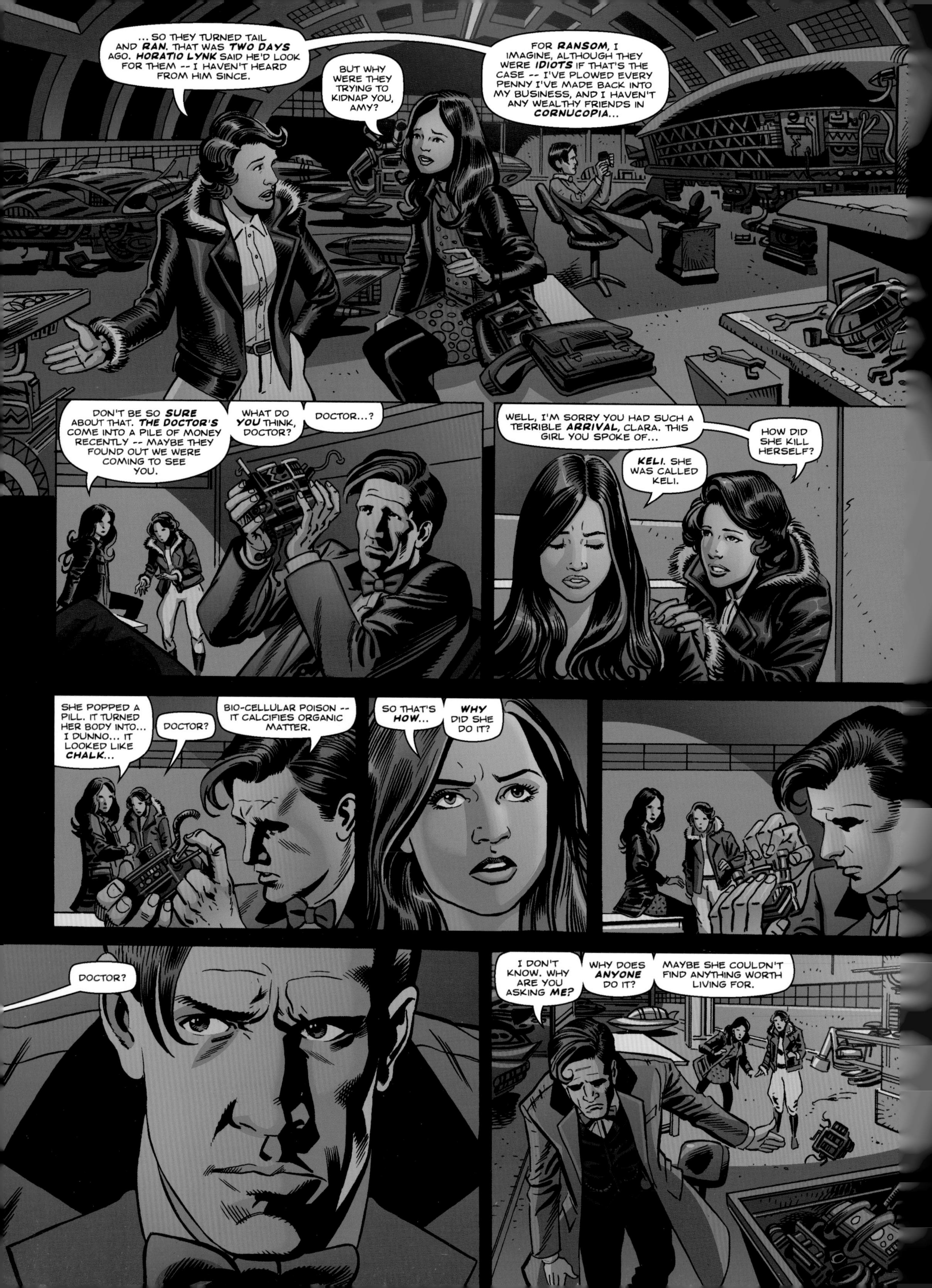
... SO THEY TURNED TAIL AND RAN. THAT WAS TWO DAYS AGO. HORATIO LYNK SAID HE'D LOOK FOR THEM -- I HAVEN'T HEARD FROM HIM SINCE.
BUT WHY WERE THEY TRYING TO KIDNAP YOU, AMY?
FOR RANSOM, I IMAGINE, ALTHOUGH THEY WERE IDIOTS IF THAT'S THE CASE -- I'VE PLOWED EVERY PENNY I'VE MADE BACK INTO MY BUSINESS, AND I HAVEN'T ANY WEALTHY FRIENDS IN CORNUCOPIA...
DON'T BE SO SURE ABOUT THAT. THE DOCTOR'S COME INTO A PILE OF MONEY RECENTLY -- MAYBE THEY FOUND OUT WE WERE COMING TO SEE YOU.
WHAT DO YOU THINK, DOCTOR?
DOCTOR...?
WELL, I'M SORRY YOU HAD SUCH A TERRIBLE ARRIVAL, CLARA. THIS GIRL YOU SPOKE OF...
KELI. SHE WAS CALLED KELI.
HOW DID SHE KILL HERSELF?
SHE POPPED A PILL. IT TURNED HER BODY INTO... I DUNNO... IT LOOKED LIKE CHALK...
DOCTOR?
BIO-CELLULAR POISON -- IT CALCIFIES ORGANIC MATTER.
SO THAT'S HOW...
WHY DID SHE DO IT?
DOCTOR?
I DON'T KNOW. WHY ARE YOU ASKING ME?
WHY DOES ANYONE DO IT?
MAYBE SHE COULDN'T FIND ANYTHING WORTH LIVING FOR.

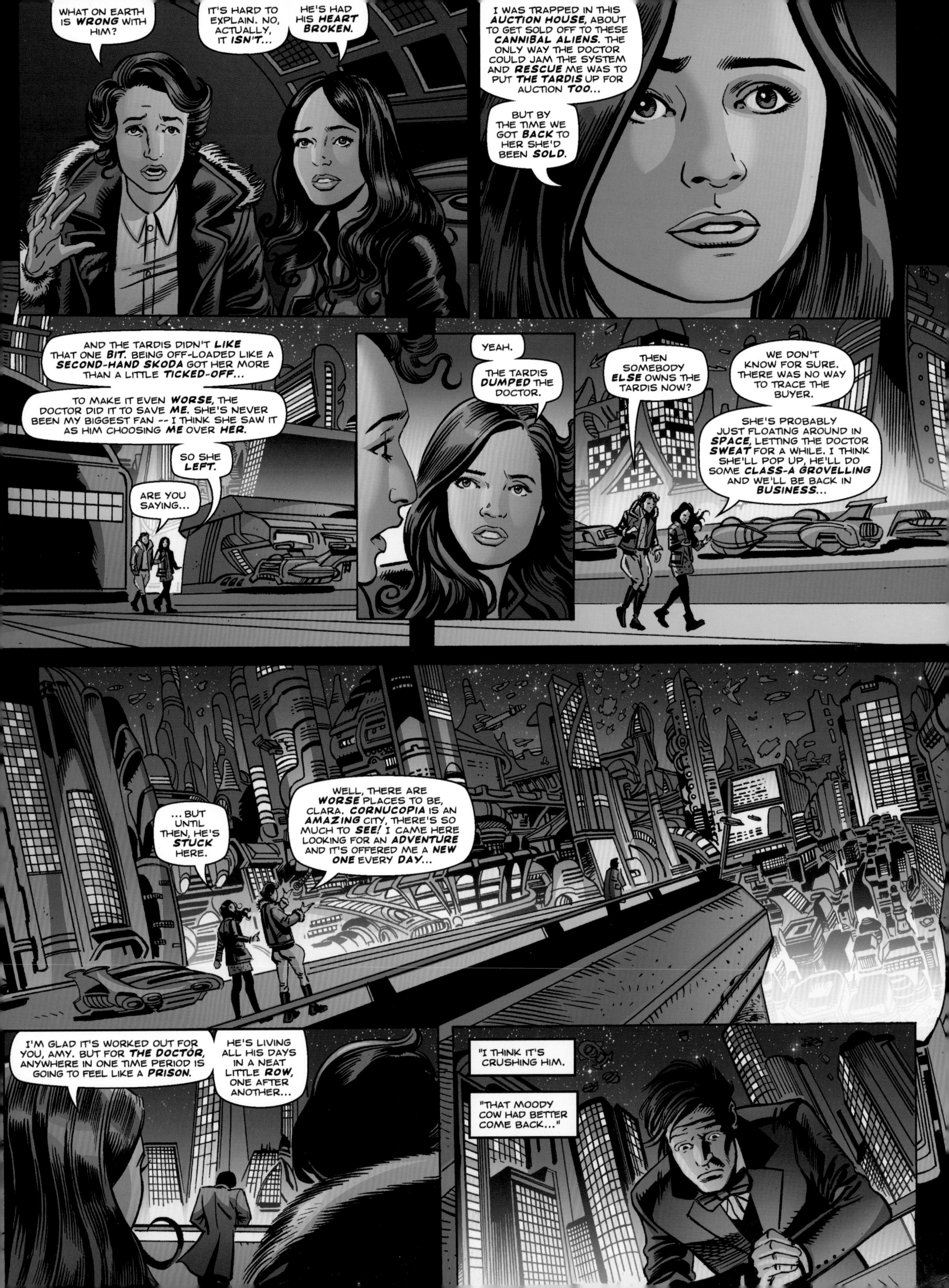
WHAT ON EARTH IS WRONG WITH HIM?
IT'S HARD TO EXPLAIN. NO, ACTUALLY, IT ISN'T...
HE'S HAD HIS HEART BROKEN.
I WAS TRAPPED IN THIS AUCTION HOUSE, ABOUT TO GET SOLD OFF TO THESE CANNIBAL ALIENS. THE ONLY WAY THE DOCTOR COULD JAM THE SYSTEM AND RESCUE ME WAS TO PUT THE TARDIS UP FOR AUCTION TOO...
BUT BY THE TIME WE GOT BACK TO HER SHE'D BEEN SOLD.
AND THE TARDIS DIDN'T LIKE THAT ONE BIT. BEING OFF-LOADED LIKE A SECOND-HAND SKODA GOT HER MORE THAN A LITTLE TICKED-OFF...
TO MAKE IT EVEN WORSE, THE DOCTOR DID IT TO SAVE ME. SHE'S NEVER BEEN MY BIGGEST FAN -- I THINK SHE SAW IT AS HIM CHOOSING ME OVER HER.
SO SHE LEFT.
ARE YOU SAYING...
YEAH.
THE TARDIS DUMPED THE DOCTOR.
THEN SOMEBODY ELSE OWNS THE TARDIS NOW?
WE DON'T KNOW FOR SURE. THERE WAS NO WAY TO TRACE THE BUYER.
SHE'S PROBABLY JUST FLOATING AROUND IN SPACE, LETTING THE DOCTOR SWEAT FOR A WHILE. I THINK SHE'LL POP UP, HE'LL DO SOME CLASS-A GROVELLING AND WE'LL BE BACK IN BUSINESS...
... BUT UNTIL THEN, HE'S STUCK HERE.
WELL, THERE ARE WORSE PLACES TO BE, CLARA. CORNUCOPIA IS AN AMAZING CITY, THERE'S SO MUCH TO SEE! I CAME HERE LOOKING FOR AN ADVENTURE AND IT'S OFFERED ME A NEW ONE EVERY DAY...
I'M GLAD IT'S WORKED OUT FOR YOU, AMY. BUT FOR THE DOCTOR, ANYWHERE IN ONE TIME PERIOD IS GOING TO FEEL LIKE A PRISON.
HE'S LIVING ALL HIS DAYS IN A NEAT LITTLE ROW, ONE AFTER ANOTHER...
"I THINK IT'S CRUSHING HIM.
"THAT MOODY COW HAD BETTER COME BACK..."

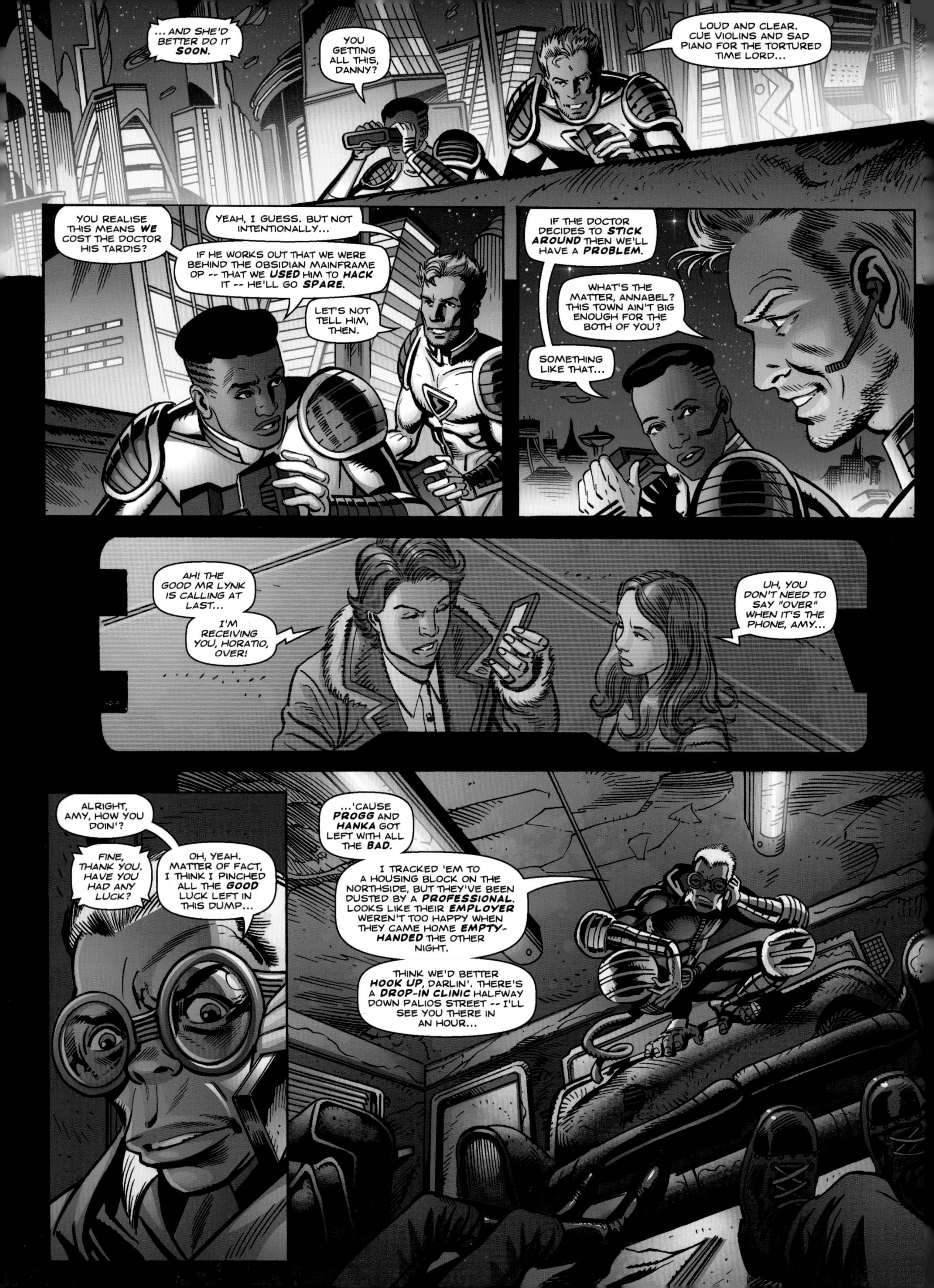
... AND SHE'D BETTER DO IT SOON.
YOU GETTING ALL THIS, DANNY?
LOUD AND CLEAR. CUE VIOLINS AND SAD PIANO FOR THE TORTURED TIME LORD...
YOU REALISE THIS MEANS WE COST THE DOCTOR HIS TARDIS?
YEAH, I GUESS. BUT NOT INTENTIONALLY...
IF HE WORKS OUT THAT WE WERE BEHIND THE OBSIDIAN MAINFRAME OP -- THAT WE USED HIM TO HACK IT -- HE'LL GO SPARE.
LET'S NOT TELL HIM, THEN.
IF THE DOCTOR DECIDES TO STICK AROUND THEN WE'LL HAVE A PROBLEM.
WHAT'S THE MATTER, ANNABEL? THIS TOWN AIN'T BIG ENOUGH FOR THE BOTH OF YOU?
SOMETHING LIKE THAT...
AH! THE GOOD MR LYNK IS CALLING AT LAST...
I'M RECEIVING YOU, HORATIO, OVER!
UH, YOU DON'T NEED TO SAY "OVER" WHEN IT'S THE PHONE, AMY...
ALRIGHT, AMY, HOW YOU DOIN'?
FINE, THANK YOU. HAVE YOU HAD ANY LUCK?
OH, YEAH. MATTER OF FACT, I THINK I PINCHED ALL THE GOOD LUCK LEFT IN THIS DUMP...
...'CAUSE PROGG AND HANKA GOT LEFT WITH ALL THE BAD.
I TRACKED 'EM TO A HOUSING BLOCK ON THE NORTHSIDE, BUT THEY'VE BEEN DUSTED BY A PROFESSIONAL. LOOKS LIKE THEIR EMPLOYER WEREN'T TOO HAPPY WHEN THEY CAME HOME EMPTY-HANDED THE OTHER NIGHT.
THINK WE'D BETTER HOOK UP, DARLIN'. THERE'S A DROP-IN CLINIC HALFWAY DOWN PALIOS STREET -- I'LL SEE YOU THERE IN AN HOUR...

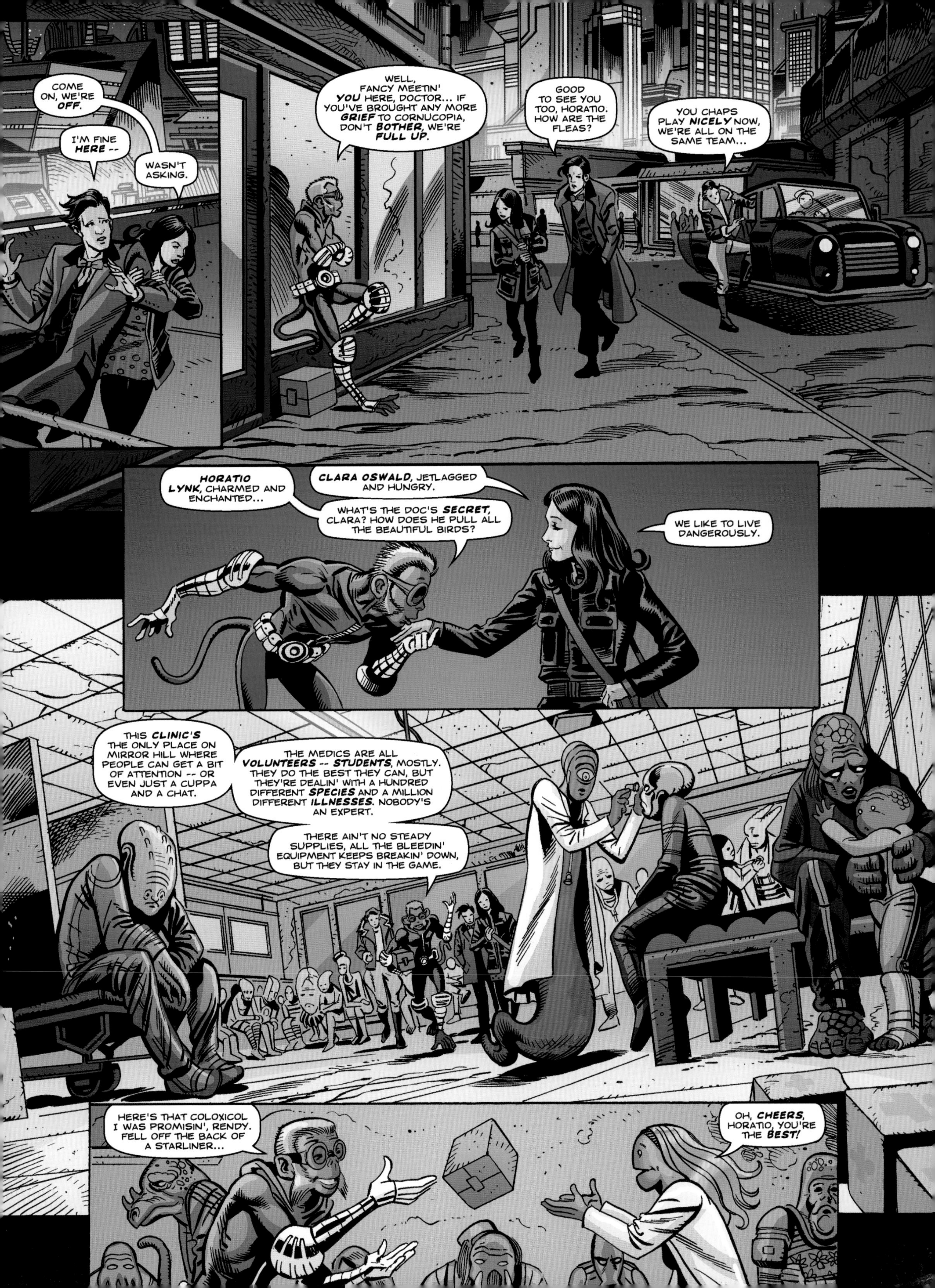
COME ON, WE'RE OFF.
I'M FINE HERE --
WASN'T ASKING.
WELL, FANCY MEETIN' YOU HERE, DOCTOR... IF YOU'VE BROUGHT ANY MORE GRIEF TO CORNUCOPIA, DON'T BOTHER, WE'RE FULL UP.
GOOD TO SEE YOU TOO, HORATIO. HOW ARE THE FLEAS?
YOU CHAPS PLAY NICELY NOW, WE'RE ALL ON THE SAME TEAM...
HORATIO LYNK, CHARMED AND ENCHANTED...
CLARA OSWALD, JETLAGGED AND HUNGRY.
WHAT'S THE DOC'S SECRET, CLARA? HOW DOES HE PULL ALL THE BEAUTIFUL BIRDS?
WE LIKE TO LIVE DANGEROUSLY.
THIS CLINIC'S THE ONLY PLACE ON MIRROR HILL WHERE PEOPLE CAN GET A BIT OF ATTENTION -- OR EVEN JUST A CUPPA AND A CHAT.
THE MEDICS ARE ALL VOLUNTEERS -- STUDENTS, MOSTLY. THEY DO THE BEST THEY CAN, BUT THEY'RE DEALIN' WITH A HUNDRED DIFFERENT SPECIES AND A MILLION DIFFERENT ILLNESSES. NOBODY'S AN EXPERT.
THERE AIN'T NO STEADY SUPPLIES, ALL THE BLEEDIN' EQUIPMENT KEEPS BREAKIN' DOWN, BUT THEY STAY IN THE GAME.
HERE'S THAT COLOXICOL I WAS PROMISIN', RENDY. FELL OFF THE BACK OF A STARLINER...
OH, CHEERS, HORATIO, YOU'RE THE BEST!

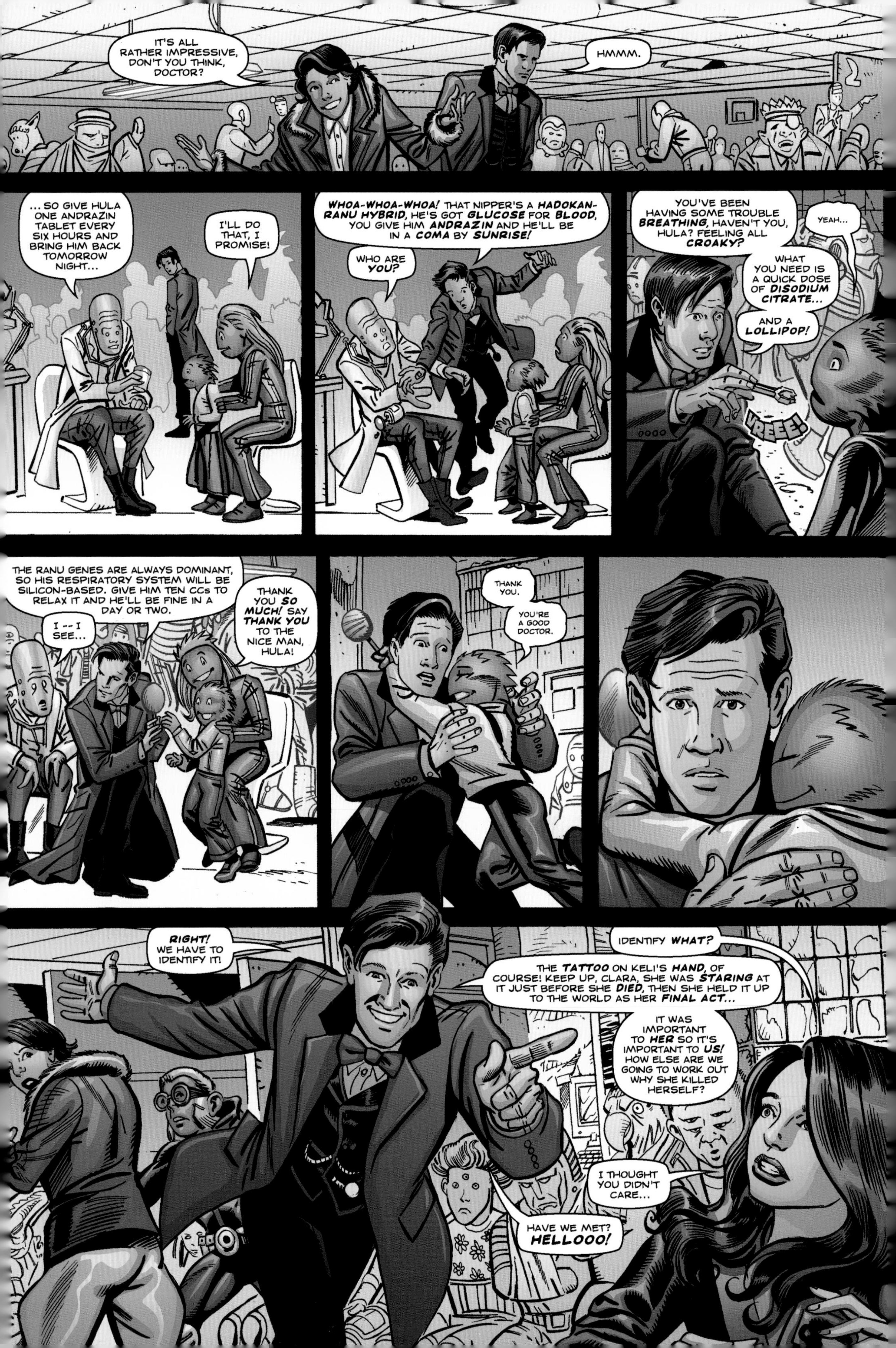

IT'S ALL RATHER IMPRESSIVE, DON'T YOU THINK, DOCTOR?
HMMM.
...SO GIVE HULA ONE ANDRAZIN TABLET EVERY SIX HOURS AND BRING HIM BACK TOMORROW NIGHT...
I'LL DO THAT, I PROMISE!
WHOA-WHOA-WHOA! THAT NIPPER'S A HADOKAN-RANU HYBRID, HE'S GOT GLUCOSE FOR BLOOD, YOU GIVE HIM ANDRAZIN AND HE'LL BE IN A COMA BY SUNRISE!
WHO ARE YOU?
YOU'VE BEEN HAVING SOME TROUBLE BREATHING, HAVEN'T YOU, HULA? FEELING ALL CROAKY?
YEAH...
WHAT YOU NEED IS A QUICK DOSE OF DISODIUM CITRATE...
AND A LOLLIPOP!
VREEE!
THE RANU GENES ARE ALWAYS DOMINANT, SO HIS RESPIRATORY SYSTEM WILL BE SILICON-BASED. GIVE HIM TEN CCs TO RELAX IT AND HE'LL BE FINE IN A DAY OR TWO.
I -- I SEE...
THANK YOU SO MUCH! SAY THANK YOU TO THE NICE MAN, HULA!
THANK YOU.
YOU'RE A GOOD DOCTOR.
RIGHT! WE HAVE TO IDENTIFY IT!
IDENTIFY WHAT?
THE TATTOO ON KELI'S HAND, OF COURSE! KEEP UP, CLARA, SHE WAS STARING AT IT JUST BEFORE SHE DIED, THEN SHE HELD IT UP TO THE WORLD AS HER FINAL ACT...
IT WAS IMPORTANT TO HER SO IT'S IMPORTANT TO US! HOW ELSE ARE WE GOING TO WORK OUT WHY SHE KILLED HERSELF?
I THOUGHT YOU DIDN'T CARE...
HAVE WE MET? HELLOOO!

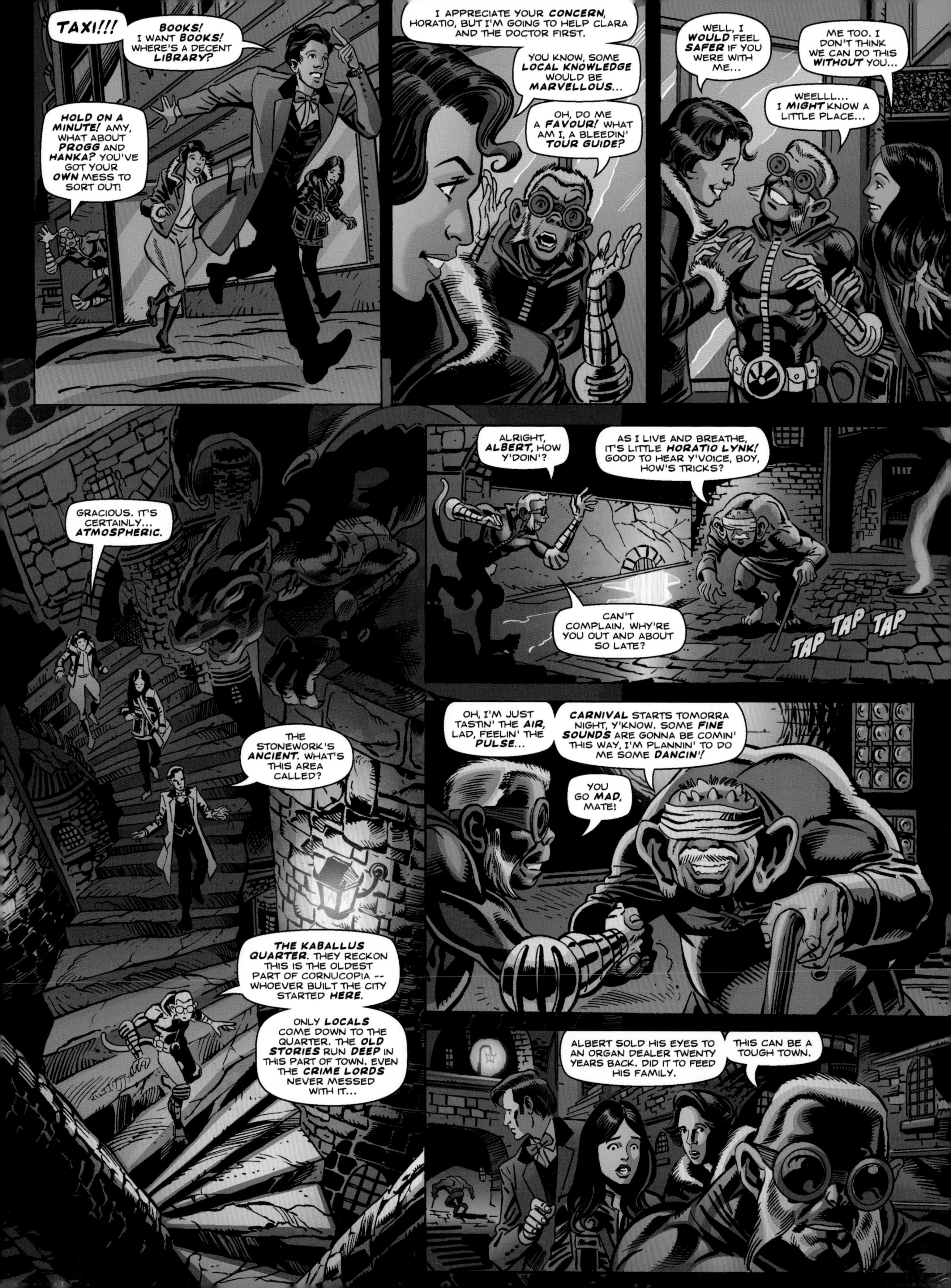
TAXI!!!
BOOKS! I WANT BOOKS! WHERE'S A DECENT LIBRARY?
HOLD ON A MINUTE! AMY, WHAT ABOUT PROGG AND HANKA? YOU'VE GOT YOUR OWN MESS TO SORT OUT!
I APPRECIATE YOUR CONCERN, HORATIO, BUT I'M GOING TO HELP CLARA AND THE DOCTOR FIRST.
YOU KNOW, SOME LOCAL KNOWLEDGE WOULD BE MARVELLOUS...
OH, DO ME A FAVOUR! WHAT AM I, A BLEEDIN' TOUR GUIDE?
WELL, I WOULD FEEL SAFER IF YOU WERE WITH ME...
ME TOO. I DON'T THINK WE CAN DO THIS WITHOUT YOU...
WEELLL... I MIGHT KNOW A LITTLE PLACE...
GRACIOUS. IT'S CERTAINLY... ATMOSPHERIC.
THE STONEWORK'S ANCIENT. WHAT'S THIS AREA CALLED?
THE KABALLUS QUARTER. THEY RECKON THIS IS THE OLDEST PART OF CORNUCOPIA -- WHOEVER BUILT THE CITY STARTED HERE.
ONLY LOCALS COME DOWN TO THE QUARTER. THE OLD STORIES RUN DEEP IN THIS PART OF TOWN. EVEN THE CRIME LORDS NEVER MESSED WITH IT...
ALRIGHT, ALBERT, HOW Y'DOIN'?
AS I LIVE AND BREATHE, IT'S LITTLE HORATIO LYNK! GOOD TO HEAR Y'VOICE, BOY, HOW'S TRICKS?
CAN'T COMPLAIN. WHY'RE YOU OUT AND ABOUT SO LATE?
TAP TAP TAP
OH, I'M JUST TASTIN' THE AIR, LAD, FEELIN' THE PULSE...
CARNIVAL STARTS TOMORRA NIGHT, Y'KNOW. SOME FINE SOUNDS ARE GONNA BE COMIN' THIS WAY, I'M PLANNIN' TO DO ME SOME DANCIN'!
YOU GO MAD, MATE!
ALBERT SOLD HIS EYES TO AN ORGAN DEALER TWENTY YEARS BACK. DID IT TO FEED HIS FAMILY.
THIS CAN BE A TOUGH TOWN.

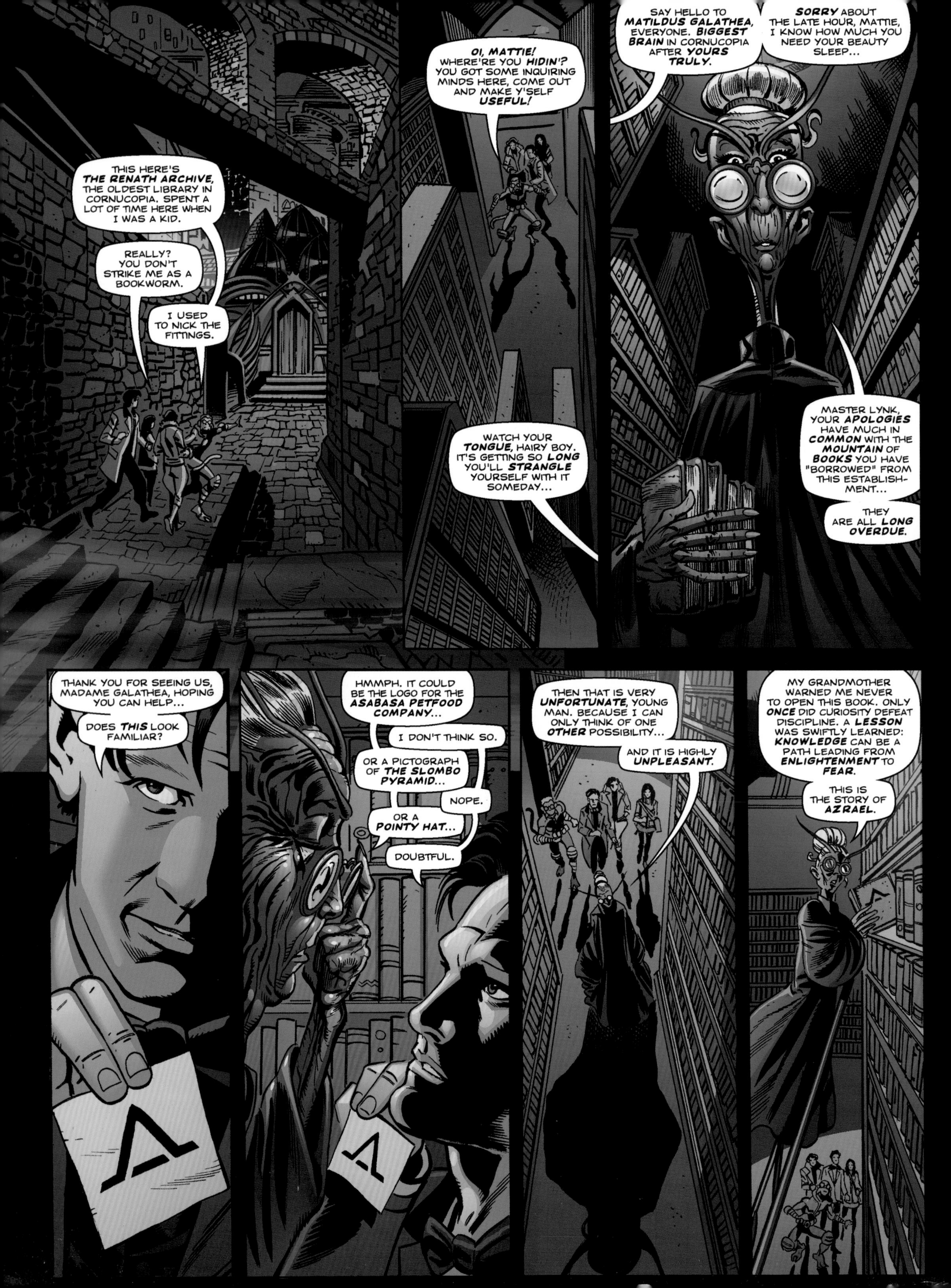
THIS HERE'S THE RENATH ARCHIVE, THE OLDEST LIBRARY IN CORNUCOPIA. SPENT A LOT OF TIME HERE WHEN I WAS A KID.
REALLY? YOU DON'T STRIKE ME AS A BOOKWORM.
I USED TO NICK THE FITTINGS.
OI, MATTIE! WHERE'RE YOU HIDIN'? YOU GOT SOME INQUIRING MINDS HERE, COME OUT AND MAKE Y'SELF USEFUL!
WATCH YOUR TONGUE, HAIRY BOY. IT'S GETTING SO LONG YOU'LL STRANGLE YOURSELF WITH IT SOMEDAY...
SAY HELLO TO MATILDUS GALATHEA, EVERYONE. BIGGEST BRAIN IN CORNUCOPIA AFTER YOURS TRULY.
SORRY ABOUT THE LATE HOUR, MATTIE, I KNOW HOW MUCH YOU NEED YOUR BEAUTY SLEEP...
MASTER LYNK, YOUR APOLOGIES HAVE MUCH IN COMMON WITH THE MOUNTAIN OF BOOKS YOU HAVE "BORROWED" FROM THIS ESTABLISH-MENT...
THEY ARE ALL LONG OVERDUE.
THANK YOU FOR SEEING US, MADAME GALATHEA, HOPING YOU CAN HELP...
DOES THIS LOOK FAMILIAR?
HMMPH. IT COULD BE THE LOGO FOR THE ASABASA PETFOOD COMPANY...
I DON'T THINK SO.
OR A PICTOGRAPH OF THE SLOMBO PYRAMID...
NOPE.
OR A POINTY HAT...
DOUBTFUL.
THEN THAT IS VERY UNFORTUNATE, YOUNG MAN. BECAUSE I CAN ONLY THINK OF ONE OTHER POSSIBILITY...
AND IT IS HIGHLY UNPLEASANT.
MY GRANDMOTHER WARNED ME NEVER TO OPEN THIS BOOK. ONLY ONCE DID CURIOSITY DEFEAT DISCIPLINE. A LESSON WAS SWIFTLY LEARNED: KNOWLEDGE CAN BE A PATH LEADING FROM ENLIGHTENMENT TO FEAR.
THIS IS THE STORY OF AZRAEL.

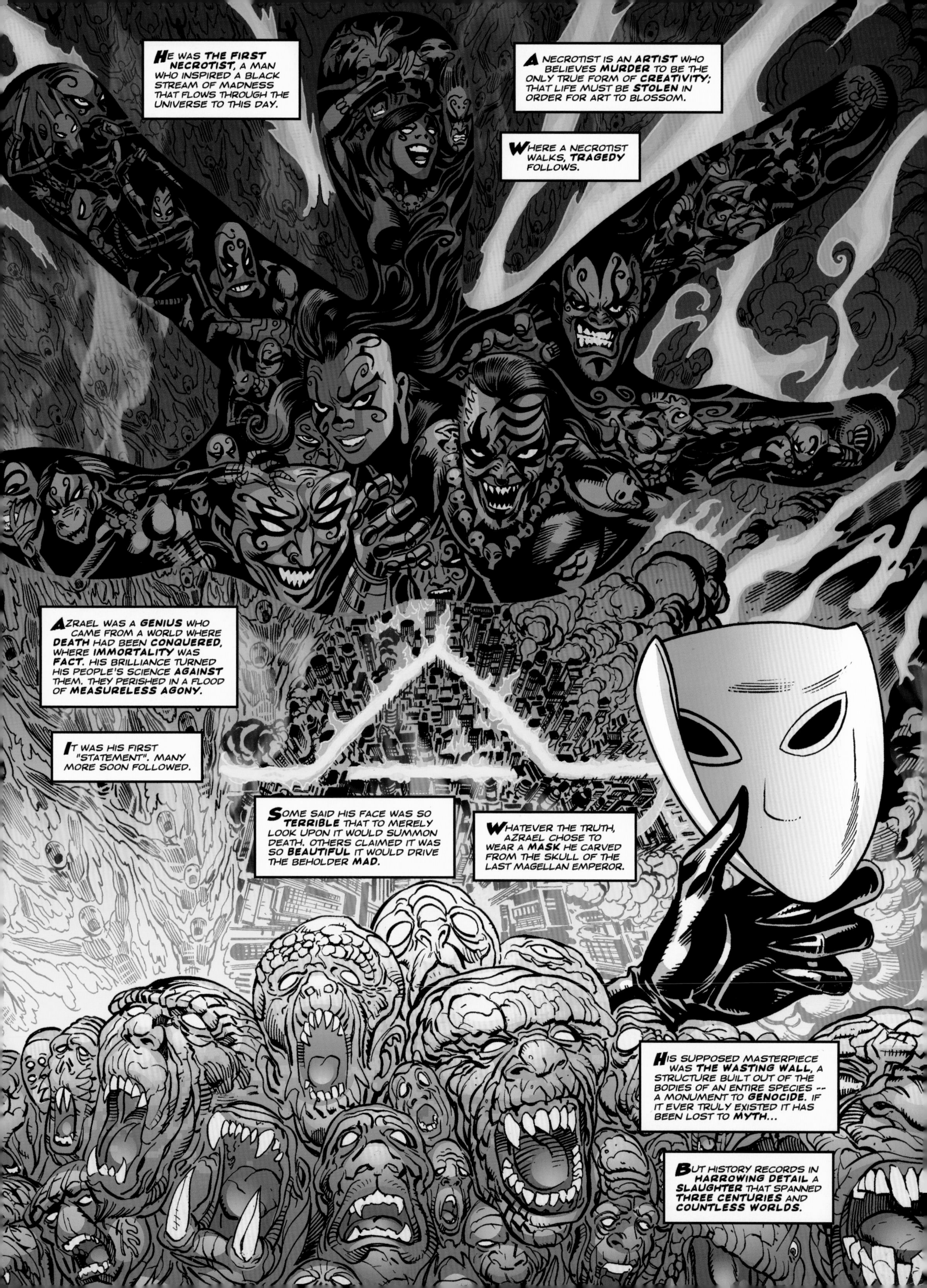

HE WAS THE FIRST NECROTIST, A MAN WHO INSPIRED A BLACK STREAM OF MADNESS THAT FLOWS THROUGH THE UNIVERSE TO THIS DAY.
A NECROTIST IS AN ARTIST WHO BELIEVES MURDER TO BE THE ONLY TRUE FORM OF CREATIVITY; THAT LIFE MUST BE STOLEN IN ORDER FOR ART TO BLOSSOM.
WHERE A NECROTIST WALKS, TRAGEDY FOLLOWS.
AZRAEL WAS A GENIUS WHO CAME FROM A WORLD WHERE DEATH HAD BEEN CONQUERED, WHERE IMMORTALITY WAS FACT. HIS BRILLIANCE TURNED HIS PEOPLE'S SCIENCE AGAINST THEM. THEY PERISHED IN A FLOOD OF MEASURELESS AGONY.
IT WAS HIS FIRST "STATEMENT". MANY MORE SOON FOLLOWED.
SOME SAID HIS FACE WAS SO TERRIBLE THAT TO MERELY LOOK UPON IT WOULD SUMMON DEATH. OTHERS CLAIMED IT WAS SO BEAUTIFUL IT WOULD DRIVE THE BEHOLDER MAD.
WHATEVER THE TRUTH, AZRAEL CHOSE TO WEAR A MASK HE CARVED FROM THE SKULL OF THE LAST MAGELLAN EMPEROR.
HIS SUPPOSED MASTERPIECE WAS THE WASTING WALL, A STRUCTURE BUILT OUT OF THE BODIES OF AN ENTIRE SPECIES -- A MONUMENT TO GENOCIDE. IF IT EVER TRULY EXISTED IT HAS BEEN LOST TO MYTH...
BUT HISTORY RECORDS IN HARROWING DETAIL A SLAUGHTER THAT SPANNED THREE CENTURIES AND COUNTLESS WORLDS.

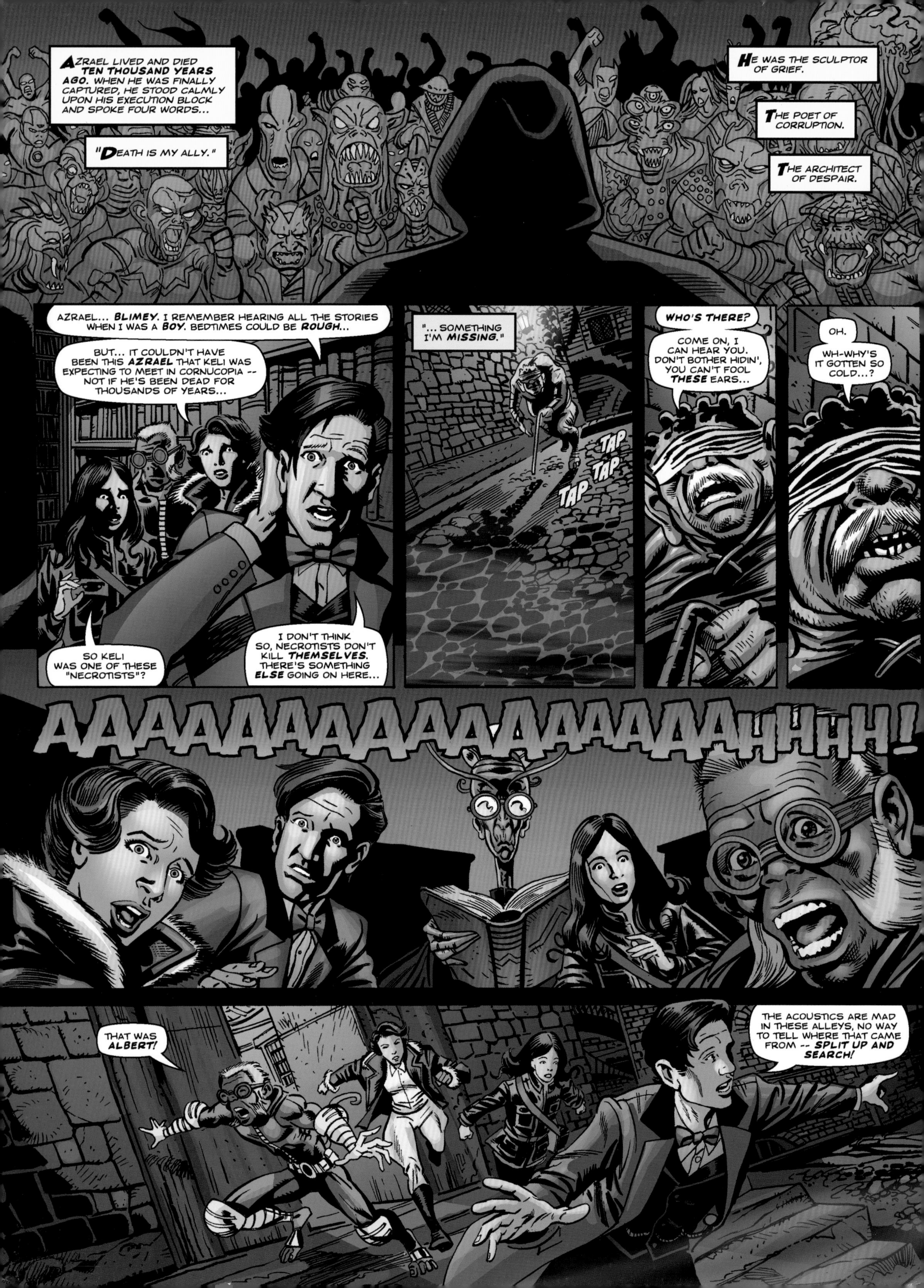
AZRAEL LIVED AND DIED TEN THOUSAND YEARS AGO. WHEN HE WAS FINALLY CAPTURED, HE STOOD CALMLY UPON HIS EXECUTION BLOCK AND SPOKE FOUR WORDS...
"DEATH IS MY ALLY."
HE WAS THE SCULPTOR OF GRIEF.
THE POET OF CORRUPTION.
THE ARCHITECT OF DESPAIR.
AZRAEL... BLIMEY. I REMEMBER HEARING ALL THE STORIES WHEN I WAS A BOY. BEDTIMES COULD BE ROUGH...
BUT... IT COULDN'T HAVE BEEN THIS AZRAEL THAT KELI WAS EXPECTING TO MEET IN CORNUCOPIA -- NOT IF HE'S BEEN DEAD FOR THOUSANDS OF YEARS...
SO KELI WAS ONE OF THESE "NECROTISTS"?
I DON'T THINK SO, NECROTISTS DON'T KILL THEMSELVES. THERE'S SOMETHING ELSE GOING ON HERE...
"... SOMETHING I'M MISSING."
TAP TAP TAP
WHO'S THERE?
COME ON, I CAN HEAR YOU. DON'T BOTHER HIDIN', YOU CAN'T FOOL THESE EARS...
OH.
WH-WHY'S IT GOTTEN SO COLD...?
AAAAAAAAAAAAAAAAHHHH!
THAT WAS ALBERT!
THE ACOUSTICS ARE MAD IN THESE ALLEYS, NO WAY TO TELL WHERE THAT CAME FROM -- SPLIT UP AND SEARCH!

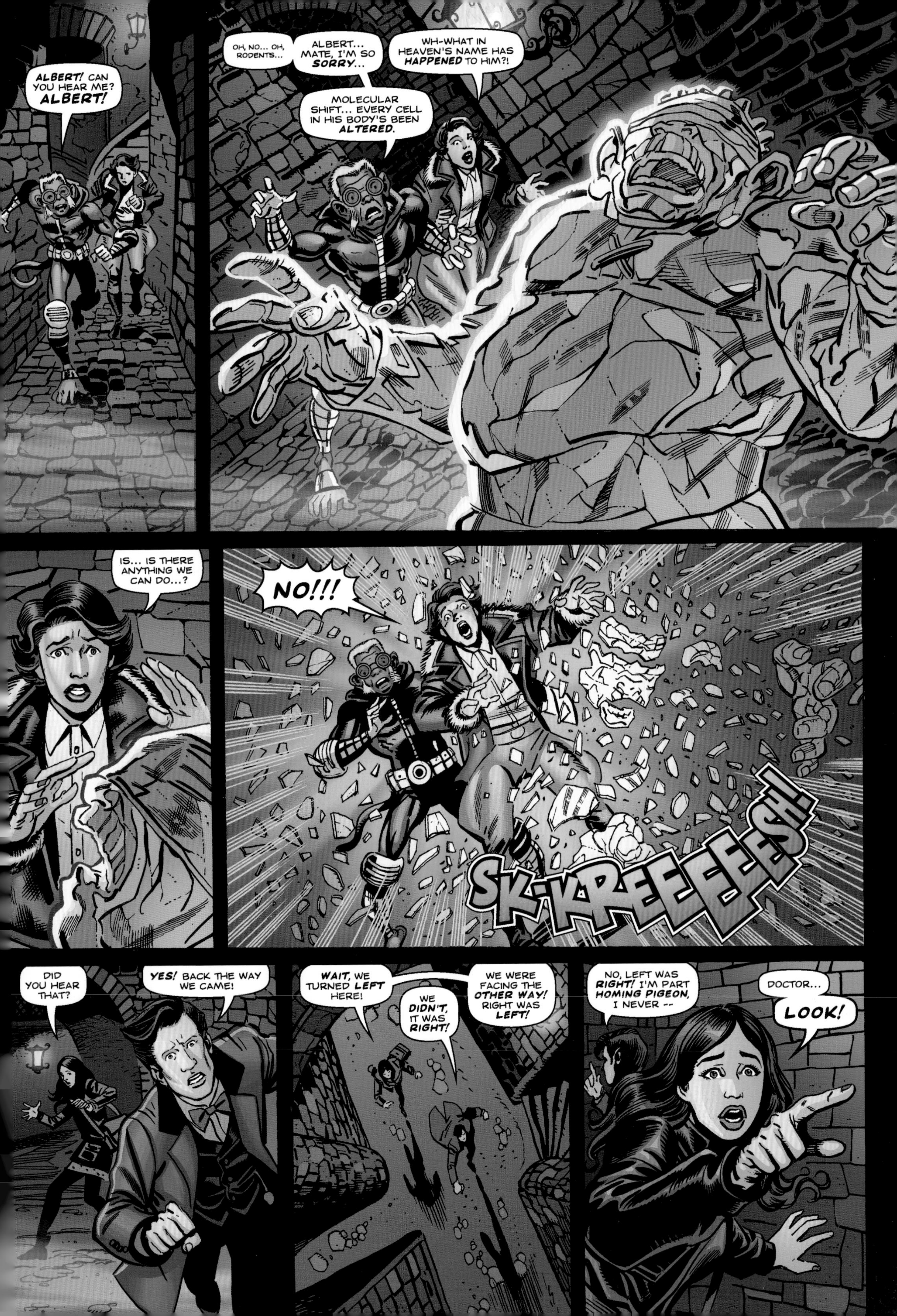
ALBERT! CAN YOU HEAR ME? ALBERT!
OH, NO... OH, RODENTS...
ALBERT... MATE, I'M SO SORRY...
WH-WHAT IN HEAVEN'S NAME HAS HAPPENED TO HIM?!
MOLECULAR SHIFT... EVERY CELL IN HIS BODY'S BEEN ALTERED.
IS... IS THERE ANYTHING WE CAN DO...?
NO!!!
SKKREEEEESH!
DID YOU HEAR THAT?
YES! BACK THE WAY WE CAME!
WAIT, WE TURNED LEFT HERE!
WE DIDN'T, IT WAS RIGHT!
WE WERE FACING THE OTHER WAY! RIGHT WAS LEFT!
NO, LEFT WAS RIGHT! I'M PART HOMING PIGEON, I NEVER --
DOCTOR... LOOK!

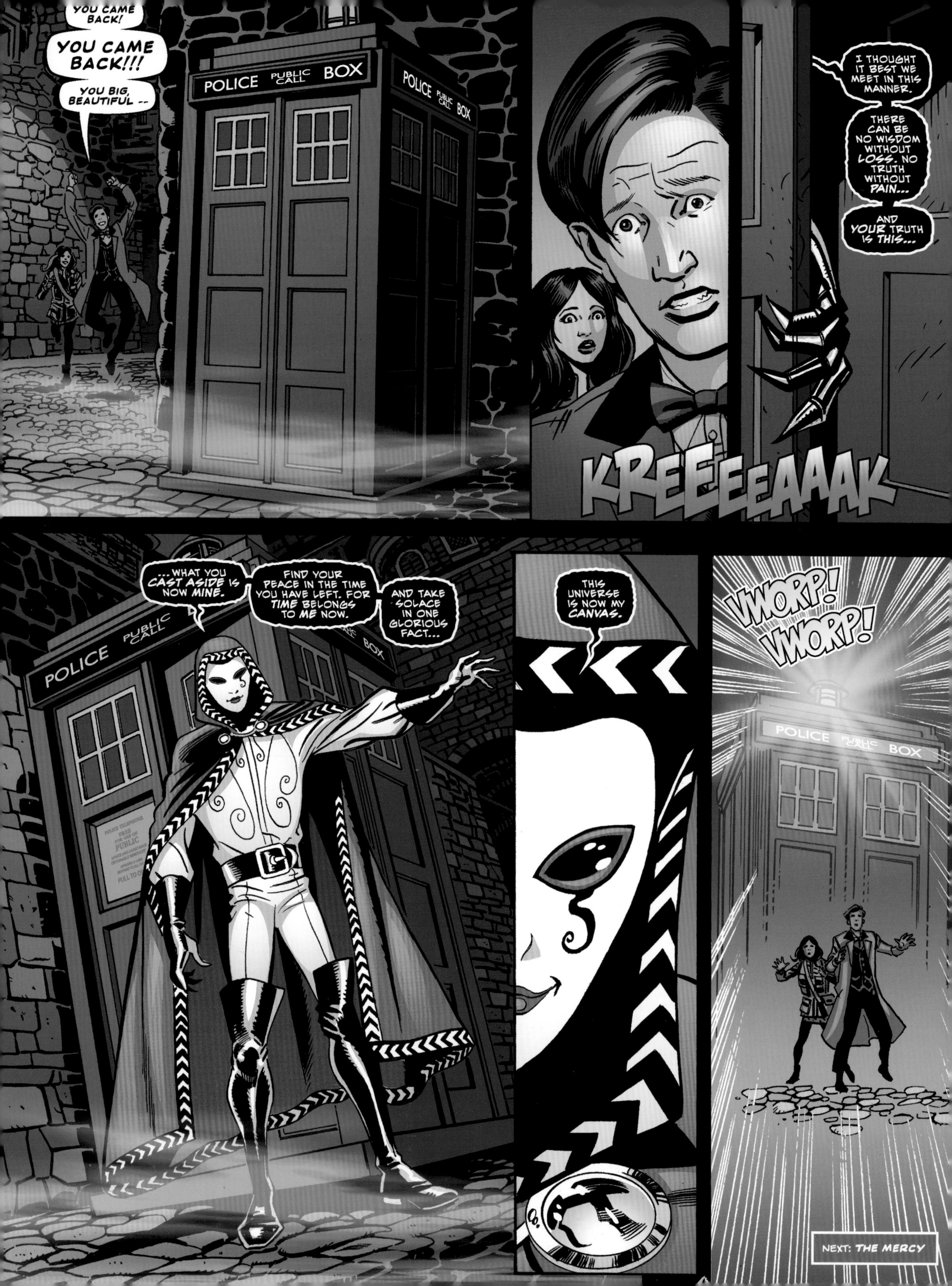
YOU CAME BACK!
YOU CAME BACK!!!
YOU BIG, BEAUTIFUL --
POLICE PUBLIC CALL BOX
I THOUGHT IT BEST WE MEET IN THIS MANNER.
THERE CAN BE NO WISDOM WITHOUT LOSS. NO TRUTH WITHOUT PAIN...
AND YOUR TRUTH IS THIS...
KREEEEAAAK
...WHAT YOU CAST ASIDE IS NOW MINE.
FIND YOUR PEACE IN THE TIME YOU HAVE LEFT. FOR TIME BELONGS TO ME NOW.
AND TAKE SOLACE IN ONE GLORIOUS FACT...
THIS UNIVERSE IS NOW MY CANVAS.
VWORP! VWORP!
POLICE PUBLIC CALL BOX
NEXT: THE MERCY

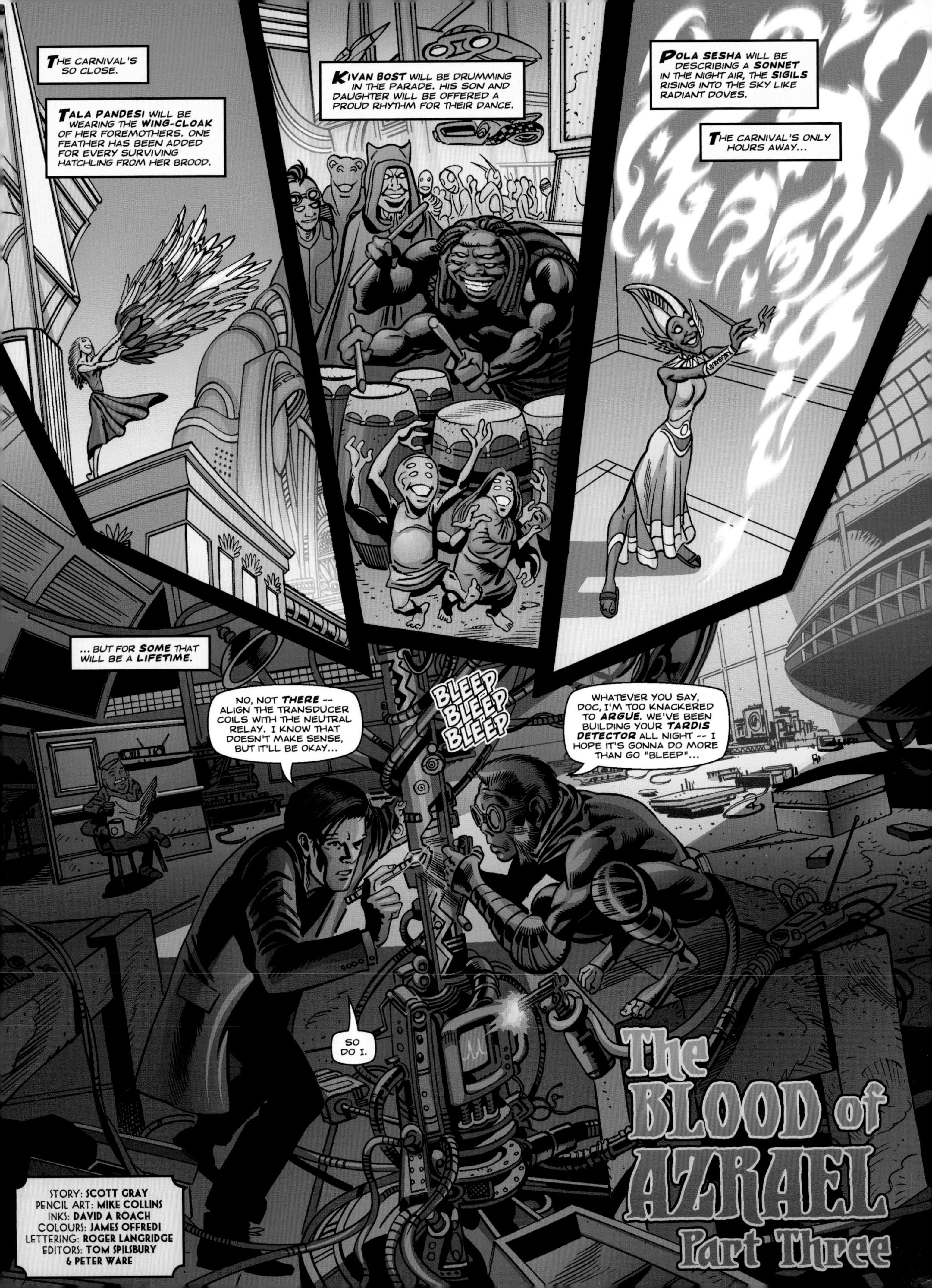
THE CARNIVAL'S SO CLOSE.
TALA PANDESI WILL BE WEARING THE WING-CLOAK OF HER FOREMOTHERS. ONE FEATHER HAS BEEN ADDED FOR EVERY SURVIVING HATCHLING FROM HER BROOD.
KIVAN BOST WILL BE DRUMMING IN THE PARADE. HIS SON AND DAUGHTER WILL BE OFFERED A PROUD RHYTHM FOR THEIR DANCE.
POLA SESHA WILL BE DESCRIBING A SONNET IN THE NIGHT AIR, THE SIGILS RISING INTO THE SKY LIKE RADIANT DOVES.
THE CARNIVAL'S ONLY HOURS AWAY...
... BUT FOR SOME THAT WILL BE A LIFETIME.
NO, NOT THERE -- ALIGN THE TRANSDUCER COILS WITH THE NEUTRAL RELAY. I KNOW THAT DOESN'T MAKE SENSE, BUT IT'LL BE OKAY...
BLEEP BLEEP BLEEP
WHATEVER YOU SAY, DOC, I'M TOO KNACKERED TO ARGUE. WE'VE BEEN BUILDING YOUR TARDIS DETECTOR ALL NIGHT -- I HOPE IT'S GONNA DO MORE THAN GO "BLEEP"...
SO DO I.
The BLOOD of AZRAEL Part Three
STORY: SCOTT GRAY
PENCIL ART: MIKE COLLINS
INKS: DAVID A ROACH
COLOURS: JAMES OFFREDI
LETTERING: ROGER LANGRIDGE
EDITORS: TOM SPILSBURY & PETER WARE

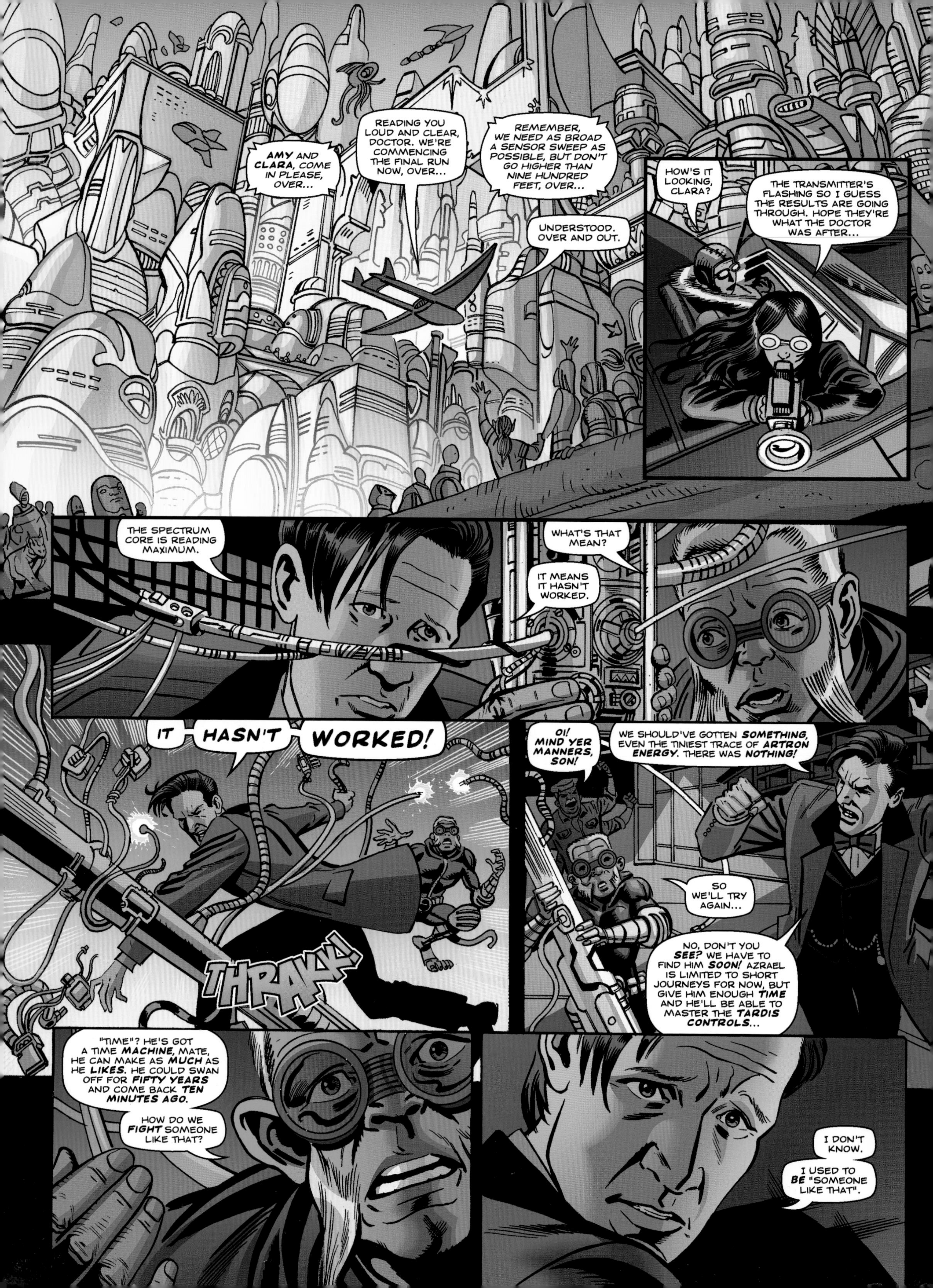
AMY AND CLARA, COME IN PLEASE, OVER...
READING YOU LOUD AND CLEAR, DOCTOR. WE'RE COMMENCING THE FINAL RUN NOW, OVER...
REMEMBER, WE NEED AS BROAD A SENSOR SWEEP AS POSSIBLE, BUT DON'T GO HIGHER THAN NINE HUNDRED FEET, OVER...
UNDERSTOOD. OVER AND OUT.
HOW'S IT LOOKING, CLARA?
THE TRANSMITTER'S FLASHING SO I GUESS THE RESULTS ARE GOING THROUGH. HOPE THEY'RE WHAT THE DOCTOR WAS AFTER...
THE SPECTRUM CORE IS READING MAXIMUM.
WHAT'S THAT MEAN?
IT MEANS IT HASN'T WORKED.
IT
HASN'T
WORKED!
THRAKK!
OI! MIND YER MANNERS, SON!
WE SHOULD'VE GOTTEN SOMETHING, EVEN THE TINIEST TRACE OF ARTRON ENERGY. THERE WAS NOTHING!
SO WE'LL TRY AGAIN...
NO, DON'T YOU SEE? WE HAVE TO FIND HIM SOON! AZRAEL IS LIMITED TO SHORT JOURNEYS FOR NOW, BUT GIVE HIM ENOUGH TIME AND HE'LL BE ABLE TO MASTER THE TARDIS CONTROLS...
"TIME"? HE'S GOT A TIME MACHINE, MATE, HE CAN MAKE AS MUCH AS HE LIKES. HE COULD SWAN OFF FOR FIFTY YEARS AND COME BACK TEN MINUTES AGO.
HOW DO WE FIGHT SOMEONE LIKE THAT?
I DON'T KNOW.
I USED TO BE "SOMEONE LIKE THAT".

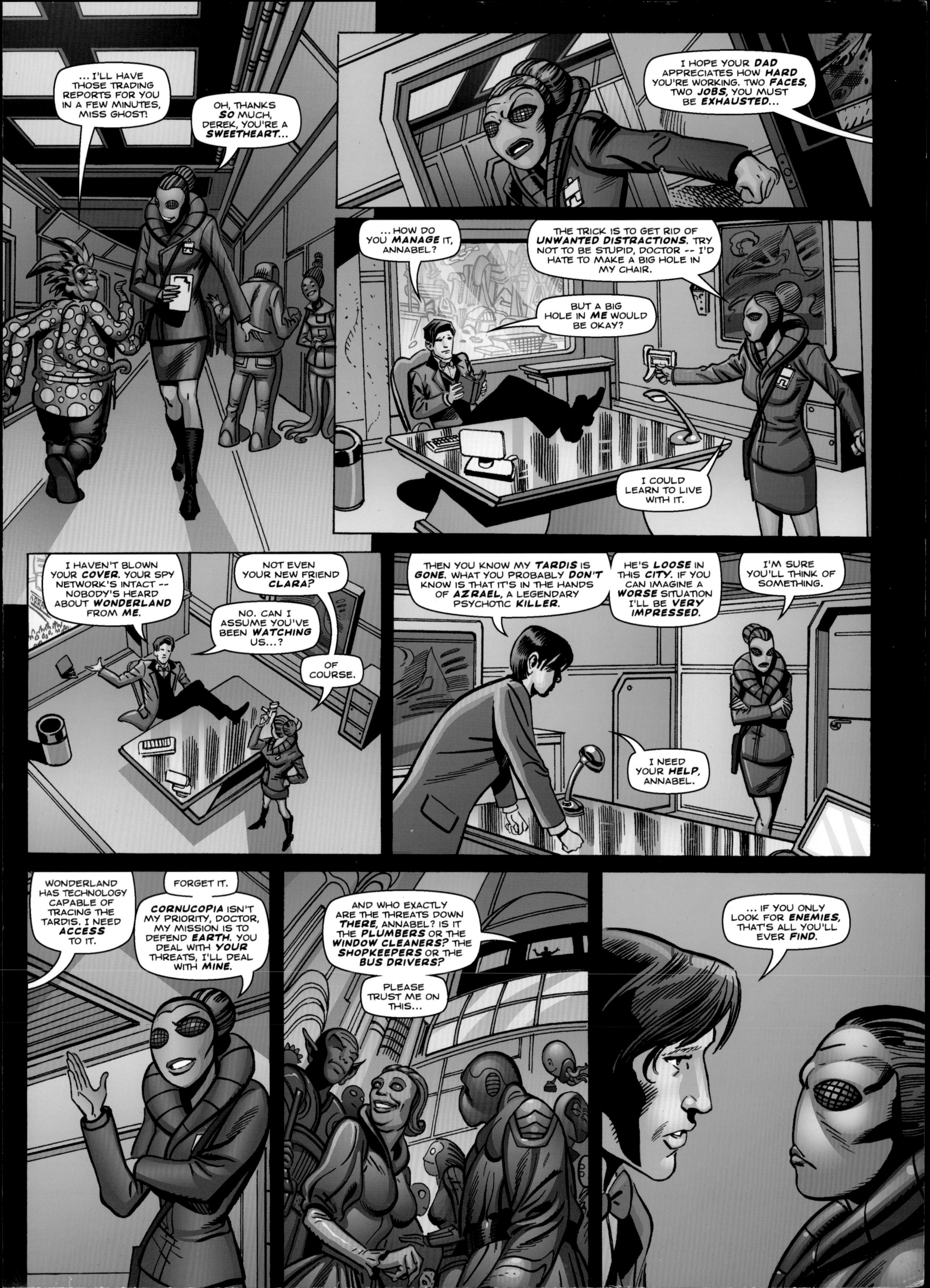
... I'LL HAVE THOSE TRADING REPORTS FOR YOU IN A FEW MINUTES, MISS GHOST!
OH, THANKS SO MUCH, DEREK, YOU'RE A SWEETHEART...
I HOPE YOUR DAD APPRECIATES HOW HARD YOU'RE WORKING. TWO FACES, TWO JOBS, YOU MUST BE EXHAUSTED...
... HOW DO YOU MANAGE IT, ANNABEL?
THE TRICK IS TO GET RID OF UNWANTED DISTRACTIONS. TRY NOT TO BE STUPID, DOCTOR -- I'D HATE TO MAKE A BIG HOLE IN MY CHAIR.
BUT A BIG HOLE IN ME WOULD BE OKAY?
I COULD LEARN TO LIVE WITH IT.
I HAVEN'T BLOWN YOUR COVER. YOUR SPY NETWORK'S INTACT -- NOBODY'S HEARD ABOUT WONDERLAND FROM ME.
NOT EVEN YOUR NEW FRIEND CLARA?
NO. CAN I ASSUME YOU'VE BEEN WATCHING US...?
OF COURSE.
THEN YOU KNOW MY TARDIS IS GONE. WHAT YOU PROBABLY DON'T KNOW IS THAT IT'S IN THE HANDS OF AZRAEL, A LEGENDARY PSYCHOTIC KILLER.
HE'S LOOSE IN THIS CITY. IF YOU CAN IMAGINE A WORSE SITUATION I'LL BE VERY IMPRESSED.
I'M SURE YOU'LL THINK OF SOMETHING.
I NEED YOUR HELP, ANNABEL.
WONDERLAND HAS TECHNOLOGY CAPABLE OF TRACING THE TARDIS. I NEED ACCESS TO IT.
FORGET IT.
CORNUCOPIA ISN'T MY PRIORITY, DOCTOR, MY MISSION IS TO DEFEND EARTH. YOU DEAL WITH YOUR THREATS, I'LL DEAL WITH MINE.
AND WHO EXACTLY ARE THE THREATS DOWN THERE, ANNABEL? IS IT THE PLUMBERS OR THE WINDOW CLEANERS? THE SHOPKEEPERS OR THE BUS DRIVERS?
PLEASE TRUST ME ON THIS...
... IF YOU ONLY LOOK FOR ENEMIES, THAT'S ALL YOU'LL EVER FIND.

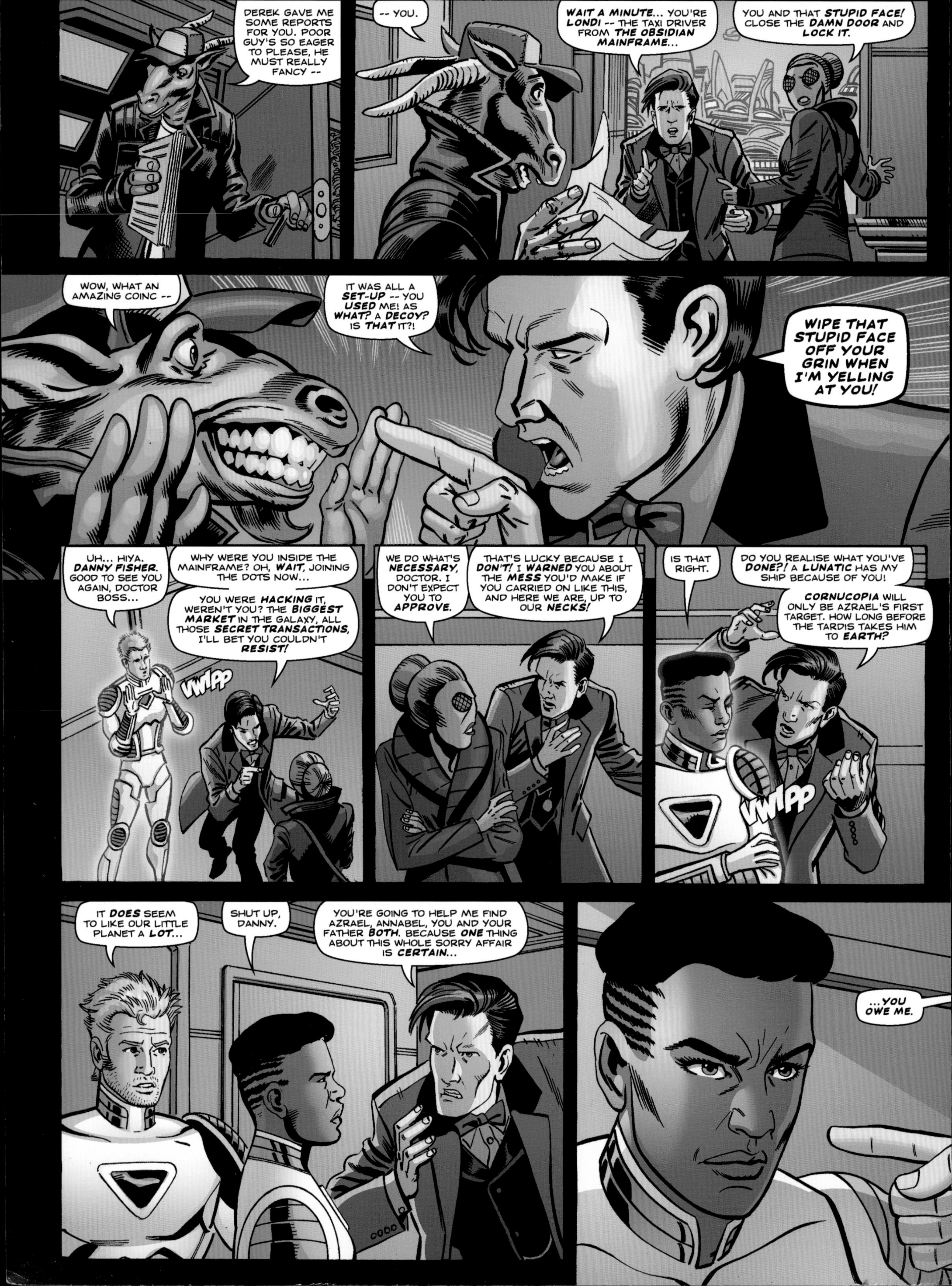

DEREK GAVE ME SOME REPORTS FOR YOU. POOR GUY'S SO EAGER TO PLEASE, HE MUST REALLY FANCY --
-- YOU.
WAIT A MINUTE... YOU'RE LONDI -- THE TAXI DRIVER FROM THE OBSIDIAN MAINFRAME...
YOU AND THAT STUPID FACE! CLOSE THE DAMN DOOR AND LOCK IT.
WOW, WHAT AN AMAZING COINC --
IT WAS ALL A SET-UP -- YOU USED ME! AS WHAT? A DECOY? IS THAT IT?!
WIPE THAT STUPID FACE OFF YOUR GRIN WHEN I'M YELLING AT YOU!
UH... HIYA. DANNY FISHER. GOOD TO SEE YOU AGAIN, DOCTOR BOSS...
WHY WERE YOU INSIDE THE MAINFRAME? OH, WAIT, JOINING THE DOTS NOW...
YOU WERE HACKING IT, WEREN'T YOU? THE BIGGEST MARKET IN THE GALAXY, ALL THOSE SECRET TRANSACTIONS, I'LL BET YOU COULDN'T RESIST!
VWIPP
WE DO WHAT'S NECESSARY, DOCTOR. I DON'T EXPECT YOU TO APPROVE.
THAT'S LUCKY BECAUSE I DON'T! I WARNED YOU ABOUT THE MESS YOU'D MAKE IF YOU CARRIED ON LIKE THIS, AND HERE WE ARE, UP TO OUR NECKS!
IS THAT RIGHT.
DO YOU REALISE WHAT YOU'VE DONE?! A LUNATIC HAS MY SHIP BECAUSE OF YOU!
CORNUCOPIA WILL ONLY BE AZRAEL'S FIRST TARGET. HOW LONG BEFORE THE TARDIS TAKES HIM TO EARTH?
VWIPP
IT DOES SEEM TO LIKE OUR LITTLE PLANET A LOT...
SHUT UP, DANNY.
YOU'RE GOING TO HELP ME FIND AZRAEL, ANNABEL, YOU AND YOUR FATHER BOTH. BECAUSE ONE THING ABOUT THIS WHOLE SORRY AFFAIR IS CERTAIN...
...YOU OWE ME.

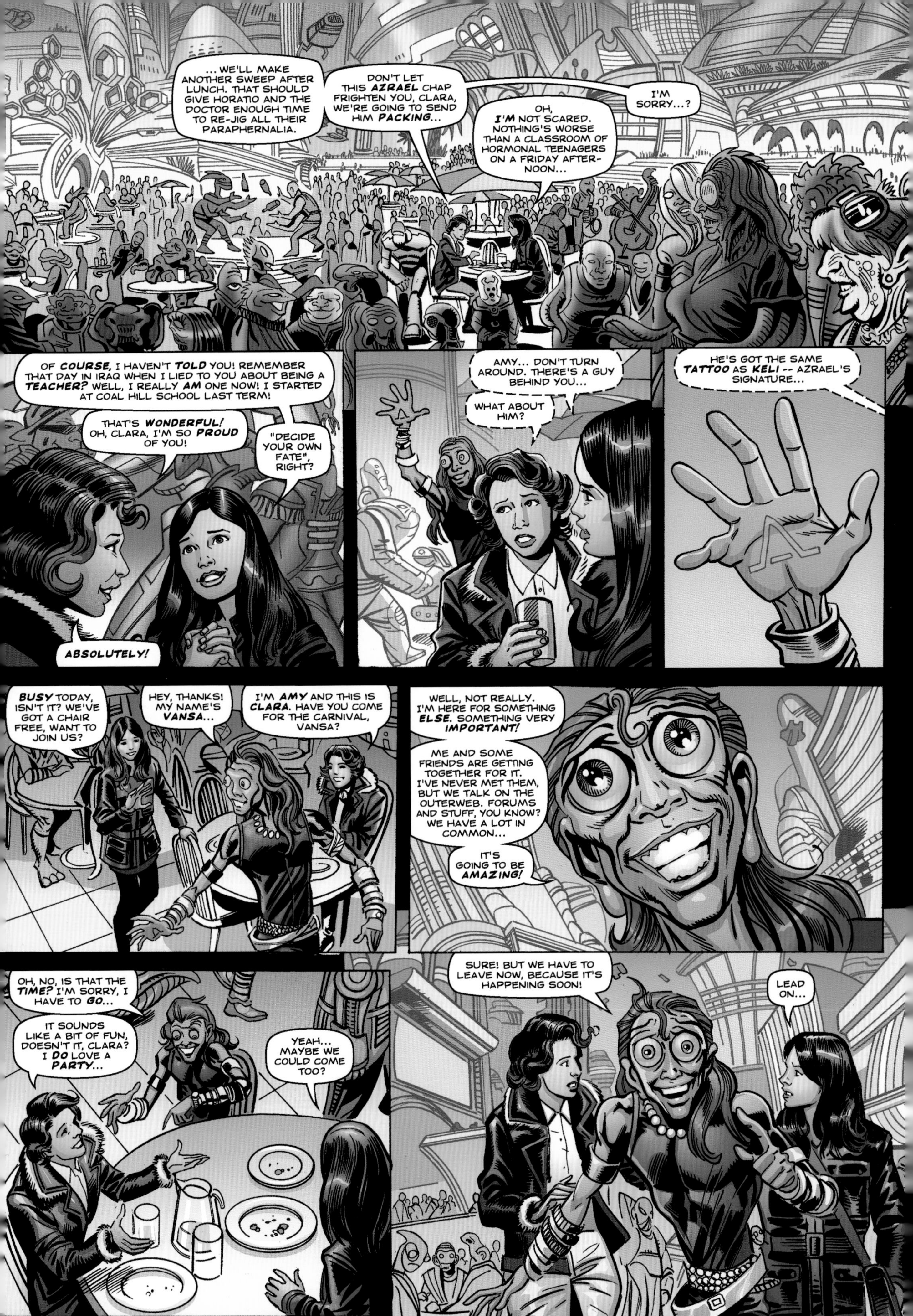
... WE'LL MAKE ANOTHER SWEEP AFTER LUNCH. THAT SHOULD GIVE HORATIO AND THE DOCTOR ENOUGH TIME TO RE-JIG ALL THEIR PARAPHERNALIA.
DON'T LET THIS AZRAEL CHAP FRIGHTEN YOU, CLARA, WE'RE GOING TO SEND HIM PACKING...
I'M SORRY...?
OH, I'M NOT SCARED. NOTHING'S WORSE THAN A CLASSROOM OF HORMONAL TEENAGERS ON A FRIDAY AFTER-NOON...
OF COURSE, I HAVEN'T TOLD YOU! REMEMBER THAT DAY IN IRAQ WHEN I LIED TO YOU ABOUT BEING A TEACHER? WELL, I REALLY AM ONE NOW! I STARTED AT COAL HILL SCHOOL LAST TERM!
THAT'S WONDERFUL! OH, CLARA, I'M SO PROUD OF YOU!
"DECIDE YOUR OWN FATE", RIGHT?
ABSOLUTELY!
AMY... DON'T TURN AROUND. THERE'S A GUY BEHIND YOU...
WHAT ABOUT HIM?
HE'S GOT THE SAME TATTOO AS KELI -- AZRAEL'S SIGNATURE...
BUSY TODAY, ISN'T IT? WE'VE GOT A CHAIR FREE, WANT TO JOIN US?
HEY, THANKS! MY NAME'S VANSA...
I'M AMY AND THIS IS CLARA. HAVE YOU COME FOR THE CARNIVAL, VANSA?
WELL, NOT REALLY. I'M HERE FOR SOMETHING ELSE. SOMETHING VERY IMPORTANT!
ME AND SOME FRIENDS ARE GETTING TOGETHER FOR IT. I'VE NEVER MET THEM, BUT WE TALK ON THE OUTERWEB. FORUMS AND STUFF, YOU KNOW? WE HAVE A LOT IN COMMON...
IT'S GOING TO BE AMAZING!
OH, NO, IS THAT THE TIME? I'M SORRY, I HAVE TO GO...
IT SOUNDS LIKE A BIT OF FUN, DOESN'T IT, CLARA? I DO LOVE A PARTY...
YEAH... MAYBE WE COULD COME TOO?
SURE! BUT WE HAVE TO LEAVE NOW, BECAUSE IT'S HAPPENING SOON!
LEAD ON...

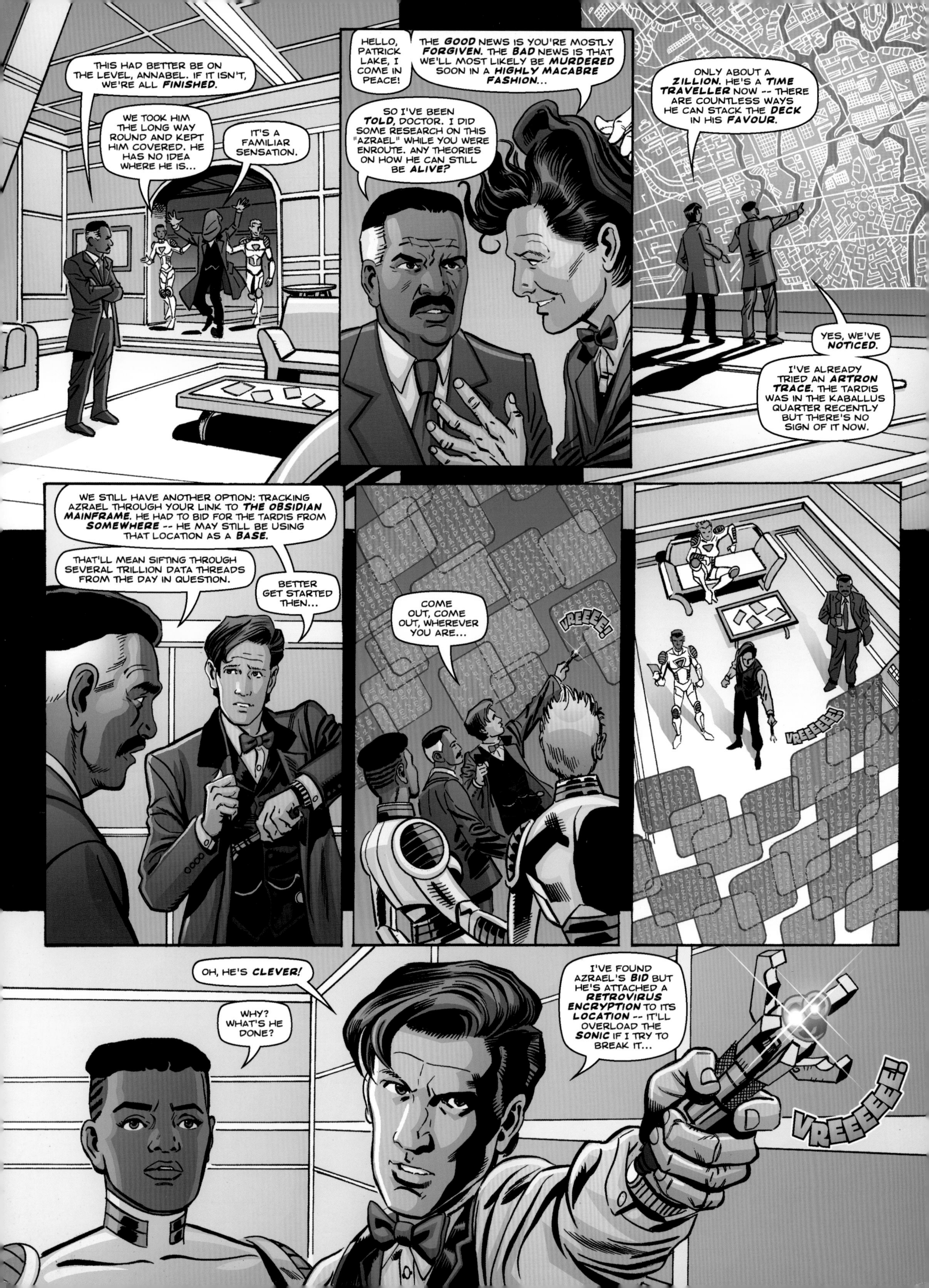
THIS HAD BETTER BE ON THE LEVEL, ANNABEL. IF IT ISN'T, WE'RE ALL FINISHED.
WE TOOK HIM THE LONG WAY ROUND AND KEPT HIM COVERED. HE HAS NO IDEA WHERE HE IS...
IT'S A FAMILIAR SENSATION.
HELLO, PATRICK LAKE, I COME IN PEACE!
THE GOOD NEWS IS YOU'RE MOSTLY FORGIVEN. THE BAD NEWS IS THAT WE'LL MOST LIKELY BE MURDERED SOON IN A HIGHLY MACABRE FASHION...
SO I'VE BEEN TOLD, DOCTOR. I DID SOME RESEARCH ON THIS "AZRAEL" WHILE YOU WERE ENROUTE. ANY THEORIES ON HOW HE CAN STILL BE ALIVE?
ONLY ABOUT A ZILLION. HE'S A TIME TRAVELLER NOW -- THERE ARE COUNTLESS WAYS HE CAN STACK THE DECK IN HIS FAVOUR.
YES, WE'VE NOTICED.
I'VE ALREADY TRIED AN ARTRON TRACE. THE TARDIS WAS IN THE KABALLUS QUARTER RECENTLY BUT THERE'S NO SIGN OF IT NOW.
WE STILL HAVE ANOTHER OPTION: TRACKING AZRAEL THROUGH YOUR LINK TO THE OBSIDIAN MAINFRAME. HE HAD TO BID FOR THE TARDIS FROM SOMEWHERE -- HE MAY STILL BE USING THAT LOCATION AS A BASE.
THAT'LL MEAN SIFTING THROUGH SEVERAL TRILLION DATA THREADS FROM THE DAY IN QUESTION.
BETTER GET STARTED THEN...
COME OUT, COME OUT, WHEREVER YOU ARE...
VREEEE!
VREEEEEE!
OH, HE'S CLEVER!
WHY? WHAT'S HE DONE?
I'VE FOUND AZRAEL'S BID BUT HE'S ATTACHED A RETROVIRUS ENCRYPTION TO ITS LOCATION -- IT'LL OVERLOAD THE SONIC IF I TRY TO BREAK IT...
VREEEEEE!

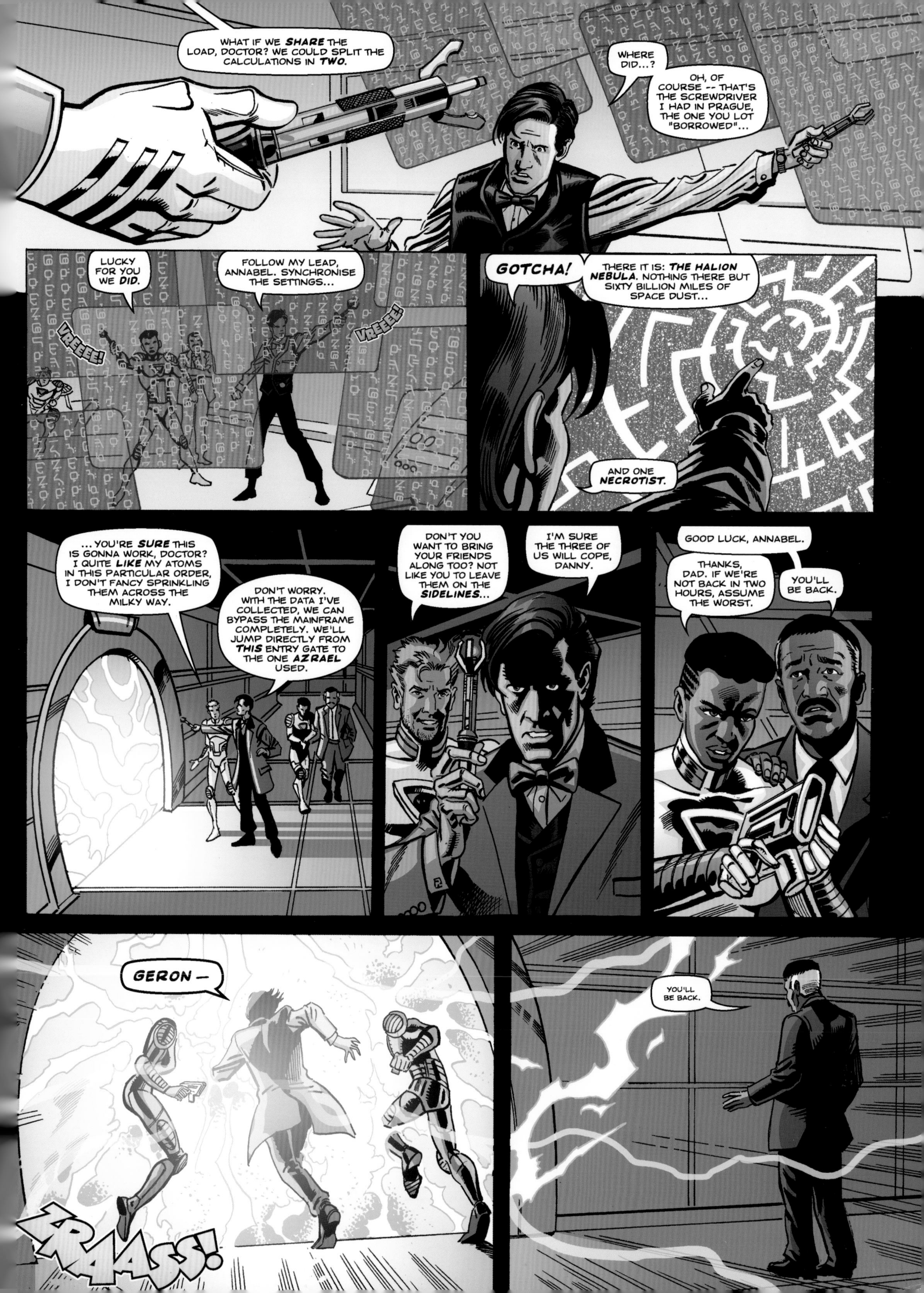

WHAT IF WE SHARE THE LOAD, DOCTOR? WE COULD SPLIT THE CALCULATIONS IN TWO.
WHERE DID...?
OH, OF COURSE -- THAT'S THE SCREWDRIVER I HAD IN PRAGUE, THE ONE YOU LOT "BORROWED"...
LUCKY FOR YOU WE DID.
FOLLOW MY LEAD, ANNABEL. SYNCHRONISE THE SETTINGS...
VREEEE!
VREEEE!
GOTCHA!
THERE IT IS: THE HALION NEBULA. NOTHING THERE BUT SIXTY BILLION MILES OF SPACE DUST...
AND ONE NECROTIST.
...YOU'RE SURE THIS IS GONNA WORK, DOCTOR? I QUITE LIKE MY ATOMS IN THIS PARTICULAR ORDER, I DON'T FANCY SPRINKLING THEM ACROSS THE MILKY WAY.
DON'T WORRY. WITH THE DATA I'VE COLLECTED, WE CAN BYPASS THE MAINFRAME COMPLETELY. WE'LL JUMP DIRECTLY FROM THIS ENTRY GATE TO THE ONE AZRAEL USED.
DON'T YOU WANT TO BRING YOUR FRIENDS ALONG TOO? NOT LIKE YOU TO LEAVE THEM ON THE SIDELINES...
I'M SURE THE THREE OF US WILL COPE, DANNY.
GOOD LUCK, ANNABEL.
THANKS, DAD. IF WE'RE NOT BACK IN TWO HOURS, ASSUME THE WORST.
YOU'LL BE BACK.
GERON —
ZRAASS!
YOU'LL BE BACK.

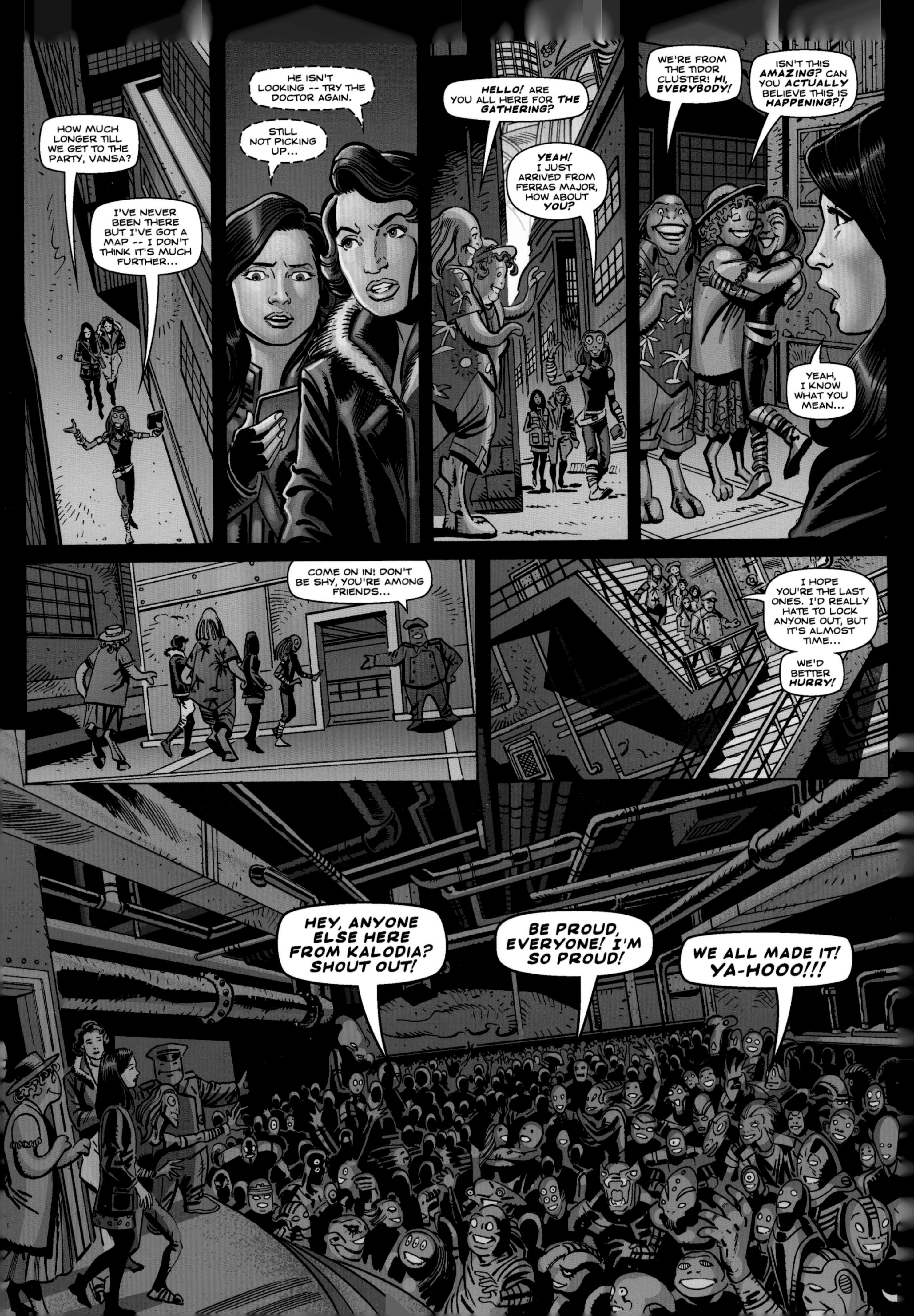
HOW MUCH LONGER TILL WE GET TO THE PARTY, VANSA?
I'VE NEVER BEEN THERE BUT I'VE GOT A MAP -- I DON'T THINK IT'S MUCH FURTHER...
HE ISN'T LOOKING -- TRY THE DOCTOR AGAIN.
STILL NOT PICKING UP...
HELLO! ARE YOU ALL HERE FOR THE GATHERING?
YEAH! I JUST ARRIVED FROM FERRAS MAJOR, HOW ABOUT YOU?
WE'RE FROM THE TIDOR CLUSTER! HI, EVERYBODY!
ISN'T THIS AMAZING? CAN YOU ACTUALLY BELIEVE THIS IS HAPPENING?!
YEAH, I KNOW WHAT YOU MEAN...
COME ON IN! DON'T BE SHY, YOU'RE AMONG FRIENDS...
I HOPE YOU'RE THE LAST ONES. I'D REALLY HATE TO LOCK ANYONE OUT, BUT IT'S ALMOST TIME...
WE'D BETTER HURRY!
HEY, ANYONE ELSE HERE FROM KALODIA? SHOUT OUT!
BE PROUD, EVERYONE! I'M SO PROUD!
WE ALL MADE IT! YA-HOOO!!!

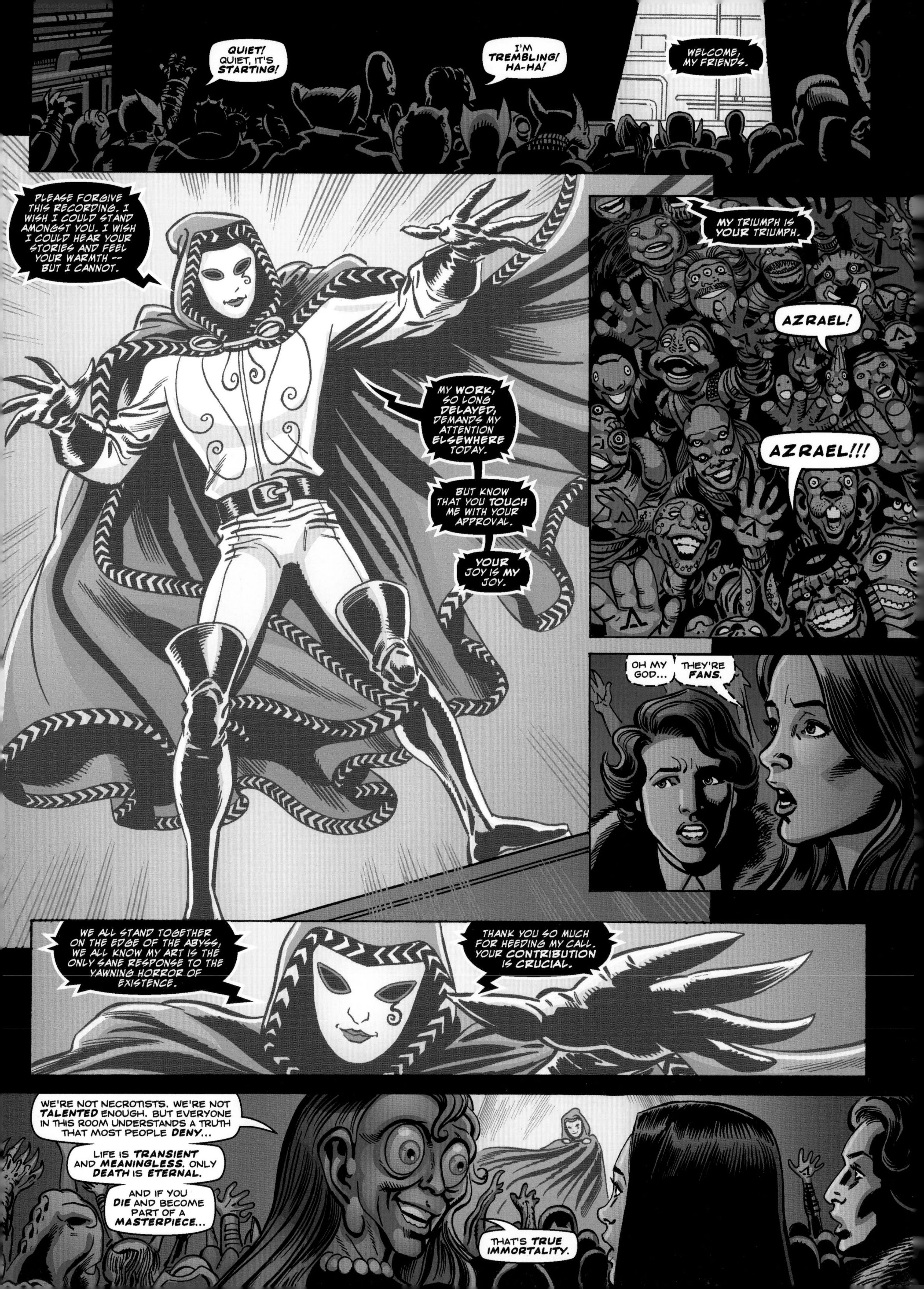
QUIET! QUIET, IT'S STARTING!
I'M TREMBLING! HA-HA!
WELCOME, MY FRIENDS.
PLEASE FORGIVE THIS RECORDING. I WISH I COULD STAND AMONGST YOU. I WISH I COULD HEAR YOUR STORIES AND FEEL YOUR WARMTH -- BUT I CANNOT.
MY WORK, SO LONG DELAYED, DEMANDS MY ATTENTION ELSEWHERE TODAY.
BUT KNOW THAT YOU TOUCH ME WITH YOUR APPROVAL.
YOUR JOY IS MY JOY.
MY TRIUMPH IS YOUR TRIUMPH.
AZRAEL!
AZRAEL!!!
OH MY GOD...
THEY'RE FANS.
WE ALL STAND TOGETHER ON THE EDGE OF THE ABYSS, WE ALL KNOW MY ART IS THE ONLY SANE RESPONSE TO THE YAWNING HORROR OF EXISTENCE.
THANK YOU SO MUCH FOR HEEDING MY CALL. YOUR CONTRIBUTION IS CRUCIAL.
WE'RE NOT NECROTISTS. WE'RE NOT TALENTED ENOUGH. BUT EVERYONE IN THIS ROOM UNDERSTANDS A TRUTH THAT MOST PEOPLE DENY...
LIFE IS TRANSIENT AND MEANINGLESS. ONLY DEATH IS ETERNAL.
AND IF YOU DIE AND BECOME PART OF A MASTERPIECE...
THAT'S TRUE IMMORTALITY.

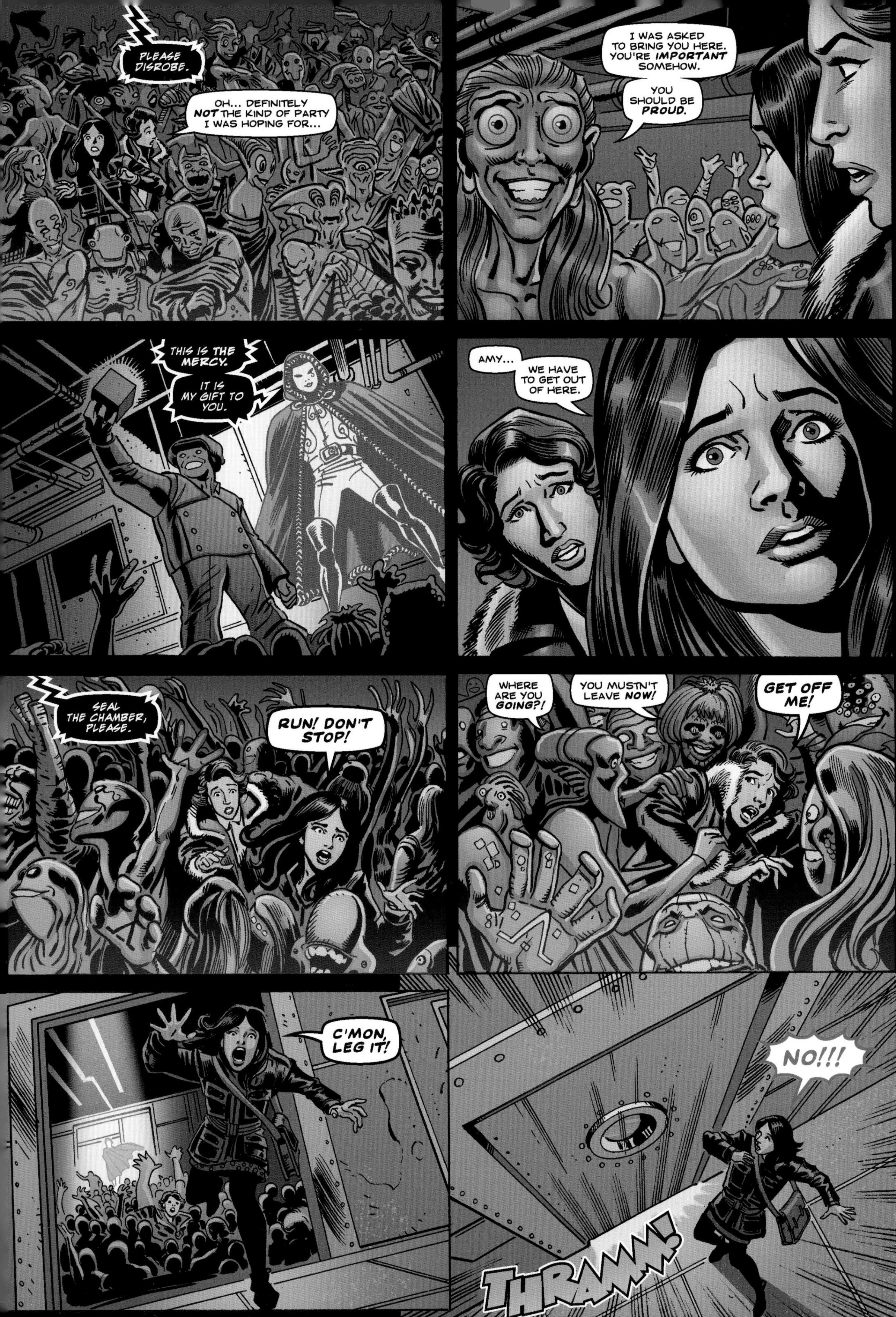

PLEASE DISROBE.
OH... DEFINITELY NOT THE KIND OF PARTY I WAS HOPING FOR...
I WAS ASKED TO BRING YOU HERE. YOU'RE IMPORTANT SOMEHOW.
YOU SHOULD BE PROUD.
THIS IS THE MERCY.
IT IS MY GIFT TO YOU.
AMY...
WE HAVE TO GET OUT OF HERE.
SEAL THE CHAMBER, PLEASE.
RUN! DON'T STOP!
WHERE ARE YOU GOING?!
YOU MUSTN'T LEAVE NOW!
GET OFF ME!
C'MON, LEG IT!
NO!!!
THRAMM!

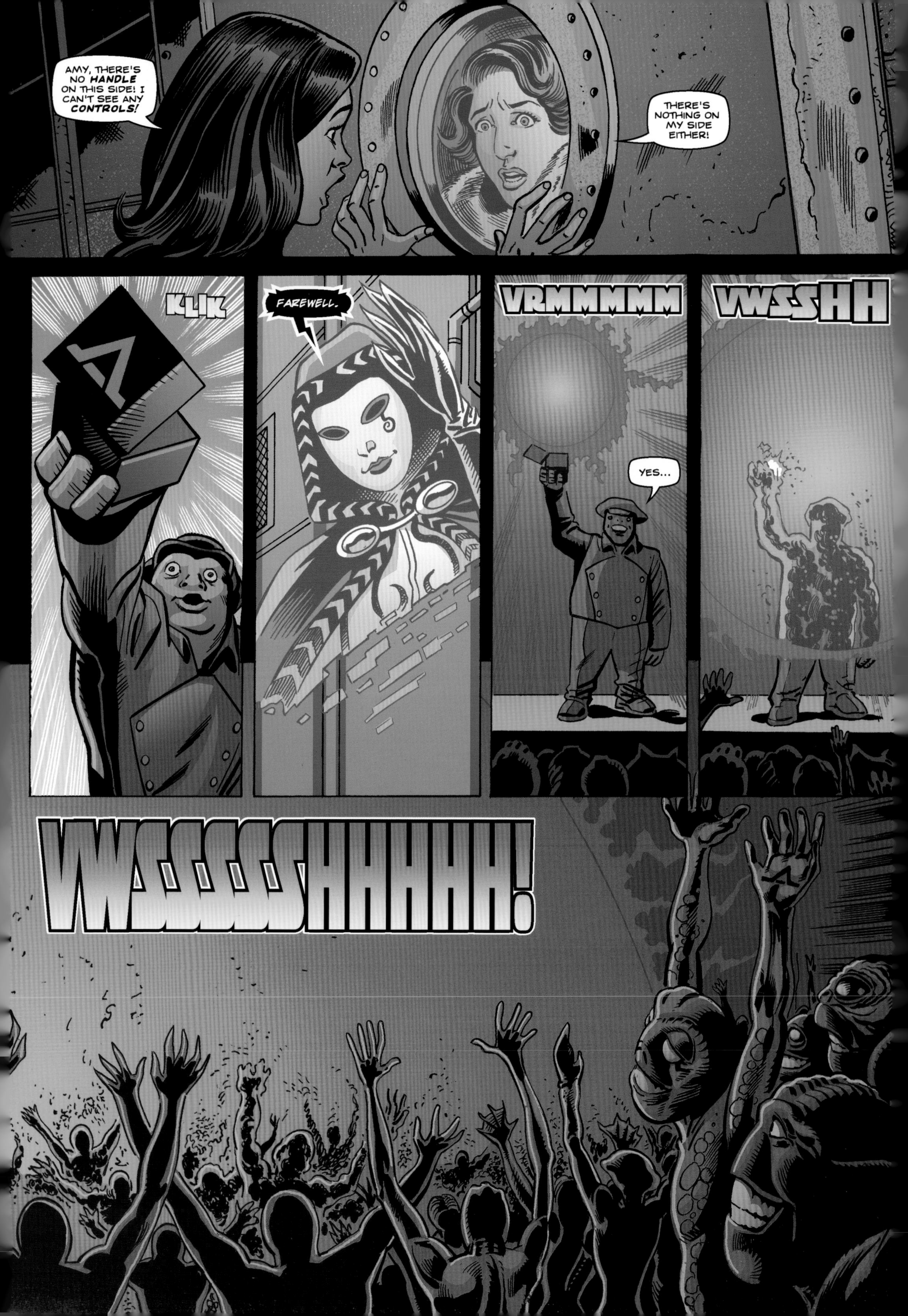
AMY, THERE'S NO HANDLE ON THIS SIDE! I CAN'T SEE ANY CONTROLS!
THERE'S NOTHING ON MY SIDE EITHER!
KLIK
FAREWELL.
VRMMMMMM
YES...
VWSSHH
VWSSSSSHHHHHH!

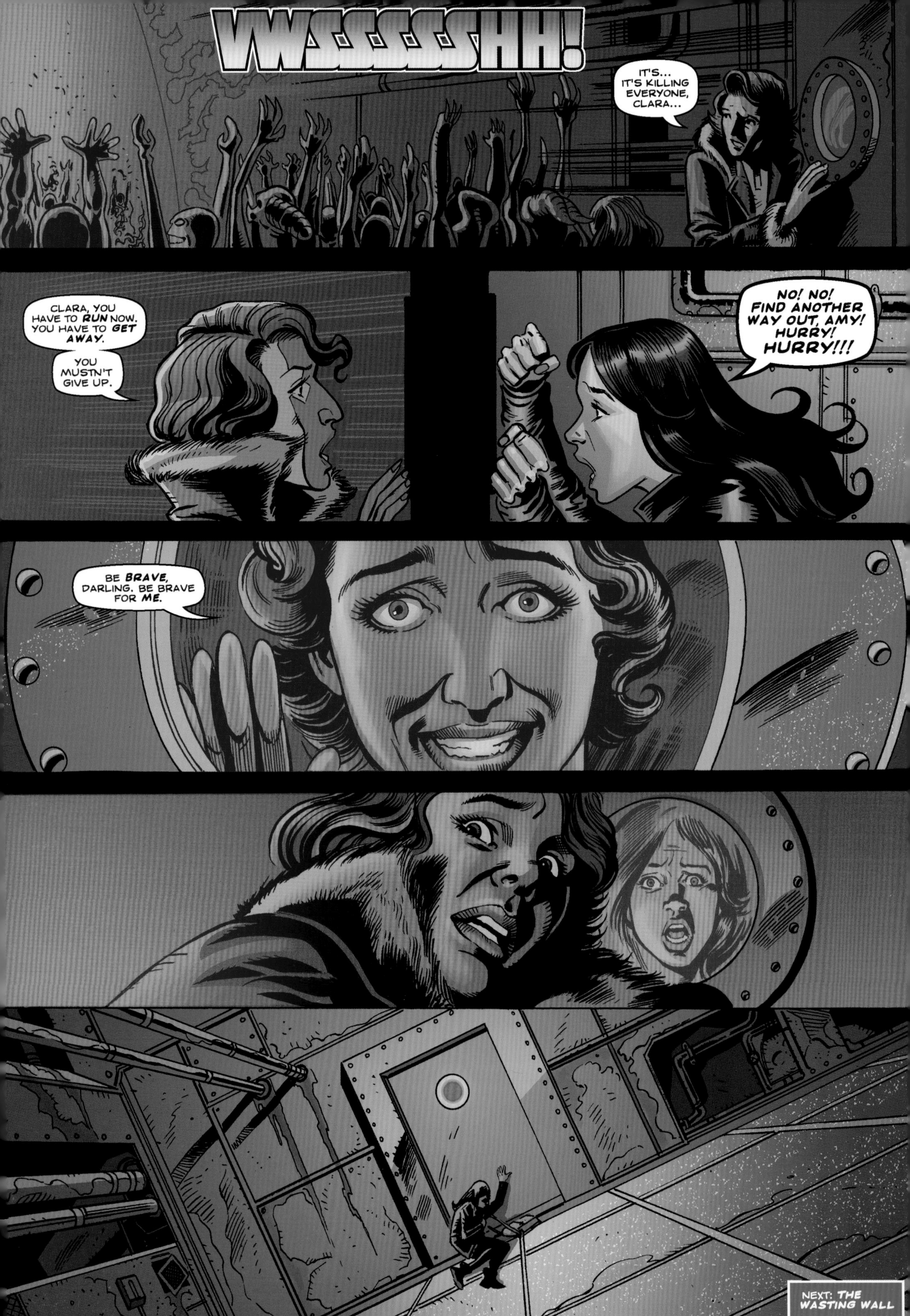
VWSSSSSSHH!
IT'S... IT'S KILLING EVERYONE, CLARA...
CLARA, YOU HAVE TO RUN NOW. YOU HAVE TO GET AWAY.
YOU MUSTN'T GIVE UP.
NO! NO! FIND ANOTHER WAY OUT, AMY! HURRY! HURRY!!!
BE BRAVE, DARLING. BE BRAVE FOR ME.
NEXT: THE WASTING WALL

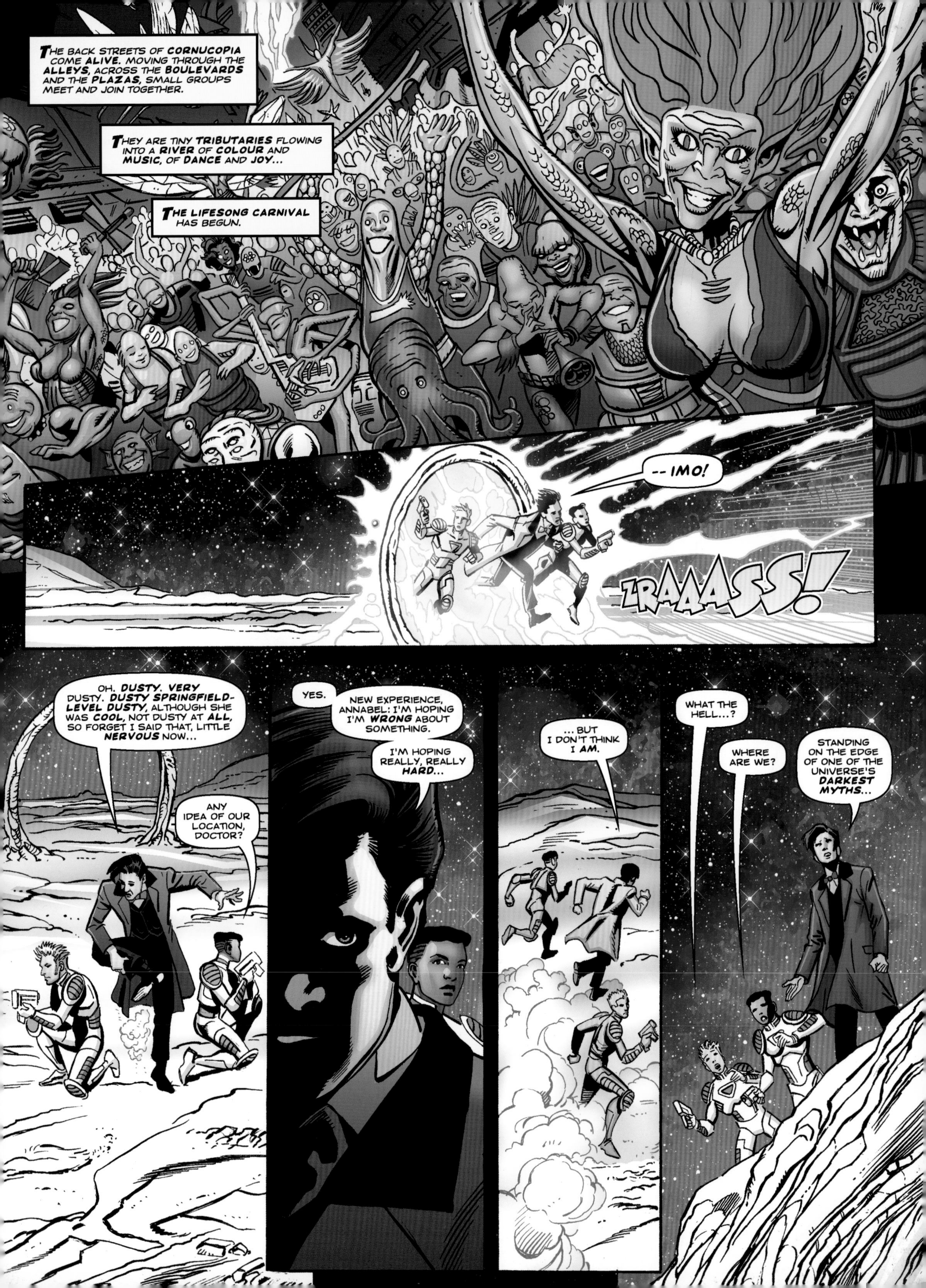
THE BACK STREETS OF CORNUCOPIA COME ALIVE. MOVING THROUGH THE ALLEYS, ACROSS THE BOULEVARDS AND THE PLAZAS, SMALL GROUPS MEET AND JOIN TOGETHER.
THEY ARE TINY TRIBUTARIES FLOWING INTO A RIVER OF COLOUR AND MUSIC, OF DANCE AND JOY...
THE LIFESONG CARNIVAL HAS BEGUN.
--IMO!
ZRAAASS!
OH. DUSTY. VERY DUSTY. DUSTY SPRINGFIELD-LEVEL DUSTY, ALTHOUGH SHE WAS COOL, NOT DUSTY AT ALL, SO FORGET I SAID THAT, LITTLE NERVOUS NOW...
ANY IDEA OF OUR LOCATION, DOCTOR?
YES.
NEW EXPERIENCE, ANNABEL: I'M HOPING I'M WRONG ABOUT SOMETHING.
I'M HOPING REALLY, REALLY HARD...
... BUT I DON'T THINK I AM.
WHAT THE HELL...?
WHERE ARE WE?
STANDING ON THE EDGE OF ONE OF THE UNIVERSE'S DARKEST MYTHS...

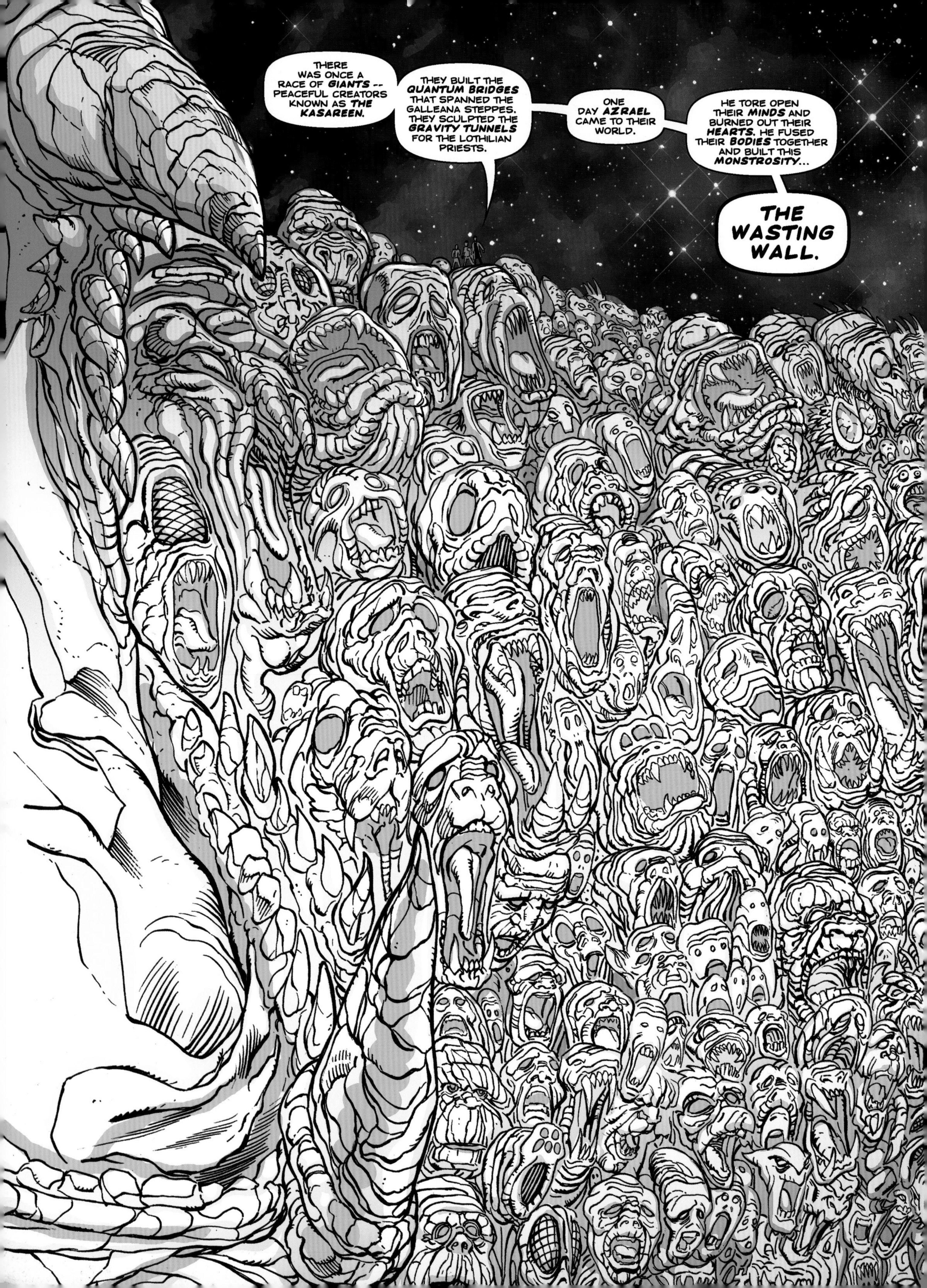
THERE WAS ONCE A RACE OF GIANTS -- PEACEFUL CREATORS KNOWN AS THE KASAREEN.
THEY BUILT THE QUANTUM BRIDGES THAT SPANNED THE GALLEANA STEPPES. THEY SCULPTED THE GRAVITY TUNNELS FOR THE LOTHILIAN PRIESTS.
ONE DAY AZRAEL CAME TO THEIR WORLD.
HE TORE OPEN THEIR MINDS AND BURNED OUT THEIR HEARTS. HE FUSED THEIR BODIES TOGETHER AND BUILT THIS MONSTROSITY...
THE WASTING WALL.

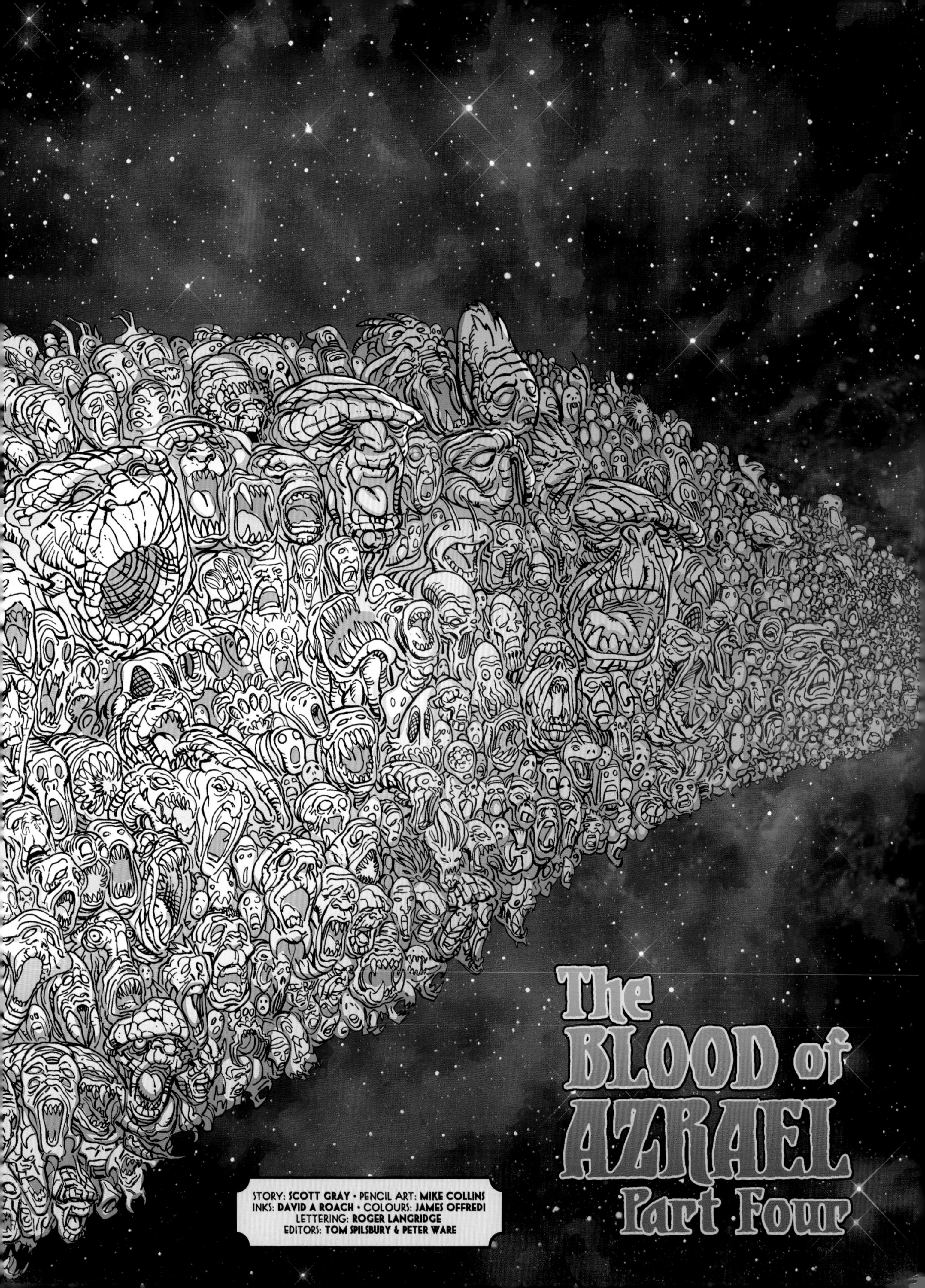
The BLOOD of AZRAEL
Part Four
STORY: SCOTT GRAY • PENCIL ART: MIKE COLLINS
INKS: DAVID A ROACH • COLOURS: JAMES OFFREDI
LETTERING: ROGER LANGRIDGE
EDITORS: TOM SPILSBURY & PETER WARE

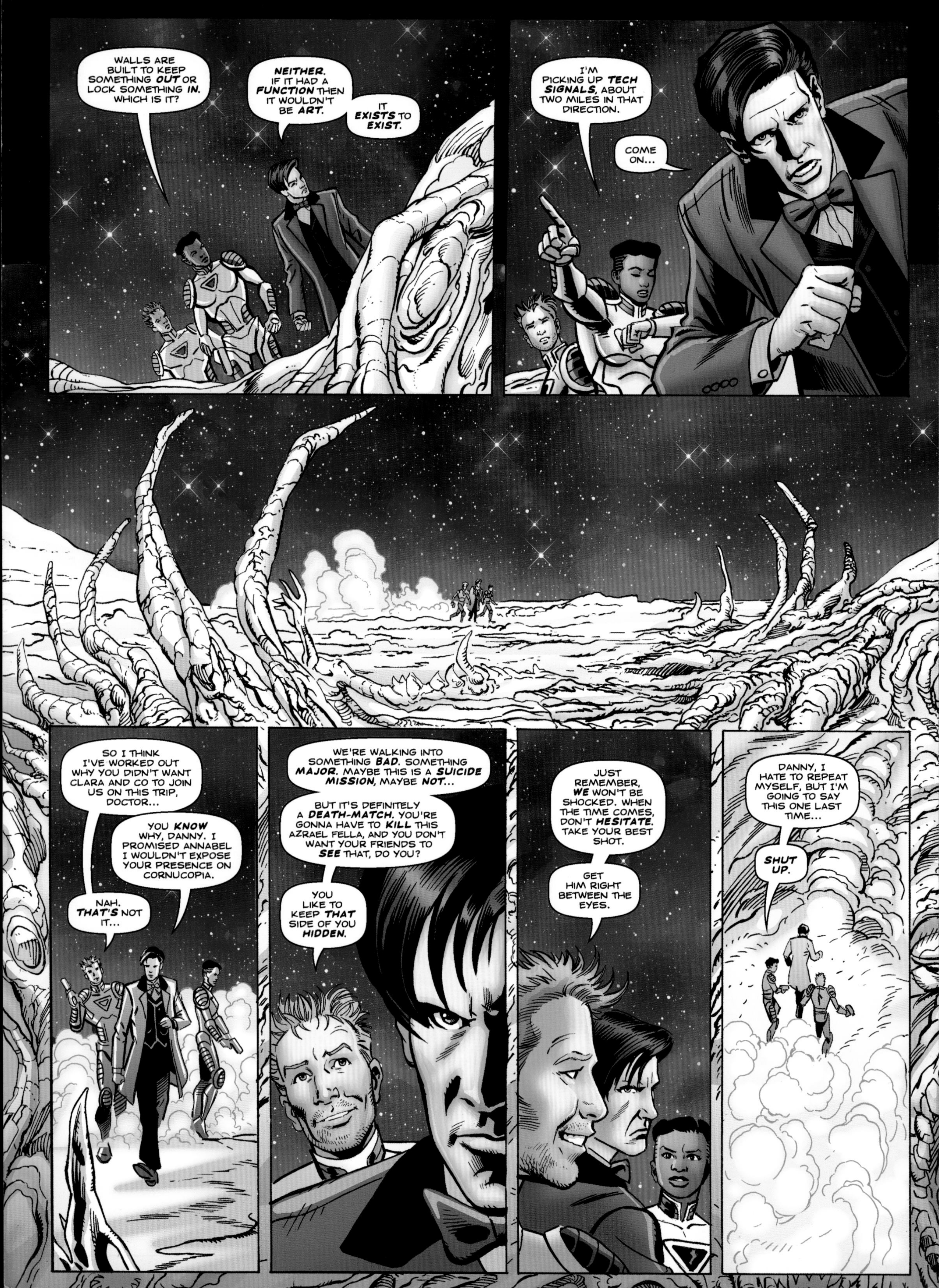
WALLS ARE BUILT TO KEEP SOMETHING OUT OR LOCK SOMETHING IN. WHICH IS IT?
NEITHER. IF IT HAD A FUNCTION THEN IT WOULDN'T BE ART.
IT EXISTS TO EXIST.
I'M PICKING UP TECH SIGNALS, ABOUT TWO MILES IN THAT DIRECTION.
COME ON...
SO I THINK I'VE WORKED OUT WHY YOU DIDN'T WANT CLARA AND CO TO JOIN US ON THIS TRIP, DOCTOR...
YOU KNOW WHY, DANNY. I PROMISED ANNABEL I WOULDN'T EXPOSE YOUR PRESENCE ON CORNUCOPIA.
NAH. THAT'S NOT IT...
WE'RE WALKING INTO SOMETHING BAD. SOMETHING MAJOR. MAYBE THIS IS A SUICIDE MISSION, MAYBE NOT...
BUT IT'S DEFINITELY A DEATH-MATCH. YOU'RE GONNA HAVE TO KILL THIS AZRAEL FELLA, AND YOU DON'T WANT YOUR FRIENDS TO SEE THAT, DO YOU?
YOU LIKE TO KEEP THAT SIDE OF YOU HIDDEN.
JUST REMEMBER, WE WON'T BE SHOCKED. WHEN THE TIME COMES, DON'T HESITATE. TAKE YOUR BEST SHOT.
GET HIM RIGHT BETWEEN THE EYES.
DANNY, I HATE TO REPEAT MYSELF, BUT I'M GOING TO SAY THIS ONE LAST TIME...
SHUT UP.

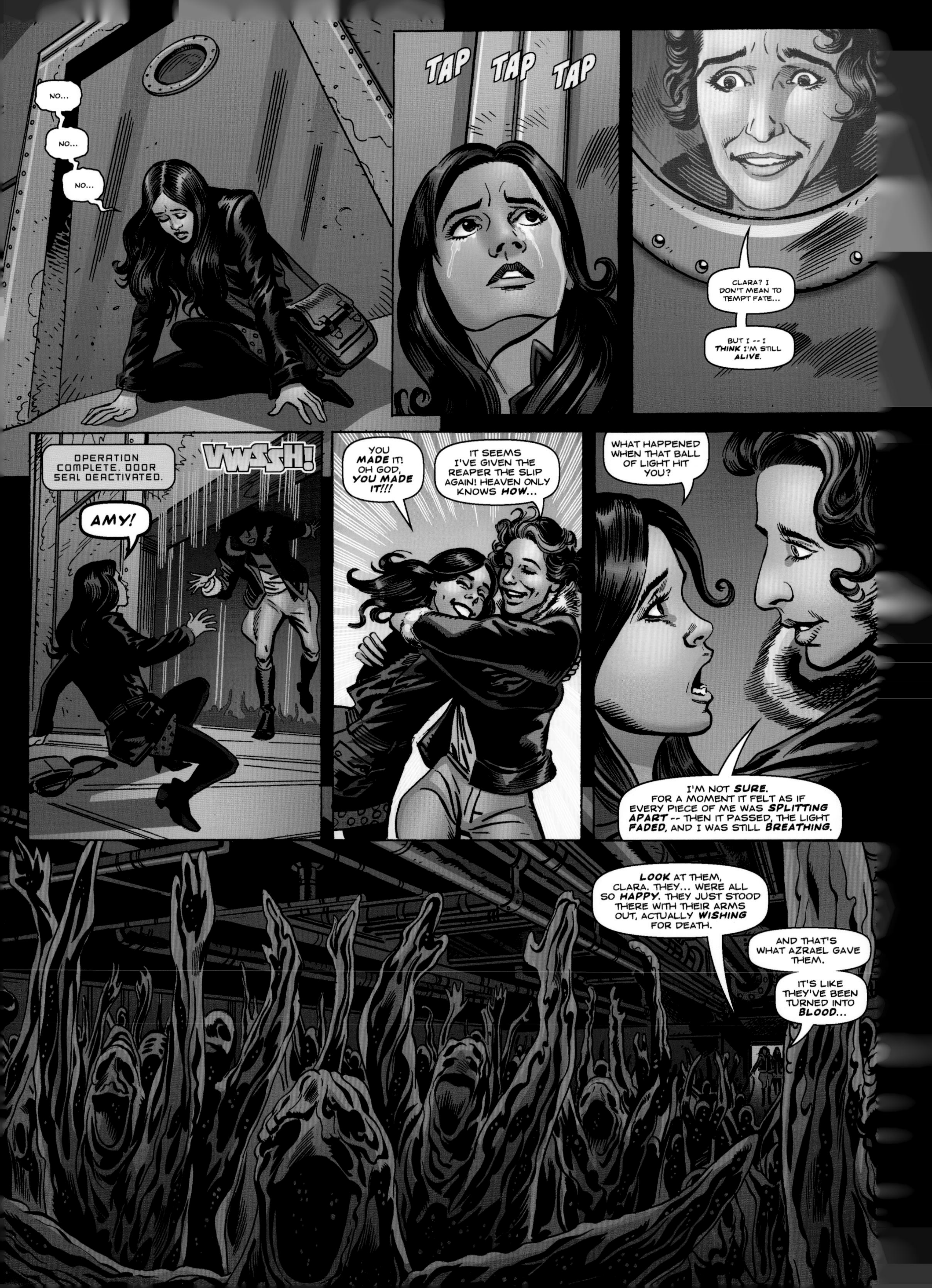
NO...
NO...
NO...
TAP TAP TAP
CLARA? I DON'T MEAN TO TEMPT FATE...
BUT I -- I THINK I'M STILL ALIVE.
OPERATION COMPLETE. DOOR SEAL DEACTIVATED.
VWASH!
AMY!
YOU MADE IT! OH GOD, YOU MADE IT!!!
IT SEEMS I'VE GIVEN THE REAPER THE SLIP AGAIN! HEAVEN ONLY KNOWS HOW...
WHAT HAPPENED WHEN THAT BALL OF LIGHT HIT YOU?
I'M NOT SURE. FOR A MOMENT IT FELT AS IF EVERY PIECE OF ME WAS SPLITTING APART -- THEN IT PASSED, THE LIGHT FADED, AND I WAS STILL BREATHING.
LOOK AT THEM, CLARA. THEY... WERE ALL SO HAPPY. THEY JUST STOOD THERE WITH THEIR ARMS OUT, ACTUALLY WISHING FOR DEATH.
AND THAT'S WHAT AZRAEL GAVE THEM.
IT'S LIKE THEY'VE BEEN TURNED INTO BLOOD...

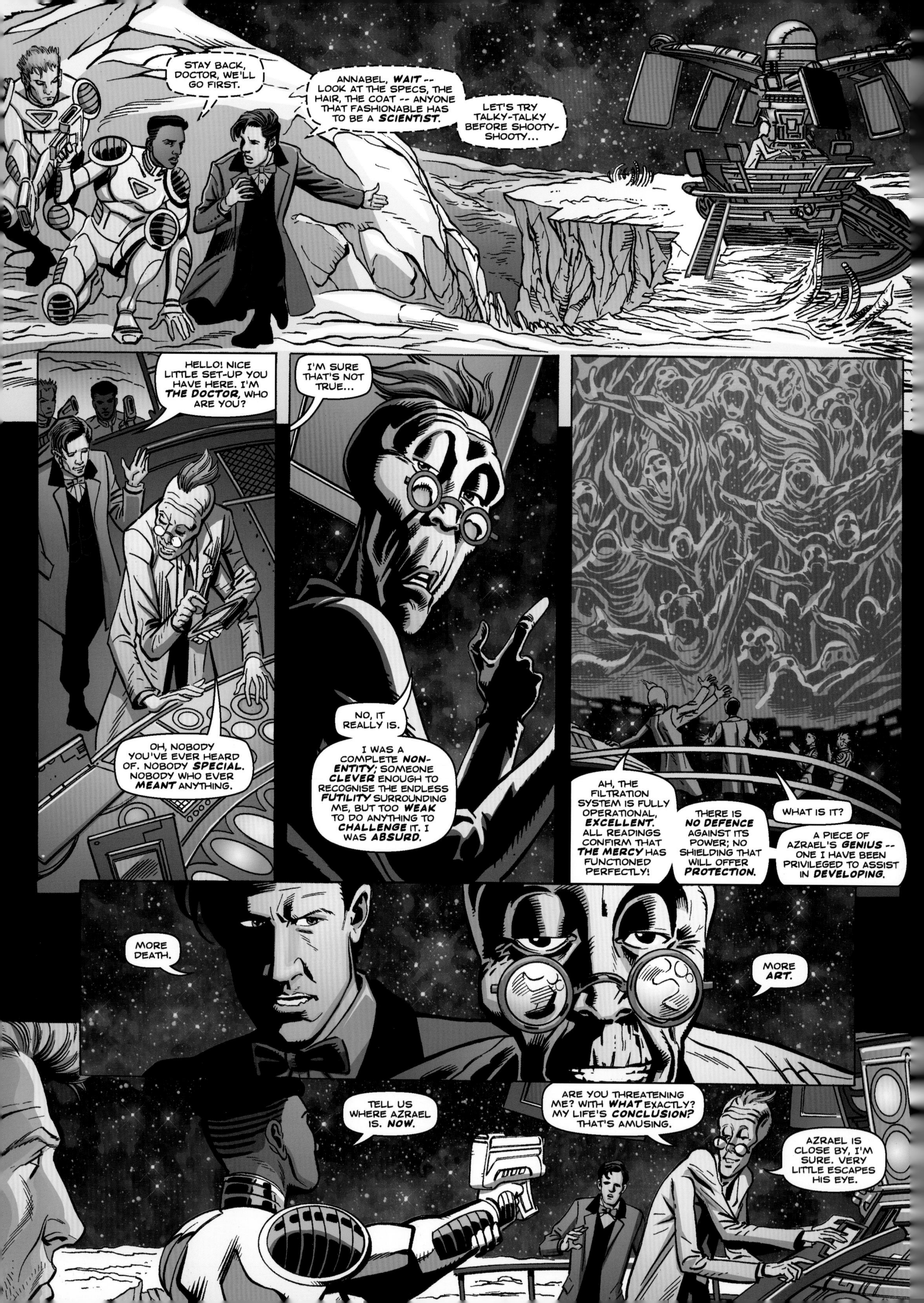
STAY BACK, DOCTOR, WE'LL GO FIRST.
ANNABEL, WAIT -- LOOK AT THE SPECS, THE HAIR, THE COAT -- ANYONE THAT FASHIONABLE HAS TO BE A SCIENTIST.
LET'S TRY TALKY-TALKY BEFORE SHOOTY-SHOOTY...
HELLO! NICE LITTLE SET-UP YOU HAVE HERE. I'M THE DOCTOR, WHO ARE YOU?
OH, NOBODY YOU'VE EVER HEARD OF. NOBODY SPECIAL. NOBODY WHO EVER MEANT ANYTHING.
I'M SURE THAT'S NOT TRUE...
NO, IT REALLY IS.
I WAS A COMPLETE NON-ENTITY; SOMEONE CLEVER ENOUGH TO RECOGNISE THE ENDLESS FUTILITY SURROUNDING ME, BUT TOO WEAK TO DO ANYTHING TO CHALLENGE IT. I WAS ABSURD.
AH, THE FILTRATION SYSTEM IS FULLY OPERATIONAL, EXCELLENT. ALL READINGS CONFIRM THAT THE MERCY HAS FUNCTIONED PERFECTLY!
THERE IS NO DEFENCE AGAINST ITS POWER; NO SHIELDING THAT WILL OFFER PROTECTION.
WHAT IS IT?
A PIECE OF AZRAEL'S GENIUS -- ONE I HAVE BEEN PRIVILEGED TO ASSIST IN DEVELOPING.
MORE DEATH.
MORE ART.
TELL US WHERE AZRAEL IS. NOW.
ARE YOU THREATENING ME? WITH WHAT EXACTLY? MY LIFE'S CONCLUSION? THAT'S AMUSING.
AZRAEL IS CLOSE BY, I'M SURE. VERY LITTLE ESCAPES HIS EYE.

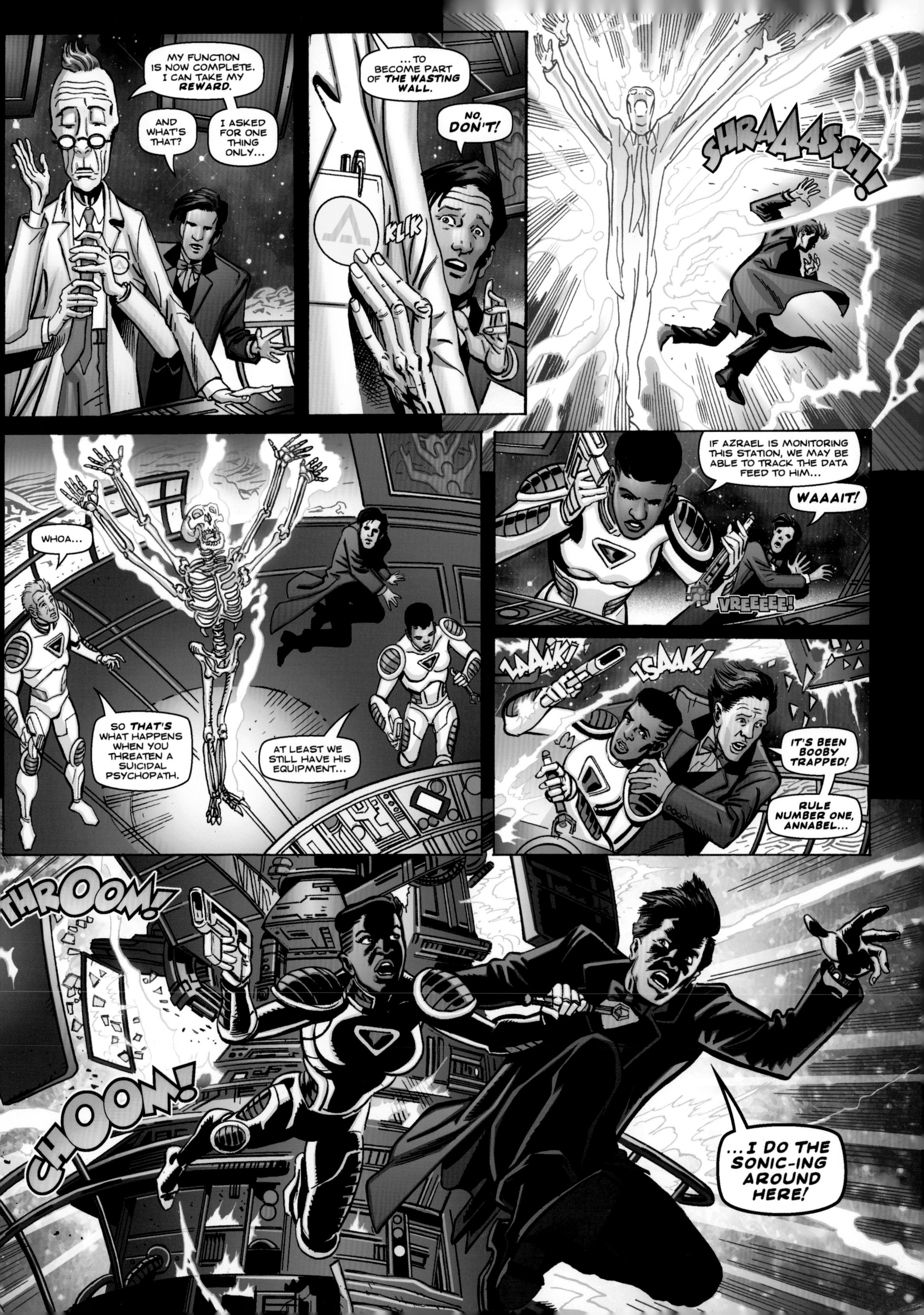

MY FUNCTION IS NOW COMPLETE. I CAN TAKE MY REWARD.
AND WHAT'S THAT?
I ASKED FOR ONE THING ONLY...
...TO BECOME PART OF THE WASTING WALL.
NO, DON'T!
KLIK
SHRAAASSH!
WHOA...
SO THAT'S WHAT HAPPENS WHEN YOU THREATEN A SUICIDAL PSYCHOPATH.
AT LEAST WE STILL HAVE HIS EQUIPMENT...
IF AZRAEL IS MONITORING THIS STATION, WE MAY BE ABLE TO TRACK THE DATA FEED TO HIM...
WAAAIT!
VREEEEE!
ZAAAK!
ZSAAK!
IT'S BEEN BOOBY TRAPPED!
RULE NUMBER ONE, ANNABEL...
THROOM!
CHOOM!
...I DO THE SONIC-ING AROUND HERE!

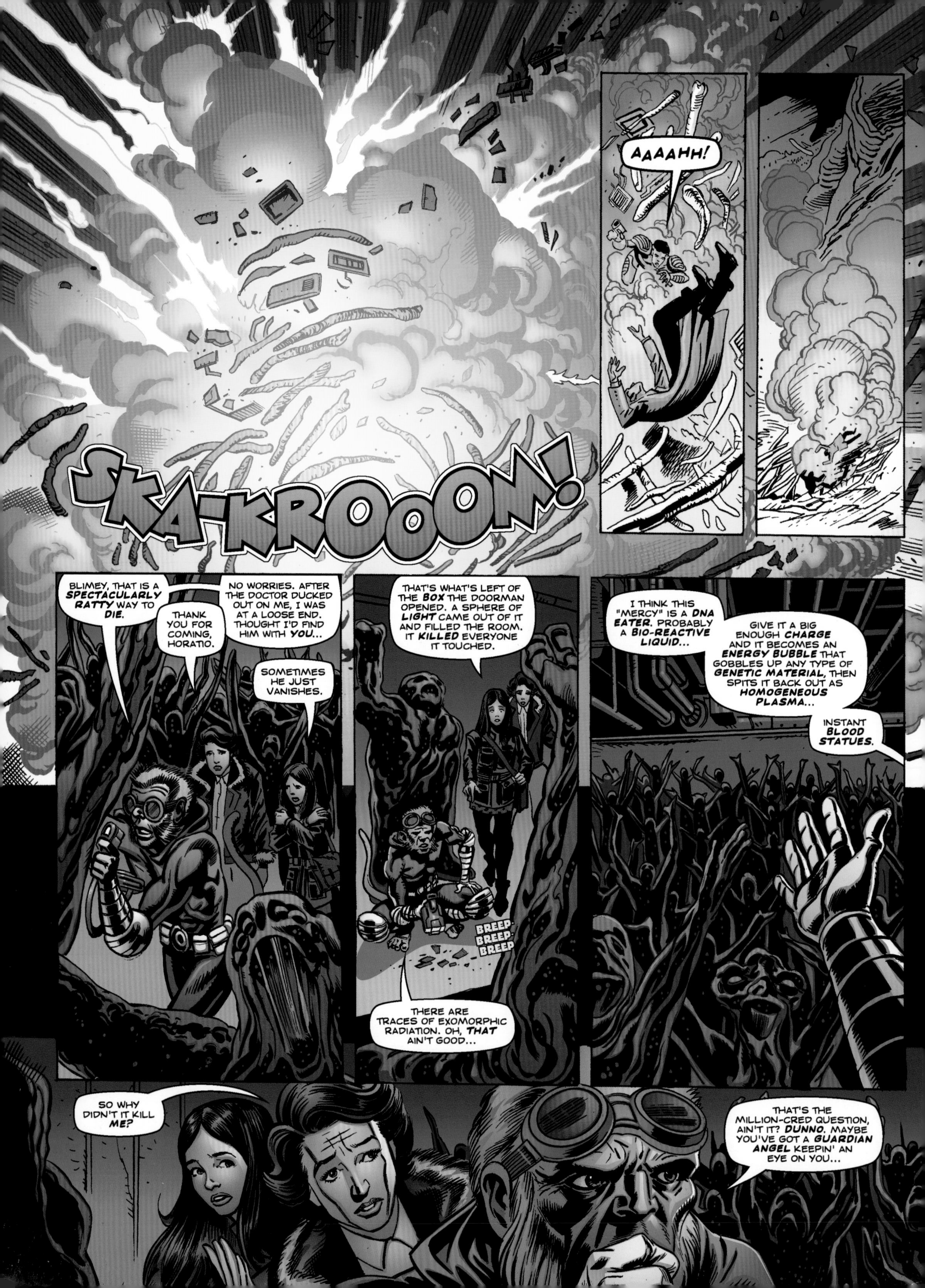
AAAAHH!
SKA-KROOOOM!
BLIMEY, THAT IS A SPECTACULARLY RATTY WAY TO DIE.
THANK YOU FOR COMING, HORATIO.
NO WORRIES. AFTER THE DOCTOR DUCKED OUT ON ME, I WAS AT A LOOSE END. THOUGHT I'D FIND HIM WITH YOU...
SOMETIMES HE JUST VANISHES.
THAT'S WHAT'S LEFT OF THE BOX THE DOORMAN OPENED. A SPHERE OF LIGHT CAME OUT OF IT AND FILLED THE ROOM. IT KILLED EVERYONE IT TOUCHED.
BREEP-BREEP-BREEP
THERE ARE TRACES OF EXOMORPHIC RADIATION. OH, THAT AIN'T GOOD...
I THINK THIS "MERCY" IS A DNA EATER. PROBABLY A BIO-REACTIVE LIQUID...
GIVE IT A BIG ENOUGH CHARGE AND IT BECOMES AN ENERGY BUBBLE THAT GOBBLES UP ANY TYPE OF GENETIC MATERIAL, THEN SPITS IT BACK OUT AS HOMOGENEOUS PLASMA...
INSTANT BLOOD STATUES.
SO WHY DIDN'T IT KILL ME?
THAT'S THE MILLION-CRED QUESTION, AIN'T IT? DUNNO. MAYBE YOU'VE GOT A GUARDIAN ANGEL KEEPIN' AN EYE ON YOU...

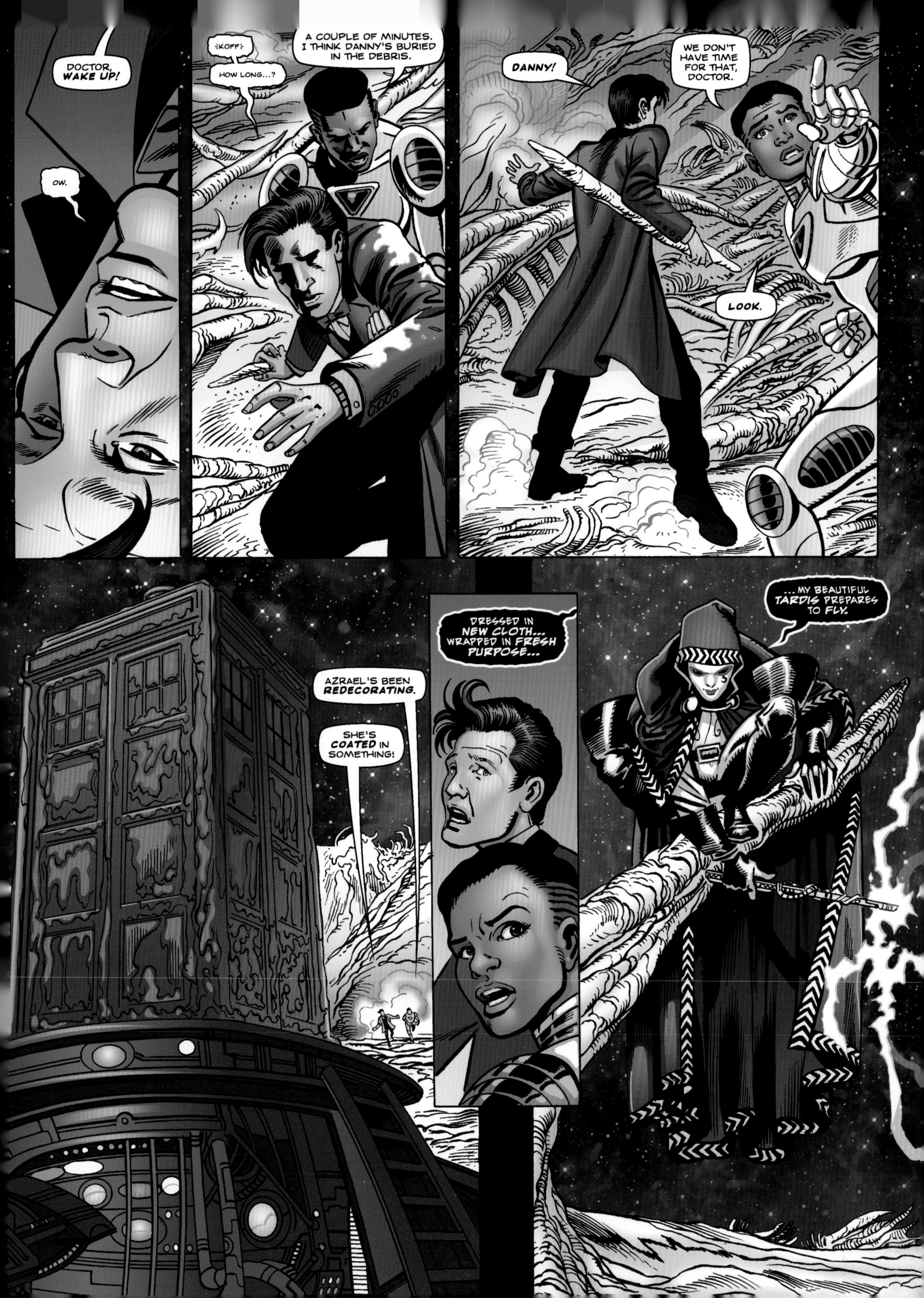

DOCTOR, WAKE UP!
OW.
KOFF
HOW LONG...?
A COUPLE OF MINUTES. I THINK DANNY'S BURIED IN THE DEBRIS.
DANNY!
WE DON'T HAVE TIME FOR THAT, DOCTOR.
LOOK.
AZRAEL'S BEEN REDECORATING.
SHE'S COATED IN SOMETHING!
DRESSED IN NEW CLOTH... WRAPPED IN FRESH PURPOSE...
...MY BEAUTIFUL TARDIS PREPARES TO FLY.

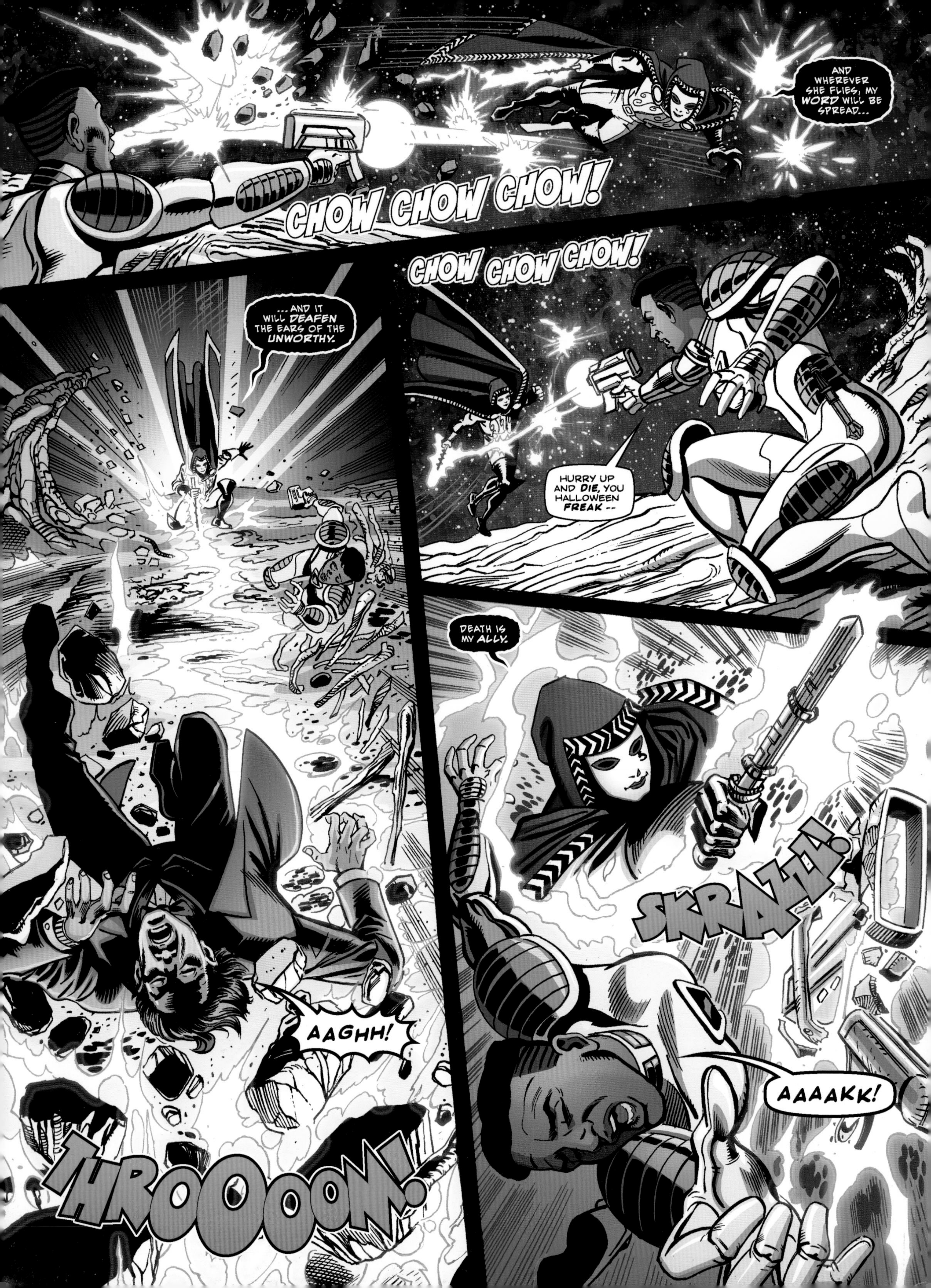

AND WHEREVER SHE FLIES, MY WORD WILL BE SPREAD...
CHOW CHOW CHOW!
...AND IT WILL DEAFEN THE EARS OF THE UNWORTHY.
CHOW CHOW CHOW!
HURRY UP AND DIE, YOU HALLOWEEN FREAK --
AAGHH!
THROOOOOM!
DEATH IS MY ALLY.
SKRAZZZ!
AAAAKK!

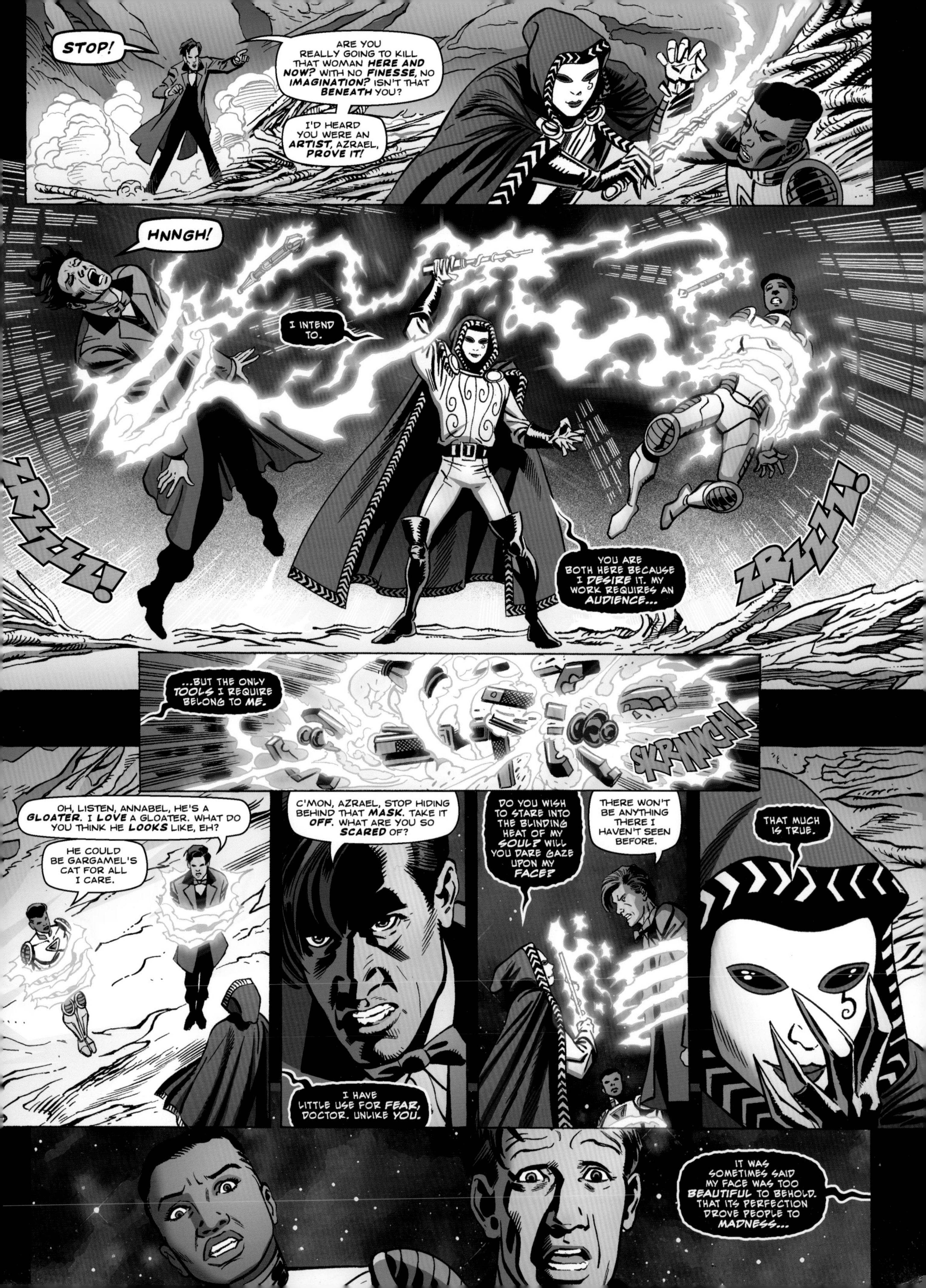
STOP!
ARE YOU REALLY GOING TO KILL THAT WOMAN HERE AND NOW? WITH NO FINESSE, NO IMAGINATION? ISN'T THAT BENEATH YOU?
I'D HEARD YOU WERE AN ARTIST, AZRAEL. PROVE IT!
HNNGH!
I INTEND TO.
ZRZZZZT!
YOU ARE BOTH HERE BECAUSE I DESIRE IT. MY WORK REQUIRES AN AUDIENCE...
ZRZZZT!
...BUT THE ONLY TOOLS I REQUIRE BELONG TO ME.
SKRANCH!
OH, LISTEN, ANNABEL, HE'S A GLOATER. I LOVE A GLOATER. WHAT DO YOU THINK HE LOOKS LIKE, EH?
HE COULD BE GARGAMEL'S CAT FOR ALL I CARE.
C'MON, AZRAEL, STOP HIDING BEHIND THAT MASK. TAKE IT OFF. WHAT ARE YOU SO SCARED OF?
I HAVE LITTLE USE FOR FEAR, DOCTOR. UNLIKE YOU.
DO YOU WISH TO STARE INTO THE BLINDING HEAT OF MY SOUL? WILL YOU DARE GAZE UPON MY FACE?
THERE WON'T BE ANYTHING THERE I HAVEN'T SEEN BEFORE.
THAT MUCH IS TRUE.
IT WAS SOMETIMES SAID MY FACE WAS TOO BEAUTIFUL TO BEHOLD. THAT ITS PERFECTION DROVE PEOPLE TO MADNESS...

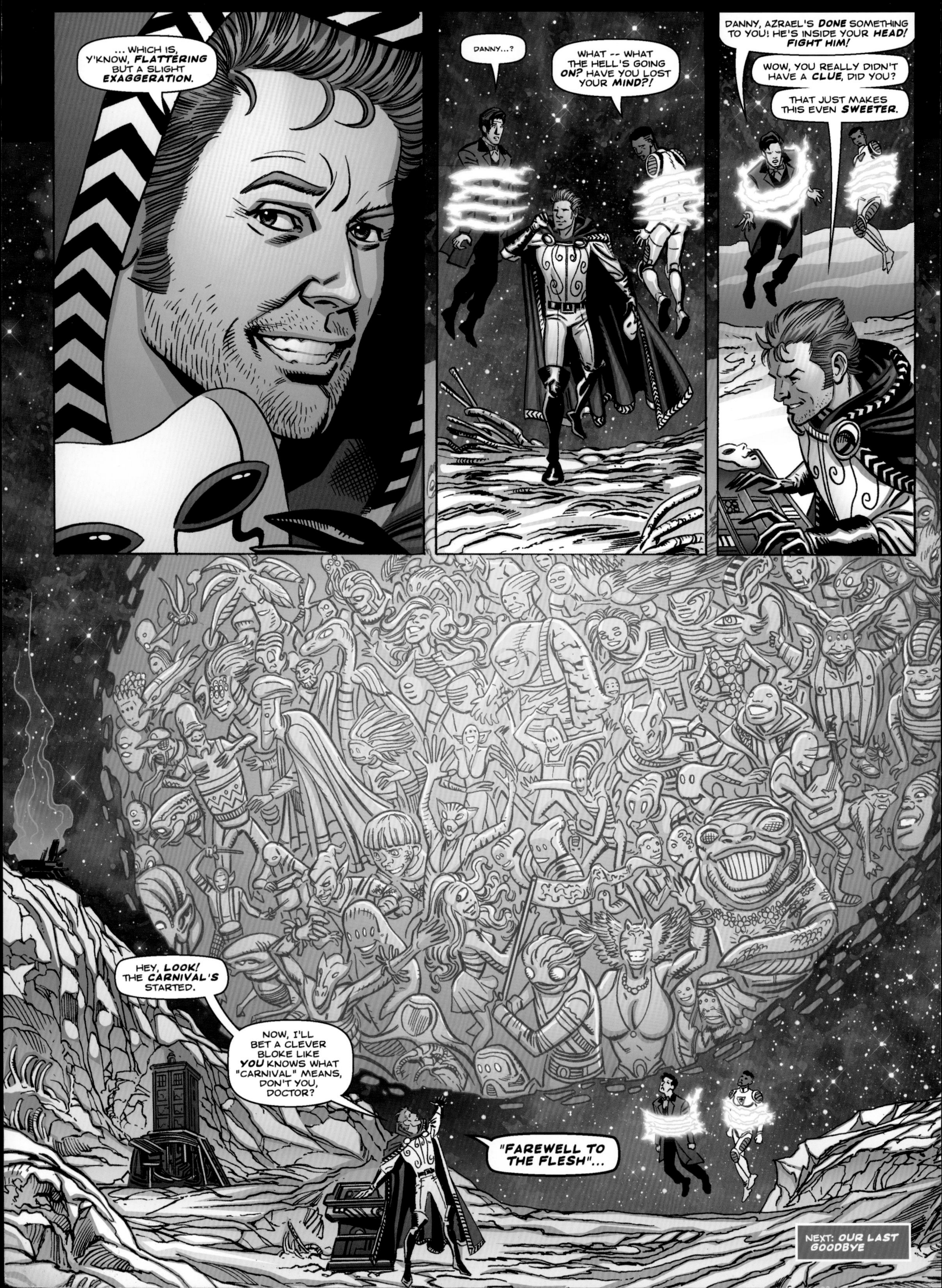

... WHICH IS, Y'KNOW, FLATTERING BUT A SLIGHT EXAGGERATION.
DANNY...?
WHAT -- WHAT THE HELL'S GOING ON? HAVE YOU LOST YOUR MIND?!
DANNY, AZRAEL'S DONE SOMETHING TO YOU! HE'S INSIDE YOUR HEAD! FIGHT HIM!
WOW, YOU REALLY DIDN'T HAVE A CLUE, DID YOU?
THAT JUST MAKES THIS EVEN SWEETER.
HEY, LOOK! THE CARNIVAL'S STARTED.
NOW, I'LL BET A CLEVER BLOKE LIKE YOU KNOWS WHAT "CARNIVAL" MEANS, DON'T YOU, DOCTOR?
"FAREWELL TO THE FLESH"...
NEXT: OUR LAST GOODBYE

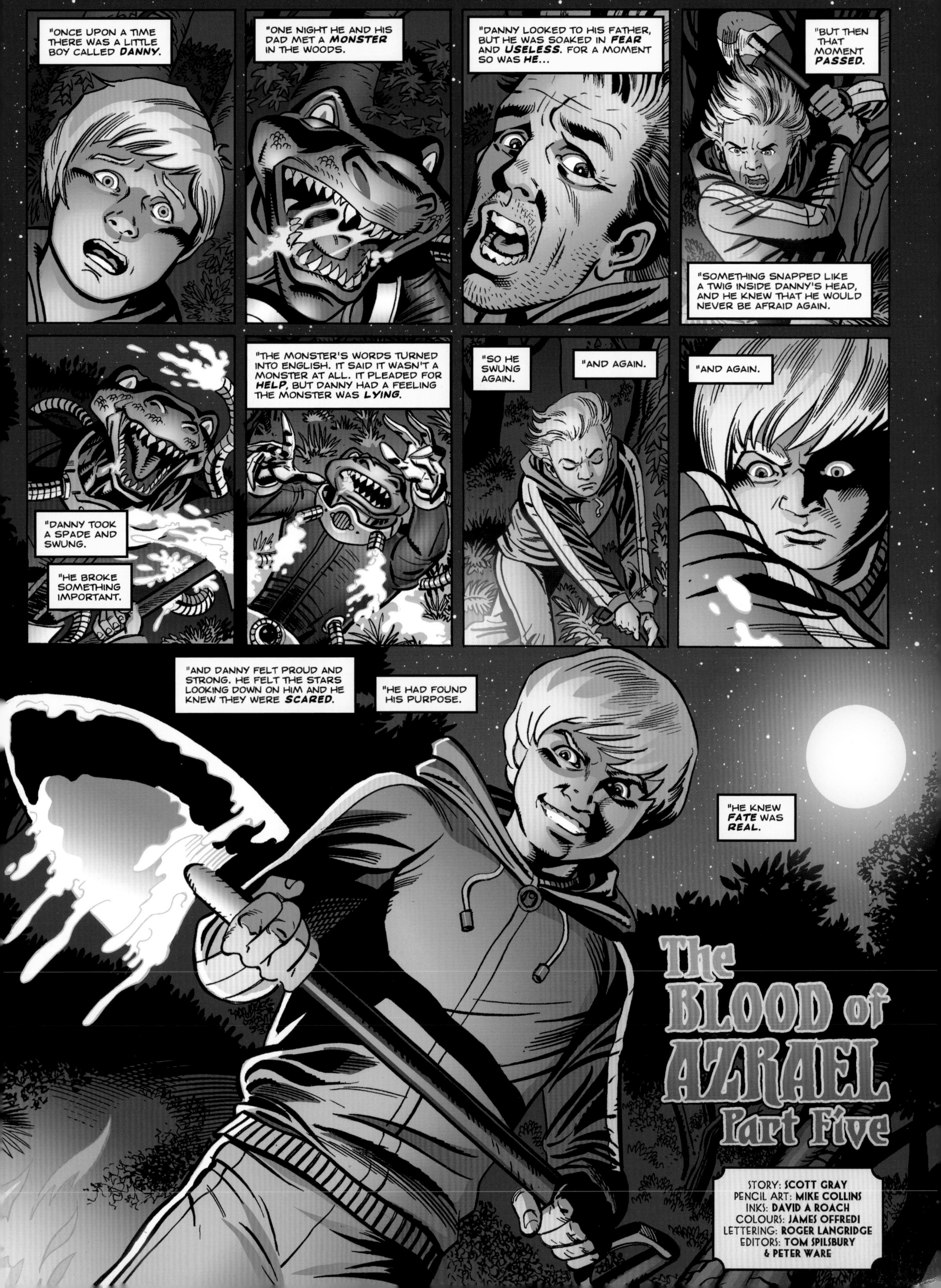
"ONCE UPON A TIME THERE WAS A LITTLE BOY CALLED DANNY.
"ONE NIGHT HE AND HIS DAD MET A MONSTER IN THE WOODS.
"DANNY LOOKED TO HIS FATHER, BUT HE WAS SOAKED IN FEAR AND USELESS. FOR A MOMENT SO WAS HE...
"BUT THEN THAT MOMENT PASSED.
"SOMETHING SNAPPED LIKE A TWIG INSIDE DANNY'S HEAD, AND HE KNEW THAT HE WOULD NEVER BE AFRAID AGAIN.
"DANNY TOOK A SPADE AND SWUNG.
"HE BROKE SOMETHING IMPORTANT.
"THE MONSTER'S WORDS TURNED INTO ENGLISH. IT SAID IT WASN'T A MONSTER AT ALL. IT PLEADED FOR HELP, BUT DANNY HAD A FEELING THE MONSTER WAS LYING.
"SO HE SWUNG AGAIN.
"AND AGAIN.
"AND AGAIN.
"AND DANNY FELT PROUD AND STRONG. HE FELT THE STARS LOOKING DOWN ON HIM AND HE KNEW THEY WERE SCARED.
"HE HAD FOUND HIS PURPOSE.
"HE KNEW FATE WAS REAL.
The BLOOD of AZRAEL Part Five
STORY: SCOTT GRAY
PENCIL ART: MIKE COLLINS
INKS: DAVID A ROACH
COLOURS: JAMES OFFREDI
LETTERING: ROGER LANGRIDGE
EDITORS: TOM SPILSBURY & PETER WARE

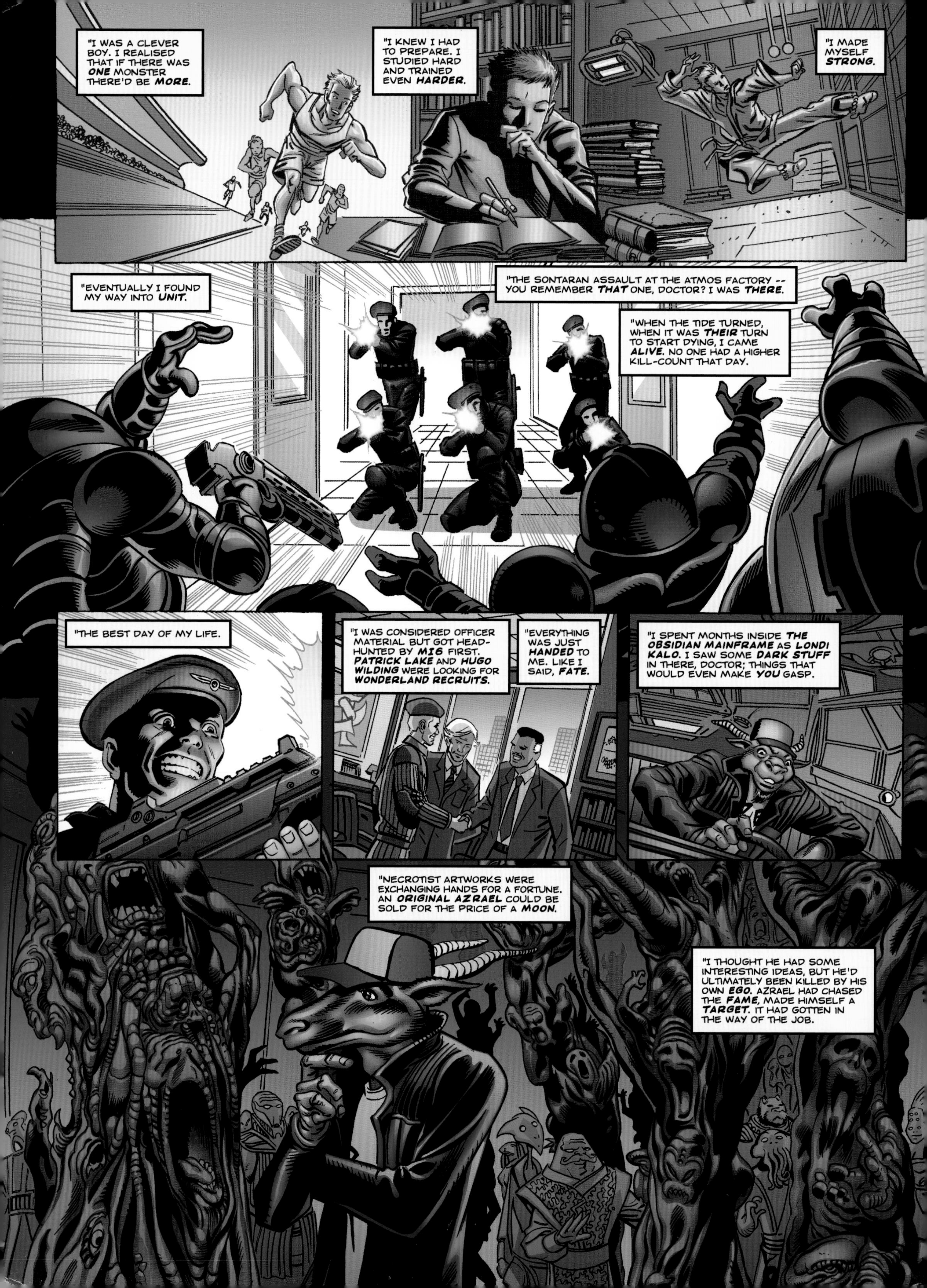
"I WAS A CLEVER BOY. I REALISED THAT IF THERE WAS ONE MONSTER THERE'D BE MORE.
"I KNEW I HAD TO PREPARE. I STUDIED HARD AND TRAINED EVEN HARDER.
"I MADE MYSELF STRONG.
"EVENTUALLY I FOUND MY WAY INTO UNIT.
"THE SONTARAN ASSAULT AT THE ATMOS FACTORY -- YOU REMEMBER THAT ONE, DOCTOR? I WAS THERE.
"WHEN THE TIDE TURNED, WHEN IT WAS THEIR TURN TO START DYING, I CAME ALIVE. NO ONE HAD A HIGHER KILL-COUNT THAT DAY.
"THE BEST DAY OF MY LIFE.
"I WAS CONSIDERED OFFICER MATERIAL BUT GOT HEAD-HUNTED BY MI6 FIRST. PATRICK LAKE AND HUGO WILDING WERE LOOKING FOR WONDERLAND RECRUITS.
"EVERYTHING WAS JUST HANDED TO ME. LIKE I SAID, FATE.
"I SPENT MONTHS INSIDE THE OBSIDIAN MAINFRAME AS LONDI KALO. I SAW SOME DARK STUFF IN THERE, DOCTOR; THINGS THAT WOULD EVEN MAKE YOU GASP.
"NECROTIST ARTWORKS WERE EXCHANGING HANDS FOR A FORTUNE. AN ORIGINAL AZRAEL COULD BE SOLD FOR THE PRICE OF A MOON.
"I THOUGHT HE HAD SOME INTERESTING IDEAS, BUT HE'D ULTIMATELY BEEN KILLED BY HIS OWN EGO. AZRAEL HAD CHASED THE FAME, MADE HIMSELF A TARGET. IT HAD GOTTEN IN THE WAY OF THE JOB.

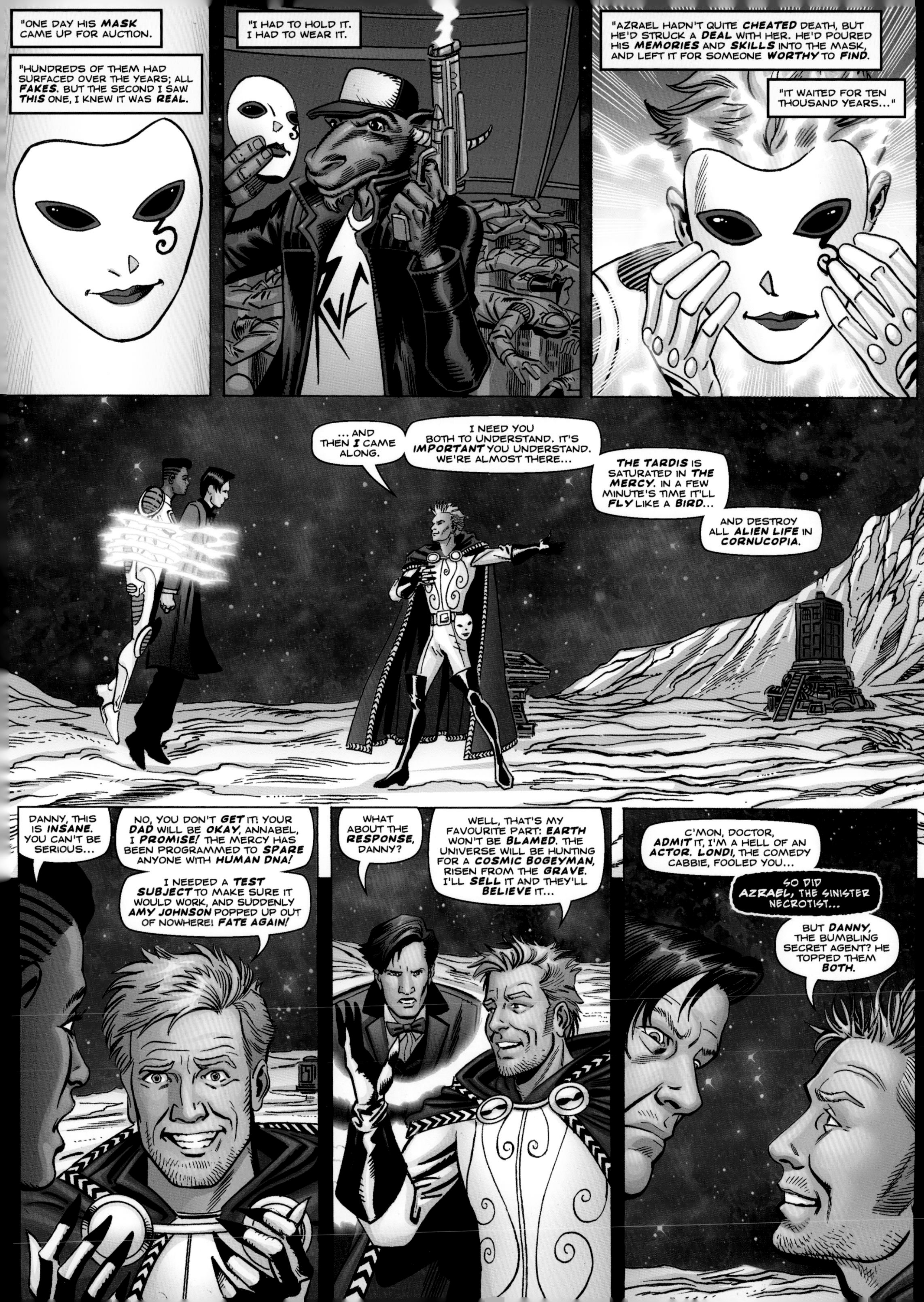
"ONE DAY HIS MASK CAME UP FOR AUCTION.
"HUNDREDS OF THEM HAD SURFACED OVER THE YEARS; ALL FAKES. BUT THE SECOND I SAW THIS ONE, I KNEW IT WAS REAL.
"I HAD TO HOLD IT. I HAD TO WEAR IT.
"AZRAEL HADN'T QUITE CHEATED DEATH, BUT HE'D STRUCK A DEAL WITH HER. HE'D POURED HIS MEMORIES AND SKILLS INTO THE MASK, AND LEFT IT FOR SOMEONE WORTHY TO FIND.
"IT WAITED FOR TEN THOUSAND YEARS..."
...AND THEN I CAME ALONG.
I NEED YOU BOTH TO UNDERSTAND. IT'S IMPORTANT YOU UNDERSTAND. WE'RE ALMOST THERE...
THE TARDIS IS SATURATED IN THE MERCY. IN A FEW MINUTE'S TIME IT'LL FLY LIKE A BIRD...
AND DESTROY ALL ALIEN LIFE IN CORNUCOPIA.
DANNY, THIS IS INSANE. YOU CAN'T BE SERIOUS...
NO, YOU DON'T GET IT! YOUR DAD WILL BE OKAY, ANNABEL, I PROMISE! THE MERCY HAS BEEN PROGRAMMED TO SPARE ANYONE WITH HUMAN DNA!
I NEEDED A TEST SUBJECT TO MAKE SURE IT WOULD WORK, AND SUDDENLY AMY JOHNSON POPPED UP OUT OF NOWHERE! FATE AGAIN!
WHAT ABOUT THE RESPONSE, DANNY?
WELL, THAT'S MY FAVOURITE PART: EARTH WON'T BE BLAMED. THE UNIVERSE WILL BE HUNTING FOR A COSMIC BOGEYMAN, RISEN FROM THE GRAVE. I'LL SELL IT AND THEY'LL BELIEVE IT...
C'MON, DOCTOR, ADMIT IT, I'M A HELL OF AN ACTOR. LONDI, THE COMEDY CABBIE, FOOLED YOU...
SO DID AZRAEL, THE SINISTER NECROTIST...
BUT DANNY, THE BUMBLING SECRET AGENT? HE TOPPED THEM BOTH.

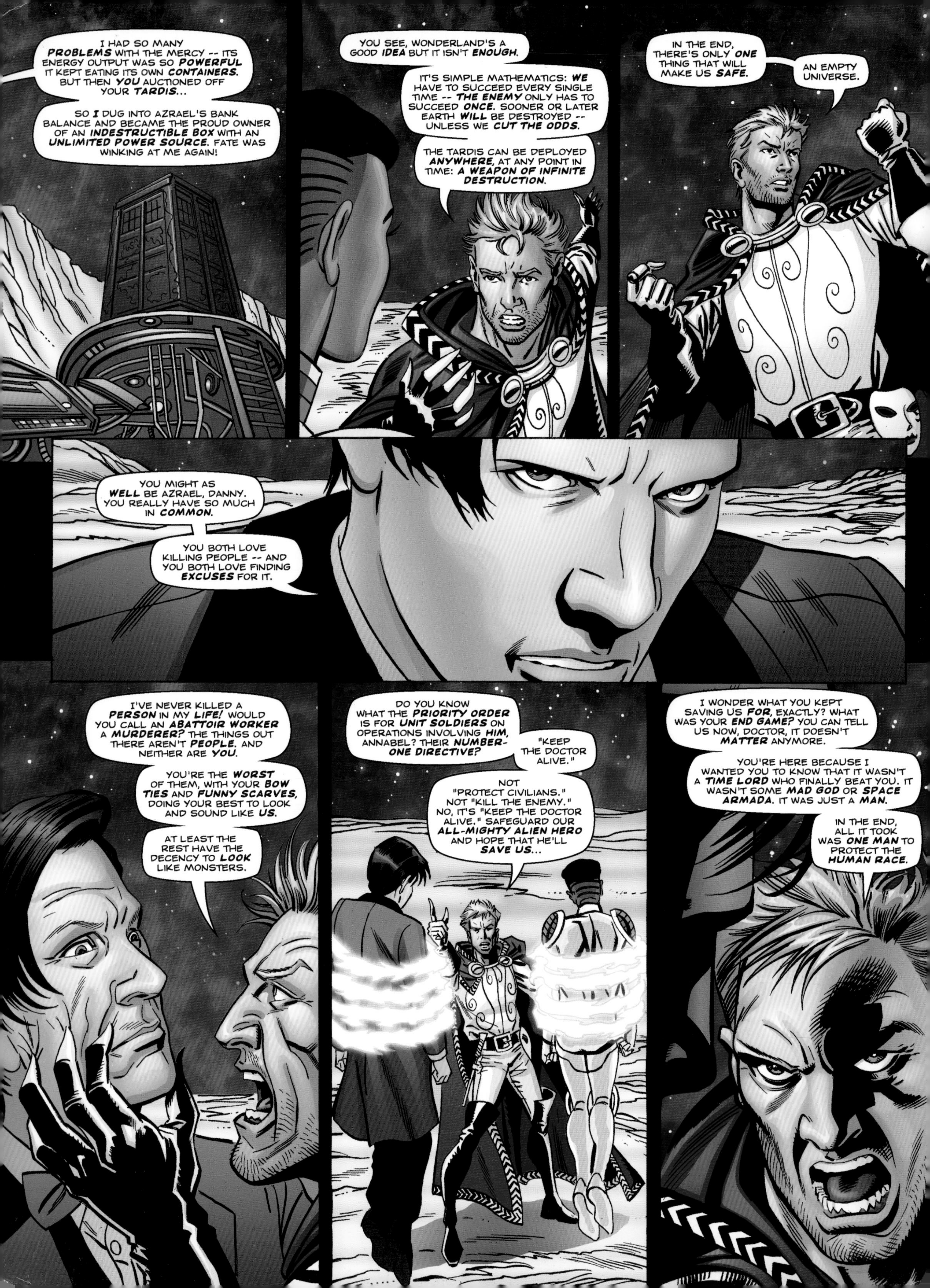
I HAD SO MANY PROBLEMS WITH THE MERCY -- ITS ENERGY OUTPUT WAS SO POWERFUL IT KEPT EATING ITS OWN CONTAINERS. BUT THEN YOU AUCTIONED OFF YOUR TARDIS...
SO I DUG INTO AZRAEL'S BANK BALANCE AND BECAME THE PROUD OWNER OF AN INDESTRUCTIBLE BOX WITH AN UNLIMITED POWER SOURCE. FATE WAS WINKING AT ME AGAIN!
YOU SEE, WONDERLAND'S A GOOD IDEA BUT IT ISN'T ENOUGH.
IT'S SIMPLE MATHEMATICS: WE HAVE TO SUCCEED EVERY SINGLE TIME -- THE ENEMY ONLY HAS TO SUCCEED ONCE. SOONER OR LATER EARTH WILL BE DESTROYED -- UNLESS WE CUT THE ODDS.
THE TARDIS CAN BE DEPLOYED ANYWHERE, AT ANY POINT IN TIME: A WEAPON OF INFINITE DESTRUCTION.
IN THE END, THERE'S ONLY ONE THING THAT WILL MAKE US SAFE.
AN EMPTY UNIVERSE.
YOU MIGHT AS WELL BE AZRAEL, DANNY. YOU REALLY HAVE SO MUCH IN COMMON.
YOU BOTH LOVE KILLING PEOPLE -- AND YOU BOTH LOVE FINDING EXCUSES FOR IT.
I'VE NEVER KILLED A PERSON IN MY LIFE! WOULD YOU CALL AN ABATTOIR WORKER A MURDERER? THE THINGS OUT THERE AREN'T PEOPLE. AND NEITHER ARE YOU.
YOU'RE THE WORST OF THEM, WITH YOUR BOW TIES AND FUNNY SCARVES, DOING YOUR BEST TO LOOK AND SOUND LIKE US.
AT LEAST THE REST HAVE THE DECENCY TO LOOK LIKE MONSTERS.
DO YOU KNOW WHAT THE PRIORITY ORDER IS FOR UNIT SOLDIERS ON OPERATIONS INVOLVING HIM, ANNABEL? THEIR NUMBER-ONE DIRECTIVE?
"KEEP THE DOCTOR ALIVE."
NOT "PROTECT CIVILIANS." NOT "KILL THE ENEMY." NO, IT'S "KEEP THE DOCTOR ALIVE." SAFEGUARD OUR ALL-MIGHTY ALIEN HERO AND HOPE THAT HE'LL SAVE US...
I WONDER WHAT YOU KEPT SAVING US FOR, EXACTLY? WHAT WAS YOUR END GAME? YOU CAN TELL US NOW, DOCTOR, IT DOESN'T MATTER ANYMORE.
YOU'RE HERE BECAUSE I WANTED YOU TO KNOW THAT IT WASN'T A TIME LORD WHO FINALLY BEAT YOU. IT WASN'T SOME MAD GOD OR SPACE ARMADA. IT WAS JUST A MAN.
IN THE END, ALL IT TOOK WAS ONE MAN TO PROTECT THE HUMAN RACE.

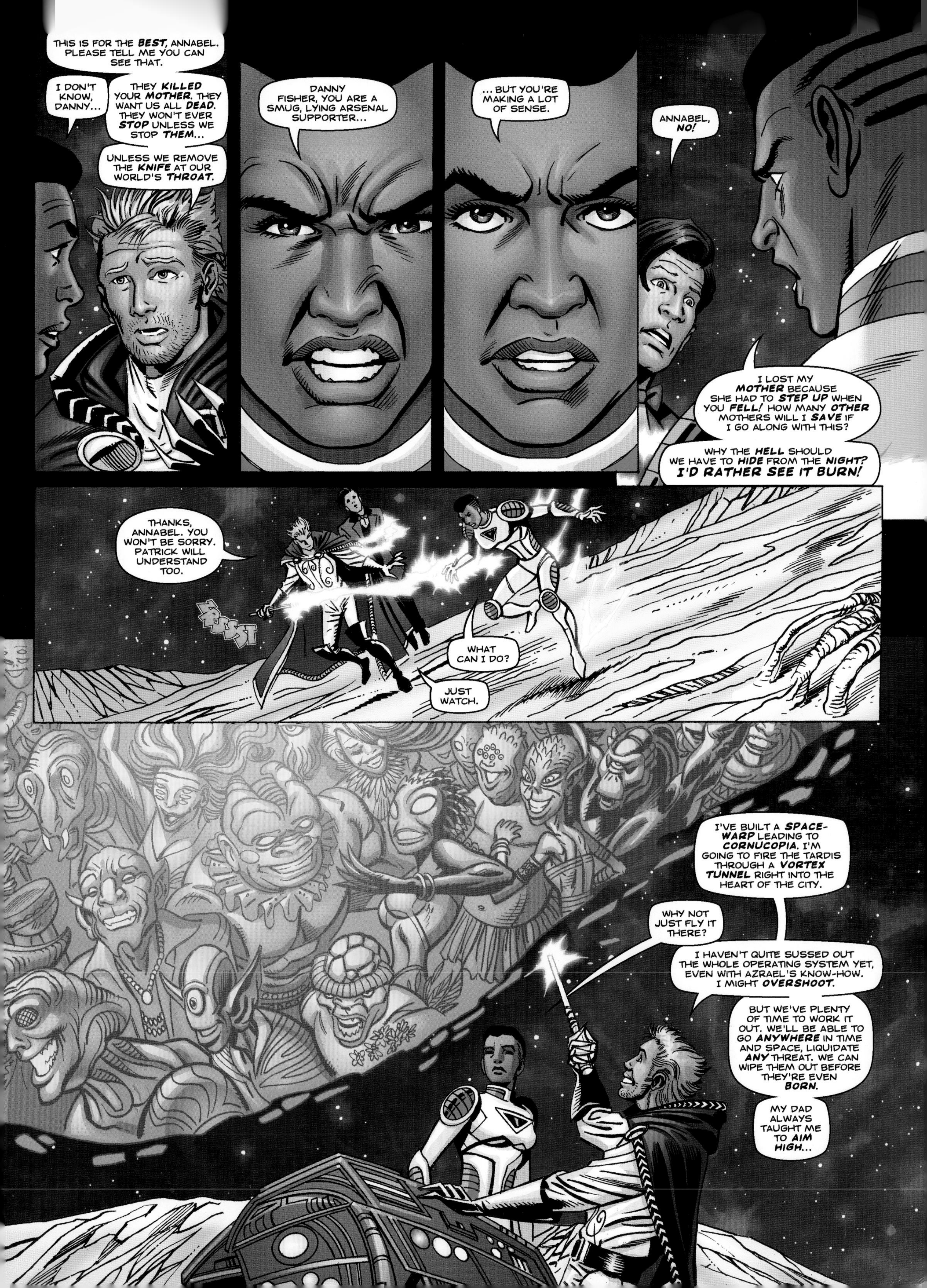
THIS IS FOR THE BEST, ANNABEL. PLEASE TELL ME YOU CAN SEE THAT.
I DON'T KNOW, DANNY...
THEY KILLED YOUR MOTHER. THEY WANT US ALL DEAD. THEY WON'T EVER STOP UNLESS WE STOP THEM...
UNLESS WE REMOVE THE KNIFE AT OUR WORLD'S THROAT.
DANNY FISHER, YOU ARE A SMUG, LYING ARSENAL SUPPORTER...
... BUT YOU'RE MAKING A LOT OF SENSE.
ANNABEL, NO!
I LOST MY MOTHER BECAUSE SHE HAD TO STEP UP WHEN YOU FELL! HOW MANY OTHER MOTHERS WILL I SAVE IF I GO ALONG WITH THIS?
WHY THE HELL SHOULD WE HAVE TO HIDE FROM THE NIGHT? I'D RATHER SEE IT BURN!
THANKS, ANNABEL. YOU WON'T BE SORRY. PATRICK WILL UNDERSTAND TOO.
ZZSST
WHAT CAN I DO?
JUST WATCH.
I'VE BUILT A SPACE-WARP LEADING TO CORNUCOPIA. I'M GOING TO FIRE THE TARDIS THROUGH A VORTEX TUNNEL RIGHT INTO THE HEART OF THE CITY.
WHY NOT JUST FLY IT THERE?
I HAVEN'T QUITE SUSSED OUT THE WHOLE OPERATING SYSTEM YET, EVEN WITH AZRAEL'S KNOW-HOW. I MIGHT OVERSHOOT.
BUT WE'VE PLENTY OF TIME TO WORK IT OUT. WE'LL BE ABLE TO GO ANYWHERE IN TIME AND SPACE, LIQUIDATE ANY THREAT. WE CAN WIPE THEM OUT BEFORE THEY'RE EVEN BORN.
MY DAD ALWAYS TAUGHT ME TO AIM HIGH...

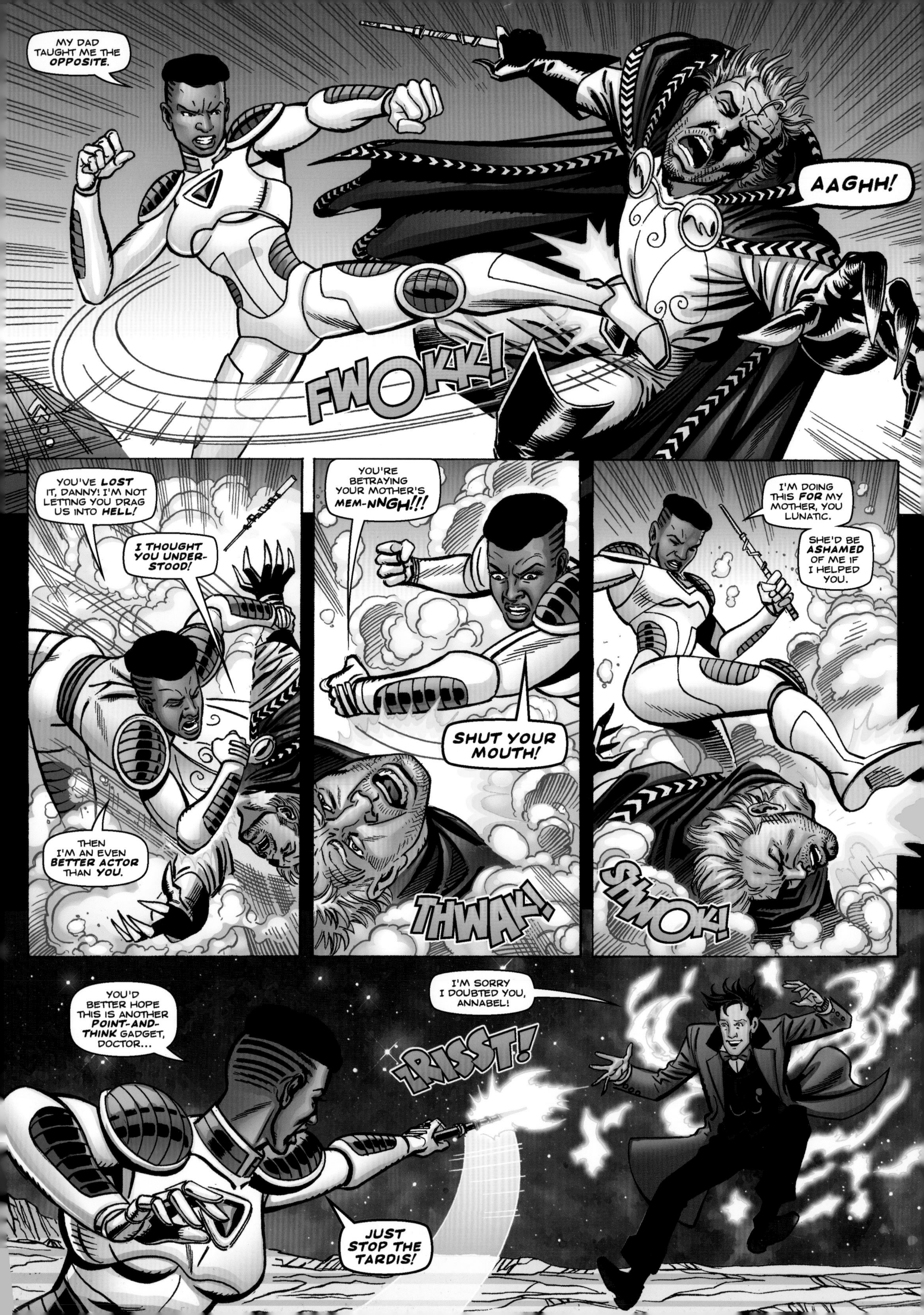
MY DAD TAUGHT ME THE OPPOSITE.
AAGHH!
FWOKK!
YOU'VE LOST IT, DANNY! I'M NOT LETTING YOU DRAG US INTO HELL!
I THOUGHT YOU UNDER-STOOD!
THEN I'M AN EVEN BETTER ACTOR THAN YOU.
YOU'RE BETRAYING YOUR MOTHER'S MEM-NNGH!!!
SHUT YOUR MOUTH!
THWAK!
I'M DOING THIS FOR MY MOTHER, YOU LUNATIC.
SHE'D BE ASHAMED OF ME IF I HELPED YOU.
SHWOK!
YOU'D BETTER HOPE THIS IS ANOTHER POINT-AND-THINK GADGET, DOCTOR...
I'M SORRY I DOUBTED YOU, ANNABEL!
TRISST!
JUST STOP THE TARDIS!

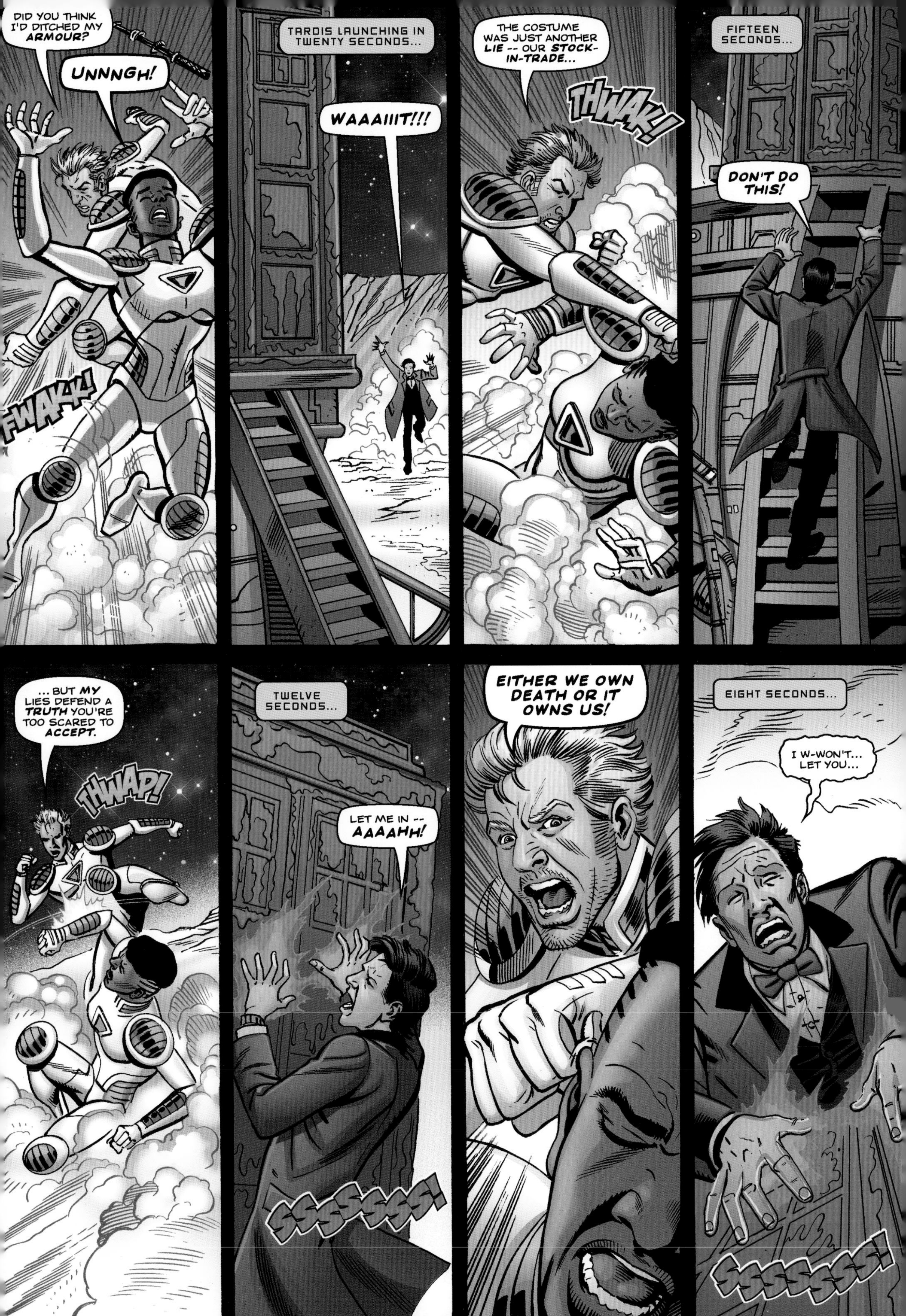
DID YOU THINK I'D DITCHED MY ARMOUR?
UNNNGH!
FWAKK!
TARDIS LAUNCHING IN TWENTY SECONDS...
WAAAIIIT!!!
THE COSTUME WAS JUST ANOTHER LIE -- OUR STOCK-IN-TRADE...
THWAK!
FIFTEEN SECONDS...
DON'T DO THIS!
... BUT MY LIES DEFEND A TRUTH YOU'RE TOO SCARED TO ACCEPT.
THWAP!
TWELVE SECONDS...
LET ME IN -- AAAAHH!
SSSSSSS!
EITHER WE OWN DEATH OR IT OWNS US!
EIGHT SECONDS...
I W-WON'T... LET YOU...
SSSSSSS!

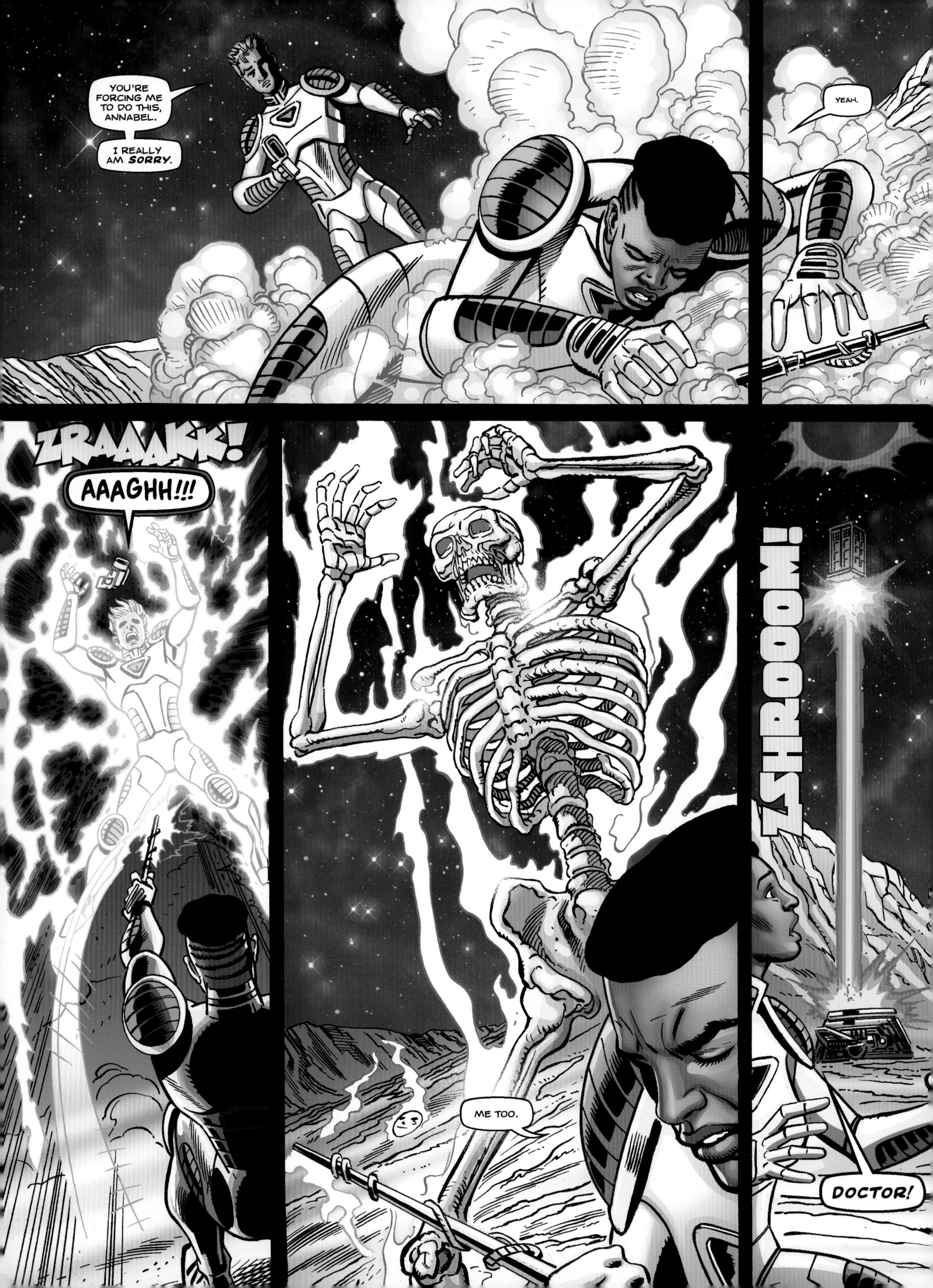
YOU'RE FORCING ME TO DO THIS, ANNABEL.
I REALLY AM SORRY.
YEAH.
ZRAAAAKK!
AAAGHH!!!
ME TOO.
TSHROOOOM!
DOCTOR!

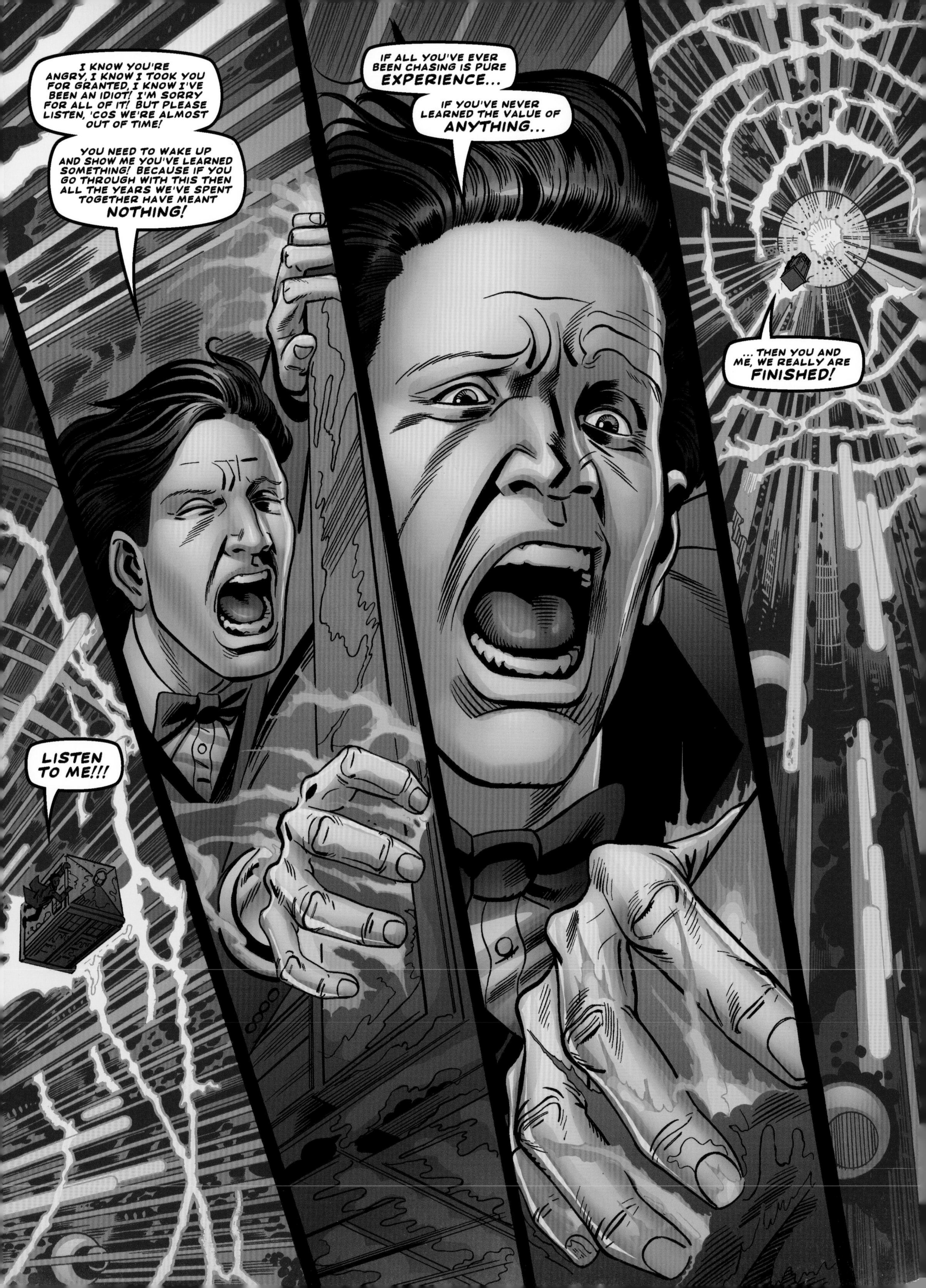
I KNOW YOU'RE ANGRY, I KNOW I TOOK YOU FOR GRANTED, I KNOW I'VE BEEN AN IDIOT! I'M SORRY FOR ALL OF IT! BUT PLEASE LISTEN, 'COS WE'RE ALMOST OUT OF TIME!
YOU NEED TO WAKE UP AND SHOW ME YOU'VE LEARNED SOMETHING! BECAUSE IF YOU GO THROUGH WITH THIS THEN ALL THE YEARS WE'VE SPENT TOGETHER HAVE MEANT NOTHING!
LISTEN TO ME!!!
IF ALL YOU'VE EVER BEEN CHASING IS PURE EXPERIENCE...
IF YOU'VE NEVER LEARNED THE VALUE OF ANYTHING...
... THEN YOU AND ME, WE REALLY ARE FINISHED!

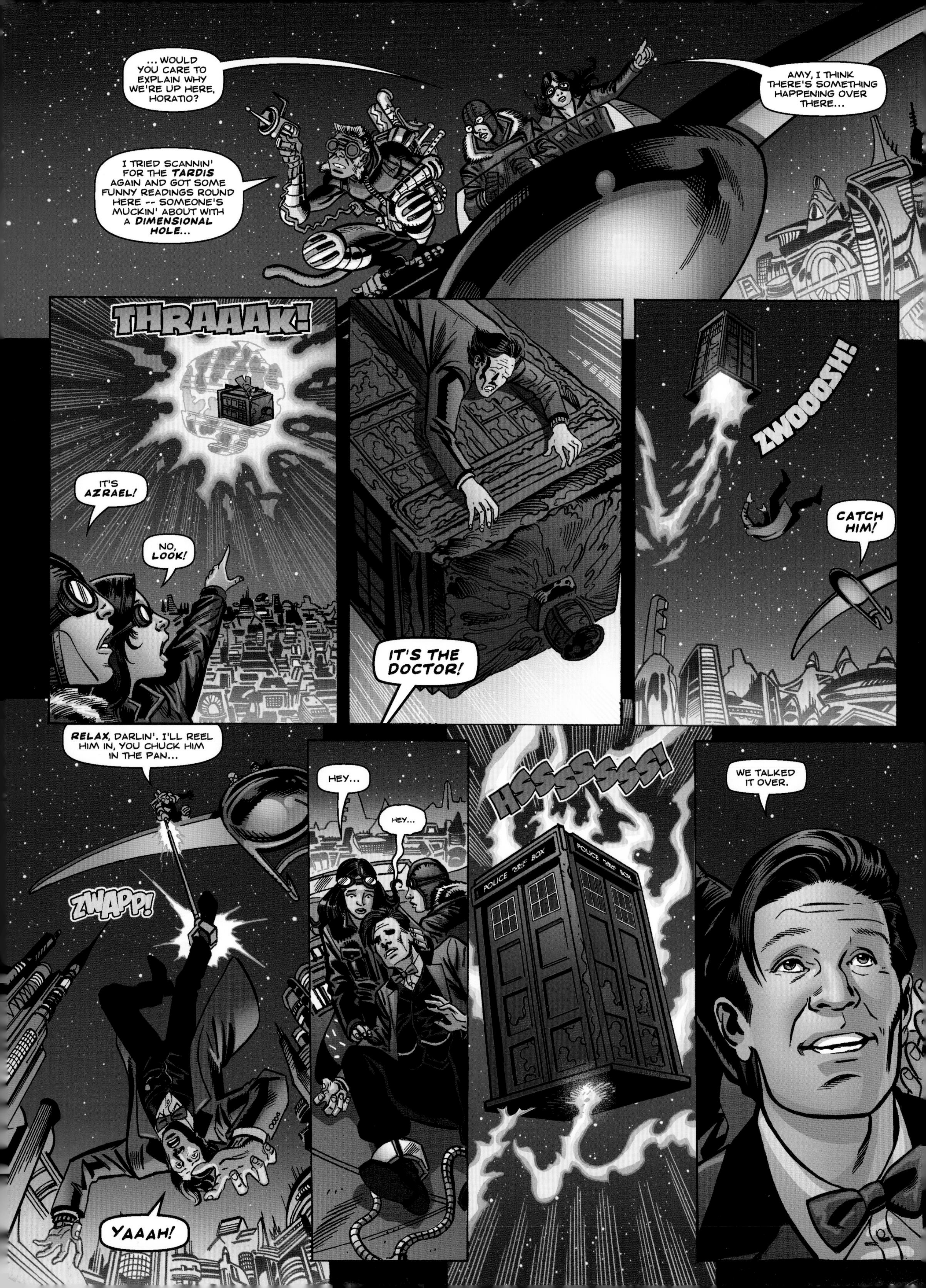

... WOULD YOU CARE TO EXPLAIN WHY WE'RE UP HERE, HORATIO?
I TRIED SCANNIN' FOR THE TARDIS AGAIN AND GOT SOME FUNNY READINGS ROUND HERE -- SOMEONE'S MUCKIN' ABOUT WITH A DIMENSIONAL HOLE...
AMY, I THINK THERE'S SOMETHING HAPPENING OVER THERE...
THRAAAK!
IT'S AZRAEL!
NO, LOOK!
IT'S THE DOCTOR!
ZWOOOSH!
CATCH HIM!
RELAX, DARLIN'. I'LL REEL HIM IN, YOU CHUCK HIM IN THE PAN...
ZWAPP!
YAAAH!
HEY...
HEY...
HSSSSSSS!
POLICE BOX
POLICE BOX
WE TALKED IT OVER.

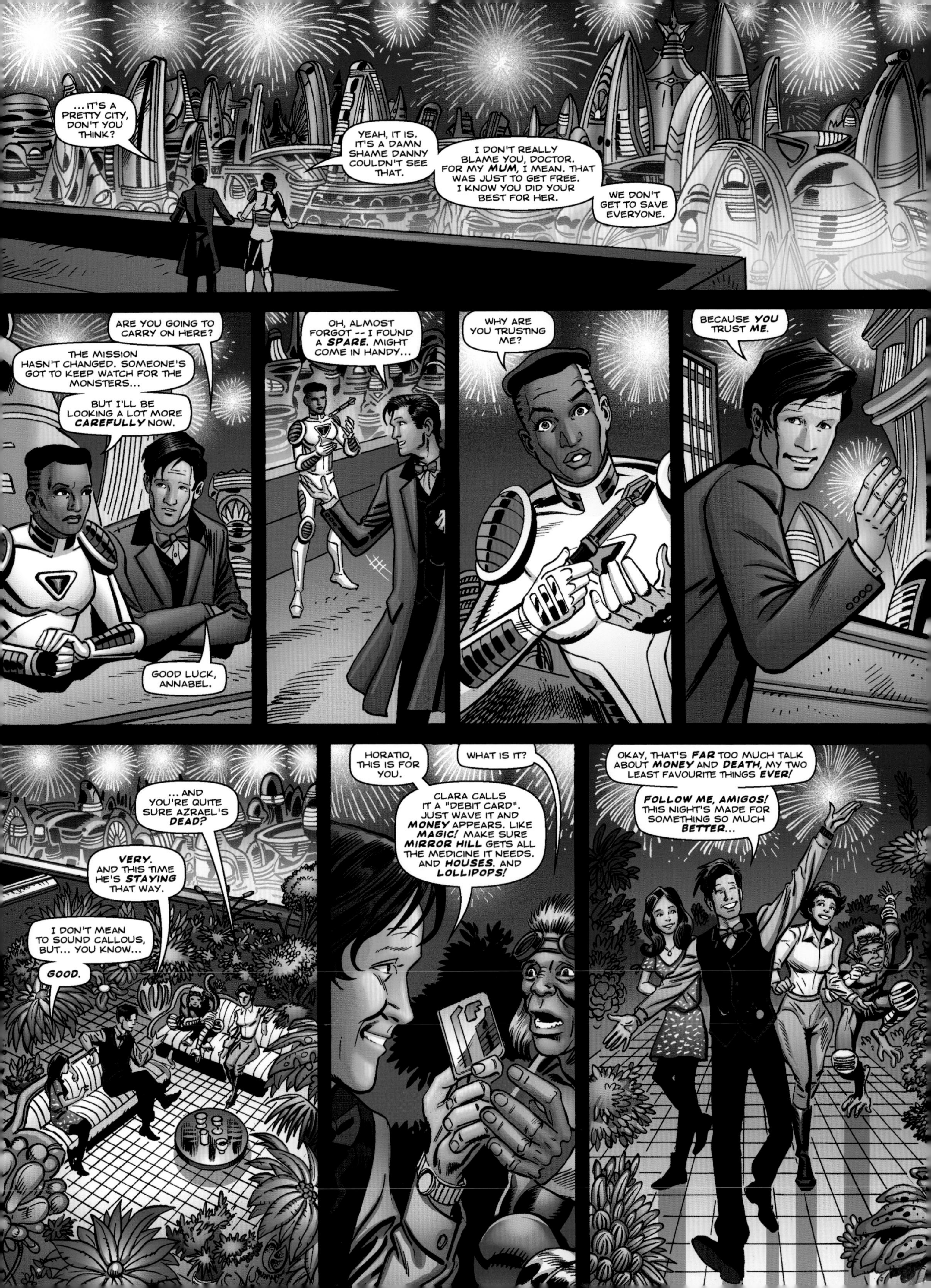
... IT'S A PRETTY CITY, DON'T YOU THINK?
YEAH, IT IS. IT'S A DAMN SHAME DANNY COULDN'T SEE THAT.
I DON'T REALLY BLAME YOU, DOCTOR. FOR MY MUM, I MEAN. THAT WAS JUST TO GET FREE. I KNOW YOU DID YOUR BEST FOR HER.
WE DON'T GET TO SAVE EVERYONE.
ARE YOU GOING TO CARRY ON HERE?
THE MISSION HASN'T CHANGED. SOMEONE'S GOT TO KEEP WATCH FOR THE MONSTERS...
BUT I'LL BE LOOKING A LOT MORE CAREFULLY NOW.
GOOD LUCK, ANNABEL.
OH, ALMOST FORGOT -- I FOUND A SPARE. MIGHT COME IN HANDY...
WHY ARE YOU TRUSTING ME?
BECAUSE YOU TRUST ME.
... AND YOU'RE QUITE SURE AZRAEL'S DEAD?
VERY. AND THIS TIME HE'S STAYING THAT WAY.
I DON'T MEAN TO SOUND CALLOUS, BUT... YOU KNOW...
GOOD.
HORATIO, THIS IS FOR YOU.
WHAT IS IT?
CLARA CALLS IT A "DEBIT CARD". JUST WAVE IT AND MONEY APPEARS. LIKE MAGIC! MAKE SURE MIRROR HILL GETS ALL THE MEDICINE IT NEEDS. AND HOUSES. AND LOLLIPOPS!
OKAY, THAT'S FAR TOO MUCH TALK ABOUT MONEY AND DEATH, MY TWO LEAST FAVOURITE THINGS EVER!
FOLLOW ME, AMIGOS! THIS NIGHT'S MADE FOR SOMETHING SO MUCH BETTER...

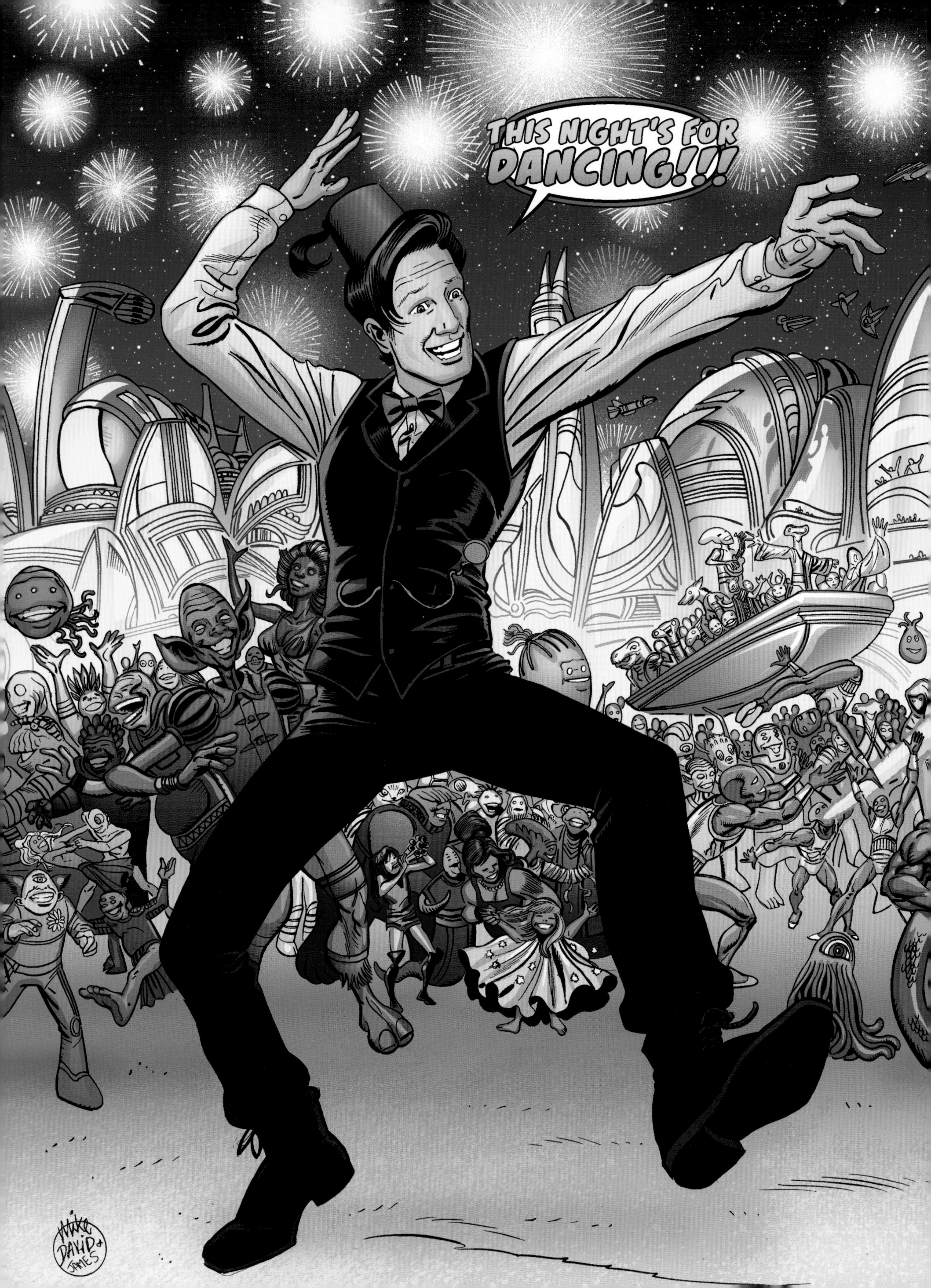
THIS NIGHT'S FOR DANCING!!!

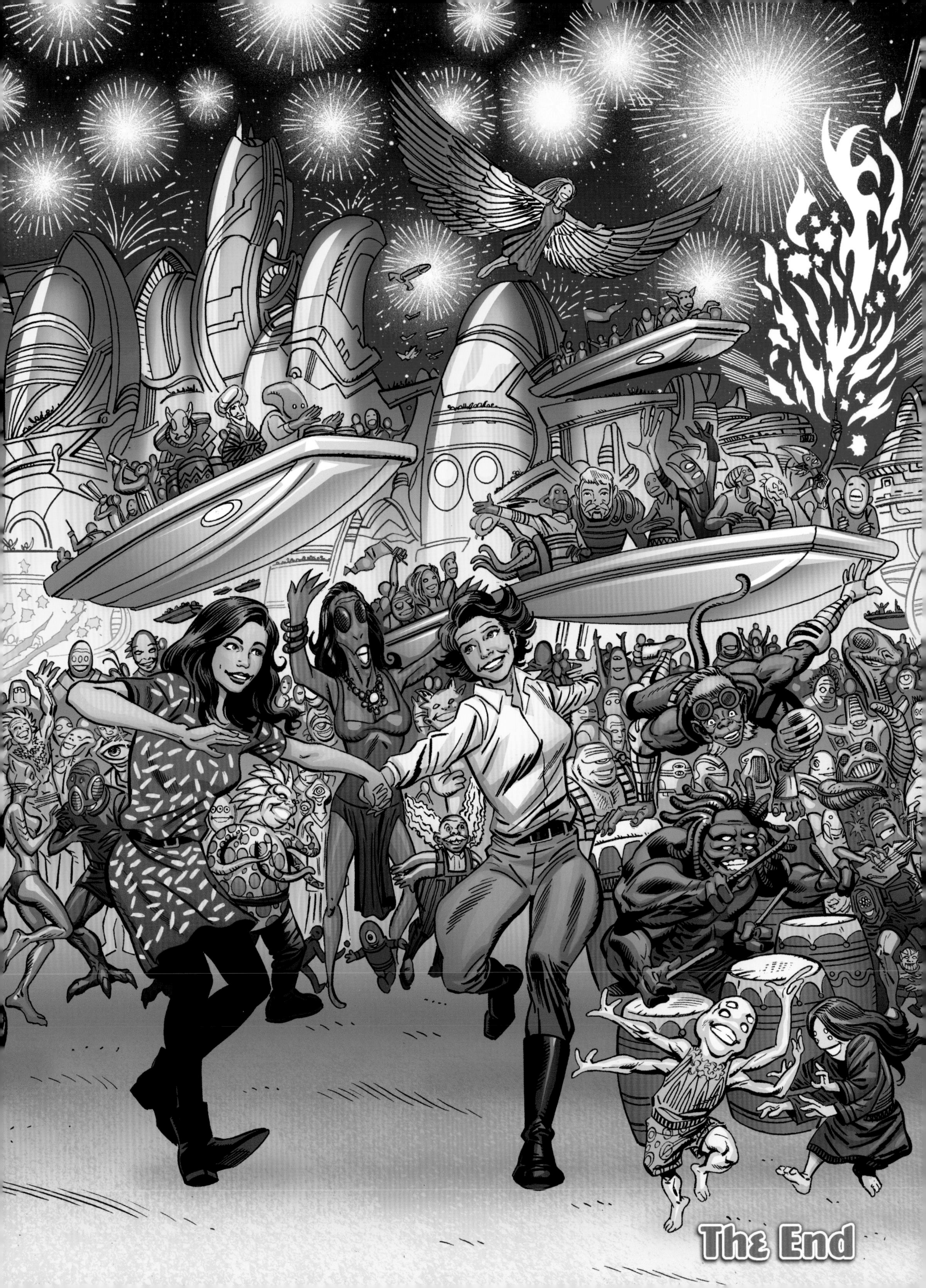
The End

COMMENTARY

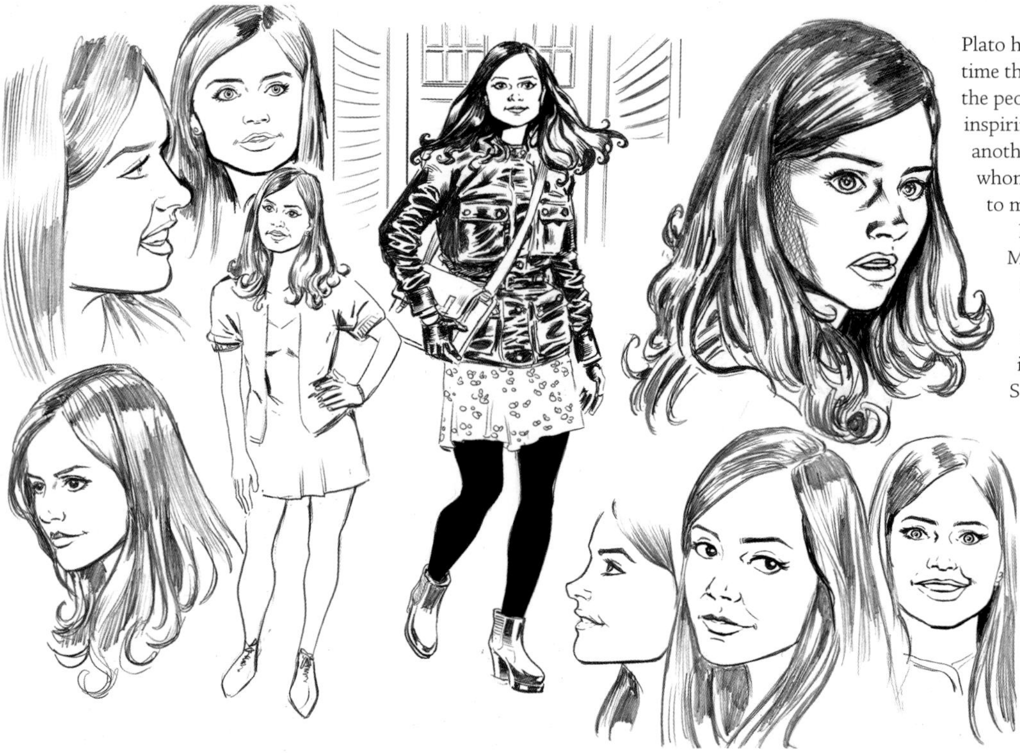

Plato had starred in *The Chains of Olympus*. Each time the story had taken shape as I researched the people in question, with details of their lives inspiring the major plot elements. I decided to try another one, and started looking for somebody whom the Doctor and Clara would be excited to meet.

I stumbled across Amy Johnson in Adam Murphy's *Corpse Talk*, a very funny regular section in the excellent kids' weekly comic *The Phoenix*. A different historical figure is literally dug up and interviewed each issue, and one week Amy was the subject. She struck me as the perfect guest star for a *Doctor Who* adventure: clever, adventurous, brave, and born into one of the most colourful eras of the twentieth century.

I didn't know a great deal about Amy, and when I quizzed other people I found that most of them were confusing her with Amelia Earhart. I collected a few books on her. By far the best was *Amy Johnson* by Constance Babington Smith which proved to be an absolute goldmine of information. Amy had been a prolific letter-writer, and Babington Smith (herself a pilot) had sought out a mountain of correspondence between Amy and her friends, family, colleagues and lovers. No-one can ever really capture a genuine flesh-and-blood person in a story, but reading so many of Amy's private thoughts allowed me the confidence to at least give her a substantial voice in *A Wing and a Prayer*.

Above: Mike Collins' initial pencil studies of Clara.

Below: The real Amy Johnson, circa 1930. © PA

Below right: Amy's biplane Jason hangs in the London Science Museum.

A Wing and a Prayer

Scott Gray Writer

Hello and welcome to the behind-the-scenes bit. Hope you enjoyed the book! Here we go...

The 'celebrity historical' is a tried and tested form of *Doctor Who* story, and one that I think tends to work very well in the **Doctor Who Magazine** comic strip. I'd used famous names in the strip a few times in the past: Frida Kahlo and Diego Rivera appeared in *The Way of All Flesh*, George Custer and Sitting Bull showed up in *Bad Blood*, and most recently Socrates and

Amy Johnson was a legal secretary from Hull who one day decided to devote her life to flight. With only 75 hours of flying experience she flew from Britain to Australia in a second-hand wooden biplane in 20 days. She went on to many other flying achievements and become one of the most famous faces of her time. She was celebrated by royalty, politicians, film stars and, most importantly, the general public. At first glance Amy would seem to be a perfect candidate to become a full-time *Doctor Who* companion but I'm not so certain of that. Companions tend to need the Doctor to come along and pull them out of their humdrum existences. Amy didn't need anyone else to provide her with an exciting life – she built one all by herself.

I went to London's Science Museum in South Kensington where Amy's plane Jason proudly hangs amongst jet fighters and spacecraft. I took a bunch of reference photos for Mike Collins as I wondered how anything so fragile could possibly have survived such an epic journey. I liked the fact that Amy developed a genuine emotional bond with Jason, echoing the Doctor's relationship with the TARDIS.

I wanted to find a specific point on Amy's first flight to Australia to place the story. She had

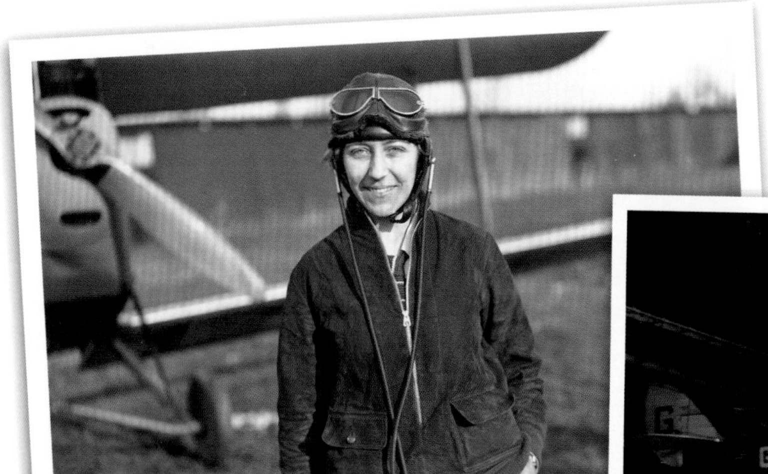

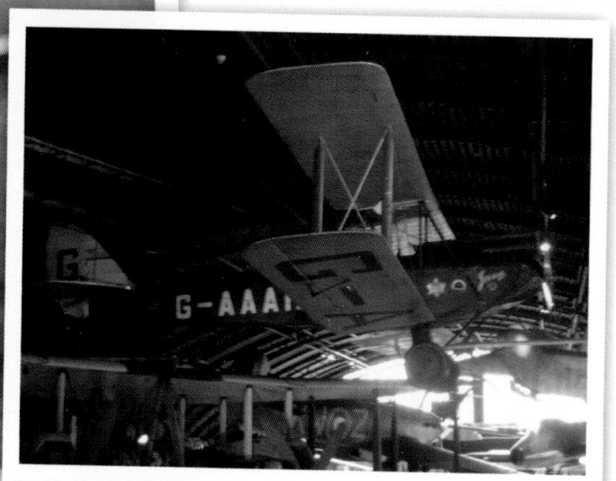

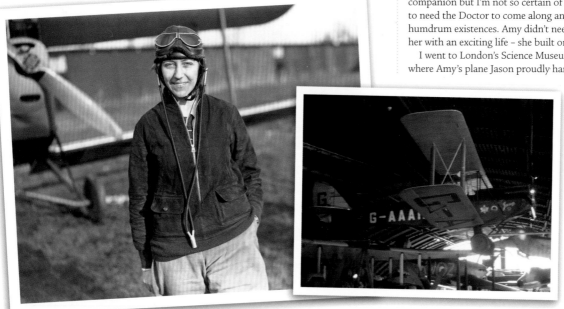

set down in several exotic locales including Turkey, Syria and Burma, but Iraq felt like the one with the most potential. Many of the details in the story are based on fact. Amy really was forced down by a sandstorm and had to wait in the desert for a few hours before carrying on to Baghdad. It seemed like an ideal moment for her to encounter Clara and the Doctor. She was genuinely armed with a revolver too.

Arnold Bradshaw is fictional. In reality, when Amy landed in Baghdad she was met by a Mr Phelps at Imperial Airways aerodrome and was treated very well. But she did travel into Baghdad for the night and had dinner on the roof of her hotel.

As with all good historicals, I knew the central figure would have to play a critical role at the end of the story. It has to be said that Amy's flying skills were still under development at this point in her life – she was no stranger to crash-landings – but people often commented on her amazing natural instinct for navigation. That inspired the thought of a hyperspace tunnel which Amy could weave her way through in the climax. Amy had a distaste for beetles which steered me towards an insect-based enemy, and her role as an early feminist heroine in turn led to her clashing with the misogynistic Arnold Bradshaw.

Looking back through my notes now, I seem to have worked out the main beats of the story quite quickly. I did toy with the idea of Bradshaw using Koragatta's telekinetic powers to remake Baghdad in the style of the British Empire – with giant sand-versions of Big Ben and Tower Bridge, *etc* – but it didn't feel very exciting and would have eaten up too much space in Part Three. The warriors pursuing Koragatta started life as big metallic insects but I much preferred the sand-forms.

A Wing and a Prayer was our first story to feature Clara. As usual we commissioned Mike Collins to produce a collection of 'audition' illustrations of her that could be checked by actor Jenna Coleman. Mike's excellent work got the thumbs-up from Jenna on the first try and we were rolling. Mike also gave us a superb villain in Koragatta with a design that would have sent any entomophobe diving behind the sofa. He also brought 1930's Baghdad to life in all its exotic glory, and he did an equally brilliant job on the hyperspace tunnel (aided as usual by the equally talented David Roach and James Offredi, of course).

I wanted Clara to be right at the heart of the action in her début comics adventure, not someone simply following the Doctor around, asking convenient questions – a trap that many an unsuspecting *Doctor Who* writer has fallen into. I admit that I was nervous writing for her at the start. Clara's onscreen character seemed to be deliberately sketchy when compared with earlier companions, entwined as she was in the whole 'Impossible Girl' mystery. But she was brave, resourceful and had dreamed of travelling since childhood, so I assumed that she'd be a feminist with one or two female role models who'd been explorers or pioneers. Amy Johnson fitted the bill perfectly. At the time I wrote *A Wing and a Prayer*, Clara was looking after those loveable scamps Artie and Angie on TV – there was no suggestion of her pursuing a career in education. It's just a lucky coincidence here that she pretends to be a teacher, so it was nice to raise the subject again when she and Amy were reunited in *The Blood of Azrael*.

Giving Clara a personal heroine (and also a best friend) seemed like a good way to help define her as a character. The fact that she'd know how Amy was going to die (and would want to save her) became the emotional backbone of the story. I very quickly realised that there was a temporal loophole wide enough for the Doctor to squeeze through and actually save Amy, which was wonderful. We got a nice letter from someone in Amy's family who was excited to see her in a *Doctor Who* story. I hope they liked the ending.

Another reader pointed out an historical inaccuracy regarding Arnold Bradshaw's rank – there were no Flight Commanders in the Royal Air Force. But my real mistake was identifying him as a former RAF officer. Bradshaw would have been part of the Royal Flying Corps (which did have Flight Commanders) at the start of the First World War. The line has been corrected for this volume. (I'll bet you're relieved.)

By the time I had finished plotting the story I knew exactly where I wanted the TARDIS to drop Amy off – Cornucopia, the exotic alien spaceport we'd previously established in *The Cornucopia Caper* and *Hunters of the Burning Stone*. Our 'season finale' was starting to take shape in my head, and I had a feeling Amy would find plenty to occupy her there...

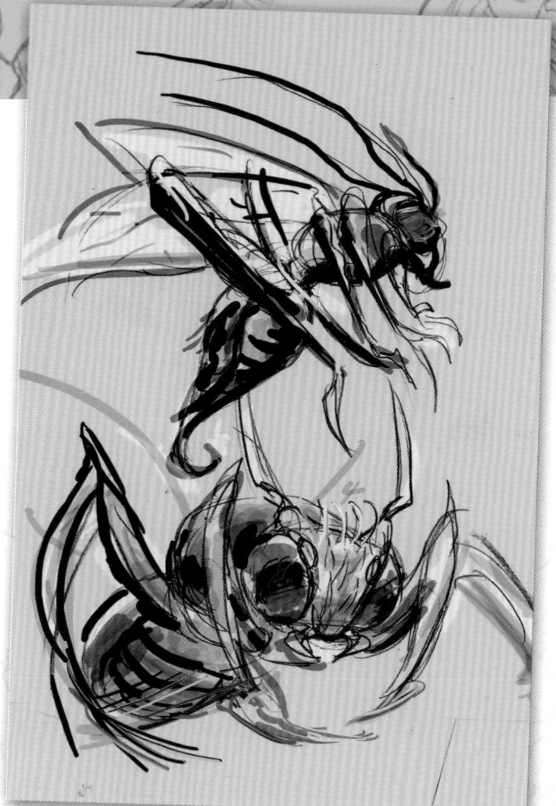

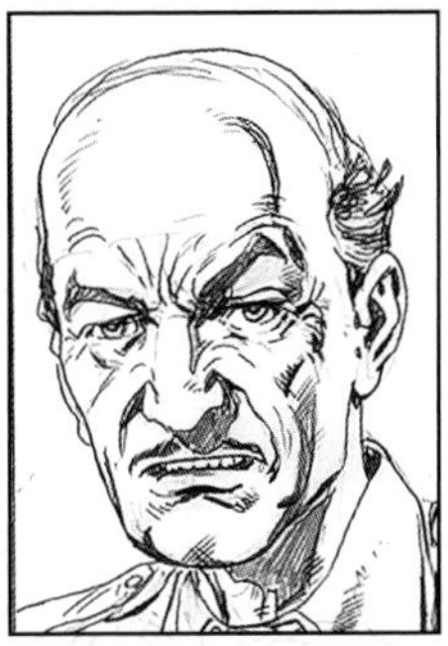

Left:
Mike's early colour sketches of Koragatta.

Below:
Arnold Bradshaw. Pencil art by Mike Collins.

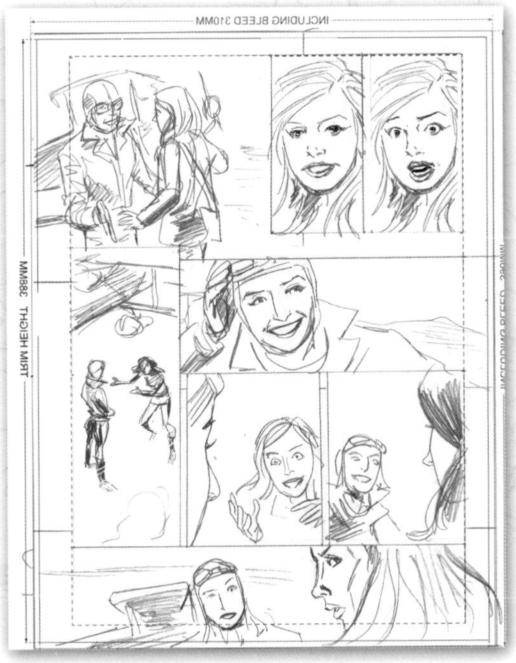

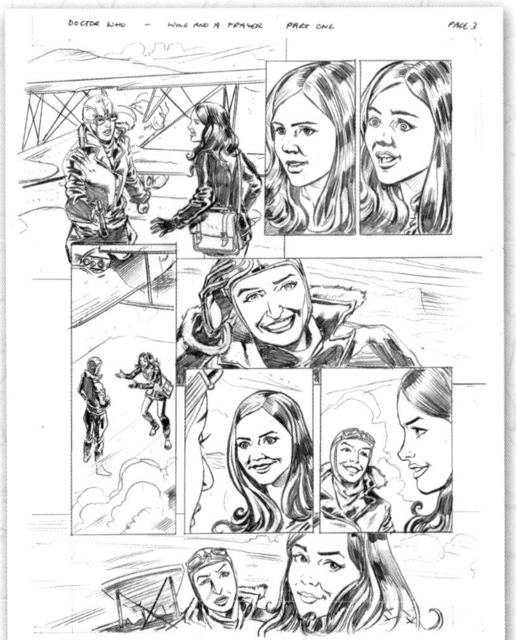

Below:
Mike's inital thumbnail layouts and finished pencils for Amy and Clara's first encounter in Part One.

Right:
Another of Mike's initial layouts and finished pencils from Part One.

Below:
John Sinclair modelled for Omar. Pencil art by Mike Collins.

Bottom:
Mike's pencils for the hyperspace tunnel scene.

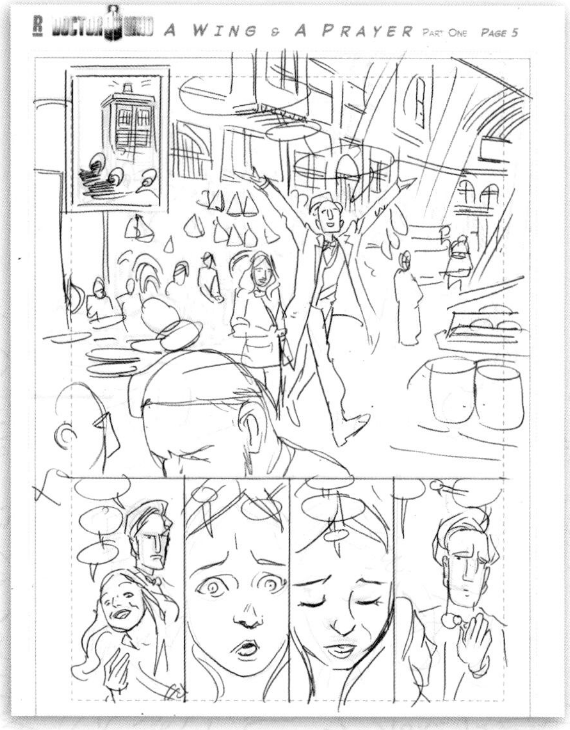
A WING & A PRAYER Part One Page 5

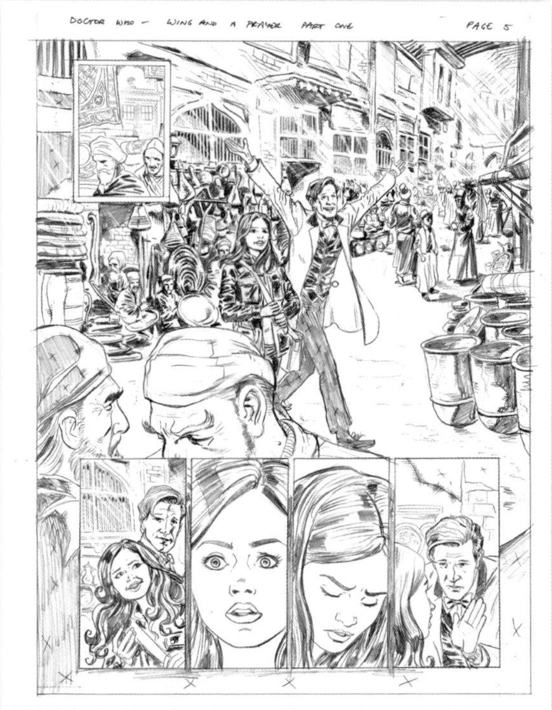

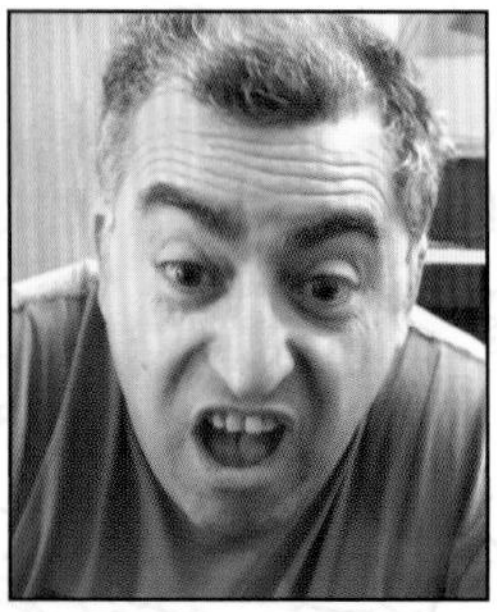

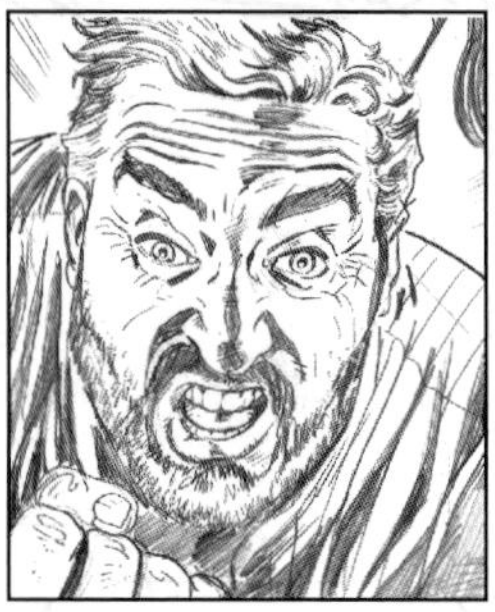

Mike Collins Artist

Scott lured me back with the chance to draw the first Clara story... and then confusingly introduced another temporary companion called Amy! I had headaches on the first few pages with her defaulting to Amy Pond in my head...

I have an abiding dislike of war comics but a love of aircraft. Unfortunately, they usually go together – here I had a chance to get my wing fixation without battlefields. Making Amy Johnson the protagonist was an inspired choice. I've always enjoyed the historical *Who* stories, and here was a genuinely unique female character who proved a great foil to Clara. Photos of Amy showed her in a couple of different looks, so I sought about to cast her as they would on TV. I came up with 'my' Amy Johnson, going through pics of the historical version – a touch Ingrid Bergman, but mostly the young Patricia Hodge (and that's the voice I heard her dialogue in). For our human antagonist I ran with Scott's suggestion of an 'evil David Niven'.

As usual, my one-off in-jokes ended up being a story point: the Fez salesman is based on a writer/actor friend John Sinclair who's appeared as a background actor in many *Who* episodes, amongst other TV and movie roles. I thought the time was right for him to 'guest' in the comic strip, assuming it was just a one-page gag... Scott hadn't sent me the full plot so I was unaware of John's pivotal role in the whole story. One for his CV!

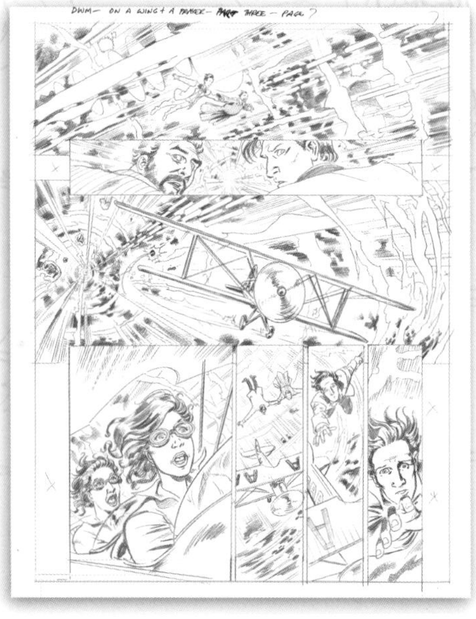

Scott did exhaustive research on Baghdad in this time period, uncovering various sites with photos which proved invaluable in grounding our story. The major element in Parts One and Two we didn't have reference for was the hotel, but – in my best BBC Locations Scout mode – I went through my old photos of a trip to Egypt I'd made a few years back, and found pictures I'd taken of the Winter Palace Hotel in Luxor. It has consciously retained its look from when Howard Carter stayed there in the 1920s (while excavating Tutankhamen's tomb). Everything was period-accurate – well, except for the sand monsters. My wife is always driven mad by my photographing everything I see but in this case it turned out to be very useful!

This was the story where I finally got to kick off on the cosmic stuff I love so much (*The Futurists* was an earlier example in the **DWM** strip where I wrote myself some out-there Jim Starlin/Steve Ditko/Jack Kirby wackiness to draw) with the tube/tunnel in the final part.

As to the monster: Scott loves bugs. I mean, he *really* loves bugs (see also *The Crystal Throne*) and they make for excellent 'alien' antagonists. The creature here is an amalgam of various insects; I spent some time trying to compose a nasty enough image, only to have Scott push to make it even more vile and more alien. I'm really happy with what we ended up with; a seriously evil-looking creature that was detailed enough to give David Roach nightmares when he came to ink it.

The epilogue is one of the most *Who*-like we've seen, with them saving Amy – the callback to the opening sequence is clever and heartfelt. I got to riff on Roy Krenkel and his fabulous city designs, my one contribution to the world of Cornucopia. Or so I thought.

This was the first story drawn to the new page dimensions of **Doctor Who Magazine** – and this caused a few problems. Over the years we've settled into a routine on the comic strip – David prefers rough 'toothier' paper to ink on, while I like to pencil on a smoother board. As there's often corrections on the art, I've taken to drawing on the smooth board, scanning in the art, making corrections then printing it out as a blue line on the toothier artboard for David to ink. In Photoshop I have presets of page sizes with bleed indicated: all was good. As long as I could print out on a sheet of A3, all was fine.

The new art paper is BIGGER than A3. Why it took so long to get a hang on this, I can't explain – I'm an artist, I generally understand visual ratios... but this took the better part of the first episode to nail down. It also meant that we didn't have two originals per page and so David had to put up with my ingrained pencil lines on smooth paper. Luckily, the art paper I use is A3+ so I didn't have to source new materials – although I did have to buy a bigger portfolio!

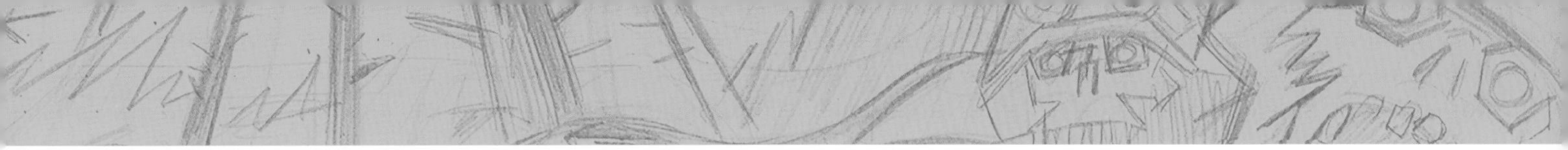

Welcome to Tickle Town

Scott Gray Writer

So we had just completed a story with a real-world setting in a specific time period, centred around a genuine historical figure. It had all been carefully studied, researched and referenced. Hmmm. No way I was doing any of *that* again in a hurry. Nope, it was time for a great big ice cream cone of total fantasy.

There was only one name on my list to illustrate this story. Any excuse to work with Adrian Salmon is always welcome – his love for both comics and *Doctor Who* is inexhaustible. Whether I'm writing or editing the **DWM** strip, I'm always on the lookout for material that might suit Ade's ultra-graphic, hyper-stylised approach. Adrian never approaches a story the same way twice – he's always experimenting with new pallettes, new techniques, new tools.

Tickle Town had two real-life inspirations: Alton Towers and Disneyland. Alton Towers is clearly a fading giant; it's looking a bit dirty and shambolic these days. My strongest memory of the place is taking my family on some rickety old indoor ride – the sort of thing where you sit in a slow-moving carriage and fire a laser gun at targets to score points. It should have been a brief trip, but one of the carriages ahead of us must have broken down (I guess – there was no announcement) and the line ground to a halt. We ended up stuck inside one of those revolving tunnels designed to confuse your equilibrium. A minute passed. Two minutes. Three. After the *fifth* minute of feeling like t-shirts in a spin cycle, the kids were just *howling*. I'm not really sure how long the whole ordeal lasted – time had started to eat itself – but when we finally staggered out into the sunlight, I remember vowing that I would use the experience somehow. Alton Bloody Towers owed me *that* much, at least.

Disneyland is the exact opposite. Both the Paris and Los Angeles incarnations are absolutely pristine, astonishingly well-organised and almost ruthlessly efficient. When we visited the Los Angeles park I noticed that it differed from its Parisian counterpart in one obvious way: there were scores of jaw-droppingly obese people everywhere. They travelled on slow-moving mobility scooters, all armed with popcorn, soft drinks and faces that flickered between blandly stoical and downright grim. Were they having fun? I couldn't say – it looked more like they were paying some sort of penance, trundling past the primary-coloured characters of their childhoods, unable to enjoy themselves but also unable to leave.

I've always been fascinated by the concept of a prison that's been disguised as some kind of idyllic community. I'm a sucker for stories like *The Truman Show*, *The Happiness Patrol* and the granddaddy of them all, *The Prisoner*. They all feature artificial societies that haven't evolved in an organic way; they arrive fully-formed, usually carved in the image of a single individual. Enjoy them – *or else*. (And if they seem impossibly far-fetched, take a quick look at North Korea sometime.) An amusement park that would let you in but never let you out again appealed to me in a big way. It felt like a natural extension of Number Six's delightfully pretty cage.

Tobias Tickle isn't really based on Walt Disney, but they do share one trait: Disney saw himself as a visionary, happily planning his communities of tomorrow, desiring to not only predict the future but to *influence* it. There's an urban myth that Disney's body is being kept in cold storage – underneath Disneyland, of course – waiting for future technology to reach the point where it is capable of resurrecting him. *Doctor Who* has only ever had one response to a good myth, of course – *use it!*

I was aware that I was writing two stories in a row where Clara would meet a childhood hero, but I reasoned that a 1930s British aviatrix and a cartoon cowboy frog were sufficiently different figures. I was again trying to flesh Clara out a little by giving her a bit of personal history; something the TV series seemed to have little interest in doing at the time.

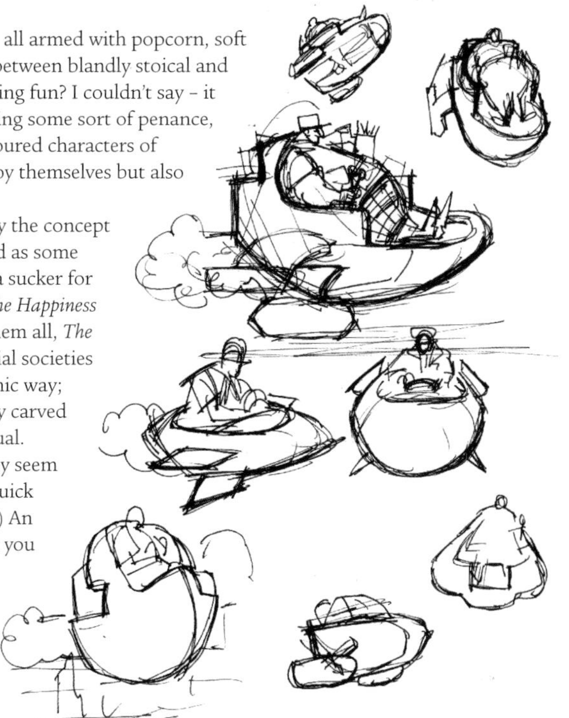

Above & below: Adrian's design sketches for the hover buggies, Sid the Stoat and Hopalong Harry.

Left: Clara and Harry meet Tobias Tickle. Pencil art by Adrian Salmon.

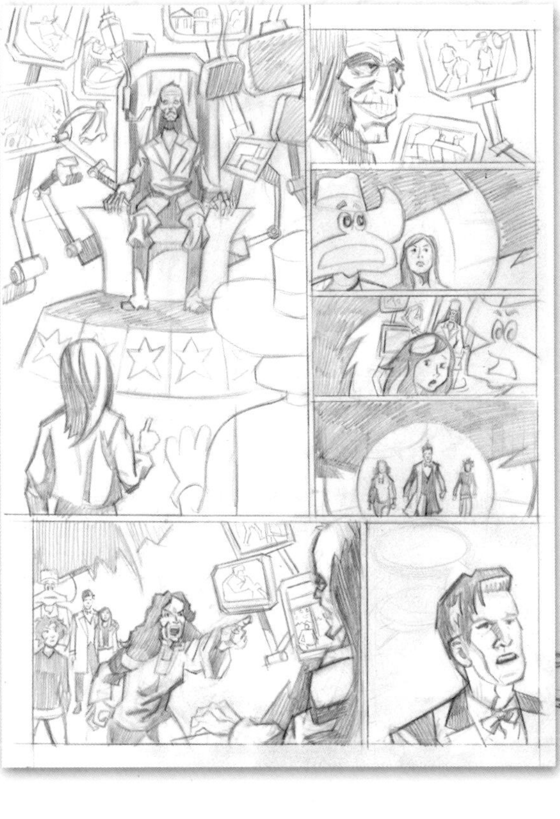

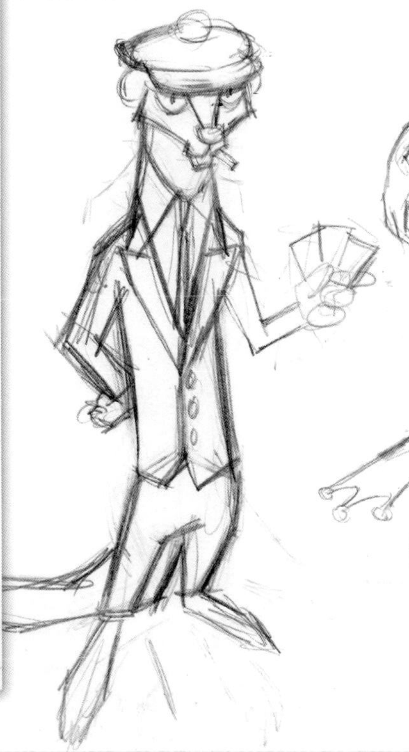

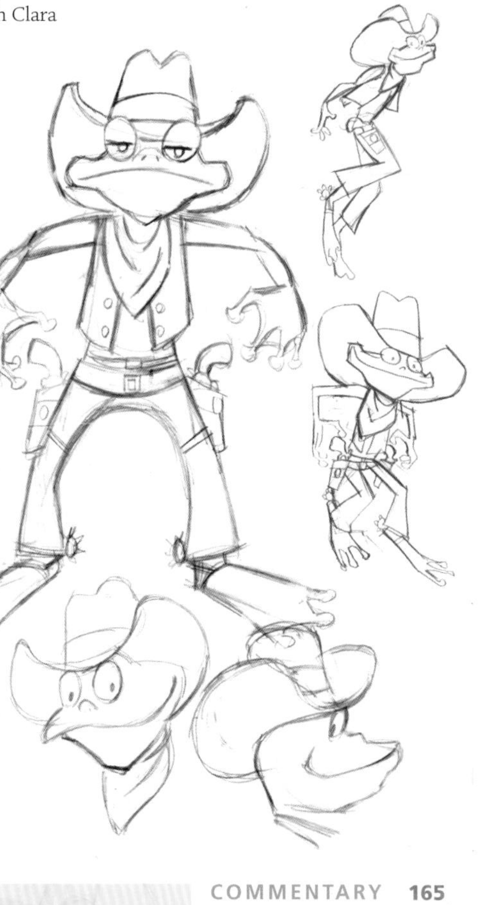

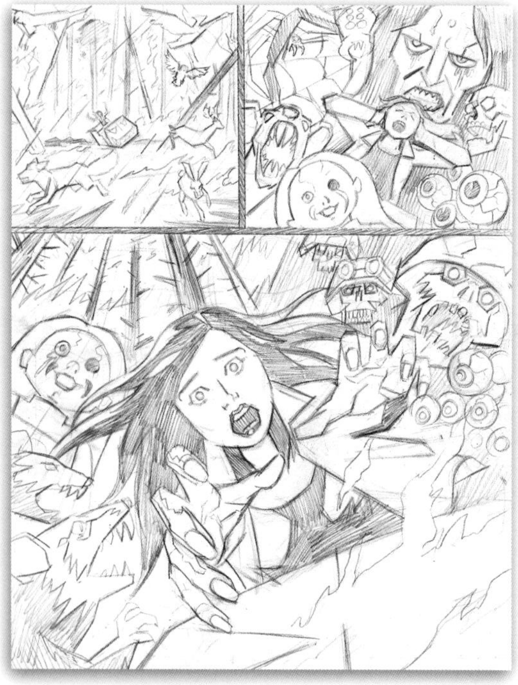

The talking animals in *Tickle Town* were initially planned to be flesh-and-blood creatures. Tobias Tickle started life as a mad scientist; a Dr Moreau-style figure who was creating strange genetic experiments. But it seemed a far more natural fit to turn them into holographic animated characters that could interact with real people in the vein of *Who Framed Roger Rabbit?*. It seemed unlikely that the TV series would be doing anything like that soon – although give it another five years and I suspect we'll see it happen.

Accidentally paralleling story elements from the TV series is an ever-present danger for the comic strip writer – there's no easier way to get a story rejected by the BBC. I did have a vertiginous moment when Neil Gaiman's *Nightmare in Silver* script arrived in the **DWM** office. The futuristic amusement park setting got my mental alarm bells clanging, but the approach and premise were thankfully very different from ours. We were safe! Even so, I decided to have Clara mention her earlier trip to a sinister funland – it just felt like a natural comment for her to make.

The plot went through a few changes along the way. The Tickle Toons (Adrian came up with the name) were originally in control of the prison, their ultimate goal being to revive their creator who was trapped in a cryogenic freezer. At the end they succeeded, but Tobias died anyway – it had all been for nothing. It felt a bit on-the-nose, however, so Tobias became the grand manipulator instead. I briefly considered splitting the Tickle Toons into two factions: slick CGI creatures who would all be nasty, and black-and-white 1930s-style animated critters who would be sympathetic.

Clara was originally going to befriend 'Basil Bulldog', a stout canine with a bowler hat and a Union Jack waistcoat. His nemesis was 'Bolshie Bear', a big Russian heavie. They didn't last long, though – Basil was soon replaced by 'Rusty Richochet', who quickly evolved into Hopalong Harry. Constable Claws was a holdover from the B&W 1930s idea – a near-colourless character from a more violent animated era. (I had Ray Winstone in mind for the voice.) Adrian did a stand-up job designing them and all the other Tickle Toons.

The big set piece was The World Outside scene, where the Alton Towers Incident finally justified itself. I was quite pleased with the accompanying song, although lyrics are hardly my greatest strength. (Special thanks to the *Penguin Rhyming Dictionary*.) I knew Adrian would unleash every weapon in his arsenal for this sequence, and boy-howdy, he did not let us down. It was just terrifyingly brilliant, jam-packed with all that stark Salmonesque imagery I've loved for years. Thanks, mate!

Adrian Salmon Artist

The most interesting aspect for me as an artist was designing the Tickle Toon characters that populated Tickle Town. Scott and I discussed early on that highly-rendered *Roger Rabbit*-style looking toons or modern approaches weren't the way we wanted to go. Scott liked the idea of basing them on the early animation look pioneered by the likes of Tex Avery and early Walt Disney. I spent a number of hours searching the internet for animation character sheets from the 1940s that would be my guide to drawing these properly. We very much liked the idea of the toons being coloured flatly like animation cells, leaving all the texturing for the background elements. That was one of those 'eureka' moments when I coloured the strip because it brought the characters instantly to life!

The Doodle Bugs that capture Winthrop and Carstairs at the start were the first I designed. I found some wonderfully animated bumblebees that fit the general look I wanted, and with the addition of those iconic pointed German Pickle Hauber helmets and bright red and white uniforms, the Doodle Bugs buzzed into life. The next character I tackled was Constable Claws who was naturally a Policeman cat. He ended up looking like a fat Sylvester the cat with comedy truncheon and razor-sharp claws! Whilst the toons might look friendly, they could be deadly too! Last of the major characters was Hopalong Harry, a timid frog sheriff with a heart of gold whom Clara

Above:
Clara suffers the torments of The World Outside ride. Pencil art by Adrian Salmon.

Below:
Adrian's character designs for Constable Claws.

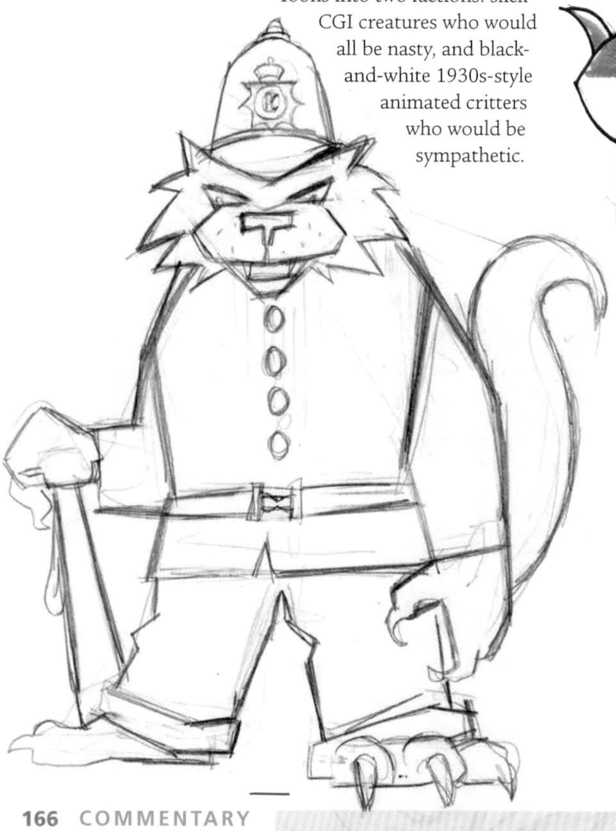

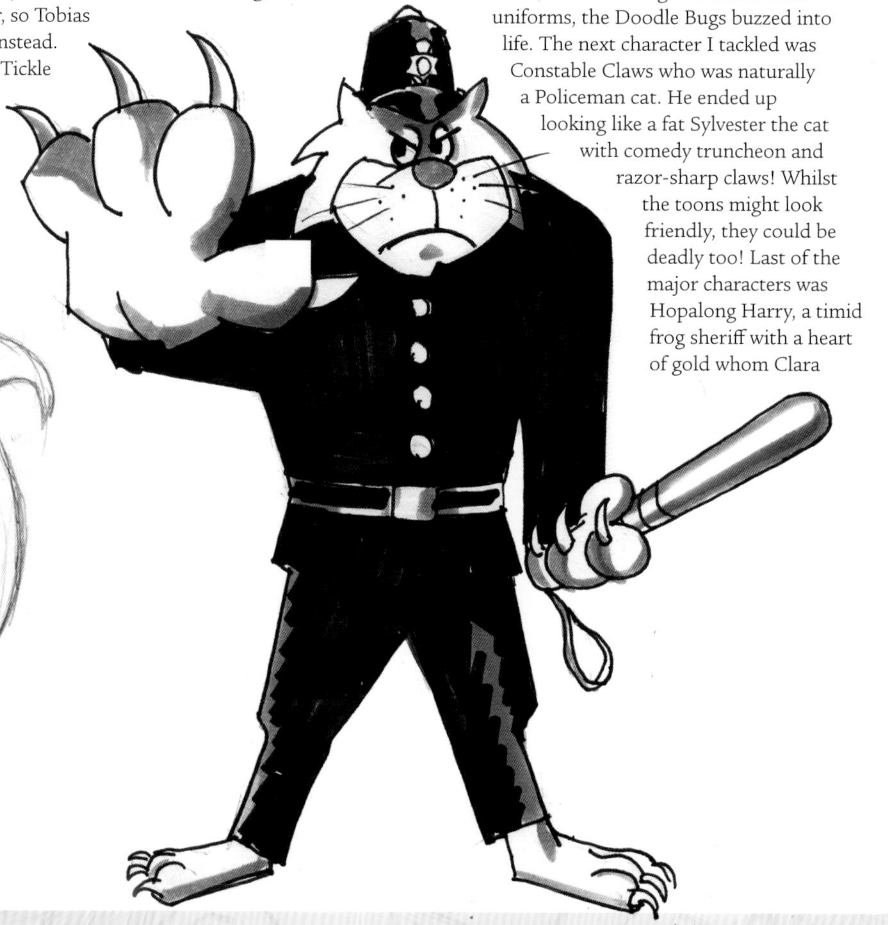

befriends. He quickly became my favourite character. He was based mostly upon Chuck Jones' animation gem, the brilliant Michigan J Frog. Jones had so brilliantly visualised what a cartoon frog should look like that I couldn't help being inspired – thanks, Chuck!

I found drawing Clara an absolute joy and dressed her in red to be instantly recognisable in a very busy strip. Scott asked for plenty of denizens of the park: Lifers (those who had given up) who were overweight and travelled around on hover buggies. In contrast there were the overtly thin Visitors who hadn't given up on escaping. I collected plenty of reference of amusement parks to inspire the various rides and sideshows that filled the park. At times I was scratching my head to think up yet *another* ride background! Though this was a futuristic strip, it still needed for the park to be rooted in reality and not be too sci-fi for reader identification.

The final pages of Part One see Clara taken prisoner by Constable Claws and brought to the globe-like World Outside ride. In the same scene we see Carstairs and Winthrop leaving the ride, their minds shattered by the experience. They were based on classic British film stars Stanley Baker and Alec Guinness. Clara rides into this world supposedly representing the horrors outside the amusement park of burned cities, mutant rats and zombie soldiers. Scott knew of my love of horror comics, and Jack Davis' fetid zombie horrors weren't far from my mind as I drew the moldering soldiers from Hell lurching towards Clara in the cliffhanger.

I wish in hindsight that I'd been a bit more creative with Tobias' underground lair, giving it a more amusement park feel. And cobwebs. When Constable Claws arrives he isn't happy, and kills Tobias off-camera – Scott had to rein in my wont for drawing a bit of blood!

In the final fight, Claws and Harry are badly hurt and Harry fades away in a cloud of pixels as Clara holds him. I loved the fact I could use a specific pixel filter in Photoshop to enhance this effect – a real **DWM** comic strip moment!

Production of Tickle Town ran very smoothly for me and in the process I learned a new appreciation of those long-gone animators of a golden era which I dedicate the strip to. Thanks, Scott, and that's all, folks!

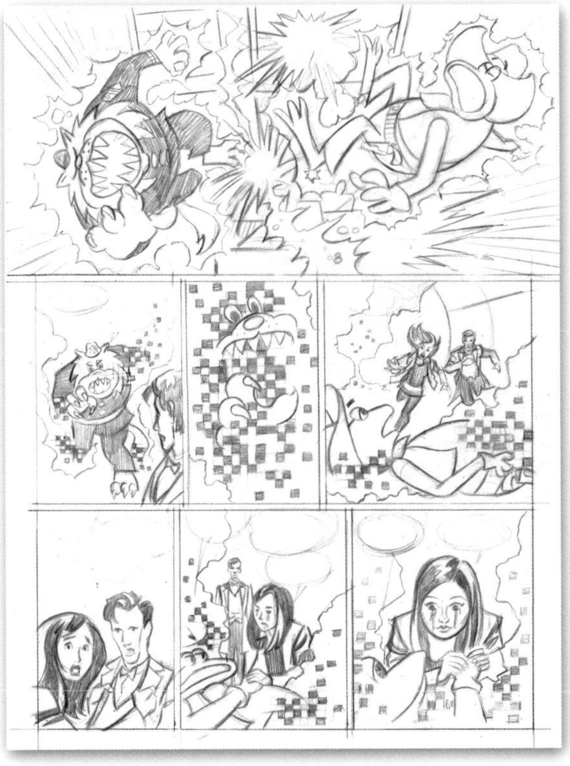

Left:
Harry meets an heroic end. Pencils by Adrian Salmon.

John Smith and the Common Men

Scott Gray Writer

I had already written a story for *Doctor Who*'s 50th anniversary celebrations – *Hunters of the Burning Stone*. It had run in **DWM** from January to June 2013, kicking off the birthday year in as big a way as I could imagine with the return of classic-era companions, old enemies, a journey into the Doctor's own history, and even a quick trip back to a familiar junkyard in Totters Lane, 1963. It couldn't have been more of a birthday bash if I had stuck 50 giant Dalek-shaped candles on it.

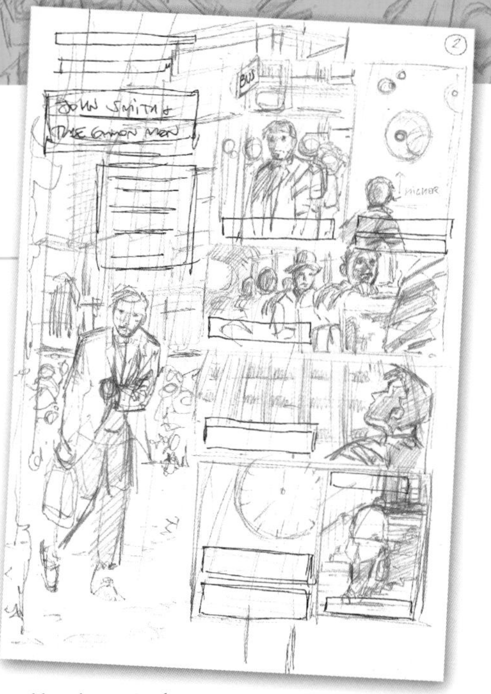

Above:
David Roach's layout for the title page of *John Smith and the Common Men*.

But it left us with a slight problem: *Hunters* had concluded well before the actual big day arrived in November. **DWM** was naturally planning a special issue for that month, and it was going to be a very big deal: an extra-large edition packed with special features, 12 art cards, a mock 1960s version of the mag, and all of it wrapped up in a sturdy cardboard envelope. So what could we do for the comic strip? I felt like I had already opened every present, popped every balloon and eaten every slice of cake. What was left?

The solution was to go smaller. *Hunters* had been a sprawling cosmic epic set in a variety of locations, all beautifully illustrated by Martin Geraghty. It was as large an event as we could make it. This second anniversary story would be much more subtle. It would be internal, concentrated, personal – it would say something, not about *Doctor Who* in general, but about the Doctor specifically.

One of the earliest ideas I had considered when beginning to plot *Hunters* was to put the Doctor and his companions (who at the start I was imagining to be Amy and Rory) into three individual 'hells' – private little fake worlds that would torture them on an emotional level. These hells would say something about their innermost fears. Rory would be turned into an intangible ghost, unable to be seen by the Doctor and Amy but forced to watch as they enjoyed a cosy life of adventuring together. The Doctor, meanwhile, would be stuck in a world of stupefying drudgery, trapped in a mundane day-by-day life, with no memory of his true self.

I didn't get as far as deciding Amy's 'hell' before moving *Hunters* in a different direction, but there was something about the image of a beaten, depressed Doctor that stayed with me. The conventional image of Hell – torture, torment, lava pits – would never be the worst thing the Doctor could experience. That would only offer him a challenge: a prison to escape, people to rescue, villains to overcome. No, for the Doctor, the ultimate fate worse than death would be *boredom*.

I was confident the concept would work. We would turn the Doctor into a miserable little man and then watch his true self fight its way back to the surface in time for a triumphant climax. The first image that came to mind was of him meekly standing in the one place sure to drive the Doctor completely insane: a queue. I described the premise to fellow editor John Ainsworth and was pleased when he got the idea immediately – we would be defining what the Doctor *was* by turning him into everything he *wasn't*.

So the Doctor became John Smith. That's a familiar name to every fan, of course: the Doctor often uses it as an alias, but always in an ironic fashion – what could be more inappropriate for this unique individual than such a bland, common name? (Apologies to any John Smiths reading this.) But in this story

PAGE SIX (10 panels)

Panel 1
John in back-shot. Clara suddenly jumps up and pleads with him over the desk, hands out, frantic, yelling! She's grabbed one of John's wrists. He's trying to pull back.

JOHN: I'M SORRY, BUT THERE'S REALLY --

CLARA: ***LISTEN!*** PLEASE ***LISTEN!*** I'VE ONLY GOT A BAG OF CLOTHES. THAT'S IT. MY ***WHOLE LIFE*** IS A ***BAG OF CLOTHES***.

CLARA 2: I SPENT THE LAST OF MY ***MONEY*** TODAY. I HAVEN'T EVEN GOT ANYWHERE TO ***SLEEP*** TONIGHT!

CLARA 3: ***PLEASE HELP ME!***

Panel 2
Tight on John. He looks down, shamed.

JOHN: THERE'S NOTHING...

JOHN 2: THERE'S NOTHING I CAN DO.

Panel 3
Clara is walking away now, towards us in the foreground, head down, still crying. She's clutching herself. John is in the far background, small, powerless. He's rubbing his wrist. He's watching her go.

BOX: She's the worst one. I can still feel her fingers digging into my wrist.

BOX 2: Why would any of these people think I could help them? Look at me.

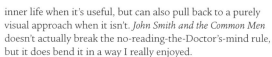

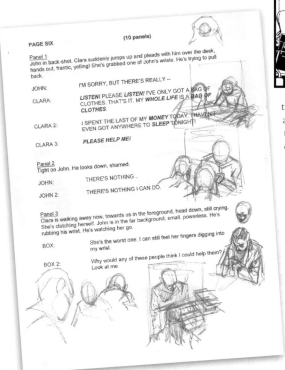

the name would fit him like a glove. He'd be a cog in the machine, faceless and ordinary, a man without a single original thought in his head. His eccentric clothes would become a mass-produced uniform. His bravery would become cowardice. Instead of challenging authority he would fear it, but also take comfort in obeying it. His burning desire to make every day of his life completely unique would be replaced with a desperate need for routine and conformity.

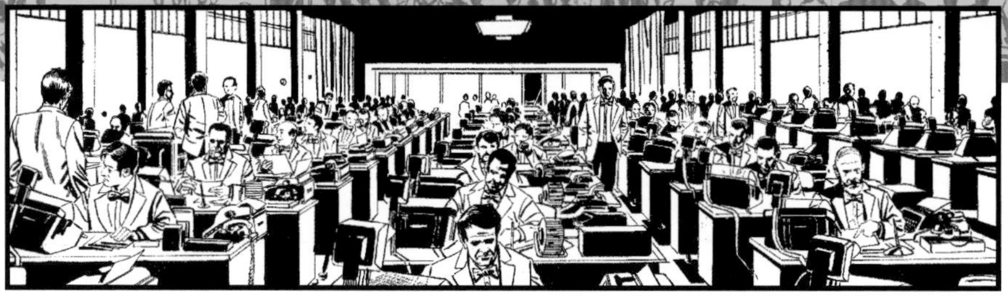

Doctor Who stories love to roam free and wild, but there's one area where they never dare to venture: the Doctor's own internal monologue. The Doctor's power lies in his mystery – he's an eternal being with a colossal, labyrinthian mind we could never hope to comprehend, and that's the way we like him. If we were ever made privvy to his private thoughts he'd be instantly brought down to our own petty human level, and the spell would be broken. That's a trap easy enough to avoid in television; it's a fundamentally superficial medium where characters only reveal themselves through their speech and actions. (That's not a dig, by the way – all mediums have different strengths and weaknesses.) It's a much harder job in prose where the novelist is expected to get under the skin of the main protagonist and explore his/her past, motivations, fears and desires. In *Doctor Who* books the companions tend to take centre-stage, filling the enigmatic gap left by our hero.

Comics, of course, are words *and* pictures. We have the best of both worlds with a medium that's equal parts literary and visual. Comics can place a magnifying glass on a character's inner life when it's useful, but can also pull back to a purely visual approach when it isn't. *John Smith and the Common Men* doesn't actually break the no-reading-the-Doctor's-mind rule, but it does bend it in a way I really enjoyed.

I quickly saw that boredom wouldn't be enough of a trial for John Smith – 12 pages of him filing accounts, answering the phone and ordering paper clips might get... well, slightly boring. So poor John was shoved into a world cut from whole cloth: George Orwell's *1984*. It was a very short hop from John Smith to Winston Smith. John's life was still filled with crushing routine but it also became one where the threat of a truncheon was always present; where there was always a watchful eye above his head and a large hand on his shoulder.

John Ainsworth suggested the title (a reference to a pop band mentioned in the TV series' first episode *An Unearthly Child*). John Smith's struggle with the clock was inspired by Harold Lloyd's classic silent movie comedy *Safety Last*. I know it's pretty obvious symbolism, but sometimes obvious is good!

I'm in awe of the level of dedication and talent that David Roach pours into his work – you can sense his love of comics in every meticulous line he places on the page. David has been inking Martin Geraghty and Mike Collins for so many years that I confess I sometimes forget what an accomplished penciller he is in his own right. David is the regular cover artist for our graphic novel line but his schedule rarely gives him the chance to illustrate the **DWM** strip. I'm so glad he found the time for this story, he did an absolutely stunning job. David loves drawing anything exotic – give him a nightmarish gothic mansion or a herd of dinosaurs or a majestic alien city and watch him go to town. So of course, I had to hand him the one story set in an office. I'm so sorry, David, but you really were the only man for the job!

We needed a hyper-real approach to the art for a number of reasons. John Smith's world had to be detailed, grimy and drab, but still visually compelling. The four past companions who appear – Harry, Jamie, Ace and the Brigadier – all had to be instantly recognisable as most of them wouldn't be name-checked in the story. Most of all, we needed an artist who could provide the subtlety of expression necessary to carry the drama. That office scene with Clara chokes me up every time, and that's all down to David. I was able to delete some captions entirely as the images were telling the story so powerfully.

James Offredi complemented David's work beautifully, making sure that the hues of John Smith's world were dull and grim before suddenly jumping to psychedelia for the climax. (I think I kept saying "*The Wizard of Oz*!" to him.) And Roger Langridge completed the package with his typically stylish calligraphy – I particularly liked the monstrous Mr Waites' word balloons at the end.

I'm very proud of this one. That issue of **DWM** stunned everyone with its huge sales – it had to go back for a second printing – and I'm glad this story was part of it.

David A Roach Artist

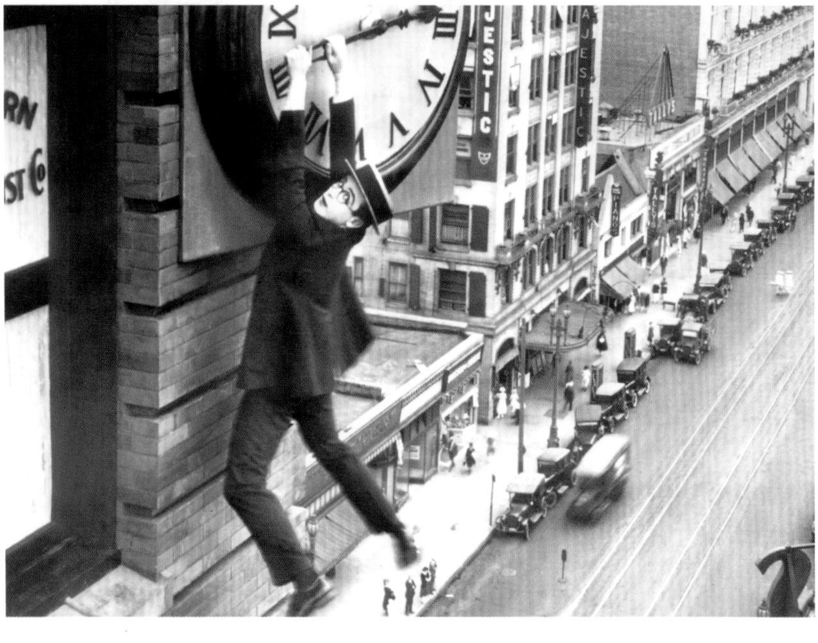

The funny thing about *Doctor Who* is that he can go anywhere in the universe, drop in on any great historical event, meet the greatest, most legendary people who have ever lived. No, really, it's quite amazing. And in the wonderful world of comic strips we're not governed by the limitations of budget or special effects; we really can take you anywhere, limited only by the breadth of our imaginations and artistic talents. So when I got the call to say that I was going to be drawing another episode of the strip, my mind started to race. I was thrilled by the infinite

Above:
David Roach's copy of the script decorated with his sketches.

Above right:
David's finished inked scene of the ultra-detailed office.

Below:
Harold Lloyd in *Safety Last* (1923), an inspiration for the story. © PA

JESTIC
JESTIC

possibilities that the strip could offer. For those of you not obsessive about credits, I should explain a little about my role on the comic; even though I've been working on it for about a decade-and-a-half, I've mostly been the inker on the strip, due to artistic commitments elsewhere on a certain Lawman of the Future, writing books and my being... ahem... a little slow at drawing. So while I get to draw all the covers to the graphic novels (including this very book you are holding in your hands) and have worked on numerous Annuals, I had only previously drawn one episode of the strip. And that was set in a nursing home. I figured that after having had my one *Doctor Who* adventure set just outside of Bristol, I was surely due something a bit more exotic or extra-terrestrial. Surely.

So imagine my excitement when this script popped into my in-box. *John Smith and the Common Men*. Hmmm, that didn't sound particularly alien, or exotic, or historical. Page One has our hero eating breakfast and washing his hair. Hmmm. Page Two has him walking through crowded streets and catching the bus. Hang on, this is looking worryingly un-intergalactic. Page Three, Panel One: 'Rows and rows of his co-workers are seated at small desks, all neatly arranged. They're all facing us. They're all typing away on clunky typewriter-computer hybrid machines.' Oh my God, I'd been sent the script from Hell! Leafing through the story, it quickly became apparent that there were pages and pages of this stuff – crowded offices, identically-dressed office workers going about their boring, repetitive, hopeless lives. We did get a hideous giant floating head on Page Ten, thank goodness, but there was a lot of work to do before we could get to that. At this point paranoia began to set in. Had I done something to offend our glorious writer? Was I perhaps atoning for some horrendous crime in a previous life? Was I ever actually going to get this thing drawn?

Deep breath. Let's read through it again. Okay, we've got the Brigadier and Ace and Jamie and Harry! Well, that's a good start. And Clara, a bit. And wouldn't you know it, the whole thing actually works. More than that, it's terrific; a beautifully-paced little epic that is genuinely moving with a really satisfying resolution (and don't be too surprised if it appears at some point in the near future on a TV screen near you).

Having accepted that the script was just too good to complain about (much), I then had the challenge of getting it all down on paper and trying to get some sort of visual template for the strip. Scott had suggested 1920s New York as reference for the city, but I actually found the tone I was looking for in American films of the 50s which were beginning to dissect the oppressive atmosphere of office life and the superficiality of consumerism. I took stills of offices and extended the lines of desks way off into infinity. Page One was a real challenge. In a strange way it's almost easier to conjure up the craziest alien vistas because quite clearly nobody knows what they look like and can't really tell if you've drawn it badly. However, we all know what it looks like to eat breakfast or wash our hair or climb a flight of stairs, so these simpler, domestic scenes need to be drawn extremely carefully. I enlisted my brother as a stand-in John Smith and stood on a chair taking photos of him washing his hair with imaginary shampoo. The Giant Floating Head was meant to be a reward of sorts for the previous nine pages of suits and desks, but since it was surrounded by 20 people lying on a circle of hi-tech slabs, surrounded by psychedelic swirls and writhing tentacles, it was not exactly a walk in the park.

In fact the high points for me were the quieter scenes where we could really explore the personalities and complexities of our characters. The Doctor shooting Harry an anxious, nervous glance. Or the Doctor lying in bed, staring bleakly up at us. Best of all was Clara, or at least this retro-future, alternative Clara, pleading for help, begging for some way out of the despair that had descended around her life. As an artist that's the sort of material I thrive on; the chance to try and convey the subtlety and intensity of raw human emotions. Looking at the script again now, it's covered in scrapped layouts, scribbled designs and endless variations of people sitting around desks as I tried out various different ways of composing each panel. Amazingly, I made the deadline, though I can't think how; the whole experience is a hazy blur of drawing, inking, rubbing-out, drawing again, correcting, replacing panels... replacing whole pages! Throughout it all I had no idea of which issue it was actually going to appear in. It never occurred to me that it was destined for the 50th anniversary issue. It never crossed my mind that it would appear in an issue with the highest print run for, what, 20, 30 years? Perhaps it's best I didn't know!

As usual, James worked his magic with the colouring, Roger supplied his typically top-quality lettering and the strip looked remarkably professional... somehow! Even if it's through gritted teeth, I suppose I have to admit that it was worth all that effort. But Scott, I've got this great idea for another episode, see what you think: the Doctor and Clara materialise on a desert planet with no buildings or cars or people or offices or buses, and they wander around being all witty and charming in a minimalist, easy-to-draw kind of way. What do you say? Sounds promising?

Oh, suit yourself...!

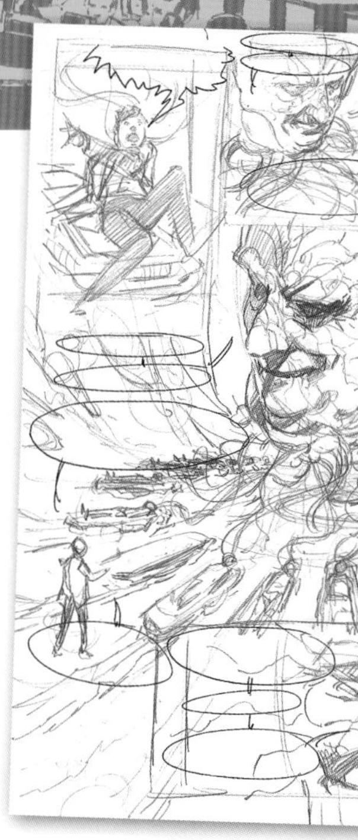

Above:
A layout of the story's climax.

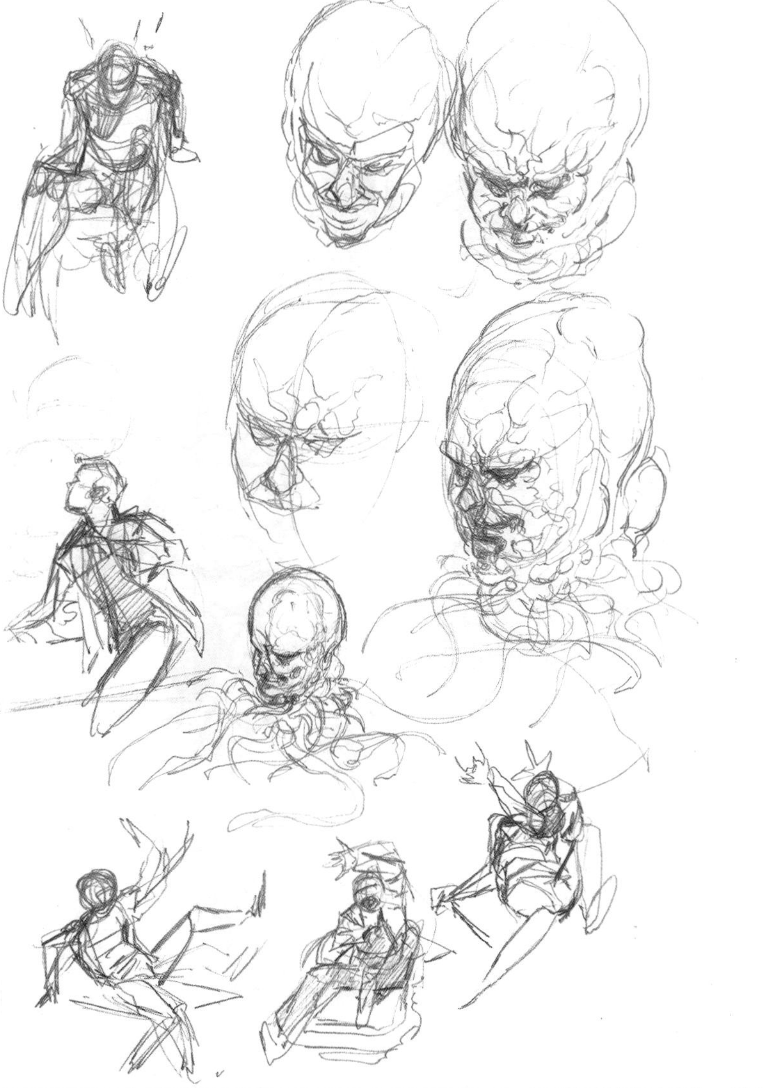

Above:
David's sketches of various characters.

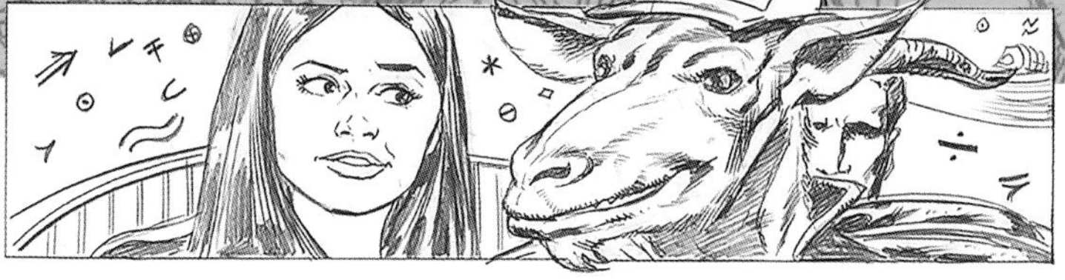

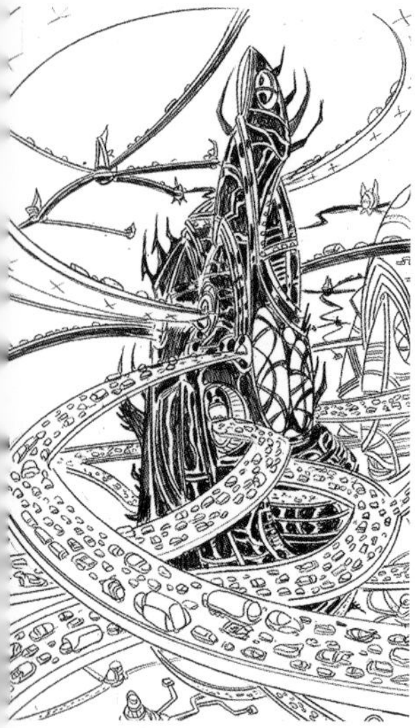

Pay the Piper

Scott Gray Writer

This one was always intended to be a bit of a tease. *Pay the Piper* was designed to look like a small, straightforward story, but right from the start it was planned as a gateway into a much larger adventure. (In the office we call them *'Utopias'*.) Nothing in *Pay the Piper* was quite what it seemed – those two twist endings were always in sight.

The Doctor's relationship with money isn't often explored. Oscar Wilde wrote that a cynic is 'a man who knows the price of everything and the value of nothing.' I think the Doctor – particularly the Eleventh Doctor – is the exact opposite of a cynic. Money means nothing to him but he has a keen awareness of what's really important in life. Clara may kid him about not knowing the price of a cup of tea, but he could give you the complete history of the drink and tell you exactly why he loves it so much. Isn't that better?

With that in mind, taking away the most important thing in his life and replacing it with a big pile of cash seemed like a wonderfully nasty piece of irony – especially as it was the result of his own recklessness.

The Obsidian Mainframe had been mentioned in *Hunters of the Burning Stone*, so I figured it was about time we got a look at it. '*Tron* meets eBay' is how I pitched it to Tom and Pete. That double-page spread at the start was magnificent – Mike, David and James were meshing better than ever. I added the vertical alien text in the sky to help give the OM an artificial feel.

I loved Mike's design for Londi Kalo. He looked like the perfect comedy sidekick, friendly and unthreatening. But 'Londi' was an onion – peel the first layer away and you'd see somebody quite different. Peel away the next and you'd find something very scary indeed. Imagine if Jar Jar Binks had revealed himself to be a Sith Lord in *Star Wars Episode Three*, stepping out of the shadows, over the bodies of a bunch of dead Jedis – c'mon, wouldn't that have been *amazing?*

'Donaria Strul' was fun to write, but I did first consider having Annabel impersonate Majenta Pryce, the high-powered businesswoman created by Dan McDaid. Majenta had travelled with the Tenth Doctor in the comic strip for a while and had been a popular companion. It would have been fun to fool the readers into thinking she had returned, but I was worried that they wouldn't have felt surprised at the end, just cheated (or worse, disappointed) when 'Majenta' turned out to be a fake.

Mr Minus was based on a Victorian carnival barker, complete with a big Jimmy Edwards-style handlebar moustache. Mike did a superlative job on his design, and I also loved his decadent auction crowd who seemed to have wandered out of King Louis XVI's court. Part One's cliffhanger was inspired by the Living Eraser, a Marvel Comics villain who had fought Giant-Man in *Tales to Astonish* #49 a million years ago. The Living Eraser was about as obscure a baddie as they come, but he had an unforgettable *modus operandi* – armed with his Dimensionizer, he could literally wipe people out of existence bit by bit (although I think he was actually teleporting them somewhere). Jack Kirby demonstrated his genius for the umpteenth time by exploiting the essential two-dimensionality of comics art to demonstrate the Eraser's power. Mr Minus doesn't delete people in quite the same way – it's a slightly more 'realistic' effect here – but that's where it comes from.

Mr Minus started life as an android enforcer for the Obsidian Mainframe before turning more organic. He became one of the Kindred quite late in the day, while I was writing Part Two's script. That bit of background made the character so much stronger. I was aware of an emerging theme in this recent run of stories; most of the villains are striving for independence. Koragatta desires to break away from the Howling Swarm. Constable Claws needs to be free of the role given him by Tobias Tickle. Mr Minus just wants to leave the Kindred and make his own way in life. In other circumstances the Doctor might applaud their goal, but unfortunately none of these blokes cares how many people get killed along the way.

Some fans have commented on the way the TARDIS has been growing more 'human' in recent years. Showrunner Steven Moffat clearly enjoys portraying the Doctor's ship as a character in its own right. The most obvious example is *The Doctor's Wife* where the TARDIS briefly gains a human body and is able to properly interact with the Doctor for the first time. Perhaps the TARDIS getting that fleeting taste of humanity has triggered some form of awakening. It – or 'she' – now seems far more prone to emotional responses – particularly jealousy.

Clara Oswald is a very important figure in the Doctor's life, having been present at a key turning point of his childhood (as seen in *Listen*), and also being seeded throughout his personal history in *The Name of the Doctor*. The TARDIS seems to perceive Clara as a rival. A vignette on *The Complete Seventh Series* DVD box set, *Clara and the TARDIS*, really drives this point home; the TARDIS taunts (and then pretty near tortures) her. She even locks Clara out at one critical moment in *The Rings of Akhaten*. When you consider that the version of Clara on Gallifrey introduced the First Doctor to his beloved time machine right at the start, you might expect the TARDIS to actually feel a little grateful to her. Nope. Not a bit of it.

I think it's in *Hide* where the TARDIS really takes the great leap forward. No, not the bit where we see it sniping at Clara through a holographic interface (a trick pulled before in *Let's Kill Hitler*). It's what happens next that left me reeling – because

Above & below: Mike's pencil art for the auction house, Londi Kalo and Donaria Strul.

Bottom: The Living Eraser from *Tales to Astonish* #49. Art by Jack Kirby. © Marvel.

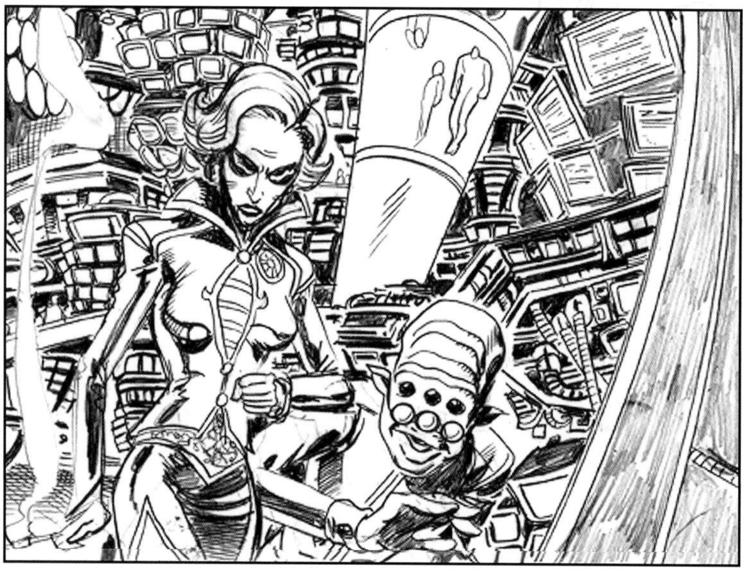

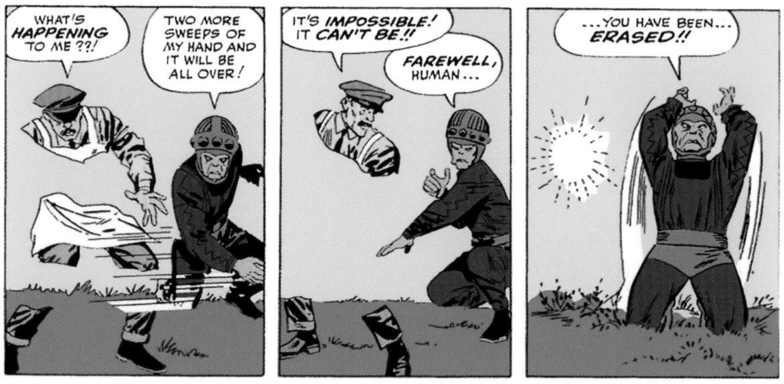
WHAT'S HAPPENING TO ME ??!
TWO MORE SWEEPS OF MY HAND AND IT WILL BE ALL OVER!
IT'S IMPOSSIBLE! IT CAN'T BE!!
FAREWELL, HUMAN...
...YOU HAVE BEEN... ERASED!!

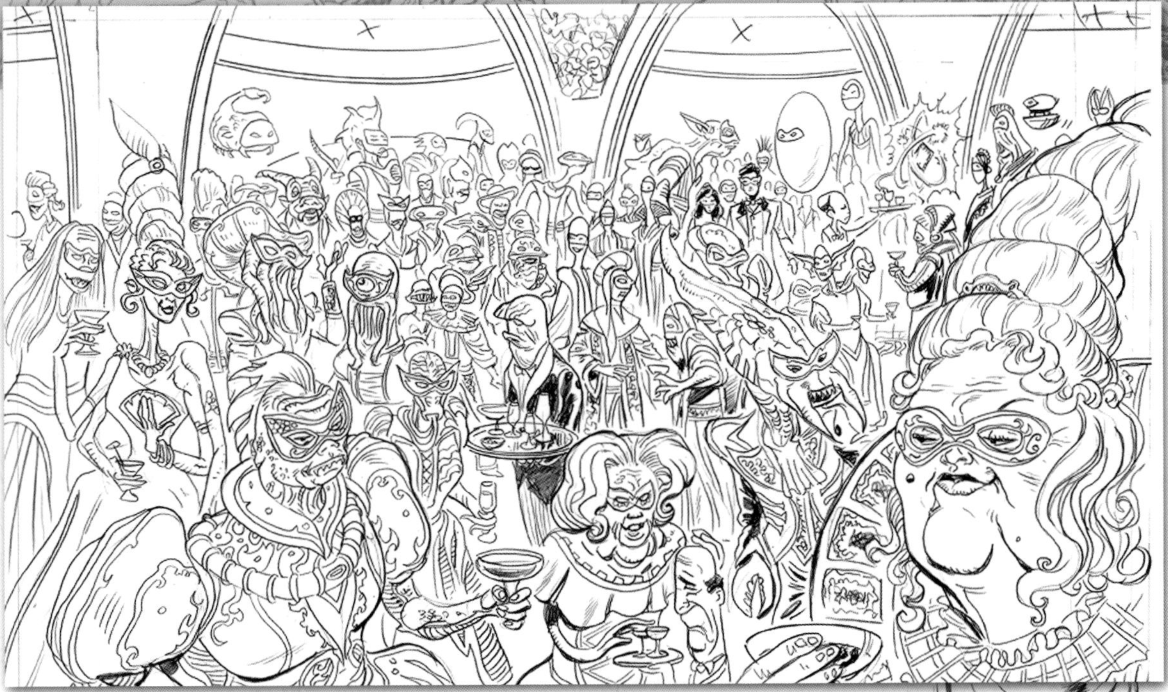

Left:
The decadent auction patrons assemble. Pencil art by Mike Collins.

for the first time in 50 years of adventure, the TARDIS *flies itself*. Think about that for a second. It definitely isn't Clara piloting the TARDIS to rescue the Doctor at the climax – the old girl is acting autonomously, zooming through a dimensional gateway all on her own to save her fella. No-one else I spoke to seemed to find that terribly remarkable, but I was gobsmacked. That was *massive!*

So the TARDIS was capable of independent thought, could pilot herself and was prone to fits of jealousy. How far could all of these elements be pushed, I wondered? What would it take for the Doctor to really screw up his relationship with the 'wife'? Would it be possible for the TARDIS to feel *so* alienated, *so* fed up, *so* taken for granted that she would actually *dump* her favourite Time Lord?

The answer was, of course, 'yes'...

Mike Collins Artist

After I'd finished on the IDW American *Doctor Who* series, Scott contacted me about doing a fun two-parter playing on the cosmic tropes I love and creating a whole raft of bizarre alien types. I had a ball visualising the initial spread of the virtual world the Obsidian Mainframe, and also the 'Wall Street cubed' look of the monitor world the Nucleus (as ever, David was not impressed by detailing that actually doubled the weight of the art board) where I really went to town on the imagery, trying to create an almost 3-D environment on the page.

The what-Cardiff-can't-afford mantra was at the fore here, with Scott pushing me to devise new and more elaborate environments. After a long period doing reality-based strips for other publishers, I seized the chance to go crazy with the design of the planet and the various species there. The world of the Mainframe had to look simultaneously alien, virtual and yet substantial. A lot of French Curve design elements. I'm pretty happy with the almost evil-Dr Seuss look to the auction house building.

The character of the taxi driver, Londi, was (I thought) a throwaway character so I based him on fellow comics artist Rufus Dayglo – certainly his build, dress sense and gestures but not in his facial features. Facially, he's a goat. Literally. (Londi, not Rufus.)

Mr Minus was fully-formed in Scott's description of him, so I think it pretty much was straight on to the page without much initial designing. The Kindred are characters-most-likely-to-be-plush-toys: friends who came by the studio while I was drawing them "awwwww'ed" and asked where they could buy one...

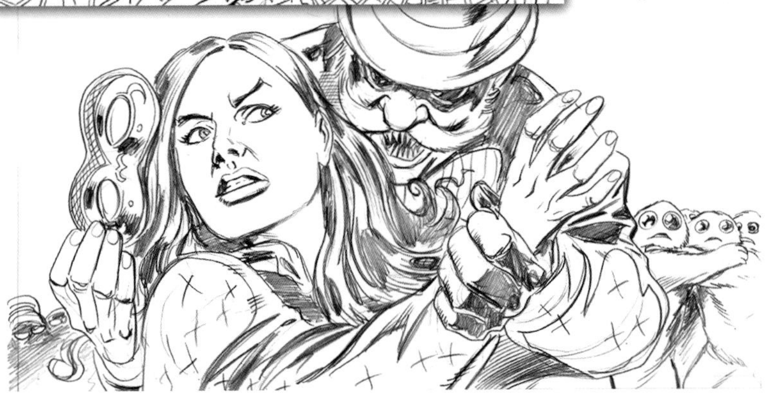

Above:
Mr Minus threatens Clara. Pencils by Mike Collins.

The way Minus wipes out the Doctor is a loving callback to old Marvel villain the Living Eraser – the layout to that page even echoes a Jack Kirby comics grid.

Part Two has some of my most 'Marvel' art for ages; the reappearance of the Doctor is riffing on Walt Simonson's amazingly kinetic style. Emotionally, the Doctor actually messing up and being shunned by the TARDIS is a deft little piece of writing on Scott's part. I spent ages nailing that shell-shocked expression of the Doctor for the final panel – it was, after all, the last time I'd draw Matt Smith's Doctor in continuity. Or so I thought...

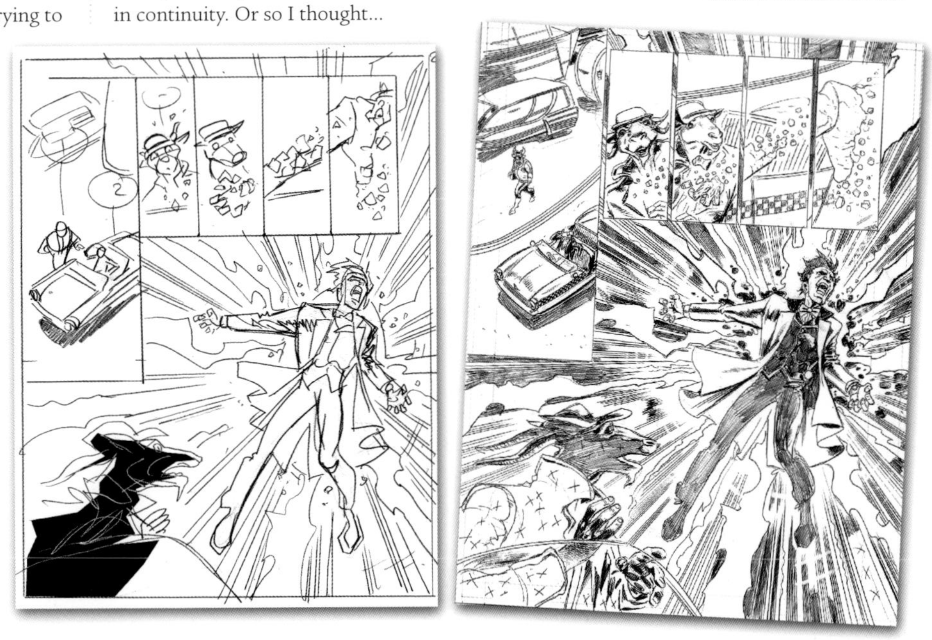

Below:
Mike's layout and finished pencils of the Doctor's resurrection in Part Two.

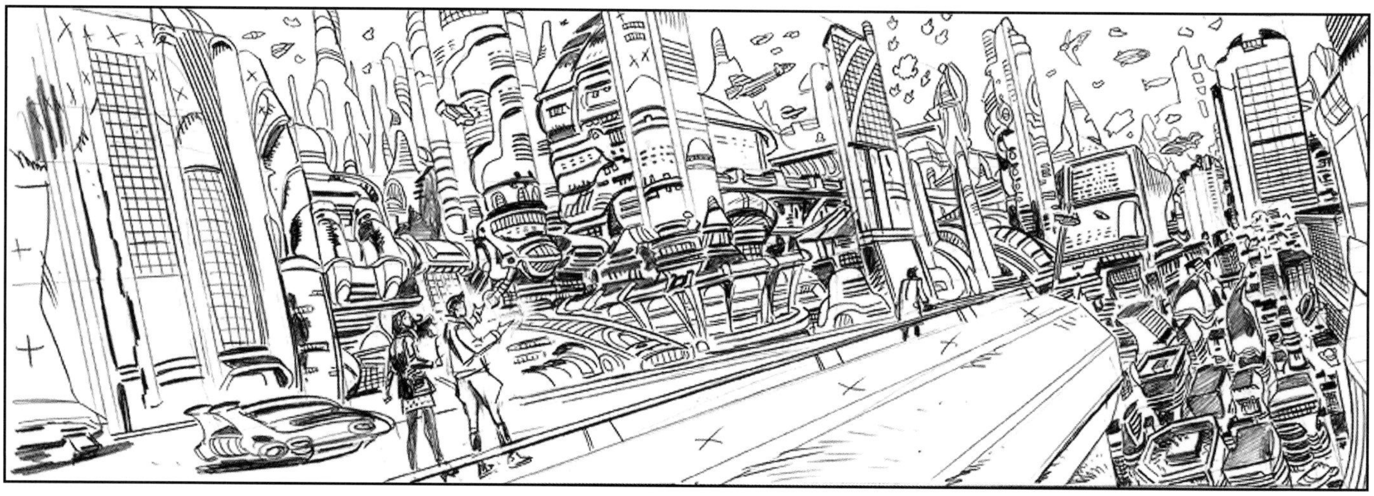

Above:
Mike Collins' detailed Cornucopia cityscape.

Below:
Mike's pencils of Miss Ghost and Londi.

Bottom:
Mike's character sketches of Progg and Hanka.

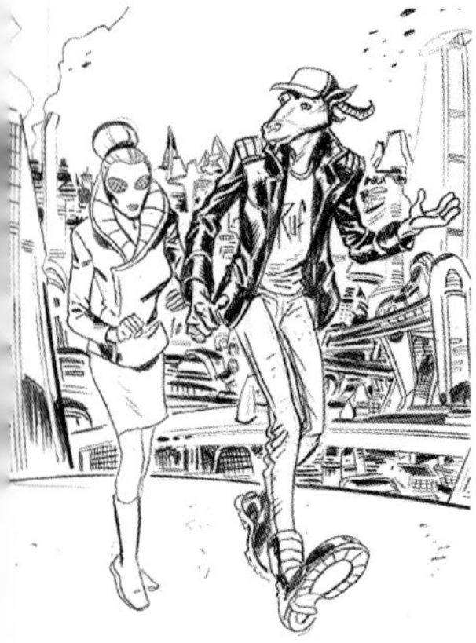

THE BLOOD OF AZRAEL

Scott Gray Writer

This was it: the final Eleventh Doctor adventure for **DWM**. I was very keen that whatever else we did with this story, his swansong would have some genuine emotional impact for the Doctor – I wanted it to be as personal a story for him as I could make it.

Martin Geraghty was originally scheduled to draw *The Blood of Azrael*, but other commitments forced him to reluctantly pass on it. Luckily Mike Collins was happy to carry on with the storyline he had started in *Pay the Piper*. Mike, David and James really went to town on this one, creating some of the most detailed cityscapes and crowd scenes ever seen in the **DWM** strip – every page had me dancing with joy.

This was our third trip to Cornucopia. For a long time I had wanted to establish a sprawling sci-fi city in the **DWM** strip that the Doctor could return to at semi-regular intervals, enabling us to chart its progress (or lack thereof) from story to story. Like any real city with a long history, Cornucopia has wildly divergent areas. In some places it's filled with gleaming Art Deco skyscrapers and walkways. In others it's all chaotic Middle Eastern marketplaces. Down the road you'll find Dickensian cobblestoned alleyways draped in eternal fog, and below that... well, you'll find out one day. Basically, Cornucopia has everything we need to make any kind of *Doctor Who* story. It's a bit like Cardiff, really.

We had a critical mass of comic strip continuity converging here: Cornucopia, Wonderland, Annabel Lake, Patrick Lake, Amy Johnson, Horatio Lynk and the Necrotists were all making return visits. I know there are some readers who would prefer it if we stuck to a steady rotation of monsters and supporting characters from the TV series, but that's never been a serious option for us. Original characters and settings help give the comic strip its own identity. It's funny, but the further the strip moves away from TV continuity and focuses on its own mythology, the more it feels like proper *Doctor Who*. (Well, to me at least. Hopefully you too.)

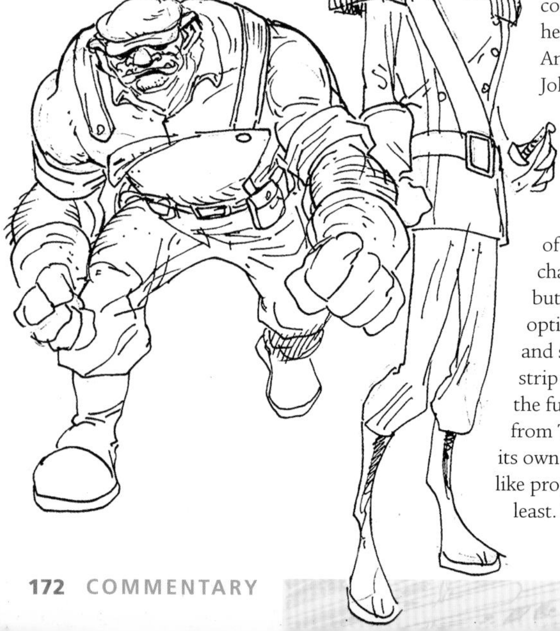

Death is a regular presence in *Doctor Who*. Sometimes it's small-scale, sometimes it's cosmic, but it's never far away. However, the TV series almost never explores the *consequences* of death; the personal impact it makes on those left behind. The TV series' nomadic nature means that we almost never revisit characters and learn how they have coped with the loss of a loved one. I wanted to address that here on a broad scale with Cornucopia's attempts to rebuild itself, and also on a personal level with Annabel Lake. We've seen Annabel as a child, watched her lose her mother and then observed as she and her father deal with their grief in a, let's face it, pretty disturbing way. Annabel's relationship with the Doctor is an evolving, unpredictable thing – I suspect that we haven't seen the last of her and her dad.

I think it's very easy to learn the wrong lesson from *Doctor Who*. Aliens are often presented as hostile, strange, unknowable creatures that want to invade our shores, take our lives and enslave us. Standing proudly in their way are the British authorities: the government, the army, UNIT, *etc.* Viewed in a superficial way, *Doctor Who* must be a very appealing show to rightwing groups like UKIP and the Murdoch press, always so eager to demonise foreigners in every possible way. (Heck, *Doctor Who* would probably look like a party political broadcast to them if it wasn't for all that 'gay agenda' malarkey.)

But when the series is observed a bit more carefully, a very different message emerges right from the beginning. Ian Chesterton nails the Daleks perfectly when he describes their "dislike for the unlike." This is followed by *The Sensorites* where the aliens at first appear to be terrifying spectres floating outside the human spacecraft – but by the end of the story are revealed to be fragile creatures being victimised by a group of desperate, paranoid humans. In *The Rescue* the peaceful Didonians are wiped out by a ruthless human. The real threat isn't alien at all. Xenophobia is the true enemy.

1970s *Doctor Who* continues the theme: the Brigadier succumbs to his fear in a catastrophic way at the end of *Doctor Who and the Silurians*. General Carrington does the same in *The Ambassadors of Death*. The Doctor challenges humanity's racial hatred in *The Sea Devils*, *The Mutants* and *Frontier in Space*. When an alien race is portrayed in *Doctor Who* as irredeemably evil, it's usually when it represents faceless, mindless conformity: Daleks, Cybermen, Sontarans, Weeping Angels, *etc.* In contrast, when aliens are portrayed as individuals they stop being 'alien' at all – they become *people*.

I'm an immigrant. I came to Britain from New Zealand in 1992 and never left. To a certain type of Briton, I'm perhaps the 'right kind' of foreigner – one who speaks English, grew up in a Commonwealth country and knows most of the words to *God Save the Queen*. My (white) face *almost* fits. But I'm still a foreigner and always will be, so to the UKIP mindset I can at best be tolerated, never welcomed. That's a very dangerous perspective to have. When times get tougher and politicians get cruder, it can lead to very dark days indeed.

All of this was much on my mind as I was writing *The Blood of Azrael*. The Doctor's discussion with Annabel in her office is a key scene. He points out that Cornucopia is populated by shopkeepers, plumbers, window cleaners and bus drivers. He can't see a single alien down there. Annabel gets the message in the end, but Danny remains blind to it. As I said, dark days...

I wanted to have the Doctor at a low ebb at the beginning, and keep him there for a while. I started by sticking him in that queue we hadn't quite found enough room to show properly in *John Smith and the Common Men*. Anyone who's ever travelled by air has at some point been trapped in a mile-long line at customs, edging forward three agonising feet every ten minutes. I'll bet you've had the same fantasy as me: arriving in a heartbeat with a triumphant VWORP! VWORP! outside the airport instead. I took an evil delight in bringing the Doctor down to our mundane level at last. His life was now moving so slowly that he almost missed Part One completely.

I was tempted to show the Doctor dealing with his newfound wealth. Financial advisors, bank accounts, stock portfolios – it would have been the most alien world he'd ever seen. I also toyed with having the Doctor set up shop in Cornucopia for a few months, working at Horatio's clinic and gradually starting to adjust to his new, stationary life. The story demanded a much faster timetable, though. I'm glad it didn't happen – it would have been too similar to the Eleventh Doctor's final TV story where he settles down to a long life on Trenzalore.

I have a pet theory about the comic strip, and I'm pretty sure it applies to every other form of storytelling too: nobody remembers the plot. Not ever. Writers can tie themselves in knots devising the most intricate, elaborate storylines with shocking reversals and surprising flashbacks and what-not, and that's fine, that's great, but people don't remember them.

No, what people remember are *characters*. Build yourself a good character (or better yet, three or four) and the plot will take care of itself. Their desires, fears and flaws will keep the audience watching. In a good story the characters drive the plot. In a bad one the plot drives the characters. When people say, "that was a great story," they really mean, "those characters felt real." They *don't* mean, "what a complex plot structure." I've always tried to make the plots for my **DWM** stories as interesting and exciting as possible, but the central characters are far more important to me. And a good villain is crucial.

One day I asked myself a question that made me laugh: "What if James Bond was a serial killer?" I mean, think about it: how would we actually *know?* What if 007 was a man with a pathological need to kill – a sociopath clever and charming enough to fool any psychiatrist, and cunning enough to maneuver himself into his dream job: a highly-paid government assassin? Once or twice a year he's called upon to save the free world. He does so with impeccable style, satisfying his homicidal desires along the way. Heck, maybe M even knows the truth and turns a blind eye!

That made me think of Dexter Morgan, the anti-hero of the *Dexter* TV series (and string of novels by Jeff Lindsay). Dexter channels his lethal urges into what he sees as a positive goal, by secretly tracking down and murdering other killers who have escaped justice. That was the spark for Danny Fisher, the man who would drive *The Blood of Azrael*: a nice, funny bloke on the surface who concealed the monster inside very, very well. Young Danny's flashback scene at the start of Part Five is about as dark as the **DWM** comic strip has ever gotten – I'm a bit surprised we got away with it, to be honest. Like Dexter, Danny justifies his murderous impulses by following a strict code. I imagined him looking like a cheeky, likeable Ewan MacGregor-type and asked Mike to think along those lines for his design.

Danny led me back to another concept I had earlier established in the strip: the Necrotists, a murderous artistic movement. I thought it would be interesting to show how they had gotten started; who their 'Picasso' had been. The idea that Necrotists could actually have fans was such a perverse notion that I couldn't resist it. The 'blood victims' in Part Four were inspired by the work of Spencer Tunick, the celebrated photographer who organises mass nude gatherings. I don't see anything perverse in that, of course – I think Tunick's work is quite beautiful – but it says something about the power of celebrity. If a complete stranger walked up to you and asked you to whip off your clothes in public so he could take your photo, you'd tell him to get lost. But if that stranger was a famous artist and was offering you the chance to become part of something permanent, something praised worldwide, you might suddenly be more amenable. There are many thousands of people who jump at the chance to become part of Tunick's portfolio. The Necrotist followers are just an example of that same attitude, dialed up to an insane, suicidal degree. They seemed horribly plausible to me.

I started off thinking that Azrael would be a conscious entity existing inside a floating mask who could talk to Danny. I ultimately decided that he wasn't necessary. Danny didn't need any help as the villain of the piece, so Azrael stayed dead. Azrael's image came from a variety of sources. I wanted him to look like a figure from a Venetian masquerade with an ivory mask, swirling cloak and the flare of a stage magician. Mike nailed him on the first pass. There was also a dash of Kabuki player there, mixed in with some *V for Vendetta*, Jack the Ripper and Doctor Strange.

Azrael was also influenced by a couple of charismatic comics villains. Stan Lee and Steve Ditko's classic *Spider-Man* baddie the Green Goblin is killed off seemingly forever back in 1973,

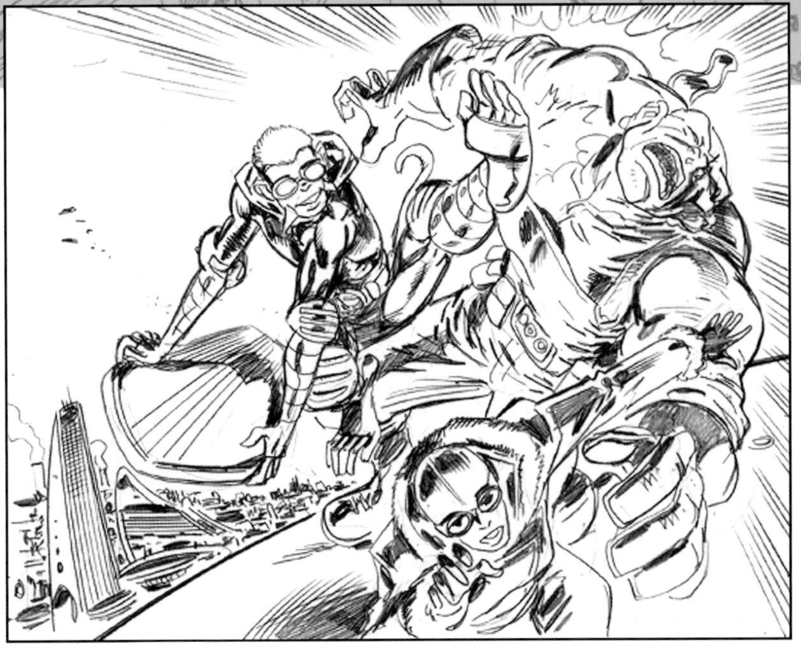

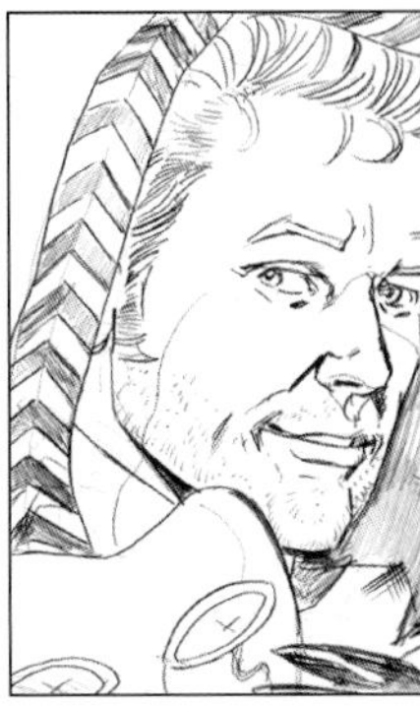

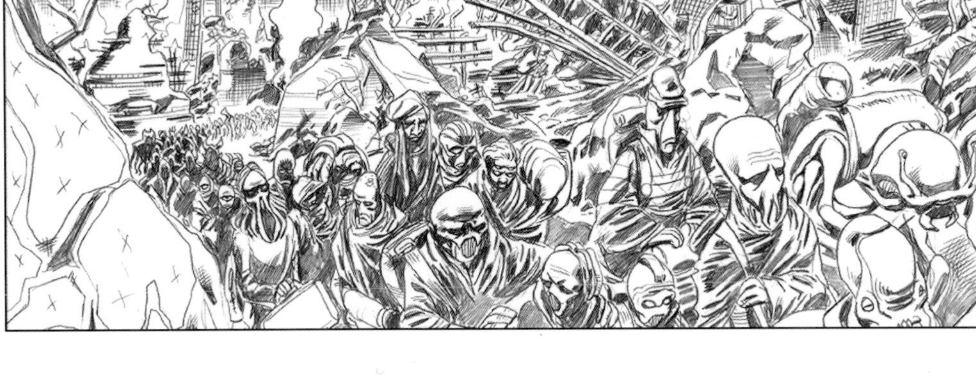

Top:
Horatio and Amy meet in Part One. Pencil art by Mike Collins.

Above:
Danny is revealed in Part Four. Pencils by Mike Collins.

Bottom:
Mike's depiction of the Cornucopia refugees in Part One.

Below:
Mike's layout for the flashback montage in Part Two.

Bottom:
Mike Collins' colour character sketches for Azrael.

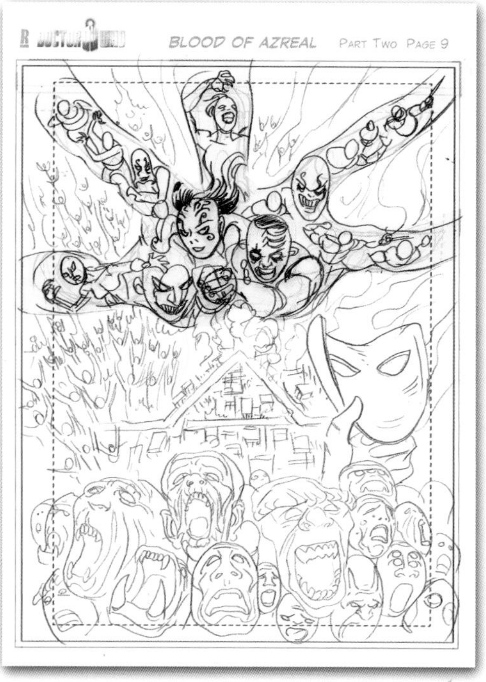
BLOOD OF AZREAL
PART TWO PAGE 9

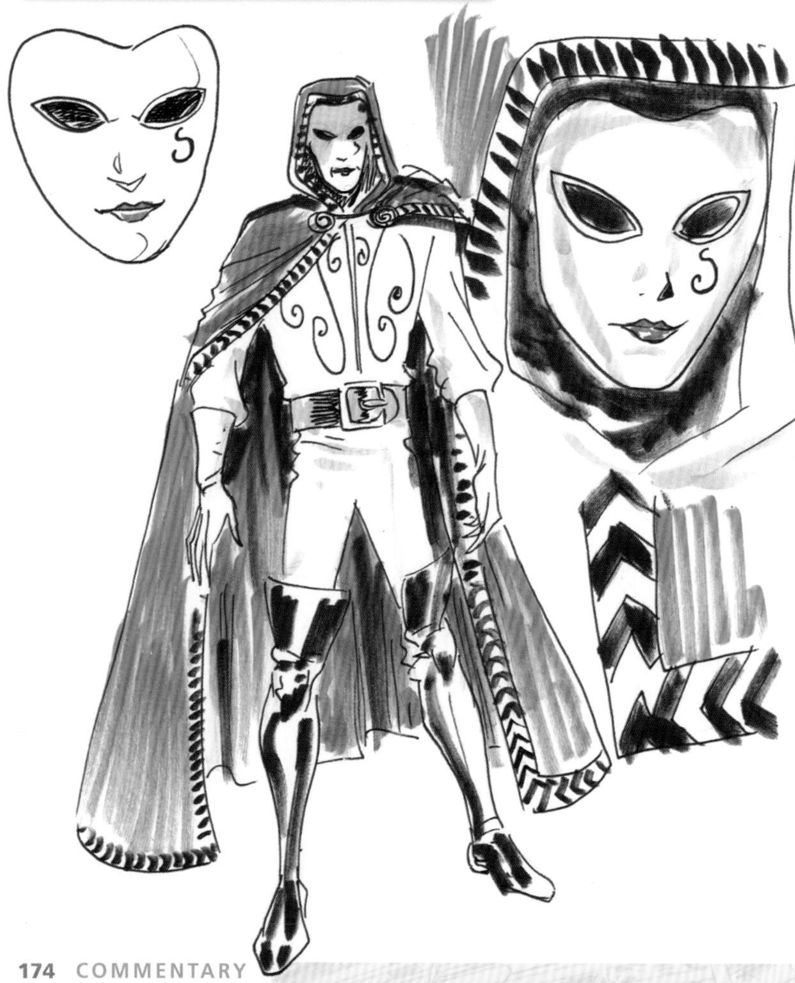

but his son is wearing the costume soon after, and several other equally disturbed people follow suit as the years pass. Another great comics villain, Matt Wagner's Grendel, dies in his very first story, but again, other people keep assuming his name and image. As a result, Grendel's 'spirit' survives for centuries. I wanted Azrael to have that kind of immortality. It's his legacy of madness that keeps him 'alive'.

Danny's base of operations, the Wasting Wall, had first been mentioned way back in 2001's *The Way of All Flesh*, the first story to feature the Necrotists. I had been waiting ever since to actually see the thing, and it did not disappoint. Mike went crazy on this one, giving us one of the most epically detailed spreads ever seen in **DWM**. (David eventually forgave him.)

Amy Johnson's return had been planned during *A Wing and a Prayer*. This Amy was 11 years older – she had experienced worldwide fame, been through a volatile marriage and learned more than a few life lessons. Her reappearance helped me ramp up the tension in a very useful way. If I had put Clara inside Azrael's death-chamber in Part Three's cliffhanger, every **DWM** reader would have just shrugged and moved on to the crossword. But Amy was a sympathetic character whom we could convincingly threaten. She had cheated death once, but there was no reason to believe her luck would continue to hold. I'm not sure why, but I hadn't given Mike a complete outline of the plot, so he wasn't aware that Amy was going to survive. He was very upset when he read Part Three's script!

The confrontation between the Doctor and the TARDIS was yet another mindblowing page from Mike, David and James. It answered another question I had been asking: the TARDIS is certainly intelligent, but had it developed any sense of morality? Could it actually *care?* I decided the answer was yes. *She* can.

And so we closed the final page on the Eleventh Doctor, so brilliantly defined by Matt Smith. I had loved writing for him. He was the most joyous Doctor of them all, so there was only one suitable way to say goodbye – with the biggest party we could possibly stage. As always, our art team provided a spectacular final image and we were done.

Hope you enjoyed the last dance!

Mike Collins Artist

So, *Piper* wasn't my last Eleventh Doctor story after all...

I was working away at various other projects (including producing art for a range of *Doctor Who* merchandise in a 70s Marvel style, and some *Horrid Henry* storyboarding for TV) and assumed I wouldn't get a call from Scott until the new Doctor came along. But then, a tentative phone call with a "So, anyway – as we left it on a cliffhanger..." and I was back.

This story was to wrap up all Scott's themes and plot ideas from his Matt Smith run, so I dived in head-first, carving my own corner of Cornucopia. I loved Dan McDaid's grubby, impressionistic feel for the place and wanted to build on that, while also mixing it with Martin Geraghty's more linear approach, creating a synthesis of styles. Scott informed me that all schools of architecture could co-exist, so I mixed and matched with glee. The 'undercity' sequence had me going to town on the pebbled streets, arches and uneven brick walls, trying to evoke a skewed recreation of a Dickensian London that never was. It also calls on gothic architecture, with gargoyles perched on walls. I pushed for a more impressionistic feel in the sequence with the Librarian, utilising negative space, though Scott reined me in when the design overtook the storytelling!

The first episode was unusual in that the Doctor is almost entirely absent until the last couple of pages. Centre-stage are the Wonderland secret-service-in-space gang. The swift introduction and establishing of Danny and his relationship with Annabel is a deft bit of writing which I hope I managed to marry up with their body language in the art. I loved how Scott introduced the strip with a seemingly random incident and then doesn't refer to it again for months – the payoff is again, |a fantastic exercise in economic writing. And after it saw print I suddenly realised in horror that two of my jobs had strangely crossed over: the young Danny looks uncomfortably like a real-world version of Horrid Henry...!

Horatio is a great character, but I was constantly forgetting his tail (I had some sort of simian blindness, assuming he was an ape, not a monkey). Scott was on tail patrol all the way through this story.

The pages where the Eleventh Doctor first turns up were actually quite challenging: one of the key words to portraying Matt Smith is 'kinetic'. He's never still, he's never stationary. Here he has to be both – stuck in a queue and closed down. They were hard to draw after the reckless hijinks with Amy and Horatio... until that final, explosive page. Again, it was a Marvel moment, in this case, me channelling classic John Byrne. It's one of the joys of *Doctor Who* that we can cover all styles and approaches in the strip and it's big enough to take it.

Each episode of this story, Scott gave me an introductory scene, separate and distinct from the body of the tale; an artist's gift – new alien environments, new aliens. I enjoyed creating the alien shanty town at the start of Part Two, the random images of Part Three, and the way it all pulls together at the start of Part Four.

This story was stressful at the time – we were constantly playing catch-up on the schedule but I was determined to produce something special, building on the jaw-dropping graphics month by month. I'm still really pleased with the 'splayed hand' page in Part Two (Page Nine) which is where I think we nailed our colours to the mast: this was going to be a VAST story, with history and scope. And consequences.

The second episode ends with the introduction of Azrael, another occasion where it came out pretty much fully-formed in Scott's script. I think I only did a couple of quick sketches and he decided we had our antagonist. There's a lovely bit of negative space going on in those last pages of Part Two with the stark TARDIS in relief from the heavily-rendered background. Well, it made me happy. It's an artist thing, I guess...

Part Three ends with one of the hardest things I've ever had to draw: the apparent death of Amy. And *no*, I didn't know she survived in the next episode. I think I spent the weekend trying to justify what Scott had done, wondering if I shouldn't ring him and argue the case for her survival. All the anguish in Clara's face is right from my reaction to that scene as I was drawing it. I'm impressed that her survival wasn't a cop-out but utterly pivotal to the plot. Good writing, that!

Part Four opens with another of Scott's 'top that' scenes, a positively Jack Kirby-esque insane spread of screaming anguished alien faces (including another Doctor – Zoidberg – search him out). It's partly down to the fact that we now have 12 pages to tell the story that we can indulge ourselves in these grand images, and totally go to town on the imagery... and it is all worth it to see David's horrified expression when he drops by to pick up the pencils...

Part Four also ends with us going all Marvel Comics in the storytelling, a full-on cosmic battle with energy blasts and earthquake eruptions! And the mangling of sonics...

Part Five opens with the resolution of the alien attack from Part One, and my inadvertent *Doctor Who/Horrid Henry* crossover, a chilling little piece. Drawing Danny's back-story gave me the excuse to re-watch the Tennant era Sontaran two-parter; research is a wonderful thing.

Scott really pushed for the cosmic here, with my inspiration for the Doctor re-bonding with the TARDIS sequence inspired by my love of late 60s Neal Adams work, particularly *X-Men* and *The Avengers*. There was always a sense of scale and wonder that I tried to emulate here.

And then, the final, most detailed splash of all, our 'goodbye' to Matt – Scott didn't want it to be wistful like the Ninth Doctor's final appearance, or sad like that fabulous last page Martin did for the Tenth, but something joyful, giddy and ridiculous, just like Eleventh's personality. I think it's (along with the splayed hand and the Wasting Wall) the longest I've ever worked on a single image.

These stories represent some of my favourite work on the strip since *The Cruel Sea*. Working on *Doctor Who* pushes you to do your finest work. It's a scary amount of pressure at the time but when we all click together, we can produce something that lasts and can hold its head up amongst the myriad splendours that make the worlds of our favourite Gallifreyan... ●

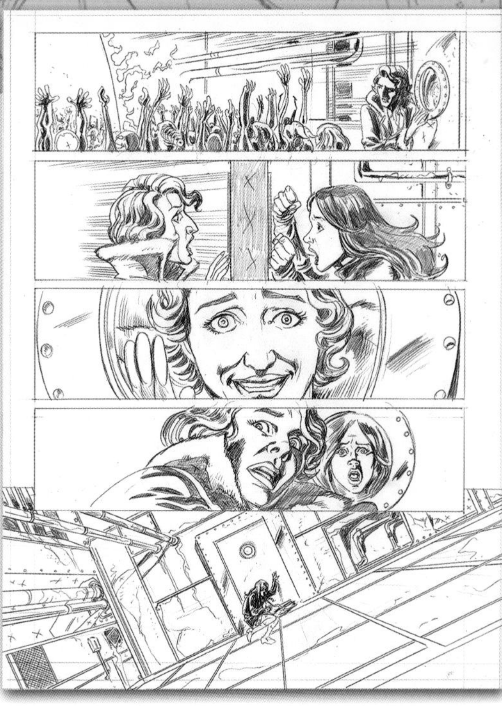

Above:
Amy Johnson faces certain doom! Pencils by Mike Collins.

Below:
The final party for the Eleventh Doctor in the **DWM** strip. Pencils by Mike Collins.

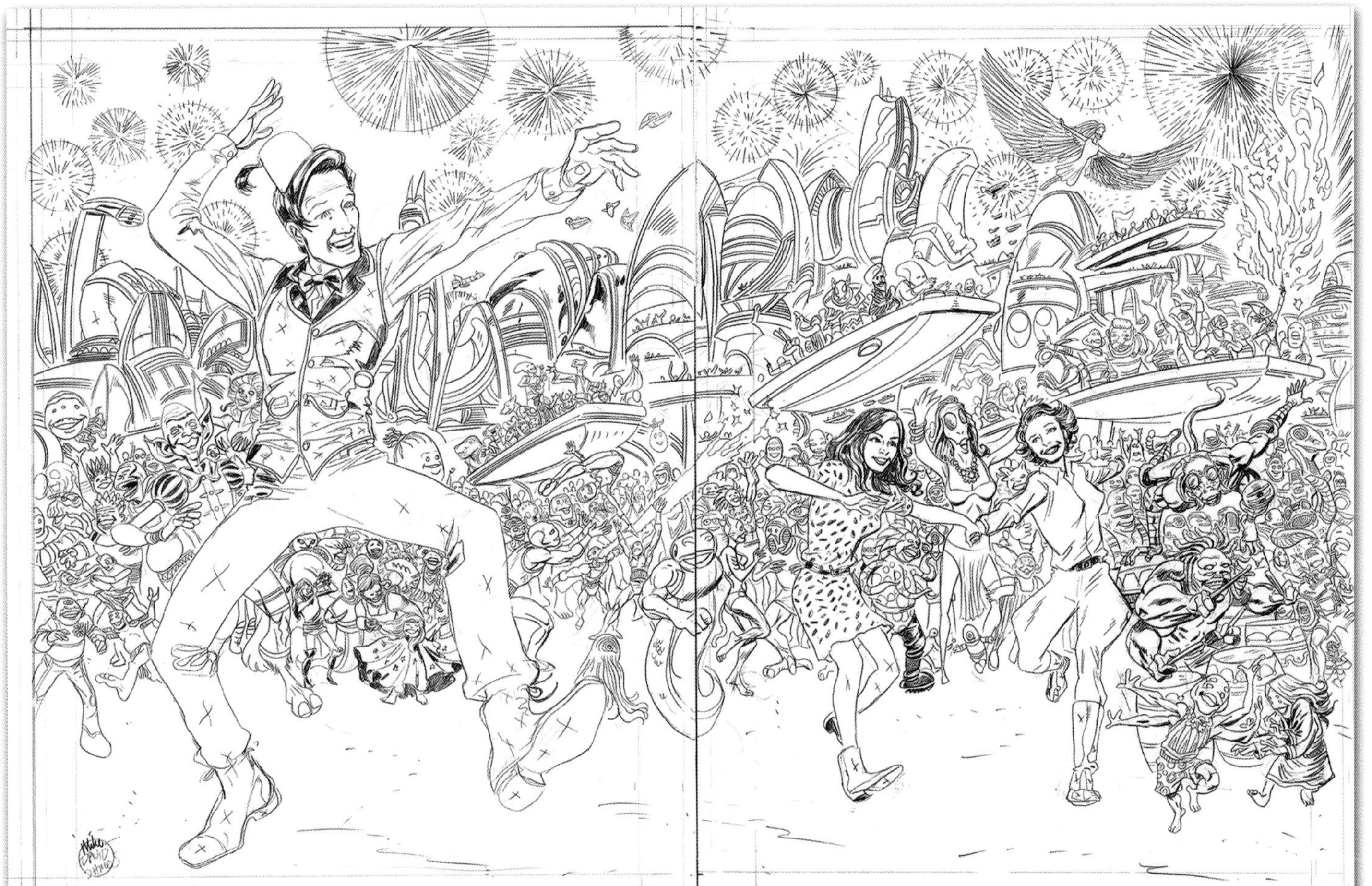

DOCTOR WHO COMIC COLLECTIONS

FOURTH, FIFTH, SIXTH & SEVENTH DOCTORS

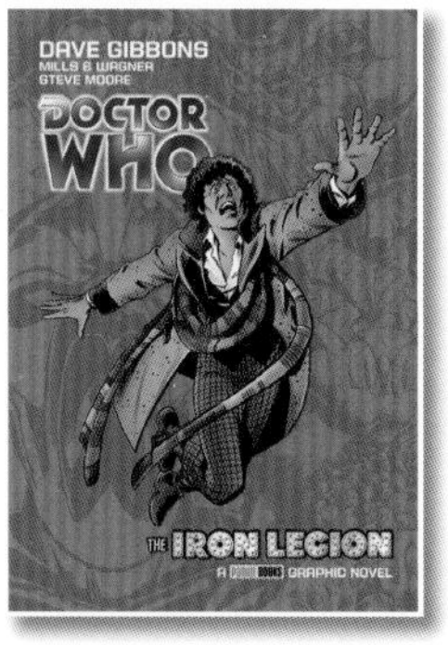
DAVE GIBBONS
DOCTOR WHO
THE IRON LEGION

Volume One of the Fourth Doctor's comic strip adventures, containing five digitally restored stories:

THE IRON LEGION, CITY OF THE DAMNED, THE STAR BEAST, THE DOGS OF DOOM and **THE TIME WITCH**!

Featuring work from **Dave Gibbons, Pat Mills, John Wagner** and **Steve Moore**

164 pages | b&w | softcover | £14.99 | $24.95 | ISBN 1-9041 59-37-0

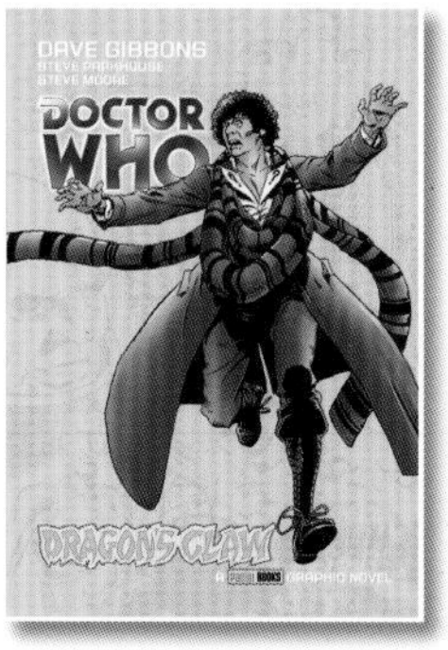
DAVE GIBBONS
DOCTOR WHO
DRAGON'S CLAW

Volume Two of the Fourth Doctor's comic strip adventures, containing 10 digitally restored stories:

DRAGON'S CLAW, THE COLLECTOR, DREAMERS OF DEATH, THE LIFE BRINGER, WAR OF THE WORDS, SPIDER-GOD, THE DEAL, END OF THE LINE, THE FREE-FALL WARRIORS, JUNKYARD DEMON and **THE NEUTRON KNIGHTS**!

164 pages | b&w | softcover | £14.99 | $24.95 | ISBN 1-9041 59-81-8

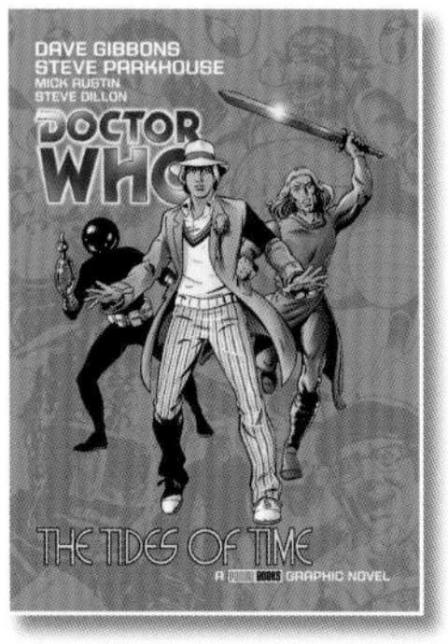
DAVE GIBBONS
STEVE PARKHOUSE
DOCTOR WHO
THE TIDES OF TIME

The Fifth Doctor's complete comic strip run, containing six digitally restored stories:

THE TIDES OF TIME, STARS FELL ON STOCKBRIDGE, THE STOCKBRIDGE HORROR, LUNAR LAGOON, 4-DIMENSIONAL VISTAS and **THE MODERATOR**!

228 pages | b&w | softcover | £14.99 | $24.95 | ISBN 1-9041 59-92-3

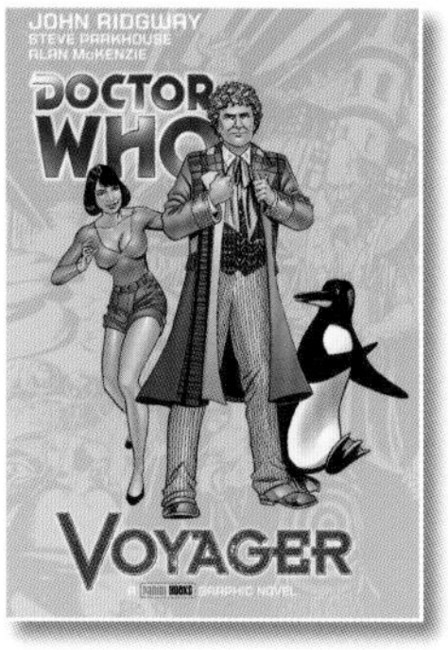
JOHN RIDGWAY
DOCTOR WHO
VOYAGER

Volume One of the Sixth Doctor's comic strip adventures containing seven digitally restored adventures:

THE SHAPE SHIFTER, VOYAGER, POLLY THE GLOT, ONCE UPON A TIME LORD, WAR-GAME, FUNHOUSE and **KANE'S STORY/ABEL'S STORY/ THE WARRIOR'S STORY/ FROBISHER'S STORY**!

172 pages | b&w softcover | £15.99 | $31.95 | ISBN 978-1-905239-71-9

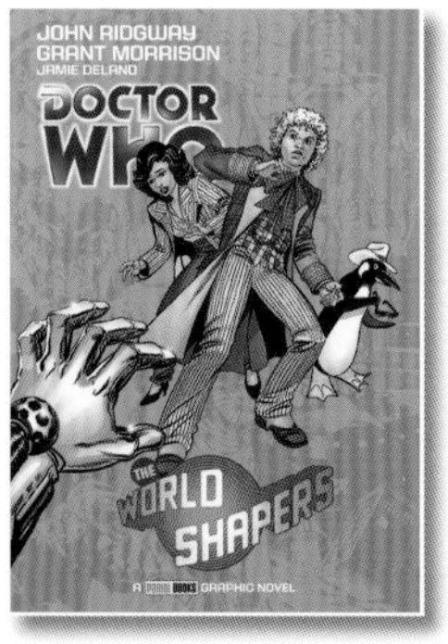
JOHN RIDGWAY
GRANT MORRISON
DOCTOR WHO
THE WORLD SHAPERS

Volume Two of the Sixth Doctor's comic strip adventures containing the following digitally restored adventures:

EXODUS, REVELATION!, GENESIS!, NATURE OF THE BEAST, TIME BOMB, SALAD DAZE, CHANGES, PROFITS OF DOOM, THE GIFT and **THE WORLD SHAPERS**!

172 pages | b&w softcover | £15.99 | $31.95 | ISBN 978-1-905239-71-9

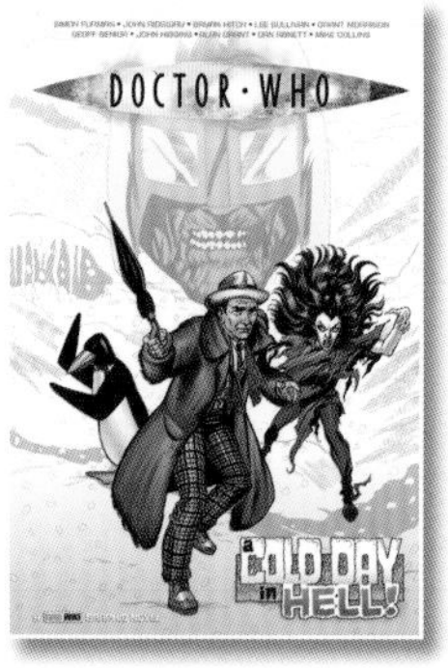
DOCTOR·WHO
A COLD DAY IN HELL!

Volume One of the Seventh Doctor's comic strip adventures containing 11 digitally restored stories:

A COLD DAY IN HELL!, REDEMPTION!, THE CROSSROADS OF TIME, CLAWS OF THE KLATHI!, CULTURE SHOCK!, KEEPSAKE, PLANET OF THE DEAD, ECHOES OF THE MOGOR!, TIME AND TIDE, FOLLOW THAT TARDIS! and **INVADERS FROM GANTAC!**

188 pages | b&w | softcover | £15.99 | $31.95 | ISBN 978-1-84653-410-2

These titles are available now from all good bookshops, specialist comic shops and online retailers

PANINI COMICS

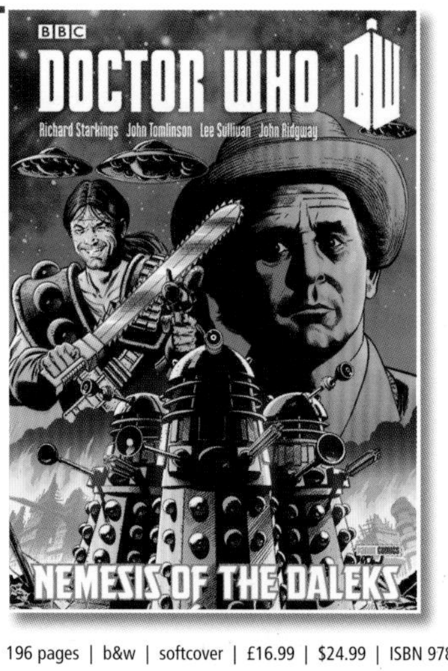
BBC
DOCTOR WHO
Richard Starkings John Tomlinson Lee Sullivan John Ridgway
NEMESIS OF THE DALEKS

Volume Two of the Seventh Doctor's complete comic strip adventures from the pages of **DWM** and *The Incredible Hulk Presents*. Contains 14 complete stories:

NEMESIS OF THE DALEKS, STAIRWAY TO HEAVEN, ONCE IN A LIFETIME, HUNGER FROM THE ENDS OF TIME!, WAR WORLD!, TECHNICAL HITCH, A SWITCH IN TIME!, THE SENTINEL!, WHO'S THAT GIRL!, THE ENLIGHTENMENT OF LI-CHEE THE WISE, SLIMMER!, NINEVEH!, TRAIN-FLIGHT, DOCTOR CONKERER! and also the adventures of Abslom Daak in **ABSLOM DAAK... DALEK KILLER** and **STAR TIGERS**!

PLUS a huge behind-the-scenes feature, including commentaries from the writers, artists and editors, cut scenes, pencil art, design sketches and much, much more.

196 pages | b&w | softcover | £16.99 | $24.99 | ISBN 978-1-84653-531-4

THE COMPLETE EIGHTH DOCTOR

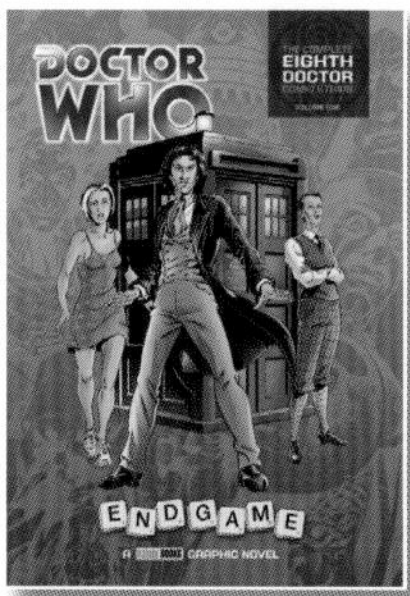
DOCTOR WHO
ENDGAME

Volume One of the Eighth Doctor's complete comic strip adventures, containing eight digitally restored stories: **ENDGAME, THE KEEP, FIRE AND BRIMSTONE, TOOTH AND CLAW, THE FINAL CHAPTER, WORMWOOD, A LIFE OF MATTER AND DEATH** and **BY HOOK OR BY CROOK**!

PLUS a 16-page behind-the-scenes feature with unused story ideas, character designs and an authors' commentary!

228 pages | b&w | softcover | £14.99 | $24.95 | ISBN 1-9052 39-09-2

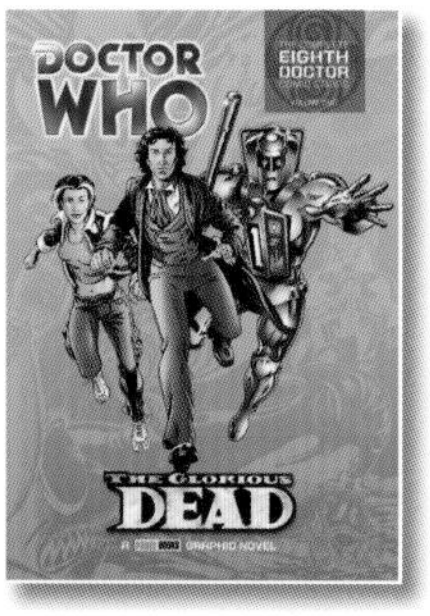
DOCTOR WHO
EIGHTH DOCTOR
THE GLORIOUS DEAD

Volume Two of the Eighth Doctor's complete comic strip adventures, containing eight digitally restored stories: **THE FALLEN, UNNATURAL BORN KILLERS, THE ROAD TO HELL, COMPANY OF THIEVES, THE GLORIOUS DEAD, THE AUTONOMY BUG, HAPPY DEATHDAY** and **TV ACTION**!

PLUS a six-page behind-the-scenes feature and two classic 1980s strips featuring Kroton the Cyberman: **THROWBACK** and **SHIP OF FOOLS**!

244 pages | b&w | softcover | £15.99 | $26.50 | ISBN 1-9052 39-44-0

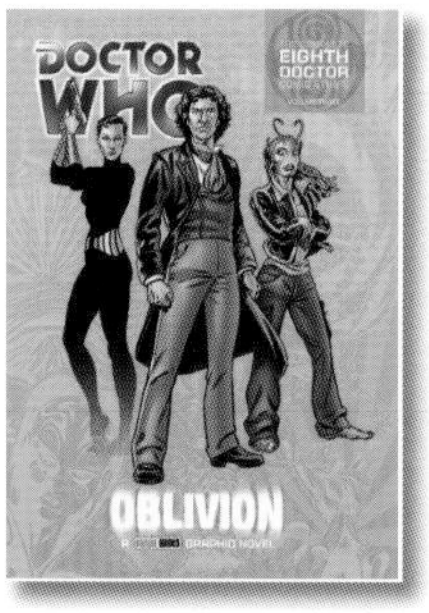
DOCTOR WHO
EIGHTH DOCTOR
OBLIVION

Volume Three of the Eighth Doctor's complete comic strip adventures, containing eight digitally restored stories: **OPHIDIUS, BEAUTIFUL FREAK, THE WAY OF ALL FLESH, CHILDREN OF THE REVOLUTION, ME AND MY SHADOW, UROBOROS** and **OBLIVION**!

PLUS a massive 22-page behind-the-scenes feature, bonus strip **CHARACTER ASSASSIN** and a newly-extended conclusion to Dalek strip **CHILDREN OF THE REVOLUTION**!

228 pages | full colour | softcover | £15.99 | $24.99 | ISBN 1-905239-45-9

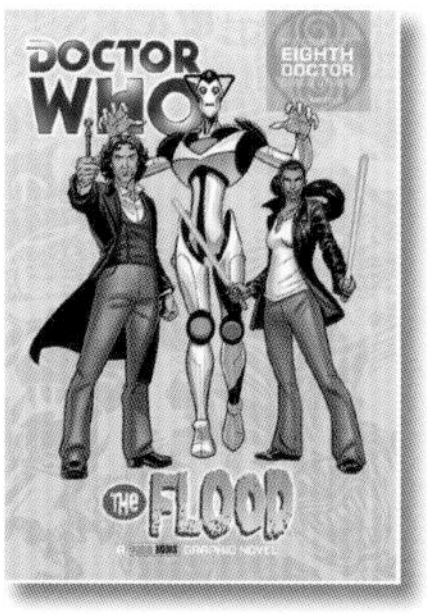
DOCTOR WHO
EIGHTH DOCTOR
THE FLOOD

Volume Four of the Eighth Doctor's complete comic strip adventures, containing eight digitally restored stories: **WHERE NOBODY KNOWS YOUR NAME, THE NIGHTMARE GAME, THE POWER OF THOUERIS!, THE CURIOUS TALE OF SPRING-HEELED JACK, THE LAND OF HAPPY ENDINGS, BAD BLOOD, SINS OF THE FATHERS** and **THE FLOOD**!

PLUS a massive 28-page behind-the-scenes feature, and a newly-extended conclusion to **THE FLOOD**!

228 pages | full colour | softcover | £15.99 | $24.99 | ISBN 978-1-905239-65-8

THE COMPLETE NINTH DOCTOR

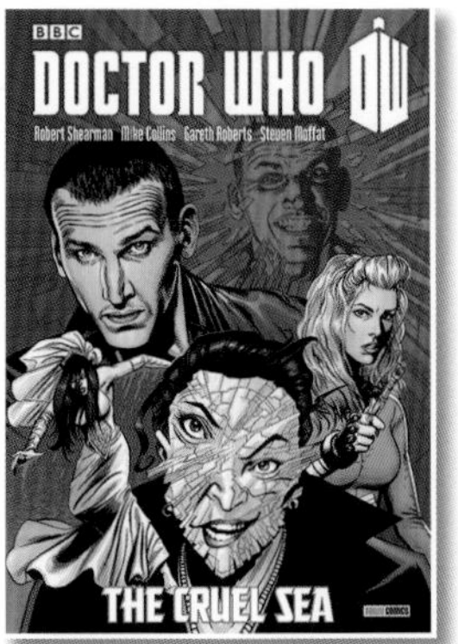
BBC
DOCTOR WHO
THE CRUEL SEA

All of the Ninth Doctor's comic strip adventures from the pages of **DWM** in one volume, containing five complete stories:

THE LOVE INVASION, ART ATTACK, THE CRUEL SEA, MR NOBODY and **A GROATSWORTH OF WIT!**

This volume also includes the Steven Moffat-written short story from the *Doctor Who Annual 2006* which inspired the TV episode *Blink*: **WHAT I DID ON MY CHRISTMAS HOLIDAYS BY SALLY SPARROW**

PLUS a massive behind-the-scenes feature, including commentaries from the writers and artists, design sketches and more.

180 pages | full colour softcover
£15.99 | $31.95 | ISBN 978-1-84653-593-2

THE COMPLETE TENTH DOCTOR

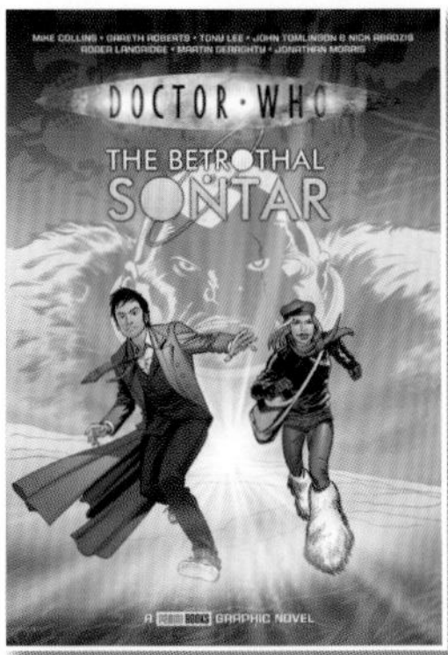
DOCTOR · WHO
THE BETROTHAL OF SONTAR

Volume One of the Tenth Doctor's comic strip adventures from the pages of **DWM**, containing eight complete stories:

THE BETROTHAL OF SONTAR, THE LODGER, F.A.Q., THE FUTURISTS, INTERSTELLAR OVERDRIVE, OPERA OF DOOM!, THE GREEN-EYED MONSTER and **THE WARKEEPER'S CROWN!**

PLUS a massive behind-the-scenes feature, including commentaries from the writers and artists, design sketches and more.

180 pages | full colour softcover
£15.99 | $24.99 | ISBN 978-1-905239-90-0

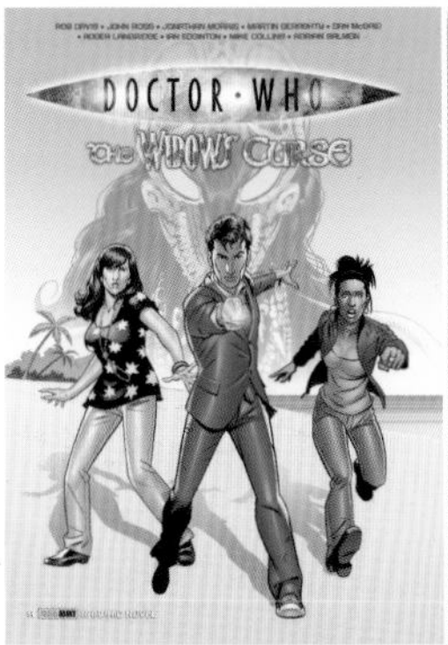
DOCTOR · WHO
THE WIDOW'S CURSE

Volume Two of the Tenth Doctor's comic strip adventures from the pages of **DWM**, containing nine complete stories:

THE WOMAN WHO SOLD THE WORLD, BUS STOP!, THE FIRST, SUN SCREEN, DEATH TO THE DOCTOR!, UNIVERSAL MONSTERS, THE WIDOW'S CURSE, THE IMMORTAL EMPEROR and **THE TIME OF MY LIFE!**

PLUS a massive behind-the-scenes feature, including commentaries from the writers and artists, design sketches and more.

220 pages | full colour | softcover
£15.99 | $31.95 | ISBN 978-1-84653-429-4

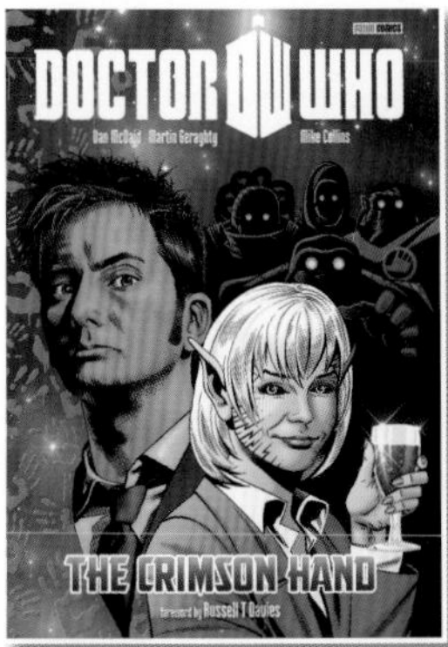
DOCTOR WHO
THE CRIMSON HAND

Volume Three of the Tenth Doctor's comic strip adventures from the pages of **DWM**, containing ten complete stories:

HOTEL HISTORIA, SPACE VIKINGS!, THINKTWICE, THE STOCKBRIDGE CHILD, MORTAL BELOVED, THE AGE OF ICE, THE DEEP HEREAFTER, ONOMATOPOEIA, GHOSTS OF THE NORTHERN LINE and **THE CRIMSON HAND!**

PLUS a massive behind-the-scenes feature, including commentaries from the writers and artists, design sketches and more.

260 pages | full colour | softcover
£15.99 | $31.95 | ISBN 978-1-84653-451-5

THE COMPLETE ELEVENTH DOCTOR

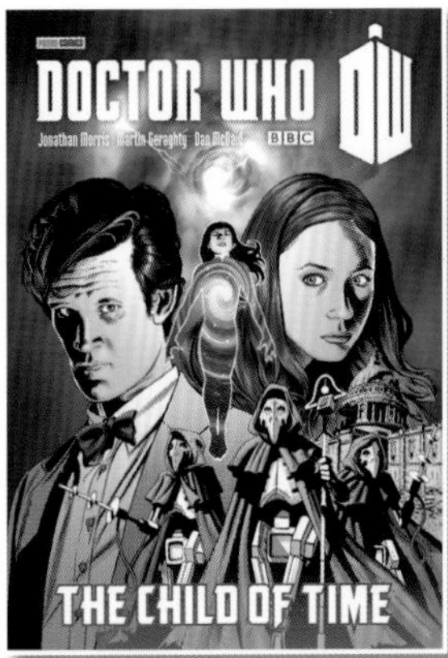
DOCTOR WHO
BBC
THE CHILD OF TIME

Volume One of the Eleventh Doctor's comic strip adventures from the pages of **DWM**, containing nine complete stories:

SUPERNATURE, PLANET BOLLYWOOD!, THE GOLDEN ONES, THE PROFESSOR, THE QUEEN AND THE BOOKSHOP, THE SCREAMS OF DEATH, DO NOT GO GENTLE INTO THAT GOOD NIGHT, FOREVER DREAMING, APOTHEOSIS and **THE CHILD OF TIME!**

PLUS a massive behind-the-scenes feature from the creators of the strips with design sketches and more.

244 pages | full colour | softcover
£16.99 | $24.99 | ISBN 978-1-84653-460-7

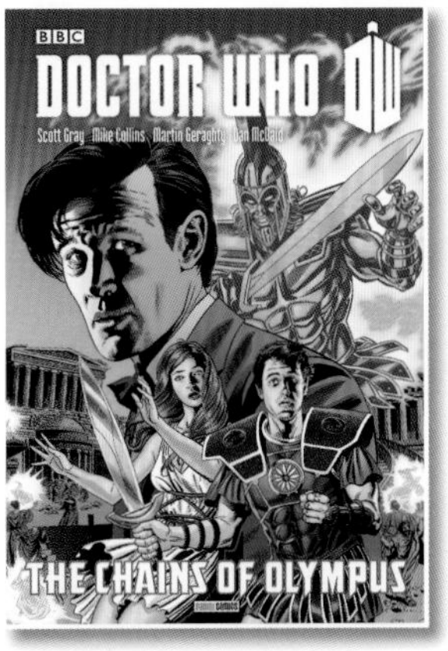
BBC
DOCTOR WHO
THE CHAINS OF OLYMPUS

Volume Two of the Eleventh Doctor's comic strip adventures from the pages of **DWM**, containing three complete stories:

THE CHAINS OF OLYMPUS, STICKS AND STONES and **THE CORNUCOPIA CAPER!**

PLUS a massive behind-the-scenes feature, including commentaries from the writers and artists, design sketches and more.

132 pages | full colour | softcover
£12.99 | $18.99 | ISBN 978-1-84653-558-1

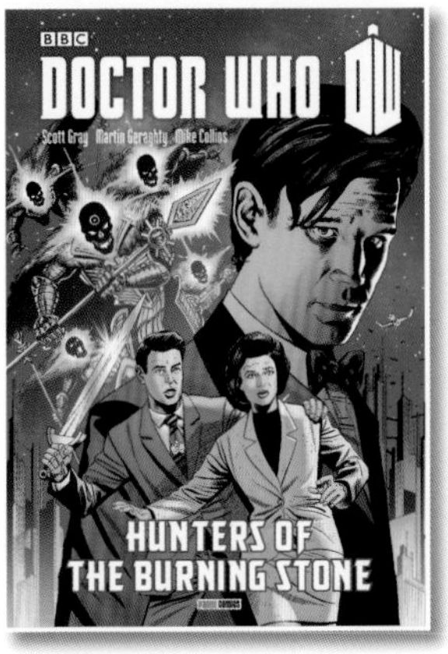
BBC
DOCTOR WHO
HUNTERS OF THE BURNING STONE

Volume Three of the Eleventh Doctor's comic strip adventures from the pages of **DWM**, containing three complete stories:

THE BROKEN MAN, IMAGINARY ENEMIES and **HUNTERS OF THE BURNING STONE!**

PLUS a massive behind-the-scenes feature, including commentaries from the writers and artists, design sketches and more.

164 pages | full colour | softcover
£13.99 | $19.99 | ISBN 978-1-84653-545-1

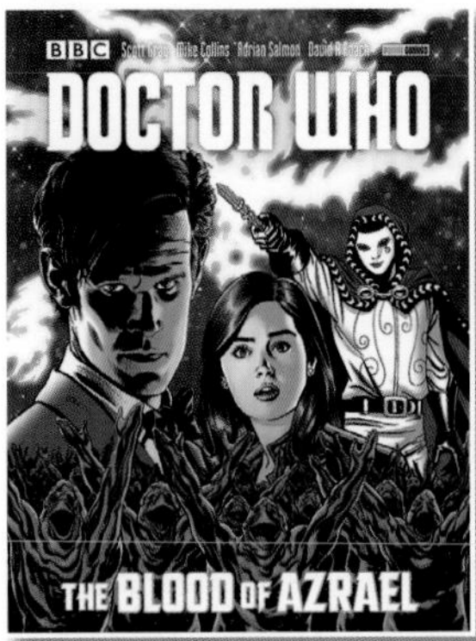
BBC
DOCTOR WHO
THE BLOOD OF AZRAEL

The fourth and final volume of the Eleventh Doctor's comic strip adventures from the pages of **DWM**, containing five complete stories:

A WING AND A PRAYER, WELCOME TO TICKLE TOWN, JOHN SMITH AND THE COMMON MEN, PAY THE PIPER and **THE BLOOD OF AZRAEL!**

PLUS a massive behind-the-scenes feature, including commentaries from the writer and artists, design sketches and more.

180 pages | full colour | softcover
£13.99 | $19.99 | ISBN 978-1-84653-625-0

COMING SOON...

THE GOOD SOLDIER

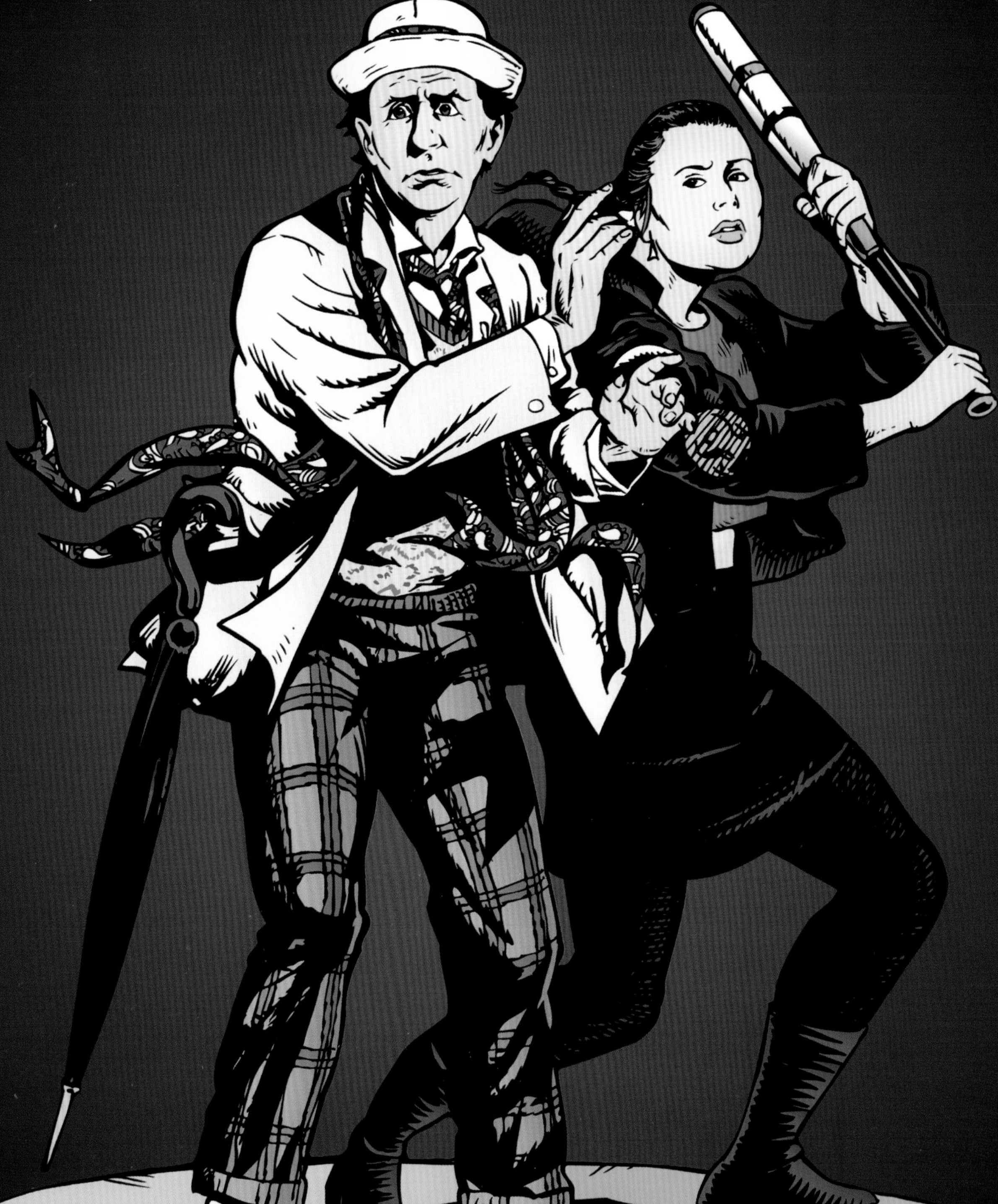

A BUMPER VOLUME OF AMAZING COMIC STRIP ADVENTURES FEATURING THE SEVENTH DOCTOR AND ACE FROM DOCTOR WHO MAGAZINE!